UPGRADING
AND REPAIRING
NETWORKS,

Second Edition

Terry William Ogletree

A Division of Macmillan USA
201 West 103rd Street,
Indianapolis, Indiana 46290

Contents at a Glance

Upgrading and Repairing Networks, Second Edition

Copyright © 1999 by Que® Corporation

International Standard Book Number: 0-7897-2034-5

Library of Congress Catalog Card Number: 99-60782

Printed in the United States of America

First Printing: December, 1999

01   00   99   4   3   2   1

Trademarks

Warning and Disclaimer

Associate Publisher
Jim Minatel

Senior Acquisitions Editor
Jenny L. Watson

Development Editors
Jill Hayden
Ben Milstead
Todd Brakke

Managing Editor
Lisa Wilson

Project Editor
Tonya Simpson

Copy Editors
Pamela Woolf
Matt Wooden
JoAnna Kremer

Indexer
Larry Sweazy

Proofreaders
Benjamin Berg
Wendy Ott

Technical Editor
Ariel Silverstone

Team Coordinator
Vicki Harding

Media Developer
Brandon Penticuff

Interior Design
Glenn Larsen

Cover Design
Karen Ruggles

Copy Writer
Eric Borgert

Production
Stacey DeRome
Ayanna Lacey
Heather Miller

Contents

32 Other Client/Server Applications   515

Part XII   Troubleshooting Internet Connections   531

33 Dial-Up Connections   533

About the Author

Terry Ogletree is a consultant currently working in New Jersey. He has worked with networked computer systems since 1980, starting out on Digital Equipment PDP computers and OpenVMS-based VAX and AlphaServer systems. He has worked with UNIX and TCP/IP since 1985 and has been involved with Windows NT since it first appeared. He is the author of *Windows NT Server 4.0 Networking*, which is volume 4 of Sams' *Windows NT Server 4 Resource Library*, and has contributed chapters to many other books published by Macmillan, including *Windows NT Server Unleashed* (and the *Professional Reference Edition*), as well as the recent *Special Edition Using UNIX, Third Edition*, published by Que. He can often be found on street corners holding a sign that reads "Will work for hundreds of thousands of dollars."

You can email him at ogletree@bellsouth.net or two@twoinc.com, or visit his home page at www.twoinc.com.

Special Thanks to...

Aaron Rogers, MCP is the network administrator at a medium-sized manufacturing company in Santa Ana, California, where is responsible for supporting all aspects of the company network and Web site. He enjoys the hardware side of the industry but has a soft side for software development and graphics work as well. Aaron has been in the computer industry as a consultant to small businesses and schools for more than five years—he has implemented small- to medium-sized Microsoft, Novell, and UNIX-based networks.

Mark Edward Soper, president of Select Systems & Associates, Inc., has been a technical writer and trainer since 1989 and has been working with business computers since 1984. He is the author of more than 100 technical articles for publications, including *WordPerfect* magazine, the *WordPerfectionist*, *PCNovice*, *PCToday*, *SmartComputing*, *PCNovice Guides*, and the *PCNovice Learning Series*. He was a contributor to the Eleventh Edition of Scott Mueller's *Upgrading and Repairing PCs* and is co-author of *Upgrading and Repairing PCs Technician's Portable Reference*, both available from Que.

For more information about customized technical reference and training materials, contact Mark at

Select Systems & Associates, Inc
1100 W. Lloyd Expy #104
Evansville, IN 47708
Phone: (812) 421-1170
Fax: (812) 468-4302
Email: mesoper@selectsystems.com
Web site: selectsystems.com

Gerry O'Brien has been using computers since the Commodore VIC-20. During this early stage of the PC, he took a course in computer programming using BASIC and was immediately hooked. He then migrated to the IBM compatible personal computer, buying his first 8086 with a whopping 40MB hard drive.

Eventually, Gerry turned his love for computers into a part-time business selling, upgrading, and repairing computers as well as providing consulting services. During this time, he also provided PC support and network administration for the Hardman Group, a property management firm. Recently he has partnered with another avid computer lover and taken his original company idea and added software development to its offerings. Gerry is also a beta tester for Microsoft, currently testing DirectX 7.0 and Windows 2000.

Gary Segler is currently a senior systems engineer at one of the industry's largest pharmaceutical companies. Gary has been working with computers since the late 1980s and has extensive experience in networking with Windows NT, Novell NetWare, and UNIX. His experience extends from the front lines of desktop support to engineering state-of-the-art servers. In addition to networking, Gary lends himself to software application development—in particular, applications to increase system administration efficiency and accuracy. Currently, Gary is involved with creating a Web-based system administration application and is maintaining the back-end network consisting of more than four dozen Novell/NT servers with more than 5,200 users connecting to them.

Acknowledgments

Without a doubt, this book could never have been completed without the consistent efforts of two editors at Macmillan Computer Publishing, who deserve as much credit as myself and the contributing authors: Jenny Watson and Jill Hayden. Of all my contacts in the publishing industry these past few years, these two determined editors made sure the result would be a quality product that the reader would be able to benefit from. The contributing authors Jenny was able to bring on board were a great help in getting this book done "almost" on time, and the chapters they produced represent the professionals that they are.

I would also like to acknowledge several people who have, in one way or another, helped me over the years in my career, which has ultimately led to the writing of this book. First, a special thanks to Jo Chamblee, who always thought I'd write something, though she was probably expecting a novel. Going way, way back to the beginning of time, I was given my first job in the computer industry by Sandra Moss and "Dusty" Dawn Morris, both of whom allowed me to explore many things that were way beyond my original job specification. This early exposure to programming and system administration only made me want to continue to learn more and more in an ever-changing environment during those early years.

Over the years I've been very lucky in choosing employers. At National Health Laboratories, Mack Brown and David Turbeville started me in technical writing, and that experience has surely been important in my latest published efforts. Rick Clayton also provided much insight into many areas that still interest me today. At Carolina Power and Light I was lucky enough to work with Les Harrison and T.C. Thomas. Les and I went on to do a few writing projects together for Sams Publishing, and we will probably be doing more later this year. T.C. has moved on and is now involved with an Internet service provider. And how can I forget Ken Arnold, who told me time and time again "it's a wiring problem…," or David Metz, who has always been a great resource for database information. When I was working on my first ethernet installation (many years ago), I found that the help and guidance from Rodney Foster made a complicated project a lot easier. We both learned a lot on that one.

During the actual writing of this book I have been working at Bristol-Myers Squibb in New Jersey. Without the infinite patience of Robert G. Venard and Paul Mullen I probably never would have been able to complete this book. Robert was also a great source for information about the early days of ethernet and local area networks. His supervisor, Tom Crayner, who is in charge of networks in our group, was also very supportive during the writing of this book.

Most of my contracting jobs during the past five years have been the result of the efforts of John Rogue of The Computer Merchant firm in Norwell, Massachusetts. The jobs he has been able to find for me not only pay the bills, but also have enabled me to greatly further my knowledge of computers and networking. His co-worker, Annette Whitty, was also a great help. And I would never have had the time to finish this book without the efforts of Michael D. Parrott of Raleigh, North Carolina, the world's best accountant. Without his hard work (above and beyond the ordinary functions an accountant usually provides), I would never have stayed financially solvent enough to do anything other than dodge bill collectors.

Finally, I would like to acknowledge my parents, who also are in possession of infinite patience, for the support they have given for everything I've ever set my mind to do.

Tell Us What You Think!

As the reader of this book, *you* are our most important critic and commentator. We value your opinion and want to know what we're doing right, what we could do better, what areas you'd like to see us publish in, and any other words of wisdom you're willing to pass our way.

As the associate publisher for this book, I welcome your comments. You can fax, email, or write me directly to let me know what you did or didn't like about this book—as well as what we can do to make our books stronger.

When you write, please be sure to include this book's title and author as well as your name and phone or fax number. I will carefully review your comments and share them with the author and editors who worked on the book.

Fax: 317-817-7070

Email: hardware@mcp.com

Mail: Macmillan Publishing USA
         201 West 103rd Street
         Indianapolis, IN 46290 USA

Although I cannot help you with technical problems related to the topics covered in this book, Terry Ogletree welcomes your technical questions. The best way to reach him is by email at

    ogletree@bellsouth.net

or

    two@twoinc.com.

Introduction

Although only a few years have passed since the first edition of this book was published, much has changed in the networking world. The Internet has grown phenomenally (and continues to do so), and the protocols and standards associated with it are becoming more important in the decisions that corporate network administrators must make today. Whether your background is in Novell NetWare, UNIX, or Windows NT, this book can be used as a reference for networking concepts applied to all these systems.

For those who are contemplating using a particular technology or are having problems with it (troubleshooting), you will find more detailed information. Thus, you will find that this book can be used as a valuable reference for subjects you are familiar with, as well as a learning tool to help you keep abreast of other technologies and emerging topics in the networking field.

Who Should Use This Book?

This book is geared toward the experienced network administrator or technician. Given the tendency for a growing network to incorporate new technologies, protocols, and components, this book can prove an invaluable reference for both problem-solving and planning. Although you might already be knowledgeable in some of the areas discussed in this book, you might find that this book can help you relate your current knowledge to other topics that you want to learn. I don't mean to exclude those who are new to the field of networking. Indeed, you also might find this book an invaluable learning and reference tool as you become acquainted with computer networks.

What You'll Find Inside

Part I of this book, "Basics of Network Troubleshooting," discusses strategies and techniques you can use when trying to solve problems with the network. Following this general introduction to problem-solving strategies is an overview of the tools, both hardware and software, that can be used when problems arise.

Part II, "Troubleshooting Hardware," covers such basic topics as network cabling and network adapter cards, along with more sophisticated network equipment such as hubs, routers, and switches, including information for ethernet and token-ring technologies. Here you will find the difference between 10Base-T and 100Base-T and what the heck 100VG AnyLAN is. There are chapters to explain the functions performed by a Multistation Access Unit (MSAU) on token-ring networks, and how they differ from hubs and switches used on ethernet.

Part III, "Ethernet Design," discusses the actual makeup of standard ethernet network frames, restrictions imposed on the LAN by the particular topology, and rules for putting together simple ethernet LANs. Frame types, from the original Ethernet II through the 802.x standards, as well as the information carried by the headers of these frames, are discussed.

Part IV, "Ethernet Problems," talks about everything from collisions and why they happen to errors that can be detected in ethernet LANs, such as late frames or short frames, and what you can do about them. Chapter 10 covers Fiber Distributed Data Interface (FDDI), an early entry into the high-speed networking market, and Chapter 11 discusses the newly emerging market for wireless networking products.

For a change of pace, Part V, "Token-Ring Design," looks at another important networking technology. Although it is not as popular, based on sheer numbers, as ethernet networks, token ring, which was introduced before ethernet, is still around today. This section gives you a good overview of how token-ring networks operate and problems to watch out for. Part VI, "Token-Ring Problems," can help you troubleshoot these kinds of networks.

Network protocols are discussed in Part VII, "Troubleshooting Protocols," starting with TCP/IP, the standard protocol used on the Internet. Chapter 18, "TCP/IP," starts with the basics of how addresses are constructed; the chapter goes on to explain subnetting, routing, and utilities that can be used to troubleshoot TCP/IP. Novell's SPX/IPX is covered next, as is NetBIOS and NetBEUI. Chapter 21, "Name Resolution," goes into detail about methods used to resolve computer names and addresses, from the LMHOSTS file to DNS to Microsoft's WINS servers.

Part VIII, "Troubleshooting Logon Problems," is next. In this section there are chapters discussing the logon procedure and methods for troubleshooting logons for Windows NT, NetWare, and UNIX/Linux clients. The Windows NT Security Accounts Manager (SAM) database is explained, as well as how to use the User Manager for Domains to manage user accounts. Chapter 23 discusses how NetWare clients can use the bindery to log on to individual NetWare servers or NDS to log on to the directory service to gain access to resources on multiple servers. UNIX and Linux are discussed as well, covering both the basic files, such as the `passwd` file, up to NIS (formerly Yellow Pages).

No book on networking would be complete without a section that covers file sharing. In Part IX, "File Sharing," one chapter reviews the protocols, from Microsoft's Server Message Block (SMB) and its spin-off in the UNIX world, SAMBA. The NetWare Core Protocol (NCP) is covered also, and there is an extensive discussion of the many protocols that make up the NFS (Network File Systems) file server technology. Along the same lines, Chapter 26, "Rights and Permissions," discusses how these file resources are protected against access. How permissions and rights are granted is examined for Windows NT, NetWare, and UNIX/Linux systems.

Part X, "Printing," covers another basic network service: printing. A chapter is devoted to the specific protocols, starting with the lpr/lpd system used on many UNIX platforms. Protocols used for Windows NT and other systems are also covered. There is also a discussion of the newly emerging Internet Printing Protocol (IPP), which is likely to be a major player in the printing field in just a few short years. Another chapter in this section discusses print servers, both hardware- and software-based, and methods for monitoring usage and troubleshooting problems that might arise.

Part XI, "Troubleshooting Network Applications," covers a diverse set of topics. There are chapters on email systems, database systems, Web servers, and other client/server applications that are used on a network. This section will be of interest to both the network administrator and the application developer.

Part XII, "Troubleshooting Internet Connections," has chapters covering simple dial-up connections, ISDN, and ASDL. Setting up PPP or SLIP connections is explained here, along with tips for setting up connections for different operating systems, from Windows NT to Linux. Troubleshooting modems and logon scripts is also covered. If you need a higher bandwidth connection than that supplied by a dial-up connection, you will find Chapter 34, "Dedicated Connections," a helpful guide to the different technologies available, from X.25 to Frame Relay and ATM.

Part XIII, "Improving Network Security," covers very important material. As networks become more interconnected, especially to the Internet, understanding how security works for the operating systems on your network is a topic that cannot be pushed to the side. In this part you will find chapters covering things such as how to create a basic security policy, tools to use to set up security mechanisms, and the auditing tools that you can use to later review the data collected by each system. Because an Internet connection is becoming almost a given for most business LANs today, Chapter 36, "Firewalls," will be of help to many readers who are about to make this connection. Another hot topic, encryption, is covered in Chapter 38.

Parts XIV, "Upgrading Hardware," XV, "Network Operating Systems," and XVI, "Hybrid Networks," cover more general topics, drawing from concepts described in earlier chapters of the book. Here you will find chapters that give you information you will need when upgrading from one hardware topology to another, such as from 10Base-T to faster ethernet technologies, or from token ring or ARCnet to an ethernet network. Next are chapters that cover migrating from one operating system to another and chapters that discuss the merits and pitfalls of integrating multiple operating systems and networking technologies in a single network.

The last part of this book consists of appendixes that contain information in a concise format that can be a valuable reference during troubleshooting or planning operations. A review of the OSI seven-layer networking reference model is explained in Appendix A, while other appendixes talk about common port assignments for the TCP and UPD protocols, cabling specifications used for different network technologies, and NetWare logon scripting commands. If you are interested in either Novell's NDS or Microsoft's Active Directory (AD), Appendix E will be a useful introduction into the X.500 and LDAP protocols that heavily influenced these products.

What's New in This Edition?

This Second Edition of *Upgrading and Repairing Networks* is a complete rewrite. Topics have been divided into chapters that concentrate on finer details than in the previous edition, making it easier to locate information when you are in a hurry. Entirely new topics have been added based on feedback to the First Edition and on many new technologies that have become important since the last publication. To assist in this, several contributing authors were brought on board to help, each a veteran in the computer book publishing field as well as experts in their areas of networking.

Part I

BASICS OF NETWORK TROUBLESHOOTING

Strategies

With network troubleshooting, as with any other form of computer troubleshooting, two approaches can be taken. One approach is reactive: Network support personnel wait until actual problems are reported before taking steps to resolve them. Because networks are made, not born, and grow over long periods of time with many changes made by many hands, this type of approach is doomed to fail.

A far better approach to network troubleshooting is a proactive approach. In a proactive approach, information about the network's physical and logical characteristics are gathered and made available to network support personnel and users before actual problems are reported. The proactive approach does not assume that a network will never fail. Instead it understands that some degree of network problems from time to time are normal and typical.

Documentation that describes the network's components accurately, network maps that chart the network's layout, FAQs that help users navigate and use network resources, structured problem-solving procedures, and project documentation are tools and techniques that can be used successfully with networks of any size to anticipate and avoid problems and make solutions to network problems easy to achieve.

Documenting the Existing Network Infrastructure

Documentation of the network is the lifeblood of any successful network troubleshooting and management strategy. To be successful, a documentation strategy needs to have the following elements:

- Default settings for workstations and servers
- Network versions and workstation software versions
- Logical map of the network
- Physical map of the network
- Cabling and patch panel information
- User and group information and permissions
- Frequently asked questions (FAQs)

In the following sections, you'll discover the best tools to document your network, the best places to store that information to allow access by the appropriate people, and who should have access to the different levels of network information.

Basic Documentation Tools

Word processors and spreadsheets are two basic documentation tools that can be used with any network of any size to gather, summarize, and report on the pieces of the network. Here is how to use a word processor to document your network.

First, use the table feature found in modern word-processing programs such as Microsoft Word and Corel WordPerfect to create a list of the items. Your table should include the items you want to record, what program or file you will use as a source for that information, and a place for notes. In Table 1.1, the items shown in boldface represent a blank table. The items in italics indicate entries you can make during the documentation process.

Table 1.1   Sample Listing of Items to Document for a Departmental Workstation

Item	Source	File	Most Recent File Date/Time
Workstation Name	*Registry via REGEDIT*	*C:\Windows\Worksta\Nameinfo.REG*	*Feb 2, 2000 11:21P*
	HKEY_LOCAL_MACHINE\System\CurrentControlSet\Services\VxD\VNETSUP		
Workstation IP Configuration	*Registry via REGEDIT*	*C:\Windows\Worksta\Ipinfo.REG*	*Feb 2, 2000 9:57P*
	HKEY_LOCAL_MACHINE\System\CurrentControlSet\Services\Class\NetTrans\0002		
Login script	*(none)*		
Network Registry Keys, INF file, and drivers	*HWDIAG.EXE*	*C:\Windows\Worksta\Netreport.rtf*	*Feb 1, 2000 6:22A*
Network Card Configuration	*Device Manager— Network Card— (print report to Generic/TextOnly printer)*	*C:\Windows\Worksta\NIC.txt*	*Feb 2, 2000 8:42P*

Next, incorporate the files you create with the appropriate tool into your master document.

Note that in the documentation list, three important sources for workstation configuration are

- The Windows 9x Registry via Regedit.exe (a standard part of Windows 95/98)
- The Hwdiag.exe utility (supplied on the Windows 95 OSR 2.x CD-ROM)
- Device Manager (report)

Regedit can output either the entire Registry or a selected branch as a file with an REG extension. This file is actually a plain-text (ANSI) file. Hwdiag.exe can output color-coded configuration information in RTF (Rich Text Format), or ANSI files. If you install a Generic/Text-Only printer and configure it to output to FILE, you can send plain-text reports out from programs that lack a File-Save option by "printing" the report to disk. If you are using a leading word-processor such as Microsoft Word or Corel WordPerfect to assemble your documentation, you can insert any of these file types into your main document through the programs' File-Insert features.

Typically, you can import or export any of the following file formats: RTF (Rich Text Format), MS Word 6.0/7.0 DOC, MS Word 97 DOC, WordPerfect 6.x WPD, and ASCII or ANSI (plain text) TXT. In some cases, you might need to perform a custom installation to add the correct import/export filter.

Automating the Document-Assembly Process

A large network will involve the assembly of many pieces of text into a whole. To make this process as simple as possible, consider using the *master document* feature of Microsoft Word and Corel WordPerfect. A master document is a skeletal document that contains links to subdocuments you specify. When you "expand" the master document, the subdocuments are incorporated into the master document, making a single document from its parts. Although both Microsoft Word and Corel WordPerfect offer this feature, the Corel WordPerfect implementation is significantly easier and faster to use, and the instructions listed here are based on it. (Microsoft Word will require you to convert the subdocuments into Word format before you can create the master document using styles.)

Detailed Procedure (Corel WordPerfect Version 8 and Above)

1. Create (or plan to create) the subdocuments. Use the programs listed earlier to create subdocuments. Any file that can be converted by WordPerfect can be used as a subdocument. Make a listing of the filenames you create or plan to create, and use the same filenames for the same data at each workstation or server whose configuration you record.

2. Create a master document. Create a document. Place headings throughout the text where you'd like to insert the contents of subdocuments.

3. Insert references to subdocuments in the master document. Place your cursor on the line following the first heading and use File, Document, Subdocument. Select a file, or enter the name of the file you want to insert. *Hint:* Because you are planning to reuse this master document over and over again, enter the names of the subdocument you want. If you don't specify a drive or folder, the reference is to a document in the same folder as the master. A small icon representing the subdocument is displayed on the left edge of the document with an arrow pointing down to it (see Figure 1.1).

   Move to the next heading, and repeat as needed until you have added references to all subdocuments. Save the master document.

4. Expand the master document with subdocuments (see Figure 1.2). Copy the master document to the folder containing the subdocuments it refers to. Start WordPerfect and open the master document. Select File, Document, Expand Master. Each subdocument will be opened. Because these documents aren't in WordPerfect format, you'll be prompted to accept the default conversion from option (ASCII/DOS Text); accept it for each document and they will be incorporated into the master document.

5. Save the expanded master document under a different name. Save the resulting expanded document under a unique name (such as the computer's name or IP address). When you close the master document, enter NO when prompted to save changes.

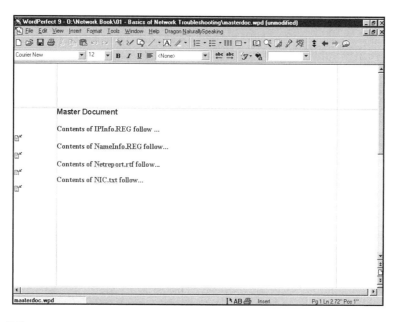

Figure 1.1 A WordPerfect 9 master document containing subdocument links. Each symbol on the left edge of the document represents a subdocument.

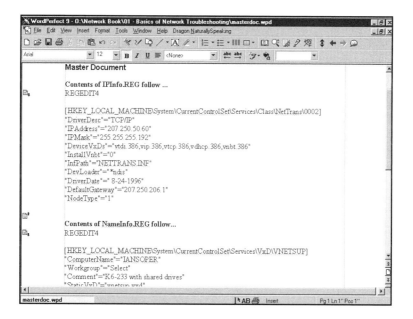

Figure 1.2 A WordPerfect 9 master document after expanding the subdocuments. The subdocument symbols are paired; each pair contains the contents of a single subdocument.

Repeat steps 4 and 5 for each system containing these documents.

Incorporating and Outputting Other Types of Network Information with Word Processors and Spreadsheets

Although some network information can be extracted in purely textual form, other types of network information useful for documentation might need to be converted to text format or incorporated into a document in their native forms.

For example, although the System Monitor feature for Windows 9x workstations is extremely useful for viewing CPU utilization, network activity, memory size, and other important factors for evaluating workstation performance, it completely lacks any report feature. To capture a snapshot of unusual system activity, you must literally take a snapshot of the System Monitor screen with the Print Screen key, paste it into a graphics program such as Microsoft Paint, and save it as a graphic file. This file can be added to a workstation report created as in the previous section. To allow the graphic to be updated as the system's condition changes, include a link to the graphic rather than including the graphic itself in your document. Then, refresh the link when a new version of the graphic has been created.

The Windows NT and Windows 2000 version of this utility, the Performance Monitor, offers both real-time graphic readouts onscreen and a log file that can be exported into tab-delimited or comma-delimited text formats, either of which can be imported into a spreadsheet or database program for further analysis or publishing.

Because of their design, spreadsheet programs such as Microsoft Excel, Lotus 1-2-3, and Quattro Pro are appropriate choices for gathering simple network information that can be exported to a database program for permanent storage (see Figure 1.3).

Because graphics from all types of sources (including screen shots, flowcharts, and network maps) can be incorporated into your master documents, spreadsheets can be imported as tables, and HTML pages (from intranet or Internet sources) can be imported and exported, you can use a word-processing program as your main documentation source.

Web Pages and Acrobat Files

After you've created network documentation for a workstation, a server, or any other part of your network, you must make it as accessible as possible. The latest versions of Microsoft Word and Corel WordPerfect can export documents into HTML and Adobe Acrobat PDF formats. These formats are widely supported and allow network documentation to be viewed by users from the network or local drives by using a Web browser (HTML) or Adobe Acrobat Reader (PDF).

HTML or Acrobat?

Which you choose is a decision that should be influenced by several factors, including

■ **How complex is the documentation?** If the documentation is primarily text-based (such as logon procedures, system configuration settings, and IP addresses) with no or limited graphics and you plan to distribute it primarily online, HTML pages will work nicely. For maximum utility, consider adding bookmarks to logical sections with hyperlinks from the beginning of the document to make navigation easier.

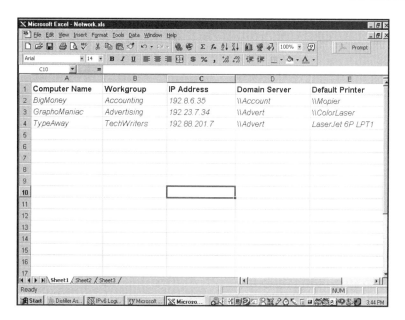

Figure 1.3   Basic network configuration data for workstations can be stored in a spreadsheet, which can then be sorted by server name, by IP address, or by other criteria.

■ **Do you want documentation for viewing only, or for printing?** Although HTML pages are easy to produce and view with any recent Web browser, keep in mind that it's difficult to print even moderately complex Web pages correctly. A "printer-friendly" Web page often loses the hybrid characteristics that make HTML pages useful (use of graphics and hyperlinking).

If the documentation contains a lot of visual elements and has complex formatting and you want to use the same document for online viewing or printing, I recommend Adobe Acrobat. Acrobat files can be generated by Corel WordPerfect 9 (part of Corel WordPerfect Office 2000) and can be viewed or printed with 100 percent fidelity across many different platforms. Acrobat pages can also be hyperlinked and can be used to launch external programs.

If you want to create both HTML and Acrobat pages, consider the work savings you can achieve by purchasing Adobe Acrobat 4, which can automatically create Acrobat PDF files from existing HTML pages.

Creating an Internal Web Site for Network Help and Troubleshooting

Here's how you can create a Web site with useful content that will help your users with networking problems. It's assumed that you have an intranet server of some sort on your network where the pages will reside.

You'll need to create the following pages available to all network users:

- FAQ page
- Troubleshooting page
- Examples page

You might also want to create a Welcome page to introduce users to the site and provide hyper-links to the other pages. This page will be displayed automatically when intranet users go to the address of the help site (such as `http://gethelp.com`). Depending on the Web-server software your network uses, this page will need to be named `default.htm`, `Index.html`, `index.htm`, or a similar name. Ask your network administrator or Webmaster for the correct name to use and for FTP (file transfer protocol) instructions to transfer the pages when complete.

Technical Considerations

These pages can be created with any HTML editor, including the HTML options built into Microsoft Word and Corel WordPerfect. Most HTML editors can convert existing Microsoft Word (DOC), WordPerfect (WPD), Rich Text Format (RTF), and plain-text (TXT) files into HTML pages, although some loss of formatting will occur. This conversion process also allows you to "recycle" existing computer data you use for tech-support and help into Web content. If you've lost (or never had) the data files for some printed help matter, scan it with OmniPage or other OCR/page-recognition software to convert it back into a data file.

Limitations of HTML

Because HTML formatting is much simpler than word-processor formatting, you should avoid elaborate document effects in your source files. Add effects and hyperlinks in your HTML editor. This loss of formatting is true even if you use your word processor as an HTML editor; WordPerfect, for example, warns that saving documents as HTML results in the loss of some document features. Microsoft Office 2000's native HTML support requires Internet Explorer 5 for its full effect. With other browsers, a complex document cannot be rendered with all its bells and whistles intact.

GIF and JPEG File Formats

The graphics in the pages must be converted into GIF or JPG files from their native file formats at a resolution of no more than 96dpi for screen use.

GIF is the preferred format for line drawings or simple color objects (such as screen captures) because it can display no more than 256 colors but does so with very small file sizes. You can control the size of the graphics file by the number of colors (16 to 256) you display. JPEG is the format to choose if you need to display photographs on your Web pages. To reduce file sizes, JPEG files can be stored with varying degrees of compression. Avoid over-compressing a JPEG file because the compression used by JPEG is *lossy*—fine image data is discarded at ever-increasing amounts as higher compression (smaller file sizes) are selected. And, the lost details can never be restored to a JPEG file.

Use programs such as CorelDraw, Adobe Photoshop 5.5, or Ulead PhotoImpact to convert images to the correct type, color depth, dimensions, and file size.

Contents of the Help Site Pages

Besides the Welcome page (typically `Index.html`), your help site on the Web should contain several other pages.

A FAQ Page

This page of frequently asked questions (FAQs) should be a listing of popular network questions and answers. See "Create Your Own FAQ List," later in this chapter for details.

A Troubleshooting Page

This page provides simple instructions for solving common problems. Solutions on this page should fall into the "first, do no harm!" category, so any discussion of using powerful, dangerous tools such as `Regedit.exe` doesn't belong here. Instead, provide instructions for using programs such as WINIPCFG, PING, and other utility programs that provide information about the workstation and the network connection.

An Examples Page

This page has a similar objective to the Troubleshooting page listed earlier but can provide step-by-step instructions for users who are unfamiliar with the programs listed on the Troubleshooting page. If you want to take the time, you could even use Lotus ScreenCam to create movies of typical processes that might be difficult for some users. To allow the movies to play back on systems lacking the native ScreenCam player, record them as either standalone EXE files (for users with Windows 9x) or as AVI files you can play back with standard media playback programs.

Each of these pages should be hyperlinked to the others, as Figure 1.4 demonstrates. In this figure, a user with a question would first pull up the FAQ page and could link from that page to the Troubleshooting page for more information on the recommended solution (along with a screen shot). A link from the Troubleshooting page can take the user to the Examples page, which provides step-by-step directions, and can even have a ScreenCam movie link, as shown here. Either page links back to the FAQ page.

It's important to offer the user a specific link to return to the original FAQ page after trying the more specific help pages.

Management and Security Considerations

As with any intranet content, the help site should be protected from unauthorized changes. FTP access to this site should be restricted to authorized help-site personnel only. To avoid a "too many cooks" syndrome, consider using a single employee to manage coordination of help files on the server.

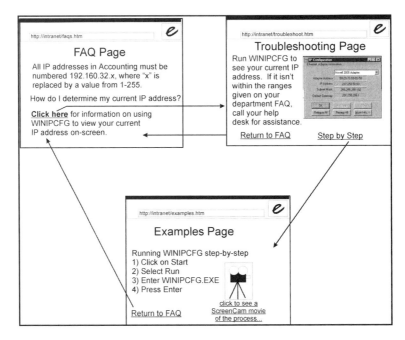

Figure 1.4   A multipage network help and troubleshooting Web site.

Securing Access to Patches and Configuration Information

Because HTML pages can be used as "containers" for virtually any type of data, it's worth considering copying the tech support sites of companies like Microsoft and others, which place technical notes on Web pages along with links to program patches and updates. This allows the information to be available from any workstation, but this type of information should be password-protected to avoid use by unauthorized personnel. Because any Web-based information must be physically downloaded to the viewing computer, technicians who access a corporate Web site with restricted information from an ordinary workstation (for reconfiguration and so on) should take the following steps after they finish using the computer:

- Use the Clear Disk Cache and Clear Memory Cache options in the browser.
- Close the browser immediately.
- Use utility software that overwrites empty/erased space to remove any traces of the secured pages. The SpeedDisk defragmenter (a part of Norton Utilities) allows this during defragmenting as an option. If such a program isn't available, defragmenting the workstation's drive with the standard Microsoft 9x defragmenter will minimize the chances of secured data being retrieved from the local hard drive.

Resources for Network Upgrading and Repairing News

Information is clearly the most valuable commodity to anyone embarking on the voyage of upgrading or repairing a network. That said, there are several resources at your disposal for staying informed about new technologies and developments.

Tap the Web

Manufacturers' Web sites are among the best sources for detailed information about any piece of network hardware and software. Advice, horror stories, tips, and tricks are also available from the Web through mailing lists, newsgroups, and user forums for products.

To get the most benefit from the vast, poorly arranged riches of the Web, use these tips:

First, make sure you know *exactly* what version of server and workstation software, hardware, operating system, BIOS, drivers, and so on, you're using. Problems with original and early releases of network operating systems, office suites, BIOSes, printer drivers, and other software and firmware are frequently solved by later releases. For example, many serious problems with Windows NT 4 can be solved by installing the latest service pack. In some cases, the latest service pack or patch isn't sufficient; you must "layer" the original release of some products with a series of service packs to achieve the desired stability, year 2000 compliance, and features. This is the case with Microsoft Office 97. You must install both SR-1 and SR-2b service packs in that order if you have the original release. Installing patches out of order could cause serious problems with software or system stability.

Find out from the vendor of your product where the version or release information is reported so you aren't looking for "solutions" to problems you don't have. Typical sources for exact release information include the dates of key DLL (dynamic link library files) for the application, the release or version number listed in "Help/About *this application*," or, in the case of Windows 9x operating systems, a VER command at a command prompt.

Second, build a database of the tech-support Web sites (or at least the main URL), telephone numbers, and fax numbers for all your hardware and software vendors. While big vendors such as Microsoft and Cisco are easy to remember, remember how unforgiving the Web is of typos and mispunctuation. To create this list with Netscape Communicator, you can bookmark the sites in your browser, retrieve your bookmark.htm file into an HTML editor, add notes, and you've got the list of sites you rely on.

Third, consider posting the most common patches and technical notes from the vendor on your own intranet. This will have several benefits, including

■ Reducing the amount of network traffic flowing to and from the Web

■ Faster retrieval of these resources from a local server than from a frequently overworked vendor server

■ Better management and control of approved patches and technical information

If you decide on this strategy, make sure you take advantage of vendor notifications and updates to keep your "mini-site" up-to-date. Microsoft Office, Internet Explorer, Outlook, and various versions of Windows are among the most frequently updated programs commonly used on networks.

Sources for Detailed Information

Reports you can generate from enterprise-management software such as Hewlett-Packard's OpenView, CA's Unicenter, IBM's Tivoli, Intel's LANDesk Manager (see Figure 1.5), and others, can be used to help give you a "big-picture" view of large networks. These products are designed to manage product compliance with SNMP (the Simple Network Management Protocol) and can report on every device with an IP address, from workstations and servers to printers, routers, and managed hubs. Because they are designed to work with products from many vendors, they might not always display the detailed information necessary for full disclosure of any particular network device. However, thanks to the advanced management features in many of today's computer systems, details of operating systems, BIOS versions, and application programs can be retrieved remotely with these programs for analysis and control from a central console.

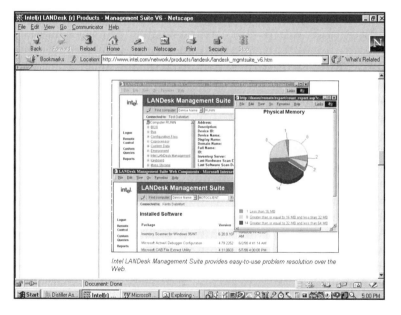

Figure 1.5 Intel's LANDesk Management Suite allows browser-based administration of networks and workstations.

For more information about network-management software, protocol analyzers, and other tools for viewing network configuration and traffic, see Chapter 2, "Tools."

Benefits of Vendor-Specific Programs for Network Component Management

When available, you might want to use the vendor-specific management programs supplied by companies such as Cisco, Intel, and many others to support their own products. For smaller networks using managed products from a single vendor, free management software tools supplied by the vendor might be more than sufficient.

For example, Intel's Device View works with a wide variety of Intel network products, including Intel Express hubs, switches, print servers, and routers. Device View provides automatic device discovery, your choice of Web-based or Windows 9x/NT workstation-based control, GUI-based views of hardware, network traffic, and support for RMON (remote monitoring) and configuration of supported devices. Device View is supplied with several Intel network products and can also be downloaded at no charge from Intel's Web site.

If your network contains managed products from a variety of vendors, you can use multiple vendor-specific management tools, or you might find it preferable to make the investment in one of the enterprise-management programs listed earlier. In addition to supporting multiple vendors' products, these programs also allow for more extensive logging and history-tracking functions, making it easier to look at the long-term changes in the condition of your network.

Some enterprise-management programs, such as LANDesk, are designed to allow you to incorporate product-specific management tools, providing you with the best of both worlds: the "big picture" of all network devices, and the most specific information possible from vendor-specific management programs.

Both enterprise-level and the more capable, single-vendor management products can be useful in determining the performance level of your network. By logging network performance over time and comparing current numbers of workstations and traffic to past values, you can use these programs to help plan for upgrades, the topic of the next section.

Lifecycle Maintenance and Budgeting

All network hardware and software have a particular life cycle. To gain the best "bang for the buck" from the network investment, it's important to understand how often upgrading hardware and software is really beneficial.

This calculation is not merely technical. Because of differences in tax laws, depreciation schedules, and whether investments can be written off the same year or must be depreciated, decisions about the hardware and software for the life-cycle of any network are financial as well as technical. Here are some general considerations that should be followed when gauging the expected life-cycle of any part of the network for budgeting purposes.

First, look at the desired performance of the component and estimate whether that component will perform adequately for one, two, or three years. To determine this, consider the following issues.

For servers, a noticeable drop in server performance as additional workstations are added is a sure sign that there is a bottleneck somewhere in the server-to-workstation link. Because this drop in performance can be caused by many factors, look carefully at all the following before adopting an upgrade strategy:

- Disk array performance
- CPU utilization
- Memory size and cache memory performance
- NIC (network interface card) performance
- Excessive number of users per network segment

You can often use utilities included with your network operating system to help you compare present and past server performance. For example, Microsoft's Performance Monitor (included with Windows NT 4.0 and Windows 2000) can be used to monitor all the potential bottlenecks listed above. Reports from the NT Performance Monitor can be output to tab-delimited or comma-delimited text formats, either of which can be imported into spreadsheet programs such as Microsoft Excel for analysis.

To get the most from a utility like Performance Monitor, it's best to run it as soon as possible after each major change to a network (initial server installation, adding workstations, and so on) to provide a baseline for determining problems and solutions later.

For workstations, determine the current CPU type and speed, operating system, and amount of RAM and compare these items to the requirements and desired levels for your favorite network-based applications. When a workstation's configuration drops below the recommended levels for your most important applications, it should be upgraded or replaced. In order of priority, memory (RAM) should be the first hardware item upgraded, followed by hard drives and video cards. CPU upgrades can be useful but tend to be very expensive for newer systems.

For more information about detecting and preventing excessive network demands and other bottlenecks, see Chapter 16, "Design Rules."

Next, look at the issue of "new" versus "needed" upgrades. While the rapid pace of hardware and software changes often encourage individual users to make frequent changes, depending on the tasks that the network must perform, this technological "churn" might not really be necessary. A review every two years of network components such as servers, switches, hubs, and routers is typical. Using network monitoring software programs referred to in earlier parts of this chapter is an important part of this review. If performance of key network components is acceptable, an upgrade is generally not needed.

The factors that must be considered in life-cycle maintenance and budgeting include the following:

- Replacement cost of each item in the budget.
- Training and deployment costs.

- Ancillary costs caused by a replacement's other components when a particular component is upgraded; for example, changing from Fast Ethernet to Gigabit Ethernet requires changing cable in wiring closets, re-qualifying other cable, changing server NICs, and so forth.

Although network gear is going through the same price revolution as other types of computer hardware, budgets should probably not be cut as a consequence. Because today's IT departments have fewer employees, less time to complete tasks, tougher requirements from end users and management, and a stream of new technology to evaluate, money spent on smarter, easier to maintain and upgrade technology is money saved in the long run. For example, many current routers and switches from a variety of vendors can be managed remotely from a Web-based or Windows-based workstation, making trips to the physical location of the device less necessary.

Some good rules of thumb to follow in life-cycle maintenance and budgeting are

- Favor stability over raw performance
- Increase performance by building on existing technologies with upgrades
- Upgrade only when true business benefits arise (such as cost savings from remote management)
- Beware of upgrades made for the sake of upgrading

These rules, applied to your network, will enable you to get the most out of your network investments.

For example, you can keep your existing Fast Ethernet server configuration but increase its throughput by adding load-balancing server NICs to your servers. This upgrade is stable, builds on existing technology, and provides a true business benefit of greater throughput for the network.

Software changes should be considered just as carefully because they will involve massive retraining of users, whether it's an operating system change, an email or network client change, or an office suite change. While Y2K fears have driven many upgrades performed in 1998 and 1999, the start of the new millennium might be a good time to jump off the "annual software change" bandwagon. If a software program really delivers improvements to basic business functionality; creates value beyond its purchase, installation, and support cost; and doesn't create hidden replacement dependencies, it's worth considering.

For example, an office suite upgrade that isn't compatible with existing file formats, uses a non-standard version of HTML for its "HTML-enabled" features, or uses a method of coping with two-digit dates for Y2K compliance that doesn't match your standard, should be approached with caution.

If you're planning a new network, consider the virtues of KISS (Keep It Simple, Stupid!) in terms of hardware and software alike. Using standardized workstations, especially if good management features are available, will enable you to "clone" a standard software configuration easily from one system to the rest and also make BIOS and firmware upgrades easier to roll out and manage. The trend toward a single protocol (TCP/IP) and away from the crazy-quilt use of multiple protocols used in the past (NetBEUI for Windows for Workgroups and Windows NT, IPX for NetWare, and TCP/IP for Internet) will also make maintenance and troubleshooting easier.

Regardless of the size of your network, avoid the temptation to buy the "NIC of the week" or the "router of the month" as you add stations. Lack of standardization here as with the workstations or servers will add layers of potential incompatibilities to your network, as well as management problems.

The Network Map

A vital tool for troubleshooting an existing network or planning upgrades is the network map. Network maps come in two forms: the *logical* and *physical*. Both types of network maps are useful and should be completed for any network, large or small.

Logical Versus Physical

The logical network map is designed to help network users and support personnel understand how the network functions. For example, a logical map typically indicates what servers use which network operating system, what parts of the network use what type of cabling, and the general relationship of switches to network servers. It can also list IP addresses or domain names. A physical map indicates the details of which routers connect to what servers, what rooms the equipment is located in, and which patch panels are connected to what equipment.

Live examples of logical and physical network maps are available online at the Florida International University's School of Computer Science Web site. Figure 1.6 shows the school's logical map as it appears online at www.cs.fiu.edu/support/netmaps/logical.

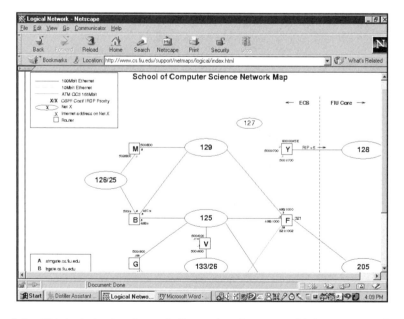

Figure 1.6 This logical network map indicates domain names with letters, uses color-coded lines to indicate different network cabling standards, and allows the viewer to click on routers for more detail.

Figure 1.7 shows the school's logical map as it appears online at
`www.cs.fiu.edu/support/netmaps/physical`.

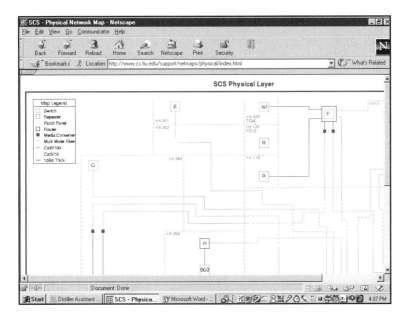

Figure 1.7   This physical network map uses color-coding to represent different network components. The viewer can click on routers for more detail.

How to Create a Logical Map of the Network

A logical map of the network can be drawn with tools as low-tech as pencil and paper, graphics programs such as Microsoft Paint or CorelDraw, or with specialized flow-chart software. Whatever tool you choose to create a logical network map, follow the rules listed here:

- Use standardized symbols to indicate workstations, routers, servers, cables, and printers, among other components. If you use a program such as Visio to create your logical map, you can take advantage of powerful database "hooks" built into the product that will help you build an accurate chart that can change as the underlying data changes.

- Label the standardized symbols clearly.

- Keep the logical map as simple as possible in its graphic design; your logical map may wind up in locations as diverse as a printout in a three-ring binder, a graphic on an HTML page, a sketch in a printed document, or in an Adobe Acrobat PDF file. Use of color, as with the maps shown earlier, is effective when color reproduction or live viewing is possible but doesn't reproduce well with monochrome inkjet or laser printers. You might need to create different versions for online and printed use.

How to Create a Physical Map of the Network

A physical map of the network deals with the hardware side of networking. While a logical map of a network should be as simple as possible to convey the information desired, a physical map of the network should be drawn in more detail. The Florida International University physical map is a typical online example, showing the approximate layout of components but lacking details about switches, hubs, or routers in use. Because a physical map of the network deals with hubs, routers, wiring closets, and other details, the user of accurate pre-drawn clip art is highly desirable. You may be able to find examples of the images needed in the vendor documentation, or at the vendor sites online. Because poorly marked cabling and sketchy physical maps are major causes of network support headaches, don't stop with a good physical map of the network. Each component of the network, from a workstation to a server to all the wiring and physical connections between them, should be clearly labeled.

Labeling Standards for the Network

Depending on the component to be labeled, there are several different methods that can be used to name the network components. Some naming methods depend on the network protocol, while others can be applied to any type of network.

On a TCP/IP-based network, the TCP/IP address can be used to label any components that use a static TCP/IP address. However, since many TCP/IP-based networks also use Dynamic Host Configuration Protocol (DHCP) to dynamically assign IP addresses, use of a friendly name (Charlie, PrintServer, and so on) is also a good idea. Table 1.2 provides recommendations for labeling network components by their type, what protocol they use, and what the label should list.

Table 1.2   **Recommended Labeling Methods for Network Components**

Component	Method	Protocol
Server, workstation, router, etc.	TCP/IP address	TCP/IP
Server, workstation, router, etc.	IPX name	IPX
Server, workstation	Unit name	NetBEUI, IPX
Any	Name	Any
Cable	Connected items	Any

Obviously, naming conventions by themselves won't help your network unless the names are attached to the components and recorded correctly. Use a label maker such as the Brother P-Touch or similar systems to create legible labels that can be attached to equipment. The following examples show recommended labels for different types of equipment:

> Workstation:
>
> NAME—Mark's Box
>
> IP Address—192.0.1.23
>
> Location—3rd floor, Suite 324
>
> OS—Windows 98 2nd Edition

Server:

NAME—The Big Kahuna

IP Address—192.0.1.0

Domain—

OS—Novell NetWare 5.0

Cable:

From—Mark's Box

To—The Big Kahuna

Create Your Own FAQ List

Thanks to the Internet, documents that contain FAQs have become a common way of distributing information about the most common questions that users have about any given topic. To help you develop your own list of FAQs, consider these issues:

- What does the user need to about the system?
- Whom should the user call or email for help?
- Where are configuration changes made that will help a user solve minor problems himself?

To develop a list of FAQs, work with the users in your organization. Keep in mind the goal of a good list of FAQs is to provide users with the answers to the most common questions.

Publishing Your FAQ

Where should FAQ information be located? One obvious answer is on the company intranet. However, if the user cannot log on to his or her system, if the FAQ list is only available online, and the answer to the question is only available online, the FAQ list can't help the user. Make sure, therefore, that users have access to technical support and common questions by other means. At the very least, every user should have the telephone number for the technical support center available. You may want to consider adding a prerecorded message that provides information on a how to successfully log on to the system.

After the FAQ list has been developed, it can be published using any of the methods discussed earlier: printed, Internet, intranet, or PDF. For Web-based FAQ lists, provide a method for users to give you feedback. Make sure that an email address is listed, and if possible, add a feedback form to the FAQ document. Providing a method for feedback will improve the quality of the FAQ list, especially if users believe that their comments are important and if you demonstrate that user comments will give rise to improvements in the FAQ contents.

FAQ Design

If your FAQ will be available via the Web (either public or intranet), design it to be easily readable. If it's longer than two screen pages, consider putting headings at the top that cross-reference to the appropriate sections beneath (using bookmarks). This design will allow the FAQs to be printed as a single document, which is better than the alternative method of creating separate FAQ documents with hyperlinks for each major topic.

Structured Problem Solving

This chapter began by discussing documentation methods, because without detailed and accurate information about the makeup of the network, fast and accurate troubleshooting is not possible. The troubleshooting method known as the *problem resolution cycle* builds on accurate information about the network to help solve and prevent problems. This method uses a question-and-answer technique to determine what Jerry Pournelle has called the key to troubleshooting, "What's changed since the last time it worked?"

The Problem Resolution Cycle

The problem resolution cycle is a method that is designed to meet two needs: solve the immediate problem that prevents the network from working and provide insights as to the cause of the failure to allow improvements in network operation in the future.

The elements of all successful structure problems always include the following:

- Accurate description of symptoms
- Complete description of symptoms
- Understanding the events happening within any and all network processes
- Solving the underlying problem rather than just working around the symptoms
- Providing a follow-up mechanism for recording and distributing solutions to problems
- Development of a problem and solution tracking system to minimize "reinventing the wheel" when solving problems

In a way, structured problem solving is a form of "digital medicine." The comparison is apt because a single symptom can be associated with more than one problem, and the more symptoms that are known about a problem, the easier it is to provide an accurate solution.

Let's take a simple example to illustrate the issue:

A user loses contact with the network. The initial symptom reported is that the user can't print to a network printer. This single symptom is not sufficient information to provide a reasoned solution.

The following is a typical structured problem-solving process for this problem:

1. Can you log on to the network? If the user can do so, the network itself can be ruled out as a cause.

2. Can the user print to other network printers? If this user can't, make sure the user has permission to use that printer, and check the workstation's printer drivers. If the user is using a Print icon found on some programs (which prints to the default printer) and the network printer is not the default, the user should either use a Print command that provides an option for choosing the target printer or set the network printer as the default.

3. Can other users print to the same network printer? If nobody can use the printer, the problem is probably at the printer itself or in the network connection to the printer.

Sometimes the first symptom reported leads to others:

1. The user tries to log on to the network, but can't. First, examine the physical connections between the workstation and the server. Are cables connected correctly? Are they damaged? If the cabling is defective, nobody will be able to use the network, so check this first.

2. Does another username work on the workstation? If so, check the username and password for the first user. Some networks are configured to allow accounts to expire after a given period of time unless they are renewed. Make sure the user is on the current list, and assign a new password if necessary. Encourage the user to change to a new password as soon as they log on.

3. Do other users of the same server have the same problem with logons? If so, determine if the users connect to the same hub or wiring closet.

By using this procedure, we determined that

- All file and print services using the given server had stopped working.
- The hub used to interconnect the server and workstations was not at fault because other workstations were able to communicate with each other.

These factors pointed to a problem with either the server or the wiring going to the server. When the server itself was examined, we found it had locked up, which caused every logon or print request to fail.

The long-term solution involves making sure the server's software is up-to-date and installed correctly, making sure there is adequate physical and virtual memory available for processing client requests, and checking memory modules and power and data cables inside and outside the drive for correct fit, corrosion, and dust.

A symptomatic approach to the problem could have led to a lot of unnecessary replacement of software and components.

Is There Really a Problem?

A big portion of network troubleshooting is understanding how to separate "glitches" from true problems. For years, I've lived by the rule that "if it happens once, it's a glitch. If it happens twice, it's a problem." Many momentary problems with an individual workstation can be "cured" by shutting down the system to power-down and restarting it.

Part of the problem resolution cycle is determining when a problem is really a problem. A good example of this happened a couple of years ago when I was working with a small network that had just converted from DOS-based clients to Windows 95-based clients. The difference in the logon process was daunting for some users. Many of the old systems that been replaced could do absolutely nothing without logging on to the network because they were diskless workstations running exclusively network-based software. The new Windows 95-based clients had hard drives and office suites, so users were able to do some of their work without logging on the network.

When users reported that they were unable to perform network tasks, a little bit of investigation determined that they had been clicking the Cancel button or pressing the Esc key during the login process for Microsoft Windows 95 instead of logging on the network. They were fooled because their new workstations now had the ability do some work without being on the network, and this was different than what they had experienced before. We determined that this was a problem by watching the users in question go through their normal startup procedure with their new workstations. We were able to replicate the problem by having them log on, which allowed them access to network resources, and watched them restart machines without logging on, which blocked access to network resources.

The ability to determine the difference between a true network problem and a case of user error is a very important one to develop. A classic joke in the computer support business is that the best solution is "restart the computer," but it's amazing how often that tip works, especially when users start up the system the way they're supposed to.

Have We Been Here Before?

Developing a means of tracking typical problems and solutions, even easy ones as in the case just described, is important to avoid the "reinventing the wheel" syndrome, in which every problem gets a brand-new solution.

Help-desk software available from many vendors can be used to automate the process of problem and solution tracking, but these so-called "expert systems" are only as good as their underlying databases. Make sure that you capture the specialized knowledge of your support personnel for re-use. You don't need anything more specialized than word-processing software to record solutions to typical problems, and you can use OCR software such as OmniPage to convert existing print-only troubleshooting information into computer format. Encourage your expert users and help desk workers to keep careful notes as they research and solve problems.

To reduce the recurrence of common problems, add the most common problems and solutions to your FAQ documents (see "Create Your Own FAQ" earlier in this chapter).

First Things First: The Process of Elimination

If you understand the process behind each network event, you can use the process of elimination to help narrow down the most likely causes of network problems, as in the example listed earlier. Now, let's take a closer look at the methods you need to use.

First, you'll want to get all the information possible about the systems in question. These types of questions were asked during the troubleshooting examples listed earlier, so we'll add the answers after the questions.

- What devices are in use?

  Case #1 (can't print): Workstation, file, and print servers

  Case #2 (no network with Win95): Workstation and file server

- What's unique about the system?

  Case #1: Nothing (system had been in use for some time)

  Case #2: New workstations with Windows 95

- What's common between this system and others?

  Case #1: Nobody can print or access files

  Case #2: Some users can use network, others can't

- What task was being performed?

  Case #1: Network printing

  Case #2: Network program and file access; printing

- Where is the system?

  This question didn't apply in either case but is useful when you suspect power-related or interference-related problems.

- What other systems share resources such as the hub, the router, the printer queue, the servers, and so on?

  Case #1: All systems shared hub, print queue, and server

  Case #2: All systems shared hub, print queue, and server

- Can the symptoms be reproduced?

  Case #1: Yes. All attempts by any user or the technician to print failed.

  Case #2: Yes and no. Initially, the answer was no because the technician (who was familiar with Win95 networking) logged in correctly and thus had access to network resources. But, after watching the user's (incorrect) startup procedures, the technician was able to reproduce the symptoms by skipping the logon prompt with the Esc key.

Look for patterns to the failure. In case #1 (can't print), the loss of all network services provided by the file/print server but the fact that others could communicate over the same hardware pointed back to the server as the most likely cause. In case #2 (no network with Windows 95), the pattern started with a new and unfamiliar operating system and logon process. When the technician was able to access network resources, it pointed toward possible user error, which was confirmed after studying the user's current startup procedure.

These examples were relatively straightforward, but often a network diagnosis isn't so simple. If a workstation uses multiple protocols, for example, does the symptom affect only IPX, only NetBEUI, only TCP/IP, or does it affect all protocols? Symptoms that affect only one or two protocols may point to problems outside an individual workstation, especially if other users report similar symptoms. Combining workstation programs such as the Windows 9x System Monitor with comparable server-based or network-based analysis programs can be useful in tracking down more complex problems at each end of the network. To isolate problems caused by cabling, use the cable-testing tools covered in Chapter 2.

Use the physical and logical maps of the network to help you determine the true cause of any given symptom. Check workstation and server configurations for the cause of protocol-dependent symptoms.

Project Documentation

Depending on whether the "project" is maintenance or a new network, there are several different approaches you can take to documenting where you've been and where you're going.

For a maintenance project (troubleshooting, upgrading, or tweaking), I like to write careful notes about existing and new configuration information as I make adjustments to a system. Windows 95 and 98 workstations have some useful tools to help record configuration information, including

WINIPCFG—Use Start, Run to launch this program, which lists the current TCP/IP configuration for the workstation, including hostname, DNS server, IP address, WINS servers, and much more. Capture the Windows-based utility screen to the Clipboard with Print Screen, paste it into Paint, and save it to keep a record.

PING—Run this from the MS-DOS prompt and enter an IP address or hostname. If you can't connect, you'll get a "Request Timed Out" for the four packets it sends by default.

You can check the loopback address to see if TCP/IP is installed properly: ping 127.0.0.1, and then try the workstation's TCP/IP address with ping. If you have problems with these, you may have a bad TCP/IP installation, a bad subnet number, or you might have forgotten to reboot after installing TCP/IP.

Device Manager, HWDIAG, and HWINFO—To check on physical settings (such as IRQs) and drivers for network or modem devices, you can use the Windows 9x Device Manager. For more complete information, some releases of Windows 95 and Internet Explorer feature the HWDIAG.EXE program, which lists hardware settings, INF files, and even registry keys for all hardware, including devices missed by the Device Manager. Windows 98 offers the similar HWINFO utility.

I like to record the changes I made to any system to create a "paper trail" for future troubleshooting. Gathering such information on previously undocumented systems should be a standard part of any routine service done to network workstations or servers.

When a new network is being installed, every component should be identified and its configuration recorded during the initial process. Depending on the component, you should record

- IP address and/or network ID
- Physical location
- Item category (server, workstation, hub, switch, router, and so on)
- Brand and model number
- Features (speeds, cable types supported, number of ports, SNMP support, and so on)
- Firmware revision and date
- Serial number
- Company-assigned identification

Detailed information like this will help make physical and logical mapping of the network easier.

Use network-testing and evaluation tools covered in Chapter 2 to determine the length of cable segments for mapping purposes.

The manuals, configuration programs, and other items that are supplied with any type of network component should be kept for future reference and clearly tagged as to which network component they belong to. When new workstations, servers, and other new equipment is being added, that's the best chance you'll ever have for recording settings, saving documentation, and creating workstation image files with programs such as Norton Ghost, ImageCast, or Drive Image.

Record and keep the information you'll need for future problem-solving before the forces of chaos "file it" in the wastebasket or on somebody's cluttered desktop.

Summary

Detailed information about all the elements of a network is vital to successful troubleshooting. As the network changes, configuration information must be updated to reflect the changes in the network. Take advantage of intranet technology to share technical support and user help information with network users to reduce the technical-support burden by helping users understand how to perform common tasks.

Tools

In a large network environment many tasks will be delegated to those who are particularly adept in a specific technology. But the administrator who sits at the top of the management ladder must understand the principles under which the network functions and the tools that are used to keep it in good working order. In this chapter, we will discuss the basic tools that are used to examine the underlying structure of the network (the cables) as well as those used to pick apart the semantics of the communication process (packets and protocols).

Basics: Testing Cables

A network consists of end user workstations connected to servers by what might appear at first to be a tangled web of wires and cables. If the building or campus is wired correctly, though, this is not a jumble of cables joined together in a spaghetti fashion, but is an orderly collection of components much like a spider's web, fanning out to connect everyone in a hierarchical manner.

When you begin to build a network, the first thing you must do is install the cables that will connect the servers and workstations. This can done when a building is being constructed, as is the case in most office buildings today. Or, it can involve placing cable ducts in ceilings and knocking out walls to install faceplates where the cables terminate. Either way, before you begin to connect end users to the network, you must test the cables that are installed to be sure that they are performing as expected.

Testing devices range from inexpensive hand-held devices that a cable installer can use to check their work to very expensive devices that require a skilled technician in order to perform their tests. Things that are usually tested include the following:

- Cable length
- Resistance
- Noise
- Attenuation
- Near-end cross-talk

Two basic instruments are used to test cables. The first is the cable checker, which is used to determine that the cable actually provides an electrical path from here to there. The second is the cable tester, which can determine whether the cable has been installed correctly to support the topology of your network, taking into consideration things such as cable length and cross-talk.

Hand-Held Cable Checkers

This inexpensive device is usually a small battery-operated unit that can be used to check STP or UTP cables.

If the cable is already attached to a network device, you will have to disconnect it and attach it to the unit. A cable checker operates by placing a voltage on a wire and determining whether it can be detected at the opposite end. This can be used to determine whether the cable has a break anywhere along its path and can be useful when trying to determine if you are looking at the same cable on both ends when several cables are traversing a single path. Most cable checkers consist of two components that you attach to opposite ends of the cable.

Cable Testers

This type of device is a step up from the basic checker. It can be used to measure near-end cross-talk, attenuation, impedance, and noise on a line. Some will even perform length measurements, both the total cable and the distance to a fault on the line. Another function you might see is wire-mapping, which checks to be sure that the correct wire pairs in a cable have been mapped to the correct pins on the terminator. In cables used for 10Base-T networks, for example, the standard specifies specific pairs of wires in the cable that must be used to transmit and receive data. If they are not correctly mapped to the pin-out on the connector specified by the standard, the cable might generate more errors due to noise or cross-talk. Figure 2.1 shows an example of a hand-held cable tester.

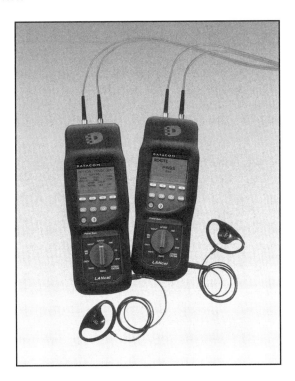

Figure 2.1   A hand-held cable tester is a useful instrument for installing network cabling.

Small hand-held instruments like these usually have LED lights that indicate a pass or fail condition for the test you are performing. They do not require a keyboard or monitor to display data. Some have a small screen that displays limited text, sometimes showing the suspected type of error that has caused a fail condition. Most are battery powered and can also use an AC-adapter, and thus are useful portable instruments to use when installing or troubleshooting cabling.

When you begin to go up the price ladder for these types of instruments, you will find some that can also perform more advanced monitoring functions, such as showing network utilization and collisions. Another useful feature to look for if you can afford the cost is the capability to log data to a memory buffer for later review. Some even have the capability to connect to a PC or printer to produce a written report. This will allow you to leave the device connected to monitor a line for a while.

Bit Error Rate Testers (BERT)

Data travels through the wire (or the fiber) as a series of signals that indicate a single bit, representing either zero or one. The statistic called Bit Error Rate (BER) is calculated as a percentage of bits that have errors when compared to the total number of bits sampled:

```
BER = number of bit errors during sampling interval
      ─────────────────────────────────────────────
          total number of bits transmitted
```

Whereas LAN analyzers operate on data captured from the wire in units of frames, a BER tester performs a more basic function to determine whether the line is capable of carrying the network signaling at the bit level with a minimum of errors. This kind of instrument is usually used when installing a connection to a network service provider, and can be used to demonstrate the quality of service that the provider establishes for your link.

The instrument used to perform this kind of error detection usually does so by generating a specific bit pattern on the line, and then checking it at another location to compare the generated signal with that which is received. A *pseudorandom binary sequence* (PRBS) of bits is produced by the instrument. It is pseudorandom because it simulates random data. However, the pattern is also known by the receiving connection so that it can make the comparison; the signal is not truly random, but instead is a predefined pattern. Other tests include sequences of specific bits, either zeros or ones, for extended periods or specific user-defined bit patterns.

When you have a line that exhibits a high bit error rate, using a slower transmission speed can usually be used to improve performance. This is because when you lower the number of errors that occur, higher-level protocols do not have to resend packets to compensate as often. One bit error might be all it takes to cause an entire frame of several hundred thousand bits to be resent.

Time Domain Reflectometers

When a signal propagates down a wire it usually does so at a constant speed, provided the impedance of the cable is the same throughout its journey. When the signal runs into a fault in the wire or reaches the end of the wire, part or all of the signal is reflected back to its origin. Similar to radar, instruments that use time domain reflectometry (TDR) to make cable measurements are based on precisely timing the signal pulse as it travels through the cable and back.

Of all the instruments that you can use to test cables, TDR is one of the most accurate and fastest methods you can use. It can help locate faults due to many things, such as

- Wires that have been spliced together
- Moisture trapped in the cable

- Cables that have been crushed or have kinks in them
- Short circuits
- Problems in the sheath surrounding a cable
- Loose connectors

You can also use TDR to measure the length of a cable that has no faults. This can be useful for inventory functions because you can even use it to measure the length of a cable while it is still on a reel to determine whether you have enough. TDR can be used to make measurements on both twisted-pair and coaxial cables.

The more expensive models of this instrument can be equipped with a CRT or LED display that shows the wave form of the signal and any reflected signals. The more common instrument will display the number of feet to the end of the cable or a fault, and might have an indicator that tells you the type of fault.

Checking Impedance

When metal conductors are placed in close proximity to each other, as in a twisted-pair or coaxial cable, the effect they have on each other is known as *impedance*. When the wires are perfectly separated by a constant distance, the impedance remains the same throughout the cable. When something happens along the way, such as damage caused by a crushed cable, the impedance changes at that point. Changes in impedance cause parts of the signal to be reflected back to where they started.

Cables that are used in local area networks (LANs) must be manufactured to strict specifications, ensuring that the dielectric material that separates the wires within the cable remains constant. If there are random variations because of poor manufacturing procedures, the cable will suffer from problems caused by signal reflections that might render it unsuitable for your network. Thus, TDR can be used not only as a fault finder when troubleshooting a wiring problem, but also to ensure that you've gotten what you paid for to upgrade or expand your network.

Setting a Pulse Width

Most of the good TDR instruments will allow you to select the pulse width, which is usually specified in nanoseconds. The larger the pulse width, the more energy is transmitted from the device and thus the farther down the wire the signal will travel.

A good tip for setting the pulse width is to start with the smallest value the instrument allows for, and make subsequent measurements, gradually increasing the value. If the fault in the cable is only a short distance away from the measuring instrument, a small pulse width will be adequate to locate it. However, if the fault is very minor, a small burst of energy might not be enough to travel to the fault and send back a reflection that can be accurately measured. By varying the pulse width and making several measurements, you can more accurately determine the location of a fault in the cable.

Comparing Velocity

Light travels at a constant speed of 186,400 miles per second. When measuring the velocity at which an electrical signal travels through a wire, it is expressed as a percentage of the speed of light, which is considered to be 100 percent, or a value of 1. For example, a twisted-pair cable that has a VOP (velocity of propagation) of .65 will conduct an electrical signal at 65 percent of the speed of light.

Manufacturers will usually supply this value to customers, and it will most likely be found on the specification sheet for the cable you are purchasing. Because TDR measures the time it takes for a signal to travel down a wire and make the return trip, you must know the VOP of the cable being tested before you can make accurate measurements.

If you have cables that you are unsure about, you can test them first to determine what the VOP is. Do this by measuring a specific length of cable and, knowing its length, use the TDR instrument to test for the length of the cable, varying the VOP until the tester reads the correct length. Of course, this assumes that the segment of cable you use for this test is in good condition.

Network and Protocol Analyzers

The first level of network testing consists of making sure that the underlying physical cabling structure is performing as expected. The next level is to monitor and test the network traffic and messages generated by the network protocols to be sure that you have a healthy network. Network analyzer products operate by monitoring the network at the data link and transport layers in the OSI reference model.

Once again you will find that the tools you can select range from the very inexpensive (free) to the very expensive. One difference between these kinds of tools and those used to check cables is that you will need to have a good understanding of the network structure and protocols used before you can make meaningful judgments about the data you collect. The LAN analyzer enables you to intercept network traffic as it passes through the wire in real time and save the data for analysis. A good analyzer should be capable of producing meaningful statistics about the traffic on the network, decoding the protocols that are used, and providing a good filtering capability so that you do not have to get bogged down in an overwhelming amount of data.

You must consider many factors when deciding on a network analyzer. The most basic is whether you want a portable device that can be transported to different sites or if you need one or more devices that can be placed at strategic locations in the network to perform continuous monitoring. Other factors will be covered later in the chapter. Some features to consider are as follows:

- **Price**—Of course this is always a factor when purchasing equipment for a network.
- **Software or hardware**—Do you need a dedicated hardware instrument that can perform intense analysis and connect to multiple segments, or can you live with a software implementation that runs on an existing network workstation?
- **Network interface**—Do you need to connect to just a 10Base-T environment, or will you need a device that connects to other topologies such as FDDI or Token Ring?
- **What protocol stacks does the device support?**—Is your network homogeneous, or does it support multiple network protocols?

- **Statistics**—What kind of statistical data does the instrument support? The most basic is frames per second; others include utilization and usage.
- **Memory and buffers**—Does the instrument provide enough buffering capacity to capture frames on a high-speed network such as 100Base-T?
- **Filters**—Does the analyzer provide sufficient filtering capabilities to allow you to look through large volumes of data to get to the frames that really matter?
- **Import and export**—Does the device allow you to save files to a disk or other medium so that you can transfer them to other workstations for further analysis?

A good LAN analyzer will allow you to monitor network traffic in real-time mode, using filters to narrow the scope of your view. You can set up capture filters and store part or all of the frames that match in a buffer and perform further analysis.

Establishing a Baseline

Before you begin to perform monitoring or analysis of the network usage and utilization, you must establish a set of baseline data. In order to interpret the statistical data that you can collect using LAN analyzers, you must have something to compare it with. Baseline data is used to define the normal operating environment for a system and provide a reference for monitoring and troubleshooting efforts.

Baseline data is also useful for deciding capacity planning and measuring the effectiveness of an upgrade. Things you should think about recording in your baseline documentation, in addition to values you monitor with a LAN analyzer, include the following:

- Location of equipment in the network
- Type of equipment in use
- The number and distribution of users
- Protocols in use

Knowing the type of equipment is important because different models of NICs, hubs, and other devices can vary widely in their performance. Knowing where each piece of equipment is located can be helpful if you must create an audit trail for troubleshooting. For example, it is common in a business environment for users and workstations to be constantly on the move.

A simple weekend move, where you take a few workstations or servers and move them to a different location, might have a dramatic impact on the network that you do not expect. Suppose you have two servers that you want to move from a departmental location to a central computer room. When they were located on the same network segment as the users that make the heaviest use of them, traffic was localized. Placing them on a different segment can cause capacity problems in a backbone link or in a device such as a switch or router that connects the network. If you keep track of hardware and statistical information about its performance and use, you can usually prevent this sort of thing from happening. At best, you can at least look back and determine where a problem lies and be in a better position to find a solution.

This same principle applies to the location of users in the network. Different users can make widely differing demands on a single workstation or server. Keep a list of users, the applications they use and, when appropriate, the time of day that they work in situations where shift work is performed.

Understanding the protocols that are used is also important. A simple problem that can at times be hard to figure out quickly is when you move a device to a different network segment, unaware that it is using a non-routable protocol. Most routers can be configured to pass these types of protocols, but you must be aware of this and configure the router accordingly before you make the move.

Finally, baseline data is never going to be something that is cast in stone and unchangeable. Modify your documentation as the network grows or changes so that the data remains a useful tool.

Statistical Data

Although most analyzers provide a wide range of statistical data, the analyzer should be capable of giving you a few general values.

First, make sure that the analyzer can give you statistics that tell you the utilization of the network. In addition to a real-time graphical display, you should also look for the capability to monitor the network and tell you when peak utilization occurs. That is, what times during the day does the network reach its busiest points? Overall utilization calculated over the average work day might not be nearly as helpful as identifying the periods of time that users are working their hardest while getting frustrated with a bogged-down network. Using peak utilization statistics, you can work to resolve the traffic problems by reallocating resources or perhaps rearranging work habits of the user base.

Another statistic that is found on most analyzers is frames per second (fps). By itself it is not a very revealing value, but when combined with data showing the size of packets traversing the network, it can produce meaningful data. The larger the packet size used by a protocol, the more efficient the protocol is likely to be. This is because each packet requires overhead necessary to implement the protocol, such as addressing and error checking information. With a larger packet size, the ratio of overhead to payload is reduced.

Protocol Decoding

The capability to take the raw bits that travel on the network and present them on a frame-by-frame basis is a powerful feature of the analyzer. Looking at a stream of byte values would not be useful when trying to troubleshoot a network problem. Looking at each frame and understanding what kinds of frames are being generated by devices on the network is a necessary component of a network analyzer.

Look for an analyzer that gives both a summary and a detailed view of the frame. The summary view will usually show the addressing and header portion of the packet, whereas the detailed view will display every byte contained in the frame.

Filtering

This is a necessary component for any network analyzer. Filtering enables you to set criteria that the analyzer uses when it captures frames, or to selectively search through a buffer of captured data to retrieve only those frames that are pertinent to your current task. Filters can usually be set to select frames by protocol type, frame type, and protocol or MAC addresses. Some allow you to search for specific data patterns throughout the entire packet.

Software-Based Analyzers

This is the cheapest route to go. Some freeware products you can find on the Web perform some or all of the functions you might need in a small network. Microsoft Windows NT 4.0 comes with a network monitor agent and tool that you can install using the Services tab in the Network applet found in the Control Panel. This monitoring and analysis tool allows the local workstation or server to monitor network traffic that is generated by or sent to the computer. The version that comes with the Systems Management Server (SMS) BackOffice component enables the network administrator to monitor all traffic on the LAN.

Novell has a software-based product called LaNalyzer, which can be used to monitor network traffic. It is a separate product that you must purchase, however, and is not included in the NetWare products.

Both products enable you to capture data on the LAN and filter through it for machine- and protocol-specific information, which is helpful for troubleshooting many kinds of problems on the LAN. Because these products run on a workstation, you can use them to collect and store large amounts of information for immediate analysis and long-term reporting. In Figure 2.2, you can see the main window of the Microsoft Network Monitor (called the Capture Windows).

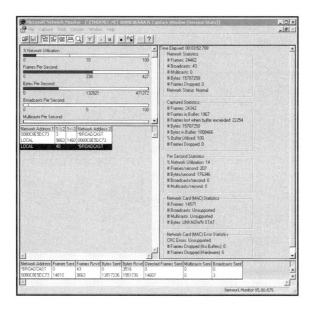

Figure 2.2 The Capture Window shows a summary of the frames that have been captured by the monitor.

To begin capturing frames on the network, use the Capture menu and select Start. You can also use the Capture menu to pause or stop the capture process. As frames are captured by the monitor, you can get an idea of what is happening on the network from the continuously updated bar graphs in the Capture Window. To view the actual data being collected, you can stop the capture process by selecting Stop from the Capture menu. From the same menu you can then select Display Captured Data to view the frames captured (see Figure 2.3).

As you can see, there is a summary line for each frame that the monitor captured. You can scroll up or down to view all frames in the buffer. At this point, the frames are stored in a temporary buffer. If you only need to view the data for immediate analysis and then discard it, you can do so from this window. If you want to store the data for later analysis, select Save As from the File menu. To view data in a stored file, use the Open option in the File menu to read the data in the file into the temporary buffer.

To examine any captured frame and view it in detail, double-click on it in the Frame Viewer window. The window opens a Detail pane that shows the kinds of data in the frame. Click the plus sign (+) to expand the list of data contained in the frame. In Figure 2.4, you can see an example of a frame being viewed. This is an ICMP frame generated during a PING operation. By highlighting the ICMP portion of the Detail pane (in the center of this figure), the monitor highlights the data pertaining to this in the data section at the bottom of the figure. By showing the bytes that make up different parts of the frame, the monitor makes your job easier.

▶▶   For more information on using PING, please see Chapter 18, "TCP/IP."

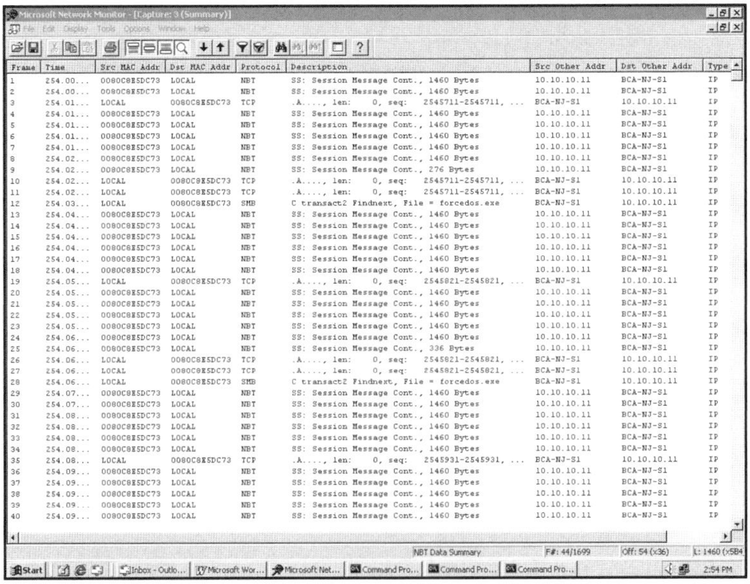

Figure 2.3   The Frame Viewer Window enables you to examine the captured data.

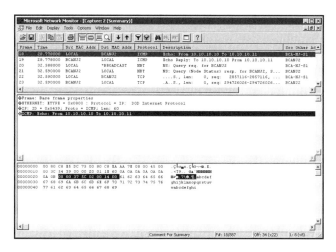

Figure 2.4 You can examine the actual contents of the frame from this view.

Capture and Display Filters

The amount of traffic that passes through even a small network can be overwhelming. However, when you use a network monitor to watch statistical information about current traffic, this does not present a problem. When you are troubleshooting, however, it is very helpful to be able to filter out the nonessential information so that you can examine only those frames which are pertinent to the problem at hand.

For this purpose, most analyzers will allow you to set up a filter that will screen out all but the frames you want to look at. A capture filter is used to create selection criteria for the frames that will be kept and stored in the temporary buffer, while a display filter can be used to further select frames from those that are captured.

In Figure 2.5, you can see the dialog box used to start creating a capture filter for the Microsoft Network Monitor.

Figure 2.5 Create a capture filter to specify which frames are copied to the temporary buffer.

For a capture filter you can specify specific protocols, address pairs, or patterns that occur in the frame itself. The following figures show how you can use Microsoft Network Monitor's capture filters to look for specific frames. This is useful when troubleshooting because you can filter for frames only going between a client and server, for example. If you are troubleshooting an application that is not communicating with the server, you can monitor the communication between the client and the server. Figure 2.6 shows the dialog box used to select address pairs. Figure 2.7 shows the dialog box used to specify a pattern.

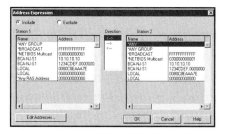

Figure 2.6   You can select the addresses that must appear in a frame in order for it to be selected for capture.

Figure 2.7   Specify a pattern and an offset value for capturing frames based on pattern matching.

When you use pattern matching, you can specify a string that must be found in the frame before it is considered a candidate for capture. You can also specify an *offset value*, which indicates a starting point for the filter in the frame when it searches for the pattern.

Capture Triggers

After you create a capture filter, you can begin to capture data based on it by selecting Start from the Capture menu. When using a very narrow filter to look for a specific problem that doesn't occur often, you can set up an event to notify you when a matching frame is finally detected instead of having to sit at the console and wait. To set a capture trigger, select Trigger from the Capture menu.

The Network Monitor enables you to monitor overall traffic on the network by watching the graphs displayed in the Capture window and look at specific frames to determine where problems exist. A good software LAN analyzer can be a valuable tool for determining network utilization or for troubleshooting specific protocol problems.

Hardware Analyzers

This type of instrument can range in price up to the tens of thousands of dollars. It can, however, provide functionality in a critical situation that cannot be obtained from a software-based product. A hardware LAN analyzer is a device that can be taken to the location where a problem exists and connected to the network. A hardware instrument will most likely be better capable of coping with a high-speed environment, such as 100Base-T, than a software application that relies on a network adapter card to get traffic from the network medium. Hardware analyzers contain special circuitry that is used to perform many functions must faster than can be done via software; they are usually more reliable as well.

Another thing to consider is that when you use a PC or workstation to act as your LAN analyzer, it can be limited as to what the NIC can do. For example, some ordinary adapter cards have built into their firmware a function that automatically discards certain kinds of packets that contain errors. If you are trying to detect what errors are causing problems on your network while troubleshooting, a software product running on a workstation might not be capable of helping you.

Also, although it is true that network adapter cards can literally see every packet on the network as it zips by, that doesn't mean they will be capable of capturing the data and passing it up to higher-level protocols. When a card does capture all frames and pass them up the protocol stack it is operating in what is called *promiscuous mode*. Some cards, especially older ones, are not capable of promiscuous mode due to the expense of the required chipset supporting promiscuous mode, so be sure to check the documentation that comes with the one you might want to use on a workstation that will host LAN-monitoring software.

Hardware analyzers are expensive because they usually do a good job. Most have built-in disk drives, including a floppy disk drive that can be used to exchange data with PC workstations. Be sure that the instrument has enough memory to buffer significant amounts of data. Also, look for a good display so that you can monitor utilization graphically and display the contents of individual frames.

There is also a hybrid type of analyzer that combines the best of the hardware and software products. This type of device implements the capturing and filtering functions in a hardware component that attaches to a workstation, which then provides the display and storage functions. The hardware component has dedicated circuitry and processing power to capture data from the wire, while a software application on the PC is used to filter, calculate, and display the data. This type of device can be external to the PC; some are implemented as cards that plug into the system's bus. This type of analyzer is more expensive but can handle analyzing much higher data rates. This is useful in high-bandwidth environments, such as fiber-optic networks.

Simple Network Management Protocol (SNMP)

Building a network today involves integrating products from a variety of vendors. In this chapter you have learned tools that can be used to locate faults in the physical elements that make up the network and tools that can be used to monitor the functioning of network protocols.

So far, the tools that have been mentioned are all limited to performing a few specific tasks, and each tool must be used as a separate entity. The Simple Network Management Protocol (SNMP) was developed to provide a *simple* method of centralizing the management of TCP/IP-based networks. The goals of the original SNMP protocols include the following:

- Keep development costs low to ease the burden of implementing the protocol for developers.
- Provide for managing devices remotely.
- Make the protocol extensible so it can adapt to new technologies.
- Make the protocol independent of the underlying architecture of the devices that are managed.
- Keep it simple.

The last goal is important. Because SNMP is meant to be incorporated into many different types of network devices, it was designed so that it would not require a lot of overhead. This makes it easy to create simple devices, such as a bridge or a hub, that can be managed by SNMP as well as a more complex device like a router or a switch. Other key factors of the protocol that stick to this goal include the use of the User Datagram Protocol (UDP) for messaging and a manager-agent architecture. UDP is easier to implement and use than a more complex protocol such as TCP. Yet, it provides enough functionality to allow a central manager to communicate with a remote agent that resides on a managed device.

The two main players in SNMP are the manager and the agent. The manager is usually a software program running on a workstation or larger computer that communicates with agent processes that run on each device being monitored. Agents can be found on bridges, routers, hubs and even user's workstations. The manager polls the agents for information and the agents respond.

Applications designed to be the manager end of the SNMP software vary both in expense and functionality. Some are simple applications that perform queries and allow an administrator to view information from devices and produce reports. Some of the other functions that a management console application can perform include

- Mapping the topology of the network
- Monitoring network traffic
- Trapping selected events and producing alarms
- Reporting variables

Some management consoles can produce trend analysis reports for capacity planning to help set long-range goals. With more advanced reporting capabilities, the administrator can produce meaningful reports that can be used to tackle a specific problem.

SNMP Primitives

Management software and device agents communicate using a limited set of operations referred to as *primitives*. These primitives are used to make requests and send information between the two. The following primitives are initiated by the management software:

- **get**—The manager uses this primitive to get a single piece of information from an agent.
- **get-next**—When the data the manager needs to get from the agent consists of more than one item, this primitive is used to sequentially retrieve data. For example, a table of values.
- **set**—The manager can use this primitive to request that the agent running on the remote device set a particular variable to a certain value.

The following primitives are used by the agent on a managed device:

- **get-response**—This primitive is used to respond to a get or a get-next request from the manager.
- **trap**—Although SNMP exchanges are usually initiated by the manager software, there are times when the agent must inform the manager of some important event. In that case, this primitive is used.

Network Objects: The Management Information Base (MIB)

The primitives are the operations that can be performed by the manager or agent processes when they exchange data. The types of data they can exchange are defined by a database called the Management Information Base (MIB). The first compilation of the objects that are stored in this database was defined by RFC 1066, "Management Information Base for Network Management of TCP/IP-based Internets." A year later this was amended by RFC 1213, "Management Information Base for Network Management of TCP/IP-based Internets: MIB-II." MIB-II clarified some of the objects that were defined in the original document and added a few new ones.

The MIB is basically a tree of information (a "virtual information store"). This hierarchical database resides on the agent, and information collected by the agent is stored in the MIB. The MIB is precisely defined, and the current Internet standard MIB contains objects for more than a thousand objects. Each object in the MIB represents some specific entity on the managed device. For example, on a hub, useful objects might collect information showing the number of packets that enter the hub for a specific port while another object might be used to track network addresses.

When making a decision about which types of objects to include, the following things are taken into consideration:

- The object must be useful for either fault or configuration management.
- The object must be "weak." This means that it should be capable of performing only a very small amount of damage if it is tampered with. Remember that in addition to reading values stored in the MIB, the management software can request that an object be set to a value.
- No object is to be allowed if it can be easily derived from other objects that already exist.

The first definition of the standard MIB hoped to keep the number of objects to 100 or fewer so it would be easier to implement. This, of course, is not now a factor.

Because the SNMP management scheme is intended to be extensible, you will find that vendors often create their own objects which can be added to the management console software so you can use them.

An object has a specific syntax associated with it, a name and a method of encoding the object. The name consists of an object identifier, which specifies the type of object to which a specific instance of that kind of object is added. The object identifier is a numeric string of decimal digits separated by periods. For example, ".3.6.1.2.1.1.1." The *instance* of an object is the same, with an additional decimal number following the original object identifier. To make things easier for humans, an object descriptor that is in a text-readable format is used.

An object can be read-only, read-write, or write-only. In addition, an object can be of a type called non-accessible. Syntax types for objects can include

- Integer
- Octet String or DisplayString
- Object Identifier
- Null
- Network Address
- Counter
- Gauge
- TimeTicks
- Opaque

In the first MIB RFC, objects are divided into only a few high-level groups:

- **System**—This group includes objects that identify a type of system (hardware or software).
- **Interfaces**—An object in this group might represent an interface number or an interface type. Other information about network interfaces, such as the largest IP datagram that can be sent or received, are included as objects in this group.
- **Address Translation**—Objects in this group are used for address translation information, such as the ARP cache.
- **IP**—Objects in this group supply information about the IP protocol, including time-to-live values, number of datagrams received from interfaces, errors, and so on.
- **ICMP**—This group includes Internet Control Management Protocol (ICMP) input and output statistics.
- **TCP**—Objects in this group are used to hold information about TCP connections. Instances of these objects exist only while the connection exists. Data contained in these objects include the number of segments sent or received, for example, or the state of a particular TCP connection (closed, listen, and so on).
- **UDP**—Objects in this group represent statistics about the User Datagram Protocol (UDP), such as the number of UDP datagrams delivered or the number of UDP datagrams received for which there is no corresponding application at the destination port.

- **EGP**—These objects are used for the Exterior Gateway Protocol (EGP) and contain information such as components of each EGP neighbor and the state of the local system with respect to a neighbor.

In MIB-II, the address translation group is declared to be *deprecated*; that is, it should still be supported but might not be in the next version. This is a means for gradually preparing for changes in the protocol. MIB-II, however, adds new objects and functionality that can be used to perform the same functions as those performed by this group, just in a different way.

MIB-II also adds new objects to the existing groups. For example, necessary information for the system group, such as a contact person, system location, and system services can now be stored in objects in this group.

New groups added by MIB-II include the following:

- **Transmission**—Related to the Interface group, this group is to be used for objects that relate to specific transmission media.
- **SNMP**—A group that was added for objects needed by the application-oriented working group to collect useful statistical information.

Proxy Agents

Not all devices are equipped with SNMP capabilities. For these devices, another device might be capable of handling those functions and acts as a *proxy agent* for the device so that it can still be managed from the SNMP management console.

SNMPv2

The original implementation of SNMP was kept simple and has been widely used throughout the industry. However, it suffers from several limitations. The get/response messaging mechanism allows for the transfer of only one piece of information at a time. The UDP packet is sufficiently large enough to accommodate more data, but the protocol was not built to allow for this. Security is also an issue with SNMP because it has no provisions for encryption or authentication.

A working committee of the IETF began work on what was to become SNMPv2 in 1994. After numerous meetings and deliberations they were unable to come to a consensus on matters regarding security and administration issues of the proposed standard. At this time, the status of SNMPv2 is still in limbo. With the need for such a standard, however, it is quite possible that something will be published in the near future to officially extend SNMP into new areas of functionality, as the current standard is widely implemented and has been found to be very useful in network management.

RMON

RMON (Remote Monitoring) is a data gathering and analysis tool that was developed to help alleviate some of the shortcomings of SNMP. RMON works in a similar manner, and its objects are defined in a MIB. It was designed to work much like the LAN Analyzer discussed earlier in this chapter. RFCs 1757 and 1513 provide the standard MIB definitions for RMON for Ethernet and Token-Ring networks, respectively.

In SNMP, the roles of the manager and agent are that of a client and server, with the agents being the client of the management console software. In RMON, the agents (often called *probes*) are the active party and become the server while one or more management consoles can be their clients. Instead of the management console performing a periodic polling process to gather data and perform analysis from agents out in the field, in RMON the agents perform intelligent analysis and can send SNMP traps to management consoles when significant events occur.

Using RMON, the administrator can get an end-to-end view of the network. The types of data collected and the alerts and actions that are associated with RMON are different than those of the standard SNMP type. The objects for RMON fall into the following MIB groups:

- **Statistics**—This group records data collected about network interfaces. A table called EtherStatsTable contains one entry for each interface to hold this data and also contains control parameters for this group. Statistics include things such as traffic volume, packet sizes, and errors.

- **History**—The control function of this group manages the statistical sampling of data. This function controls the frequency at which data is sampled on the network. The historyControlTable is associated with this group. The history function of this group of objects records the statistical data and places the data in a table called the etherHistoryTable.

- **Hosts**—This group tracks hosts on the network by MAC addresses. Information in the hostControlTable specifies parameters for the monitoring operations, and a table called the hostTimeTable records the time a host was discovered on the network.

- **HostTopN**—This group is used to rank hosts by a statistical value, such as the number of errors generated or "top talkers." TopNControlTable contains the control parameters for this group, and HostTopNTable keeps track of the data.

- **Matrix**—Data recorded by this group involves the exchange of frames between hosts on the network. Statistics are kept here for data traveling in both directions between hosts.

- **Filter**—This group specifies the types of packets that the RMON probe will capture, such as frame size.

- **Capture**—While the Filter group specifies the parameters that are evaluated for capturing packets, this group is responsible for capturing packets based on those parameters.

- **Alarm**—This group is used to set up alarms for events that are described in the Event group. Here you can set the sampling intervals and thresholds that will trigger an alarm. This group reads statistics that have been gathered, and when they exceed the threshold an event is generated.

- **Event**—When a variable exceeds a threshold defined by an alarm, an event is generated. This group can generate an SNMP trap to notify a network management station or record the information in a log. The Event Table is used to define the notification action that will be taken for an event, and the Log Table is used to record information.

As this list shows, RMON provides a great deal of functionality to SNMP. It allows for the collection of statistical data from all levels of the OSI reference model, including applications at the top in RMON2.

Because ethernet and token-ring networks operate in a fundamentally different way, additional groups defined in RFC 1513 are specific to token-ring networks:

- **Token-Ring Statistics**—A group to store information about the behavior of the ring, from traffic volume to the number of beacons occurring, ring purges, and other information specific to Token Ring.

- **Token-Ring History**—Similar to the History group used for Ethernet, this group keeps track of events on a historical basis.

- **Token-Ring Station**—Detailed information about each station on the ring can be found here.

- **Station Order**—The physical order of stations in the ring can be determined by information stored in this group.

- **Station Config**—Configuration information for stations is stored here.

- **Source Routing**—Monitors information about token-ring source routing for inter-ring traffic.

Alarms and Events

RMON agents can be programmed to take actions when specific things happen on the network. The Alarms and Events group provides an important intelligence function.

Configuring an alarm consists of specifying a variable to be watched, the sampling interval, and the event that will be performed when a threshold is crossed. The threshold can be a rising or a falling threshold, or both. For example, this means that an alarm can be set to notify you when something begins to go awry and also when the situation gets better.

An event that is generated by an alarm can be configured to send an SNMP trap message to one or more management consoles and store the event in the Log Table. The management station can then take the actions it deems necessary, including retrieving information from the Log Table.

Establish a Baseline

When making decisions on how to set up alarms and the events they generate, you should consider how the network functions normally. First monitor the network using RMON agents over a long period of time, noting when variations in traffic or errors occur. Note any fluctuations that regularly occur for specific dates or for a particular time of day.

Different network segments might require different sampling intervals and thresholds. For example, a local LAN segment might be subject to wide variations depending on only a small number of users, while a major backbone might fluctuate much less as traffic from many segments is blended together. When deciding on a sampling period, it is best to use a shorter interval for a segment that experiences frequent fluctuations and a longer interval for a segment that behaves in a more stable manner.

Response to alarms can be in the form of immediate corrective action, as in the case of a defective device, or a long-term solution, such as additional capacity or equipment. Regularly review the baseline values you set and change them as network usage or topology changes. If alarms and events are not configured to reflect activity that is of a genuine concern, network operators might begin to ignore them, much like what happened to the boy who cried "wolf."

Summary

The tools needed to manage a network successfully, both for installation and troubleshooting purposes, are many. They can be hardware or software-based products. Becoming familiar with the tools that are available will make you better able to cope with change or crisis when it happens. These tools include network analyzers, network monitoring software, and SNMP-capable hardware.

Network analyzers play an important role in both monitoring and troubleshooting networks. Using these devices allows a technician to filter network traffic and analyze packets from specific systems. This is useful for identifying the heaviest traffic producers and troubleshooting connection problems.

Network monitoring software and SNMP-capable hardware provide the capability to monitor and troubleshoot specific network components, such as hubs, routers, and gateways. This allows an entire network to be monitored from a central location.

Finally, we discussed how to implement alarms and events for network monitoring, and discussed the importance of gathering a usage baseline to reference against.

In the next chapter, we will look at some of the standards that have come about with regard to the physical network medium as well as the methods of transmitting data on the network. Understanding the physical layer of the network will give you a better understanding of how to use the tools described in this chapter.

Part II

TROUBLESHOOTING HARDWARE

Testing Cables

SOME OF THE MAIN TOPICS IN THIS CHAPTER ARE

Conformance to Standards

10Base-2 and 10Base-5

10Base-T

100Base-T

100VG-AnyLAN

Fiber Optics

Gigabit Ethernet

Incorrect Wiring

Connectors

Other Problems

CHAPTER 3

Although wireless computer networks are now beginning to make inroads into the modern business environment, the most common method of connecting computers is still by a physical medium of some sort. The connection can be a cable made up of metal wires or of fiber-optic strands. In this chapter you will learn about the most common types of cables in use today, and you will see an overview of the standards that have been developed for sending data across the different types of media. In addition, some common problems and troubleshooting methods are discussed.

Conformance to Standards

Without standards, the computer industry would not have gotten very far during the last two decades. At one time, computer hardware and operating systems were highly proprietary designs, usually optimized for specific business or scientific functions. It was typical for a company to be an "IBM Shop" or a "Digital Shop," for example, using hardware and software components from only one vendor to provide solutions for a wide range of business needs. As third-party suppliers began to make inroads into the computer industry, supplying peripherals such as printers, modems, and other devices, it became more important for each manufacturer to pay closer attention to standards.

Standards Organizations

Wiring a network to support computer and telecommunication devices from multiple vendors using many different protocols used to be a challenge for the network or communications professional. In today's fast-paced technological environment it is quite possible—and highly probable—that by the time a new building is designed, built, and ready to be occupied, the computer and telephone equipment that were planned for the site are out-of-date. You only have to imagine how difficult it would be to use electrical appliances if every time a new vendor came to the market they brought with them a new kind of proprietary wiring system and plug design. We would be constantly tearing out walls and putting in new cables and wall sockets. Or would we? It is more likely that it would be more difficult to get new products to market because of the high infrastructure costs associated with them.

Thus, it is important that you leverage everything you can to make sure that the physical plant you install today will be capable of adapting to newer technologies a few years down the road.

ISO Seven-Layer Networking Model

Before beginning a discussion of the various standards that have been adopted by most vendors for networking, it is important to understand that underlying modern networking protocols is a *reference model* that was developed by the International Standards Organization (ISO) for its Open Systems Interconnect (OSI) networking protocols.

This seven-layer model separates the tasks of networking into functionally different components and defines the tasks to be performed at each layer. For example, the *Physical Layer* includes such items as the network cables, whereas the *Transport Layer* is concerned with protocols that are responsible for moving data across the network.

The important thing to know about this model is that it enables interaction between current and emerging hardware and software technologies. Although most networking protocols—aside from the OSI networking suite developed by the ISO—do not strictly adhere to all seven layers, there is a general adoption of the concept. For example, in some protocols several layers are collapsed together and the functions provided by the separate layers are performed as a single task. In others, a layer can be divided into two or more functional sections. Still, this model has made it possible for vendors to produce products that interact well with those from other vendors and allow for innovation in new products, because components at one layer can be modified or enhanced without the need to reinvent the entire protocol stack or hardware associated with it.

Understanding the functionality of the ISO seven-layer model is not critical to managing a network today. It will, however, give you more insight into why certain standards evolved into what they are. This knowledge can also help you when using troubleshooting tools. For example, if you only know about TCP/IP addresses (which belong in the Network Layer) on your network and are not cognizant of MAC addresses (used at the Physical Layer) you will have difficulty using a protocol analyzer while trying to trace a problem to a particular node on the network.

For a more detailed discussion of this reference model, see Appendix A, "The OSI Seven-Layer Networking Model."

IEEE 802.3

Because of the pace at which technology continues to advance in this field, it is a good idea to be cognizant of the 802.3 standards. This is not just so that you can understand the technology you are already using in your LAN, but so you can better plan for future expansion when upgrading or repairing your network today.

In the 1980s, small computers began to work their way into almost every major business organization. Users who found the traditional multiuser minicomputer or mainframe system difficult to use or access could accomplish a lot of work by using a small *personal computer*. In the beginning, most corporate computer departments ignored these "toys" and wished they would just go away.

After the computer industry began to stabilize on the IBM-compatible PC platform, it became possible for many vendors to jump in and create computers, expansion cards, and software. Early attempts at PC networking were not as successful as those used in the minicomputer arena (such as DECnet), but they did allow PCs to further proliferate in the business environment because small department LANs allowed multiple users to share programs and exchange data without the usual expensive overhead associated with minicomputers, technical staff, and maintenance costs.

It became inevitable that standard methods and protocols had to be established to make these networks manageable.

Robert M. Metcalfe, working at the Xerox Palo Alto Research Center (X-PARC), had pioneered networking by developing the first ethernet network, which transferred data from one computer to another at a blazingly fast speed of 3Mbps.

In 1980 a group of vendors made up of Digital Equipment Corporation (DEC), Intel, and Xerox released a standard (named DIX for the companies' initials) for a 10Mbps network based on the ethernet technology. This technology, which is still called Ethernet by most users, was standardized by the Institute of Electrical and Electronics Engineers (IEEE, pronounced *I Triple E*) in 1985, and was officially called the "IEEE 802.3 Carrier Sense Multiple Access With Collision Detection (CSMA/CD) Access Method and Physical Layer Specifications." That's a big name for what is now called the 802.3 standard. Another standard—IEEE 802.5—was also developed, based on networking technology developed by IBM for its token-ring networks.

Since then there have been many additions to the standard, including the adoption of different cable types (from *thicknet* coaxial cable to twisted-pair wiring) and faster speeds (from 10Mbps to the now evolving standard of Gigabit Ethernet).

The IEEE 802.3 and 802.5 standards that will be discussed in this chapter include

- **IEEE 802.3**—The first 10Mbps Ethernet. This includes 10Base-2, 10Base-5, and 10Base-T.
- **IEEE 802.3u**—The specification for "Fast Ethernet," or the 100Base-T standard for 100Mbps networks.
- **IEEE 802.3z**—The specification for Gigabit Ethernet, which includes 1000Base-T, 1000Base-SX, 1000Base-CX, and 1000Base-LX.
- **IEEE 802.5**—The standard that is used for 4 or 16Mbps token-ring networks.

Structured Wiring: EIA/TIA 568

Placing a networked computer workstation on each user's desktop is not as simple a task as you might expect. Just as the telephone system needs to be carefully planned and implemented in a structured manner, so does a computer network. Installing cables and interconnecting tens or hundreds (and sometimes thousands) of small computers in a large building or on a college or business campus needs to be done in a way that allows for easy management and expansion. In 1985, a task force was formed by the Electronics Industries Association (EIA) and the Telecommunications Industry Association (TIA) to establish standards for installing network wiring in buildings.

The first draft was finished in 1991 and is known as EIA/TIA-568. The current revision is called TIA/EIA-568A. This document defines a standard for structured wiring that covers the cables used, network topology, connectors, and other items necessary to connect end users to the network. The equivalent document in Canada is known as CSA T529. The International Organization for Standardization (ISO) is currently working on a cabling standard for international use. This document is known as ISO/IEC 11801 (Generic Cabling for Customer Premises Cabling).

Although you might never have heard of EIA/TIA-568A, the results of this effort are easily identifiable in almost any computer network today. The main topics covered by this standard are

- **Work Area**—From the *information outlet* (faceplate on the wall) to the user's workstation, including any connectors. The Work Area must have at least two information outlets: one for voice and one for data connections.
- **Horizontal Wiring**—The cable running from the faceplate in the user's work area to the telecommunications closet. This includes the patch and jumper cables housed inside the closet. The maximum length of the horizontal wiring needs to be no more than 90 meters,

with up to an additional 10 meter length of patch or jumper cables in the closet or work area.

- **Telecommunications Closets and the Equipment Room**—A telecommunications closet is the place where the wiring that comes from the user's work area terminates. The ANSI/EIA/TIA-569 standard is to be used when building the telecommunications closet. An *equipment room* is generally more complex than a telecommunications closet, and is the place where a backbone that connects to the closets terminates.

- **Backbone Wiring**—Typically runs "vertically" up through the floors of a building and is used to connect equipment rooms and telecommunications closets.

- **Entrance Facility**—The point at which hardware and cables connect the building's cabling to outside services.

- **Star Topology**—A hierarchical star topology is used to connect the various telecommunications closets and equipment rooms. Between the horizontal cross-connect (where the horizontal wiring terminates), there can be only one additional cross-connect before reaching the main cross-connect.

- **Cables**—Unshielded twisted-pair (UTP), shielded twisted-pair (STP), and fiber-optic cables.

Standards for Telecommunications Pathways and Spaces—EIA/TIA 569

Whereas EIA/TIA 568 covers how the elements of a structured wiring environment should fit together, another standard—EIA/TIA 569—addresses the details about the physical pathways that cables take through the building and the spaces used to house network equipment, such as the telecommunications closet or equipment room. For example, for the telecommunications closet, the EIA/TIA 569 specifies that there will be at least one per floor of the building served. There will be additional closets when the floor area served exceeds 10,000 square feet, or when the horizontal distance on the floor exceeds the 90-meter maximum to a user's workplace. This standard also governs the amount of wall space used for the termination of lines at the entrance facilities portion of the building.

Testing Standards: TSB 67 (Telecommunications System Bulletin 67)

Another important standard that has come from TIA is TSB 67. This standard defines uniform methods that will be used when testing wiring installations based on TIA/EIA 568-A (field testing) to ensure that installations are done correctly. This standard provides for channel testing (from the user's cable to the termination in the wiring closet) and link testing (individual segments in the channel). Standard methods include testing for length, wire mapping, attenuation, and NEXT (near-end cross talk). TSB 67 also specifies how each test is to be performed.

Before TSB 67, it was common to experience different results when using test equipment from different vendors or when using different methodologies for testing.

CSMA/CD Versus Token Ring

As mentioned at the beginning of this chapter, standards enable manufacturers to build equipment that can interoperate with equipment from other manufacturers. The items contained within a standard such as cable lengths, however, are not simply arbitrary decisions by some standards committee. Cabling standards are designed around the underlying technology for which they are intended. An electrical signal, for example, loses strength as it travels farther distances, and the trip through the wire is not instantaneous. Most networking technologies allow multiple systems to use the same, shared network medium. Thus, a standard method must be used to enable users to access the network medium, and there must be an agreement on the maximum distances to be covered so that timing issues can be uniform.

The original Ethernet network, later formalized in the 802.3 standards, used a signaling technology that allowed each computer on the network to have equal access to the network medium. This can be likened to a crowded room, where one person talks and everyone else listens. However, sometimes more than one person begins to speak, and confusion results. When more than one person talks and a miscommunication occurs, a method has to be found to decide which person gets to talk first.

CSMA/CD stands for *carrier sense multiple access/collision detection.* In this type of network, a workstation first listens to determine whether any other computer is transmitting data at that moment. If nothing is heard, the workstation can begin to transmit. Hopefully, the data will get through to its intended recipient. However, it is quite possible that more than one workstation will listen and then start to transmit at the same time. When this happens, the data on the shared wire gets garbled and a collision occurs. The workstation can sense this event and knows that it must retransmit the data.

Instead of simply sending the data out on the wire again, a backoff algorithm is used so that each of the workstations involved in the collision will not try to retransmit immediately, thus causing another collision. Instead, a random interval timer is used and each workstation waits, based on this random interval, before attempting to transmit again. On a busy network, it is quite possible that the second attempt at transmission will also result in a collision.

To provide for this possibility, the workstation will increase the amount of time before it begins to retransmit, and will try as many as 16 times to get the data successfully through the wire. If it is not successful in transmitting a packet after 16 attempts, it will finally give up and discard the packet.

Because this standard allows for the possibility that a packet will not be transmitted successfully every time, it is called a *best-effort* protocol. This does not mean that computer networks that use ethernet protocols are unreliable; it just means that at this level of the networking stack, guaranteed delivery is not part of the process. It is up to higher level protocols (those that perform functions further up in the OSI seven-layer model) to determine whether data is getting through, and to compensate for this.

The Collision Domain

One important concept to remember is that there is a limit to how large a network can be when you are using CSMA/CD. It's a matter of timing; a workstation cannot just wait forever to determine if a packet has been sent successfully to another workstation. Timing is very important, and is measured in microseconds. Therefore, the 802.3 standards define the maximum size that a *collision domain* can be, depending on the specific network technologies used.

A collision domain is defined as any network in which it is possible for any two attached workstations to experience a collision (and detect the collision) when they both try to transmit. The length of the network medium (copper cable or fiber optics) is limited by the time it takes a signal to travel from one end of the network and back (the round trip time). If the cable exceeds the maximum length allowed, the round trip timer expires before the signal has completed the trip, causing the workstation to transmit again.

Although you can use a *repeater* when you need to connect multiple segments of a particular medium to create a larger network, this will not bypass the limitations of a collision domain. Because the repeater simply sends an incoming signal back out to the other segments, and because the total round trip time for the signal cannot be exceeded, the network is limited to a set size. The network can be expanded by *switches* that interconnect collision domains. However, it is very important to remember that each workgroup LAN that is connected via a repeater hub is limited in the number of workstations it can support and in the total amount of network cable that can be used.

Multiple Access

Another feature of CSMA/CD is that it is a very democratic system. Each workstation on the network has the same chance of making use of the transmission medium; no workstation is given a priority over another. This does not mean that every workstation will be allocated the same amount of network bandwidth on a proportional basis—it only means that each workstation can listen to the network and make the attempt when no one else is transmitting. There is no central controller that dictates which workstation is allowed to use the network.

Token Ring

The Token-Ring network specification (IEEE 802.5), however, *does* provide a controlling mechanism. In this type of network, each workstation is connected in a logical star topology to a central device called a Multistation Access Unit (MSAU). Instead of making transmission attempts and then checking for collisions on the network medium, a token frame is passed around from one computer to the next, in round-robin fashion, and only the computer that has current possession of the token is allowed to transmit. All data packets are sent around the network and eventually return to the workstation that began the transmission.

This chapter concentrates on the standards used for networks that evolved from the original Ethernet specifications. These types of networks make up the majority of installed LANs today. For more information on token-ring technology, see Chapter 14, "Token-Passing Technology."

Physical Cable Types

Much of the content of specifications used for ethernet and token-ring networks is based on the composition of the physical infrastructure that connects the network: cables and the wires and other components that make them up. You must understand the type of cable, the number of wires it contains, whether it is shielded or unshielded, and other related factors when discussing the standards that have evolved over the years. The type of cable that is used will also dictate such things as the number of nodes that can be placed on a cable segment and the number of segments that can be used in a single LAN. When troubleshooting network problems, this kind of information is invaluable.

Two important factors that limit the performance of any particular cable are *attenuation* and *cross-talk*.

Attenuation occurs when an electrical signal travels down the wire and slowly begins to lose strength. There are several causes of attenuation. First, consider the way an electrical signal travels through the wire. You might think that it is spread evenly through the entire diameter of the wire; however, that is not the case. Instead, the signal tends to flow more freely near the outside perimeter of the wire rather than at the center. This effect is more pronounced at higher frequencies. Attenuation can also happen when part of the signal is absorbed by the supposed nonconducting substance that surrounds it. A very small amount of the signal can be picked up by the nonconductor; this effect is more pronounced at higher temperatures.

Cross-talk occurs when the electrical field of one wire in a cable interferes with the electrical signal in another wire. Twisted-pair cables are twisted because it helps reduce cross-talk among the wires that make up the pairs.

The first ethernet networks used coaxial cables to make connections between workstations. In the beginning there was *thickwire* (10Base-5), which was difficult to handle and rather expensive to purchase and install. The next generation of ethernets used *thinwire* (10Base-2), which was easier to install and a little cheaper than thicknet.

Coaxial Cables

If you look at the cut end of a coaxial cable (commonly called *coax*) you will see that it has several layers, much like the rings in a tree (see Figure 3.1).

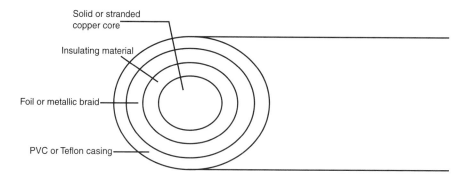

Figure 3.1   Coaxial cables are composed of several layers.

The center is composed of either a single solid wire or a collection of wire strands that are used to conduct a signal. This metal core is surrounded by a dielectric material—a substance that does not conduct electricity. Next comes a layer of either aluminum foil or a metallic braid, or possibly both, which is used as the ground for the cable. This outer metallic layer also helps to shield the inner wire core from electrical interference. The name *coaxial* reflects that these two conductors (the inner core and the outer metallic layer) center around a common axis. Finally, the cable is encased in an insulating jacket, which is usually composed of PVC or Teflon. The Teflon variety is used in installing cables in the *plenum*—the air handling parts of a building, such as the space between the ceiling and the next floor above. This is done to protect people from the toxic fumes created by PVC if a fire breaks out.

Thickwire Ethernet uses coaxial cables that are about 1 cm (0.4 inches) in diameter; it also usually has a solid wire core. This type of coax is very inflexible compared to the thinner variety, and it cannot be installed in places that require sharp bends. Thinwire Ethernet is a smaller coaxial cable of approximately 0.5 cm (3/16 inches) in diameter. It has a stranded wire for the inner core, which, along with its smaller diameter, makes it less rigid than thickwire, and therefore easier to handle.

Coaxial cable must be manufactured to strictspecifications and have a 50-ohm impedance rating. This results in cable that can be used over longer distances and that is more resistant to electrical interference than twisted-pair copper cables.

Copper Cables

Twisted-pair copper cables have been used for many years in the telephone industry. Each cable pair consists of two copper wires, which are twisted together to reduce electrical interference. The number of twists per foot is important, and directly relates to the speed at which a signal can be sent through a particular cable with minimal electrical interference.

Unshielded twisted-pair cables (UTP) are presently classified into five basic categories, based on their performance and usage. Only Category 3 and higher cables are to be used in modern networks, and standards are currently being defined for Categories 6 and 7. UTP cables are now the most widely used cables for connecting individual workstations to a network.

Category 1 and 2 cables are generally not suited for most networking purposes. Category 1 was used for POTS (Plain Old Telephone System) voice-grade service. Category 2 was used for connecting terminals to multiuser computer systems, as well as for some early attempts at networking, such as ARCnet. Category 3 cabling (using four twists per foot) is meant to operate at speeds of up to 16MHz. Category 4 isn't actually much different than Category 3; it is rated for speeds of up to 20MHz. Category 5 (with four twists per inch) is designed for speeds of up to 100MHz.

Shielded twisted-pair cables (STP) are mostly used in token-ring networks, though they are being put to some use in higher speed ethernet networks.

10Base-2 and 10Base-5

The 10Base-2 specification is more commonly called Thinwire Ethernet, thinnet, or—to use a more descriptive phrase—*cheapernet*. The last term refers to the fact that 10Base-2 is cheaper to install and use than its predecessor, 10Base-5. It is also much easier to handle.

When you dissect the name 10Base-2, you will find

- A network pipe that runs at 10MHz
- Baseband signaling over RG-58 coaxial cables
- A maximum distance of about 200 meters (actually 186 meters, or about 607 feet) for a single segment

- A maximum distance through the LAN (collision domain) connecting segments using repeaters of 925 meters, or about 3,035 feet

To connect a computer to a 10Base-2 cable, a BNC connector is used. This type of connector has both male and female counterparts that twist-lock together. A barrel connector of this type can be used to connect two cable segments together. A T-connector (shown in Figure 3.2) is used to connect a workstation to the network.

Note

A BNC (Bayonet Neil-Concelman) connector is made up of two parts. The "male" part contains a centered pin that connects to the coaxial cable's conducting wire. The "female" end consists of a receptacle, connected to the conducting wire on the segment to be joined, into which this pin is plugged.

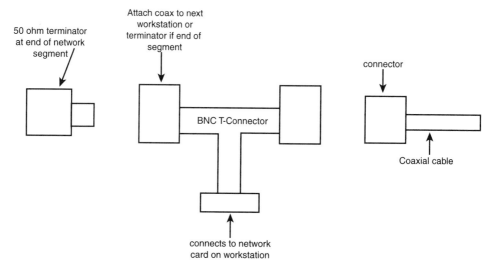

Figure 3.2   A T-connector is used to attach a workstation to a 10Base-2 thinnet coaxial cable.

Figure 3.3 shows how a simple bus topology is employed to connect computers. The network segment is terminated at each end with a 50-ohm terminator, one of which is grounded. Notice that in addition to the maximum segment length, there is also a *minimum* length that is enforced between each node on the bus of 0.5 meters (about 23 inches). The terminators serve to absorb the signal when it reaches the end of a segment so that it is not reflected back, causing errors.

One major disadvantage of using a bus topology and coaxial cables is that the cable becomes a single point of failure. For example, if you have 10 workstations daisy-chained along a single cable and something happens to damage the cable, all workstations on that cable are unable to communicate on the network. The T-connectors enable you to attach or detach any workstation from the bus without causing disruption, but you cannot detach the cable from any of the T-connectors on the bus (including the terminator at the end of the cable) without causing a disruption of service. In many cases, the end user is not well acquainted with the technology. A common problem with this type of network is a user moving their computer and disconnecting the coaxial cables in the process, bringing the entire network to a halt.

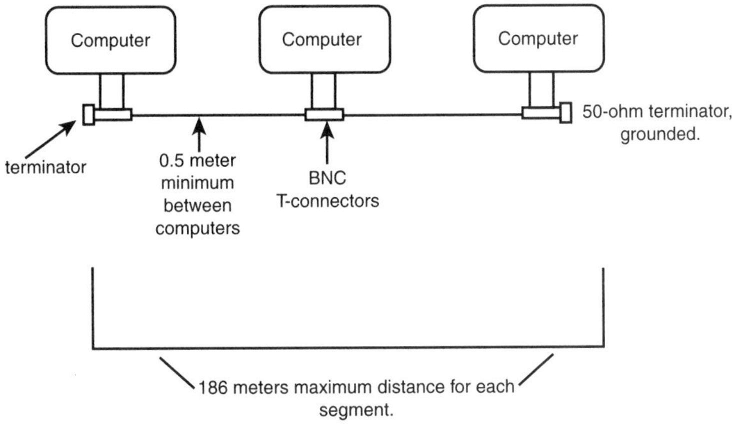

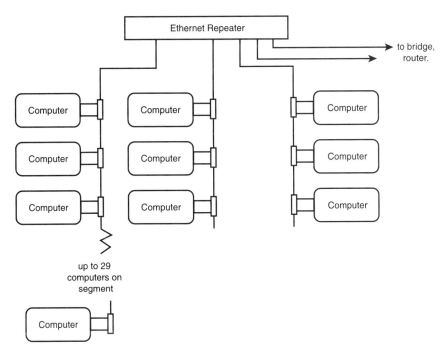

Figure 3.3 Simple bus topology network using 10Base-2.

You can place up to 30 computers on a network segment of this type. To create a larger network, you can use a repeater to join segments. In Figure 3.4, there are three network segments. With a network of this type, there can be a maximum of 29 computers on each network segment because the repeater itself is also counted. Additionally, although up to five segments can be connected to the repeater, only three of them can be used to connect computers. The other two segments can be used to connect to other repeaters or to a switch.

Figure 3.4 An ethernet repeater joins multiple segments together.

Also note that in a 10Base-2 network there must be only one ground connection. When more than one ground connection exists, noise can be generated on the coaxial cable, causing disruptions. Coaxial cables are shielded cables, and thus are more immune to outside electrical interference than are twisted-pair cables. Furthermore, they can be used over longer distances than twisted-pair cables. However, twisted-pair cables allow for much greater speeds of data transmission and are the preferred method for building a network today.

10Base-5 thicknet cables are larger and more difficult to install than 10Base-2 cables. This type of cable uses a DIX (Digital, Intel, and Xerox) or an AUI (attachment unit interface) connector. Whereas thinnet cables can be connected using BNC connectors that make a connection to the computer or repeater using a simple twist-lock motion, the method used for thicknet cables is called a *tap*, or sometimes a *vampire tap*. A hole is drilled into the cable and the connector is literally clamped onto it to make a connection to the solid wire core inside.

Thicknet cables allow a larger segment length than thinnet (about 500 meters). There must be at least 2.5 meters (8 feet) between each tap, and from the tap to the computer there can be no more than 50 meters (about 164 feet). Like 10Base-2, 10Base-5 networks can be joined using repeaters with a maximum collision domain distance of 2,406 meters (about 8,200 feet), with up to 100 computers placed on each segment.

You might find that thicknet is still being used as a backbone cable in some networks, but with the advent of newer, faster technologies such as fiber optics, it is not the method of choice in new installations. If the cabling is already installed in your building, you can save money up front by using thicknet. But to plan for future expansion, you probably want to expend the necessary funds to provide a faster pipeline for your backbone. Optical fiber has dropped dramatically in price recently and is a better choice.

10Base-T

The 10Base-T specification is perhaps the most widely used for modern computer networks. Unshielded twisted-pair cables (categories 3, 4, and 5) are used to connect each computer to a central *hub*, which serves as a wiring concentrator for the LAN. Each computer can be placed up to 100 meters (328 feet) from the hub. As was noted earlier in this chapter, the length of the horizontal wiring is usually up to 90 meters from the hub to the faceplate in the user's work area. The remaining 10 meters are for the patch cables used at the work area to attach the computer to the faceplate, and for any patch cables used in the wiring closet in which the hub resides. Although you only need Category 3 twisted-pair cabling, you can prepare yourself for the eventual upgrade to faster network technologies by installing Category 5 instead.

As you can tell from the name, 10Base-T also uses a data rate of 10Mbps, and uses baseband signaling just like 10Base-2. The major differences between the two standards are the cables used and the network topology. The *T* stands for *twisted-pair*.

10Base-T networks do not use the bus topology. Instead, these networks consist of computers connected in a star formation (see Figure 3.5), with hubs arranged in a hierarchical fashion. There is only one workstation on each cable, rather than a daisy chain of stations strung out in bus fashion. This prevents a broken cable from becoming a major point of failure because only one workstation will suffer from such an event rather than a string of workstations along a single cable.

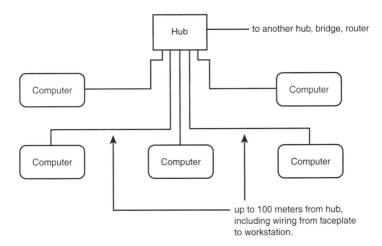

Figure 3.5 10Base-T networks use a star topology instead of a bus.

Connectors and Cables

10Base-T networks are much cheaper to construct than those based on 10Base-2. The cables are cheaper and less prone to abuse in handling. The connectors that are used are called modular 8 or RJ-45 connectors (*Registered Jack*, using pin numbering design 45); these connectors are similar to those used to connect a modular phone to the faceplate, but they are a little larger. They snap in and out easily. Although you can buy the connectors and cables and use an RJ crimping tool to make your own cables, it is simpler to buy pre-made cables from a vendor.

Twisted-pair cables are not made up of a single core of wire, unlike coaxial cable. Instead, there are multiple pairs of wires, with one pair being used to send data and another being used to receive data. Each workstation sends and receives data to and from the hub, which in turn sends the data back out (repeats) on the other segments that are connected to it. Another advantage this has over thinnet coaxial cables is that you can unplug the cable from the workstation or the hub at any time without disrupting the network. To add a new workstation to the network, you simply plug it into an available port on the hub. There is no need to splice a new T-connector into a cable segment.

If you examine a Category 3–5 cable, you'll see that there are eight individual wires, or four sets of two. These wire pairs are color-coded so that the installer can identify the pairs at each end of the cable. One of the wires in a pair will be a solid color; the other wire will be that same color, in a stripe against a white background.

The usual color-coding scheme is based on either the EIA/TIA 568A or 568B standard. The 568B wire pairs are color-coded as follows:

- **Pair number 1**—Blue and blue stripe on white.
- **Pair number 2**—Orange and orange stripe on white.

- **Pair number 3**—Green and green stripe on white.
- **Pair number 4**—Brown and brown stripe on white.

In a 10Base-T cable only the second and third wire pairs (orange and green) are actually used. That might be simple enough to remember if each wire was connected to the RJ-45 pins in the same order. But they are not. Instead, as you can see in Figure 3.6, the *pinout* (which wires from the cable connect to which pins on the connector) for the connector has pins 1 and 2 connected to the transmit wires and pins 3 and 6 connected to the receiving wires.

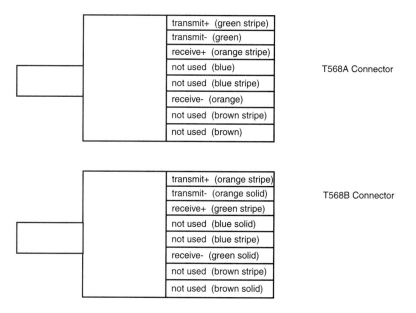

Figure 3.6   A pinout of the RJ-45 connector.

Caution

When making your own cables, you might think it's easier to simply pinout the wires into the RJ-45 jack in the order that they are in the cable. Don't do this! Because of the electrical properties of the cables, it is important that the transmit wires be paired together and the receive wires be paired together. If you decide to separate the receive pair by using one wire from the green set and one wire from the blue set, thus separating the receive and transmit wires, you might create network performance problems.

Cross-Over Cables

Because the transmit and receive wire pairs are terminated on the same pins on both sides of the cable, the hub is usually responsible for switching the send and receive signals before sending them back out to other workstations on the network. However, it is easy to create a cross-over cable if you only need to connect two workstations. This might be useful in a computer laboratory type of situation where you are just experimenting with a new operating system or application; or it can be an inexpensive method of connecting two computers at home.

To create a cross-over cable, you simply have to reverse the transmit and receive pairs on one end of the cable, in the following manner (based on the 568B color-codes):

- Transmit + (orange stripe) on pin 3
- Transmit - (orange solid) on pin 6
- Receive + (green stripe) on pin 1
- Receive - (green solid) on pin 2

Tip

The prices of small workgroup-LAN hubs have dropped dramatically in the past few years. You can now find a five-port ethernet hub at most consumer computer stores for less than $75. In fact, with a rebate coupon, hubs have recently been advertised at only $29. If you are networking a small office and are starting out with just two workstations, buy a small hub instead of using a cross-over cable. A small hub gives you the capability to add a few more workstations later. If your needs escalate faster than you expect and you outgrow a five-port hub, you can still make use of it by connecting it to another hub of the same or greater capacity.

10Base-T Specifications

You can create a hierarchical network of workstations by connecting up to 12 hubs to a central hub. In a 10Base-T LAN you can have up to 1,024 workstations, but you can extend your network by attaching to an ethernet switch or by using a bridge to join multiple collision domains.

100Base-T

As its name implies, 100Base-T operates at a data rate of 100Mbps. Another common name for this standard is Fast Ethernet. You will find that there are two competing standards for networks that run at this speed: Fast Ethernet and 100VG-AnyLAN, which is discussed later in this chapter.

Fast Ethernet was designed to be compatible with existing 10Base-T networks. It uses the same frame format, and it still uses the CSMA/CD medium access method that is defined in the 802.3 standard. What makes it even nicer as an upgrade path for an existing network is that it can interoperate on the same wiring as 10Base-T. That is, with an intelligent hub that can detect the speed being used by a particular workstation's network adapter card, you can use both types on the same network and they can talk to each other. The hub will take care of the speed difference between the communicating workstations. If you are installing a 10Base-T network at this time and are planning to migrate later to a 100Base-T network, you can also find network adapter cards that operate at both speeds.

One of the nice things about migrating to 100Base-T is that you can use existing wiring if the building has Category 3 cabling already in place. The 100Base-T standard is defined for use with either twisted-pair wiring (100Base-TX and 100Base-T4) or optical fiber (100Base-FX). 100Base-T4 also allows for the use of Category 3 wiring, so an upgrade path exists for those who cannot afford the expense of rewiring a building at this time.

There is an important difference between 100Base-T4 and 100Base-TX: They do not use the same cable pairs to transmit and receive data. 100Base-T4 uses all four cable pairs and a different signaling technique.

100Base-TX

For sites that were forward-thinking and installed Category 5 cables when creating a 10Base-T network, upgrading to a 100Mbps network will prove that the investment was worthwhile. This twisted-pair version of the 100Base-T specification can be used on this cabling or on the shielded twisted-pair (STP) cables that are usually found on token-ring networks. The 100Base-TX standard is based on the ANSI TP-PMD (Twisted-Pair Physical Medium Dependent) specification. The maximum segment length is 100 meters, but again you must remember to include the distance from where the horizontal wiring terminates at the work area faceplate to the workstation.

The total distance through the LAN can be up to 200 meters, incorporating up to two hubs. There are two classes of hubs.

Class I Hubs

A standard 10Base-T hub receives data from a segment and outputs the same signal on the other segments that are attached to its ports. Because there are three different formats used by 100Base-T, a standard hub limits a particular LAN to having only one type of 100Base-T segment. A Class I hub solves this problem by translating the incoming signals from one format to another before sending the signal back out on the other ports. Because of the overhead involved in the signal processing, the standard limits a network to using only one Class I hub.

Class II Hubs

A Class II hub operates with only one media type—100Base-TX. It performs no signal translation and acts as a simple multipoint repeater. There can be a maximum of two Class II hubs in the collision domain.

100Base-T4

For those networks that have a heavily installed base of Category 3 or Category 4 cabling, this version of 100Base-T provides an upgrade path. This standard uses half-duplex signaling on four pairs of wires, as opposed to the two pairs used by 10Base-T and 100Base-TX. Three of the wire pairs are used for actual data transmission, and the fourth pair is used for collision detection. The three pairs used in transmission each operate at only 33.3Mbps, for a total of 100Mbps (called the 4T+ signaling scheme). Additionally, a three-level encoding scheme is used on the wire instead of the two-level scheme used for most other media. Because 100Base-T4 requires special hardware, such as network adapter cards and hubs, and because it operates only in half-duplex mode, it shouldn't be considered for a new installation, but only a possible upgrade path when other options cannot be justified.

100Base-FX

Fiber-optic cable provides the greatest distance for Fast Ethernet. 100Base-FX, using a two-strand cable (one strand for transmission and one for receiving data and detecting collisions), can achieve a distance of up to two kilometers.

Tip

The measurements 62.5 and 125 microns do not imply that there are two different sizes of fiber-optic cable, like the coaxial cables used in 10Base-2 and 10Base-5. Instead, they refer to the size of the glass core (62.5 microns) and the diameter of the full cable (125 microns).

Fiber is a good choice for use as a backbone in the network. Unlike copper wire cables, which use electrical impulses for communications, fiber uses pulses of light. This also makes fiber cable a better choice in an environment with a lot of electrical interference. Because fiber-optic cable emits no electrical signals itself (which can be intercepted to eavesdrop on the network), it is also ideal in a situation in which security is a great concern. Finally, optical fiber provides a built-in capability that will certainly be pushed to greater transmission speeds as new standards develop.

100VG-AnyLAN

This type of network is documented in the IEEE 802.12 standard. The name 100VG-AnyLAN gives some clues as to how it functions:

- 100 indicates that the speed of the network is 100Mbps.
- VG stands for *voice grade*, meaning that the transmission can be done on ordinary Category 3 voice grade cables.
- AnyLAN refers to the capability to transmit both 802.3 Ethernet frames and 802.5 token-ring frames.

At this time, one of the most limiting factors to consider before adopting 100VG-AnyLAN is the lack of vendors who supply the technology. It was originally developed by the Hewlett Packard Company, and then was standardized by the IEEE in 1995. Since then there has not been a great rush from a lot of vendors to this market. This means that prices remain higher for this equipment than for related technologies such as 1000Base-T products.

However, 100VG-AnyLAN *does* have many good features that make it attractive.

Cabling

The rules for cabling for 100VG-AnyLAN are similar to those used for 10Base-T. An important difference is that instead of using two wire pairs for transmitting data (one to transmit and one for receiving), four pairs are used, and all four pairs can be used for either transmitting or receiving. Each wire pair uses a 25MHz signal, giving a bandwidth of 100MHz across all four pairs. The low frequency allows 100VG-AnyLAN to be used with lower voice grade cables without causing FCC concerns.

Of course, you can always use a higher grade of cable, such as Category 4 or 5. But the point is that this is not necessary due to the lower frequencies used in transmitting data. If you use existing cable that is already installed, however, you need to examine each connector to be sure that all four wire pairs are terminated in the connector, rather than just those two that were previously used on a 10Base-T network.

100VG-AnyLAN can also be used over fiber-optic cable, giving it the capability to operate over greater distances.

According to the 802.12 standard, the following distance limitations need to be observed for node-to-hub connections or hub-to-hub connections:

- **Category 3 or 4 cable**—100 meters.
- **Category 5 cable**—200 meters.
- **Fiber-optic cable**—500 meters (800nm transceivers) and 2 kilometers (1300nm transceivers).

Hubs can be cascaded up to five levels. One drawback to this, however, is that adding a level of hubs to the network effectively shortens the total radius (from root hub to end node) of the network.

Note

One thing you cannot do when using 100VG-AnyLAN that you can do in a 10Base-T or 100Base-T network is connect two workstations with a cross-over cable. Why? There are a couple of reasons. The first is that there are no distinct transmit or receive wire pairs. The second—and perhaps most important—is that the hub is the point of transmission control. There must be a hub to synchronize which workstation gets to transmit.

Demand Priority Access

The 802.3 and 802.5 Ethernet frames are retained by this standard, but the CSMA/CD medium access protocol is not. Indeed, one of the better aspects of 100VG-AnyLAN is that no collisions occur. Instead, an access scheme is implemented, whereby a root hub grants to each port, or each cascaded hub, the right to make transmissions. The root hub grants this right using a round-robin polling method, but allows also for two kinds of priorities: normal and high priority. High priority request should only be enabled on ports that need this type of access, such as one that transmits video information.

The root hub (see Figure 3.7) is responsible for controlling who can transmit in the network. The root hub starts at port 1 and polls each of its ports in order. When no transmissions are occurring, workstations and hubs exchange an idle signal. When a workstation needs to transmit a packet, it sends a transmission request to the hub. This request includes the type of priority it wants to use. If the hub is the root hub of the network, it will grant the workstation the right to transmit one packet when its turn comes in the polling sequence. If it is not the root hub, it will pass the transmission request up to the next hub. If the next hub is not the root hub, it too will pass the transmission request up the hub hierarchy.

When the request reaches the root hub, it grants the originating hub, when its polling sequence arrives, the right to transmit the packet. When the root hub polls a particular port and that port is connected to a lower-level hub, the ports on the lower-level hub are polled in order, and so on down the line. In this manner, all ports are granted an equal right to transmit data on the network in an orderly fashion.

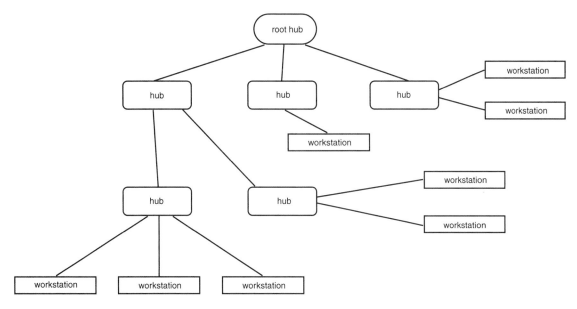

Figure 3.7 The root hub controls all transmissions in the network.

However, when a high priority request occurs on the network, it preempts normal requests. Control is transferred to the hub that originated the high priority request, and afterward control returns to the hub that was preempted. To prevent high priority requests from totally locking out other ports, a normal priority request is elevated to a high priority request when it has been waiting for 300ns.

Security Concerns

In an ethernet network, all workstations in the collision domain can see all the packets. Each workstation usually intercepts only those packets that were destined for it for further processing. It is possible, however, to intercept all packets in this type of network by putting the network adapter into *promiscuous mode*, therefore compromising security.

In 100VG-AnyLAN, this security concern is not so marked. The 100VG-AnyLAN hub will only transmit a packet to ports that lead to the destination of the packet. Although it is still possible for a clever individual to intercept the traffic, it is much more difficult to do so.

Fiber Optics

Fiber-optic cable has many advantages over copper wire cables. Now that the costs associated with fiber-optic cable have dropped dramatically, it is being adopted widely as a networking medium—not just in backbone implementations, but also to the desktop. In Figure 3.8 you can see that the components of a fiber-optic cable are simple. There is a center core that is made up of either glass or plastic. This is surrounded by a cladding material that serves to reflect light back into the core. Surrounding the cladding is a plastic buffer material, which is then encased in a stronger material (usually DuPont Kevlar) that adds strength to the cable. The outside jacket is usually made of PVC.

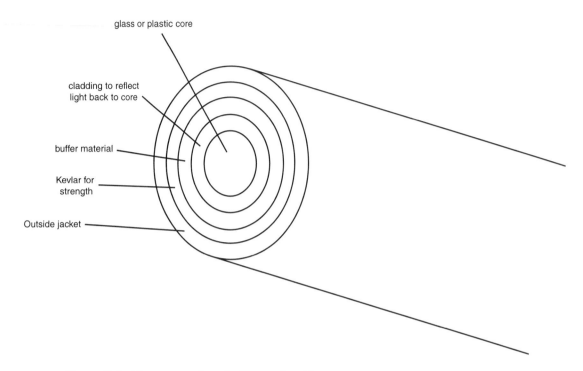

glass or plastic core

cladding to reflect
light back to core

buffer material

Kevlar for
strength

Outside jacket

Figure 3.8   The construction of a fiber-optic cable.

Single- and Multi-Mode Fiber

Fiber-optic cables come in two major varieties: single-mode and multi-mode. It is most likely that you will use multi-mode cables instead of the more expensive single-mode, but you want to understand the difference between the two.

Single-mode fiber uses a very narrow core of only 8 or 9 microns in diameter. This type of cable has a very low rate of attenuation (loss of signal strength) and can be used over great distances. The data to be transmitted is sent through the cable encoded by pulses of light, produced by lasers. This type of cable is usually used by telephone companies because of its distance and high bandwidth capabilities. It is called single-mode because only one frequency of light is used in the transmission.

Multi-mode fiber uses an inner core that is usually 62.5 microns in diameter, though it can be found with a 50 micron core. Instead of lasers, light-emitting diodes (LEDs) are used. Multiple light frequencies are used for transmitting data—hence the name. Multi-mode cables are much cheaper to use than single-mode cables. Most multi-mode fiber installations use light at either 850nm or 1300nm wavelengths. If you are not sure which wavelength will be used when you are installing cables, be sure to have the installer test the cable for both.

Two basic devices used to test optical cables are the power meter and the optical time domain reflectometer (OTDR). The power meter produces readings in decibels (dB) and is used first at the transmitter end to establish a reference reading, and then at the receiving end of the cable. The difference between these two measurements should be compared to the expected loss for the particular cable and the connectors and splices that make it up. As a general guideline, the loss you can expect for the individual components are 0.5 dB for each connector and 0.2 dB for each splice in the cable.

In addition, the length of the cable should be factored in. For multi-mode fiber you can expect a loss of 0.1 dB per 100 feet when using a light source of 850 nm or 0.1 dB per 300 feet when using a light source of 1,300 nm. For multi-mode fiber you can expect a loss of about 0.1 dB for each 600–700 feet.

If the measurements the installer makes disagree significantly with your calculations, you should begin to inspect each component individually to locate any problems.

The OTDR is best suited for testing the installed cables to locate problems. It operates by measuring light that is reflected back due to things such as excessive bends, faulty connectors, and so on.

◄◄ For more information about tools, refer to Chapter 2.

With fiber, there must be two paths that the light can take: one for transmitting and one for receiving. You will often find cables that hold both paths.

Advantages of Fiber

When compared to copper wire cables, fiber almost always comes out on top. It has superior bandwidth capabilities and can be used on very long cable runs. Other advantages include

- Resistant to EMI and RFI because the signal travels using light waves instead of electricity.
- Better security. Because fiber does not radiate electromagnetic waves, it is less susceptible to being tapped.
- Reduced signal attenuation in single-mode fiber.

Gigabit Ethernet

The next standard to be finalized for ethernet will be the Gigabit Ethernet standard. There are two groups working on this faster standard: the IEEE 802.3z task group and a group known as the Gigabit Ethernet Alliance. In 1998, the 802.3z standard was finished and includes the following:

- **1000Base-SX**—Using multi-mode fiber for short distances. Up to 300 meters when using 50-micron multi-mode fiber or 550 meters when using 62.5-micron multi-mode fiber.
- **1000Base-LX**—Using single-mode fiber for distances up to 3,000 meters, or using multi-mode fiber for up to 550 meters.
- **1000Base-CX**—Using twisted-pair copper cables rated for high performance for up to 25 meters. Intended for use in wiring closets.
- **1000Base-T**—For use over Category 5 twisted-pair cables for a maximum distance of up to 100 meters.

The last two specifications are still under development.

When finalized, Gigabit Ethernet is expected to mesh well with 10/100Mbps networks. It will use the same CSMA/CD medium access protocol and the same frame format and size. It will be ideally suited for use as a network backbone to connect routers and hubs or other types of repeaters, because of its compatibility with existing technology and the speeds of transmission that can be accomplished. For example, another feature that will enhance this use is the capability to run in full-duplex mode on non-shared connections. In this mode there will be two connections used to send data so that collision detection will not be needed. This will enable faster data transmissions between a high-end server and a hub or between hubs.

Will Gigabit Ethernet ever reach the desktop, or is it destined to serve only to interconnect other high-speed devices? At first it might seem that the speed will not be needed any time soon on the desktop. Indeed, most of today's operating systems and equipment cannot handle the speeds envisioned by this standard. Furthermore, when integrating other types of transmission such as video or multimedia, Gigabit Ethernet might not fare as well as other technologies, such as ATM, which have built-in quality of service techniques. However, the RSVP (Resource Reservation Protocol) might be able to take up the slack in this area as the technology is further developed and deployed.

Note

To keep track of current developments by the Gigabit Ethernet Alliance, you can go its Web page: `www.gigabit-ethernet.org`. There you will find several informative white papers and other documents.

Incorrect Wiring

It has been estimated by many surveys that most network downtime (up to 50 percent) is due to wiring problems. Sometimes this is because a network was installed and the wiring that was already in place was used. Sometimes it is because the installers of a new cable plant have not carefully adhered to the standards. Rapid personnel changes in businesses today are resulting in frequent additions and changes to the network. Each time a workstation is moved or a new cable strung, the possibility of failure creeps in. This is why it is so important to document your network and keep close track of changes. When it's time to troubleshoot, a network map is an invaluable tool.

Cable Lengths

If you buy your cables in standard lengths, with connectors attached, and if you stick to the standards concerning the number of workstations and hubs for the type of network you are using, you will probably not have any problems that result from cables being too long.

Although you can probably get away with using a cable that is slightly longer than the specification for 10Base-T networking, you won't be so lucky when it comes to faster networks such as 100Base-T. The degradation of the signal as it travels through the wire (attenuation) might not be significant enough to make the network packets unreadable, but in faster networks it might cause problems in timing, resulting in packets being dropped. Remember that in 100Base-T networks the timing intervals are 10 times less than those in 10Base-T networks, and the amount of data is 10 times greater. Those shorter round-trip times are necessary when operating at this speed.

You can measure cable length using a simple cable tester or a time domain reflectometer. If you find that a cable suffers from a large degree of attenuation, the most likely cause is that the cable is too long.

When using a cable tester, you might also find that a cable appears to be shorter than it actually is. This can be due to reflections caused by punch blocks or other intervening connections. If the cable still functions and other tests look okay, you probably don't need to worry about this further.

Checking for Terminations

Remember that coaxial cables need to be terminated with a 50 ohm terminator at each end of the bus. One of these terminators needs to be grounded. If a particular segment of the network suddenly begins to behave erratically, check each end to be sure that the terminators are in place. Check the last workstation on the bus to see if the user has possibly moved the computer recently and tampered with the T-connector. Make sure than only one terminator on the bus is grounded.

Crossed Wires

Most cable testers can perform a wire map function, which can show you which wires are terminating on which pins. If you make your own cables, it is easy to get confused when installing a large number of network drops at a single time. If you keep a stockroom full of cables, label those that are wired to be cross-over cables so that they are not mistakenly used on a patch panel or at a user's work area.

Another common problem is using the wrong type of cable. For example, a cable that has been wired for token ring will use a different set of wires than that wired for 10Base-T.

Bending, Breaking, and Stretching Cables

It is very important that you make sure that cables are not stressed when they are installed. If you break a wire inside the cable, you will probably notice the effect as soon as you install it. If you leave loose cables dangling around in the user's work area, they can be stressed by the user. Simply stepping on a cable can be enough to cause a breakage if the cable has already been stressed, and rolling a chair over a cable certainly won't do it any good.

Locating a cable that is causing problems because of a breakage or bending problem isn't too difficult if you only have one computer on the link, as in a 10Base-T or 100Base-T network. You simply need to examine the cable used by the workstation that is experiencing problems. If the cable is one used to connect hubs, however, the problem can be much more difficult to track down. For that reason, be sure that you follow the standards when installing cables, particularly when it comes to bending. A cable should be bent no more than a radius that is 10 times the diameter of the entire cable. Cables that are bent or that have been compressed can suffer from excessive crosstalk.

Mixing Different Cable Types

Never mix different grades of cable in a network. The cable used in the path from the hub to a workstation needs to be consistent. The entire path is only as good as its weakest member. If you are running a 100Base-T network and use Category 3 cables at the patch panel, you will experience a lot of problems. Also, never use Category 1 or 2 cabling to wire a connection. These grades of cable are not suitable for most modern network devices.

You want to also try to buy your cable from the same manufacturer whenever possible. Cables from different manufacturers can vary in quality. In the early 1990s, a shortage of the material used to make cables safer during fires (fluorinated ethylene propylene) caused manufacturers to substitute other materials in some cases. Mixing cables that were made with one substance with those made with another can cause problems with noise on the network.

Connectors

The quality of the cable you use is important, so it is obvious that the connectors that are used at each end of the cable also need to be of a consistent quality. Just as you should not mix different categories of cables in the network, you also need to be aware that there are different categories of connectors, faceplates, and so on. If you are using Category 5 cables, use connectors that are also rated Category 5.

Use the Same Type

Modular 8 plugs come in several types. One is used for solid core cables and the other is used for stranded core cables, and each uses a different method of attaching to the wire. The jack used for solid-core wires has two tines that lock on to the solid wire. The type used for stranded wire cables merely punctures the wire to make a connection. Some manufacturers do make another type of jack that can be used with either solid or stranded cables, but be careful when buying connectors because using the wrong kind can lead to communication problems that might be difficult to track down.

EMI and RFI

There are two types of electrical interference: Electromagnetic Interference (EMI) and Radio Frequency Interference (RFI). Remember that the higher the frequency used on the cable, the greater the tendency for the current to flow more rapidly at the outer surface of the wire than in the center. If the frequency is great enough, it will cause the wire to radiate energy at a 90-degree angle to the flow of the current in the wire. This energy can affect the signal in another wire that is close by, causing distortion in its signal. Other devices, such as fluorescent lights, can also contribute to this effect.

RFI is caused when two signals with similar properties affect each other. This is why thinnet cables are terminated: to prevent the signal from bouncing back and interfering with the original signal.

There are a few obvious sources for EMI and RFI that you can look for if you suspect them to be the cause of noise on your network:

- Power cables
- Florescent lights
- Machinery that contains electrical motors (especially in a factory environment)
- Transformers
- Radio transmitters (including cell phones)

If you suspect one of these sources, simply move the cables a few feet further away to see if that solves the problem. With florescent lights, you might try replacing the light because they can perform erratically as they near the end of their usable lifetime.

NEXT (Near End Cross-Talk)

When using twisted-pair cables, it is very important to make sure that the twists in the wire are maintained throughout the length of the wire. This includes the connector. Per the standard, you do not want to untwist more than 1/2 inch at the end of the cable when attaching it to the connector. Failure to follow this guideline can result in a condition called *near end cross-talk*, or *NEXT*. NEXT results when the signal in one wire interferes with the signal in an adjacent wire. By twisting the wires in the proper way, it is usually possible to cancel out the effect. The higher the frequency that will be used on the cable, the more twists per length that need to be used. This is one of the reasons you need to always try to use the highest category of cable when you are going to use 100Base-T or Gigabit Ethernet.

If the twists are not maintained correctly at the end of the cable where you attach the connector, NEXT will probably occur. Specifically, NEXT occurs when the stronger transmit signal interferes with the much weaker signal traveling on the receive wire. Because these wires are reversed on the hub and workstation side, you must, when testing for NEXT, be sure to test both ends of the cable. Other possible places to look when trying to diagnose NEXT problems include

- Patch cables: *Never* use ribbon cable (sometimes called silver satin cable) on a patch panel.
- Low category wiring (that is, voice grade instead of Category 3 or 5).
- Old 66 punch down blocks.
- Connectors that are not rated for the category of cable you are using.

Another practice to avoid is connecting two cables using a female-to-female connector. It's tempting to do so, but it's safer to just get the right length of cable to begin with.

Other Problems

There are many different things that can go wrong with the physical aspects of the network. Cabling problems are usually the most suspect because they undergo modification more often than other parts of the network. As cables age and are handled frequently, they can deteriorate because of bending and other stresses. It's cheaper to throw out a suspect cable and replace it than it is to wait for another failure and start the troubleshooting process over again. Remember to use the most basic troubleshooting tool when a network segment starts to misbehave: What has changed on that segment?

Summary

Many different types of cables are used in modern networks to transmit data. Multiple standards define methods of using these cables for networking. When planning a new installation or performing a major upgrade to an existing network, always try to use cables that are rated superior to those that are required. This will give your installed physical cable plant a longer lifetime because it is almost inevitable that you will change out network components for newer, faster ones as the years go by. Laying network cables can be labor intensive and expensive. Provide for more capacity at the beginning, and you might save money in the long run.

Network Interface Cards

SOME OF THE MAIN TOPICS IN THIS CHAPTER ARE

Choosing a Hardware Bus Type: PCI, ISA, or EISA?

Software Drivers

Multihomed Systems

IRQs

Base I/O Ports

Troubleshooting Network Cards

The *network interface card* (*NIC*) is the piece of hardware that links your computer or workstation to the network media. The NIC resides at the physical level of the OSI Seven Layer reference model and is the device that is responsible for translating data into zeros and ones for transmission on the transmission media for the network. The driver software for the card interfaces with the hardware elements of the card and the protocol stack that runs on the computer to send data to and from other computers. Although many cards manufactured today support Plug-and-Play, not all operating systems do. So, although you might find that installing a new workstation or upgrading an old one with a new network adapter card is an easy task, this might not always be the case. In this chapter, you will look at the items that are typically configurable for NICs and list some of the methods you can use to troubleshoot cards that do not function as expected.

Choosing a Hardware Bus Type: PCI, ISA, or EISA?

The ISA bus is an older architecture that has been slowly going away as manufacturers move to EISA bus computers. The newest bus is the PCI, or Peripheral Component Interconnect, bus. This bus has many advantages over previous standards, including dramatically faster data transfer rates and 32- or 64-bit wide data paths. Devices on the PCI bus can also use a feature called bus mastering, whereby they can take control of the bus and directly transfer large amounts of data to system memory without involving the CPU. Microsoft and major PC vendors are likely to begin ending support for older ISA and EISA products in the next year or two. For that reason, you might want to consider purchasing network cards that fit into a PCI slot in your computer rather than an older *legacy* card, as ISA and EISA cards will be called in the near future.

Software Drivers

When networks were composed of mainly proprietary solutions for a particular vendor's systems, the vendor could write a simple software driver that could handle all the functions for the protocols that the vendor chose to implement. In networks today, it is usually necessary to use more than one type of protocol on a network, so now software drivers must be capable of handling more than one protocol.

In the case of servers or routers, another factor to consider is a system that has multiple network cards installed. The driver software must be capable of distinguishing the different NICs, as well as the protocols supported on each.

The two main types of NIC software drivers that you will find today are called ODI and NDIS. Predating both of these, however, is a type of driver called a Packet Driver, which was developed by FTP Software in 1986. Because different operating systems or networking software might work with only a specific kind of driver, you must be aware of the kinds of drivers that a network card can be used with if you are planning to upgrade NICs or, perhaps, undergo a more complex change such as migrating to a new operating system. For example, if you are thinking of migrating to a Novell network, you should concentrate on devices that support DI drivers. In a Microsoft networking environment, you would need to be looking for devices that support NDIS.

Packet Drivers

In the early days of networking, one of the main problems with network cards and protocol stacks was that they were too closely interrelated; that is, purchasing a network protocol software package meant you had to be sure it supported the network card you were using. The code to interface with the card was provided by the specific protocol package instead of by the operating system. This, of course, meant that developers of protocol stacks had to spend lots of time developing code to support the many different types of network cards that were on the market.

The Packet Driver was developed by FTP Software to create an interface that protocols could use to access functions provided by the network card. Protocol stacks that use the Packet Driver can exist on the computer and use the network card at the same time. Previously, network drivers were tightly bound to the network card at boot time, and you had to reboot the computer each time you wanted to use a different network protocol.

ODI

Open Data-Link Interface (ODI) was developed by Novell and Apple Computer in 1989 with the goal of providing a seamless interface at the network, transport, and data-link levels, as shown in the OSI Reference Model. The ODI specification can be divided into three main components:

- **Multi-Link Interface Driver (MLID)**—This component controls communication between the network card and the link support layer. It consists of a section of code written by Novell called the Media Support Module (MSM) and the Hardware-Specific Module (HSM), written by the card vendor. The MSM provides the functions that implement standard network functions for the media types that are supported by ODI. The HSM code is written by the vendor to handle the details of its particular card; the HSM code communicates with the MSM.

- **Link Support Layer (LSL)**—This layer enables multiple protocols to exist on a single network card. The LSL is a gateway that determines which protocol stack a packet belongs to and sends it on its way.

- **Protocol Stack**—This component gets packets from the LSL and sends the packet on to another higher-level protocol or application.

Because ODI is modular, it makes writing protocol stacks or software drivers easier for third-party vendors. The code developer who works on the software to implement a protocol must only write to the specifications of the ODI interface, without regard to the underlying network card or the network media. The network card vendor must simply worry about writing code that can communicate with the MSM to implement the functions that are implemented by the card's hardware.

NDIS

Network Driver Interface Specification (NDIS) was initially developed by Microsoft and 3Com Corporation, and more recent versions have been developed by Microsoft. NDIS serves the same purpose, more or less, that ODI does in that it allows the development of software for multiple protocol stacks to exist on multiple network adapters in a single computer. The actual implementation details, however, are quite different.

In Windows NT, transport protocols span a portion of the Transport Layer, the Network Layer, and a portion of the Data-Link Layer. Transport protocols such as NetBEUI Frame (NBF) and TCP are implemented by calling services in the NDIS interface. NDIS doesn't completely hide the underlying network media from the protocol stack in the way that ODI does. This limits most drivers to using Ethernet 802.3 or Token Ring 802.5. Drivers for ARCnet, for example, are written to take this into account and make the media look like ethernet or token ring to the software layers above.

Both ODI and NDIS provide support for each other. ODI provides a program called ODINSUP to support NDIS drivers. Windows NT comes with NWLink, which is Microsoft's implementation of the IPX/SPX protocols. Windows NT also comes with Client Services for NetWare, which allows Windows NT clients to access resources on NetWare servers. Gateway Services for NetWare performs similar functions by using a single Windows NT computer as a gateway to the NetWare services. A separate product called File and Print Services for NetWare is available from Microsoft and can be used on a NetWare client to give it access to resources in a Windows NT network.

Multihomed Systems

Some computers need more than one network card. For example, if you have two subnets in your LAN that both need to connect to the same server, the server computer will need more than one network adapter. Some operating systems enable a server to route packets between subnets when more than one network card is installed. It is also possible, depending on the type of computer, to attach more than one network card to the same subnet. In either case, each network card must be set up with its own network address and host name.

For example, a high-performance server might be used on an intranet to provide a WWW service and an FTP service to clients. If the server is capable of processing the requests at the required rate but the network adapter card is a limiting factor, you can install multiple cards and assign an address and host name for each service.

IRQs

Although many new NICs support *plug-and-play* capabilities, which means they can be automatically detected and configured by the operating system, this capability is not implemented in all operating systems, such as many UNIX variants. Because of this, you might find yourself having to configure a card manually when upgrading a system with a new card or when adding other devices that might conflict with the NIC. The two main items you will commonly have to modify are the values for the IRQ (Interrupt ReQuest Line) and the base I/O port.

When a device on the computer's bus needs to get the attention of the CPU, it uses a hardware mechanism called the *Interrupt ReQuest Line*, or *IRQ*. Hardware interrupts are executed by signaling the CPU through a set of wires that is connected to the pins that attach the CPU to the motherboard. It is a direct connection. Because there is a variety of devices that might need to get the CPU's attention at any particular time, one IRQ is not sufficient. Instead, in most cases each device has its own interrupt line. When a device signals the CPU using an interrupt, it is telling the CPU that it has a processing request that needs to be satisfied as quickly as possible.

When the CPU receives an interrupt, it grants the device its attention for a short period of time—as long as it is not currently servicing another interrupt that is of a higher priority. It is also possible that the CPU is performing some task that is too critical to allow for an interrupt. When that is the case, the CPU does not allow a hardware interrupt to distract it. For that reason, this type of interrupt is called a *maskable interrupt*. This means that the CPU can be put into a mode in which it masks out these interrupts while it is busy on an ultra important task, and then reenables the interrupts when it is again capable of processing them.

The number of IRQs that is available on the system depends on the system bus type. Early PCs that were based on the ISA (Industry Standard Architecture) bus type had only eight hardware interrupts, numbered from 0–7, as shown in Table 4.1.

Table 4.1   ISA Bus Hardware Interrupts

IRQ	Function
0	System Timer
1	Keyboard Controller
2	Available
3	Serial Port 2 and 4 (COM2:, COM4:)
4	Serial Port 1 and 3 (COM1:, COM3:)
5	Hard Disk Drive Controller
6	Floppy Diskette Drive Controller
7	Parallel Port 1 (LPT1:)

This small set of IRQs was sufficient for a small system with few devices. As you can see, only one IRQ—2—is available for an additional device in this layout. When the EISA (Extended Industry Standard Architecture) bus was developed, the number of interrupts was doubled to 16. However, to do this, two interrupt controllers were needed on the system; one of them funnels its interrupts through IRQ2. This means that there are actually only 15 interrupts available for use by other devices on the system. Table 4.2 shows the devices that usually make use of these IRQs.

Table 4.2   ISA Bus Hardware Interrupts

IRQ	Function
0	System Timer
1	Keyboard Controller
2	Second Interrupt Controller
8	Real-time clock
9	Network Card
10	Available
11	SCSI card
12	Motherboard mouse port
13	Math coprocessor

(continues)

Table 4.2   Continued

IRQ	Function
14	Primary IDE (Hard Disk Drive) controller
15	Secondary IDE (Hard Disk Drive) controller
3	Serial Port 2 and 4 (COM2:, COM4:)
4	Serial Port 1 and 3 (COM1:, COM3:)
5	Sound card or parallel port 2 (lpt2:)
6	Floppy Disk Drive Controller
7	Parallel Port 1 (LPT1:)

Notice that the IRQ numbers in Table 4.2 are not in numerical order. Instead, they are listed in order of priority, with those at the top of the table having a higher priority than those at the bottom. Because the additional eight IRQs were added by a mechanism that uses the original IRQ2, those IRQs all have a higher priority than IRQs 3–7. On some systems, IRQ9 is used to perform the same functions that were done by IRQ2 in the earlier design. For this reason, you might see this IRQ on a card labeled as 2, 9, or possibly IRQ 2/9.

If your computer is a plug-and-play system, you might find that you do not need to make any changes to the card or the system software to select the IRQ. If you do, however, be sure to consult the documentation that comes with the card to determine which interrupts it can use and how they are set. IRQs are usually set by jumpers on the card. A jumper consists of a set of pins that can be connected together to form a complete circuit by placing a connector between them.

Base I/O Ports

Again, if you find yourself in a situation where your computer's operating system does not provide plug-and-play capabilities, you might have to manually configure the value of the memory address that the network card uses to transfer data to and from the system. After the network card signals to the CPU that processing must be done, it uses a memory address called the *base I/O port address* for this purpose. Because many devices in the system might use memory port addresses, it is important to configure each device to use a different address so that any data transfers performed do not conflict with each other.

On most systems, 64K of memory is set up to be used for I/O ports, so they do not represent a limited resource like the IRQ does. Consult your operating system documentation to determine how to display the current memory assignments for this area of memory. For example, in Microsoft Windows, a utility called Microsoft Diagnostics can be used to display a wide variety of hardware and software configurations. In Figure 4.1 you can see the utility, displaying the I/O ports on a Windows NT Server computer. Note that at the bottom of the display are buttons you can use to view other device-related information, such as IRQs and Memory allocations.

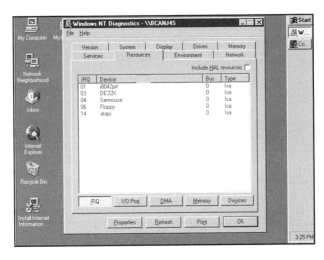

Figure 4.1   The Microsoft Diagnostics utility can show you how I/O ports are assigned.

In addition to the base I/O port, some devices use a section of memory to buffer data temporarily. For this, they require a *base memory address*, which points to the start of the buffer. Your network card may or may not make use of the computer's RAM, so check the documentation carefully if a conflict arises.

Troubleshooting Network Cards

When you install or replace a network adapter card and find that it does not function, there are several things you can examine to locate the problem. The cause might be due to a hardware problem with the card itself, the computer, or possibly the hub or cable that links the card to the hub. It might be a simple problem of changing the configuration for the device. If you're having a bad day, it might even be a combination of these things!

When adding a new network card to a workstation, you want to first review the documentation that comes with the card to determine what values you can use for the IRQ, base I/O port address, and so on. You might also need to look at documentation for other devices on the system because resolving a conflict might require you to change some other device instead of the network card.

Check the LEDs

Network cards usually have one LED (light emitting diode) that you can see from outside the computer. Some cards might have two LEDs. Generally, if the card has only one LED, it should be lit if the card is capable of communicating with the hub. Most hubs also have an LED status light for each port, so it is a good idea to check the hub also. The problem can be in the hub, the network card, or possibly the cable that connects them. Of course, you should be sure to review the documentation for the card to determine the actual meaning of any LEDs it might have. For example, some 3Com cards have one light that is used to indicate the link status. If the light is on, the link is okay. If the light is flashing, there is a problem with the transmit/receive wires in the cable used (reversed polarity). Another LED is used to indicate when the network card is sending or receiving data.

If it appears that there is a problem with the link, try to localize the problem and determine where the fault is by trying the following:

- Check all connectors to be sure they are firmly plugged into their sockets.
- Try another port on the hub.
- Try a different cable, preferably one that you know is in good working condition.
- Try moving the network adapter to a different slot in the computer.
- Substitute a card that you know is good to see if the problem still presents itself.

If none of these options seem to work, try the card in another computer where no problem exists. If it works there, the problem obviously does not lie in the NIC.

Run the Adapter's Diagnostic Program

Most cards, even those labeled as Plug and Play, come with a floppy disk that contains software drivers and a diagnostic program. Usually, you will find that it is necessary to boot the computer into MS-DOS to run the diagnostic program, and indeed some cards come with a floppy disk that is also MS-DOS bootable. When using a diagnostic program like this, be sure that no other drivers or memory managers are loaded when you perform the test to help eliminate conflicts that can result in inaccurate results. Note that "MS-DOS" does not mean a command prompt window in Windows 98 or Windows NT; it means booting the computer into the actual MS-DOS operating system.

The kinds of tests that can be run will vary, but you will probably get a menu that enables you to run one or all the tests that the program is capable of. This can include simple hardware-specific checks and loopback tests. Some cards provide for an echo test in which two cards from the same manufacturer can send and receive packets from each other for a diagnostic test. If the card cannot pass all the diagnostic tests supplied by the vendor, and if you are sure there are no other problems (such as a bad slot in the computer's system bus), you probably have a bad card and need to replace it.

Configuration Conflicts

If the card passes the vendor's diagnostic tests and you can find nothing wrong with the physical components of the card, computer system, or the hub, it is time to check into the configuration of the card. Earlier in this chapter, in the section "Base I/O Ports," you saw how the Microsoft Diagnostics utility under Windows NT can be used to determine which memory address a device is configured to use. This utility can also be used to determine the IRQ and other configuration information for the devices installed in the computer. In Figure 4.2, you can see this utility as it executes under Windows 98. In this version, the Resources tab has been used after the network device was selected.

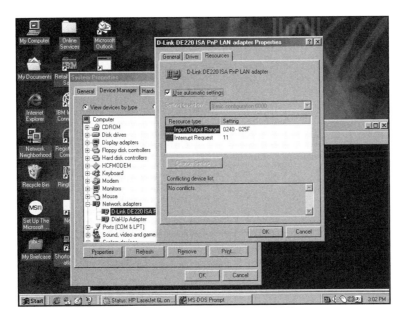

Figure 4.2 Under Windows 98, you can check for device conflicts easily by using the Microsoft Diagnostic utility.

At the bottom of this figure is a field titled Conflicting Device List. Fortunately for me, no other hardware devices are listed here. If you find that, in your case, other devices are shown here, you can take the appropriate action and reassign the IRQs or memory addresses as needed until all devices are functioning correctly.

For UNIX users, the situation is more complicated. In many cases, adding new hardware requires that you recompile the kernel and reboot. Many systems will recognize well-known hardware components and configure them automatically, but this is not always the case. Depending on the version of UNIX, you might be able to examine configuration files to determine the interrupts and memory addresses used by a particular device. Check your system documentation for further information.

Preventive Steps to Take

Keeping track of system information for the computers in your network can make troubleshooting tasks a lot easier. For example, a spreadsheet that lists all the nodes on your network, along with configuration information, is very useful when you need to upgrade or replace a particular component. If you have this information already available before a problem arises, you will be able to devote more of your time to solving the problem.

This kind of information can also be used to help you make purchasing decisions. For example, if you know the number of ISA and PCI slots that are built into a workstation, and if you know which of these have already been populated, you won't make the mistake of buying an ISA card when there are no slots left that you can use it in.

Summary

Network interface cards are an important piece of the network puzzle. When you have properly configured a card for a workstation or server, you will probably not have to deal with it further. However, to make troubleshooting (and replacement) easier, it is a good idea to keep a record of the configuration information—such as the IRQ and the base I/O address—that was available on the system to use the card.

When choosing a network card, be sure that the manufacturer has a driver that will work with the computer and network operating system you will be using. Most NICs come with industry standard drivers that are ODI- or NDIS-compliant. If a new version of the operating system is in your near future, check with vendors to be sure you will be able to obtain a driver that will work.

Bridges, Routers, Switches, and Repeaters

SOME OF THE MAIN TOPICS IN THIS CHAPTER ARE

Repeaters

Bridges

Switches

Routers

Summary

Every ethernet network topology has two basic underlying factors: You can only go so far with one cable and you can only connect so many workstations to the LAN before it will begin to suffer from excessive collisions. A *collision* occurs when two or more nodes attempt to send a signal at the same time.

▶▶ For more information on collisions, see Chapter 12, "Collision Rates."

In a bus topology such as 10Base-2 or 10Base-5 there are limits to how long the cable segment that forms the bus can be and a limit to how many workstations you can put on the cable. In a 10Base-T hub-based network you can only chain together so many hubs and attach so many workstations before the same problems begin to apply—too long or too many, you might say.

When you need to expand your LAN you can take several upgrade paths, each of which progressively solves one or both of these problems to a degree. Each involves using a specialized device, which is the subject of this chapter.

Repeaters

Repeaters are the simplest and least expensive method of joining multiple network segments. In a 10Base-T network, a simple hub operates as a multiport repeater, transmitting any incoming signal on all other ports so that every connected Ethernet node can receive the signal. In the case of a hub, however, the total size of the network does not change. It is still bound by the limitations imposed by the standard for distance and the number of nodes that can be connected.

A *repeater* is a device that can join two physical segments and functions by amplifying the signal it receives on one port before transmitting it out the other port to the next network segment. Because a repeater only amplifies the electrical signal and does not perform any actions on the actual information represented by the signal, it is totally ignorant of any addressing or routing information that might be encapsulated in the frame. This results in the repeater amplifying not only good frames that are transmitted on the network, but also background noise as well.

In a small network, this kind of device can be used advantageously to increase the size of a network based on a bus topology. For example, a Thinnet network (10Base-2) is limited to cable segment lengths of only 185 meters, or about 607 feet. The specifications for this kind of network enable you to join up to five cable segments using four repeaters, which gives an overall length to the network of about 3,000 feet, as is shown in Figure 5.1. Remember also that in this kind of network you can attach workstations to only three of the five segments. The other two segments can be used to extend the length of the LAN. In Figure 5.1, one segment is used to extend the LAN between floors in the building and another is used on the first floor to add extra distance to get to the location of the users.

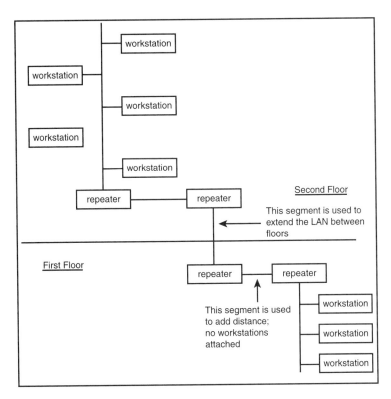

Figure 5.1 Repeaters can extend the network beyond the length allowed for one cable segment.

Advantages to using simple repeaters include price and simplicity. They are usually relatively inexpensive devices when compared to bridges or switches, and they require no management console or intervention by the administrator for configuration. A repeater can be used as a quick remedy when your small LAN segment needs to be extended before you need to explore further upgrade options. The main disadvantage of the repeater as compared to other devices discussed in this chapter is that it does nothing to reduce network traffic as you add more nodes to the local broadcast domain.

Bridges

Whereas repeaters operate at the Physical Layer of the OSI layered networking reference model, another device, called a *bridge*, can be useful when joining cable segments. A bridge operates at the Data Link Layer and does a little more than just amplifying the incoming signal and sending it out the remaining ports.

A bridge is basically a repeater with a little intelligence. At the Data Link Layer the Media Access Control (MAC) address is used to distinguish each network device on the LAN. When a bridge is used to connect cable segments, it examines the frame and determines the source and destination MAC addresses. It adds these values to a table that it keeps so that it can learn which devices are attached to which ports. Because a bridge becomes aware of which devices are attached to its ports, it can make decisions when it comes to transmitting an incoming frame on the other ports so that the frame is sent out only over the port that will get it to its eventual destination.

In Figure 5.2 you can see a simple network, consisting of two cable segments separated by a bridge. On each of these segments there is a hub to which workstations are attached.

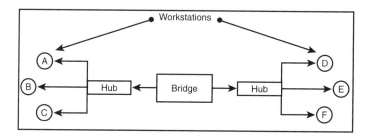

Figure 5.2   A bridge can be used to connect network segments.

When the bridge is first powered up it has no knowledge of the layout of the network. There is no information in its internal tables telling it which devices are on the network, much less which cable segment they are attached to. This information is built up over a period of time as the bridge learns. Consider the following scenario:

- Workstation A sends out a packet that it wants delivered to workstation C.
- The hub to which workstation A is attached repeats the frame on its other ports, one of which is connected to the cable to which the bridge is attached. The bridge also creates an entry in its internal table, recording the MAC address for workstation A and noting which port it came from.
- The bridge does not yet know which segment workstation C is attached to, so it repeats the frame on its other port. Workstation C recognizes that the frame is addressed to it, and communication between workstation D and workstation A continues. However, when the bridge sees the first packet from workstation C, addressed to workstation A, it does not repeat the frame on the other ports because it now knows that workstation A is on the same segment as C. It also makes an entry in its table for workstation C so that future communications on this segment from A to C will not be repeated on the other port.
- Workstation C sends a packet destined for workstation F. Again, the hub notes the port and MAC address for workstation C—because it has not heard of it before—and makes an entry into its table. The frame is repeated on to the segment that is attached to the other port.
- When workstation F receives the frame, it sends a frame back to workstation C. When the hub sees the destination MAC address, it recognizes the address as one stored in its table and repeats the frame on to the port that has workstation C attached.

As you can see, every time the bridge sees a packet that has a source address that is not in its table, it makes an entry so that in the future it will know whether it needs to forward packets that are destined for that MAC address on to other segments. As things progress, the bridge eventually learns all the MAC addresses for active workstations on the segments to which it is connected. When the bridge receives a frame whose destination address it does not recognize, it repeats the frame on to the other port by default.

Note

Because this type of bridge forwards frames without having to interact with the source or destination nodes, they are not aware of the fact that a bridge might exist between them. For this reason, this type of bridge is usually referred to as a *transparent bridge*.

The benefits of a bridge over a simple repeater are obvious. The bridge cuts down on unnecessary broadcasts because it does not forward a frame after it learns which port a MAC address is attached to unless it is necessary to get the frame delivered to its destination.

Segmenting a LAN

Bridges can be used to take a simple network and divide it into segments to help isolate broadcast traffic. The 80/20 rule states that you need to segment a LAN with bridges so that 80 percent of the traffic is destined for devices attached to the local segment, whereas 20 percent might need to pass through a bridge to reach its destination.

By taking a single LAN and placing a bridge between nodes that do very little communication, you effectively increase the available bandwidth because the entire LAN does not have to hear broadcast traffic for every single node. If you have one set of users who make heavy use of a particular server and another set of users who rarely use the server but send a lot of print jobs to a print server, separating these two groups with a bridge cuts down on the overall network traffic, while still allowing every workstation to exchange data.

So far only the connection of two LAN segments has been discussed. In most situations, the network is more complicated than that. You can use multiple bridges to break a LAN into more than two broadcast domains. In Figure 5.3, users in segment A make heavy use of the file and print servers located on their segment. Occasionally, however, they need to access the file server that resides on the other side of a bridge in segment B. Users in segment C make the most demand on the print server on their segment, but sometimes need to access the file server located on segment B also.

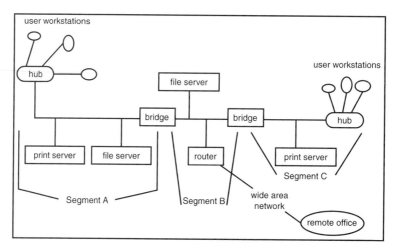

Figure 5.3   You can use multiple bridges to break a LAN into smaller network segments.

Still, both groups of users need to exchange data with a remote office on a periodic basis, and it is accessible through a router connected to segment B. By placing the router on this segment, you keep down the level of traffic the router must process because it does not see every packet that contends for network bandwidth on segments A and C. Because the file server on segment B is used by both groups of users, but not on a frequent basis, the traffic to and from it is not likely to place a strain on the router's capability to process packets.

The Spanning Tree Algorithm

It is also possible to connect two network segments with more than a single bridge. This can be done to provide for fault tolerance. If one bridge ceases to function properly, another path exists between the segments so that users are unaffected, as you can see in Figure 5.4.

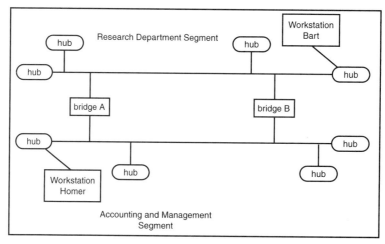

Figure 5.4   You can use more than one bridge to connect the same segments.

However, using multiple bridges can result in a lot of confusion if the bridges are not configured to cooperate. For example, consider the following situation:

- If the workstation named Homer sends out a frame that has the workstation Bart as its destination, both bridges A and B see the frame on the segment used by the accounting and management divisions. They both retransmit the frame onto the segment used by the research department.

- Both bridges then add an entry into their internal tables so that they will remember that Homer is connected to the accounting and management segment.

- When bridge B sees the frame that bridge A transmitted onto the research segment, it does not understand that this frame is a duplicate of the one that it also transmitted. Instead, because the bridge only looks at the MAC address, the bridge sees the frame as if it were just broadcast by Homer on this segment.

- Bridge B then decides that Homer must have been moved, and changes its internal table so that Homer now is attached to the Research segment. Bridge A suffers the same fate, based on the frame that was originally retransmitted by bridge B.

Depending on timing issues, it is also possible that Bart might try to send a frame to Homer. If it is detected by either bridge while they still have Homer listed incorrectly in their internal tables, Homer will never get the frame because the bridges assume that workstation Homer is on the same cable segment as workstation Bart, and there is no need to send a copy of the frame over to the segment that Homer is actually located on.

But it can still get worse. After both bridges have retransmitted the other's retransmitted frame back to the first segment, they again see the other bridge's newly retransmitted packet and once again make changes to their internal tables, once again forwarding the duplicate frames back to the research department's LAN segment!

Note

A bridge does not maintain an entry for a node in its internal table forever. In actuality, each bridge has a time-to-live (TTL) value that it uses. When an entry has been in the table longer than this value without being refreshed by the bridge again seeing it in a source address, the entry is removed.

This infinite looping makes it impractical to use more than one bridge to connect two segments. In a large environment, chaos can result if an administrator accidentally connects two segments with a second router without realizing the problem. This chaos is usually referred to as a *broadcast storm*.

▶▶ For more information on broadcast storms, see Chapter 13, "Ethernet Errors."

To prevent just this type of situation, the IEEE 802.1D specification defines the *spanning tree algorithm*. This specification allows bridges to interact with each other to initially create and then maintain a loop-free network. Although there might be many routes that a frame can take through a multiple bridged network, the spanning tree algorithm establishes only one route that a frame can take between any two points. When a new bridge is added to or a bridge is removed from the network, the bridges recalculate the paths and nodes can still communicate, provided more than one bridge can be used to forward the frame.

Several values are used to provide the information needed by the algorithm to calculate the paths that are to make up the tree. The administrator of the network can assign these values. They are

- **Bridge ID**—A unique identifier for each bridge.
- **Port ID**—A unique identifier for each port on each bridge.
- **Port priority**—A relative value designating a port's priority.
- **Port cost**—A value that designates a "cost" for a port. The higher the bandwidth of the link, the lower the cost for the port.

When a bridge is added to the network, it multicasts a message called a Bridge Protocol Data Unit (BPDU); this contains information, including the ID and cost information of the bridge. The bridges in the network evaluate these messages to calculate the correct paths that make up the tree of bridges.

The root bridge is selected based on the bridge ID value. The bridge that has the lowest bridge ID value becomes the root bridge. If two bridges both have been assigned the same ID, the one that has the lowest MAC address becomes the root bridge.

Every other bridge then has to calculate the lowest cost path that will connect it to the root bridge. The port that provides the lowest cost path to the root bridge is designated the root port for that bridge. In a case in which there are two ports that have an equal cost path to the root bridge, the one with the lowest priority to the root bridge is designated to be the root port.

For each LAN, a designated bridge must bespecified. If only one bridge is connected to the LAN, it obviously becomes the designated bridge. If more than one bridge is connected, the bridge that has the lowest cost path to the root bridge becomes the designated bridge for that LAN.

For bridges that are not the designated bridge for a LAN, each port that is not a root port on the bridge is set to a blocked state so that it does not transmit any data. These blocked ports still listen for BDPU messages, however, so that when the network topology changes they can be used to begin the tree calculating process again. Bridges continue to exchange BDPU messages on a periodic basis. When bridges detect that a designated bridge has failed because they do not receive a BDPU message from it within the specified time limit, they begin to recalculate the tree topology.

When to Bridge

Bridges do more than just join segments together. They are inexpensive devices that can be used to help grow a network until you reach the point where a switch or router makes more sense. By limiting the area in which a frame can travel, you can use them for

- **Reducing network congestion**—Grouping workstations that frequently interact with each other reduces the total number of frames broadcast throughout the entire network.
- **Extend the length of the network**—Bridges enable you to connect multiple segments together until you reach the limit for the particular topology.

- **Security purposes**—Place all workstations that exchange confidential data on a single network segment and use a bridge to connect them to the rest of the LAN. This way, only those workstations on that local segment can intercept the packets that are exchanged. A network sniffer on another segment, for example, cannot intercept these packets because they never get to that segment.

- **Fault containment**—One malfunctioning device on the LAN is less likely to cause a problem beyond the segment to which it is connected.

However, in many cases a bridge only makes sense when used in a moderately sized network, unless it is used in conjunction with other devices such as switches or routers to limit traffic on a few segments. When the network outgrows the distances imposed by the topology limitations, you must use other means as an upgrade path.

Switches

Think back to the simple passive hub: Remember that it functions by repeating incoming traffic on the other ports so that each node connected to the hub hears all packets that are broadcast throughout the LAN. A hub has many advantages over the bus topology network in that wiring is centralized and a cable break does not bring down the entire LAN. However, a simple passive hub does nothing to reduce the total traffic on the LAN.

As discussed in the previous section, a bridge can be used to join segments together to help compartmentalize traffic on specific segments and reduce the total amount of packets that traverse the entire LAN. However, it is terribly expensive to use a bridge for each and every workstation on the network.

Using a *switch*, however, you can achieve almost the same effect. A switch operates like a hub, with each port being used to connect to a workstation. The difference, however, is that a switch does not repeat each broadcast packet on all the other ports. Instead, a switch outputs the packet only onto the port to which the destination device is connected. Like a bridge, a switch learns the locations of specific devices by examining the source address of a packet when a workstation first sends out a transmission. After the switch builds a table of workstation addresses, it is no longer necessary to send a packet to all ports.

Technical Note

Here we are discussing how a basic switch works with individual workstations. There are also switches that connect LAN segments that have more than one workstation attached to a port. There are switches to which you can attach a single workstation, or a LAN segment to each port, depending on your needs. For the purposes of this discussion, the concept has been simplified so that it is easier to understand.

In Figure 5.5 you can see an example of a LAN connected by a switch rather than a hub. In this LAN, when workstation A wants to send a packet to workstation D, neither of the other workstations is burdened with having to examine the packet header to determine if it is destined for them. This is because they never see the packet. This means that the available bandwidth on each workstation's connection to the switch has increased because only two nodes exist on that segment: the switch and the workstation. This dramatically reduces the broadcast domain seen by each workstation in a large network.

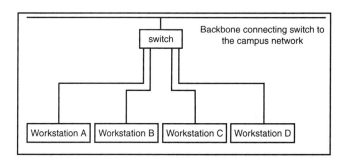

Figure 5.5   Only the switch and each end node communicate on a segment.

Full-Duplex Ethernet

The switch makes possible another new concept in ethernet technology: *full-duplex*. Remember that in a standard Ethernet implementation, each device must contend with all others that want to make use of the transmission medium. The CSMA/CD mechanism is used so that only one device successfully ends up talking on the wire at any particular time. The more stations that are added to the collision domain, the lower the total throughput as collisions increase and retransmissions become more frequent.

When you have a situation in which a single workstation is connected to a switch, there are only two stations in the local collision domain: the switch and the workstation. Because the transmit and receive functions are performed by separate wires, it is possible to do both at once. Because there are no competing devices, the switch and the workstation can send and receive from each other at the same time, the result of which is a full-duplex operation. Because there is no contention for the wire, there are no collisions. You can come close to achieving the actual 10Mbps throughput of the wire. Actually, when you consider the capability to transmit and receive, you can achieve a total throughput of close to 20Mbps on a 10Mbps network!

This isn't done without some extra expense, though. Ordinary ethernet cards are not fashioned to operate in this mode, so if you want to upgrade to a switch and allow for full-duplex operation, you also have to purchase new network adapter cards. This might make sense in some situations, though not for all devices on your network. For example, you upgrade and replace a hub with a switch that is capable of full-duplex operation. Most of the workstations are for ordinary users, none of which individually generates a whole lot of network traffic.

On this same network you have a high-end server that is capable of processing many end-user requests rapidly, but the bottleneck is the network adapter card, which is a standard Ethernet card capable of sending or receiving—but not both at the same time.

By replacing the network card on the server with a full-duplex card and plugging it into a port on the switch that supports full-duplex operations, you can increase the availability of the server to its clients and incur only the expense of a new network card for the server.

Switch Types

There are many different architectures used for switching at this time. Because it is a hot technology, many different approaches are being tried. Some involve software that makes decisions much like a router and sends frames on their merry way. Others are hardware-based and can perform better because no single component such as a CPU can be bogged down when too much traffic passes through the switch.

There are also two modes of operation that can be used by a switch when it forwards a packet out of a selected port: cut-through mode and store-and-forward mode.

Cut-Through Mode

In this type of switch, the switch begins transmitting the incoming packet on the outgoing port after it receives the header information (or about 20 or 30 bytes). All the switch needs to determine which port to output the frame on is the destination address, which is contained in the header. The switch continues to receive information and transmit it until the frame has been "switched" from one port to another. The advantage to this mode of operation is speed. As long as nothing else goes wrong, the packet gets on its way to its destination at a very fast pace, with little time involved in the switch.

There are several disadvantages to this method, however. The switch begins to send the packet out before it knows if the frame is damaged in any way. If the frame has corrupted data, the switch cannot detect it unless it first receives the entire frame and then computes the CRC value stored in the frame check sequence field. If a frame is badly malformed, as when a NIC sends out a frame that is too long, a cut-through switch might think it is a broadcast packet and send it out of all ports, causing unnecessary traffic and congestion.

Store-and-Forward Mode

In the store-and-forward mode of operation, the switch buffers the frame in its own memory before beginning to send it out the appropriate port. There are two main advantages to this technique:

- The switch can connect two different topologies, such as 10Mbps and 100Mbps networks, without having to worry about the different speeds.
- The switch can operate like a bridge and check the integrity of the frame, allowing it to discard damaged frames and not propagate them onto other network segments.

Although this increases the latency factor, this delay is usually not a big concern when you consider the increased throughput you can achieve with a switch.

When to Switch

In general, you can say that a switch will probably increase your network performance if your network makes a lot of use of hubs and you have network traffic problems. In most cases, a switch is an excellent choice for an upgrade path when other options require a larger expense that you cannot justify at this time.

Do not think of a switch as simply a replacement for a hub. There are some circumstances in which a switch does not do much to improve performance. For example, in Figure 5.6 you can see a small departmental LAN where each workstation is connected to a switch, which in turn has a server attached to a port.

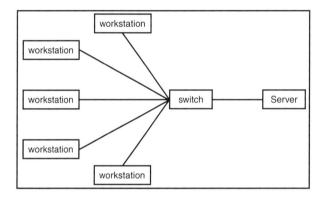

Figure 5.6   A switch might not improve performance when all workstations need to access the same local resource.

Because all the workstations that access this server are in the same location as the server, the switch merely serves to allow one workstation to converse with the server at a time. This achieves about the same throughput as putting the server and the workstations on a hub.

If you increase the number of ports on the switch that are connected to the server, however, the situation changes (see Figure 5.7).

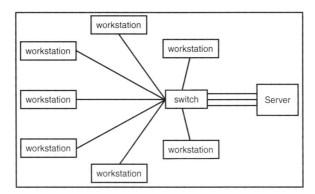

Figure 5.7   Connecting a busy server to a switch via multiple ports might improve performance.

Now the switch can simultaneously handle up to three data exchanges between the workstations and the server. As long as the server itself is of sufficient capacity to handle the exchange, throughput increases and users will notice a faster response from the server.

In general, a switch works best when connecting multiple users to multiple resources. In the example shown in Figure 5.7, the single server becomes a multiple resource because it has multiple pathways connecting it to the switch.

When considering whether a segment connected to a switch should have one computer or multiple computers attached to it, think about the type of traffic that will be generated by the computers. If you have several workstations that make little demand on the network resources, put them on a single segment and connect it to the switch. If you are connecting a multimedia server that generates a lot of network traffic, put it on a segment by itself and connect it to the switch.

When you are evaluating different switch products, there are several things you must consider. What is the forwarding rate from one port to another? What is the latency? Also remember to inquire about the total bandwidth that can pass through a switch at one time, not just a port-to-port value. Does the switch support any kind of flow control? Some models use a mechanism similar to the CSMCS/CD mechanism and simulate collisions on the port to which the sending station is attached. Will this work in your situation?

Performance is not the only criteria you need to consider. For example, what kind of management capabilities are provided? For the most part, a switch is a plug-and-play type of device like a hub and requires little management. However, when troubleshooting, you will be grateful for any tools provided by the vendor. Does the switch have a proprietary console mode accessed by a specific port, or can it be managed using SNMP? Can you easily integrate its management functions into your current environment?

Routers

Routers are another step up from the repeater and bridge concept. Routers are also intelligent repeaters, but operate a little further up the network model. Whereas bridges operate at the Data Link Layer, basing decisions on MAC addresses, routers operate at the Network Layer and use higher level protocol addresses, such as TCP/IP addresses, instead of the MAC address. Whereas a bridge must keep a table of information telling it which MAC addresses are located on which port, the router builds a table that tells it which port can be used to eventually deliver a frame to a particular network.

Also separating bridges and switches from routers are the various routing protocols that are used. Not every router operates in the same way when making decisions about where to send a packet of information. Routers are also generally much slower, or have a higher degree of *latency*, than the other devices that have been discussed in this chapter because they must process more information.

Note

The terms *gateway* and *router* are often used to mean the same thing. For example, when configuring TCP/IP on a client, one of the pieces of information you usually have to supply is the *default gateway*. This default route is a router to which packets that are not destined for hosts of the local network are sent. More specifically, however, the term *gateway* has come to mean a device that functions as a router, but also performs some kind of protocol translation, connecting two different kinds of networks.

There are two general types of routing protocols: interior and exterior protocols. Interior protocols perform routing functions within autonomous networks (node-to-node communication). Exterior routing protocols (router-to-router communication) handle the routing functions between autonomous networks and glue the Internet together. These routing types are more formally referred to as *Interior Gateway Protocols* (*IGPs*) and *Exterior Gateway Protocols* (*EGPs*). The network you manage for your business is an independent domain that functions internally as a unit. It is an autonomous system within which you can make decisions about which hosts use a particular address and how routing is done. When you connect your network to the Internet, the ISP or other provider manages routers that allow your autonomous system to exchange information with other autonomous systems throughout the Internet.

For the most part, the network administrator is concerned with IGP types of protocols. Of these, two are most often used: RIP and OSPF.

Note

Another IGP you might hear about occasionally is the HELLO protocol. This protocol is mentioned here mostly for historical purposes because it is not employed very much anymore. HELLO was used during the early days of the NFS-NET backbone and uses a round-trip, or delay time, to calculate routes.

RIP Routing

RIP is the acronym for *Routing Information Protocol*. It is the most common routing protocol for autonomous systems in use today, though that doesn't mean it's the best. It is a distance-vector protocol, which means that it judges the best route to a destination based on a table of information that contains the distance (in hops) and vector (direction) to the destination.

In Figure 5.8, there are two company sites that are connected through two links that have routers between them. The user on workstation A wants to connect to a resource in the remote network that resides on server A.

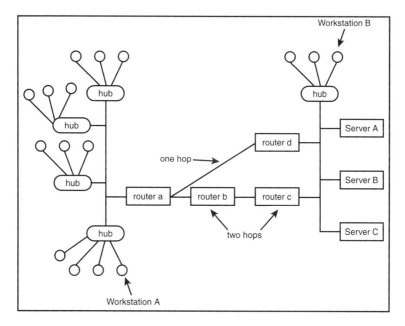

Figure 5.8 RIP decides the best route based on the number of hops between two nodes.

When router A sees the first packet from workstation A and realizes that it cannot be delivered on the local network, it consults its routing tables to first determine if it can find a path that will get the data to its destination. If more than one path exists, as is the case here, the router makes a decision as to which path to take. A simplified version of the routing table information looks like this:

Destination	Next Hop	Metric
Server A	Router D	1
Server A	Router B	2

Router A has two paths that it can use to get the packet delivered. The routing table it keeps in memory doesn't tell it the actual names of the servers, as is shown here. Instead, it uses network addresses. It also doesn't show every single router through which the packet passes on its route to its destination. It only shows the next router to send the packet to and the total number of routers through which the package must pass.

RIP routing makes simple decisions based solely on the metric called a *hop count*. In this case, RIP would decide to send the packet to Router D because with that route the packet must pass through only one additional router to reach its destination. Routing the packet through Router B would take two hops.

Technical Note

The number of hops to a destination cannot be infinite. In RIP routing, the maximum number of hops that will be considered is 15. If a destination lies more than 15 hops away from the router, it is considered to be an unreachable destination and the router does not attempt to send a packet (if it knows that this is the case).

As simple and straightforward as this might seem, RIP routing might not be the best solution. One of the problems of RIP routing is that it never takes into consideration the bandwidth of the route. It might be that the path from router A to router C is made up of high-speed T1 links and the line between router A and router D is a slower ISDN connection. For small simple packets, such as an email delivery, this might not make a great deal of difference to the end user. For a large amount of traffic, though, this can make a difference.

Another problem with RIP is that it doesn't load-balance. If there are a lot of users trying to reach the remote system, it will not use both of the available routes and divide up the traffic. RIP continues to select what it considers the best route and just send the packets on their way.

Router Updates

RIP routers periodically exchange data with each other so that each router can maintain a table of routing information that is more or less up-to-date. In earlier versions of RIP a router broadcast its entire routing table. Newer versions only allow routers to send changes or to respond to routing requests from other routers (called *triggered RIP*).

The traffic generated by routers can be significant in a large network. RIP routers update their routing tables every 30 seconds by requesting information from neighboring routers. They also announce their existence every 180 seconds. If a router fails to announce itself within this time, other routers consider it to be down and modify their routing tables.

Disadvantages of RIP

RIP is a good routing protocol for use in small networks, but it doesn't scale very well. It became quite popular early on because it was distributed as part of the Berkeley version of UNIX, in the form of the routed daemon. Following are the major disadvantages of RIP:

- The broadcast messages used to update routing tables can use up a lot of network bandwidth.
- There is no general method to prevent loops from occurring.

- For larger networks, 15 hops might not be enough to consider a destination unreachable.

- Update messages propagate across the network slowly from one router to the next, hop by hop (called *slow convergence*), so inconsistencies in routing tables might cause a router to send a packet using a route that no longer exists.

OSPF

OSPF is the acronym for *Open Shortest Path First*. Whereas RIP is a vector-distance protocol, OSPF uses a link-state algorithm. OSPF routers maintain a routing table in memory just as RIP routers do, but instead of sending out the entire routing table in a broadcast every 30 seconds, OSPF routers exchange link-state information every 30 minutes. In that interval, very short link-state advertisements (LSAs) are used to send changes to other routers.

OSPF was developed by the Internet Engineering Task Force (IETF) and was meant to solve most of the problems associated with RIP. Instead of using a simple hop count metric, OSPF also takes into consideration other cost metrics such as the speed of a route, the traffic on the route, and the reliability of the route. Also, OSPF does not suffer from the 15 hop limitation that RIP employs. You can place as many routers between end nodes as required by your network topology. Another difference between RIP and OSPF is that RIP does not use subnet masks, whereas OSPF does.

Although OSPF functions more efficiently than RIP, in a large network the exchange of information between many routers can still consume a lot of bandwidth. The time spent recalculating routes can add to network delay. Because of this, OSPF incorporates an idea called an *area*, which is used to divide the network. Routers within a specific area (usually a geographical area such as a building or campus) exchange LSAs about routing information within their area.

A router that is used to connect the areas with a backbone of other routers is called a *border router*. A hierarchy of routing information is built using this method so that every router does not have to maintain a huge database showing the route to every possible destination. Instead, a border router advertises a range of addresses that exist within its area. Other border routers store this information and therefore only have to process a portion of an address instead of the entire address when making a routing decision. Border routers store this higher level of routing information as well as the information for routes in their area.

In Figure 5.9 you can see a network that has four major areas, each of which has routers that maintain a database of information about their specific area. These routers exchange information with each other, which keeps them updated. Each area has a border router that is part of the area and the backbone area. These border routers exchange summary information about their respective areas with other border routers that are part of the backbone area.

OSPF has the drawback of administrative overhead. Also, low-end routers might not be able to cope with the amount of information a border router needs to manage.

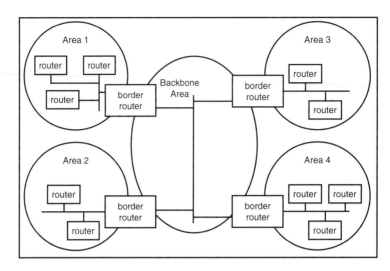

Figure 5.9 OSPF routers are responsible for their area.

When to Use Routers

Whereas bridges are used to segment physical parts of the network, routers are used to segment the network based on logical components, such as IP network addresses. Routers also provide other important functions that can make them a good choice when upgrading your network.

The filtering capability can do a lot to reduce network traffic. In an environment where a lot of broadcast messages are used—for example, an environment that uses a NetBIOS-based protocol—routers can be used to separate subnets by department and limit the broadcasts to their local areas. Windows NT Servers enable you to place backup domain controllers on separate subnets to provide local authentication for clients. You can also use WINS or the LMHOSTS file to specify the address of a domain controller or other important server that resides on the other side of a router. Thus, though you might be using only NetBEUI for communications, you can still use routers to divide the network and reduce the overall broadcast traffic on the network.

▶▶ For more information on NetBIOS, WINS and LMHOSTS, see Chapter 21, "Name Resolution."

▶▶ For more information on Windows NT domains, see Chapter 22, "Windows NT Domains."

Perhaps one of the most important functions that routers serve now that the Internet is becoming an invaluable resource is to create firewalls. Routers can filter traffic based on protocol, frame type, and even source or destination addresses. Using routers for security purposes makes sense even in a closed environment such as an intranet—you can use it to keep prying eyes out of confidential servers, for example those in the payroll department.

Summary

When you outgrow a small departmental LAN or when you need to interconnect more than one network, you must use specialized devices such as bridges, switches, or routers to do so. The device you use depends on the type of segments you want to connect and the amount and type of traffic on the network. Organizing a network or an internetwork involves more than just physical connections and means that you need routers to logically organize the network end nodes according to the network protocol in use.

Routers are the basis of interconnecting networks to each other and the Internet. As a network administrator, you must become familiar with routing within your network, the autonomous system. Understanding the underlying physical topology, including the types of links and number of users on any particular segment, will aid you in deciding which type of router or protocol to use.

Media Access Units (MAUs) and Multistation Access Units (MSAUs)

SOME OF THE MAIN TOPICS IN THIS CHAPTER ARE

MAUs, CAUs, and LAMs

Ring-In and Ring-Out Ports

Insert and Bypass Functions

Configuring and Troubleshooting MAUs

Token-ring networks are composed of stations that are wired in a star-ring fashion. Each workstation is connected to a central wiring concentrator, similar to the hub that is used in ethernet networks. However, the devices used for this purpose in a token-ring network—commonly called MAUs *(media access unit)* and MSAUs *(multistation access unit)*—function much differently than a hub. The term *MAU* will be used throughout this chapter for the sake of simplicity because an MSAU is just a bigger version (more ports) of a MAU. In this chapter we examine these devices, related equipment, and the functions they perform for the network. This information will help you with upgrading to or repairing a token-ring network because the MAU/MSAU provides the physical focal point of the network.

MAUs, CAUs, and LAMs

Although token-ring workstations are attached to the MSAU in a star fashion, the electrical circuitry inside the device connects the workstations into a physical ring. Whereas an rthernet hub takes incoming signals and rebroadcasts them on all other ports, the MAU connects the incoming transmission cable from one workstation to the receiving cable of the next station in the ring. This would appear to create a linear topology, but instead a ring is formed because the transmission cable from the last workstation is connected to the receiving cable of the first.

In Figure 6.1 you can see that although the workstations are connected to a central device—a star topology—the logical topology created inside the MAU when it makes connections between workstations is really a ring. Data frames, like token frames, are passed around the ring from one workstation to the other until they arrive at their eventual destination.

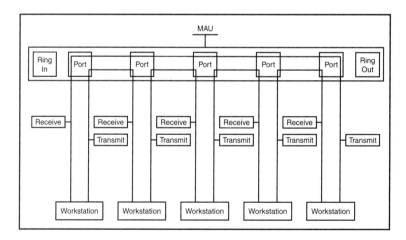

Figure 6.1 The MAU connects the transmit cable from one workstation to the receive cable of the next workstation in the ring.

In this diagram you can see that the last workstation that is connected to the MAU has its transmit cable routed back to the receive cable of the first workstation, thus creating a ring.

Note

An advantage of token-ring networks, which is directly related to the ring topology and token-passing mechanism, is that every workstation is guaranteed access to the network medium within a known amount of time. When using Ethernet technology, one or more workstations transmitting heavy loads onto the network can end up causing excessive signal collisions and prevent other nodes from getting equal-time access.

The two basic kinds of MAUs are *passive* and *active*. A simple passive MAU provides the necessary electrical wiring and relays that are used to connect stations into the ring and pass data through the network. An active MAU provides other circuitry that can enhance or amplify the signal, enabling you to create a LAN that is larger than that which can be created using a passive MAU.

MAUs come in a variety of styles, with capacities generally ranging from 8–16 ports, though you will also find more expensive MAUs that support more workstations than this.

More sophisticated MAUs have an additional feature: remote management. These *controlled access units* (or CAUs) allow the network administrator to remotely manage stations connected to the ring. Workstations do not directly connect to the CAU, however. Instead, a *lobe attachment module* (LAM) is used to connect workstations to the CAU. Generally, LAMs support 20 individual workstations, and you can connect up to four LAMs to a CAU.

Ring-In and Ring-Out Ports

In addition to the ports that are used to connect workstations to a MAU, each MAU also has two other ports: ring-in and ring-out. These ports are used to connect multiple MAUs together to create a larger LAN. As you can see in Figure 6.2, the connected MAUs create a ring topology when connected, similar to the ring created inside each MAU for the workstations it manages.

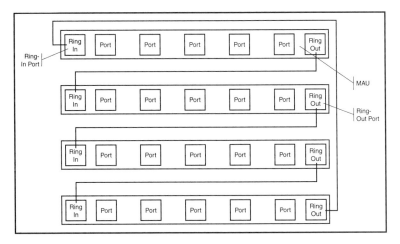

Figure 6.2 Ring-in and ring-out ports connect multiple MAUs to form a larger LAN.

Insert and Bypass Functions

Each workstation that attaches to the MAU is initially in what is called a *loopback mode*. When the workstation is first connected to the MAU, the circuitry inside the device connects the workstation's transmitting cables with it's own receiving cables. After the station's network adapter card has performed self-tests, it applies a voltage to the transmission cable called a *phantom voltage*. The term "phantom" is used because the voltage does not affect data communications on the ring, but is used instead to tell the MSAU that the station is ready to be inserted into the ring.

When the MAU detects the phantom voltage, it activates an internal relay that physically connects the workstation into the ring. This is done by connecting the workstation's transmitting cable to the receiving cable of the next workstation in the ring (its downstream neighbor) and its receiving cable to the transmitting cable of the workstation that precedes it in the ring (its upstream neighbor).

Note

Because token-ring MAUs use electrical relays and phantom voltage to insert a workstation into the ring, a workstation that is suddenly powered off is automatically removed from the ring.

When errors are detected by members of the ring, a process is started that is used to try to detect the workstation that is malfunctioning. When a workstation receives notification that it is suspect, it will initiate a process whereby it removes itself from the ring so that it can perform self-testing again. This is known as *bypass functioning*. For more information about the error-detection process and how individual workstations can be isolated to prevent disruption to the network, see Chapter 14, "Token-Passing Technology."

Note

In a typical Ethernet LAN, you can set up a two-node LAN by directly connecting two workstations. Using 10Base-2 cables this is easy because the topology is a linear bus. Using 10Base-T this can be accomplished by building a cable that crosses the transmit and receive wires, commonly called a *crossover cable*. Because of the physical process of inserting and removing a workstation from the ring, it is not possible to directly connect two workstations together that use token-ring technology.

Configuring and Troubleshooting MAUs

MAUs, like hubs, generally require no configuration. They are connectivity devices that provide a central location which is used to connect workstations to the network. However, some more advanced models, which can offer management features such as SNMP or RMON, might require that the administrator perform some configuration tasks. Carefully study the documentation for the MAU to ensure that you understand its capabilities and how to use any advanced features the vendor has supplied.

Troubleshooting a standard MAU is a lot like troubleshooting an Ethernet hub. Most models have LED lights that indicate error conditions you can use to localize problems with faulty ports. More advanced models that incorporate management features can have additional software tools that you can use. If you find a workstation is incapable of participating in the ring and you are not sure whether the trouble lies with the network adapter or the MAU, try connecting the workstation to another port to see if it is capable of seeing the network. If not, the problem is most likely with the network adapter, or it is a configuration issue with the networking software on the workstation itself. If it does work, the problem is most likely with the port.

Because token-ring networks have built-in functionality that allows them to recover from some kinds of errors, you might find yourself at a disadvantage if you are not aware of the errors that are occurring on the ring. In each ring one workstation functions as an active monitor, which means that it is the workstation that starts the token-passing process and performs monitoring functions for other processes. All other workstations act as standby monitors ready to take over if the active monitor fails.

Although not required, most token-ring implementations enable you to load additional software onto a workstation and have it function as a Ring Error Monitor (REM). This software does not perform any error-correcting functions, but does maintain a list of errors that have occurred on the ring. Using an REM, the administrator can at least be made aware of how well the ring is functioning and take preemptive action when it looks like a particular workstation or cable segment is involved in excessive errors.

Summary

Token-ring networks use the MSAU as a connection point for workstations attached to the network. The MAU is similar to an Ethernet hub in the functions it provides, but the mechanisms are different and the two cannot be used interchangeably. Little administrative effort is needed to manage a hub other than to physically connect the lobe cables used to connect the workstation. The next chapter provides a look at hubs and how they function.

Hubs

CHAPTER 7

In the earliest Ethernet networks, computers were connected in a linear fashion along a single wire. This bus topology worked fine in small networks. The major problem with the bus, however, is that any break in the cable will result in network down time for all computers located on that segment. Network segments can be joined into a larger network using a multiport repeater, a bridge, or a router. The multiport repeater is a simple device. Each segment is connected to a port on the repeater, which takes incoming signals and retransmits them on all ports. Each segment can consist of multiple computers daisy-chained along the segment, or you can use the repeater to gather together cables, each of which services only a single computer.

Using the multiport repeater to join segments that each had only one computer eliminated a major limitation of the bus topology. If any cable becomes faulty or a terminator is removed from the end of the segment, for example, only the computer on that segment will be disconnected from the network.

When ethernet networking was developed to operate on twisted-pair wiring, this idea became central to the concept, and the *hub* was born.

Choosing the Right Kind of Hub

Like servers and workstations, making decisions about which kind of hub (or hubs) to use in your network is a task that should be based on your knowledge of how the network is currently configured and what kind of performance you want to achieve when you make changes or additions. At the low end of the spectrum you can find small workgroup hubs with no management capabilities that work fine in a very small environment. At the upper end you will find devices that provide management features such as SNMP and RMON.

A simple hub is a multiport repeater. Each port on the hub is used to connect a single computer to the network. The hub operates at the Physical Layer of the OSI reference model. It does no addressing or framing; instead, it simply receives data signals and sends them out to all other ports. Because incoming signals are retransmitted on all the other ports, every computer in the broadcast domain can receive the data. This kind of hub is ideal for a very small LAN. There are more advanced hubs available today, however, which provide functions above and beyond the simple repeater.

In Figure 7.1, you can see that the hub creates a network based on a star topology from the physical point of view. However, from a logical view, the network still resembles the bus topology because each workstation in the subnet can intercept every packet that is broadcast on the network.

Advantages of the Star Topology

The most basic function that a hub provides is that of a wiring concentrator. However, because of the star topology that it imposes on the LAN, there are several other advantages you can achieve with a hub that are not found when using the bus topology. These include

- Only a single workstation will suffer if a cable problem develops. In a LAN that uses the bus topology, problems with one workstation can bring down the entire LAN.

- A hub makes it easy to move computers because the entire network does not have to be disrupted when a computer is moved. When using a 10Base-2 cable type, you have to *break* the cable and install a T-connector to add a computer at a new point in the network. Using a hub, you can add or remove workstations as you need to with no effect on the other nodes in the LAN.

- The hub centralizes wiring. Instead of having a single coaxial cable snaking throughout the office or building, each workstation is connected by an easy-to-install twisted-pair cable. This can make troubleshooting much easier. If only one workstation is having problems, you can localize the problem to that workstation and its connection to the hub. Troubleshooting problems on a LAN based on the bus topology can be tedious as you move from one workstation to another performing tests.

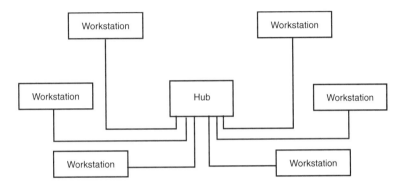

Figure 7.1   The simple hub creates a network with a physical star topology.

What Kind of Hub Do You Need?

In general, hubs can be classified by their function or by their construction. By physical construction, you can classify hubs as follows:

- Standalone
- Stackable
- Modular

Standalone hubs are small units that can be used to build a very small workgroup LAN. These are the most inexpensive hubs, and can be purchased as a commodity item at most computer stores. These are small devices that usually have a small number of ports (2–10).

For larger LANs, stackable hubs provide for easy expansion as the network grows because they can be linked together. When you link stackable hubs, they operate together much like a single hub and can usually be managed as a unit. Depending on the vendor, you can find stackable hubs that need only one unit with management functionality that can be linked to lower-cost units that provide additional ports. As you can see in Figure 7.2, creating additional ports is a simple matter of connecting another stackable hub unit to the existing units.

For networks that support multiple technologies, such as mixed token ring and ethernet, modular hubs might be the solution you are looking for. Like stackable hubs, this kind of hub can also be easily linked together. Instead of separate units that need to be linked together by short lengths of cable, the modular hub consists of a *cage* or *chassis* with a *backplane* or *motherboard*. Hubs are implemented as cards, with ports that can be inserted into the backplane. This type of hub can be quite sophisticated, incorporating ethernet ports, token-ring ports (MAUs), management modules, and other devices (see Figure 7.3). Whereas stackable hubs each have a separate power supply and therefore require a separate plug in the wiring closing, a modular chassis unit provides a common power supply for all the cards it holds.

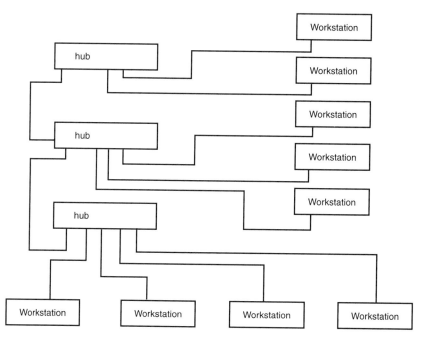

Figure 7.2   Stackable hubs make it easy to expand the network.

Some modular hubs use a standard backplane, which consists of a single bus that is shared by all the cards that are inserted into the chassis. Some modular hubs house multiple buses, with each bus being specific to a particular network segment or LAN. A segment bus is similar to the multiple bus design, but the administrator can configure ports to be part of different LANs (*virtual LANs*). Finally, a multiplexed bus allows for a multiple bus design using a single bus, with each separate LAN multiplexed on a separate channel. These last two types make it easier to move a workstation from one LAN to another. The administrator must only use the hub's management software to reconfigure the port to be on the new virtual LAN. This is much simpler than having to physically move the cable from one port to another or from one hub to another.

In spite of the advanced features of a modular hub, you might find that stackable hubs are better suited to your situation. Considering the fact that all cards in the modular hub share a common power supply, you can potentially lose more clients when a power supply malfunctions. Although an easy solution to this problem is to purchase a modular hub that has dual-redundant power supplies, you cannot plan for all possible disasters when using one piece of equipment to house so many things.

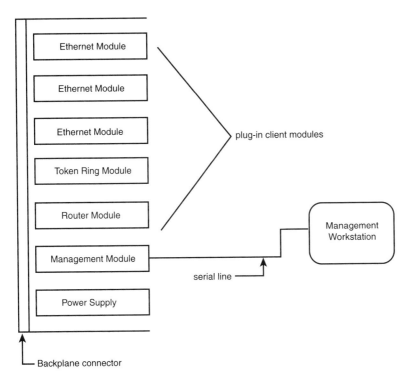

Figure 7.3 A modular hub can house cards for different network types.

With stackable hubs, you can patch around a malfunctioning hub and keep your most important clients connected. Also, modular hubs are meant to be space-savers. Some of the features you expect on a hub, such as the LEDs that indicate the status or error condition, might not exist on individual cards that make up a modular hub.

Classifying Hubs by Functionality

After you have considered the physical aspects of a hub, you must determine what, if any, management capabilities the hub should support. The range of features you will find is quite broad. For example, small standalone hubs that sell for less than $75 might not have any management capabilities at all, whereas modular or stackable hubs can support SNMP or provide management software that you can access via a console port or TCP/IP. If you manage a large network, the ability to remotely manage or troubleshoot hubs is almost a necessity. Management capabilities are not the only functionality you should look for in a hub. For example, some hubs have the capability to correct minor errors or isolate a misbehaving port so it does not interfere with other users on the LAN.

By function, hubs can be classified into three major types:

- Passive
- Active
- Intelligent

Passive Hubs

This is the simplest hub, and it does not perform actual data processing. This type of hub simply repeats incoming messages on all other ports. No signal processing is done when using this type of hub, so you need to be sure to stick with the cable lengths specified by the standard (such as 10Base-T/100Base-T).

In a small business office that has no need to connect to a larger network, the standalone hub is an excellent choice. If you only need to connect 2–10 workstations, you can use this type of hub. For home networking, most computer stores also sell these hubs in a kit format ("network in a box") that includes the hub, two network cards, and the cables you need to connect the computers to the hub. For $30 –$100, you can set up a network at home or in a small office in less than an hour.

Active Hubs

Attenuation and other factors cause the signal to degrade as it passes through the wire. An active hub has electronic components that can amplify or clean up the signal it receives from a port before sending the data out on the remaining ports; this process is called *signal regeneration*. Some active hubs also have a capability called *store and forward*, in which individual packets can be examined and some simple corrections can be made to damaged packets.

Active hubs can also help compensate for ports that are connected to cables or workstations that are more likely to produce timing errors. Packet loss can be compensated for on these slower links because the active hub can retime their delivery. This might at first seem like a bad idea because it effectively slows down communications when faster nodes communicate with the slower one; however, an advantage can be gained because the error-prone computer does not have to make repeated attempts to rebroadcast packets.

Be aware that simple basic hubs, which do not contain the sophisticated circuitry to correct packets that have errors or to retime the signal, might regenerate the signal before passing it on to the other ports. In this case, any noise on the line will also be amplified and broadcast on these ports. More expensive hubs will actually dissect the packet and re-create it before putting it out on the LAN, avoiding this problem.

Intelligent Hubs

The signal regeneration function of an active hub is included in an intelligent hub. Network management functions, which enable the administrator to gather information about the hub or each port on the hub, are also included. Statistical data about network traffic and error detection can make a big difference when you are troubleshooting. Some vendors provide their own proprietary management software. If you work in an environment in which the network is expected to keep growing, look to a vendor that supports industry standards such as the Simple Network Management Protocol (SNMP) so that other devices you add later can be incorporated into the management structure.

Note

The SNMP is a standard protocol that enables management software to manage and monitor devices throughout the network. SNMP provides a communication path between Management Stations and Management Agents that reside on the network device. For more information about SNMP, see Appendix D, "SNMP Commands."

Intelligent hubs often include not only monitoring features, but also management features that enable you to do things such as shut down an individual port that has a computer that is causing problems on the network. For example, if a device on the network is malfunctioning and sending out a storm of broadcast packets, you can detect which port is causing the problem, and then selectively disconnect it from the network until the problem is fixed.

Hub Ports

The most typical hub has a row of sockets for the RJ45 connector, which is a popular connector that is used for cables that connect workstations and network devices to a hub. When linking hubs to create a larger network, twisted-pair wiring might not be the cabling of choice if you need to span a distance longer than UTP can support. For this reason, you will find additional sockets on most hubs that can be used to connect the hub to a backbone.

It is important that you understand the physical topology of your network when you need to purchase additional hubs to expand the network. If the hub doesn't provide the type of port that you need to make the connection to the backbone, it will be of little use to you. For example, you probably won't find a small workgroup basic hub that has a port for fiber-optic cable. It is more likely that this kind of hub will provide an Uplink port with a socket that is intended for an RJ45 connector to be used to link to the larger network (another hub) via twisted-pair cabling.

UTP, AUI, and BNC Ports

UTP ports are used with RJ45 jacks to connect twisted-pair wiring to the hub. For connecting a hub to a network backbone, some hubs come with an AUI port, which can connect an Ethernet transceiver to 10Base-5 thicknet cabling. More common is the BNC port, which can be used to connect the hub to a 10Base-2 thinnet cable.

You can find more advanced hubs that have connectors for other cabling, such as fiber-optic cabling. Indeed, there are hubs that are used for fiber-optic networks that use mirrors to split signals instead of electronics, as is done with a standard hub.

For management purposes, you might find a port for a DB9 connector that is used to attach a management terminal to the hub. This type of asynchronous port is used either for the exchange of simple ASCII characters between the hub and a terminal when performing monitoring or management functions, or to connect the hub to a central unit that manages multiple hubs.

Note

A hub doesn't have to have a serial port that can be used to attach a management console. In fact, some advanced hubs can be configured with an IP address so that management applications can make use of Telnet and other utilities to perform management and monitoring functions.

Cross-Over Ports

Cross-over ports can be used to connect one hub to another to expand the LAN broadcast area. Sometimes referred to as an Uplink port, this port is wired differently from the others so that the send and receive lines match up when communicating between hubs. Some hubs have a switch next to the cross-over port so that you can toggle it to work as a regular port. This feature can be used to connect an additional workstation to the hub if you don't need to attach it to another hub. When it comes time to expand the network, toggle the switch, link the hubs, and use the next hub to connect additional clients.

Troubleshooting Hub Problems

Because a hub acts as a wiring concentrator for the LAN, it can sometimes be difficult to determine where the fault lies when a problem crops up. Suppose, for example, that you have a user's workstation that suddenly cannot communicate on the network. Is there a problem with the hub port, or is the problem the cable that connects the workstation to the hub? Has the user changed the network configuration on the workstation? It is probably best to start your efforts with the physical aspects of the link by checking the hub, the NIC, and the cable. If these prove to be in good working order, you can expand your search to networking software and configuration issues.

Check the LEDs

The simplest check that you can make is to visually inspect the hub. There should be an LED status indicator for each port. When lit, the hub is communicating with the attached workstation in a normal manner. This does not mean that the network traffic being exchanged is okay, just that the link exists and some kind of packets can be exchanged.

If the hub LED is not lit, the first step is to try another port, preferably one that you know is currently in good working order. If that works, the problem is indeed with the hub port. If you are using an inexpensive workgroup hub, it is not practical to make a repair. Instead, use another available port or replace the hub. More expensive models can usually be repaired, and you should contact the vendor or the party responsible for providing support.

If you find that the workstation is still incapable of communicating while you are using a port that is known to be good, concentrate your efforts on testing the cable and the user's NIC to find the fault. You can use a hand-held cable tester to test the cable. If the workstation is in close proximity to the hub, it might be easier to again perform a simple substitution and use a cable that you know is good to make this kind of check.

Check New Connections

If you are having problems connecting a new workstation to the hub, perform the LED check and try another port if you experience problems. If that fails, proceed to check the cable and the user's NIC. One of the most common problems encountered with new connections results from excessive cable length or sources of electrical interference somewhere along the path that the cable takes to the workstation. Remember that the maximum distance that the cable can be extended from the hub to the faceplate in the user's work area is 90 meters, with another

10-meter cable running from the faceplate to the workstation. In addition, don't forget that Category 5 twisted-pair cables are the preferred wiring for 10Base-T and faster technologies. If you are still using Category 3 cables and are having problems, use a shorter cable length or, better yet, upgrade to Category 5.

Remember also that a very common source of electrical interference is florescent lighting fixtures or high-voltage electrical wiring. Try relocating the path of the cable to avoid such sources of interference.

Check the Hub or Port Configuration

Sometimes the problems you find in a hub are not due to failure of the hardware components, but instead to improper configuration. During a recent experience I had trouble figuring out the half-duplex/full-duplex setting on a hub. It should be obvious that both the workstation's NIC and the hub's port must be set to the same thing. However, in some instances one person manages the hub while another performs an installation or upgrade to the NIC on the user's workstation, and a miscommunication can result in improper configuration. In the situation I found the NIC was set to full duplex but the hub was set to half duplex. The confusion still allowed for some communication to get through but resulted in extremely high levels of collisions.

In addition, although a hub might be designed to auto sense the full- or half-duplex condition, or possibly the network speed (10Mbps or 100Mbps), it might not do so correctly all the time. To fix this kind of problem, you should set the port to match the NIC's capabilities. This is usually done by using the management software that accompanies the hub.

Use the Hub's Management Software

If the hub manufacturer has provided management software, you will most likely find that in addition to configuration commands there are several commands that you can use to troubleshoot individual ports or the hub overall. You can access this kind of application via a serial console port, and in many cases via a network connection. It is a good idea to review the documentation and become familiar with the commands before trouble happens. Some vendors adhere to standards such as SNMP, and you can use third-party applications to manage many hubs. Others take a proprietary approach and provide management software that can be used only for their products. If you are managing a large network, look for products that are built according to industry standards so that management tasks can be centralized for all the hubs you use.

General Hub Failure

Many problems you will encounter with hubs involve only the failure of a single port. However, occasionally the entire hub will cease to function. One of the more common reasons for this is temperature. All electronic equipment has a maximum temperature beyond which it will not operate properly. If you suspect that this is the problem, try leaving the unit powered off for a half hour so it can cool off, and try powering it up again. If this solves the problem, examine the physical space in which the hub resides. Have you recently placed additional equipment on top of or next to the hub? Is there adequate room for air to circulate between the devices? Has the air conditioning in the room recently been changed?

If the hub appears outwardly to be functioning—LEDs are lit, for example—but in reality does not perform properly, power it off and power it on again. Most hubs will run through a power-on self test (POST) program that checks vital system components when it is powered on. Depending on the hub, you will be able to determine the problem by looking for a sequence of LEDs lighting up, or possibly flashing, or by looking at error information using the management software supplied with the hub.

If temperature is not the problem and the hub does not respond, even to management software, you should suspect the power supply. If the power supply is external, this can be checked by once again using the simple substitution method: Try another power supply. If this is not the problem, or if the power supply is internal, it will probably be necessary to have the hub serviced by a technician to troubleshoot the components inside to make a problem determination.

Summary

Hubs can range from simple wiring concentrators to advanced systems that aid the network administrator by gathering statistical data and supplying a management application that can be used to administer the hub. Since hubs range from the extremely low end—for example, a two-port workgroup hub—to modular or stackable hubs that can accommodate hundreds or thousands of workstations, you want to use a hub-based network rather than the legacy 10Base-2 or 10Base-5 bus type of network. Even a simple network that has only two computers can be connected using a minihub that can typically be purchased for under $50.

When troubleshooting hub problems, don't forget that the problem might not be in the hub, but in the user's NIC or the cable that links it to the hub. If your initial troubleshooting efforts reveal no problems with the hub, concentrate your efforts on these components instead. Using the process of elimination, you will eventually get to the source of the problem.

Part III

ETHERNET DESIGN

Ethernet Frame Types

CHAPTER 8

When referring to the data that is transmitted through the network, it is a common practice to call the bundles of data *packets*. However, the actual terminology for the containers of data exchanged between systems on a network varies, depending on which level of the OSI seven-layer model is being referenced. For example, at the network layer, a packet of data is called a *datagram*. At the Data Link Layer, these datagrams are usually referred to as *frames*. Each frame contains the information that is required for it to be transmitted successfully across the network media, as well as the data that is being exchanged.

The data portion of the frame usually consists of bytes of information that were packaged by a higher level protocol and then delivered to the Data Link layer for transmission in an ethernet frame. For example, the IP protocol specifies the header information used by that protocol, as well as the data that is being carried by the IP packet. When the IP packet passes down to the data link layer, however, all this information is contained in the data portion of the ethernet frame.

The composition of the frame depends on the type of network. The original Ethernet frame format and Ethernet II format differ only a little from the IEEE 802.3 frame format, and the IEEE 802.5 (Token Ring) standard defines a frame that is far different from these two. This is because ethernet and token ring have different methods for granting access to the network media and for exchanging data between network nodes. The 100VG-AnyLAN network is designed to work with either the 802.3 frame or the Token-Ring frame format.

In this chapter, we explore several frame types as they evolved with the technology. When heavy-duty troubleshooting is involved, you will need to get down to this nuts-and-bolts information in order to understand just what is happening on the wire.

XEROX PARC Ethernet and Ethernet II

The original Ethernet network that was developed at Xerox PARC was further developed by Digital Equipment Corporation, Intel, and Xerox (hence the "DIX" name used in older documentation) into the Ethernet II standard. The original Ethernet frame had defined several fields that were still used in the Ethernet II specification. These fields include the following:

- **Preamble**—This is an 8-byte sequence of zeros and ones that is used to announce the start of a frame and to help synchronize the transmission.

- **Destination MAC address**—This is a 6-byte address, usually expressed in hexadecimal format.

- **Senders MAC address**—Another 6-byte field, specifying the address of the workstation that originates the frame.

- **Type field**—This was a 2-byte field used to indicate the client protocol (such as IPX, IP, DECnet, and so on) that can be found in the data field.

- **Data field**—A field of unspecified length that holds the actual data.

In this original frame, it was left up to the higher-level protocol to determine the length of the field. Because of this, the Type field was an important part of the frame.

Technical Note

The term *MAC address* stands for *Media Access Control address*. This is a 48-bit address that is hardwired into the network adapter when it is manufactured. The MAC address (sometimes called the *hardware address* or *physical address*) is usually expressed as a string of 12 hexadecimal digits, two for each byte, separated by dashes; for example, 08-00-2B-EA-77-AE. The first three pairs are unique to vendors that manufacture ethernet equipment, and the last three hexadecimal pairs are a unique number assigned by the manufacturer. Knowing a manufacturer's three-pair MAC digits can be a useful tool when troubleshooting network problems.

An address of FF-FF-FF-FF-FF-FF is used as a broadcast address, which is used to send a single message that all nodes on the network will read.

CSMA/CD

In the original PARC Ethernet, the method used to exchange data on the network media was called *Carrier Sense, Multiple Access (CSMA)*. The Ethernet II specification added *Collision Detect (CSMA/CD)* to this technique. A collision occurs when two stations on the network both sense that the network is idle and both start to send data at approximately the same time, resulting in a garbled transmission. The Manchester encoding scheme that was used on early Ethernet implementations used an electrical signal that varied from +0.85V to -0.85V. Collisions could be detected when this voltage varied by an amount considerably more than that allowed by this range.

However, in order to detect that a collision had occurred, the station transmitting a frame on the wire had to transmit data for at least as long as the worst-case round-trip time for the signal to traverse the wire. The round-trip time is not meant to indicate that the frame travels to the end of the network bus and is then reflected back again. Indeed, on the original ethernet implementations, each end of the bus is terminated with 50 ohm terminators that are meant to absorb the signal and prevent a reflection.

The round-trip time is meant to keep the wire active (that is, non-idle) for the amount of time it takes the signal to be heard by all stations on the network, including that at the farthest end. In addition, the wire must remain active for the amount of time it takes the first station to sense if the station at the farthest end had started a transmission just before receiving the first station's transmission—in other words, to sense whether a collision has occurred.

In other words, the station could not start to transmit yet another packet until enough time had elapsed for the following:

- Its first packet to travel all the way to the network node that is located at the furthermost end of the collision domain.
- Time for any packet transmitted by the furthermost node to reach the first node if the furthermost node started transmitting *just before* receiving the first data transmission.

The point of all this is that the round-trip time requires that a frame meet a minimum size standard. Because the Ethernet II standard specified a 10Mbps network speed, the round-trip time was specified to be a maximum of 50 microseconds.

In order to provide for this, the minimum amount of data that needs to be transmitted is 500 bits, or 62.5 bytes, which was rounded up to 64 bytes to give the minimum size of an Ethernet II frame. If the data that was appended to the frame as its data portion resulted in a frame that was less than 64 bytes, the remainder of the frame was padded with zeros to make up the difference.

A maximum size for the frame was also added by the Ethernet II specification, resulting in a frame size with a minimum of 64 bytes and a maximum size of 1,500 bytes.

Note

Actually, the term *byte*, used in this chapter to specify the length of a field in an Ethernet frame, is not the most specific term that could have been used by those who designed these specifications. Instead, the term *octet*, which means "eight bits," is the term you see in most of the standard documentation. For purposes of clarity, however, the term *byte* is used here because most readers are familiar with its meaning and are less likely to be confused by another term.

In Figure 8.1, you can see the layout used for the original Ethernet frame.

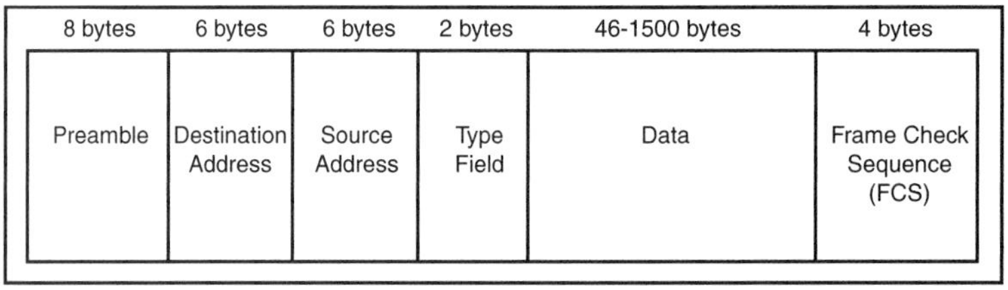

8 bytes	6 bytes	6 bytes	2 bytes	46-1500 bytes	4 bytes
Preamble	Destination Address	Source Address	Type Field	Data	Frame Check Sequence (FCS)

Figure 8.1   The layout of the original Ethernet II frame.

802.3

When the IEEE 802 project defined a frame format, it kept most of the features found in the Ethernet II frame. There are some important differences, however. In Figure 8.2, you can see the layout of the 802.3 Ethernet frame.

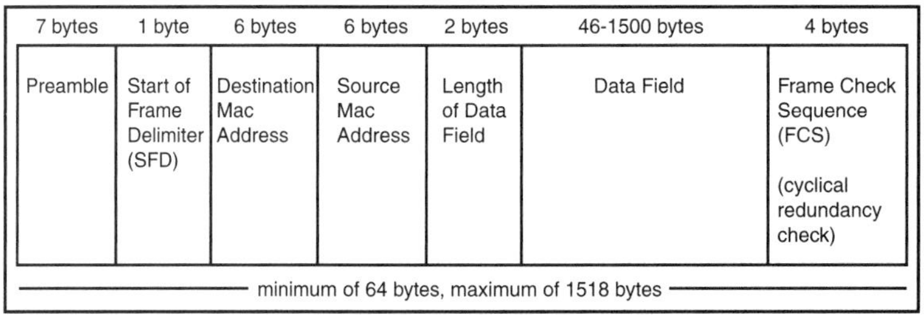

7 bytes	1 byte	6 bytes	6 bytes	2 bytes	46-1500 bytes	4 bytes
Preamble	Start of Frame Delimiter (SFD)	Destination Mac Address	Source Mac Address	Length of Data Field	Data Field	Frame Check Sequence (FCS) (cyclical redundancy check)

minimum of 64 bytes, maximum of 1518 bytes

Figure 8.2   The IEEE 802.3 frame format replaces the Type field.

The major changes of the project included the replacement of the Type field with an entirely new field. These two bytes are now used to specify the length of the data field that follows it. When the value in this field is 1500 or less, you can tell it is being used as a Length field. If the value is 1536 or larger, the frame is being used to define a protocol type.

Additionally, the preamble was reduced from eight bytes to seven, and is now followed by a 1-byte Start of Frame Delimiter (SFD). The SFD is composed of a bit configuration of 10101011 (the last byte of the earlier preamble has 10 for the last two bits).

The last part of the frame is a 4-byte Frame Check Sequence (FCS). This is used to store a cyclical redundancy check value that is calculated on the frame. The transmitting station calculates this value based on the other bits in the frame, and the receiving station calculates the CRC based on the frame's bits and compares it to this value. If they are not identical, the frame must have suffered some damage in transit and must be retransmitted.

802.2 Logical Link Control (LLC)

In the OSI seven-layer reference model, the two lower layers are the Physical Layer and the Data Link Layer. When the IEEE designed its reference model, it took a slightly different approach. In Figure 8.3, you can see that the IEEE version includes a Logical Link Control sublayer and a Media Access Control sublayer on top of the Physical Layer, with the Media Access Control Layer straddling the boundary of the Physical and Data Link Layers as defined by the OSI model.

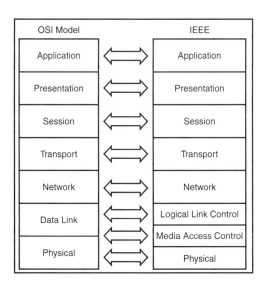

Figure 8.3 The IEEE model differs from the OSI reference model.

There is a rationale for incorporating some of the functionality of the OSI Physical Layer into the media access control layer and dividing up the Data Link Layer to provide for a Logical Link Control sublayer: to allow different types of transmission media and methods of media access to exist on the same network.

The LLC Subheader

The media access control sublayer is responsible for making use of the services provided by the Physical Layer to get data transferred to and from remote stations on the network. This includes functions such as basic error checking and local addressing with physical or MAC addresses.

The LLC sublayer offers services to the layers above it, and these services can be classified into the following three types:

- **Unacknowledged connectionless**—Some upper-level protocols (such as TCP) already provide flow control and acknowledgment functions that check whether a packet was successfully sent. There is no need to duplicate those functions here.

- **Connection-oriented**—This service keeps track of active connections and can be used by devices on the network that do not implement the full OSI layers in their protocols.

- **Acknowledged connectionless**—This service is a mix of the other two. It provides acknowledgement of packets sent and received but does not keep track of links between network stations. This kind of service is useful in an environment where overhead—memory—is in very short supply, such as factory automation devices. Error detection is accomplished by acknowledgment, but each message is an independent communication.

To implement these LLC functions, the IEEE 802.2 protocol specifies a subheader that is placed into the frame directly before the data field. This LLC subheader field consists of three bytes. The first is the Destination Service Access Point (DSAP), the second is the Source Service Access Point (SSAP), and the last is the Control field.

The LLC Ethernet Frame

In Figure 8.4, you can see that when the LLC subheader is combined with the standard 802.3 frame, the overall size of the frame doesn't change, but the amount of space remaining in the data portion of the frame does.

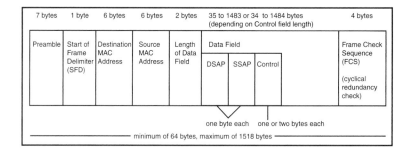

Figure 8.4   Including the LLC subheader with the 802.3 frame cuts the size of the data portion of the frame.

802.3 SNAP

In the earlier Xerox PARC and Ethernet II frame formats, the 2-byte Type field was used to indicate the higher-level protocol for which the frame was being used. When the 802.3 frame was delineated, this field was replaced with the Length field, which indicates the length of the Data field.

The SNAP subframe was introduced to provide for backward compatibility with earlier networks that still need something in the frame to identify the protocol that will be used. The term *SNAP* stands for *Sub-Network Access Protocol*. The SNAP subframe is constructed by adding additional fields to the LLC subheader. The following additional fields are added after the LLC fields:

- Organizationally Unique Identifier Field (three bytes)
- Protocol Type (two bytes)

The SNAP extensions must be used with the LLC subheader fields. There are no provisions for a SNAP subheader without the LLC subheader. Figure 8.5 shows the full 802.3 frame, including the SNAP fields.

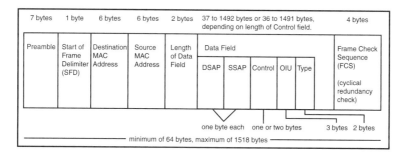

Figure 8.5   The 802.3 frame, which includes SNAP extensions, must also include the LLC subheader.

Looking Ahead

The 802.5 specification defined the frame format used for token-ring networks. Token-ring networks are fundamentally different from Ethernet networks not only in their frame formats, but also in the methods they use to grant access to the network media. For information on the format of the token-ring frame, see Chapter 14, "Token-Passing Technology."

New Developments

Networking technology is an evolving process. As newer and faster products are brought to market, the standards must also adapt. In 1998, the IEEE 802.3z standard for Gigabit Ethernet added another field to the basic 802.3 frame: the Extension field. This field is appended to the frame after the Frame Check Sequence field, and is used to pad the frame so that its minimum size will be 512 bytes instead of the 64 bytes used by slower standards. This increased size is needed only when operating Gigabit Ethernet in half-duplex mode, where collision detection is still involved. In full-duplex mode, this field is not needed.

Another way to make faster transmissions with Gigabit Ethernet is to reduce the overhead created by using CSMA/CD for every single frame that is sent on the network. A mode of operation called *burst mode* was added in the 802.3z standard; burst mode provides for sending multiple frames, one after the other, after gaining access to the network media. This is accomplished by inserting special *extension bits* in the interframe gaps between normal frames. These extension bits keep the wire active so that other stations do not think it is idle.

Tip

Another proposal that is being considered by many companies is called *jumbo frames*. This proposal, the work of Alteon Networks, Inc., raises the overall length of an Ethernet frame (on a full-duplex mode link) to 9000 bytes. You can download the specifications for jumbo frames (in Adobe PDF format) from their Web site: **www.alteon.com**.

Summary

This chapter introduces you to the formats used to exchange data on ethernet networks. Understanding the components of these frames can be invaluable when diagnosing protocol problems using a network protocol analyzer. This understanding will also help you better understand the different functions performed by devices such as hubs, bridges, and routers, and how these devices make decisions about the paths taken by data packets as they move through the network.

Ethernet Topology Restrictions

SOME OF THE MAIN TOPICS IN THIS CHAPTER ARE

Limiting Factors

Implementing a Bus Topology

Using a Star Topology

Hybrid LAN Topologies

Using a Backbone to Connect the Enterprise

The topology of a *local area network (LAN)* can be described in two ways. The first is the *physical topology*, which describes the physical layout of the network media and the devices that connect to it. The second is to describe a *logical topology*, which is not concerned with the actual physical connections, but with the logical path through the network that data can take from one place to another. This chapter discusses the topologies used in ethernet networks and what factors to consider when upgrading to ethernet or a new topology. These factors include the number of workstations on the network and the length between segments of the network.

Limiting Factors

The two basic topologies that can be used to form an Ethernet local area network are the *bus* and *star*. By using interconnecting devices such as routers and switches, a larger network can be constructed, building on the bus and star to create a more complex network topology.

The restrictions that are imposed by a particular topology generally have to do with several factors:

- **The network transmission media**—Imposes length and speed restrictions.
- **Interconnecting devices**—Used to join together different physical segments.
- **The number of devices on the network**—Because Ethernet uses a broadcast method for data exchange, too many devices on the network can cause congestion problems that can rapidly degrade performance.
- **Media access mechanisms**—How the individual devices compete for or obtain access to the network media. In Ethernet networks, each workstation contends for access to the local media.

Interconnecting Devices and Cable Segment Length

These are the most basic limiting factors for a local area network. As cables grow longer, the signal tends to degrade until eventually it cannot be understood by another device attached to the same media. Even if you were to insert devices to strengthen or regenerate the signal at regular intervals, as is done with the telephone system, the length of the cable would be a problem because ethernet networks rely on round-trip timing to determine if a packet has been properly sent.

The length of a cable segment depends on the type of cable. For 10Base-2 (Thinnet coaxial cable), a segment can be up to 186 meters, or 607 feet. With repeaters, the total diameter of the network is limited to 925 meters, or 3,035 feet.

For 10Base-T, the workstation must be within 100 meters (328 feet) of the hub. For Fast Ethernet environments, you can use different types of cable, from twisted-pair to fiber optic, and each of the Fast Ethernet specifications have different cable length limitations.

For Fast Ethernet, the 100 meter limit for any segment still applies for 100Base-TX and 100Base-T4 segments, but there can be up to 250 meters from one node to another. 100Base-FX (fiber optic cable) has a maximum segment distance of about 2 kilometers. The distance advantage the 100Base-FX has over the other cabling methods makes it more suitable for use as a network backbone medium.

If you are upgrading from another network type, such as Token Ring or Arcnet, it is best to implement the 10Base-T topology. This is the most widely used ethernet topology and provides the best fault-tolerance. It is also easier to upgrade to 100Base-T at a later time for less cost.

The only times you should consider using the 10Base-2 bus topology are if all the systems are close together and the cost prohibits cabling to each machine in a star configuration, or when you require a network segment to be over 100 meters.

The 5-4-3 Rule

There is an easy way to remember what you can place between any two nodes on an Ethernet LAN. The *5-4-3 rule* means that there can be

- A maximum of five cable segments on the LAN.
- A maximum of four repeaters or concentrators.
- Only three segments containing cable that has nodes attached.

This is a general rule that you should stick to when planning your network upgrade. Note, however, that the last part of the rule applies only to coaxial cable, such as 10Base-2 or 10Base-5. When connecting nodes using a hub and twisted-pair wiring, each node has its own cable and can vary from a small workgroup of just a few computers to a much larger one supported by stacked hubs.

Implementing a Bus Topology

The bus topology was the first type used in ethernet networks. It is a series of workstations or devices connected to a single cable (see Figure 9.1). This is the topology used for networks that are composed of 10Base-2 or 10Base-5 cabling.

The 10Base-5 bus topology is considered obsolete and is not recommended for upgrading a network.

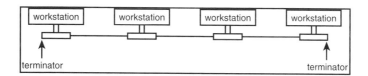

Figure 9.1 The bus topology consists of multiple devices connected to a single cable segment.

Connecting workstations along a single cable is commonly referred to as *daisy-chaining*.

The bus topology, although simple to implement, has a few problems, including the following:

- The cable itself is a single point of failure for the LAN. One break or loose terminator can disrupt the entire LAN.

- Because all workstations or devices share a common cable, tracking down a node that is causing problems on the network can be very time-consuming. For example, a loose terminator or connector on a single workstation can disrupt the entire LAN, and you might spend hours going from one node to the next checking connections.

- Bus topologies for ethernet are usually built using coaxial cable (10Base-2 and 10Base-5). Although less cable is used than in a star topology, these cables are more expensive than simple twisted-pair cables. In the case of 10Base-5, the cable is not very flexible and can be difficult to route through wall or ceiling structures.

In spite of its limitations when used to connect individual workstations into a LAN, the bus is a method that has often been used to join together smaller groups of computers.

When repairing a bus topology network, one of the first things to look for is a cable that has been disconnected within the network. This can happen frequently for different reasons, such as furniture being moved and pulling the cable apart, or users moving their computers and not connecting the cables back together.

If you encounter intermittent problems with a 10Base-2 network, one of the first things to check is that the network is terminated properly. Not using a terminator or using the wrong kind can cause intermittent connection problems.

Using a Star Topology

Chapter 7, "Hubs," discusses the technology that was introduced into Ethernet networking when 10Base-T was developed. Instead of linking workstations together in a linear fashion along a single cable, the hub acts as a wiring concentrator, providing a central point in the network where all nodes connect. Figure 9.2 shows a simple LAN connected to a hub from a star.

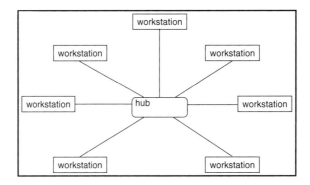

Figure 9.2   Workstations connect to a central hub in a star formation.

All data that travels from one node to another must pass through the hub. A simple hub merely repeats incoming transmissions on all other ports, whereas more complex hubs can perform functions that strengthen the signal or correct minor problems. The star topology has only a few shortcomings when compared to the bus: More cabling is required, and the hub becomes a single point of failure.

However, the benefits that the star topology has over the bus are many:

- Installing wiring for this type of network is easier than for the bus. Although more cable is required, the cables are less expensive and more flexible for routing throughout a building.

- It is easier to detect errors in the LAN through LEDs on the hub or by using a hub that incorporates management software.

- One workstation or cabling segment that experiences problems does not disrupt the entire network.

- Adding and removing nodes from this type of LAN is a simple matter of plugging in the cable to a free socket on the hub.

- If a hub fails, it can be replaced quickly with a spare by unplugging cables and inserting them into the new hub.

The star topology most closely mirrors the physical topology of token ring, and would be a good choice when upgrading to ethernet.

When repairing a star ethernet network, the first thing to verify is that the hub is active and whether the segment you are encountering problems with shows activity on the hub.

Hybrid LAN Topologies

The hub is a simple method that can be used to create small workgroup LANs. By using structured wiring methods, it is also easy to connect hubs together to create larger LANs. Two popular methods used to do this are the *Tree* and the *Hierarchical Star*.

Tree

Figure 9.3 shows a combination topology that groups workstations together in a star and joins the stars together along a linear bus. The majority of the problems of the bus are eliminated because a single workstation cannot bring the entire LAN to a halt. You can still add or change workstations by plugging them into a different port on the same hub, or on another hub. If one hub malfunctions, it only disables the workstations that are attached to it from communicating on the network. The remaining workstations on the other hubs can continue to function normally.

This is an inexpensive method that can be used to join different work departments in a building. Each local workgroup can have an administrative person who is responsible for managing the connections on the local hub. The network administrator can regulate when and where new hubs are attached to the network.

The major problem with this type of hybrid topology, however, is that if there is a problem with the backbone bus cable, the network becomes segmented into individual hubs. Workstations on each hub can communicate with each other, but data transfers through the network to workstations on other hubs will be disrupted until the cable problem is diagnosed and corrected.

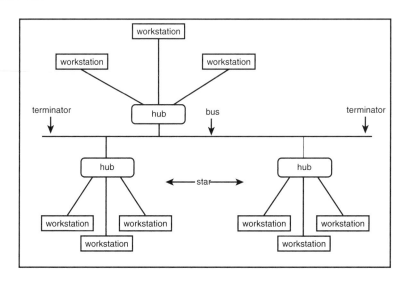

Figure 9.3 The tree topology connects star formations along a linear bus.

Hierarchical Star

Another method that can be used to connect hubs is a Hierarchical Star. This method, shown in Figure 9.4, uses a central hub to link hubs that have workstations attached.

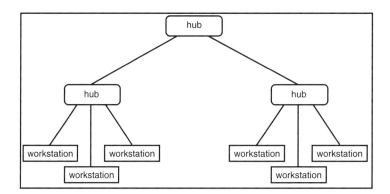

Figure 9.4 Hubs can be used to form hierarchies of star networks.

This method can be used to attach up to 12 hubs to a central hub, creating a large LAN. Without using a bridge, you can connect up to 1,024 workstations into a LAN using this method. Remembering the 5-4-3 rule, there can be only four repeaters in the path between any two nodes in the network.

Using a Backbone to Connect the Enterprise

Up to this point, I have discussed how to connect individual workstations together in an Ethernet LAN. The local LAN is a broadcast domain where all connected stations must be capable of receiving a data transmission from all other workstations in the LAN. This requirement of the CSMA/CD technique—used by ethernet for contention and access to the network media—limits the size of the total LAN in distance. For practical purposes, the number of workstations you can attach to an Ethernet LAN is also restricted because the more workstations there are—and therefore the more network traffic there is—performance begins to degrade as more and more computers experience collisions when trying to gain access to the network at the same time.

If other technologies were not available, it would not be possible to have the Internet, which is growing so rapidly today. Indeed, by using bridges, routers, and other devices, it is possible to interconnect individual network segments to form a larger network.

Chapter 5, "Bridges, Routers, Switches, and Repeaters," covers devices that join LANs and the functions they perform in more detail. To put it succinctly, these devices can create a larger network because each segment they join together is a broadcast domain in itself, subject to the limitations of their individual cabling and protocol requirements. These internetworking devices make decisions about sending packets to other networks, and do not operate using the CSMA/CD method.

Using an Ethernet Switch to Limit the Broadcast Domain

Routers operate by determining if a packet is destined for a different network segment based on its IP address. For this reason, routers are not used to join segments containing workstations that all use the same TCP/IP subnet. Instead, to create a larger network with workstations that all reside in the same subnet address space, you can connect segments using a special device called a *switching hub*, also called an *ethernet switch*—or just *switch* for simplicity (see Figure 9.5).

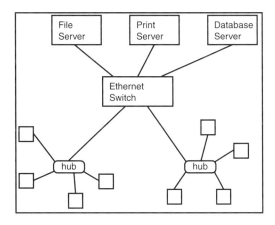

Figure 9.5 An ethernet switch can join segments that have the same IP subnet.

The switch can help solve network problems in many ways. It does not operate like an ordinary hub, broadcasting all incoming traffic on the remaining ports. Instead, a switch "learns" MAC addresses, and when it needs to transfer data between two nodes, it can set up a *circuit* so that only those two nodes see the packets. In Figure 9.5, several hubs are connected to the switch and are used to connect individual users' workstations.

You can also see from this figure that a high-volume server, such as a database server or print server, can be segmented from the other network segments. The switch can set up pathways for data going to and coming from these devices. By simply adding more hubs to this picture, or by placing workstations on the switch, you can limit the problem that would occur if all these devices existed in the same broadcast domain and had to suffer from an overloaded segment.

Using Routers to Join Networks

A router can also enable you to segment a network into smaller subnets, or to join networks together to create larger internets. Routers operate by determining the path a data packet needs to take to get to its final destination, and by sending it on the best possible route. A packet might pass through more than one router to get to its final destination.

In Figure 9.6, a router is used to join two networks. In this case, they are geographically separated. One network uses a high-speed backbone to which the router is attached. Hubs that have workstations attached are also connected to the backbone. The router takes care of sending and receiving data to and from the other network.

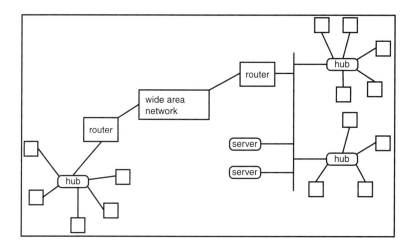

Figure 9.6 A router can be used to join different subnets or networks.

Routers do not have to be used just to cross great distances; they can be used on an intranet to join an address space that has been subnetted into smaller subnetworks. Each subnetwork is its own broadcast domain, and devices attached to the subnet contend for access to the local network media. The router, however, does not pass broadcast messages by default, so you can use it to break up an address space into units that are grouped by function or location.

Summary

The simplest topologies you can use to create an Ethernet LAN are the bus and the star topology. The bus topology is used primarily in 10Base-2 and 10Base-5 networks, but can also be used to connect stars into a broadcast domain. Hardware devices such as switches and routers can extend the area covered by your network, but routers can only connect different subnets. Ethernet switches can be used to broaden the area covered by a broadcast domain because they can learn where workstations are located and limit the traffic that is sent out on each physical cable segment.

Part IV

ETHERNET PROBLEMS

FDDI

FDDI stands for *Fiber Distributed Data Interface*. Work was started on FDDI in the early 1980s to provide a reliable, high-speed method of networking to connect the faster workstations and computers that were becoming commonly available that time. While ethernet and token-ring networks were operating at that time at maximum speeds of 10Mbps, FDDI was designed to provide a 100Mbps bandwidth, which was a substantial increase of existing technologies. Because of the development of other high-speed networking technologies (such as Gigabit Ethernet) and protocols that provide better control and quality of service (such as Frame Relay and ATM), basic FDDI is not as popular as it once was.

However, when used for the backbone in a network, it can still be a viable option for the network administrator to consider. The technology is mature, and you can find a large number of vendors and installers for FDDI. When adding a new building to an existing network that already contains FDDI segments, it might be more cost-effective to use FDDI than to incorporate newer technologies. If you are planning a complete overhaul of your network or are in the process of building a new one from scratch, the upgrade path for newer networking techniques, such as Gigabit Ethernet, might be a better choice.

A very important feature that can make FDDI an attractive networking solution is the security features inherent in using optical fiber as a network medium. Unlike topologies based on copper wire cables, optical fiber has no electrical properties and emits no signals that can be detected outside the cable.

In this chapter we will look at the components that make up the FDDI protocol and the methods used to transmit data and perform maintenance functions on an FDDI ring, and examine some typical configurations.

FDDI Dual-Ring Topology

Two of the main goals for FDDI during its development were speed and reliability. Optical fiber was selected as the network transmission medium because of its capability to transmit data at high speeds. The topology chosen was the ring topology, similar to token-ring networks. However, to provide enhanced reliability, a dual-ring topology was developed that uses two rings which transmit data in opposite directions (counter-rotating rings). Figure 10.1 shows the layout of a simple FDDI dual ring.

By using a dual-ring topology, with one ring operating as the primary ring and the other as a secondary backup ring, a simple failure of one fiber cable segment is less likely to cause disruption of the entire network. In Figure 10.1 you can see that each station on this ring has two ports, labeled A and B, which connect it to the ring. At first glance it might appear that one port is used for each ring. However, that is not the case. Instead, on the primary ring the A port receives data from its neighbor, which is transmitting the signal on its B port. On the backup secondary ring, the A port transmits data to its neighbor in the opposite direction and the neighbor receives the data on its B port.

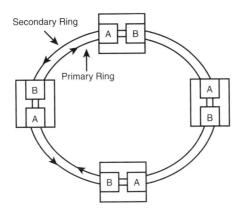

Figure 10.1 FDDI uses the dual counter-rotating ring topology.

Ports and Stations

The first example of a simple FDDI ring that we have looked at consists of stations that have two ports, labeled A and B. This kind of station is called a *dual-attached station*. This topology is called a *dual-attached ring*. Other ports that you might find on a FDDI network are

- M or *master* port
- S or *slave* port

These ports enable you to connect other kinds of stations to the FDDI ring, specifically a concentrator or a *single-attached station* (SAS). Single-attached stations do not have an A or B port, but instead have an S port. In this case the SAS is not directly attached to the dual ring, but is connected via an M port on a concentrator. In Figure 10.2, you can see an example of a concentrator that consists of both A, B, and M ports. The M ports are used to connect multiple workstations to the ring via their S ports.

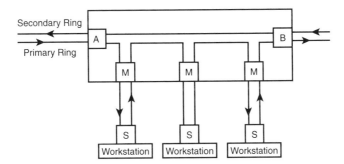

Figure 10.2 Concentrators can be used to connect single-attached stations to an FDDI ring.

Using this concentrator-based ring topology can aid in reducing network outages due to problems with workstations attached to the ring. The concentrator can act in a manner similar to the ethernet hub or token-ring MSAU and isolate individual workstations that fail, preventing them from causing problems for other nodes in the ring. For dual-attached stations, however, even a simple power-down of the unit can cause problems because the node, which is powered off, no longer is capable of receiving or retransmitting data, causing a break in the ring.

Ring Wrap

The *dual-ring* topology allows FDDI to heal itself when faced with simple failures of one node. When a station fails or if a cable between two stations is damaged, other stations detect the failure and the ring is automatically wrapped back onto itself to form a single ring. Figure 10.3 shows four network nodes (dual-attached stations) operating normally in a dual-ring topology.

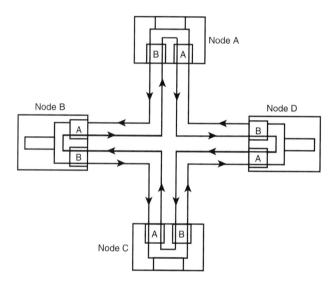

Figure 10.3   During normal operation, FDDI uses a dual-ring topology with one ring serving as the primary network medium.

In Figure 10.4 you can see what happens when a single node on the ring fails. Here Node C has failed and no longer participates in ring communications. Instead, Nodes B and D have internally wrapped the ring back onto itself. That is, the cable that was used for the secondary ring has been joined in these nodes to the primary ring, creating a single ring consisting of Nodes A, B, and D.

This self-repair method works well when only one node on the ring has failed. If more than one node fails, ring-wrapping might result in two or more separate rings. For this reason, it is preferable to use concentrators to join individual workstations to a ring rather than make each workstation or PC a dual-attached station. The concentrator itself becomes a single point of failure, and if it fails it can take all workstations connected to it down. However, because even something as simple as powering down a workstation that is dual-attached can cause a break in the ring, it is generally more likely that a workstation or PC will be the point of failure rather than a concentrator that is safely tucked away in a wiring closet.

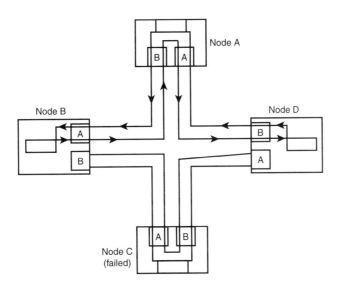

Figure 10.4 When a node on the ring fails, the Media Access Control Layer forms a single ring to isolate the malfunctioning node so that the other nodes can continue to operate.

Another consideration to think about is that because ring wrapping increases the actual distance information must travel around the ring, you must plan the maximum size of the ring accordingly. In a large LAN it would be impractical to size the ring to be able to accommodate a large number of failures. However, for a ring that is rated as a highly available network, you should plan to limit the maximum size to account for at least two to four simultaneous failures.

Optical Bypass Switches

Another device that you can use to help prevent ring failures is called an *optical bypass switch*. This device can prevent ring-wrap from happening if the station that is attached to it fails. This is accomplished in the bypass switch by an optical relay that causes the signal to bypass the failed station and continue on to its neighbor in the ring. However, these kinds of switches are expensive and result in a small amount of signal loss. Using them for each station on a large ring can cause signal degradation that can make network performance suffer noticeably.

Dual-Homing Important Devices

Some network nodes are usually considered to be more important than others. For example, a user might think that his or her workstation is the most important device on the network, but the failure of a router or file server that is also attached to the local ring can cause more than one user to be affected. Important devices can be made less susceptible to network failure by a technique called *dual-homing*. In this situation an important device is attached to two separate concentrators that are then attached to the ring. Only one of the links is active, while the other acts as a standby. If the active connection made to the first concentrator becomes unavailable, the device can then use the secondary connection to continue operations.

FDDI Protocol Standards

FDDI is defined by standards from the American National Standard Institute (ANSI) and the International Organization for Standardization (ISO). The four key components of FDDI are as follows:

- Media Access Control (MAC) Layer
- Physical (PHY) Layer
- Physical Media Dependent (PMD) Layer
- Station Management (SMT) Protocol

The MAC Layer interfaces with higher-level protocols, such as TCP/IP, and passes their protocol data units (PDUs) to the PHY Layer after repackaging them into packets of up to 4,500 bytes. Other functions performed by the MAC Layer are addressing, scheduling, and routing. The MAC specification defines the frame format and takes care of error recovery. It also is responsible for calculating the CRC value and token handling procedures.

The PHY Layer is responsible for the actual encoding and decoding of the packet data into the format used by the transmission media. The method used for encoding is called *4B/5B* encoding, which means that 4 bits of information are encoded into 5-bit groups. This encoding technique is used to ensure that under normal circumstances the bit stream, which is transmitted by FDDI, will never contain four 0 bits in a row, which is important from a timing standpoint. FDDI has no Active Monitor like a token-ring network, and each station has its own clock and must be capable of synchronizing with other stations.

While we normally think of 8-bit values (a byte) when encoding data, the 4B/5B technique concentrates on units of only 4 bits in length. The 4B/5B technique uses data symbols to represent the actual data that is being transmitted (labeled 0–9 and A–F), and eight control symbols used for things such as indicating the state of the link (symbols I, H, and Q) or as frame delimiters (symbols J, K, and T), among other things.

In Table 10.1 you can see the symbols used for data, along with the actual binary value each symbol represents. The last column shows the actual bits transmitted for this symbol on the FDDI ring.

Table 10.1 4B/5B Encoding Values for Data Symbols

Actual Binary Value	Symbol Name	Symbol Bits
0000	0	11110
0001	1	01001
0010	2	10100
0011	3	10101
0100	4	01010
0101	5	01011
0110	6	01110
0111	7	01111

Actual Binary Value	Symbol Name	Symbol Bits
1000	8	10010
1001	9	10011
1010	A	10110
1011	B	10111
1100	C	11010
1101	D	11011
1110	E	11100
1111	F	11101

As you can see, a binary value of 0000 would be transmitted as 11110, while the binary value of 1111 would be transmitted as 11101. In the actual bits transmitted, no symbol contains more than two 0 in a row, so when combined with other symbols the bit stream will not contain more than four 0 in a row.

The PMD Layer does the actual physical signaling on the transmission media, which is fiber optic cable for FDDI. To make it easier to attached common devices such as PCs and workstations to an FDDI network, the CDDI (Copper Distributed Data Interface) specification allows the PMD Layer to also transmit data using copper wires as the network medium.

The SMT protocol is the component that is responsible for managing the ring. Similar to token-ring networks, SMT functions include neighbor identification, detection of faults, and reconfiguration of the ring due to faults or insertion or removal of a station from the ring.

FDDI can extend for up to 100Km when using multi-mode fiber, with stations being up to 2Km from each other. When using single-mode fiber, stations can be up to 20Km in distance from each other. The maximum number of stations on the ring is 500.

Transmitting Data on an FDDI Ring

The method used by FDDI to transmit information across optical fiber is light. Two kinds of fiber-optic cables can be used; they are classified as either *single-mode* or *multi-mode*. Single-mode fiber uses a laser as its source of light and can be used over longer distances than multi-mode fiber. Multi-mode fiber cables allow multiple rays of light, entering the cable at different angles, to carry signals through the cable and uses a light-emitting diode (LED) as its light source.

Using Light to Encode Bits

A station on the ring will look at the state of the light beam on the fiber about every eight nanoseconds. The only possibilities are that the station will either sense that light is present or that it is not. To determine whether a 0 or a 1 is being sent, the station will compare the current sampling with the one immediately before it. If the state of the fiber has changed—that is, it has gone from no light detected to light detected, or vice versa—it is determined that a bit representing a 1 has been transmitted. If no change between this sampling period and the 1 immediately previous to it is detected, a 0 bit has been transmitted. This technique for signaling is known as *nonreturn to zero with inversion (NRZI)* modulation.

FDDI Frames

FDDI frames are similar to token-ring frames. A token frame (shown in Figure 10.5) is passed from one station in the ring to the next. When a station on the ring has data that it needs to transmit, it seizes the token, adds addressing information and data to the frame, and then transmits the data frame (see Figure 10.6).

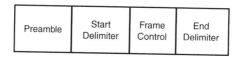

Figure 10.5   The token frame is used to mediate access to the ring.

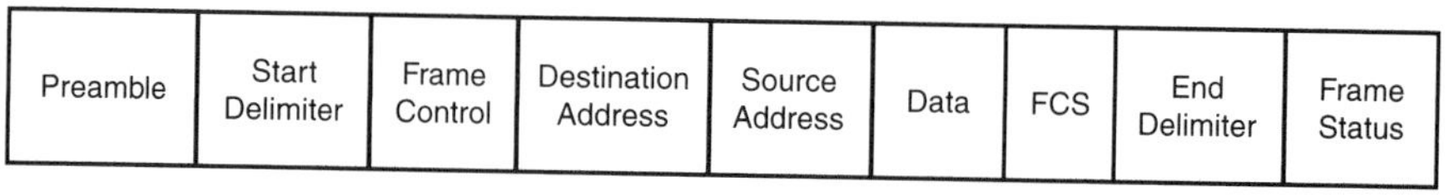

Preamble	Start Delimiter	Frame Control	Destination Address	Source Address	Data	FCS	End Delimiter	Frame Status

Figure 10.6   The data frame contains the same fields as the token frame, but addressing information and data are also included.

The fields that are shown in Figures 10.5 and 10.6 are used for the following functions:

- **Preamble**—This field indicates that a frame is arriving at the station so that the adapter can prepare to receive it.
- **Start delimiter**—Designates the start of the frame.
- **Frame control**—Specifies the size of the address fields and other control information.
- **Destination address**—The 6-byte address of the destination of the frame. This can also be a multicast address such as a broadcast or group address.
- **Source address**—This field contains the 6-byte address of the station that originated the data frame.
- **Data**—Control information or data that is destined for a higher-level protocol, such as TCP/IP.
- **Frame check sequence (FCS)**—A 32-bit CRC value used to check the integrity of the frame when it arrives at its destination.
- **End delimiter**—Designates the end of the frame.
- **Frame status**—Contains bits used to indicate errors, address recognized and frame copied.

The token frame is passed around the ring in an orderly fashion. When a node on the ring wants to transmit data, it grabs the token. That is, instead of retransmitting the token frame to its neighbor, it transmits one or more data frames. Data frames can be used to send information that is destined for a higher-level protocol, or it can be control information used in ring maintenance procedures.

Some of the more important FDDI management frames are as follows:

- **Neighbor Information Frame (NIF)**—This frame is sent around the ring periodically (usually from 2–30 seconds) and is used to exchange information about stations and their neighbors on the ring.

- **Status Information Frame (SIF)**—This frame gives stations configuration information and operation information stored in a *MIB (Management Information Base)*.

- **Parameter Management Frame**—This frame is used to read information from or write information to the MIB.

- **Status Report Frame**—Uses a multicast address and is used to give status information to management applications.

The Target Token Rotation Timer and the Claim Process

When the ring is first initialized, the Target Token Rotation Time (TTRT) is determined. The Token Rotation Timer (TRT) is initially set to this value. If the TRT expires before a station receives a token, it assumes that some kind of error has occurred and it starts the claim process.

During this process the stations also negotiate to determine which one will be responsible for generating the first token on the ring. Each station is assigned a value for TTRT. During the claim process, each station compares the value for TTRT that was set by the previous station in the ring. If the TTRT it receives from its neighbor is longer than its own value, it substitutes its own value and retransmits the claim frame. If the received TTRT value is shorter than its own, it retransmits the frame. If its value is the same as that it receives from its neighbor, the station with the highest address wins. When a station receives the claim frame back and recognizes that it is the winner, it sets the TTRT for the ring and generates the first token.

After normal operations begin, each node on the ring monitors the ring and frames passing around it to check for errors.

When a station transmits a data frame, the frame travels around the ring and is read by each node and retransmitted to the next node on the ring. When a node recognizes itself as the destination address of the frame, it copies the address to a buffer and sets the address recognized and frame copied bits in the Frame Status field before retransmitting it. When the frame arrives back at the station from which it was originally generated, the station can determine whether the frame was received by checking these bits. If the error bit is set, it can take actions to resend the data.

When a station begins to transmit frames on the ring, it can continue to do so for as long as the rules negotiated with other stations allow. This time is monitored at each station by a timer called the *Token Holding Timer*.

Beaconing

When a station on the ring fails to receive a frame (either token or data) from its neighbor, it begins the beaconing process by transmitting a beacon frame. Each station in the ring retransmits the beacon frame to the next station in the ring. If the beacon frame travels around the ring back to the station where it originated, the station stops transmitting beacon frames because it assumes that the fault has been repaired.

If it does not receive the beacon frame back after about 10 seconds, it will start a trace process. During this process the station will use the secondary ring instead of the primary ring to communicate with its upstream neighbor. Both nodes will remove themselves from the ring and test the connections between them. If no fault is found, both stations will rejoin the ring. If one of the stations encounters an error, it stays out of the ring and the other station will perform the ring-wrap function so that other nodes on the ring can continue to operate.

Common Problems Using FDDI

Although FDDI rings perform some basic maintenance functions to help take care of problems, it is still necessary to monitor the LAN periodically to ensure that the network is operating optimally. Also, many problems can't be corrected by software, such as faulty network adapters or network cables. Tools you can use for monitoring and troubleshooting efforts include a cable tester (one intended for use with fiber-optic cable) and a standard LAN protocol analyzer. Most FDDI vendors will also provide a station management application that can be used to examine ring functionality and gather statistics and error information. It is a good idea to get a thorough understanding of station management software so that you are better prepared when problems occur.

Ring Wrapping

This process allows for a malfunctioning node to be isolated from the other nodes in the ring. To restore the ring to normal functioning it is necessary to track down the offending node and determine the cause of the failure. Station management software can provide the information you need to determine which station has left the ring. Perhaps the most common reason why ring wrapping occurs is a simple power failure. This can result from a faulty power supply in one of the attached workstations or in a concentrator on the ring. It can also result from human error when someone who doesn't understand how the ring operates mistakenly powers down a station.

Other possible causes include all the associated hardware, from the cable to the connectors to the interface card that is installed in the workstation. Be sure to check that all connectors are correctly fastened and are not loose. Check for crushed or otherwise damaged cables. Fiber-optic cable is not as forgiving as twisted-pair can be, so it should be handled with care.

If all else fails, check the interface card on the computer. Use the vendor-supplied diagnostic software to determine if the card is in good working order. If the card passes all the vendor's tests, try using it in a different slot on the computer bus or swapping it out for a card that is known to be working at this time.

Ring Initializations and Frame Check Sequence (FCS) Errors

Errors in the transmission of bits (causing FCS errors) or a high number of ring initializations (beacon or claim frames) may indicate problems with the light signal strength. It is easy to introduce dust, fingerprints, or other obstacles to the light signal when handling connectors. Connectors that are not tightly fastened can also lead to problems with the quality of the light signal and promote these kinds of errors. A cable tester designed for fiber-optic cabling can be used to test the signal strength for each segment.

Exceeding the maximum distance specifications for FDDI can also cause problems resulting in FCS errors or frequent ring initializations. Although a ring might be capable of continuing functioning if a single node is removed from the ring through ring wrapping, the removal of more than one can cause the total distance through the ring to be in excess of the specifications, resulting in a poor signal. If you are using optical bypass switches to help prevent ring wrapping, you can still experience these problems because each optical bypass switch can introduce a two-decibel reduction in the signal strength.

Although not as common, a faulty network interface card or port on a concentrator can be the cause of these problems. Other possible sources that can affect signal quality include low quality fiber-optic cable and imperfect splices in the cable. You can track down a faulty network adapter using the station management software or by using a LAN analyzer and looking for the station that is starting the claim process. Look at this station's upstream neighbor to find out if a faulty card is causing the problem.

Making Repairs

Fiber-optic cabling is more expensive than copper wire cabling and requires a skilled technician for installation and repairs. Tasks such as replacing a network adapter or moving a node to a different port on a concentrator can be easily performed by a network administrator. Splicing fiber-optic cables or attaching connectors, however, should be done by someone who is well trained in the techniques. For all but large shops this usually means an outside vendor or contractor.

In addition to the introduction of obstructions like dust or fingerprints, the light signal can also become degraded due to incorrect polishing when the cable is cut and attached to a connector. This doesn't mean that you cannot make such repairs yourself. If the size of the network warrants the expense, purchasing the tools and training an employee in the necessary techniques might be appropriate.

Summary

FDDI is similar in many ways to token ring. It mediates access to the network medium by passing a token frame from station to station and uses the address recognized and frame copied bits in a data frame to tell the sending station that its data was received at its destination. Because of its high transmission rate (100Mbps), FDDI is usually employed as a backbone in a network. Other technologies, which are generally less expensive than FDDI, are usually used to connect individual workstations or PCs to the network. Newer high-speed protocols, such as Frame Relay or ATM, which provide enhanced features not found in FDDI, are making FDDI a less attractive choice for new network implementations.

Wireless Networking

SOME OF THE MAIN TOPICS IN THIS CHAPTER ARE

Uses for Wireless LANs

Wireless Topology

Wireless Standards

Other Wireless Developments

While the installed base of networked computers today is mainly composed of technologies using copper wire and fiber-optic cable, the growing market for wireless technologies cannot be underestimated. The popularity and rapid growth of the cellular telephone market, for both personal and business applications, attests to this fact. Ten years ago, cellular telephones were a high-priced item used mainly by top business executives. Today they are sold in shopping malls and it is common to see teenagers walking around with one stuck to their head. In a few more years it will be hard to imagine how we ever got along without them.

Laptop computers provided the first true mobility for computer users. Linking these powerful platforms to a computer network can be accomplished easily either by means of a PCMCIA network adapter card or a docking station. By using DHCP to assign network configuration information it is easy to move a portable computer from one location to another and still provide a simple connection to the network. However this kind of mobility still depends on a wired connection of some sort, either a direct connection to the network or possibly a dial-up connection for remote access. Wireless networking, although not widely deployed at this time, may provide a better solution to the problem of mobility for computers and other similar devices.

Uses for Wireless LANs

For a technology to grow it must solve some kind of problem. That is, it must be useful in some way. Wireless LANs have primarily found their niche in vertical markets, such as healthcare services and the factory floor. The most obvious benefit this kind of networking provides is mobility. Other benefits that you may get from wireless networking include

- Faster installation
- Adaptability in a dynamic environment
- Reduced costs in certain situations

In a typical LAN setup it is necessary to install and configure the networking software on the client computer and also provide the wiring from the network hub or switch to the user's work area. With a wireless LAN you only need to configure the computer's networking software. There is no need to string cables through the building for each user. In an environment that changes rapidly, this can be an advantage. For example, point-of-sale terminals in a large store can be easily reconfigured for seasonal adjustments such as the end of the year Christmas buying spree. In a warehouse the floor layout may change during the year for similar kinds of reasons. Being able to relocate computers in this kind of situation is much easier if there are no cables to contend with. After the initial investment is made in wireless LAN devices, the ability to reconfigure the physical network topology can result, in many cases, in reduced costs over time.

In addition to these kinds of environments, you will find wireless LANs increasingly being used in situations such as

- **Hospitals**—Patient information can be easily obtained using a laptop computer or specialized terminal. Instead of having to return to a central location, such as the nurses' station on the hospital floor, doctors and nurses can get information quickly from a laptop computer or hand-held device as they make their patient rounds.

- **Older buildings**—In some cases it can be difficult to wire the premises for a traditional network. Some older buildings that do not have plenum areas in the ceiling can be difficult to adapt. Using wireless communications makes networking in this kind of environment an easy task.

- **Temporary setups**—A consulting group sent onsite to a customer's premises can quickly set up their own local area network (LAN) without having to make use of the customer's equipment. In a trade show, where the network is usually set up for only a few days, the computers can be configured ahead of time so that the only thing the user has to do is turn them on.

- **Warehouse and factory floors**—Laptop computers and hand-held bar code scanners that use wireless LAN technology can quickly return the investment needed for their implementation.

Note

When discussing the applications of wireless networking, the dialogue should not be limited to just computers. By enabling data collection devices, such as bar code scanners or hand-held data entry terminals with wireless networking connections, many more practical uses for wireless communications will develop in the next few years.

Wireless Topology

Most of the wireless products on the market today can be used to connect mobile computing devices to the standard wired network. They can also be used to create a simple peer-to-peer network, as shown in Figure 11.1. This kind of workgroup LAN can be useful when only a few stations need to communicate in a small geographical area.

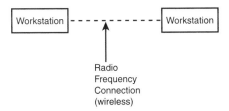

Figure 11.1 A simple peer-to-peer network can be accomplished easily with wireless LAN equipment.

However, when a connection to the larger wired network is required, additional equipment is used to provide an *access point* that allows the mobile computers to communicate among themselves and with other nodes on the network (see Figure 11.2).

Because multiple access points can be placed throughout the network, this topology allows for a wider geographical range for mobile users. An *access point* is a device that connects to the wired network and provides a transmitter/receiver that can be used to communicate with mobile users' workstations. In addition to providing the wireless communications service, an access point typically is also responsible for buffering data between the wireless clients and the wired network. It can also be responsible for mediating communications between wireless clients that operate within range of the same access point.

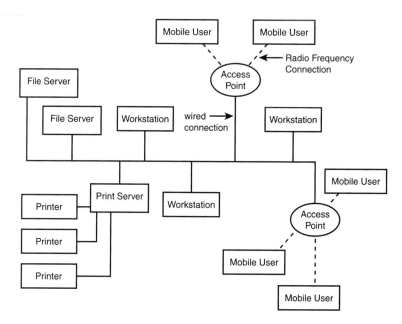

Figure 11.2   Access points provide the connection to the wired network for mobile users.

An access point device can also be used without a connection to a wired network. In this setup, shown in Figure 11.3, the access point serves as a *base station* that mediates communications between several wireless clients. Note that by placing an access point between two clients you can effectively double the maximum distance between the two clients because the access point serves as a sort of hub.

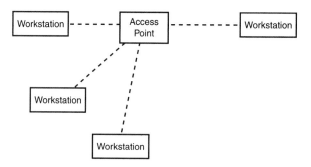

Figure 11.3   An access point can be used to create a simple wireless network.

Most devices on the market today will support from 10–50 wireless clients on a single access point at any given time.

Communication Methods

Several methods can be used to provide the wireless connection. The infrared and radio wave transmission methods are discussed here.

The Infrared Method

The infrared (IR) method uses light just below the visible spectrum for communications. It is limited, though, to a small area and cannot be used when it is necessary to communicate through a physical medium such as a wall or other obstruction. However, this limiting factor can also be used as a security advantage. Since the network signal cannot be detected beyond a certain area or outside of the building, it can provide a good method for creating a secure LAN, especially when used with other techniques such as encryption.

Radio Wave Transmissions

The most popular method for providing a communications medium for a wireless LAN is typical radio wave transmissions. The Federal Communications Commission (FCC) allocated a radio spectrum in 1985 that is called the Industrial, Scientific and Medical (ISM) band. It operates in the 2.400 to 2.483 GHz range and does not require the end user to obtain any kind of license. Similar agencies in other countries have followed suit and set aside this range for the same use. When developing products for wireless networking using this range, a technique called spread-spectrum broadcasting is used.

Spread-Spectrum Technology

During World War II the military began development of a radio transmission technology called *spread spectrum*. A normal radio signal, such as those you pick up on your car radio, are called *narrowband* because they concentrate all their transmitting power on a single frequency. Spread-spectrum technology uses a much larger bandwidth instead and can be deployed using two basic methods: Direct Sequence Spread Spectrum (DSSS) or Frequency Hopping Spread Spectrum (FHSS). Spread-spectrum techniques are attractive to manufacturers of wireless equipment for many reasons. One of the more important reasons is that they are difficult to detect or intercept. Additionally, from a security standpoint, they are very difficult to "jam" or interfere with.

The two main aspects of any spread-spectrum technique are

- The signal that is transmitted is of a greater bandwidth than the actual transmitted information's bandwidth.
- The resulting bandwidth is determined by some method other than the information being transmitted.

For commercial systems, the actual bandwidth used may be from 20–200 times the bandwidth of the actual information that is being transmitted, perhaps even larger. Some systems use a bandwidth that is up to a thousand times larger than the information. Because the signal is spread out over a larger bandwidth, it can occupy the same bands as ordinary narrowband transmissions with little interference.

DSSS systems use a signal that is composed of a pseudo-noise signal combined with the actual information modulated on an RF carrier. This results in a signal with a wide bandwidth that appears to be noise. At the receiving end the pseudo-noise signal is used to mask out the actual information signal.

FHSS employs a much simpler technique. It uses a narrowband carrier that continually changes frequencies. The transmitter and receiver must both be synchronized to know which frequencies are used, and in what order, for this to work. The FCC dictates that at least 75 or more frequencies must be used for this technique, and any single frequency cannot be used for a burst of data longer than 400ms. Some methods of FHSS employ a simple pattern of switching from one frequency to the next. Others use a technique where certain frequencies are skipped.

Wireless Standards

The main standard for wireless LANs is the IEEE 802.11 standard. It was first drawn up in 1990 and has gone through several drafts since then. The final draft was approved in 1997 and includes definitions for the Physical Layer (PHY) and the MAC Layer protocol. The standard envisions two kinds of clients: ad hoc and client/server. The ad hoc client method involves a peer-to-peer network between clients located close to each other without the need for an access point. The client/server method uses an access point device to mediate network communications and possibly provide a connection to a wired network.

The Physical Layer

The Physical Layer of a network involves the mechanisms used to actually transmit the signal on the network medium. In this case, the medium is infrared, FHSS, or DSSS. When using FHSS the data rate is 1Mbps. For DSSS, the standard defines both 1Mbps and 2Mbps techniques. For infrared, the standard also supports both 1 and 2Mbps data rates.

Note

While the standard defines both spread spectrum and IR methods at the Physical Layer, wireless clients using different Physical Layer components cannot interoperate.

The MAC Layer

For the MAC Layer the standard is very similar to the 802.3 standard for traditional ethernet networks. However, while ethernet uses the CSMA/CD method that "detects" collisions, the MAC Layer of the 802.11 standard uses CSMA/CA, where the CA stands for *collision avoidance*. In an RF network it is difficult for the sending station to accurately detect a collision. When using the collision avoidance technique, a station that wants to transmit measures the RF signal coming from the antenna and, if it is below a specified threshold, the channel is available for use. If it is above the threshold, the channel is already in use. For the actual transmission of data, several informational frames are used: RTS, CTS, and ACK.

To send data, the station first transmits a request to send (RTS) frame. This frame contains information about the amount of data the station wants to send (the amount of time it needs to transmit the data) and the destination. The receiving station sends back a clear to send (CTS) frame. All other stations detect these frames and "back off" for the amount of time the sending station has requested. After the actual data transmission the receiving station sends an acknowledgement frame (ACK). If the sending station does not receive the CTS frame after it requests transmission time, it does not transmit data, avoiding a collision.

The MAC Layer also provides other services, such as *association* and *reassociation*. An access point and its clients make up a Basic Service Set (BSS) in the network. A client is associated with a particular BSS. When a client moves from one BSS to another, reassociation takes place. While the 802.11 standard provides for the concept of reassociation, the actual mechanism for this function is not specified in the standard.

Security in Wireless Networks

An option to the 802.11 standard is called Wired Equivalent Privacy (WEP). WEP is a shared key system that can be used to validate clients on the wireless network. In order to become associated with an access point (AP) the client must possess the shared key valid for that AP. The option uses the RC4 encryption algorithm. Data communications between clients and the AP are also encrypted using the shared key, making it difficult for an eavesdropper to penetrate the network.

Other Wireless Developments

The IEEE 802.11 standard was a good start toward defining wireless networking. However, it lacks some features that are needed to make it more complete so that multiple vendors will be able to make products that can fully interoperate with each other's equipment. The Wireless LAN Interoperability Forum was formed in 1996 and has set forth the OpenAir standard as an alternative to 802.11. OpenAir uses the FHSS spread spectrum method and provides additional security and other features not found in 802.11. For more information on this forum, visit their Web site at www.wlif.com.

Wireless Application Protocol (WAP)

Another interesting related development is the Wireless Application Protocol (WAP), which was created by the Wireless Application Protocol Forum. The WAP V1.0 specification was published by the forum in April of 1998. This standard aims at providing information services on devices such as mobile phones and remote terminals. The information can be something such as Internet access or a distributed application, such as a data collection system. The programming model that this standard uses closely resembles the World Wide Web protocols. For example, WAP uses HTTP 1.1 for interacting with Web servers.

To get more information about this developing technology, visit the forum's Web site at www.wapforum.org.

Bluetooth

A more recent development in wireless networking that goes by the strange name of Bluetooth (named after an early Danish king who only infrequently visited a dentist) might turn out to be the most widely deployed wireless technology in the near future. Advanced by vendors such as Intel, Nokia, IBM, and Toshiba, Bluetooth targets more than computers and similar data processing devices. The Bluetooth specification is intended to be a replacement for cables for almost any kind of electronic device, including telephones, pagers, radios, personal digital assistants (PDAs), and so on. The Bluetooth chip is a small device, only 9×9 mm, and is expected to be produced for a very low cost due to the large market that is anticipated for it.

Bluetooth uses low-power transmissions and therefore is very limited in the distance it can cover, up to about 10 meters, broadcasting in the 2.4GHz (ISM) band. Frequency hopping is also used, but at a much faster rate than other wireless networking products: 1,600 hops per second using 79 hops separated by 1MHz over the total spectrum. Both asynchronous communication (at 721Kb/second) and synchronous communication (at 432.6Kb/second) are supported to provide for both voice and data transmissions. The initial Bluetooth specification also provides techniques for authentication and encryption.

Piconets and Scatternets

The ad hoc nature of Bluetooth networking minimizes the need for management or administrative functions for networks made up of Bluetooth-capable devices. The concept of a *personal area network*, in which devices in close proximity can form a small network (called a piconet) without user intervention, enables users to transfer data between a cellular phone and a laptop computer, for example, simply by coming within range.

A piquant is formed when two or more devices discover each other and begin to communicate. A piconet can have up to eight devices connected, with one device acting as a master, the remaining devices as slaves. The first device to initiate transmission will become the master, though there are provisions in the specification for a master and slave unit to exchange roles. Within each piconet, a specific frequency hopping sequence is used by all devices in the piconet. A scatternet is formed when devices participate in more than one piconet.

Before a piconet is formed, devices are in the *standby* mode, in which it will listen for messages every 1.28 seconds. To initiate a connection with another device, an *inquiry* message can be sent, which is used to find other Bluetooth devices. If the address of the device to which a connection is desired is already known, a *page* message is used instead to initiate communications.

Sniff, Hold, and Park Modes

Many of the devices that are ideal candidates for Bluetooth technology are low-power devices. Unlike a traditional network adapter card used for desktop PCs, the Bluetooth device does not continuously listen to all traffic on the medium. Instead, there are several modes of operation:

- **Hold**—A master unit can put a slave unit into hold mode, or the slave unit can request that it be placed into this mode. This is a power-saving mode in which the unit no longer actively exchanges data with other devices.

- **Sniff**—In this mode, the device does not actively participate in communications with other devices, but it does "wake up" and listen for messages frequently. The frequency with which it wakes up and listens is dependent on the particular application the device is used for and is programmed by the manufacturer.

- **Park**—In this low-power mode, the device is still considered to be part of a piconet but no longer has a MAC address associated with it. The device will listen for broadcast messages and resynchronize its clock with the master but does not actively communicate.

Because it is so flexible, it is very likely that Bluetooth will become an industry standard in a short time. The capability to handle both voice and data communications to form intimate networks with little or no user intervention and the relatively low cost of the hardware make Bluetooth an interesting technology to watch.

Summary

In the near future you can expect to see a much larger market for wireless networking devices. As standards continue to evolve, the interoperability of different manufacturers' devices will make vendors more competitive and cause the initial investment in the technology to be significantly less than it is today. However, for the problems that a wireless network can solve, by providing flexibility and mobility to the network, the costs may already be sufficiently low when compared to the functionality achieved. As newer devices, such as hand-held terminals and advanced mobile phones are developed, entirely new applications for wireless networking will certainly be developed.

Collision Rates

CHAPTER 12

Keeping the network healthy requires that you make sure that all physical components are functioning normally and at optimal levels of performance. However, you still need to monitor the network to be sure that other factors are not limiting the amount of real data that can travel through the network.

Although collisions are a normal event, and indeed are expected for a network based on ethernet technology, it is always possible for excessive collisions to cause a significant degradation of performance that will be noticeable to end users.

Why Collisions Happen: CSMA/CD

Let's quickly review why collisions occur. The term *collision* itself seems to imply that something is wrong. In some technical literature, this kind of event is called a *stochastic arbitration event*, or *SAE*, which sounds much less like an error than does *collision*.

The acronym *CSMA/CD* is used to describe the method used by Ethernet devices to access the network medium. It stands for *Carrier Sense Multiple Access with Collision Detection*. When you take these words and examine exactly what they mean, you can obtain a better understanding of what a collision is. The method that a device uses is described in the following steps:

1. Listen to the network to determine if any other device is currently transmitting (Carrier Sense).

2. If no other transmission is detected, start transmitting.

3. If more than one device senses that no transmission is occurring, both can start transmitting at the same time. The network physical connection is a shared medium (Multiple Access).

4. When two devices start transmitting at the same time, the signal becomes garbled and the devices detect this (Collision Detection).

5. When a collision is detected, a device sends out a jamming signal of a few bytes of arbitrary data to inform other devices on the network.

6. The device pauses for a short amount of time (a few milliseconds), listens to the network to see if it is in use, and then tries the transmission again.

Because ethernet enables more than one device to use the same transmission medium, with no central controller or token dictating which node can transmit, collisions can occur. When this happens, as explained in the next section, each node "backs off" for a certain amount of time before attempting retransmission. This doesn't happen on token-ring networks. Instead, access to the network is granted in a controlled manner by passing a certain frame (the token frame) from one station to another. A station that needs to transmit data does so after it receives the token frame. When it is finished transmitting, it sends the token frame to the next station on the network. Thus, token ring is a deterministic network and guarantees each station on the ring the capability to transmit within a specified time. Ethernet, however, is a more competitive environment in which each station on the LAN must contend with any other station that wants to transmit at the same time.

The Backoff Algorithm

When a collision happens, the device that detects it will stop and then try once again to transmit its data onto the network. If a collision is caused because two stations try to transmit at about the same time, they might continue to cause collisions because both will pause and then start transmitting at the same time again.

The backoff algorithm is an essential component of CSMA/CD. Instead of waiting for a set amount of time when a device backs off and stops transmitting, a random value is calculated and is used to set the amount of time for which the device delays transmission.

The calculation used to determine this time value is called the *Truncated Binary Exponential Backoff Algorithm*. Each time a collision occurs for an attempted transmission for a particular frame, the device will pause for an amount of time that increases with each collision. The device will try up to 16 times to transmit the data. If it finds that it cannot put the information onto the network medium after 16 attempts, it drops the frame and notifies a higher-level component in the protocol stack.

Note

A method similar to CSMA/CD is CSMA/CA, where the last two letters, CA, stand for collision avoidance. Networks that use this method for accessing the physical medium—such as AppleTalk—listen to the network just as an Ethernet device does. However, before sending out a frame on the network, networks using CSMA/CA first send out a small packet indicating to other stations that they are about to transmit. This method helps to greatly reduce collisions, but is not widely used because of the overhead that is produced when its networks send out the informational packet.

Relating Collisions to Packet Size

The rules used to create Ethernet networks are not simply arbitrary decisions made by some committee; they relate to the characteristics of the physical devices used to create the network. When using a collision detection mechanism to arbitrate access to the network, the transmitting device needs to know how long it will take, in the worst case, for its transmission to travel to the furthermost device that resides on the same segment.

Why is this? Consider what happens when a device starts transmitting. Because the signal moves through the wire at a non-instantaneous speed, it will take some amount of time before all devices on the same segment sense that the cable is being used. At the furthermost end of the cable, it is possible for another device that has not detected the first transmission to listen and then start signaling its own data onto the network, just before the first signal reaches it. The result is a collision. The first station that initiated a transmission will not detect that a collision has occurred until the signal travels back to it, hence the round trip timer value.

A 10Mbps Ethernet network signals at a speed of 10 million bits per second. The standard says that the round trip time can be no more than 51.2 milliseconds. This is the amount of time it takes to transmit about 64 bytes of data at 10Mbps. Thus, the rules state that a device must continue to transmit for the amount of time it would take for its signal to travel to the most distant point in the network and back—the round trip time.

If the device does not continue transmitting for the duration of the round trip time, it is not capable of detecting that a collision occurred with that frame before it began to transmit another frame.

If a frame that needs to be transmitted is less than 64 bytes in length, the sending node will pad it with zeros to bring it up to this minimum length.

Collisions and Network Utilization

When a device begins to experience collisions at a rate that is one percent of the total network traffic, you might have a problem. Another statistic to watch when monitoring the network is utilization. In theory, you might expect that a network operating at 10 million bits per second would actually be capable of transmitting that much data on a continuous basis. However, that is not the case. In most ethernet networks, the actual utilization rate is only 40 percent before performance begins to degrade rapidly. As utilization rises, so do collisions.

If the network topology rules are followed and the network utilization is low, excessive collisions might be due to a faulty network card that is not listening to the network.

Detecting Collisions

A simple method for determining how many collisions are occurring is to look at the LED lights on the hub. Most hubs have an LED that lights up when a collision is detected. If you notice that this light is flashing continuously or very frequently, investigate further to determine if the rate is excessive. If it is, take actions to reduce it.

LAN analyzers and monitoring tools can aid you in counting the number of collisions that are occurring. Management consoles that employ SNMP and RMON probes can be useful for collecting statistical information that can be used to localize segments in the network that experience high collision rates. The historical data maintained by RMON can be analyzed and stored for use in creating baseline data that you can use to judge network performance.

Collision Types

A good network analyzer will give you a lot of statistical information. When it comes to collisions, there will most likely be more than one kind of statistic to help point out the cause of the collision.

Local Collision

A *local collision* (also called an *early* collision) is a collision that happens on the local segment during the transmission of the first 64 bytes of a frame. This is the most common type of collision you will see on a network segment, and usually does not indicate a hardware problem. This type of collision happens when two different stations on the LAN detect that nothing is being transmitted on the wire, and both begin to transmit at about the same time. The result is a frame called a *runt*, named because only part of the frame was transmitted successfully before the collision event occurred. The ethernet specifications take into consideration this expected event, and both stations use the backoff algorithm to delay transmission.

When high levels of early collisions are occurring, look to see if the utilization on the segment is nearing or surpassing 40 percent. If this is the case on a regular basis, the segment is probably overloaded. Consider using a switch to limit collisions. If you can identify a particular node that is experiencing a high rate of local collisions, there may be a hardware problem. Check the connectors that join it to the network; if no fault is found there, try replacing the network adapter card to see if that is the problem.

Late Collisions

A *late collision* occurs when two devices on the network start to transmit at the same time and do not detect the collision immediately. This kind of collision is usually caused by a network segment that is too long. If the time it takes to put the frame on the network is shorter than the amount of time it takes for the frame to travel to the node that is the greatest distance away, neither device will know that the other has started transmitting until after the first 64 bytes (the minimum frame size) have been put on the wire.

For example, suppose workstation A begins to transmit a frame and finishes transmitting before the signal reaches workstation B, which has been cabled to the network at a distance that exceeds the specs. Workstation B, thinking that the wire is clear, begins to transmit its frame just before the signal from workstation A reaches it. Of course, because workstation B is closest to the collision event, it detects the collision. However, because workstation A has finished transmitting the frame it has also stopped listening to detect whether a collision has occurred. The end result is that workstation A thinks it was capable of successfully transmitting the frame. It has no idea that a collision has occurred.

Late collisions do not cause a frame to be retransmitted, simply because the NIC does not know that a collision has occurred. It is up to a higher-level protocol to determine that something has caused an error and to request retransmission.

If the LAN is experiencing high levels of late collision events, check for topology problems. This includes not only excessive cable lengths, but also using too many repeaters or other devices. If no apparent problems can be found and the network appears up to specifications, there is probably a hardware problem. Try to locate the offending NIC or cable by looking at the addressing information decoded by a LAN analyzer.

Sampling Intervals

When monitoring for collisions, don't jump to conclusions when you only see sporadic increases. Take samples several times during the work day, and try to correlate them with the functions being performed by users on the network at that time. Sometimes it is the actual day that matters, and not the time. For example, at the end of a month or a quarter, many business functions are performed—such as accounting reports—that generate large amounts of network use.

An overall average of the number of collisions that occur per second, along with the network utilization rate, is useful in determining if the network is becoming saturated. Information about peak levels is useful for designing user work patterns so that the network is used more efficiently.

Reducing Collisions

There are several reasons why collisions will occur at excessive rates. Some of those reasons include ignoring topology rules, faulty hardware, and an overloaded segment (too many users).

Incorrect Network Topology

If you use segments that exceed the length permitted by your network topology, some devices on the network might not detect that the network is in use until a transmission by another node is well underway. Check your cable lengths and make sure they are within the standards. When it comes time to expand the LAN, you should never haphazardly add new segments by simply attaching a new repeater, hub, or bridge to the network. It is important to keep an up-to-date map of the physical topology of the network so you can plan additions before you implement them.

Remember that 10Base-T workstations can be no more than 100 meters apart. In addition, the 5-4-3 rule states that there can be a maximum of 5 cable segments on the LAN, with a maximum of 4 repeaters or concentrators, and only 3 segments can have nodes attached.

Faulty Network Adapters

One particular problem is an adapter that does not sense the carrier signal due to faulty hardware, and begins to transmit whenever it wants to, thinking that the wire is available. In Chapter 4, "Network Interface Cards," you will find a more detailed discussion of troubleshooting NICs. However, a basic strategy to follow is to replace the suspect device and, if that does not solve the problem, try using a different cable to connect the NIC to the network or try reseating the NIC in another slot in the computer. When replacing the device, be sure to use a substitute that is known to be in good working order. The same goes for replacement cables. Another troubleshooting tactic is to use the diagnostic software provided by the network adapter's manufacturer.

The most common problem relating to collisions caused by a faulty NIC is late collisions. These occur when a network adapter malfunctions and becomes incapable of hearing other traffic on the wire. Its transmissions can be responsible for both late and early collision events. However, if the network topology has been verified to be within specifications and late collision events are occurring, suspect a faulty NIC, the cable, and the connectors.

Top Talkers

There are only so many devices you can place on a network in the same broadcast domain before performance will begin to suffer. A small number of high-performance computers that generate a lot of network traffic can produce the same result. Remember that as utilization rises, so do collisions. So, when you are experiencing a high collision rate and the network segment's utilization approaches or exceeds the 40 percent mark, it's time to consider segmenting the LAN using a switch or another similar device. A switch, which can be used to give high-end servers a full-duplex connection, is an ideal choice when a local segment contains both end users and powerful servers that are "top talkers."

Summary

Collisions are normal occurrences on an Ethernet network. When network utilization rises, collisions typically do the same. Collisions can be caused by ignoring topology rules and creating a broadcast domain that is too large, or by faulty equipment. You can solve excessive collision problems by determining the cause and remedying it. Fix the topology problem, replace the equipment, or, when the network is growing either in number of nodes or in traffic generated, segment the network.

To reduce the collision rate, determine the main reason for its occurrence and tackle the problem there. For example, if the problem is the result of normal growth and the network has become too large for the number of users, segment the network into smaller broadcast domains using bridges, switches, or routers. Using ethernet switches for high-performance servers can solve a lot of problems. Even if you use other ports on the switch to connect segments that contain multiple workstations, you can distribute network nodes in a manner that prevents the server from saturating a particular segment on a continual basis.

Ethernet Errors

A lot of things can go wrong when you send hundreds of thousands of bits out on a copper wire, hoping they arrive at their destination in the proper order and with no changes. With the higher speeds that are being achieved with new technologies, detecting errors is becoming increasingly more important.

The simplest method for error detection is called a *parity check*. An example of this method is transmitting characters using the ASCII 7-bit character set with an eighth bit added. If *even parity* is being used, the eighth bit is set to zero or one, whichever makes the number of one bits an even number. If *odd parity* is being used, the eighth bit is selected to make the number of one bits an odd number. The receiving station can calculate what the parity bit should be by examining the first seven characters and making a simple calculation. This scheme easily breaks down, however, if more than one bit was transmitted in error.

Also, this type of error checking operates at the byte level and is not very useful for determining if an error exists in a frame of data that is 1518 bytes in length. Ethernet frames use the *Frame Check Sequence (FCS)* to check the integrity of the frame. Higher-level protocols employ other methods to ensure that packets arrive intact and in the correct order. In addition to errors involving corrupted frames that can be detected using the FCS, there are other types of common Ethernet errors. This chapter takes a quick look at the most common errors and their possible causes.

Bad FCS and Misaligned Frames

The most obvious place to start is the Frame Check Sequence (FCS) error. The MAC layer computes a cyclic redundancy check (CRC) value, based on the contents of the frame, and places this value in the FCS field. The receive station can perform the same calculation and, by checking its result against that stored by the transmitting station, can determine whether the frame has been damaged in transit.

The frame could be damaged for any of the following reasons:

- The FCS value was incorrectly computed by the sending station due to a hardware problem where this MAC layer function is performed.

- The adapter that is sending out this frame is experiencing some other kind of problem and is not correctly transmitting the bits on the wire.

- There is a problem with the cables that are connecting the network, such as a bad connector or electromagnetic interference.

When you monitor a level of bad FCS errors that exceeds two or three percent of the total utilization of bandwidth on the network, you should begin troubleshooting to find the offending device. Using a LAN analyzer, you can usually locate the source address of the faulty device and take corrective action.

To determine whether the suspected device is indeed the source of the error, first power it off and continue to monitor the network. If errors continue to occur, but another address appears to be the source, there might be cabling problems on the network. If the errors disappear when the device is powered off, you can troubleshoot it further to locate the cause. You should look for the following:

- **Bad connector**—Check the connector that attaches the network cable to the workstation's adapter card.

- **Bad port**—If the workstation is connected to a hub or a switch, the port on that device might be causing the problem. Also, be sure to check the connector on that end of the cable segment.

- **Malfunctioning network card**—Finally, replace the network adapter card on the workstation to see if this clears up the problem.

Because a frame is composed of bytes—units of eight bits—the resulting frame should be evenly divisible by eight when it reaches its destination. If it isn't, something has gone wrong. This type of error is called a misaligned frame, and the frame usually also has a bad FCS. The most common reason for this type of error is electrical interference on the network or a collision. Another common cause is an incorrect network topology, where more than two multiport repeaters are used in a cascaded fashion.

You can troubleshoot this type of problem using the same methods as for a bad FCS error. Of course, if you are aware of a topology problem, you already know where the problem is.

Short Frames (Runts)

A *runt* is an Ethernet frame that is smaller than the minimum size of 64 bytes. Remember that the transmitting NIC must transmit a packet for an amount of time that allows it to make a round trip in the local broadcast domain before it stops transmitting. Otherwise, the transmitting NIC cannot effectively detect a collision. The maximum propagation time for Ethernet segments is 51.2 microseconds, which is the amount of time it takes to transmit 64 bytes. This minimum frame size does not include the preamble.

There are many reasons why *short frame errors* can occur on the network wire. Some of these short frames stem from

- **Collisions**—For more information, see Chapter 12, "Collision Rates."

- **Faulty network adapters**—For more information, see Chapter 4, "Network Interface Cards."

- **Topology errors**—For more information, see Chapter 9, "Ethernet Topology Restrictions."

If a runt frame has a valid FCS value, which indicates that the frame appears to be internally valid, the problem is most likely in the network card that generated the frame. If the FCS value is not correct for the frame's contents, the problem is most likely due to collisions or topology.

Collisions are a normal event for Ethernet. Sometimes, however, the byproduct of a collision results in signals on the wire that are interpreted as a short frame. If you are experiencing a lot of errors that indicate short frames, check the utilization statistics for the segment. If the peak utilization is heavy, but ordinary overall utilization is acceptable, try to rearrange user workloads so that some tasks are delayed to a time when the network is less busy. Another solution is to either segment the network using a switched hub or upgrade to 100Base-T.

If the utilization values for the segment are low, you might want to investigate further to determine the workstation or device that is originating the short frames, and subject the NIC to diagnostic testing to determine if it is at fault. This can often be a difficult task because a lot of errors of this type occur with frames so short that you cannot determine the source address.

Ignoring the topology rules of Ethernet can also produce short frames. A common error is to use more than four repeaters for a single collision domain, which can result in short frames appearing on the wire. The Ethernet 5-4-3 rule allows only four repeaters to be used, with five network segments total.

▶▶ For more information on Ethernet topology rules, see Chapter 9, "Ethernet Topology Restrictions."

Giant Frames and Jabber

Sometimes, a network adapter produces frames that are larger than the maximum allowable size. The opposite of a short frame error is a *giant frame error*. According to the rules that govern Ethernet communications, the maximum size that a frame can be is 1518 bytes, excluding the preamble bits. Reasons that oversized frame errors appear on the wire include

- A defective NIC that is transmitting continuously.
- Bits indicating the length of the frame have been corrupted and indicate that the frame is larger than it actually is.
- There is noise on the wire. Random noise on a faltering cable can be interpreted as part of a frame, but this is not a very common reason why oversized frame errors occur.

Finding the location of a device that is malfunctioning might be simple if the LAN analyzer you are using is capable of detecting a source address. You can power off or disconnect the suspected node to determine if it is the cause of the problem. It is possible that you will not be capable of detecting the address of the NIC if the malfunctioning card is repeatedly sending out meaningless signals. In that case, you need to look at each workstation on the segment, one by one, and try removing them from the network to see if the condition clears up.

The term *jabber* is sometimes used to refer to oversized frames, but is really just a catch-all term used to indicate that a device on the network is not following the rules and is behaving improperly when it comes to signaling on the network. A defective NIC might be sending out frames that are larger than is allowed, or it might be signaling continuously.

This type of error can literally bring down an entire segment because an adapter that continuously transmits does not give any other station a chance to use the wire. Because stations are supposed to check the network medium to see if it is busy before transmitting, the workstations that are functioning normally simply wait until the network becomes available.

Multiple Errors

Depending on the tool used to monitor the network, the number of different error types you see can vary. For example, misaligned frame errors usually have a bad FCS field as well. Some analyzers record two errors for one event, whereas others might record the error as one type or the other.

Check the documentation for the product you use to determine if this is true for your particular product.

Broadcast Storms

Broadcast storms usually occur when devices on the network generate traffic that causes even more traffic to be generated. Although this additional traffic might be due to physical problems in the network devices or the network media, it is usually caused by higher-level protocols. The problem with trying to detect the cause of this type of situation is that when it occurs, you are usually unable to access the network. Broadcast storms can slow down network access dramatically, and can sometimes bring it to a halt.

When monitoring the network for broadcast activity, you normally see a rate of 100 broadcast frames per second or less. When this value increases to more than 100 per second on an ongoing basis, there might be a problem with a network card, or you need to segment the collision domain into smaller parts. You can use routers to do this because they do not pass broadcast frames unless they are configured to do so. Many bridges can also be configured to detect excessive broadcasts and to drop broadcast packets until the storm subsides.

Broadcast storms usually result from poor network design. For example, if NetBIOS is being used on a WAN with bridges when a user tries to view the entire network, the resulting network requests generated can cause a broadcast storm. Email can also be a likely culprit when used in this scenario, such as if a user sends a global email. This is why using NetBIOS and bridging is not recommended for WANs.

Monitoring Errors

There are many tools you can use to monitor errors on the network. A *network analyzer*, for example Network Sniffer from Network General, displays information about frames that contain errors, including runts, CRC, and alignment errors. Some software-based applications, such as the Network Monitor tool included in Windows NT Server or Microsoft's System Management Server, allow you to view statistics about frames dropped, CRC errors, and broadcasts. Simpler hand-held tools might also provide functionality that allows you to detect when these errors are occurring.

For a network that requires centralized management and control, an SNMP management console application, using RMON, can be used to both monitor the network for Ethernet errors and to set up alerts that trigger notifications so you can become aware of problems immediately. The history group of RMON objects allows you to record error counts over a period of time and use them for later analysis to assist in troubleshooting.

Depending on the vendor, many internetworking devices—such as routers and intelligent hubs—are equipped with management software than can be tapped to display error statistics when you do not need a more extensive application (such as a management console). Checking statistical information on a regular basis and keeping a log of it is a good idea. When you keep track of error conditions on a regular basis, you can begin to solve problems more quickly because you can determine if the current situation matches a previous problem.

Summary

In order to determine if the network is functioning at optimal levels, periodically monitor the devices and cable segments that make up the network. Waiting for a problem to show itself—for example, when a user complains that the network is slow—might make the problem more difficult to troubleshoot. When making changes to the network or when upgrading to new equipment, be sure to understand the topology of the existing system, and do not violate any of the rules when adding new components. Carefully documenting the devices and pathways that make up the network also puts you in a better position to determine where problems exist when something goes wrong.

Part V

TOKEN-RING DESIGN

Token-Passing Technology

SOME OF THE MAIN TOPICS IN THIS CHAPTER ARE

CHAPTER 14

This chapter provides a quick overview of how token-ring networks function, which is essential if you are to be responsible for troubleshooting problems on this kind of network. If you are considering upgrading a network that consists of token-ring LANs, the information in this chapter will help you decide if it would be better to continue with your present technology or possibly make a switch to ethernet.

Today, most local area networks are based on ethernet technology, which consists of multiple computers or devices on a shared network medium, each contending for a share of the bandwidth. Ethernet has been implemented in many different ways, from the bus technology at the beginning to the 10Base-T hub that is the most widespread today. What all the different ethernet topologies and cabling schemes have in common, though, are the frame type and the CSMA/CD contention method used to gain access to the network medium and to transmit data.

Token-ring networks were originated by IBM and later standardized by IEEE 802.5. Token-ring networks were from the beginning, however, much different than ethernet. In this type of network, there are no collisions or back-off algorithms. Network access is not something that each workstation has to contend for. Instead, access to a token-ring network is done in a controlled, orderly fashion, using a frame that is passed from workstation to workstation, possession of which is required in order to begin transmitting data on the network. This "permission" frame is called a *token*. It passes through the network in a logical ring topology. Hence, the name token ring is used for this technology.

Overview of Token-Ring Networking

In Figure 14.1, you can see that the logical layout of a token-ring network is a ring. Each computer in the ring connects to two other computers, affectionately referred to as *neighbors*. The upstream neighbor is the computer from which a station will receive the token or data frame. The downstream neighbor is the one to whom the station will pass the frame.

If the workstations were actually wired in this manner, however, it would be quite a problem to add new stations or move them around. Doing so would break the chain of cables and the network would grind to a halt. To prevent this from happening, each device on the ring is actually connected by two sets of wires to a hub-like device called a media access unit (MAU) or a multistation access unit (MSAU). The MSAU looks very similar to a hub. It is usually tucked away in a wiring closet like a hub and, in some versions, uses RJ-45 connectors and twisted-pair wiring just like ethernet networks do.

Unlike an ethernet hub, however, the MAU does not repeat incoming traffic on all other ports. Instead, using electrical relays, the MAU connects the receiving wires from one station to the transmitting wires of the previous station in the ring.

A frame called a *token* is continuously passed from one station to another around the ring. When a workstation receives the token frame, it retransmits it to the next station in the ring. When a station needs to transmit data to another station on the ring, it "seizes" the token. That is, instead of immediately retransmitting the token frame, the workstation modifies a bit in the frame, appends the data it wants to transmit and the destination address, and transmits the new frame to its neighbor instead.

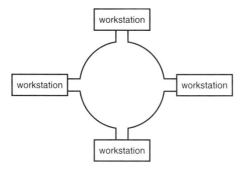

Figure 14.1   Token-ring networks are wired to form a ring.

This data frame is passed from station to station until it reaches its destination or returns to the sender. Each station in the ring checks the destination address to determine if it received the frame. If the station recognizes the address, it sends the frame up the protocol stack for further processing. It also retransmits the data frame to the next workstation on the ring, after changing a bit that indicates that it has received the data.

When the data frame returns to its original sender, it is *stripped* from the ring. The originating station checks to see if the destination workstation has acknowledged receiving the data and, if it has, starts the process over again by sending a token frame to its neighbor.

This simple process describes how data is exchanged between computers that are attached to the network. For a complete understanding of how the technology works, a few other questions need to be answered:

- What controls this orderly process? Where does the first token come from when the network is first started?
- How does a station join a ring?
- What does a token frame look like? A data frame?
- How are errors detected and fixed?

Before answering these questions, it will be helpful to first look at the format of the frames used on token ring networks to gain an understanding of how these problems can be addressed using the types of information that can be sent between stations.

Token Ring Frames

There are three kinds of frames used in token rings. One is the token frame that is passed around the idle network. This frame is only 3 bytes long, and is seized by a computer when it wants to transmit data on the network. The other two frames are longer, and contain either data or commands used to manage the network. Token-ring adapters use the MAC frame when communicating with each other. When sending data that is destined for a higher level protocol, such as IP or IPX packets, the LLC frame format is used.

The Token Frame

The first type of frame to discuss is the token frame itself. This is a 3-byte frame that circles the ring until a station decides that it needs to transmit data. In Figure 14.2, the token frame format is shown. Only 1 byte is really worthy of discussion: the access control byte.

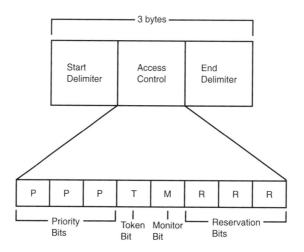

Figure 14.2   The token frame is only 3 bytes long.

The access control field contains several important values that are all stored in only 1 byte. These values represent the priority bits, the token bit, the monitor bit, and the reservation bits.

The Token Bit

The *token bit* is used to indicate that the token is free and the workstation receiving it can transmit. In this mode the token bit is zero. When a station wants to transmit data, however, it changes the token bit to a 1. It then copies this byte to a buffer, adds addressing information to create a larger frame, and then transmits the larger frame to its downstream neighbor. The workstation can continue transmitting until it is finished, or until the token-holding timer expires. When the computer has transmitted the last frame that it needs to for the time being and the frame has circled the ring and arrived back at its starting point, a new token is generated—with the token bit set to zero—and released to the ring.

The Monitor Bit

The *monitor bit* is used by a workstation that acts as the *active monitor* for the ring to determine when a frame has been around the ring more than once. This workstation performs other important functions for the ring, which are discussed later in this chapter. It is important to understand that although any workstation that generates a token frame sets the value of this bit to zero, only the active monitor can change it to a 1, which it does when it sees a data frame for the first time. If the frame continues to circle the ring without ever reaching its destination, the active monitor can detect this, remove the frame from the ring, and start the process over again. The monitor bit, therefore, is used to prevent a data frame from circling the ring endlessly. This might happen when a computer is taken out of the ring, for example.

Priority and Reservation Bits

Token-ring networks have the capability to enable individual workstations to take priority over others when it comes to claiming a token and beginning a transmission. In some applications, such as real-time factory-floor automation environments, this can be a major advantage over Ethernet's contention method for network access. This is done by using *priority bits* and *reservation bits*.

The priority bits are the first 3 bits of the access control byte. Counting in binary, this gives eight possible levels (000–111) of priority values.

The reservation bits are also used to specify a priority value between 000 and 111, in binary. A station that wants to reserve the token for its use will set these bits to the priority it expects to use, provided it is a higher value than the current priority bits represent. When the token is regenerated by a station, it will set the priority bits to this value so that the reserving station will be capable of seizing the token when it passes by again on its way around the ring. The reservation doesn't guarantee that the station will get the token on the next pass, however, because another workstation with a higher priority might intervene.

LLC and MAC Frames

In Figure 14.3, you can see that the frame type used to send a command or transmit data is much longer than the 3-byte token frame. Indeed, because token ring networks do not limit the overall length of the frame to a small value (like Ethernet frames), this frame can potentially be quite large.

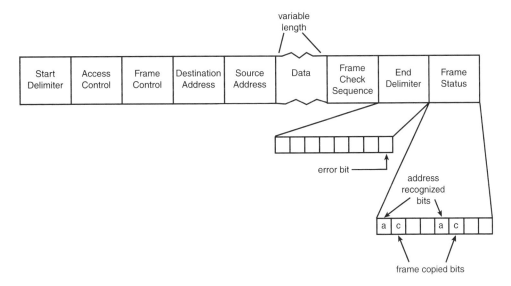

Figure 14.3 Data and command frames can become quite large.

The access control field for this frame type is copied from the token that the workstation has just seized, but the token bit's value is changed to 1 to distinguish it from a token frame. The source and destination addresses are each 6 bytes long. The frame check sequence field is 4 bytes long and is used to store a cyclic redundancy check (CRC) value that can be used to validate the integrity of the frame as it travels from one workstation to another.

All other fields, except for the data field, are 1 byte long.

The end delimiter field is 1 bit (the last bit) that serves an important function. When a station determines that the frame has been damaged or corrupted in transit, it sets this last bit—the error bit—to a 1.

The last field is called the frame status field. This is where the station that originates a data frame checks to see if it was received properly by the destination computer. Remember that the frame will circle the ring until it arrives back at its point of origin.

When a station receives a frame that contains its address in the destination address field, it sets the address-recognized bits to 1. If it is capable of copying the frame to a buffer successfully, it also sets the frame-copied bits to 1.

The originating station can interpret these bits when the frame circles around to it as follows:

- If the address-recognized bits and the frame-copied bits are all zero, the frame was never received by the destination computer. This means that the computer does not exist or is not active on the ring at this time.

- If the address-recognized fields are set to ones, but the frame-copied fields are still set to zeros, the destination computer was unable for some reason to copy the frame into its internal buffer for further processing.

- If both the address-recognized bits and the frame-copied bits are set to ones, then the frame was successfully received and copied by the destination computer.

Technical Note

If the frame arrives back at the originating station with the error bit set to 1, it does not necessarily mean that the destination did not successfully receive the information. If the frame copied bits are set to 1, the target workstation *did* receive the frame and successfully copied the data. Thus, if the frame-copied bits are set to 1, and the error flag is set to one, the sending workstation does not consider this an error. It indicates that the frame was corrupted *after* it was received by the target workstation, so there is no need to retransmit the frame.

The frame control byte is used to define the type of frame. If the first 2 bits of this frame are both zeros, it is a media access control frame. If they read 01, it is a logical link control frame.

If the frame is carrying data—an LLC frame—the destination computer will pass it up to the next layer in the protocol stack for further processing. The LLC header information, such as the DSAP and SSAP bits, is found at the beginning of the data field.

If it is a command frame—a MAC frame—the data field will contain a 16-bit field called a vector identifier. The types of commands that can be stored in this field and their values are shown in Table 14.1.

Table 14.1   Access Control Frame Functions

Value	Description
00000000	Duplicate address test
00000010	Beacon frame
00000011	Claim token frame
00000100	Purge ring
00000101	Active monitor present
00000110	Standby monitor present

Each command serves a specific purpose that is used to either notify other stations that everything is functioning well—the active and standby monitor commands—or to perform maintenance functions when something appears to have gone awry.

Active and Standby Monitors

Not every station on a token-ring network is equal to the others; some computers serve specific roles in the network. For example, when the network is started, someone has to send the first token frame through the ring.

This is done by a station called the *active monitor*. The active monitor is the station that manages the ring. Although any workstation can be the active monitor, there can be only one active monitor in the ring, and all other stations attached to the ring act as *standby monitors*. If the active monitor fails or is taken off the network, one of the standby monitors takes over the role and becomes the new active monitor. The major functions of the active monitor are

- Initializing the first token when the network is powered up.
- Initiating *neighbor notification*, whereby all stations in the ring learn the names (addresses) of their upstream and downstream neighbors.
- Providing a master clock that all other stations use for timing purposes.
- Providing ring delay.
- Detecting *lost* tokens and frames.

The clocking function provided by the active monitor is important in a deterministic network such as token-ring. All other stations synchronize their clocks to the clocking signal provided by the active monitor. Stations do not have to listen for a set of *preamble bits* as they do in an Ethernet network. The network is precisely clocked so that a computer knows when to expect the token or a data frame. This timing mechanism enables a computer to detect that a problem exists on the network if a token does not arrive on time, and causes error detection procedures to begin.

Ring Polling (Neighbor Notification)

Each station on the ring must know the address of the station immediately upstream from it. This station is called its *Nearest Active Upstream Neighbor*, or *NAUN* for short. Knowing the address of its NAUN enables a station to detect errors and begin a correction process when it notices that its neighbor has failed in some way.

The active monitor begins a process called neighbor notification when the network is first started. This process is also called *ring polling*. There are two types of frames that are used in this process: active monitor present and standby monitor present.

To begin the process, the active monitor broadcasts an active monitor present control frame around the network. (Remember that the address-recognized and frame-copied bits in the frame status field are initially set to zeros.) Because this frame is a broadcast frame, it will be recognized by any station that receives it, which will be the station immediately downstream from the workstation that is acting as the active monitor.

The station that receives the broadcast frame will reset its timer, using the value supplied by the active monitor. It will copy the source address—its upstream neighbor's address—into memory for future reference. The address-recognized and frame-copied bits in the frame status field are set to ones, and the frame is sent on its way to the next workstation. Other stations on the ring will not copy this frame because the appropriate bits have already been set. The frame circles the ring until it arrives back at the active monitor, which strips it from the network.

When the second station in the ring retransmits the active monitor present frame with its bits set, it also sets a 20 millisecond timer. This is done to give the active monitor present frame enough time to move around the ring. When this timer expires, it will send out a frame similar the one it just received. However, this frame is a *standby monitor present* frame. It serves the same type of function as the previous frame to the next workstation downstream because its address-recognized and frame-copied bits are initialized to zero.

When the next station downstream receives the standby monitor present frame it recognizes it as a broadcast frame and, because the appropriate bits are set to zero, it realizes that it has just received the frame from its immediate upstream neighbor. It stores this neighbor's address in memory for future use, sets the address-recognized and frame-copied bits to ones, and retransmits the frame to the next workstation. It also sets a 20 millisecond timer, and when the timer expires, it repeats the process by sending its own standby monitor present frame to the next workstation downstream.

Finally, when the active monitor receives a standby monitor present frame with the address-recognized and frame-copied bits set to zeros, it knows that the neighbor notification process has completed successfully.

So that all members of the ring will be kept updated about potential new members in the ring or other changes, the active monitor will send out an *active monitor present* frame every 7 seconds. If any station in the ring does not receive the frame at least every 15 seconds, it will initiate a process called *monitor contention* so that a new active monitor can be designated for the ring.

How the Network Repairs Itself When the Active Monitor Fails

Each station other than the active monitor is designated to be a standby monitor. These stations expect that every 2.6 seconds, either a token frame or a data frame will pass their way. They also expect that at least every 15 seconds, an active monitor present frame will arrive. If any of these events fail to occur, it is assumed that the active monitor has been taken offline, or has failed in some manner. To remedy the situation, the first standby monitor that notices this situation initiates a process called monitor contention, in which a new active monitor is designated to manage the network.

All stations except for the current active monitor will participate in the "election" of a new monitor. The current active monitor, if it is still present on the network, assumes that it is not functioning correctly because another station has begun the monitor contention process.

The station that begins the process puts itself into Claim Token Transmit mode and sends out frames called *claim token frames*. These frames contain the station's own DLC address. The next station downstream receives this frame and compares the address to its own. If its own address is of a higher numerical value, it substitutes its own address for the one put into the frame by its upstream neighbor, retransmits the frame, and puts itself into Claim Token Transmit mode. Otherwise, it puts itself into the Claim Token Repeat mode and forwards the frame to the next station so that it can make the comparison.

After a short time, only one station will remain in Claim Token Transmit mode. When a station receives its own Claim Token Transmit mode back from circling the ring three times in a row, it will decide that it has won the election and begin operating as the active monitor for the ring.

To begin its new duties, the new active monitor will

- Take over the clocking functions for the ring.
- Send out a *ring purge frame*.
- Begin ring polling (neighbor notification).
- Transmit a free token so that the network can resume normal operation.

The ring purge sets the ring back to an initial state, causing stations that receive the frame to reset their timer clocks and to abort any other task that they were in the process of doing. When the frame has circled the ring, the active monitor can send out the new token and stations can again resume normal processing.

The Active Monitor Watches for Problems

The active monitor guards the overall health of the network by constantly monitoring activity on the ring. It expects its own active monitor present frame to return, along with the standby monitor present frames generated by other stations (received every 7 seconds). It watches to determine if a station has raised the priority of a token, but failed to lower it, thus making the token unusable by other stations. All in all, the active monitor expects to see a good token every 10 milliseconds, and will take steps to repair the network if it does not arrive on time.

When a token frame or data frame passes by the active monitor, it sets a timer. If the timer expires before it sees another frame, it assumes that the frame has been lost, purges the ring, and initiates a new token.

The monitor bit is set only by the active monitor when it first sees a frame. If it sees the same frame again—which it can determine because no other station can set this bit to a value of 1—it will assume that the frame is circling the ring endlessly and will strip it from the ring.

When the active monitor detects errors in a frame based on the CRC value, it purges the ring and, if the purge frame returns to the active monitor undamaged, initiates a new token so that processing can resume.

Because token ring networks are so small, the token can travel around from station to station quite quickly. Thus, it is possible for a station to begin stripping bits off a frame before it has finished transmitting the entire frame. To prevent this from happening, a latency factor is introduced by the active monitor. The latency buffer is a minimum of 24 bits and is used to introduce this delay. This value is used because the token frame itself is 24 bits in length (3 bytes).

Detecting Errors on the Ring

One of the nice things about token-ring networks is that they are somewhat capable of detecting errors—such as a malfunctioning upstream neighbor—and in many cases can make corrections that will keep the network functioning. When a station detects that it has a problem with its upstream neighbor, it starts a process called *beaconing* to inform the other downstream stations so that the process of isolating the error can begin.

Transmitter Failures

Each station has already learned the address of its upstream neighbor because of the ring polling process. When a station determines that it is no longer receiving frames from its NAUN, it begins to send out beaconing frames that contain its own address and the address of the neighbor that it assumes has malfunctioned. Other stations receiving these frames enter an error correction mode, and other traffic on the ring stops until the beaconing process is complete.

Eventually, if there are no other problems in the network, the beacon frames arrive back at the upstream neighbor, which recognizes that its address is present in the frame. Because another station is complaining, the station removes itself from the network ring and performs a self-test, just as it does when it joins a ring. If it does not pass its own self-test, it remains off the ring until an administrator can diagnose the problem and repair it. If it passes the test, it reinserts itself into the ring. All these actions are performed without the intervention of the administrator. However, network management software, such as SMTP- or RMON-based products or ring management software provided by the vendor, can be used to detect or monitor this kind of situation.

If the problem station stays removed from the ring, the relays in the MSAU reconfigure the wiring connections so that the station is bypassed, as is shown in Figure 14.4. Thus, the station that is issuing the beaconing frames is connected to a neighbor that is one further upstream from it than the one that was removed. If all is functioning normally, the station that first detected the failure begins to receive the beaconing frames it originated to probe the problem. It then stops transmitting the frames and waits for the active monitor to restore the network to normal functioning, which the active monitor does by issuing a new token.

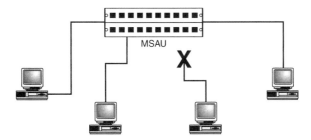

Figure 14.4   A malfunctioning station can be physically disconnected from the ring at the MSAU.

Receiver Failures

In the situation just described, you can see how a station with a faulty network adapter that cannot transmit will be automatically removed from the ring.

However, when a station can no longer hear frames from its upstream neighbor, the problem doesn't have to be in that neighbor's adapter card. Instead, the problem might lie in this station's card, which might be malfunctioning, making it unable to receive the data properly.

This type of malfunction will also be detected by stations on the ring and the offending station will be isolated.

When a station starts transmitting beaconing frames to let others know that it cannot hear its upstream neighbor, it sets a timer. This timer is of a sufficient value to enable the upstream neighbor to self-test and remove itself from the ring. If the timer expires, the beaconing station will suspect its own receiving capability, remove itself from the ring, and perform the self-test. If it fails the test, it knows that it is the malfunctioning unit and stays disconnected from the ring.

In this case, the upstream neighbor will have passed its self-test and reconnected to the ring.

Technical Note

Not all hardware problems can be resolved in this manner. For example, when a cable that connects two MSAUs together breaks, the intervention of an administrator is required to correct the problem. Chapter 3, "Testing Cables," discusses some of the problems that can arise because of faulty cabling. For more information about cables used specifically for token-ring networks and how they are used, refer to Chapter 9, "Ethernet Topology Restrictions," and Chapter 16, "Design Rules."

What Is Early Token Release?

Token-ring networks operate at either 4Mbps or 16Mbps. When operating at 4Mbps, a station will release a new token on the network after it has received a data frame that has finished circling the ring. When the network speed is 16Mbps, this fact introduces a significant delay factor that prevents the available bandwidth from being efficiently used—a frame circling at 16Mbps takes less time to circle the ring. On a ring that holds a large number of stations, very short frames introduce a significant amount of idle time on the ring.

To increase the use of available bandwidth, 16Mbps stations can be configured to release a token shortly after they release their data frame. Thus, a station downstream can begin to transmit data more quickly than if it had to wait for the data frame to circle the ring. This is called *early token release*, and is the default operation for token ring adapters operating at 16Mbps. Thus, upgrading from 4Mbps hardware to 16Mbps token ring can improve network throughput because of both the faster signaling method used by 16Mbps token ring and the more efficient communications that result from early token release.

Adding a Station to the Ring

Now that I have covered the mechanics of how a token-ring network operates, you might wonder how a new workstation joins a ring that is already functioning. The process doesn't require that the entire network be brought down and restarted. However, for a short period of time, the new workstation checks out its own capability to transmit and receive data, and then announces itself to the network.

Remember that the MSAU contains electrical relays that can be used to add or remove a station from the ring. When a station is first connected, the relay connects the station's transmit wires to its receive wires. Thus, at this point in time, it can only talk to itself.

The process of inserting a new member into the ring consists of the following steps:

1. The token-ring card runs its own self-diagnostics tests and sends a signal on its transmit wires. Because the transmit and receive wires are being connected by the MSAU, it receives its own signal back. It compares this to what it sent to determine if it is functioning correctly.

2. If everything appears to be in working order, the adapter will then apply a voltage, called a *phantom voltage*, to the transmit wires. This causes the MSAU to activate the relay that is connecting the transmit and receive wires. The relay will then physically connect the station to its neighbor's transmit and receive wires, inserting it into the active ring.

3. The new node will wait up to 18 seconds while it monitors incoming signals to determine if an active monitor present frame is circling the ring. If it does not see one, it will initiate the contention process so that a new active monitor will be designated for the ring.

4. Assuming that the active monitor present frame was received, the station will then send out a frame called the Duplicate Address Test frame. This frame contains its own address and circles the ring so that other stations can examine it to determine if the address already exists on the ring. If the frame arrives back at the station with the address-recognized bits in the frame status field set to ones, it will realize that the address is already in use and remove itself from the ring until an administrator can remedy the problem.

5. If it determines that it has a unique address, the station participates in the next ring poll, learning the address of its upstream neighbor and informing its downstream neighbor of its address.

After these steps, the station is a functioning member of the ring. Other housekeeping functions might be performed, such as the learning of certain ring parameters, for example ring number and other configurable values. The duplicate address problem is easy to detect if you are attaching a new station to the ring. The station does not join the ring and, in most cases, returns an error message. You can quickly review your documentation to determine the correct address and correct the problem.

This problem can also creep in unknowingly, however. For example, a server or workstation might be powered off for a length of time for maintenance or repair. While it is off the ring, a mistake is made and its address is used by a new workstation that is connected to the ring. When the original server is powered up, it detects that it has a duplicate address and cannot join the ring. To monitor such situations it is important that network documentation always be kept up-to-date and available to those responsible for maintenance functions. Also, ring management software or other network management software that can decode token-ring management frames can help you detect these kinds of situations.

Choosing Between Token Ring and Ethernet

Token-ring advocates and those who champion ethernet have argued for many years over which technology best serves the market. There are advantages and disadvantages to both. It is interesting to note, however, that as ethernet technologies are expanded to higher network speeds, they are incorporating some techniques that are already present in token-ring technology.

Because token-ring techniques can guarantee an equal access to the network within a specified time limit, token-ring networks are more suited to environments that require a specific response time. Ethernet networks are fine for many network applications, but can become bogged down when too many workstations try to flood the wire with a lot of information at the same time. A lot of processing power can be spent simply by the contention method that involves collisions and back-off algorithms.

Ethernet networks use a relatively small packet size, which can be a up to a maximum of only 1,518 bytes. This size was originally conceived to work in the 10Mbps environment, and has been kept as ethernet speeds have advanced to 100Mbps. With the exception of Jumbo Frames—proposed by Alteon Networks (see Chapter 8, "Ethernet Frame Types")—most ethernet networks waste valuable bandwidth due to the overhead of these small frames. In 16Mbps token-ring networks, the maximum frame size is controlled by a timer and can reach sizes of up to 18KB, although 4KB is more common in actual practice at this time. This is a considerable improvement!

Other areas in which token ring excels over ethernet include the priority and reservation fields, which can be used to provide a quality of service functionality. By using source route, bridging token-ring clients can specify multiple routes to a particular destination, which is not allowed under the spanning tree routing technologies.

One disadvantage, however, is that token ring is usually more expensive than ethernet to implement. Token-ring adapters are made by very few companies and, because of their complexity, cost more to produce. MSAUs are more complex than their passive hub cousins, and also are more expensive. Also, because the MSAU is a required component of a token-ring network, you cannot simply create a crossover cable to connect two workstations as you can with ethernet. However, because a two-node network is not a common implementation except in a very small business or a home environment, this is not a large disadvantage.

The two technologies can operate together, each being used for what it does best. There are switches, routers, and adapters that can be used to connect the two types of networks so that workstations can communicate throughout a larger network. As higher-speed Ethernet networks continue to evolve and make use of token passing techniques, it becomes clear that token-ring technology, while by no means state-of-the art, is not about to fade away.

Summary

Token-ring networks have been around for many years and operate in a manner very different from ethernet networks. Token rings operate in an orderly manner and are a good choice when a deterministic network model is needed to ensure that each station is always granted access to the network within a specified time. Their capability to correct some physical errors without bringing down the network can be an advantage in many cases.

Although the technology has not been as widely adapted as ethernet, there is still a future for token ring. Token ring is still well-suited for some networks, such as those in the manufacturing industry where precise timing on the factory floor is crucial.

The next chapter covers the different topologies that can make up a token-ring network, and looks at other high-speed networks, such as FDDI, that use the same principles.

Token-Ring Topology Restrictions

SOME OF THE MAIN TOPICS IN THIS CHAPTER ARE

The Star Topology

Hierarchical Topologies

Variations on a Ring: Token-Bus Networks

Token-ring networks operate in fundamentally different ways than LANs based on Ethernet technology. Instead of competing for access to the network bandwidth by a listen-and-try method, members of a token-ring network take turns in an orderly fashion, passing a permission frame called a *token* from one member to the next. Because the token is passed from network node to network node in a round robin fashion, the topology that the protocol dictates is a ring—hence the name.

This chapter examines the basic ring structure for this type of network and looks at some of the methods for joining smaller units to create larger LANs.

The Star Topology

The name token ring implies that the workstations on the LAN are organized in a circular fashion, with one station connection to a neighbor on the left and right, and with the last workstation connecting back to the first, as shown in Figure 15.1. This is indeed the actual *logical* formation for a token-ring LAN.

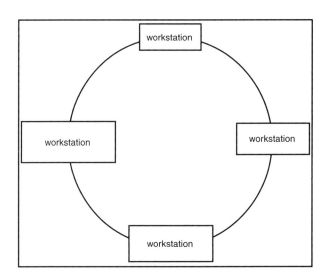

Figure 15.1 Token-ring networks form a logical ring.

Looking at this figure, it appears that the ring is simply a bus topology that has been joined back onto itself. You can almost imagine a T-connector attaching the cable to each workstation, with each end of the connector attaching to a cable that joins the station to its two neighbors in the ring.

If this were the *physical* method used, however, it would defeat one of the main benefits that token ring has over its rival networking technology. That is, a break anywhere on the cable would bring down the entire LAN because the token, not to mention the data frames, would no longer be capable of completing the circuit.

Multistation Access Units

Token-ring LANs are a *logical ring* in that communications only transpire between a station and its upstream and downstream neighbors. A workstation receives a frame on one set of wires and retransmits it on another set of wires. The transmit cables from one station carry the signal to the receiving pins on its neighboring network adapter, first passing through a device called a Multistation Access Unit.

The Media or Multistation Access Unit (MAU or MSAU) appears to be very much like a hub, and indeed, it is a device used to centralize wiring. In Figure 15.2, you can see that, like a 10Base-T network, token-ring LANs appear to be wired as a star.

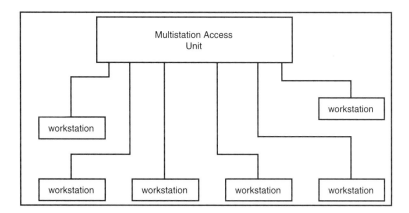

Figure 15.2 Token-ring LANs are physically wired in a star formation from the MAU/MSAU but logically communicate in a ring formation.

The main difference between a hub and a MAU is that the MAU does not provide a central location to rebroadcast a frame to every port simultaneously. Instead, the inner workings of the MAU provide a physical connection for the transmit and receive wires from one workstation to the next in the logical ring, as shown in Figure 15.3. You can think of a star-wired token ring as a collapsed "ring in a box" because the ring portion of the wiring is accomplished inside the MAU, and not throughout the physical cable plant of the building.

The simplest MAU devices do nothing more than provide electrical relays that connect the wires together in the proper fashion. More advanced devices can actually perform other functions, such as signal regeneration. The basic function of the MAU, however, remains the same: to provide a central wiring location to connect diverse workstations on the LAN into a logical ring, physical star topology. For a more in-depth discussion of MAUs, see Chapter 6, "Media Access Units (MAUs) and Multistation Access Units (MSAUs)."

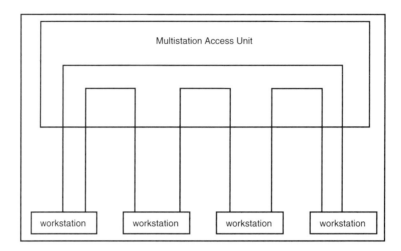

Figure 15.3   The MSAU connects the stations into a ring.

Connecting MAUs to Create a Larger LAN

Getting back to the logical ring concept, look at what happens when you need to connect more than one MAU to the network. When two or more MAUs are connected, the logical ring structure still must be maintained in the LAN. The token must still be circulated from one station to the next until it arrives back at the originating station, no matter which MAU a workstation is attached to. In Figure 15.4, you can see that the MAUs are connected in a ring just as the workstations are.

In some cases, there are primary and secondary paths between each MAU to help reduce network down time when a problem occurs in the connection between MAUs.

Hierarchical Topologies

As with all LANs, there comes a time when you have too many workstations to connect, or when the distance between the furthermost workstations becomes too great. When this happens, you must segment the network using devices such as bridges, switches, or routers. Chapter 5, "Bridges, Routers, Switches, and Repeaters," covers these devices in detail, mostly in the context of an Ethernet network. When it comes to bridges and switches, operation in a token-ring environment is a little different.

Source Route Bridging

Bridges are used to combine smaller LANs into larger ones. Bridges are an advance from simple repeaters that send a signal from one cable segment out onto another without making any decisions based on information contained in the frame. Source-route bridging is used in token-ring networks to connect rings to or from a larger network. As the name implies, the source first determines what route the data exchange should take through the network before beginning to exchange actual data with a remote system.

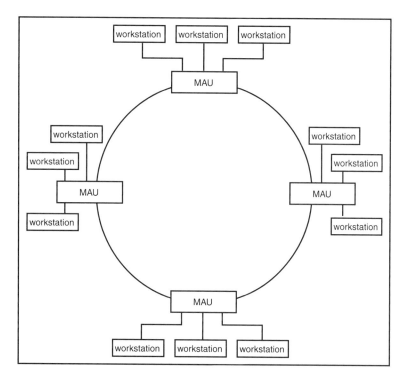

Figure 15.4   MAUs are joined together into a ring.

The basic process can be described in a few simple steps:

1. The source workstation sends out a test frame that is used to determine whether the destination workstation is on the same local ring.

2. If the source workstation doesn't receive a response to its test, it assumes that the destination is on another ring.

3. The source workstation sends out a frame called an *All Routes Explorer (ARE)* frame. This is a broadcast frame that bridges typically forward to all other rings in the network.

4. As the ARE frame passes through each bridge, information is added to the frame, indicating the path it is taking. This includes the ring number and an identifier that is used to identify the bridge.

5. The ARE frame eventually makes its way to the destination computer, which returns a directed reply. It is not necessary to send a broadcast frame for the reply because the destination computer can read the routing information in the ARE frame to see the path it has taken.

6. The originating workstation receives one or more replies from the destination computer. If there is only one route to the destination, only one reply is received. If more than one route exists, a reply is received, showing each route.

The workstation that sent out the original ARE frame makes a judgment on which path to use, and then sends directed frames that use that path for further communications with the remote system. In the simplest case, the workstation uses the path specified by the first reply that is received.

This type of bridging is different from *transparent bridging* used in Ethernet networks. In transparent bridges, the spanning tree algorithm is used to set up a network of bridges where there is only one possible path a frame can take to its destination, even though there might be multiple physical pathways between any two stations. The spanning tree algorithm calculates the path a frame will take and changes it only when a particular path becomes unavailable, at which time the entire bridging tree formation is recalculated. Another difference between token ring and Ethernet bridges is that Ethernet bridges make decisions based on MAC addresses, learning which addresses are on which ports. Token ring bridges do not need to keep a table of MAC addresses, and instead use a field called the *Routing Information Field (RIF)*. If a frame does not contain this field, it does not need to cross the router.

The ARE frame contains the RIF that is used to store information about each step the route takes. The size of this field generally limits the number of bridges a frame can pass through. On networks built to IBM specifications, this number is usually 7. For networks based on IEEE 802.4 specifications, this number might be as large as 13. In Figure 15.5, you can see how the routing information is stored in an 802.5 MAC frame.

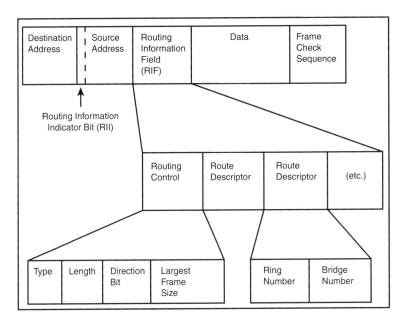

Figure 15.5 Routing information in an 802.5 MAC frame.

The usual fields are still there, such as the source and destination addresses. However, the first bit of the source address is called the *Routing Information Indicator (RII)* bit, and is used to indicate that this is a frame that contains routing information. The other field of importance here is the Routing Information Field, which is divided into several other components. The Routing Control component consists of the following:

- **Type**—The type of routing. This can indicate an ARE frame, a specifically-routed frame, or a spanning-tree explorer frame.

- **Length**—Specifies the total length of the RIF field, which can include multiple route descriptor fields.

- **Direction Bit**—The direction of the bit, forward or reverse. When the station that originated the routing request frame receives this frame back, it can reverse this bit so the routing descriptor fields are read in a reverse manner to reach the destination station.

- **Largest Frame Size**—This field contains the size of the largest frame that can be sent via this route. In other words, it indicates the smallest frame size encountered during its journey, which becomes the common denominator for the route.

The Routing Control field can be followed by multiple Route Descriptor fields—from 7 to 13, depending on the type of network, IEEE 802.5 or IBM. Each field contains the ring number and bridge number for each bridge or ring the frame passes through during route discovery.

As you can see, this format makes it easy for devices between the two workstations to route the packet. The direction bit can be turned on or off by each end of the connection to cause intervening bridges to interpret the route descriptor fields in the opposite direction, depending on the direction of the communication.

When compared with transparent bridges, which are configured with parameters by network administrators that control the various paths through the network, source routing bridges are less complex. They do not have to exchange information among themselves to calculate a spanning tree because it is the source of the data communication that decides the path that will be taken. Because of this, however, there is a little more latency on the part of this type of bridge.

Note

IEEE standards define a type of bridge called a *Source-Route Transparent Bridge*. This type of bridge forwards packets that contain a RIF based on the information in that particular RIF. If the packet does not contain a RIF, the MAC address is used instead.

Gateways

When a network is composed of more than one technology, some sort of device is needed to translate between the different formats and protocols used. A *gateway* can be used to connect ethernet and token-ring LANs. A standard bridge simply forwards the same frame it receives based on the MAC address in the frame. A gateway operates up into the Logical Link Control (LLC) Layer of the OSI reference model, takes the information it receives in one format, and repackages it into a different format, depending on the kinds of networks it is bridging (see Figure 15.6).

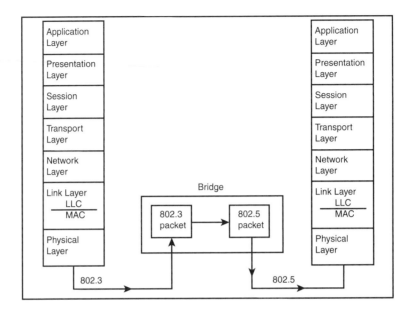

Figure 15.6 Gateways can be used to join different network types.

Note

At one time, gateways were also referred to as *translational bridges.*

In this example, the gateway strips off the 802.3 MAC sublayer information from the incoming Ethernet packet and decides where the packet should be sent at the LLC sublayer. It then repackages the packet in an 802.5 frame and sends it back down to the Physical Layer for retransmission on the 802.5 Token-Ring network.

End user workstations do not need to be aware that this translation is being done. Each continues to receive a frame in the format of the network on which it resides. This is one of the benefits of using a model such as the OSI reference model. Instead of having to write a complex program to allow for the interchange of data between two diverse networks, only a simple repackaging step is needed in the gateway device.

Token-Ring Switching

Switching is a method used to speed up the connection between two network nodes. It provides for a direct, dedicated path that does not involve contention for the network medium, either by CSMA/CD or by possession of a token. The usual means for joining together multiple rings in a token-ring environment is a bridge or router. When you have users who make a lot of use of a particular server, about the only thing you can do to decrease latency and increase access time is to place the server on the ring that the users are on. In a larger environment, you can end up with servers distributed throughout the network, which makes them more difficult to manage.

Unlike bridges, switches enable you to attach a ring segment, an individual workstation, or a server directly. When a server is directly attached to a port on a switch, it does not have to wait for a token to come its way before it can transmit data. Likewise, the switch does not have to wait for a token when it wants to output frames on the port to which the server is connected. Thus, by connecting high-performance servers to a switch, and then using the switch to connect to other workstations or network segments, you can increase the total throughput for the network.

Just as a switch provides a dedicated path for Ethernet networks, allowing for full-duplex Ethernet connections, a switch can also be used to double the bandwidth of a token-ring connection. This technique is called *Dedicated Token Ring (DTR)*. A token-ring adapter uses two pairs of wires—one pair to transmit and the other pair to receive. After you eliminate the token passing function of the protocol, both of these wire pairs can be used at the same time.

Troubleshooting Bridges

Individual token rings contain many mechanisms, both physical and software based, that can be used to help detect and temporarily fix many problems. When a network adapter on a workstation begins to malfunction, it is possible for other workstations to detect this and force the offending workstation to disconnect itself from the ring and perform a self-test. Administrators can usually diagnose and fix problems that occur within the local ring without a lot of time spent investigating the problem.

When you begin to connect LANs to a larger network, however, connectivity between two workstations that reside on different rings can be troublesome and time-consuming. You need to know what types of devices are installed between the workstations, and understand how they are used.

For example, *SRT bridges*, which are used for transparent or source route bridging, might be dropping packets that have a Routing Information Field (RIF) when connecting with an Ethernet segment. You can use a network analyzer to determine whether packets are being forwarded through the network. By checking the source address on packets output by the bridge—looking for a high-order bit set to one to indicate RIF—you can determine if it is passing RIF frames.

You might think a certain path handles all types of traffic on your network, but you might be unaware that a particular device is misconfigured or malfunctioning. Check the fields that show the ring numbers on packets that pass through the bridge to be sure they are correct. Also, check the bridge ID itself to be sure you don't have two bridges in the network set to the same value.

When the number of network clients increases suddenly, a bridge might begin to degrade in performance. Remember that bridges used in a small network might not have the capacity to buffer a traffic load when you begin to upgrade your network with higher-capacity servers or additional workstations that generate a lot of traffic. Consider installing a switch to relieve these types of congestion problems. Using a switch, you can isolate high-performance machines from those low capacity ones while still maintaining connectivity.

Finally, remember that not all vendors' equipment works with everyone else's. When making purchasing decisions, be sure to investigate the documentation and sales literature to be sure that the bridge or device you are planning to add to your network will work as you expect.

Variations on a Ring: Token-Bus Networks

One of the main differences between the star and bus topologies is that all workstations connected to a bus can hear all transmissions that are made. Even when Ethernet networks are connected to a hub in a star-wired fashion, the hub repeats the incoming frames on the other ports so that the basic function of a bus remains.

The MAU in a token-ring network does not create a bus topology when it concentrates the process of connecting a ring together in one location. However, there is a variation on token-ring technology that does use a bus. This is referred to as a *Token-Passing Bus*. In this type of token ring implementation, the token frame is logically passed from one workstation to another, although all workstations are connected by a bus cable and can hear every transmission. The MAP (Manufacturing Automation Protocol) uses this technique for connecting equipment on the factory floor.

The IEEE 802.4 Committee set forth the standards for the token-bus network. Each station on the bus has a numerical address that determines the order in which it is granted the token. In Figure 15.7, you can see that the order in which stations are attached to the bus is unimportant because the token is passed according to station address.

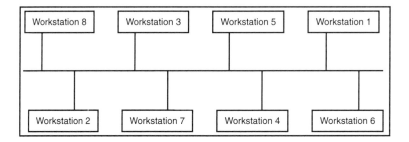

Figure 15.7   In an 802.4 Token-Bus network, a logical ring is formed by the stations' addresses.

You can see that the workstations are connected along the bus in no particular order. Workstation 8 is the first on the bus and is followed by workstations 2 and 3, with workstations 1 and 6 attached side-by-side at the end of the bus. You can move a station from one point in the network to another without having to change its address. The token, however, is passed in order of address from one station to the next, and the token is still the method used to grant access to the network medium for transmission of data frames.

Note

Within a single MAU, a token-ring network operates as bus, with both ends open. The last node on the network (determined by node number, not physical location) passes the token back to the first station.

Technical Note

Another token-passing network technology, known as *ARCnet (Attached Resource Computing Network)*, also uses a bus topology. ARCnet is one of the oldest LAN technologies still in use today. Although it employs a bus and uses the token-passing method to grant access to the cable, it does not conform to the IEEE 802.4 specifications.

Summary

Token-ring networks are based on a simple topology: a ring. How these rings are connected together to from a larger LAN, however, can become quite complicated. Bridging can be used to extend the network, as can routers, and both can be used in the local environment or for wide area networking. Switches can be used to upgrade from standard MAUs to provide dedicated links for high-performance machines.

The next chapter discusses some of the factors you want to take into consideration when laying out the topology of your network, such as the geographical distances you can achieve with different cable types and the number of devices you can place on a segment.

Design Rules

CHAPTER 16

There are two basic types of cables that are used to connect token-ring networks. Workstations are connected to the *Multistation Access Unit* (*MAU* or *MSAU*) by means of a *lobe* cable. The MAU is similar to a hub that is used in Ethernet technology, but acts to connect workstations into a physical ring and does not repeat signals on all ports simultaneously. To create larger LANs, MAUs are connected using a Ring In/Ring Out cable.

Adjusted Ring Length

The distances you can cover with a token-ring network depend on the type of cable used, the number of workstations and other devices in the ring, and the vendor who manufactures the equipment.

The term *Adjusted Ring Length* (*ARL*) is used to specify the worst case distance between any two stations in the ring. It is calculated as follows:

```
ARL = lengths of all MAU to MAU cables - shortest MAU-MAU cable.
```

In some implementations you do not have to count cables that are 3 meters or shorter and used in the same wiring closet to connect MAUs. Other devices, including surge suppressors and punch down connectors, might need to also be figured into the calculation. Be sure to review the vendor's specifications carefully when making a purchasing decision.

Rules for STP and UTP Cables

Both shielded and unshielded twisted-pair cables can be used with token-ring networks. In many token-ring networks you will find that cables are usually classified according to a scheme devised by IBM back in 1982: the *IBM Common Cabling Standard* (*CCS*). CCS defined eight levels of cable types, as well as a system of using ducts to conduct cables through buildings, with terminations at faceplates in the user's workspace. This was an early attempt to create a procedure for wiring a building so that various devices used to process data and voice communications could be connected in a standard and consistent manner.

Note

Taking into consideration these cable definitions, there are several types of cables that are now standard in token-ring networks. In the discussions that follow, the standard lengths that are quoted apply when the LAN is composed of more than one MAU. In a small workgroup LAN it is usually possible to achieve a greater distance.

Type 1 Cables

Type 1 cables consist of two pairs of solid 22 AWG wires. Each pair is shielded by a layer of foil, and the entire cable is surrounded by a braided metal shield, encased in PVC. This type of cable is usually used for trunk connections: joining together MAUs that are distributed throughout an office building, for example.

These cables are used in places such as the walls of office buildings, and they connect wiring closets and distribution panels that are usually found in the same building. The maximum distance for this type of cable is 101 meters, or 331 feet.

Note

A cable designated as Type 9 is similar to the Type 1 cable, except that it uses a plenum jacket for use in air handling spaces to satisfy the requirements of fire codes.

This type of cable can be used to connect up to 260 devices, using 12 or less wiring closets and up to 32 MAUs.

Type 2 Cables

Type 2 cables are similar to Type 1, except that they also include additional unshielded twisted-pair cables that can be used for voice or other transmissions. This means that there are six twisted pairs in the same cable. The cable can be used to provide both voice and data connections, using only one cable strung between end points. The maximum distance for this type of cable is 100 meters, or 328 feet.

Larger token-ring networks are usually constructed using STP (either Type 1 or Type 2), and can support up to 260 workstations and up to 32 MAUs.

Token-ring networks of both 4Mbs and 16Mbs can be run on Type 1 and Type 2 cables.

Type 3 Cables

This cable type is much less expensive than are the first two. Types 1 and 2 are made of shielded twisted-pairs, whereas this type is made up of unshielded twisted-pair (UTP) cables with a minimum of two twists per inch, using 22 or 24 AWG solid wires. Remember that the more twists that are used for any given length of cable, the less crosstalk between the wires. The entire cable is encased in PVC.

This UTP cable is more flexible than the other types and thus is easier to route around corners and in tight places. This cable type is generally only used on 4Mbs networks and has a distance of up to 45 meters (148 feet), according to IBM standards. Some vendors publish specifications that use this cable type for distances of up to 150 meters.

This is the most popular type of cable and can support up to about 72 workstations. If repeaters are used, subtract one from this value for each repeater. Depending on the vendor, this cable type can be used in between two and six wiring closets.

Type 6 Cables

To connect MAUs, a patch cable that is usually referred to as Level 6, or Type 6, is used. This is a shielded twisted-pair cable made up of two pairs of stranded wire with both foil and braided shielding. It is encased in a rigid PVC jacket.

These patch cables can be purchased in standard lengths of 8, 30, 75, and 150 feet, and can be special ordered in custom lengths if required.

This cable is a little more flexible than the Type 1 cable and can be used to connect MAUs and to connect individual stations to the MAU. When used to connect stations, it is usually used only in a small network with around 12 MAUs, which are usually of the IBM Model 8228 type.

Lobe Cables

The cables that connect individual workstations to the central MAU device are called lobe cables. Each cable uses four wires for communications. Two are used for transmitting data to the MAU, and two are used for receiving data. For the standard STP cable (Type 1 and Type 2), an IBM Type A data connector is used at one end to connect the cable to the MAU, and a 9-pin connector is used at the other end to connect to the token-ring network card.

If the cable type is UTP (Type 3), the connectors are usually RJ-11 or RJ-45, although the RJ-11 type is an older model that is not often used today. Most token-ring adapters that are currently being manufactured have both a 9-pin and RJ45 socket to provide for different cable types.

Ring In/Ring Out Cables

These cables are used to connect MAUs in order to form a larger LAN. When you join MAUs, you connect the Ring In port of one MAU to the Ring Out port of another, with the end result forming a ring so that the last MAU is connected back to the first.

Although a malfunction of a lobe cable will only cause the attached workstation to be dropped from the LAN, the failure of a cable that connects two MAUs is a more serious problem. Saying that a Token Ring LAN is "self-healing" refers to its capability to lock out a malfunctioning workstation, not a break between MAUs.

Fiber-Optic Connections

Fiber-optic cable (sometimes called Type 5) has been used in token-ring networks for many years. One of the benefits of this cable is that it enables you to greatly extend the distances covered by the LAN. When computing the ARL, for example, fiber-optic cable usually counts as a zero length cable. This means that if you use fiber-optic cable for all the MAUs in the ring, only the lengths of the lobe cables from the MAU to the workstation need to be figured in.

Connectors

When using IBM Type 1 cables, the standard connector is called an *IBM-type Data Connector (IDC)*, or a *Universal Data Connector (UDC)*. These connectors are not like RJ-45 connectors, where the cable consists of a male connector that plugs into a female socket. Instead, these connectors are blade-type and interlock into each other.

UDC connectors use the color coding scheme shown in Table 16.1.

Table 16.1   Color Codes for UDC Connectors

Wire Color	Use	Polarity
Red	Receive data	+
Green	Receive data	-
Orange	Transmit data	+
Black	Transmit data	-

A DB-9 connector contains nine pins for terminating wires, but only four are used by token-ring networks. Table 16.2 shows the pinout for this connector and the wire color coding scheme that is used.

Table 16.2   Color Codes for DB-9 Connectors

Pin Number	Wire Color	Use	Polarity
Pin no. 1	Red	Receive data	+
Pin no. 5	Black	Transmit data	-
Pin no. 6	Green	Receive data	-
Pin no. 9	Orange	Transmit data	+

You can also use RJ-45 connectors; this is the type of connector most often seen in 10Base-T Ethernet networks. This type of connector is similar to the modular connector used on most telephones today. The color coding and pins that are used with this connector for token-ring networks are shown in Table 16.3.

Table 16.3   Color Codes for RJ-45 Connectors

Pin Number	Wire Color	Use	Polarity
Pin no. 3	Blue/White	Transmit data	-
Pin no. 4	White/Orange	Receive data	+
Pin no. 5	Orange/White	Receive data	-
Pin no. 6	White/Blue	Transmit data	+

Another modular connector that is used, although not as often as the others discussed here, is the RJ-11 connector. This connector type is usually used with older network adapters. Table 16.4 lists the color codes and pins used for this type.

Table 16.4   Color Codes and Pinout for RJ-11 Connectors

Pin Number	Wire Color	Use	Polarity
Pin no. 2	Blue/White	Transmit data	-
Pin no. 3	White/Orange	Receive data	+
Pin no. 4	Orange/White	Receive data	-
Pin no. 5	White/Blue	Transmit data	+

Media Filters

If you have older token-ring adapters that only have a 9-pin connector, you can find media filters that can be used to join them to an RJ-45 connector. Various vendors produce these inexpensively. Ethernet cards are, for all practical purposes, a commodity item that can be replaced cheaply. Token-ring adapters are more expensive, so using a media filter to attach an older card to a new cabling standard for your network might be a good idea, economically, if you have a lot of stations.

Cabling Scenarios

Now let's look at some cabling scenarios and types of cable to use. The general specifications that you must analyze are ring speed, maximum distance between any workstation and the MAU, number of workstations, and whether a voice connection is going to be carried over the LAN cabling.

Scenario #1

Ring speed: 16mps

Maximum distance: 35 meters

Number of workstations: 62

Voice connection: No

Solution—This scenario will require Type 1 cabling. Even though the number of workstations and maximum distance require only Type 3, the requirement of 16mps speed necessitates using Type 1.

Scenario #2

Ring speed: 16mps

Maximum distance: 85 meters

Number of workstations: 185

Voice connection: Yes

Solution—This scenario will require Type 2 cabling. The ring speed, maximum distance, and number of workstations can be implemented using Type 1 or 2, but the voice requirement can be handled only using Type 2 cabling.

Scenario #3

Ring speed: 4mps

Maximum distance: 35 meters

Number of workstations: 25

Voice connection: No

Solution—This scenario requires only Type 3 cabling due to the low requirements. This type of cabling is the cheapest and easiest to install, and is the best choice on a small LAN.

Summary

The number of stations you can connect to a token-ring network and the distances you can achieve depend on the type of equipment and cables that are used, as well as the specifications supplied by the manufacturer. You can join token-ring LANs by using token-ring bridges, as described in Chapter 15, "Token-Ring Topology Restrictions," but be careful not to exceed the limitations imposed by the architecture when designing a ring.

In the next chapter, some of the common problems with token-ring networks are discussed, along with methods used to monitor the network.

Part VI

TOKEN-RING PROBLEMS

Monitoring Token-Ring Utilization

SOME OF THE MAIN TOPICS IN THIS CHAPTER ARE

Token-Ring Statistics

Using Network and Protocol Analyzers

**Token-Ring Extensions to the Remote Network
Monitoring MIB**

Troubleshooting Tips

Because of the fundamental difference between ethernet and token-ring technologies, the statistics that you use to monitor the separate network topologies are quite different. For example, an Ethernet network operating at 10Mbps will begin to degrade rapidly when overall utilization of the network media rises above 50 percent. This is primarily because of the access method used, which allows for collisions to occur when more than one station attempts to transmit at about the same time. Token-ring networks operating at 4 or 16Mbps can actually use a much larger percentage of the network bandwidth because only one station is normally transmitting at a time. The mechanisms that token ring uses to grant access to the network (the Token frame) and other functions used to maintain network functionality (that is, ring polling and beaconing), and the kinds of information available to the administrator are different than those on an ethernet network.

This chapter briefly looks at some of the statistics and errors that the administrator should look for and discusses methods for troubleshooting problems in a token-ring environment.

Token-Ring Statistics

Two kinds of frames are used on a token-ring network. The *logical link control* (*LLC*) frame is used to carry data that a station on the ring wants to send to another station. Most of the frames that will be generated on a token-ring network will be of this type. The network adapters, however, use another type of frame, called the *media access control* (*MAC*) frame to communicate with each other and perform ring management functions. MAC frames are not generated by higher-level protocols. The data portion of an LLC frame carries data from one station to the other. The data portion of a MAC frame carries ring management information from one adapter to another.

Technical Note

Because MAC frames on the token-ring network are used for local ring management functions, they are not normally passed by bridges, routers, or switches. For a more detailed discussion of MAC frames and LLC frames, see Chapter 14, "Token-Passing Technology."

The most basic MAC frames that you will see are the *active monitor present* (*AMP*) and *standby monitor present* (*SMP*) frames. The AMP frame is normally passed around the ring every seven seconds. It is used to tell other stations which monitor is the active monitor. Other stations on the ring are considered to be standby monitors and will decide on a new active monitor if the AMP frame fails to arrive on time.

Network analyzers, both hardware and software, usually enable you to collect and display statistics about the functions performed by these ring management frames. They also can show you statistical information about errors that occur on the ring.

Remember that the token-ring topology is not like the broadcast collision domain that is used in Ethernet networks. Each station on the ring will receive a frame from its nearest upstream neighbor. This is not necessarily the neighbor that is plugged into the next port on the MAU; it is the nearest upstream neighbor that is currently active on the ring, hence the term *NAUN* for *nearest active upstream neighbor*.

A typical monitoring program will show statistics such as

- Beacons
- Token claims
- Ring purges
- Broadcasts
- Stations

Monitoring beacon frames is important for maintaining a healthy network. These frames are sent to downstream neighbors when an adapter fails to detect any data or MAC frames from its nearest upstream neighbor, usually indicating that the upstream neighbor is malfunctioning or possibly a cable fault. If the process works as it should, the upstream neighbor receives the beacon frames after they travel around the ring and detaches itself from the ring to perform diagnostics. If the upstream neighbor is seriously impaired, it might not be capable of receiving the beacon frames or responding. In that case, the ring will stay in a beaconing mode, incapable of transmitting user data, until the network administrator steps in and solves the problem.

Obviously, if you notice that the ring is experiencing a high level of beacon frames, it might be an indication that an adapter or possibly a cable is unstable and should be looked at immediately.

Token claims can result from something as simple as a new station joining the ring or a problem that causes the active monitor to leave the ring. Ring purge frames are used to set the ring back to a known state when something has gone wrong and can also be used when the active monitor leaves the ring and a new one is elected or when the active monitor detects some other kind of error condition and needs to reset the ring. When a station receives a ring purge frame, it stops its current processing and resets its timers. If the ring is experiencing a high level of ring purges, you should study other error or statistical information to determine the cause.

For example, a good monitoring program will show you the current number of active stations on the ring. It will usually also show you the maximum number of stations that have been on the ring since the monitor began recording data, and possibly an average number of stations. If the average number of stations on the ring is significantly lower than the maximum, check to determine why stations are leaving and rejoining the ring. If you are moving equipment around or rearranging workstations on the network, this might not present a problem.

Error Detection and the Fault Domain

Each station on the ring expects to receive network frames from its NAUN. When it does not, something must be wrong. In a sense you might say that stations upstream watch out for their downstream neighbor and when they sense a problem, they attempt to notify other stations and try to locate the error, which is called the *fault domain*. The fault domain is defined by the beacon frame, which contains the address of the station that is reporting a failure on the ring and the address of its NAUN, which it suspects is having a problem. The fault domain includes these two stations and anything that might lie between them, such as the lobe cables and the ports they use on the MAU.

The reconfiguration process triggered by beaconing should be capable of isolating the malfunctioning station that caused it to be bypassed in the MAU. If it does not succeed, manual intervention by the administrator will be required.

The Ring Error Monitor

An optional software component that many administrators will find useful for troubleshooting is the Ring Error Monitor software. Every ring has an AMP, and the remaining workstations are designated as standby monitors. The Ring Error Monitor is a station that does nothing more than receive error reports from other stations as they detect them. It keeps a running list that the administrator can review when trouble is suspected on the ring.

When a station on the ring detects that an error has occurred, it will wait for a few seconds (two seconds by default) and listen to the network to see whether any further errors occur. After the wait interval has expired, the station will send a report of the errors it has seen to the Ring Error Monitor. If you are using a Ring Error Monitor on your network, review the error data it collects on a regular basis. Even simple errors that do not cause down time for the ring can indicate that a component is unstable and prone to more severe failure in the near future. Taking proactive steps to diagnose and fix a small problem can prevent a much larger problem from disrupting other users later.

Token-Ring Errors

Errors can be classified into two broad categories: hard and soft. *Soft errors* can occur during normal ring operation, but they do not bring down the local ring. *Hard errors* are caused by such things as broken or malfunctioning cables or ports on the MAU that can possibly stop normal functioning of the ring.

Soft errors can be described as either isolating or non-isolating errors. An *isolating* error is an error that can be traced back to a single station on the ring, while a *non-isolating* error cannot. Simply put, an isolating soft error usually indicates an error condition with a particular station on the ring. That is, it can be isolated to a particular station. A non-isolating error usually indicates a problem with the ring itself and not necessarily a particular workstation.

The IEEE 802.5 specification that sets the standards for Token-Ring networks defines several error types:

- **Burst**—This error indicates that there is noise on the network media. It occurs when a station detects three bits without a clocking bit in the middle. The source of the noise can be environmental, such as a strong electrical field near a network cable, or might result from faulty hardware. This error can also happen when a station is inserting itself into the ring or taking itself out of the ring. The burst error is probably the most frequent error you will see on a Token Ring.

- **Line**—This kind of error is similar to a burst error and usually indicates that one is about to happen. It can be generated when a station receives a frame and calculates that the CRC value does not match the contents of the frame. When a station detects this kind of error it sets the error bit in the frame to 1 so that other stations do not report the error. In general, you will see a ratio of one line error for every 10 burst errors detected.

■ **Lost Frame**—When a station transmits a frame, it sets a timer that tells it how long it should expect to wait until the frame travels around the ring back to it. If this timer expires, a lost frame error is generated, which causes the active monitor to generate a new token.

■ **Token**—The active monitor sets a timer each time it sees a valid frame on the ring. Because the monitor knows how long it takes for the frame to travel the distance around the ring, it assumes an error has occurred if this timer expires before it sees another frame. This can result from noise on the line. The active monitor generates a new token when this condition is observed.

■ **Internal**—An internal error occurs when a station detects an internal parity error when using DMA (direct memory access) to exchange data with the workstation's memory. To determine whether the network adapter card is the problem, you can install it in a different workstation and see if the error occurs. If it does not, try power-cycling the original workstation to see if the error can be corrected.

■ **Frequency**—When the frequency on the network media detected by a station differs significantly from that which is expected, a frequency error is recorded. A standby monitor on the ring can detect this error, which usually results from a problem with the active monitor that generates the clocking signal. To determine whether the active monitor is problematic, remove it from the ring and see if this problem still occurs.

■ **AC**—This error type indicates that a station received more than one AMP or SMP frame with both the address recognized and frame copied fields set to zero. This error occurs when the nearest upstream neighbor of the station does not properly set these bits. Check the upstream station when troubleshooting.

■ **FC or Frame Copied**—A station generates this error type when it receives a MAC frame that is addressed to it, yet the address recognized bit is already set to 1, which is an indication that another station also thought that this frame was destined for it. This can be the result of a problem on the line or possibly indicate that two stations on the ring have the same address. Note that the duplicate address problem will exist at the frame level and is not indicative of a duplicate address of a higher-level protocol.

■ **Abort Delimiter Transmitted**—This error type happens when a station transmits an abort delimiter while it is transmitting. It happens when a station, while transmitting, receives a claim token or beacon frame, which causes it to abort its transmission.

■ **Receive Congestion**—When a station receives a frame that is destined for it but does not have enough buffer space to copy the frame, a receive congestion error occurs.

Some of the problems causing these errors can be easily fixed. For example, if you notice a large number of frame copied errors—indicating a possible duplicate address—and you have just installed a new workstation on the ring, recheck the new workstation to be sure you correctly configured its address. Congestion errors can be solved by replacing older network adapters that might not be capable of keeping up with the traffic on the ring. Congestion errors can also indicate that an adapter is having problems and is about to fail. Replace the adapter to see whether the error persists. Burst errors and token errors can lead you to check the cabling or connectors for all stations on the ring. If cabling has recently been moved or new cabling was installed, check for sources of electrical interference.

Internal errors should direct you to examine the adapter or workstation from which they originate. Replace the adapter to see if the problem subsides, and if not, perform diagnostics on the workstation itself.

Using Network and Protocol Analyzers

In addition, the error recording functions of the Ring Error Monitor and a good protocol analyzer can be a big help in troubleshooting problems on a ring. The protocol decode function provided by the analyzer should be capable of decoding frames specific to token-ring networks (that is, the MAC frames used for ring maintenance), as well as higher-level protocols such as TCP/IP or IPX/SPX.

When using a protocol analyzer, it is important to understand how your network works during the normal workday. At certain times of the day there will normally be peaks during which activity is high on the ring, while at other times utilization is quite low. If you are unfamiliar with these times, you might not fully understand the voluminous data that you can get using a protocol analyzer. Some soft errors are to be expected, such as those caused when a station is inserted or removed from the ring. If you are not familiar with the pattern of utilization on the ring and the usual error activity, you might judge the ring to be in worse shape than it is!

Token-Ring Extensions to the Remote Network Monitoring MIB

The objects defined in previous RFCs for monitoring network activity, such as those defined in RFC 1271, are separated into nine groups. Some of these groups, such as the statistical groups, are designed with the assumption that the underlying network technology at the Data Link Layer is Ethernet. In order to fully implement SNMP and RMON technology for devices that are used for token-ring networks, additions had to be made.

Tip

RFC stands for *Request for Comments* and is a mechanism used on the Internet in the process of defining standards. *SNMP* stands for the *Simple Network Monitoring Protocol*, which is a technology that allows for monitoring of network components remotely by the network administrator. RMON is similar to SNMP but extends its functionality. *MIB* stands for *Management Information Base* and is a collection of objects that define the kinds of data collected and functions that can be performed by RMON. For more information, see Chapter 2, "Tools".

RFC 1513 defines extension to the MIB, which was defined in previous RFCs, and describes how existing object groups will be used for monitoring token-ring networks. These changes are

- **Host Group**—Only isolating errors will cause error counters in this group to be incremented. These are line errors, burst errors, AC errors, internal errors, and abort errors.

- **Matrix Group**—No error counters will be incremented in this group for Token-Ring networks.

- **Filter Group**—Conditions are defined for how the bitmask is used in this group.

In addition, the RFC provides additional groups of objects that are specific to token-ring networks. In particular, RFC 1513 defines four additional object groups:

- **Ring Station**—This group provides information about each station on the local ring and also status information about each ring that is being monitored.

- **Ring Station Order**—The order of stations in the ring is contained in this group.

- **Ring Station Configuration**—This group is used to manage stations by active means. Objects in this group can be used to remove a station from the ring and download configuration information from a station.

- **Source Routing Statistics**—Utilization statistics about source routing is contained in this group.

Whereas the Ring Error Monitor can provide useful information collected on the local ring, SNMP and RMON can enable you to centralize monitoring for larger networks, making the troubleshooting process much easier. In addition, RMON provides for alarm functions that can be set to trigger when certain events occur, giving you a heads-up before a situation becomes more serious.

When upgrading network components, check to be sure that they provide SNMP and RMON functionality.

Troubleshooting Tips

As you can see, a lot of different kinds of information can tell you how well your token-ring network is functioning. However, too much information can be useless if you don't understand how to interpret it. The best thing you can do to keep yourself prepared is to monitor the network on a frequent basis and keep track of normal usage patterns. In other words, determine a baseline for the network and use the baseline data when analyzing or troubleshooting.

The following are a few general things that should apply to most rings, however:

- Every seven seconds the active monitor present frame should be seen circling the ring. This ring polling mechanism allows each station to determine what its nearest active upstream neighbor is. It also lets each station know that the ring is functioning normally and that the active monitor is watching for token and other errors. Following shortly after the AMP frame, you should notice a standby monitor present frame.

- Soft errors and ring purge frames are expected events when a station is inserted or removed from the ring, and should not be a cause for alarm. Soft errors that are not associated with insertion or removal should be less than 0.1 percent of the total number of packets transmitted.

- Insertion and removal of a station can also cause burst errors, line errors, and possibly token errors. If these errors are not associated with the time frame during which an insertion or removal was performed, they might indicate a problem unless they are sporadic.

- Utilization on a Token-Ring network above 70 percent can cause slower response for end users. Normally, response times should be around one tenth of a second. Peak utilization of 100 percent does not indicate a problem unless it is happening frequently.

Summary

Token-ring networks use a network access mechanism that is different than that used on Ethernet LANs. For this reason, the kinds of statistics you should monitor and the kinds of errors you will usually see are different. Still, there are tools that can provide you with the information you need to maintain a healthy network.

In the next chapter we look at the TCP/IP protocol suite and examine some of the methods used for troubleshooting its components.

Part VII

TROUBLESHOOTING PROTOCOLS

TCP/IP

CHAPTER 18

The TCP/IP network protocol suite has become the standard networking protocol for today's LAN and WAN installations, and is the primary protocol for the Internet. TCP/IP is referred to as a *suite* because the term applies to a group of protocols and the utilities that were designed around them. The acronym TCP/IP stands for *Transmission Control Protocol/Internet Protocol*.

This chapter briefly reviews the major protocols used in the TCP/IP protocol suite, examines the nature of IP addressing, and, finally, discusses tools that you can use when trying to troubleshoot problems on a TCP/IP network.

Underlying Protocols

When you see the term TCP/IP, it is important to understand that TCP and IP are two distinct protocols, each defined and developed by numerous Request For Comments (RFCs) documents. Each is concerned with specific functions, but they work together to provide the network connection between two computers. These two protocols are the basis for transmitting data from one host to another on the Internet. However, two other protocols—UDP (User Data Protocol) and ICMP (Internet Control Message Protocol)—are also important, especially from a troubleshooting and administrative standpoint.

Internet Protocol (IP)

The *IP protocol* provides a connectionless unacknowledged network service. It is responsible for getting data packets from one host to another. IP has no mechanisms for checking to see that a packet actually arrives at its destination—unacknowledged delivery—and it doesn't concern itself with the path the packet takes through the internetwork. IP doesn't even guarantee that the packets will arrive in the order they were sent, and therefore is termed connectionless. IP does perform functions such as fragmenting data packets into smaller ones and reassembling them, so it is capable of sending packets through networks and devices of many different types. A checksum value is calculated for the header information of an IP packet, but the data portion is not protected by this protocol.

When encapsulated in an Ethernet frame, the type field of the Ethernet packet is set to 0x0800 to identify it as an IP packet. When encapsulated in frames that use IEEE 802 Logical Link Control (LLC), the value of 0xAA is used for the DSAP and SSAP field, and the value of 00-00-00-08-00 is used in the SNAP ID field.

▶▶ For more information about the construction of Ethernet and IEEE 802 frames, see Chapter 8, "Ethernet Frame Types".

Transmission Control Protocol (TCP)

TCP uses IP to provide a reliable connection service between two hosts on the Internet. Whereas IP simply sends packets on their way, unconcerned about their fate, TCP provides the mechanisms that make sure the packets are actually received intact and that they can be put back into the correct order at the destination computer.

It is through the TCP protocol that checksums are done on the actual data that is transmitted. TCP also has mechanisms that regulate the flow of data to avoid problems associated with congestion. It attempts to make efficient use of the network by trying to create packets that contain more than just a few bytes of information.

Address Resolution Protocol (ARP)

IP addresses are used to route a packet to its destination. If the packet is destined for a network other than the one on which it originated, it is passed to a router, which in turn sends it on its way to the correct network segment, or perhaps to yet another router that can perform this function. When a packet finally arrives at the correct network segment, it must be determined what MAC address is used by the destination computer. Remember that on the wire, the actual address used to communicate between two devices—whether they are computers, routers, or whatever—is the built-in MAC address.

The *Address Resolution Protocol (ARP)* was developed for this purpose. When a device wants to send a packet to another device and does not know the MAC address, it will instead send out a broadcast message that every computer on the local segment can see. This ARP message contains the originating computer's own MAC address and the IP address of the computer it wants to talk to. When the destination computer sees this message, it sends a packet back to the originator and includes its own MAC address. After that, each computer knows the MAC address of the other, and further transmissions take place using these.

Each host keeps a table of MAC addresses for some time so that it can use this table when it needs to communicate again, making repeated broadcasts unnecessary if the communication takes place before the address is aged out of the table.

User Datagram Protocol

User Datagram Protocol (UDP) is similar in function to TCP in that it uses the IP protocol to actually move packets through the network. However, unlike TCP, UDP does not have an acknowledgment mechanism, so it provides a connectionless service. This protocol is used by applications that do not require the guaranteed delivery mechanisms of TCP and the overhead associated with it. For example, the Domain Name Service (DNS) uses UDP packets to exchange information with computers in a quick, efficient manner.

Internet Control Message Protocol (ICMP)

Internet Control Message Protocol (ICMP) is used for maintenance and diagnostic purposes, and is therefore valuable when troubleshooting network problems. Like TCP and UDP, this protocol makes use of the IP protocol, which does the actual moving of data through the network.

ICMP defines certain message formats that are used by utilities such as PING and TRACEROUTE to perform their functions. You might not hear a lot about this protocol, but it is a required part of any TCP/IP implementation, and the functions it performs are very important not only to host computers, but also to routers and other network devices that communicate via TCP/IP.

Each ICMP packet has a field that defines the message type. The types of messages carried by this protocol are shown in Table 18.1. Each ICMP packet also contains a code field that is used to further delineate the type of message.

Table 18.1   ICMP Message Types

Message Type	Description
0	Echo Reply
3	Destination Unreachable
4	Source Quench
5	Redirect Message
8	Echo Request
11	Time Exceeded
12	Parameter Problem
13	Timestamp Request
14	Timestamp Reply
15	Information Request (no longer used)
16	Information Reply (no longer used)
17	Address Mask Request
18	Address Mask Reply

The most common use of ICMP messages is the PING command, which uses the ECHO request and ECHO reply messages to establish if simple connectivity exists between systems. However, this protocol is used for functions of much greater importance. The source quench message is sent to tell a sending host that the destination host cannot keep up with the speed at which it is sending packets. The destination host will keep sending these quench packets until the sender cuts back its transmissions to an acceptable rate.

A router uses ICMP to tell another device that it knows of a better path to the destination, using redirect messages. Routers use the time-exceeded messages to indicate why a packet was discarded; it either exceeded the hop count or timed out during reassembly.

For example, like routers and other intermediary devices, hosts can use ICMP to determine routing. For example, when a computer boots and does not know what the network mask is, the local LAN can generate an address mask request message. Another device on the network can reply to assist the computer.

Note

The Information Request and Information Reply message types are shown only for completeness. Their functionality was to enable a host to obtain an IP address, but this type of function is now supplied by the bootp protocol and by the Dynamic Host Configuration Protocol (DHCP).

IP Addressing

Network adapter cards, commonly referred to as *NICs* (for *Network Interface Cards*), come from the manufacturer with a hard-coded network address, which is burned in during the process of manufacturing the card. When frames are sent through the network media from one station to the next, it is this Media Access Control address that is actually used for the source and destination addresses embedded in the ethernet frame. Other terms commonly used for MAC addresses are *physical addresses* or *hardware addresses*.

The MAC address that is assigned to each NIC is unique. It is a 6-byte address that is usually expressed in hexadecimal numbers to make it easier to write. For example, it is much easier to write 00-80-C8-EA-AA-7E than to express the same address in binary—what the network sees—which would be a string of zeros and ones, 48 characters in length (see Table 18.2).

Table 18.2   Hexadecimal to Binary

Hexadecimal Value	Binary Value
00	00000000
80	10000000
C8	11001000
EA	11101010
AA	10101010
7E	11111110

The first three bytes of the MAC address identify the manufacturer of the card. Each manufacturer then uses the next six bytes of the address range to incrementally assign a unique number to each NIC card produced. The remaining three bytes are used by the manufacturer to uniquely identify each device they manufacture.

You might wonder, "If each network card that is produced already has a unique address, why is it necessary for a network protocol to assign yet another address? Instead of learning the ins and outs of IP addresses, why don't I just use the built-in MAC address instead?"

The reason is simple: It is so that network administrators can better organize the workstations and servers in their networks, and so that routers and other network devices can determine what path a data packet should take when it flows through the network. The remaining sections of this chapter explain how IP addresses are constructed and how their composition implies a hierarchical network structure.

As you recall, the initials TCP/IP stand for *Transmission Control Protocol/Internet Protocol*. The Internet Protocol is the subject of this chapter. The term *Internet* indicates that this protocol is used for exchanging data between networks; this can be seen in the make up of IP addresses, which contain bits that specify the network and bits that specify the individual computer or workstation on that particular network.

If there were no need to connect smaller networks into a larger structure, addressing could be quite simple. Either the MAC address or a simple numbering scheme (1, 2, 3...) could be used to uniquely identify each computer on the network. However, the IP protocol allows computers on diverse types of networks to exchange data.

The IP address consists of four bytes of information, or 32 consecutive bits. Whereas MAC addresses are usually expressed in hexadecimal notation, IP addresses are typically written in what is termed dotted-decimal notation. That is, each byte is converted to its decimal representation, and the four bytes of the address are separated by periods. Table 18.3 shows how the decimal values relate to the binary value in the 32-bit address 10001100101100001101100110010100.

Table 18.3   IP Addresses Expressed in Decimal Notation

Decimal Value	Binary Value
140	10001100
176	10110000
217	11011001
148	10010100

As you can see, it is much easier to write the address as 140.176.217.148 than to use the binary equivalent.

Part of an IP address identifies the network, and part of the address identifies the computer. It should be a simple question to ask which part is which. Well, it depends. IP addresses are divided into three major classes—A, B, and C—and two less familiar ones—D and E). Each class uses a different number of bits in the IP address to specify a network address. Because the total number of bits available for addressing is always constant—32—this implies that some classes will have the capability to identify more networks than others and some will have the capability to identify more workstations.

You can tell which class an address belongs to by examining the first four bits of the address. Table 18.4 lists the IP address classes, showing the bit values for the first four bits. In this table, the bit positions that are marked with an x indicate that this value does not matter.

Table 18.4   IP Address Classes, Determined by the First Four Bits of the Address

Column Heading	Column Heading
Class A	0xxx
Class B	10xx
Class C	110x
Class D	111x
Class E	1111

As you can see in Table 18.4, any IP address that has a zero for its first bit will be a Class A address, no matter what the values are for the remaining bits of the next three bits—or of the entire address, for that matter. Any address that has 10 for the first two bits of the address will be a Class B address, and so on.

Class A Addresses

Possible Class A addresses range from a binary value of zero for all 32 bits to a binary value of zero in the first position, with the remaining bits being ones. If you take each byte of the address and convert it into decimal, you see that Class A addresses, when expressed in dotted-decimal notation, can range from 0.0.0.0 to 127.255.255.255.

Tip

For those who are not so familiar with binary notation, the value of a byte with all ones—11111111—is 255 in decimal notation. You can gather from this that no IP address can ever have a value for any of its four bytes that is greater than this value. For example, the address 140.176.123.256 is not a valid IP address because the last byte is larger than 255 decimal. It is not possible to express the value of 256 in binary when using only eight bits.

In this class of addresses, the first byte is used to represent the network portion of the address, and the remaining three bytes are used to identify each workstation on the network. A little math shows that there can be only 127 network addresses—binary 01111111—in a Class A network. There can't be 128 network addresses in this class because to express 128 in binary, the value is 10000000, which indicates a Class B address.

Because only the first byte is used to identify network addresses, this leaves three bytes that can be used to identify individual computers on the network. In binary, the maximum value you can store in three bytes is a string of 24 ones; this value in decimal is 16,777,215. If you count zero, this means that a total of 16,777,216 (2 to the 24th power) addresses can be expressed using three bytes.

Thus, there can be a total of 128 Class A networks, and each can have up to 16,777,216 unique addresses. In dotted-decimal notation, this value ranges from 0.0.0.0 to 127.255.255.255. When you see an address that falls in this range, you can be sure that it is a Class A address.

Class B Addresses

Class B addresses must have the first two bits set to 10. That's 1 and 0 in binary, not *10*. This means that a Class B address, expressed in binary, can range from 1 followed by 31 zeros to 10 followed by 30 ones. When expressed in dotted-decimal notation, the minimum and maximum values for Class B addressing are 128.0.0.0 and 191.255.255.255, respectively. The value of 128 decimal is 10000000 in binary. The value 191 decimal is 10111111 in binary.

Class B addresses use the first two bytes of the address to identify the network and the last two bytes to identify computers on each network. When using two bytes, there can be a maximum of 16,384 possible network addresses in this class (from 128.0 to 191.255) and 65,536 (2 to the 16th power) individual computers on each Class B network. At first glance, you might think that because both the network and the host portion of the address use the same number of bytes, there should be an equal number of network addresses and host computer addresses. Remember, however, that although the first two bytes are used to specify the network address, not all the possible values of these first two bytes can be used. Some of these values represent network addresses from other classes of addresses.

In summary, Class B addresses can range in value from 128.0.0.0 to 191.255.255.255.

Class C Addresses

Class C addresses always begin with the value of 110 in the first three bits. If you convert this to decimal, you can see that a Class C network address can range from 192.0.0.0 to 223.255.255.255. You have probably guessed by now that a Class C address uses the first three bytes to represent the network address and only the last byte to represent the host portion of the address.

The calculations will tell you that there can be up to 2,097,152 Class C networks, each having up to 256 host computers. This class has a significantly smaller number of host addresses, but the number of networks allowed is huge.

Classes D and E

Classes D and E are used differently than the first three classes. Class D addresses are reserved for multicast group usage. *Multicasting* is the process of sending a network packet to more than one host computer. Class D addresses range, in decimal, from 224.0.0.0 to 239.255.255.255.

In this class of addresses, there are no specific bytes allocated to the network or host portion of the address. This leaves a total of 268,435,456 possible unique addresses that can be created in the Class D address space.

Class E addresses begin with ones in the first four bit positions. If you convert the minimum and maximum values for this class to dotted-decimal notation, you can see that a Class E address falls between 240.0.0.0 and 255.255.255.255, which is the maximum value you can specify in binary when using only 32 bits.

Class E addresses are reserved for future use and are not normally seen on networks that interconnect via the Internet.

Unicast, Broadcast, and Multicast Addresses

When examining the possible ranges of addresses that can be calculated for the A, B, and C IP address classes, the discussion centers on using an address to specify one unique host system. An address that uniquely identifies a single host—or one adapter on a host—is called a unicast address. This type of address is used for point-to-point communication between devices on the network.

However, there are special cases that limit the total number of unicast addresses in any of the classes. For example, any address with 127 for the first byte is not a valid address outside the local host computer. The address 127.0.0.1—technically a Class A address—is commonly called a *loopback address* and can be used to test the TCP/IP stack on the computer. When you send a packet to this address (using the `PING` command, for example) it never leaves the local network adapter to be delivered on the network. Instead, the packet merely travels down through the protocol stack and back up again to verify that the local computer is properly configured.

This address can be used with TCP/IP utilities other than `PING`. For example, you can telnet to your local computer using this address if you want to test the functionality of a local telnet server.

In general, do not use the value of zero or 255 for any of the four octets of an IP address. When used in the network portion of an address, zeros imply "the current network," and the value of 255 is used in the last octet of IP addresses to specify a broadcast message. This type of message is sent out only once but can be received by more than one host. Broadcasts can be used to send a packet to all computers on a particular network or subnet. For example, the address 10.11.255.255 would be received by all hosts in the network defined by 10.11.

Table 18.5 shows the actual number of addresses for Classes A–C that remain after the special case addresses have been subtracted.

Table 18.5   IP Addresses Available for Use

Class	Number of Networks	Number of Hosts
A	126	16,777,214
B	16,384	65,534
C	2,097,152	254

Subnet Masks and Subnetting

By specifying both a network and host address in an IP address, a hierarchical address space is created that has an organizational advantage over the flat address space created by MAC addresses. However, in many cases it is not convenient to use the entire range of assigned host addresses on a single subnet. For example, a network that has been assigned a Class B address space would find it very difficult to put 65,534 host computers on one network segment.

Another level has been added to TCP/IP addressing that enables the local administrator of an address space to further divide that space to create *subnets*. This is accomplished by using a *subnet mask*.

Subnetting can be used to solve many administrative problems, including

- **Joining different networking technologies**—You can subnet the address space, allocate one subnet to a token-ring network and another to an ethernet network, join the two using a router.

- **Reducing network congestion**—Rather than putting all 254 hosts of a Class C network on a network segment, you can subnet the address space into two or four distinct subnets, put each into its own collision domain, and thus reduce contention on each segment.

- **Allocating the address space over geographical distances**—If you have multiple branch offices, each with only a small number of computers, it is wasteful to allocate a full Class C address to each location. Instead, you can subnet a single address space into equal amounts, and use one subnet for each location.

Class A, B, and C Netmasks

In the discussion of IP address classes, I noted that a portion of each address specifies the network address and the remaining portion of the address is used to identify a host computer on that network. To subdivide a particular network address into subnets, it is necessary to borrow a few bits from the host portion of the address and use them to identify the network or subnet. The subnet mask is a value expressed in dotted decimal format, just like an IP address, and its purpose is to mask out the portion of the IP address that specifies the network and subnet part of the address.

For example, the A, B, and C address classes that were just described each have a specific mask associated with them. The Class A address mask is 255.0.0.0. Since 255 in binary is equal to a string of 8 ones, the binary representation would be 11111111000000000000000000000000. Boolean logic is used to find out the network address. When using the AND operator in Boolean logic, the TRUE result will be obtained only when both arguments are TRUE.

If TRUE is represented by the number 1 and FALSE is represented by the number 0, it is easy for a computer or a router to apply the mask to the IP address to obtain the network portion of the address. Table 18.6 shows how the final values are obtained.

Table 18.6   Boolean Logic Is Used for the Subnet Mask

IP Address Value	Mask Value	Result
1	1	1
1	0	0
0	1	0
0	0	0

Thus, when you apply the subnet mask of 255.0.0.0 to a Class A address, the only portion of the IP address that is selected to be the network address is that portion contained in the first byte.

It is easy to see from this that the subnet mask for a Class B address would be 255.255.0.0, and 255.255.255.0 for a Class C address.

Subdividing an Address Using Subnet Masks

So far, I have shown how the subnet mask can be used to mask off portions of the address that are already understood to be network addresses by the class structure. In fact, subnetting becomes useful when you use it to take a particular network address space and further divide it into separate subnets.

For example, the subnet mask 255.255.255.128 can be used to subnet a Class C address space into two distinct subnets. If this mask is applied against a network address of 192.113.255, you end up with one subnet with host addresses ranging from 192.113.255.1 to 192.113.255.128, and second subnet with host addresses ranging from 192.113.255.129 to 192.113.255.254. Note in this example that addresses that end in all zeros or all ones have been eliminated. Remember that those addresses are special cases and are generally not allowed as host addresses (192.113.255.0, for example).

To carry the example further, you can see that a subnet mask of 255.255.255.192 would divide a Class C network address space into four subnets, and each would have 62 host addresses available. The binary representation of 192 is 11000000, so this leaves only six bits that you can use for host addresses. The largest number you can store in six bits is 63. Because you cannot use a host address with all ones or all zeros, this leaves only 1–62 for host addressing.

In Figure 18.1, you can see that the IP address now consists of three parts: the network address, the subnet address, and the host address.

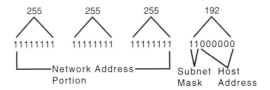

Figure 18.1   The mask defines the network address, subnet address, and host portions of the IP address.

Subnet Calculations

When you are deciding to subnet your address space, it might be easier to sit down with a pencil, paper, and a calculator that can translate between decimal and binary. Decide on the number of host addresses you will need in each subnet and express that amount in binary. This will show you how many bits you need for the host portion of the address space. Subtract that from the number of bits available (eight if you're subnetting the last byte of a Class C address). Then, calculate the decimal equivalent for a binary number that contains that number of left-most bits set to one.

For example, if you want 30 host addresses in each subnet, the binary value of 30 is 11110, which takes five bits to write in binary. That leaves three bit positions that need to be masked off for the subnet mask portion of the address (8–5=3). A binary representation of the required mask would be 11100000, which is 224 in decimal.

Because the subnet mask is only three bits in length, the largest number you can express here is 7 (111 binary = 7 decimal). If you include zero, you can create eight possible subnet addresses.

This means that you can have eight subnets, each with 30 host addresses, when you use 255.255.255.224 to subnet a Class C IP address. So far it seems easy, but what would the actual host address be for each subnet? Again, get out the calculator and do the math. The first subnet address is 000. Because the IP address is expressed in dotted-decimal notation, calculate how many addresses you can store in an eight-bit binary value that always begins with 000, and then translate that to decimal as follows: 00000001 to 00011110, which is 1–30 in decimal. The addresses of 00000000 and 00011111 are not valid because they result in a host address of all zeros or all ones. If this mask were applied to a Class C network address of 192.113.255.0, hosts in the first subnet would range from 192.113.255.1 to 192.113.255.30.

The second subnet address is 001. The range of host addresses that could be created for this subnet is 00100001 to 00111110, which is 33–62 in decimal. When applied to the network address of 192.113.255.0, the hosts on the second subnet range from 192.113.255.33 to 192.113.255.62.

The third subnet address is 010. The range of host addresses is 01000001 to 01011110, or 65–94 in decimal. The range of hosts on this third subnet is from 192.113.255.65 to 192.113.255.94.

If you continue to do the math for the remaining subnets—011 to 111—you will find that you will have eight subnets, each with 30 available host addresses.

You can subdivide the address space further by using up to six bits for the subnet mask. This leaves only two host addresses available—because you can use all zeros or all ones—and is more of a mathematical exercise than a practical application of subnetting.

Name Resolution and Routing Issues

So far I have covered the two basic addresses that are used on the TCP/IP network. The MAC address is the actual address used by the hardware level to communicate. The IP address is a logical hierarchy of addresses that are assigned to particular MAC addresses for administrative and management purposes. There is still one more level of abstraction that is used, which moves us even further away from the MAC address: the hostname.

Hostname Resolution

Computers on a network are given names because it is much easier for a human to remember a name than a hexadecimal MAC address or an IP dotted-decimal address. Names can be meaningful—for example, Atlanta or Toronto, which indicate the computer's location—or they can be totally arbitrary, as when the more technical among us choose to name computers after Star Wars characters. The important issue is not the name itself, but rather that the name be something the end user can relate to and remember.

The ARP protocol is used on the local network to resolve TCP/IP addresses to MAC addresses. There are several methods to perform this translation function between hostnames and IP addresses, from simple text files to the ever-evolving directory services that are now the current rage.

Files

The simplest method of resolving a hostname to an IP address is to use a text file. This is the method that was used when TCP/IP networks were just beginning. The file is usually called HOSTS or HOSTS.TXT, depending on the operating system or the vendor of the TCP/IP software for a particular computer. In the Berkeley Software Distribution (BSD) version of UNIX, this file is \etc\hosts. In Windows NT 4.0, this file is found in \<systemroot>\System32\Drivers\Etc\hosts.

The file is simple. Each line in the file contains an IP address, followed by one or more spaces and then the hostname. You can also follow the hostname with a third column of comments, but comments must be prefixed with the # character. For example, lines in a HOSTS file would resemble the following:

        192.113.252.13 yoko.ono.com   #Tim's workstation

        192.113.252.14 Karma.ono.com #Sally's workstation

This method works best in small networks for two very important reasons. First, it is difficult to keep the host files synchronized on a large number of computers when a change needs to be made. Second, there are much better methods for performing address-to-name translations today.

Note

The larger the network, the larger the HOSTS file must be. If you expect each computer on your network to be capable of contacting every other computer on your network, each HOSTS file must contain every single address-to-name translation for every single host on the network. Imagine stuffing every single address and hostname used on the Internet into a single text file and then trying to place that file on every computer connected to the Internet. Then, imagine coordinating the thousands of changes that occur every day. The HOSTS file has outlived its usefulness as the Internet has grown from a small network connecting a few universities, government agencies, and businesses. It is mentioned here only for historical purposes and because it might still be in use in a few small legacy networks.

DNS and Directory Services

The *Domain Name System (DNS)* was created to centralize the task of making changes to network name-to-address assignments, and to automate the task of performing translation functions. In the early days of the Internet, a central location—SRI NIC at Stanford Research Institute in California—was responsible for maintaining a HOSTS file that contained the name of every host on the Internet, along with its address. Administrators had to communicate changes to SRI NIC, and these changes were incorporated into the file periodically. Of course, this meant that the file had to be distributed to every single host so that they could have the updated version.

The disadvantages of this system included the volume of data and the time wasted on keeping it synchronized. The use of the centralized HOSTS file also pointed out a fundamental problem in the naming scheme: Sooner or later, they would run out of hostnames. That is because in the beginning, every hostname had to be unique in this file. In 1984, the Domain Name System (DNS) was put in place to handle this chore. In addition to making it easier to update the database of name-to-address translations, a hierarchical domain structure was adopted. Instead of using a single name for a host, each host was associated with a name that identified a network or subnetwork.

For example, instead of clunker, you might instead see clunker.dunker.com as a hostname. This would be the unique name for the computer named clunker, which resides in the dunker.com domain. By using a hierarchical naming system, it is possible to have more than one computer named clunker. For example, clunker.acme.com is not the same as clunker.dunker.com.

To put it as briefly as possible, DNS is a hierarchical structure that is spread across many computers throughout the Internet. There is a root server that holds information about top-level domains such as .COM, .EDU, and .GOV, and each domain throughout the Internet has a domain name server that is responsible for the computer names and addresses used in that domain. Client computers query DNS servers when they need to get the address for a hostname. If the local DNS knows the address, it returns the address to the client computer. If it does not, it sends the query up the chain of DNS servers until one is found that can resolve the name, provided it is indeed a valid name.

▶▶ This is only a brief explanation of DNS. For a further examination of the Domain Name System, see Chapter 21, "Name Resolution."

Routing Tables

In the discussion of Ethernet LANs, you learned that there is a maximum size to which a LAN can grow—depending on the network media used—because timing issues require that a station be capable of detecting collisions with another workstation within a set amount of time. This LAN was defined to be a collision domain. In other networking technologies, there are factors that make the size of any particular network segment a set value and still allow all computers to directly exchange packets of information.

However, the Internet itself now consists of millions of computers and doubles in size every few years. How is this possible if a network can grow only to a finite size?

Routing is used to perform this function. When I discussed the importance of IP addressing, one of the key features was the fact that it provided a hierarchical structure for segmenting networks. With a network address that is separate from a host computer address, it is possible to address either the host computer or a particular network.

When a workstation exchanges data with another computer on the same LAN segment, it does so directly, using the MAC address to make the connection. To get a data packet from a computer on another network segment, a router is used. In TCP/IP configurations, you are asked to specify a *gateway*. This is the address to which a packet will be sent when it is determined by the local computer that its destination is not on the local segment. The router can then either forward the packet directly to a router that is connected to the destination network segment, or to another router that knows what path to take.

In Figure 18.2, the workstations that are connected to the hub on Network A can each communicate using their MAC addresses via the hub. However, in order to send a packet to a workstation on Network B, the hub forwards the packet to a router. The router on Network A has an address stored in its memory, which tells it that the destination network can be reached via Router B; so it forwards the packet to Router B, which then sends the packet to the correct network segment for final delivery.

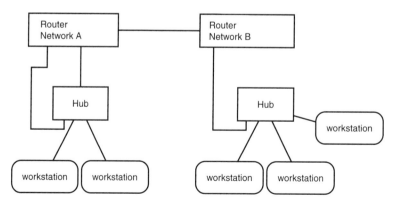

Figure 18.2   Routers connect LANs into a larger network.

A packet can travel through several routers before it gets to its final destination. After the packet arrives at the router, which is connected to the destination network, that router will place the MAC address of the target computer into the packet, and it will finally be delivered.

In order to perform these functions, routers keep a list of addresses, known as a *routing table*. The format of the table depends on the routing protocol in use, and can vary from one router or computer to another. However, the routing table is basically just a list of network addresses and an address that can be used to forward data for that network. Some routing tables include a *hop count*, which is the number of other devices between the current router and its destination network. The hop count can also be used to calculate the best path for a packet to take when there is more than one route that can get it delivered.

Routing tables are also kept on the local computer. This is necessary because there can be more than one router connected to the local network. In addition to the default gateway, an administrator can place static entries into the routing table. When the destination of an outgoing packet is not the local network, the routing table is searched. If the address of the destination network is found, the packet is forwarded according to that entry in the routing table. If it is not found, the packet is forwarded to the default gateway.

This brief discussion of routing is meant to show you that addressing in TCP/IP is necessary to create a hierarchical network structure. If MAC addresses were used instead of network addresses, maintaining a table that contained the route to every single computer on a network—much less on the Internet—would be a nightmare.

You need this information when you plan to install or upgrade a network to use TCP/IP as the network protocol because you will need to assign IP addresses to each computer on the network and configure the subnets for each network segment. It also is necessary to understand how routing works to properly troubleshoot networking problems when they appear.

▶▶ For more information on routers and how they function, including a discussion of popular routing technologies, see Chapter 5, "Bridges, Routers, and Repeaters."

Troubleshooting Commands

TCP/IP includes not only the protocols that have been discussed in this chapter, but also many useful utilities such as FTP and Telnet. To simplify administrative and troubleshooting tasks, the suite also includes several utilities for that purpose.

Using *PING* to Check Connectivity

When you first start to troubleshoot a problem with connectivity on the network, the PING command is the best place to begin because it verifies that TCP/IP is installed and functional on the system.

PING stands for *Packet Internet Groper*, which doesn't make a whole lot of sense at first glance. This utility is used to test connectivity between two systems on the network. The ICMP protocol is used by PING to exchange packets with the remote system. The remote system sends the packets back to their source, and the round trip is timed. PING tells you how long (in milliseconds) the trip took, and it tells you when packets do not make it back successfully.

The PING syntax can vary depending on the operating system, and even between different variants of UNIX. However, its basic use is simply PING hostname or PING ip address. The syntax for a Linux PING follows:

```
ping [-R] [-c number] [-d] [-I seconds] host
```

The options include

- **-c**—Specifies the number of ICMP ECHO_REQUESTS that are sent.
- **-d**—Causes PING to send packets as fast as they are echoed back from the remote system, or up to 100 times per second. Exercise caution when using this option regularly in order to avoid generating high volumes of traffic on a busy network.
- **-I**—This option enables you to specify the number of seconds between each packet sent; the default is =1 second. This option cannot be used with the -R option.
- **-R**—Records the route taken by the packet.

The same command has a much different syntax when used with the Windows NT operating system:

```
ping [-t] [-a] [-n count] [-l size] [-f] [-i TTL] [-v TOS]
     [-r count] [-s count] [[-j host-list] ¦ [-k host-list]
     [-w timeout] destination-list
```

The options include

- **-t**—Continue PINGing until explicitly stopped by Ctrl+C. Statistics are displayed after you stop the command.
- **-a**—Resolves addresses to hostnames.
- **-n count**—Specifies the number of ICMP ECHO_REQUEST packets to send.
- **-l size**—Sends buffer size.
- **-f**—Sets the don't fragment flag in the packet. Useful to determine whether a device is changing the packet size between nodes.
- **-i TTL**—Time to Live value.
- **-v TOS**—Type of Service.
- **-r count**—Displays route for count hops.
- **-s count**—Displays a time stamp for each hop.
- **-j host-list**—Loose source route along host-list.
- **-k host-list**—Strict source route along host-list.
- **-w timeout**—Timeout value to wait for each reply (in milliseconds).

As you can see, the syntax can vary widely between implementations, as can the usefulness of PING as a diagnostic tool.

Following is an example of a simple use of the PING command:

```
F:\>ping 10.10.10.11

Pinging 10.10.10.11 with 32 bytes of data:
Reply from 10.10.10.11: bytes=32 time=10ms TTL=128
```

```
Reply from 10.10.10.11: bytes=32 time<10ms TTL=128
Reply from 10.10.10.11: bytes=32 time<10ms TTL=128
Reply from 10.10.10.11: bytes=32 time<10ms TTL=128
Ping statistics for 10.10.10.11:

Packets: Sent = 4, Received = 4, Lost = 0 (0% loss),
Approximate round trip times in milliseconds:
Minimum = 0ms, Maximum =  10ms, Average =  2ms
```

In this example, the computer is responding well. There is zero percent packet loss in the transmissions, and the reply time was 10 milliseconds or less. The size of the packet sent was 32 bytes.

Technical Note

The inability to PING a remote node is not a guarantee that the node is disconnected physically from the network. In other words, you cannot simply assume that a PING failure indicates a wiring problem. It might be that an intermediary device, such as a router or bridge, is malfunctioning. This is one of the reasons you need to keep a detailed map of your network: When you have to troubleshoot, you can check not just the end nodes, but also every device and cable along the path between them.

The *TRACEROUTE* Command

This diagnostic command is similar to PING in that it uses ICMP to try to locate each device through which a packet passes in order to reach its destination. This can provide useful information if you are not sure about the route being taken when you are trying to diagnose a sluggish response from PING. It can also help you find where along the network path the network is failing by showing each hop up until it fails.

TRACEROUTE—called tracert in the Windows NT version—does this by setting the TTL (time to live) value in the packet, hoping to receive an ICMP TIME_EXCEEDED message from each hop the data packet takes on its path. The TTL value is the allowable number of hops a packet can take before it is discarded. Thus, by increasing this value, starting with one and incrementing by one for each pass, TRACEROUTE can get the TIME_EXCEEDED message from each router or other device through which the packet must pass. For each attempt, three packets are sent.

The syntax for using TRACEROUTE in Windows NT is

```
tracert [-d] [-h maximum_hops] [-j host-list] [-w timeout]

        target_name
```

The options include

- **-d**—Do not resolve hostnames to addresses.
- **-h maximum_hops**—Maximum number of hops to search for target.
- **-j host-list**—Loose source route along host-list.
- **-w timeout**—Wait timeout milliseconds for each reply.

Following is the output from executing the Windows NT version of TRACEROUTE:

```
D:> tracert www.bellsouth.net
Tracing route to www.bellsouth.net [205.152.0.46]
over a maximum of 30 hops:
  1   231 ms   200 ms   220 ms   envlnjewsap02.bellatlantic.net. [192.168.125.189]
  2   261 ms   160 ms   160 ms   192.168.125.158
  3   180 ms   200 ms   181 ms   206.125.199.71
  4   181 ms   160 ms   180 ms   Hssi4-1-0.border2.teb1.IConNet.NET. [209.3.188.201]
  5   241 ms   180 ms   180 ms   POS10-0-0.core2.teb1.IConNet.NET. [204.245.71.221]
  6   180 ms   181 ms   280 ms   Hssi0-0-0.peer1.psk1.IConNet.NET. [204.245.69.174]
  7   180 ms   181 ms   180 ms   BR1.PSK1.Alter.net. [192.157.69.60]
  8   180 ms   181 ms   240 ms   Hssi0-1-0.hr1.nyc1.alter.net. [137.39.100.2]
  9   180 ms   181 ms   200 ms   101.ATM2-0.XR2.NYC1.ALTER.NET. [146.188.177.90]
 10   240 ms   181 ms   200 ms   194.ATM3-0.TR2.EWR1.ALTER.NET. [146.188.178.230]
 11   301 ms   200 ms   200 ms   105.ATM6-0.TR2.ATL1.ALTER.NET. [146.188.136.37]
 12   241 ms   220 ms   180 ms   198.ATM7-0.XR2.ATL1.ALTER.NET. [146.188.232.101]
 13   201 ms   200 ms   220 ms   194.ATM11-0-0.GW2.ATL1.ALTER.NET. [146.188.232.69]
 14   321 ms   200 ms   220 ms   bs2-atl-gw.customer.alter.net. [157.130.69.106]
 15   220 ms   220 ms   221 ms   205.152.2.178
 16   200 ms   281 ms   200 ms   205.152.3.74
 17   220 ms   220 ms   201 ms   www.bellsouth.net. [205.152.0.46]
Trace complete.
```

As you can see, you can gain a lot of information about how your network functions by using this command. There are three columns showing how long it took each of the three attempts to reach the particular node for that hop. An asterisk character that is displayed in any of these time columns indicates that the ICMP packet was not returned. The hostname and address are displayed by default. If the command fails at any point, you can start tracing the network fault at the last successful hop to determine where the fault lies.

Use *ipconfig* and *ifconfig* to Check Host Configurations

The ipconfig command is useful for checking the TCP/IP configuration of a Windows NT Server or Windows NT Workstation computer. A similar command on UNIX workstations is ifconfig. On Windows 95/98 systems, you can use the winipcfg command.

ipconfig for Windows NT

Using ipconfig with no parameters displays network configuration information about each adapter on the system, as well as for PPP connections. The basic information includes

- IP address
- Subnet Mask
- Default Gateway
- DNS Servers
- NT Domain

With the /all parameter, you can also obtain the hardware (MAC) address and DHCP information.

These commands can also be used to modify some of the configuration information:

- **ipconfig /release**—Releases an IP address that was configured via DHCP.
- **ipconfig /renew**—Renews an IP address that was configured via DHCP.
- **ipconfig /flushdns**—Purges the DNS resolver cache.
- **ipconfig /registerdns**—Refreshes all leases granted by DHCP for the adapter and re-registers DNS names.
- **ipconfig/displaydns**—Shows the contents of the DNS resolver cache.

Obviously, this command is extremely useful when you are trying to solve problems related to DNS and DHCP functions. The quantity of information you can show is useful when constructing a spreadsheet or other document for help desk use. One method that will help you keep up with current configuration information is placing the following command in a login script or startup file:

```
ipconfig /all > <network drive>%computername%.config
```

The %computername% environment variable will be replaced with the computer name that is assigned to the system, and a text file will be created. By placing the output file on a central network drive, you can have it available for use by administrative or help desk staff.

ifconfig *for UNIX*

On UNIX systems, ifconfig is a very powerful command. You can use it not only to display IP configuration information, but also to make changes to the configuration. The ifconfig command is used during the boot sequence to perform the initial configuration for network adapters that are attached to the system. After the system is up and running, only the superuser can use this command to change the configuration. For troubleshooting, it is a quick way to get the information you need to determine if the system was properly configured.

To simply display the current configuration information, you can execute the command with no parameters. For the superuser, the following commands can be used to modify the configuration:

- **ifconfig arp**—Enables the Address Resolution Protocol. Use ifconfig -arp to disable.
- **ifconfig dhcp (or ifconfig auto-dhcp)**—Use DHCP to acquire an address for the adapter.
- **ifconfig down**—Marks the interface as down, effectively shutting down network communications using this adapter.
- **ifconfig metric** value—Changes the routing metric for this interface.
- **ifconfig netmask** mask—Sets the subnet mask for this adapter.

The *NETSTAT* and *ROUTE* Commands

On UNIX systems, the netstat command is used to obtain statistics about the TCP/IP protocols. This command is most useful when you are trying to debug routing problems. netstat can also be found on Windows NT and Windows 95/98 computers.

```
netstat -r
```

will display the routing table that is maintained on the current host. For example, on Windows NT, you can also use the command ROUTE PRINT to display the routing table information. Following is an example of the routing table and an explanation of the data that is shown:

```
netstat -r
Route Table
Active Routes:
Network Address          Netmask          Gateway         Interface     Metric
        0.0.0.0          0.0.0.0     151.204.200.25   151.204.200.25        1
       10.10.0.0      255.255.0.0      10.10.10.10      10.10.10.10        1
     10.10.10.10  255.255.255.255        127.0.0.1        127.0.0.1        1
   10.255.255.255  255.255.255.255      10.10.10.10      10.10.10.10        1
        127.0.0.0        255.0.0.0        127.0.0.1        127.0.0.1        1
   151.204.200.25  255.255.255.255        127.0.0.1        127.0.0.1        1
   151.204.200.25  255.255.255.255   151.204.200.25   151.204.200.25        1
   151.204.255.255  255.255.255.255   151.204.200.25   151.204.200.25        1
        224.0.0.0        224.0.0.0      10.10.10.10      10.10.10.10        1
        224.0.0.0        224.0.0.0   151.204.200.25   151.204.200.25        1
   255.255.255.255  255.255.255.255      10.10.10.10      10.10.10.10        1
```

Each line in this display starts with a destination address. When deciding where to send a packet, this table is consulted to see if one of these destination addresses matches the destination address of the packet in question. In the first line, the address of 0.0.0.0 might not seem to make sense. This is the entry, or the *default gateway*. That is, if a packet cannot be routed to its destination using any of the remaining entries in the route table, it will be sent to this address.

The second column shows the netmask for this route entry. Like a subnet mask, this mask is used to mask out portions of the destination address when a routing decision is to be made. The netmask is converted to binary. When deciding if a packet matches the destination address, the portions of the destination address that are in the same position as a 1 must match the packet's destination address exactly. A netmask of 255.255.255.255 is a string of 32 ones in binary. This is used for a host address, and the packet must match the address exactly to be routed by this entry.

The next column shows the gateway. Packets that match this entry will be sent to this address. The next column—Interface—is the address of the network card or PPP adapter that the packet will be sent through. The last column—Metric—shows the number of hops the packet will take to reach its final destination.

The syntax for the netstat command varies depending on which UNIX implementation you are using.

Other uses for the netstat command include showing the current state of TCP/IP ports and sockets (netstat -a) or showing the ARP table (use netstat -p on UNIX or the arp command on Windows NT).

To see statistics about the specific protocols—UDP, ICMP, TCP, or IP—use the `netstat -s` command. This is especially helpful when you are trying to diagnose connectivity problems that are intermittent or might be due to network congestion. The output is quite lengthy, so you might want to pipe the results to a text file (`netstat -s > stats.txt`). Following is an example of the data you can obtain by using the `-s` option with this command:

```
netstat -s
IP Statistics
  Packets Received                      = 19942
  Received Header Errors                = 0
  Received Address Errors               = 2
  Datagrams Forwarded                   = 0
  Unknown Protocols Received            = 0
  Received Packets Discarded            = 0
  Received Packets Delivered            = 19942
  Output Requests                       = 19682
  Routing Discards                      = 0
  Discarded Output Packets              = 0
  Output Packet No Route                = 0
  Reassembly Required                   = 0
  Reassembly Successful                 = 0
  Reassembly Failures                   = 0
  Datagrams Successfully Fragmented     = 0
  Datagrams Failing Fragmentation       = 0
  Fragments Created                     = 0

ICMP Statistics
                           Received     Sent
  Messages                 341          257
  Errors                   0            0
  Destination Unreachable  30           16
  Time Exceeded            142          0
  Parameter Problems       0            0
  Source Quenches          0            0
  Redirects                91           0
  Echos                    34           189
  Echo Replies             44           34
  Time stamps              0            0
  Time stamp Replies       0            0
  Address Masks            0            0
  Address Mask Replies     0            0
TCP Statistics
  Active Opens                          = 454
  Passive Opens                         = 0
  Failed Connection Attempts            = 4
  Reset Connections                     = 33
  Current Connections                   = 0
  Segments Received                     = 6399
  Segments Sent                         = 6359
  Segments Retransmitted                = 14

UDP Statistics
  Datagrams Received       = 13184
  No Ports                 = 325
  Receive Errors           = 0
  Datagrams Sent           = 13048
```

The `route` command is used to make modifications to the routing table. You can use it to add routes, to delete routes for individual hosts or networks, or to modify the default route or gateway. In Chapter 5, the `route` command is covered in more detail, along with the more popular routing protocols in use on the Internet today.

The *arp* Command

IP addresses and hostnames are used for the convenience of humans so we can configure and manage a network in an orderly manner. At the lowest level, however, it is the hardware MAC address that network cards use when they talk to each other. Remember that a computer finds out the hardware address of another computer on the local segment by using the Address Resolution Protocol (ARP). Just as a host computer keeps a table of routing information, it also keeps a table of MAC-to-IP address translations known as the *arp table*.

The arp command enables you to view the arp table and to add or delete entries within it. Again, the syntax varies between different systems, but the following should work for most:

- `arp -a`—Displays the current contents of the arp table.
- `arp -d` IP_address—Deletes the entry for the specified host.
- `arp -s IP_address ether_address`—*Adds an entry to the table.*

For example, to add an entry, you use the following syntax:

```
arp -s 192.123.111.2    08-00-2b-34-c1-01
```

The *tcpdump* Utility

If you are extremely knowledgeable about TCP/IP and are capable of understanding the bits and bytes of IP frames, you can use the `tcpdump` utility to capture header information from packets as they pass through the network. Because there can be a potential security problem with being able to view this information, it is not a utility that the ordinary UNIX user can use. It is generally restricted to the root user or must be installed with setuid to root.

There are many command-line parameters associated with this utility, and you can create complex expressions that are used to evaluate which packets to intercept. You cannot supply selection criteria, and all packets will be dumped.

Some of the command options for `tcpdump` are

- `-a`—Try to convert network and broadcast addresses to names.
- `-c count`—Exit after receiving *count* number of packets.
- `-e`—Display the link level header information on each line (the Ethernet header information).
- `-f file`—Use the text found in file for the selection expression. If you use this option, any expression given on the command line is ignored.
- `-i interface`—Specifies the interface to monitor. If you do not specify this, `tcpdump` will select the lowest numbered configured interface, excluding `loopback`.

- **-n**—Don't convert host addresses, port numbers, and so on to names.
- **-N**—Don't display domain name qualification of names.
- **-q**—Limit the amount of information displayed for a briefer listing.
- **-t**—Don't print time stamp on each line.
- **-v or -vv**—Give additional information from each packet. Both of these cause the output to be more verbose.

The selection expression criteria can be quite complex, and you should consult the man pages for your UNIX system to get the full listing and examples. A few simple uses follow:

```
tcpdump host hercules
```

This shows packets that are going to or coming from the system named hercules.

```
tcpdump ip host venus and not hercules
```

This shows packets going to or coming from the system named venus, unless they are coming from or going to hercules. The output displayed by this command depends on the protocol of the packet that is intercepted.

Other Useful Commands

The TCP/IP suite consists of several protocols and utilities that have been developed over the years. Other commands can be useful for troubleshooting. For example, the `telnet` command is used to establish a remote terminal session on another computer. If you are having trouble with a workstation, you can always `telnet` to it and perform diagnostic functions directly. This is very convenient when the network is dispersed geographically. The `ftp` command can be used to move files to and from a remote system. This can be useful to retrieve the output of a diagnostic command, a log file, or perhaps a configuration file, so that you can examine or edit it locally.

The `nslookup` command is used with the Domain Name System (DNS). This command and its use are covered in Chapter 21, along with other tools you can use for the various name resolution solutions that exist today.

Summary

TCP/IP is the most widely used networking protocol suite in the world today, implemented on almost every major operating system from PCs to mainframes. Understanding the underlying protocols and utilities will greatly assist the network manager in diagnosing and repairing network problems.

There are many standard utilities that are part of the TCP/IP suite, including `ping`, `netstat`, and `tracert` (to name a few). Becoming proficient in the use of these tools will make your job a lot easier. Understanding the ins and outs of IP addresses, including the task of subnetting a network address space, is not as difficult as it might seem at first pass.

IPX/SPX

SOME OF THE MAIN TOPICS IN THIS CHAPTER ARE

IPX

SPX

NCP (NetWare Core Protocol)

CHAPTER 19

The IPX/SPX protocol suite was designed by Novell for use with NetWare networks. This protocol stack was based on the Xerox XNS protocols and was the basis of client/server communication in Novell networks until Novell decided to adopt TCP/IP. Microsoft has also developed a similar protocol suite called NWLink, which behaves exactly like Novell's IPX/SPX suite but with a different name to avoid trademark conflicts. In this chapter, we quickly examine the IPX/SPX protocols. An understanding of the underlying protocols will enable you to make better decisions expanding or modifying an existing network, or when you find yourself troubleshooting network connectivity problems.

IPX

IPX is short for *Internetworking Packet Exchange*. It is a routable, connectionless-oriented protocol that runs at the Network Layer of the OSI reference model (see Figure 19.1), similar to the Internet Protocol (IP) of the TCP/IP stack. Because it is a connectionless protocol, IPX packets are not acknowledged by their destination workstations. If a packet is lost, the application that is sending or receiving the packet is responsible for recognizing the situation and requesting a duplicate packet to make up for the lost packet. IPX is also responsible for the addressing scheme of this protocol suite. With TCP/IP, addresses are manually or dynamically assigned to workstations and other devices on the network. With IPX, addresses are always dynamically assigned; workstation address configuration is not required.

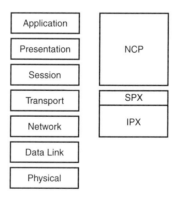

Figure 19.1 IPX/SPX protocol suite compared to the OSI reference model.

IPX uses the node's hard-coded network interface board number (the Media Access Control, or MAC address) along with a network number and a socket number. This scheme ensures uniqueness among the stations on the network.

Note

Connectionless means that when a node on a network uses IPX to communicate with a server or another node on the network, a connection or "handshake" is never established. So, when IPX packets are addressed and sent to their destinations, a verification or acknowledgement packet is never sent back to the sending node. Each packet is independent of each other as far as the protocol is concerned. It is up to higher level protocols or applications that use a connectionless protocol to make provisions for detecting errors in transmission.

IPX creates its own internetwork addressing scheme by utilizing the unique physical address of the network interface card (MAC address) along with a unique network segment number and a socket number to identify each device on the network. A complete IPX network address is a 12-byte hexadecimal number that consists of the following parts:

- A 4-byte network number
- A 6-byte node number (MAC address)
- A 2-byte socket number or process ID

An example of an IPX network address is 8CB064 0090276DC341 1859. This number can be found in the IPX packet header and defines the destination network, node, and socket. The *network number* defines the address of the network on which the node it wants to talk to is located. If the node is on the same segment as the node sending the packet, the node name is used. The *socket number*, sometimes referred to as the process number, is the process ID on the destination node that it is using to process the information contained in the packet.

Network Number

The 4-byte hexadecimal network number's sole purpose is for routing. A network segment on an internetwork is assigned a unique network number to bridge separate networks together. One physical network with 100 nodes on it might be assigned number 8CB064 and another might be assigned number 8CB034. The network router that connects these two networks uses these numbers to route packets between them.

A network number can be assigned freely with some limitations. A network number can contain up to eight digits, including zeros. The numbers 0 and 0xFFFFFFFF cannot be used; they are reserved by IPX to serve special purposes.

Note

Leading zeros are not normally displayed when showing an IPX address.

Node Number

The *node number* is a 6-byte hexadecimal number that identifies the device or node on an IPX network. The node can be a workstation, printer, router, or server. The node number is identical to the MAC address assigned to the network interface card embedded by the manufacturer of the card.

The node number must be unique within the network number segment. This should never be a problem when using MAC addresses because every network interface card manufactured should have a unique physical address assigned to it by the manufacturer. If your network is using LAA (Locally Assigned Address) node numbers, usually used only on token-ring networks, the possibility of duplicate node numbers is much greater.

Socket Number

The 2-byte socket number identifies the ultimate destination of an IPX packet within the node. The destination is normally the process that operates on the node. A process can be a routing process, a printing process, or any other process that is executing on the destination node. Because there is normally more than one process executing at any given time and using a network connection, a socket number provides a way of distinguishing which process the packet is for. Although each connection between any two devices on the network will use the same address for the destination computer, the sessions can be distinguished from one another by use of a socket number to identify a unique process on a computer.

The IPX Header

An IPX header will always be 30 bytes, and the very beginning of every IPX header will begin with a hexadecimal value of 0xFFFF. IPX headers follow the MAC frame but come before the actual data in the packet. In Figure 19.2 you can see the layout of an IPX header. A breakdown of each field and its function follows:

- **Checksum**—In most cases, the Checksum field is not used; the 2-byte value of xFFFF is used in the field. A checksum is already done on the packet and frame so Novell opted not to use the Checksum field in the IPX header. However, it is possible to turn on the checksum, though it is not advisable. Turning on the Checksum field decreases network performance because both the sending and receiving nodes must process the packet for accuracy.

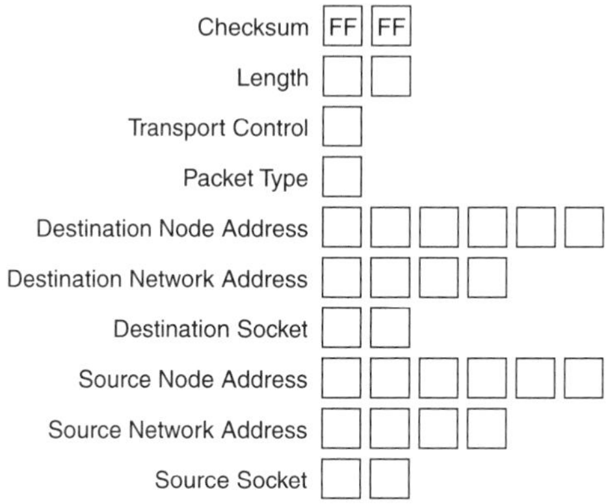

Figure 19.2 An IPX header format showing each field and its length.

- **Length**—The Length field has a value equal to the entire size of the packet, including the IPX header. The Length value does not include the size of the ethernet frame length.

- **Transport Control**—IPX routers on the network use this field to indicate how many routers the IPX packet has crossed (the number of hops). The station or node sending the packet sets the field to zero. As IPX packets are routed, each router increments the field by one. After the field has reached 16, the packet is discarded. Thus, an IPX packet can go through only 15 routers.

- **Packet Type**—The Packet Type field should consist of one of the following: 0, 4, 5, or 17. The number in the field represents which type of service the packet is using. 0 or 4 is IPX-based communication, 5 is SPX-based communications, and 17 is NCP communications.

- **Destination Network**—The 4-byte network number discussed earlier is placed in this field. If you analyze the network wire (using a LAN Analyzer or a "sniffer," for example) and come across packets that have 0x-00-00-00-00, the network the packet is destined for is the same network or segment of the node that is sending the packet. The router does not route the packets that have a null address in the Destination Network field. If the packet is destined to a NetWare 3.x or 4.x server on another segment of your internetwork, the unique 4-byte network number of the segment is placed in the field.

- **Destination Node**—The Destination Node field is the 6-byte network number also mentioned earlier. If the packet is destined for a NetWare server, the field will contain 0x-00-00-00-00-00-01. The address of the server is contained in the ethernet frame header and will route appropriately. If the packet is meant to be broadcast throughout the segment or internetwork, the value of 0XFF-FF-FF-FF-FF-FF will be in the Destination Node field.

- **Destination Socket**—The 2-byte socket number that the node's process is using is placed in this field.

- **Source Network**—The sending node's network number is contained in this field.

- **Source Node**—The Source Node field contains the 6-byte node address of the node sending the packet.

SPX

SPX (Sequenced Packet Exchange) protocol is a routable, connection-oriented protocol that runs at the Transport Layer of the OSI reference model. SPX is similar to the Transport Control Protocol (TCP) of the TCP/IP stack. SPX verifies delivery on all packets sent to the network. Whereas TCP uses IP for delivery of its packets, SPX uses IPX in a similar manner. IPX provides addressing functions for the protocol stack while SPX provides the capability to maintain sessions and reliably transfer information.

Note

Networks using SPX-based communications are limited to a 574-byte maximum packet size. With SPX's header size being 42 bytes, that leaves only 534 bytes for the data. Because today's ethernet and token-ring technology can support larger sizes, you should consider using SPX II on your Novell network. Novell introduced SPX II in March 1992 with much fanfare from the SPX developers. SPX II can effectively transmit and receive 1,518 bytes of data in a single packet, thus providing a very efficient data exchange.

The SPX Header

The SPX header (see Figure 19.3) is 42 bytes in length and includes the 30-byte header of IPX. The 12 extra bytes that SPX tacks on is for the sequencing and acknowledgement of each packet. Although SPX packets are ensured guaranteed delivery, this protocol is slower because of the overhead of flow control, sequencing, and packet acknowledgement. It's not the extra 12 bytes that slows SPX down, it's the acknowledgement, or "SPX handshake," which puts more packets on the wire than when using just IPX. IPX does its best to send its packets to ensure delivery but does not require packets to be acknowledged and sends packets in any order. Typical uses of the SPX protocol are for applications such as Novell's RCONSOLE (Remote Console) and Novell's PSERVER (Print Server).

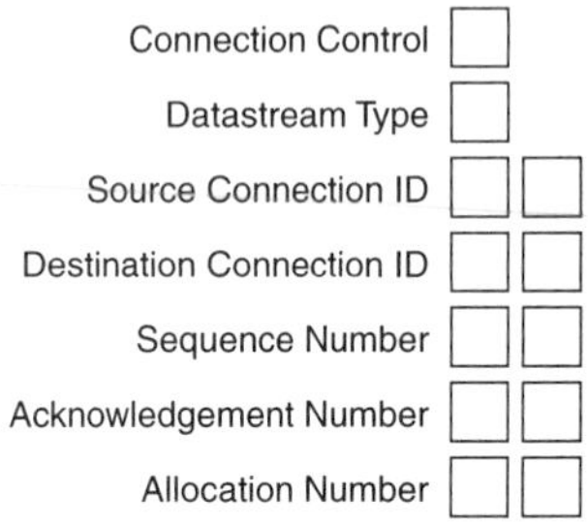

Figure 19.3   An SPX header format showing each field and its length.

The IPX header length field that is included in the SPX header includes the entire 42-byte SPX header information and the data in the packet. The fields that make up the SPX header include

- **Connection Control**—The 1-byte value in the Connection Control field is for bidirectional flow control of the packet. For example, a value of 0×10 signals the destination node that the sending node wants to end the communication session. A value of 0×40 tells the destination node that an acknowledgement is required by the sending node.

- **Datastream Type**—The Datastream field is 1 byte and indicates the type of data that is sent with the packet. Generally, the value is defined by the client but can contain a request from the sending node to end the connection by placing the value of 0×FE. To acknowledge the receipt of this request, the receiver sends a value of 0×FF.

- **Source Connection ID**—More than one node on the network can use the same socket; the field value is the virtual connection number of the socket. The value is also contained in the Destination Connection ID field after it is assigned by the node with the process being used.

- **Destination Connection ID**—The 2-byte entry in the Destination Connection ID field is the session (connection) ID number of the node to which the original node is sending packets. The value is set to 0xFFFF because the source node does not know the destination's connection ID yet.

- **Sequence Number**—The Sequence Number field indicates the number of packets transmitted from a node on the network. The value increments when the sending node receives an acknowledgement packet from the destination node. The value does not increment when it sends an acknowledgement packet.

- **Acknowledgement Number**—During normal network traffic, data packets that travel across the network can be lost because of collisions or overloaded buffers. The acknowledgement number is the packet sequence number that ensures the delivery of the packet. When the destination node receives an SPX packet, it checks the Acknowledgement field for the expected sequence number. When it does not get the sequence number it expects, the Acknowledgement field assumes that the packet has been lost or an error has occurred.

- **Allocation Number**—The Allocation Number field contains the value of the receive buffer at the node. The higher the buffer, the more data packets the receiving station can hold before the workstation processes the data in the packet. The Allocation Number decreases if the processing workstation is too busy processing data. The lower the allocation number, the busier the workstation is.

NCP (NetWare Core Protocol)

This chapter would not be complete without mentioning NCP. Other than SAP broadcasts, NCP is the most common packet you'll find in a NetWare environment. NCP is NetWare's principal protocol for transmitting data between NetWare servers and workstations with NetWare's client software installed. NCP is responsible for logon authentication requests and many other types of requests to the file servers and print servers, and IPX is the underlying protocol that carries these data transmissions.

▶▶ For a more in-depth discussion of NCP see Chapter 25, "File-Server Protocols."

Summary

The native protocol suite for use with NetWare is IPX/SPX. However, with NetWare v5.x, the TCP/IP suite is the preferred protocol. IPX/SPX is much easier to install and administer overall but does have a bit more overhead. IPX is a self-addressing and connectionless-oriented network protocol. IPX uses network interface hardware addresses and assigned network addresses to create a unique node addressing scheme. SPX, the sister protocol of IPX, is a connection-oriented protocol that maintains the communication session of two communicating nodes on the network. IPX sends packets over the wire without any acknowledgement from the destination node. It is the responsibility of the destination node to check for corrupted or lost packets and request a retransmission. SPX creates a communication session between two nodes and ensures delivery of all packets.

In the next chapter, we look at another early entry into LAN protocols: NetBIOS and NetBEUI.

NetBIOS and NetBEUI

CHAPTER 20

Perhaps one of the most often confused collection of network protocols that were developed mainly for use in PC networks are those that are referred to—usually interchangeably—as NetBIOS and NetBEUI. Then there is NetBIOS over TCP/IP, or NetBT, and NetBIOS over IPX, developed for Novell networks. The common factor in all these protocols is the NetBIOS interface.

An interface is not a network transfer protocol. It is a method of accessing underlying software and hardware mechanisms from a higher level, for example at the application programming level. The NetBIOS interface was originally developed for IBM as an *Application Programming Interface (API)* for use in networking PCs. If you extend the name *NetBIOS* into its original full-length name, you get *Network Basic I/O System.* Just as the BIOS (basic input/output system) you find on your computer motherboard is a collection of software routines that make writing code easier for operating system and application developers, NetBIOS makes it easier to write applications that require network communications. By making use of an API, the programmer doesn't have to get down to the bits and bytes of the underlying hardware or network protocols.

This chapter explains the NetBIOS interface and then looks at the other protocols that were developed to work with or extend NetBIOS. Although the TCP/IP protocol dominates the Internet today, NetBIOS and its related protocols played an important part in computer networking and are still widely used.

A Brief Historical Look at NetBIOS

NetBIOS was originally developed for IBM in 1983 by Sytec, Inc. It was designed for use in small departmental LANs of about 20–200 computers and provided peer-to-peer networking capabilities. It was first employed on IBM's PC Network. At that time, the PC revolution had barely begun and in the business world this was a generous estimate for a large network. Larger networks could be built using gateways or other devices to join these smaller LANs.

In 1985 the *NetBIOS Extended User Interface (NetBEUI)* was released. This allowed more functionality for networking with NetBIOS. NetBEUI, which was used extensively by Microsoft, made a clearer distinction between the protocol functionality and the programming interface. This was in line with trends in the computer networking industry toward standards, in particular the OSI seven-layer reference model. Rather than lumping all network functions together into one large definition, modularizing specific functions into components that provide services to layers that are above and below allows for the easy replacement of layers that use different methods to accomplish that functionality.

Novell released its Advanced NetWare 2.0 in 1986 with a NetBIOS emulator. This enabled programmers to write applications that used NetBIOS calls, yet the underlying transport mechanisms were Novell's own IPX and SPX protocols. Subsequent versions of NetWare have continued to provide a NetBIOS interface, even with NetWare 5, which uses TCP/IP as its core network transport rather than the company's own protocols.

When token-ring networks were developed by IBM, an emulator for NetBIOS was created. NetBIOS could now be used on both Ethernet and token-ring networks. The underlying transport, again, is not really relevant. Providing a common programming interface to top-level applications enabled PC networking to grow faster than it had when proprietary solutions were employed by each vendor.

There have been many other implementations of PC networking software that made use of the NetBIOS interface. Pathworks (Digital Equipment Corporation) was an implementation of a LAN Manager 2.x network running on Digital's DECnet networks. Furthermore, Microsoft has used NetBEUI in LAN Manager since 1987, and it has been integral to networking in Windows for Workgroups and Windows NT to version 4.0. Although Windows 2000 includes support for NetBEUI, it is no longer required, and is not the preferred network protocol.

RFC 1001, "Protocol Standard for a NetBIOS Service On a TCP/UDP Transport: Concepts and Methods," was finished in 1987 and delineates a method of using NetBIOS as an interface with TCP/IP as the network transport. Another, RFC 1002, details the specifics for this proposal, including descriptions of the contents of packets, the format of names, and pseudo code that shows different mechanisms that can be used to resolve names in this environment.

There have been many other networking products that made use of NetBIOS and NetBEUI. Because the specifications were not exacting—as they are in other established network protocols, such as TCP/IP—many LAN products were released from various vendors that could not interoperate. Still, until the Internet became a dominate force in both LANs and WANs, NetBIOS and NetBEUI were used by almost every major PC network product.

The important point to gather from this historical perspective is that NetBIOS was the first widely-adopted attempt at a networking standard, even though it might not have been as "clean" as the standards that are being developed and used today. The advantages that came from using NetBIOS and NetBEUI helped formulate a desire for network components that could work together instead of the proprietary traps that major computer vendors used before PCs came along.

NetBIOS Names

Most network protocols require a network address—usually a numeric value—to identify the different computers and processes that run on them. For example, in the TCP/IP protocol suite, IP addresses are used to identify computers and other devices, and ports are used to address specific applications or processes on those computers. NetBIOS, however, is used to establish a logical communication path based on names.

NetBIOS names can be classified into two categories: *unique names* and *groupnames*. A unique name can be used by only one workstation in the local broadcast network, whereas groupnames can be shared by many computers. A NetBIOS name is 16 bytes in length, and if a shorter name is used, it is padded so that it is 16 bytes long. In some implementations, the 16th byte is given a special meaning. Unlike DNS names, NetBIOS names can be made up of almost any type of character, but cannot start with the asterisk character (*).

Each computer that participates in the network has a unique name that identifies it. A computer can hold more than one unique name. In order for a computer to lay claim to its name, it must broadcast that desire to the rest of the network and wait to see if another participant challenges it.

The Sixteenth Character

Although NetBIOS names can be 16 characters in length, in many cases (as with Microsoft and IBM products) they are limited to 15 actual characters. The first 15 characters can be anything the administrator wants to use, but the sixteenth character is used to differentiate between different types of names. This character is often called the NetBIOS suffix, and it qualifies the function of the resource represented by the name. In Table 20.1 is a listing of most of the NetBIOS name types employed by Microsoft. Note that the last character in the name does not have to be in the range of printable ASCII characters. For this reason, the hexadecimal value is shown instead. In the Type column, the letter *U* indicates that the name is a unique name, and *G* indicates that the name is a groupname that can be registered by multiple computers.

Table 20.1   NetBIOS Names

NetBIOS Name	Type	Suffix	Description
<computername>	U	00	Workstation Service
<computername>	U	01	Messenger Service
<\\-_MSBROWSE_>	G	01	Master Browser
<computername>	U	03	Messenger Service
<computername>	U	06	RAS Server Service
<computername>	U	1F	NetDDE Service
<computername>	U	20	File Server Service
<computername>	U	21	RAS Client Service
<computername>	U	22	Microsoft Exchange Interchange
<computername>	U	23	Microsoft Exchange Store
<computername>	U	24	Microsoft Exchange Directory
<computername>	U	30	Modem Sharing Server Service
<computername>	U	31	Modem Sharing Client Service
<computername>	U	43	SMS Clients Remote Control
<computername>	U	44	SMS Administrators Remote Control Tool
<computername>	U	45	SMS Clients Remote Chat
<computername>	U	46	SMS Clients Remote Transfer
<computername>	U	4C	DEC Pathworks TCPIP Service on Windows NT
<computername>	U	52	DEC Pathworks TCPIP Service on Windows NT
<computername>	U	87	Microsoft Exchange MTA
<computername>	U	6A	Microsoft Exchange IMC
<computername>	U	BE	Network Monitor Agent
<computername>	U	BF	Network Monitor Application
<username>	U	03	Messenger Service
<domain>	U	00	Domain Name
<domain>	U	1B	Domain Master Browser
<domain>	U	1C	Domain Controllers
<domain>	U	1D	Master Browser
<domain>	U	1E	Browser Service Elections

NetBIOS Name	Type	Suffix	Description
<Inet~Services>	U	1C	IIS
<IS~computername>	U	00	IIS

NetBIOS Scope ID

When using NetBIOS over TCP/IP, the NetBIOS Scope identifier can be used within a WAN to uniquely identify groups of computers. This identifier is composed of a string of characters that conform to the rules used to construct DNS names. By using a scope identifier, it is possible to use the same unique NetBIOS name on a network more than once (which is strongly discouraged). The different systems that use the same unique name are differentiated by the scope ID.

For example, the NetBIOS name popeye can be used to uniquely identify a computer on a LAN in the accounting department in the San Francisco office. The same name can also be used to identify a computer in the New York office. Each is qualified by its scope ID, so the names popeye.sf.achme.com will not be confused with popeye.ny.acme.com.

However, use the NetBIOS Scope ID with reservation because workstations that have a scope ID can only communicate with other nodes that have the same scope ID. This feature is useful for providing the capability to allow users to communicate only with machines within a specific group.

Node Types

RFC 1001 defined three end-node types, based on the method used to register and resolve NetBIOS names: b-node, p-node, and m-node. An additional h-node has been formalized and is used in Microsoft's Windows networks. Deciding which node type is implemented depends on your network configuration and number of computers.

B-Node (Broadcast)

This type of node uses broadcasts on the local network to register and resolve names. This mode of operation has two major drawbacks. First, in anything but a very small network, a lot of bandwidth can be taken up by broadcast messages. Second, most routers do not forward broadcast messages by default. Even if you have a router that can be configured to forward broadcast messages, you probably don't want to do so except in a special case where nothing else can be done. You will end up loading multiple network segments with broadcast messages.

This type of node might work well in a very small network, such as a home network. In such a situation, where the volume of network traffic is quite low, broadcast messages are an insignificant matter. In any other type of networking environment, where there are a large number of computers and network bandwidth is a commodity to be monitored and used wisely, setting up a computer to operate as a b-node is unacceptable.

P-Node (Point-to-Point)

A p-node communicates with a *NetBIOS Name Service* (NBNS) to register and resolve names. RFCs 1001 and 1002 describe the functions performed by an NBNS. Microsoft's implementation of the name server is called WINS, for Windows Internet Name Server. WINS operates much like a DNS server, except that it maps NetBIOS names to IP addresses, whereas DNS maps TCP/IP names to IP addresses. WINS also differs from DNS in that it is a dynamic database. Nodes register unique names and groupnames when they boot up by sending directed datagrams to the WINS server. Dynamic name registration techniques for DNS servers are described in quite a few RFCs, but are not widely implemented at this time.

The main advantages that the p-node has over the broadcast method are obvious: No broadcast messages propagate through the network, and by using the IP address or point-to-point communication with a name server, this type of node can talk with a name server on the other side of a router. Thus, it reduces network traffic and scales better for a larger network.

There are drawbacks, however. You must configure each client computer to know the address of the name server because this is the computer it needs to contact both to register its own names and to resolve other names. If the name server is down, the client computers cannot register any new names or resolve names for nodes with which they want to communicate.

Microsoft has addressed both of these issues in Windows NT networks by adopting DHCP so that client nodes can be configured automatically when they boot, and by allowing for multiple WINS servers to replicate data so that if one goes down the others can fill the void.

M-Node (Mixed: Broadcast and Point-to-Point)

The m-node was designed to address the problems inherent to both the b-node and p-node methods. A computer configured as an m-node first attempts to use broadcast messages to register or resolve NetBIOS names. If that fails, it resorts to point-to-point communication with a name server. The advantage this has over the previous nodes is that if the name server is down, computers within the same broadcast domain can still communicate to resolve names among themselves. Resolving names for computers or resources in other subnetworks, however, is hampered until the name server returns to service.

H-Node (Hybrid)

The h-node was not included in the RFC 1001 specification, but has been adopted by Microsoft in its Windows operating systems. This node is basically the opposite of the m-node. It first tries point-to-point communications with a name server and, if that fails, it operates as a b-node and attempts name registration and resolution using broadcast methods.

The advantage this node type has over the p-node is the same advantage that the m-node has: It can continue to register and resolve names in the local broadcast domain if communication with the name server fails. The advantage this type has over the m-node, however, is that it limits the use of broadcast messages. As long as the name server is available and can answer the queries the client submits, broadcast messages do not consume network bandwidth.

Another advantage the h-node has over the other three types is that it can be configured to consult the lmhosts (LAN Manager Hosts) file. This file is similar to the hosts file used by TCP/IP clients to translate TCP/IP hostnames to IP addresses. The lmhosts file, however, is used to translate NetBIOS names to IP addresses.

Technical Note

It is important to understand the differences between b-nodes and p-nodes. Because one uses only a broadcast method to register and resolve names and the other uses only a name server, these two node types cannot interact with each other in the name resolution process. There is no common point of reference between the two. It is possible for m-nodes and h-nodes to interact with nodes that use only broadcast methods.

The NetBIOS Namespace

Unlike the TCP/IP namespace, the NetBIOS namespace is flat, with no hierarchical organization. *Flat* means that employing a name is not much different from using the MAC address. There is nothing in the MAC address or a NetBIOS name that enables the administrator to organize networked computers and resources into a meaningful structure. TCP/IP names represent a hierarchical structure. Computer names are qualified by the domain or subdomain in which they exist. For example, bob.ny.acme.com is immediately identified as a unique computer that is in the subdomain ny that is part of the acme.com domain. The same Acme company can have many different locations and can address computers or resources in each location by the subdomain in which they reside.

The use of scope identifiers seems to overcome this problem with NetBIOS names. However, this is not part of the original NetBIOS implementation; instead, it uses the organization inherent in TCP/IP and the domain name system. It is generally not recommended to use scope IDs unless absolutely necessary. One reason would be if you are upgrading a large network with many duplicate names and cannot adopt unique names at this time. The main drawback to the scope ID is that the computers can communicate only with other computers within their own scope. If your network requires the computers with duplicate names to communicate with each other, new unique names will need to be assigned.

Representing NetBIOS Names in the Domain Name System

Because NetBIOS names can consist of characters that are not used in the *Domain Name System* (*DNS*), a method needs to be used to construct a name that is acceptable to DNS when using NetBIOS with an underlying TCP/IP transport mechanism. RFC 1001 defines such a method, which takes the 16-character name and transforms it into a 32-character name that consists of all uppercase ASCII characters. This process is termed *reversible, half-ASCII, biased encoding*. After the name has undergone this first-level encoding, it is subject to the same compression techniques used by DNS as described in RFC 883.

To perform first-level encoding, each byte of the NetBIOS name is split into two 4-bit values. Each of these 4-bit values are right-filled with zeros to produce a full byte. The hexadecimal representation of the ASCII value for the uppercase letter *A* is then added to each of these new bytes to produce the final value. This produces an uppercase ASCII character in the range of A–P, all of which are valid characters in a DNS name.

For example, the space character (ASCII value 32 decimal, 20 hexadecimal) is not valid in a DNS name. The binary representation of this ASCII value is "100000". This value is split into two half-bytes (sometimes called *nibbles*) of "0010" and "0000". These nibbles are reconstructed into two separate bytes by right-filling them with zeros. The resulting bytes are "00000010" and "00000000".

Finally, add 41 (hexadecimal) to each of these bytes to get the final byte value for each of these characters:

"00000010" + "01000001" = "01000011" or 43 hexadecimal

"00000000" + "01000001" = "00000001" or 41 hexadecimal

The ASCII character representation of a byte that has a hexadecimal value of 43 is C. The ASCII character represented by the hexadecimal value 41, of course, is A. Thus, the space character of a NetBIOS name is represented as CA when it is transformed into the 32-byte DNS-compatible string.

Before the NetBIOS name can be stored in a DNS database, however, it must have its scope ID appended to it to form a valid DNS fully-qualified name. For example, if the NetBIOS name is The NetBIOS name, and the scope ID is ACME.COM, the fully-qualified DNS name, after encoding, is FEEIEFCAEOEFFEECEJEPFDCAEOEBENEF.ACME.COM. It might not make a lot of sense when you look at it, but this encoding method does get around the limitations imposed by DNS name rules, allowing DNS servers to be used to resolve NetBIOS names.

NetBIOS Services

NetBIOS provides services to the programmer. The name services have already been discussed. But if all NetBIOS provided was the capability to register and resolve a name on the network, it would not be of much use. The functionality that is missing is communications. NetBIOS (and NetBEUI and other implementations of NetBIOS) provide communications services between NetBIOS names, which can be of three basic types:

- **Datagram**—This is an unreliable connectionless service. A datagram can be sent to a unique name or a groupname. Each datagram is considered independent of others. Because there is no ongoing exchange of data in a logical sequence between computers, it is considered to be "connectionless." Because there is no acknowledgement, the sending computer does not know if the message is ever received (hence, it is unreliable). The datagram method is the fastest method of sending information by NetBIOS. The size of the message is limited to 512 bytes in most implementations.

- **Broadcast**—Similar to the datagram service, the broadcast service also provides an unreliable connectionless service. The main difference is that the broadcast message can be picked up by all computers in the broadcast domain and is not limited to a specific unique or groupname.

- **Session**—The session service provides a connection-oriented service in full duplex mode. A session ID is used to identify the session, and communications can flow in both directions. Because NetBIOS was intended for small networks, there are no provisions for flow control. Messages using the session service can be up to 64KB in length.

For any of these services to work, both nodes must cooperate. That is, when an application wants to send data, it issues a send or call command. Computers that want to receive these messages must have outstanding receive commands in order to process any incoming messages.

Locating Network Resources: Browsing

When a Windows client uses the Network Neighborhood icon on the desktop to view the resources available on the network, the display that is shown is constructed from a list of servers that make up the *browse list*. You can also use the NET VIEW command from the MS-DOS command prompt to display this list.

Microsoft networks use a method called browsing to enumerate (list) resources on the network and make a list available to clients that need to locate these resources. The browser was first created for use in Windows For Workgroups, but has continued on in other Microsoft products including LAN Manager and the Windows 95, Windows 98, and Windows NT operating systems.

Computers that can offer services to the network use NetBIOS names to announce themselves. The computer does not have to be a Windows NT Server computer to offer services. For example, a Windows 95 or Windows 98 computer will announce the file and print services it can offer if you allow it to do so when you are configuring its network properties. When the computer boots, it sends a *server announcement* to the master browser or the domain master browser.

The browser system has three main components that can be summarized as follows:

- **Master Browsers**—The computer that is the master browser is responsible for compiling the master browse list, which contains a list of servers, workgroups, and domains. The master browser is an elected position, though certain types of computers are more likely to become the master browser than others. If the network contains domains and the domain extends over more than one subnet, the master browser keeps the browse list for the domain members on its subnet.

- **Backup Browsers**—Computers that operate as backup browsers poll the master browser every 15 minutes to obtain an updated copy of the browse list. If for any reason a backup browser cannot communicate with the master browser, it forces an election.

- **Browse List**—The list of servers that the master or backup browser can maintain is limited to 64K of data. This limits the number of entries to between 2,000 and 3,000, more or less. If a computer is elected to be the master browser and finds that its browse list is empty, it sends out a request datagram asking servers on the network to send it a server announcement. Computers that receive this request respond during a random interval within 30 seconds. The random delay factor is used to minimize network traffic that occurs if a large number of computers respond at the same time.

The list of servers that is maintained in the browse list does not mean just Windows NT Servers. A server is any node that provides a network and uses NetBIOS names for sharing them.

Client Computers

A client computer first contacts the master browser for a list of backup browsers when an application first makes a NetServerEnum API call. It uses the QueryBrowserServers directed datagram to the NetBIOS name *<domain name>*\0x1d to do this. This API call is used by the application to obtain the browse list (list of computers on the network).

When the master browser on the client's subnet detects this datagram, it sends the client a list of browsers for the workgroup or domain that the client requests. The client selects three names from this list, randomly selects one of these browsers, and sends a request to it for the browse list.

The Domain Master Browser

A special type of master browser is the domain master browser. This browser service runs *only* on the domain's primary domain controller. When the domain spans more than one subnet, each master browser that is responsible for a subnet portion of the domain announces itself to the domain master browser. The domain master browser obtains a list of servers from each master browser and compiles the domain browser list. This list is updated every 15 minutes. This domain-wide browse list is then solicited by each master browser so that its clients can browse the entire domain.

If the network is composed of only Windows for Workgroups computers and no domain mechanism is in place, each subnet functions as a separate browsing entity. It makes no difference if you use the same workgroup name on each subnet. It is the domain master browser that provides the capability of maintaining a browse list that extends across subnets.

When Servers or Browsers Fail

When a node that provides a service or a computer that is operating as a browser fails, the names of the servers or services are not immediately removed from the browse list. This is because the updates that are made to the list are not done in real-time, but rather at regular intervals.

Backup browsers and computers that provide a NetBIOS service but that are not browsers announce themselves every 12 minutes on the network. If the master browser does not receive an announcement for three consecutive time periods from a server, it removes the server's name from the browse list. Because backup browsers receive updates from the master browser every 15 minutes, it can take up to 51 minutes for a server to be removed from the list of resources ($3\times12 +15=51$).

Because backup browsers expect to receive updates every 15 minutes from the master browser, the failure of a master browser will be noticed more quickly. If any backup browser cannot contact the master browser, it begins the election process. If a client computer detects the failure (that is, in its first attempt to get a list of backup browser from the master browser), it begins the election process.

When the domain master browser fails, each master browser can only maintain a list for the servers on its subnet. Thus, if the domain master browser is not restored, the domain resources on other subnets are removed from the browse list after a short period of time.

Browser Elections

Whether a computer can become the master browser depends on several factors. It is an "elected" position. Almost any computer running a Windows-based operating system can become a browser. Unless the browser service is configured not to start, it automatically does so when the computer boots. Some computers serve as master browsers, others as backup browsers. If there is more than one subnet, there is at least one master browser for each subnet, and there is a domain master browser if domains are in use.

The election of a master browser occurs when

- A computer boots and finds that it cannot locate the master browser.

- A computer that has already booted loses communication with the master browser. A client tries to contact the list of backup browsers it knows about first, and then the master browser. When it fails to find any of them, it forces an election.

- A computer that is running Windows NT Server is booted. These computers are *preferred* master browsers.

When any of these events occurs, the computer that is involved sends out an *election datagram*. This datagram contains two important pieces of information that are used to evaluate which computer will become the master browser: election version and election criteria.

Election version data consists of a fixed value that is 16 bits in length. It specifies the version of the browser election protocol running on the computer. The election criteria value is a 32-bit value, which is divided into four hexadecimal values of two bytes each (as shown in Figure 20.1).

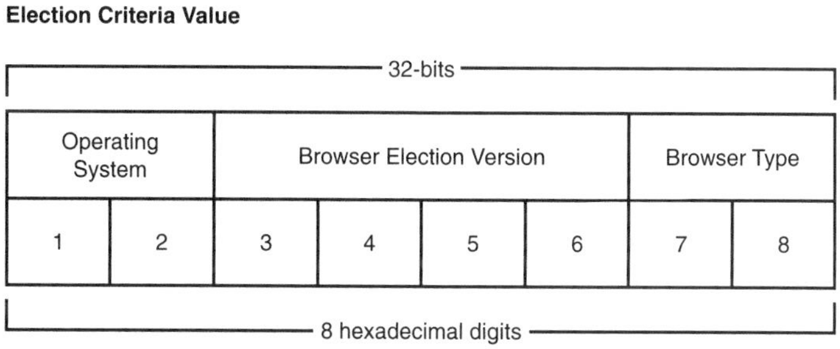

Election Criteria Value

Figure 20.1 Election criteria for master browser elections.

The first two bytes indicate which version of the operating system the computer is running. This value (in hex) is 20 for Windows NT Server, 10 for Windows NT Workstation, and 01 for Windows for Workgroups or Windows 95.

The last two bytes are used to obtain further information about the computer's suitability to become the master browser:

- **80**—This computer is a primary domain controller.
- **20**—This computer is a WINS client.
- **08**—This computer is a preferred master browser.
- **04**—This computer is already a running master browser.
- **02**—The Registry for this computer indicates that it has the MaintainServerList value or the BrowseMaster value set to Yes.
- **01**—This computer is a running backup browser.

When a computer receives the election datagram, it compares the datagram to its own values. The first comparison is made of the election version. If the computer has an election version higher than that found in the election datagram, it wins the election at this point and does not bother to process the remaining election criteria.

Otherwise, a comparison is made of the election criteria. If the computer that receives the datagram has a higher value for the election criteria, it joins the election by sending out an election datagram itself. Otherwise it attempts to determine which other computer will become the master browser.

There can be a tie when evaluating the election criteria. The ties are resolved as follows:

- The computer that has been running the longest wins, or
- The computer with the lower lexical (numerical, then alphabetical) name wins.

When a computer determines that it has won the election based on the datagram it has evaluated, it enters the running state and broadcasts up to four election datagrams. If it receives no election datagram from any other computer indicating that it should not be the winner, it promotes itself to become the master browser. If it receives an election datagram indicating that another computer will win, it demotes itself to become a backup browser. The delay for sending out the election datagrams is different, depending on the current status of the computer:

- 200 milliseconds for a computer that is a master browser.
- 400 milliseconds for a computer that is a backup browser.
- 800 milliseconds for all others.

If a computer that is running in the election receives an election datagram that shows it cannot possibly win the election, it does not continue to send out the remainder of the four election datagrams because doing so would not change the outcome of the election.

The Server Message Block Protocol (SMB)

So far I have discussed the construction of NetBIOS names and how Microsoft clients that use them locate resources on the network. After a client locates a resource, however, the client must be able to make use of the service the resource provides. The *Server Message Block* protocol (*SMB*) was originally developed at IBM, with later development done at Microsoft. SMB is used to create file and print services, among others, and is an important protocol to understand because it is also used to provide non-Microsoft and non-IBM clients with connectivity to these networks also.

For example, SAMBA is a suite of applications that allow SMB clients to make use of resources that reside on UNIX systems. Banyan VINES networking protocols are another example of using SMB to implement network files and print sharing.

SMB is a request-response type of protocol. An application formats its message into a data structure called a *Network Control Block* (*NCB*) and sends the message to the server. SMB messages can be grouped into four basic categories:

- **Session Control**—Messages used to create or delete connections to a network resource.
- **File**—Messages that control accessing file system resources on a network resource.
- **Printer**—Messages used to send files to a print resource and to monitor the status of the print job.
- **Message**—Messages, such as unicast or broadcast messages, used to exchange information between network nodes.

Further development of SMB is continuing under the name *Common Internet File System* (*CIFS*). This enhanced version of SMB will be an open standard that can be ported to many different operating system platforms and provide a common means for file sharing on the Internet.

An in-depth examination of the SMB protocol and CIFS and how they are used can be found in Chapter 25, "File-Server Protocols."

Summary

What's in a name? Well, if you are using NetBEUI on your network, a lot. NetBIOS names are used to identify computers and the resources they provide on a local area network. NetBEUI is ideal for a small network where fast response time is required. Because it is not a routable protocol, though, it is not suited for use on large networks or internetworks such as the Internet where computers spend a lot of time communicating with resources on different subnets or networks. Because they are broadcast-intensive, the troubleshooting of NetBIOS protocols can be time consuming when you are trying to locate a particular node that is misbehaving. The large amount of broadcast traffic also makes NetBIOS-based protocols a bad choice for network applications that require the use of a large amount of bandwidth.

NetBIOS computers use computers that are designated as browsers to find out which resources are available. In the next chapter, the topic of name resolution will be explored, showing how b-, p-, m-, and h-nodes determine the actual hardware addresses for the resources to which they connect.

Name Resolution

Computers use hardware addresses when exchanging data on the local network. Depending on the type of protocol in use, additional layers of addresses or names are added to make networks function more efficiently and to ease administration chores. Names are convenient for use by humans who have to operate computers, but computers need to exchange data on a network. Hence, they must first translate these user-friendly names to protocol addresses and then to hardware addresses before a final delivery can be made.

Understanding how name resolution works on your network will make you better prepared to troubleshoot problems users encounter when trying to locate resources.

Hardware Versus Protocol Addresses

When communicating on the same network segment, computers can directly communicate by sending directed datagrams to another computer and specifying the Media Access Control (MAC) address that is assigned to the network card when it is manufactured. In TCP/IP networks, the Address Resolution Protocol (ARP) is used in a local broadcast domain to determine the hardware address of another computer by sending out a broadcast packet that contains the computer's IP address.

Most major networking products now support the TCP/IP protocol suite in some way or another. NetBIOS has been adapted to run over IP, and the newer NetWare 5 networking software has adopted this as its underlying protocol as well.

This chapter discusses name resolution techniques used to translate user-friendly computer hostnames to IP addresses and some of the methods for troubleshooting problems you might encounter.

NetBIOS

In Chapter 20, "NetBIOS and NetBEUI," the NetBIOS and NetBEUI protocols were described. Although its original specifications were only sufficient for use on very small LANs (under 200 nodes), NetBIOS has been a mainstay in most Microsoft network products and until Windows 2000, NetBIOS names were integral to the Windows operating systems' management functions. For example, domain names and hostnames are made up of NetBIOS names. The Server Message Block (SMB) protocol that is used for resource access and administrative duties in LAN Manager and the Windows operating systems' networking software modules are based on NetBIOS names.

The LMHOSTS File

In the directory `\%systemroot%\SYSTEM32\DRIVERS\ETC` is a file called `LMHOSTS.SAM`. For Windows 95 and Windows 98 clients, this file is found in the `\WINDOWS` directory. It is used to map NetBIOS names to IP addresses. The `.SAM` filename extension indicates that this is a sample file. If you are going to use the file, you will have to copy it or rename it `LMHOSTS`, with no extension. Because it's always a good idea to keep the original copy in case things become confused along the way, making a copy is a good choice.

The Windows 98 and the Windows NT files are the same, except for a few of the comment lines. Following is the Windows NT file from Windows 2000 Advanced Server:

```
# Copyright (c) 1993-1999 Microsoft Corp.
#
# This is a sample LMHOSTS file used by the Microsoft TCP/IP for Windows.
#
# This file contains the mappings of IP addresses to computernames
# (NetBIOS) names.  Each entry should be kept on an individual line.
# The IP address should be placed in the first column followed by the
# corresponding computername. The address and the computername
# should be separated by at least one space or tab. The "#" character
# is generally used to denote the start of a comment (see the exceptions
# below).
#
# This file is compatible with Microsoft LAN Manager 2.x TCP/IP lmhosts
# files and offers the following extensions:
#
#      #PRE
#      #DOM:<domain>
#      #INCLUDE <filename>
#      #BEGIN_ALTERNATE
#      #END_ALTERNATE
#      \0xnn (non-printing character support)
#
# Following any entry in the file with the characters "#PRE" will cause
# the entry to be preloaded into the name cache. By default, entries are
# not preloaded, but are parsed only after dynamic name resolution fails.
#
# Following an entry with the "#DOM:<domain>" tag will associate the
# entry with the domain specified by <domain>. This affects how the
# browser and logon services behave in TCP/IP environments. To preload
# the hostname associated with #DOM entry, it is necessary to also add a
# #PRE to the line. The <domain> is always preloaded although it will not
# be shown when the name cache is viewed.
#
# Specifying "#INCLUDE <filename>" will force the RFC NetBIOS (NBT)
# software to seek the specified <filename> and parse it as if it were
# local. <filename> is generally a UNC-based name, allowing a
# centralized lmhosts file to be maintained on a server.
# It is ALWAYS necessary to provide a mapping for the IP address of the
# server prior to the #INCLUDE. This mapping must use the #PRE directive.
# In addition the share "public" in the example below must be in the
# LanManServer list of "NullSessionShares" in order for client machines to
# be able to read the lmhosts file successfully. This key is under
# \machine\system\currentcontrolset\services\lanmanserver\
#  ➥parameters\nullsessionshares
# in the registry. Simply add "public" to the list found there.
#
# The #BEGIN_ and #END_ALTERNATE keywords allow multiple #INCLUDE
# statements to be grouped together. Any single successful include
# will cause the group to succeed.
#
# Finally, non-printing characters can be embedded in mappings by
# first surrounding the NetBIOS name in quotations, then using the
# \0xnn notation to specify a hex value for a non-printing character.
#
# The following example illustrates all these extensions:
#
```

```
# 102.54.94.97     rhino            #PRE #DOM:networking   #net group's DC
# 102.54.94.102    "appname   \0x14"                       #special app server
# 102.54.94.123    popular          #PRE                   #source server
# 102.54.94.117    localsrv         #PRE                   #needed for the include
#
# #BEGIN_ALTERNATE
# #INCLUDE \\localsrv\public\lmhosts
# #INCLUDE \\rhino\public\lmhosts
# #END_ALTERNATE
#
# In the above example, the "appname" server contains a special
# character in its name, the "popular" and "localsrv" server names are
# preloaded, and the "rhino" server name is specified so it can be used
# to later #INCLUDE a centrally maintained lmhosts file if the "localsrv"
# system is unavailable.
#
# Note that the whole file is parsed including comments on each lookup,
# so keeping the number of comments to a minimum will improve performance.
# Therefore it is not advisable to simply add lmhosts file entries onto the
# end of this file.
```

As you can see from the sample file, you can place comments anywhere on a line by using the # character. Using comments will aid in managing the file when there are multiple administrators. However, as the last bit of text explains, the entire file is parsed (read) each time it is consulted for a name lookup. If this file becomes huge and full of both name translations and comments, it has probably outgrown its usefulness and you need to look to another means of name resolution, such as WINS.

The # character can also be used to specify several keywords that have very specific functions when used in this file. The keywords are

- **#PRE**—Load this entry into the NetBIOS name cache.
- **#DOM**—This entry is a domain controller.
- **#INCLUDE**—Use the filename following this keyword to get name-to-address mappings.
- **#BEGIN_ALTERNATE** and **#END_ALTERNATE**—The #INCLUDE commands within this block are to be processed in order until one of them succeeds.

For small networks that have several subnets separated by a router, using the #DOM keyword for an entry can enable a client to locate a domain controller on another subnet. Although it is preferable to have a backup domain controller on each subnet, this workaround can be helpful for special conditions.

In Figure 21.1, you can see the logical steps that a b-node goes through when trying to resolve a name to an IP address. The NetBIOS name cache is first consulted, followed by broadcasting. Finally, if these two methods fail, the LMHOSTS file is checked.

The in-memory NetBIOS name cache is always consulted first. This cache can hold up to 100 entries. When a name is successfully resolved by the broadcast method or by lookup in the LMHOSTS file, it is added to the name cache and can be resolved there from that point onward.

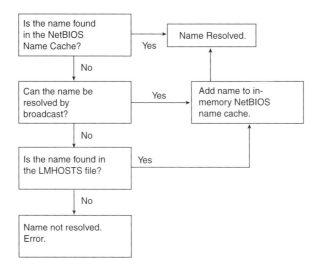

Figure 21.1   In Microsoft networks, a b-node consults the LMHOSTS file when other methods fail.

You can ensure that an entry will be placed in the name cache when the workstation boots by using the #PRE keyword for that entry in the LMHOSTS file:

```
175.110.32.31       kyoko.ono.com       #PRE
```

Tip

You can force an update to the NetBIOS cache by using the command **nbtstat** **-R** to reload the cache from the LMHOSTS file.

Windows Internet Name Service (WINS)

WINS is Microsoft's NetBIOS Name Server (NBNS) developed according to the details set forth in RFCs 1001 and 1002 and is based on a client-server architecture. Only Windows NT Server computers can run the WINS service, and the server does not have to be a domain controller. In the traditional DNS server, an administrator is responsible for editing files to maintain address-to-name mappings. WINS is a dynamic database and name registrations are performed by unicast messages between the server and the WINS client. Because the WINS server does not have to be on the same network segment as the client, and because no broadcast messages clutter up the network medium, WINS is a more efficient method of name resolution when compared to b-node functionality.

The following are some of the important benefits of using WINS:

■ **Ease of Administration**—Updates to the database are dynamic. When a computer is moved to a different location and acquires a new address, it updates the WINS server when it boots. If DHCP is used on the network, moving the client computer requires nothing more than hooking it up to the network.

- **Interaction with DNS**—In Windows NT 4.0, WINS has the capability of interacting with Microsoft's DNS server. If properly configured, a non-Windows client can query the DNS server, which can then query the WINS server to obtain the address of a NetBIOS client.

- **Static Mappings**—If WINS is not set up to interact with the DNS server, you can place static mappings in the database for clients that do not have WINS client functionality.

- **Replication**—Though not specified in the RFCs, WINS servers are typically set up with replication partners. This means that over a given convergence time, all WINS servers in the network are updated with changes made on any one of them.

- **Fault-Tolerance**—Clients are typically configured to locate a primary WINS server and a secondary WINS server. Because the database is replicated at intervals, the secondary WINS server can continue to service all clients until the primary server is brought back online.

Client Name Registration and Release

For a client computer to register a name with the WINS server, it sends a Name Registration Request to the server. This is a directed message, not a broadcast message. If the name is not found in the database, the WINS server returns a Positive Name Registration Response to the client. The record is given a time stamp, and a renewal interval is also recorded in the record. The record is also given an Owner ID, which identifies the WINS server that originates the record. When the record is replicated to other WINS servers, they use this ID to identify the original server.

After half the renewal period has elapsed, a Windows NT client attempts to reregister its ownership of the name by sending the server a Name Refresh Request. The reregistration process functions the same as the initial registration. By setting a Time to Live (TTL) value on each record, the WINS database can eventually be purged of records that are no longer valid.

The state of the name record changes over time depending on the status of the client. At any time, a record is either in the active state or it can be marked as released or extinct. At each state, a time-out value is marked on the record and is used to determine when to change it to the next state.

A name can be released in two ways:

- The name can be released explicitly if the client computer is shut down in a proper manner. The client sends a message to the server telling it to release the name.

- The name is set to a released state by the WINS server if it does not receive Name Refresh Request before the renewal period expires.

When the name is released, the WINS server does not yet delete the record from the database. Instead, it marks the record as released, adds another timestamp (showing the time of the release), and then adds an Extinction Interval to the record. If the WINS server that receives the release is the original owner of the record, it does not propagate a record update to other WINS servers. This reduces replication traffic. If another WINS server—that still has a record showing the name is active—receives a request from another computer to use the name, it tries to contact the original owner and find out at that time if the name can be reused.

At certain intervals, the WINS server scavenges the database. If it finds a record whose extinction interval has expired, it marks the record as extinct. This state is often referred to as the *tombstone state*. When a record is marked as extinct, it receives another timestamp and an extinction time-out value. If a record has not been reregistered by the end of this final time-out interval, the scavenge process will finally remove it from the database.

If a WINS server receives an explicit release request from a client, and the server is not the original owner of the record, it makes itself the new owner of the record. Instead of placing the record into the released state, it proceeds directly to the extinct state. Unlike records in the released state, records in the extinct state do get replicated at replication time. The reason a WINS server immediately marks a record it does not own as extinct is so that the record will be quickly replicated and will get back to the WINS server that originated the record.

If a name is already in the database, the client can still be awarded ownership of it, depending on certain factors. If the name is in the released or extinct state, the server knows that it can reassign the name because the previous owner has released it. If it is in the active state, the WINS server tries to contact the original owner. If the original owner does not respond, the WINS server reassigns the name to the node that is requesting it.

Note

In general, static entries made to the WINS database are not subject to the scavenge process and remain in the database. However, the administrator can configure the server to operate differently by setting the Migrate On switch (in the WINS Administrator Utility). If this switch is set, the static entry can be overwritten by a new name request if the original owner does not answer a challenge from the WINS server. The Migrate On switch is meant to be used when migrating a network from static entries to dynamic entries. This might be the case when you are upgrading your network with new client software, for example, and relieves the administrator of the burden of having to remove the static entries manually.

When a client workstation is moved to a new subnet and receives a new address, it sends a Name Registration Request to the WINS server. The WINS server queries the old IP address, determines that the name is no longer in use, and then grants the name to the new IP address.

Static Name Entries

You can enter static entries into the WINS database using the WINS Manager utility. This is usually done for non-WINS clients, such as UNIX workstations. Although you can configure the Windows client to use DNS to resolve these names, a static entry into the WINS database does two things. It makes name resolution faster because the client only has to query the WINS server. It also helps to prevent errors by preventing a WINS client from registering a name already in use by a non-WINS enabled client.

Name Queries

In Figure 21.2, you can see the process that a client computer goes through when trying to resolve a name using WINS servers. The steps it takes depend on whether it has one or two WINS servers in its configuration (Primary and Secondary WINS servers) and whether the node is configured as a p-node or an h-node.

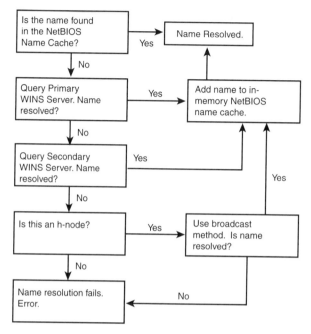

Figure 21.2 Name resolution using WINS servers for p-node and h-node clients.

When a WINS server receives a Name Query Request from a node, it returns a Positive Name Response with one or more IP addresses associated with the NetBIOS name to the requestor via a UDP packet. If the WINS server does not have a record for the name, it sends a Negative Name Response. If the client is configured with the address of a secondary WINS server, it attempts to resolve the name by contacting that server.

Technical Note

In earlier WINS implementations, clients only resorted to the secondary WINS server when the primary server did not respond. Microsoft changed this in Windows NT 3.51 so the secondary server functions as a backup for the primary WINS server and also as a secondary search possibility. Clients that can make use of this new search procedure include Windows 95/98 and Windows for Workgroups 3.11 clients that use TCP/IP-32 for Windows for Workgroups version 3.11b and the updated redirector file.

If the secondary server also returns a Negative Name Response, the client either fails to resolve the name (if it is a p-node) or it uses a broadcast message as a last resort (if it is an h-node). If the computer the client wants to contact is on the local network segment, the broadcast can succeed. If not, the client is unable to resolve the name to an IP address and will be unable to contact the other computer.

The WINS Proxy Agent

To provide access to the WINS server information for b-nodes that cannot query the WINS server directly, the concept of a proxy server was created. These servers listen to broadcast messages issued by a b-node on the local network segment and if the name being sought is in the proxy server's name cache, it returns a response to the b-node. If the name is not in the proxy server's cache, it queries the WINS servers it knows.

When a proxy server is also configured to monitor name registration broadcast messages it listens for these messages and sends a negative response to a b-node that attempts to register a name that exists in the WINS database. The proxy server does not, however, make name registrations into the WINS database for a b-node. It merely responds to name registrations that conflict with the database.

To resolve names for b-nodes, the proxy server examines the subnet address of the b-node that is performing the name query. This is done so that the proxy server does not respond to name queries for nodes that are on the local subnet, which can respond for themselves.

Configuring WINS Servers and Clients

To set up a Windows NT Server computer to be a WINS server, you need to install the WINS service by using the Network applet in the Control Panel. In the Network applet, click on the Services tab and select the Add button. This brings up the Select Network Service dialog box (see Figure 21.3), where you can select the Windows Internet Name Service.

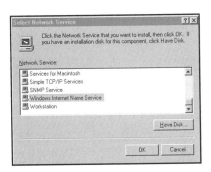

Figure 21.3   Select the Window Internet Name Service entry to install WINS.

After you click the OK button, you are prompted for the location of the Windows NT source files. They are usually in your CD-ROM drive. When the installation procedure has finished copying the files it needs, it tells you that you must reboot for the installation to complete. When the computer has rebooted, you are capable of starting the WINS Manager found in the Administrative Tools folder. Alternatively, at the Command Prompt, you can start the WINS Manager by entering the command:

```
START WINSADMN <IP address>
```

As you can see from the syntax of this command, you can run the WINS Manager utility and select the WINS server you want to manage. In Figure 21.4, you can see the main window of the utility, which shows statistical information about the server you have selected.

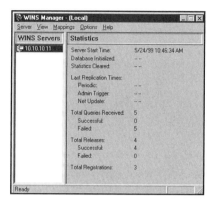

Figure 21.4 The WINS Server Manager utility.

To manage WINS servers on other computers, use the Server menu. The options you can perform under this menu are

- **Add WINS Server**—You are prompted to enter the IP address of another WINS server to add to the list of servers you are managing with the utility.

- **Delete WINS Server**—To delete a WINS server, you can highlight it in the WINS Server window and the select this function. Note that this does not delete the WINS service from the remote computer, but merely removes it from the list of servers you are managing at this time.

- **Detailed Information**—This option brings up a window that shows more detailed information about the selected server.

- **Configuration**—Use this option when you want to change the configuration of the WINS server. From this selection, you can modify renewal and extinction time-out values, event logging parameters, and the Migrate On/Off switch, among other things.

- **Replication Partners**—This selection brings up a window where you can control replication. You can add or remove WINS servers that are replication partners and you can configure the replication interval time value. You can also use this option to force replication to begin immediately if you have a need to propagate changes to other partners without waiting for the next scheduled replication time.

Using the Configuration option, you can modify four time-out values. These timers have been set by Microsoft to optimal values, but you can make changes to accommodate your network configuration. For example, you might want make the renewal interval longer if the computers in your network are rarely moved. The times you can modify are

- **Renewal Interval**—This is the amount of time that the name remains active before a client has to refresh it. A Windows NT client usually refreshes its name registration after one half of this interval has passed. The default for WINS servers under Windows NT 4.0 is six days.

- **Extinction Interval**—After a name has been released, it stays in that state until this interval has passed, at which time it is marked extinct. The default value for this timer under Windows NT 4.0 is six days.

- **Extinction Time-Out**—After a record is marked as extinct, this amount of time must pass before it is eligible to be scavenged from the database.

- **Verify Interval**—This value is used to time-stamp active entries on the pulling replication server. At verify time, the server examines all active records for those that are older than the Verify Interval allows, and then queries the originating server to see if the records are still valid. This periodic checking helps to keep the databases synchronized among the replicating servers when errors creep in. For example, if an extinct record is removed from the database before being replicated to other servers, it remains as active on other servers, when in fact it is no longer valid. This type of thing can happen when servers are off the network during replication. The default value for this timer is 24 days.

Caution

The values for these timers is not absolute—under certain conditions, WINS will alter them. The default values given here are for Windows NT 4.0. They were different in Windows NT 3.* systems, and are likely to be changed by developers in future operating system updates or patches. Use them as guidelines for configuring your system, but do not depend on them completely when troubleshooting WINS database problems.

You can update the statistics shown in the main display of the WINS Manager by selecting the View menu and then Refresh. You also find a selection here that can be used the clear the statistics. The Mappings menu enables you to view the IP address-to-name mappings, manage static mappings, or back up the database. You can also choose to begin the scavenging process from this menu if you have made a lot of changes to the database and do not want to wait for the next scavenging interval to expire.

In Figure 21.5, you can see the Show Database window. Under Owner, the Show All Mappings radio button has been selected to view the entire database. You can change the sort order by making a selection under Sort Order or you can use the Set Filter button to mask out certain entries (and the Clear Filter button to remove the filter).

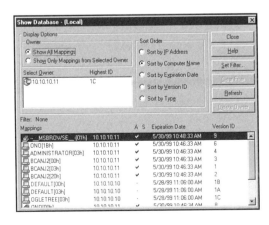

Figure 21.5   The Show Database window can be configured to show mappings in several different ways.

This look into the database can be a quick way to troubleshoot problems in the network when computers cannot resolve names of remote workstations. If you do not find the entry for the disputed name, you can begin to check the remote workstation to be sure that it is connected to the network. You can reboot it to force a name reregistration.

Using WINS with DHCP

Two major tasks are associated with managing a network that undergoes frequent changes. One is assigning and keeping track of addressing information for each node and the other is providing a method for name resolution. WINS is designed to solve problems with the second task. The Dynamic Host Configuration Protocol (DHCP) operates to make the initial assignment of addressing information automatic and can be used to remedy the first task.

DHCP typically provides a client with an IP address and a subnet address. However, DHCP can be configured to provide other options, such as the addresses of WINS servers the client should use. If you are using Microsoft's DHCP Service, you can run the DHCP Manager (found in the Administrative Tools folder) and select Global from the DHCP Options menu. In Figure 21.6, the dialog box used to add DHCP options and their values are shown.

Figure 21.6 DHCP options can be configured to supply clients with WINS server addresses.

Under Active Options, you see that DHCP options 044 (WINS/NBNS Servers) and 046 (WINS/NBT Node Type) have been selected. Option 044 is used to specify the addresses of the WINS server(s). To add IP addresses to be dispensed from DHCP, select the Value button and click the Edit Array button. In Figure 21.7, you can see the dialog box that enables you to manage the IP addresses for WINS servers.

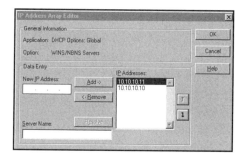

Figure 21.7 Use the Array Editor to enter WINS server option information.

For the clients of the DHCP server to make use of the WINS servers, you want to also add DHCP option 046 and set it to one of the following hexadecimal values:

- **0×2**—p-node
- **0×4**—m-node
- **0×8**—h-node

This option sets the node type of the client computer. If you use the value of 0×1, the node is configured to be a b-node, uses broadcast messages for name registration and resolution, and does not use the WINS servers.

Recovering a Corrupt WINS Database

A WINS server can be set up to automatically create a backup of the database every three hours, using the WINS Manager utility select Backup Database from the Mappings menu. You then select a directory to use for the backup files. Note that the directory used for the backup files must be on a disk local to the system. You cannot use a network drive.

To restore the database, you again use the WINS Manager, selecting Restore Database from the Mappings menu.

TCP/IP Names

The address space for IP addresses is a hierarchical one that allows computers to be grouped into networks and subnetworks. The flat address space created by MAC addresses do not allow for any kind of grouping because they only provide an address for the host physical adapter and do no distinguish the network. It is also possible to create a hierarchical name space for nodes on a TCP/IP network by concatenating the hostname with a domain name. For example, the host computer named jack in the domain named acme.com is jack.acme.com as a fully-qualified name.

Names are more convenient for humans than the numerical address format implemented in the TCP/IP suite. Just as the numerical address space is a hierarchical one, so is the name space. However, it is important to understand that the two do not have to be directly related on a one-to-one basis. For example, suppose a computer named printserver.ono.com has an address of 193.220.113.10. This is a class C IP address, so the network portion of the address is 193.220.113. You might be inclined to think, then, that a computer with a name of fileserver.ono.com is also located in the same network and has an address that begins with 193.220.113. However, there is no direct relation between the two.

Not that there can't be. It might be very convenient to set up a small network with a few subnets and create host computer names that all match up to a particular network address or subnet. In practical terms, however, this is hard to maintain as the network grows and changes.

Instead, use the TCP/IP name space to create a logical arrangement of computers that matches some kind of business layout or other type of function. It makes sense to use names such as the following:

```
susan.accounting.ono.com
heather.accounting.ono.com
jack.shipping.ono.com
holly.shipping.ono.com
```

It is clear from these names that the company or organization is called Ono, and that there are computers in the accounting and shipping departments. In this case, however, it might be that Susan works out of the company's office located in the heart of downtown, whereas Heather works in a suburban office. Their TCP/IP hostnames reflect the business organizational unit in which they work. Their IP addresses, however, can be on completely different subnets or networks, depending on the physical location or other factors.

The rules for creating a hostname are not as carefree as those used for NetBIOS names. You cannot use spaces in a TCP/IP name, for example. The following rules must be followed when creating the name:

- You can use alphabetical characters (a–z) or numeric characters (0–9), and the first character of the name *must* be alphabetical or a digit.

- You can use the minus sign (dash), but this cannot be the last character in the name.

- Periods are allowed, but are used to separate hostnames from domain or subdomain portions of the name. This is covered in RFC 921, "Domain Name System Implementation Schedule." Because the period is used to separate components, it cannot be the last character in the name either.

- Names are case-insensitive. Capital A is the same as lowercase a.

- The host portion of the name should not be longer than 24 characters. In practice, you can exceed this limit most of the time, but it is not a good idea if you are connected to the Internet where there are other computers and devices that do stick to the strict limit.

Note

These restrictions apply to names you enter in the HOSTS file. When using a Domain Name System (DNS) server, the restrictions are a little different, as is explained in the following sections about DNS.

Although you can use names in the TCP/IP networking environment to conveniently organize your host computers, once again there needs to be a mechanism for resolving these names to the actual IP addresses that are associated with the computer. TCP/IP provides the HOSTS file, which was originally a central file maintained by a central authority and periodically distributed to nodes throughout the Internet. You can probably guess that this method—such as the LMHOSTS file used on NetBIOS networks—has been outgrown by the rapid growth of the Internet, and is now used only on small networks or for special cases.

The Domain Name Service (DNS) is now the primary means for resolving IP address to hostnames on the Internet. In some UNIX shops, the Network Information System (NIS) is used. NIS was originally called Yellow Pages but had to change its name due to a trademark infringement.

The HOSTS File

On UNIX systems, the HOSTS file is usually found in the `/etc` or the `/etc/inet` directory. Like the LMHOSTS file, it has no filename extension. It is a text file that contains IP addresses followed by the hostname or names associated with the address. The # character is used to denote comments. Each line should have only one IP address, followed by a space or tab character, and then the hostname. You can place more than one name on the line (each separated by a space or tab character) to provide multiple names for a host (sometimes called nicknames). For example

```
#This is the HOSTS file
#
127.0.0.1       localhost
10.1.22.13      pkd.ubik.com            # Server at Atlanta office.
10.1.22.46      psi.ubik.ocm            # Joe's workstation.
192.208.46.158  www.digital.com         # Digital's homepage.
```

Note that the first entry in the file is the loopback address for the local adapter. You will find this in many HOSTS files, but it is not a requirement.

The HOSTS file has the same limitations as the LMHOSTS file. Mainly, it doesn't scale very well. Each time a change is made in the network, you need to update the file on each machine to reflect the change. This makes it easy to get different copies out-of-sync on a larger network.

In a very small network that doesn't change very often, using the HOSTS file can be preferable to using DNS, but for a growing network or for one in a fast-paced business environment where employees are always on the move, use DNS or NIS instead.

Domain Name System (DNS)

When TCP/IP became the standard protocol used on ARPAnet (which became the Internet), the HOSTS file was maintained by SRI-NIC at a central location. Periodically, changes were made to the file as administrators emailed requests to SRI-NIC. The updated HOSTS file then had to be distributed to every node, making the maintenance of this file a major administrative chore.

In 1984, the Domain Name System was adopted for the Internet. DNS is not only a hierarchical database, but also a distributed one. WINS servers use replication with partners to keep a full copy of the WINS database on each WINS server. On the Internet, each registered domain (that is, `acme.com` or `microsoft.com`) has a DNS server that is responsible for managing the database of hostnames within that domain or subdomains. This distribution of the database makes it easier to scale to a larger size than with the WINS model. Administration can also be delegated so that no central management of the entire database is needed.

Tip

One of the first implementations of DNS was developed at Berkeley for their BSD UNIX (version 4.3) operating system. Thus, you will often hear the term BIND (Berkeley Internet Name Domain) used in place of DNS.

The topmost entry in the DNS hierarchy is called the root domain and is represented by the period character (.). Underneath this root domain are the top-level directories that fall into two groups: geographical and organizational. Geographical domains are used to specify specific countries. For example, .au for Australia and .uk or the United Kingdom. Under each of the geographical domains, you might find organizational domains. Organizational domains you might be familiar with include

- **com or co**—Used for commercial organizations.
- **edu**—Used for educational institutions.
- **gov**—Used for U.S. Government entities.
- **mil**—Used for U.S military organizations.
- **int**—Used for international organizations.
- **net**—Used for network organizations such as Internet service providers.
- **org**—Used for nonprofit organizations.
- **arpa**—Used for inverse address lookups.

The structure of the Domain Name System is similar to an inverted tree. In Figure 21.8, you can see that at the top is the root domain with the com through arpa domains underneath. Under the com domain are individual business organizations that each have their own domain. Under any particular domain there can be subdomains.

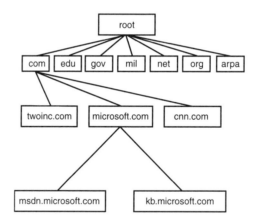

Figure 21.8   The Domain Name System is a distributed, hierarchical structure.

At each level, a fully-qualified domain name (FQDN) is created by concatenating the local name with the names of the entities above it in the hierarchy. Thus, msdn.microsoft.com is used to name the msdn subdomain in the Microsoft domain that falls under the com domain. By using the FQDN, it is possible for a hostname to be used multiple times, as long as it is produces a unique FQDN. For example, fileserver.twoinc.com names a host called fileserver. This host cannot become confused with another host of the same name that resides in a different domain such as fileserver.acme.com.

There are several restrictions to the names you can use in the DNS system:

- The maximum length of a domain name or a host label is 63 characters.
- The maximum length for the FQDN is 255 characters.
- There can be up to 127 subdomains.
- All text is not case sensitive.

Primary, Secondary, and Caching Only Name Servers

For each domain on the Internet, there must be a primary server and a secondary server. The primary DNS server for the domain contains a collection of *resource records* that contain the address mappings for hostnames in the domain. The primary DNS server is the final authority for these mappings. The secondary DNS server contains a copy of the database maintained by the primary server and can continue to resolve names when the primary server is offline. It is important to note that the primary DNS server is where changes are made to the database. Through the use of the *zone transfer* mechanism, the data is copied to secondary servers.

In many cases, a DNS server answers name queries for domains for which it is not the authority. In this case, the DNS server contacts a DNS server further up the hierarchy until one is found that can resolve the name translation, or that can point to another DNS server that is the authority for the name. The DNS server maintains a cache of names that have been resolved by this method so that it does not have to continually poll other servers for names that are frequently queried.

A third type of DNS server is a caching-only server. This type of server does not maintain a database for a particular zone. To put it in other terms, it is not authoritative for any zone or domain and does not use the zone transfer mechanism to keep a current copy of the entire database. Instead, a caching-only name server has to contact another DNS server to initially resolve a name, but like the other servers it maintains a cache of names it has resolved so that it does not have to keep forwarding the query to another server. This type of server is usually used on a network segment connected to the rest of the network by a slower link (or a more expensive one) and is used to reduce network traffic.

Zones

In many cases, it is not efficient to have a single server maintain the database for an entire domain. Instead, a primary DNS server can be authoritative for only a zone in the domain. A *zone* is a partition of the domain into subdomains. For example, one DNS server might be the authority for the zone biz.twoinc.com, whereas another might serve as the authority for the zone research.twoinc.com. Both subdomains exist within the same domain: twoinc.com. However, by dividing the domain into subdomains, it becomes easier to manage not only the DNS servers but also the individual business or organizational units that the domain services.

A *zone transfer* occurs when a secondary DNS server contacts a server that is primary for the zone, and finds that it needs to obtain changes to the database. This is accomplished by using serial numbers contained in the database. If the secondary server has a lower serial number, a new copy of the database is copied to it.

DNS Database Files

There are four basic types of files used by DNS servers. In most DNS implementations, you need to use a text editor to make changes to these files. Some newer DNS servers, such as Microsoft's DNS server, provide a graphical interface that can be used for adding or changing information in the DNS files. The basic files are

- **The Database File**—This is the file that stores the resource records for the zone(s) that the DNS server is responsible for. The first record in this file is the Start of Authority (SOA) record.

- **The Cache File**—This file contains information for other name servers that can be used to resolve queries that are outside the zone or domain that the server is responsible for.

- **The Reverse Lookup File**—This file is used to provide a hostname when the client only knows the IP address. This can be useful for security purposes. For example, a Web server that receives a request from a client can query the DNS with the name of the client to find out if the hostname associated with the IP address is correct.

Resource Records

DNS databases are usually composed of ASCII text files containing records that can be used to translate a name to an IP address. There are several types of records that can be used in the database, each representing a specific type of resource, such as a computer hostname or a mailserver name.

When representing a domain name in DNS, a specific syntax is used. The term label is used in RFC 1035, "Domain Names - Implementation and Specification," when describing this syntax. A *label* is a one-byte length field followed by a data field. The length field indicates the number of characters in the data field. A domain name is represented by a series of labels and the entire domain name string is terminated with a length field of zero. For example, Figure 21.9 shows the layout of a series of labels that would be used to define the domain name zira.twoinc.com.

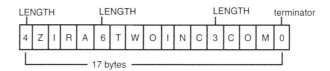

Figure 21.9 The domain name is represented by a series of labels in DNS.

Although the string is only 13 bytes long, excluding the periods, it takes 17 bytes to represent it in the database because of the length fields and the terminator field. To avoid repetition for domain names that are used a lot in the database, a pointer record can be used.

The general format used for a resource record contains the following fields:

- **Name**—The owner name. This is the name of the domain to which this record belongs.
- **Type**—A two-byte field that specifies the resource record type code.
- **Class**—A two-byte field that specifies the resource record class code.

- **TTL**—A 32-bit signed integer that specifies the time-to-live value. The TTL value specifies the amount of time a record can be cached before its value needs to be refreshed from the authoritative source. Zero indicates that the record cannot be cached.

- **RDLENGTH**—An unsigned 16-bit integer that indicates the length of the data field that follows.

- **RDATA**—The data field. This part of the record describes the resource. The contents depend on the values of the TYPE and CLASS fields.

The type field indicates the type of resource record. Table 21.1 contains a list of the record types along with a description of their use.

Table 21.1   DNS Resource Records

Record Type	Description
A	Host IP Address
AAAA	Host IP Address (Ipv6)
NS	Name Server Record
PTR	Pointer to another Domain Name Record
SOA	Start of a zone of authority
WKS	Well-Known Service
HINFO	Host Information
MX	"Mail Exchanger" for the domain
MINFO	Mailbox or Mail list information
TXT	Text entry for miscellaneous information
CNAME	Canonical Name for an Alias

In earlier implementations of DNS, other record types were also used. For example, MD and MF were used to specify Mail Destination and Mail Forwarder records. RFC 1035 made obsolete three other RFCs: 882, 883 and 973. Four other types that are considered experimental are

- **MB**—Mailbox domain name
- **MG**—Mail group member
- **MR**—Mail rename domain name
- **NULL**—Null resource record

The Start of Authority (SOA) record is used at the beginning of the database and is used to describe the database. It is used mostly by secondary DNS servers to get zone information. The fields in this record are

- **Domain name**—Name of the domain for which this database is the authority.
- **IN**—The class type of Internet.
- **SOA**—The Start of Authority record type indicator.
- **Primary server**—The FQDN of the primary DNS server for this domain.
- **Email address**—The email address of a person who is responsible for this domain.

- **Serial number**—A 32-bit value that shows the revision number of the database file. It is incremented each time a change is made to the database so that secondary servers can detect the change.

- **Refresh Rate**—A 32-bit value used by secondary servers. After this interval has elapsed, the data for a record must be checked again in the primary server database.

- **Retry Rate**—A 32-bit value indicating the amount of time to wait before retrying to refresh data after a failed attempt.

- **Expire Rate**—A 32-bit value indicating the maximum amount of time a secondary server is to try to refresh data before it stops processing DNS data for this zone.

- **Minimum TTL**—The minimum amount of time for a resource record's TTL. This value can be overridden by the TTL value specified in the record itself.

All time values in the SOA record are in seconds.

The NS record type can be used to indicate that another name server is authoritative for this subdomain. For example, the record

```
Zork.twoinc.com    IN    NS    zira.twoinc.com
```

indicates that the name server whose FQDN hostname is zira.twoinc.com is the authoritative name server to get information from about the subdomain zork.twoinc.com. To get the address of the name server zira.twoinc.com, an "A" type record is needed:

```
Zira.twoinc.com    IN    A    216.65.33.219
```

The CNAME record is used to specify aliases or nicknames that can be used in addition to a hostname, for example

```
ftp.zira.twoinc.com    IN    CNAME    zira.twoinc.com
```

Pointer records (PTR class) are used to get the name that is associated with an IP address—a reverse translation. For example

```
219.33.65.216    IN    PTR    zira.twoinc.com
```

can be used to perform a query to get the name of this host when only the IP address is known. Notice, however, that the IP address has been reversed. It is represented in a pointer record as 219.33.65.216 instead of 216.65.33.219. The reverse format is used to make a key-lookup in the database function properly. The special domain called IN-ADDR.ARPA contains the data used when a server needs to look up the hostname for an address in the domain.

The Class field is generally IN, which stands for Internet. The numeric value for this code is 1. In addition to this class type, you might see references to CS, which stands for the obsolete CSNET class. The CH class stands for the CHAOS class and the HS class code stands for the Hesiod class.

Configuring a UNIX DNS Server

On most UNIX systems, configuring a DNS server involves editing ASCII text files and making the appropriate entries. The actual files to edit depend on the brand of UNIX you are using. The most common is the Berkeley Internet Name Domain (BIND) implementation. This server uses a daemon called `in.named`.

In addition to the actual zone database files you also have to edit

- **/etc/named.boot**—This file provides information for the in.named daemon when it starts up. The Directory directive specifies the directory that holds the zone database files (usually /var/named). The Cache directive tells the server to load a cache of initial hostnames. The directive Primary tells the server that it will function as the primary DNS server for the zone and the directive Secondary tells the server that it will function as the secondary DNS server for the zone.

- **/var/named/db.cache**—This is the usual name for the cache file. To obtain a copy of the latest records for the top-level DNS name servers, you can ftp a copy.

To start the BIND service daemon after you have edited all the appropriate files, you only need to enter the command in.named at the system command prompt. If you have edited the /etc/named/boot file, the server automatically starts the next time the system is booted.

The most time-consuming task is the editing of the zone database files, making entries for the hosts in the domain.

Configuring Microsoft DNS Server

Microsoft DNS Server must be installed on the system in a manner similar to the WINS server: by using the Network applet in the Control Panel to add a service. After you select the Microsoft DNS Server service, you have to reboot the system before the installation completes.

Upon rebooting, you can bring up the DNS Server graphical interface by selecting Start, Programs, Administrative Tools, DNS Server. When the utility first starts up, no servers are defined, so select New Server from the DNS drop-down menu to get to the Add DNS Server dialog box, shown in Figure 21.10.

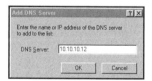

Figure 21.10   You must first add the name or IP address of a server to begin configuring the Microsoft DNS Server.

To configure a DNS server on the local node, enter the IP address for that node in the dialog box. If you want to connect to a DNS server that has been installed on another server, enter its address instead.

After you add the server to the list of DNS servers, create a zone. Making sure that the server is highlighted in the Server List, select New Zone from the DNS menu. The first dialog box prompts you to create a Primary or a Secondary zone type. Click the Next button after your selection. If you are creating a secondary zone, you also have to enter the name of that zone and the name of the server where primary server resides.

The next dialog box prompts for the name of the zone and the name of the database file that is to be used to hold the records (see Figure 21.11).

Figure 21.11   The DNS Wizard prompts for the name of the zone and the database file to be created.

The database file for the new zone is created, and you can then begin populating the file. For example, enter a host record, select the zone name in the Server List, and from the DNS menu select New Host. A dialog box (shown in Figure 21.12) prompts you to enter the name of the new host and the IP address for the host. Only enter the actual hostname, not the fully qualified host-name. For example, enter zira instead of zira.twoinc.com. Because the database is for a particular zone, you must enter host records for that zone.

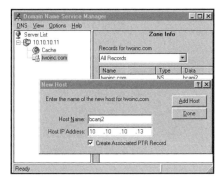

Figure 21.12   Enter the hostnames and the IP address in this dialog box.

When you are finished entering hostnames, click the Done button. In Figure 21.13, you can see the Domain Name Service Manager with a populated database file.

To view details about any record or to make modifications, double-click it. To delete a record, right-click on the record and select Delete.

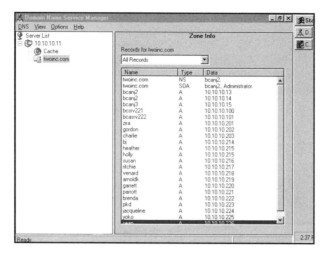

Figure 21.13   The Domain Name Service Manager provides a graphical interface into the zone database.

Configuring DNS Clients

UNIX clients get their information about name servers from the file /etc/resolv.conf. To configure the client, edit this file. To place comments in this file, you can use the semi-colon (;) character. The three directives that you configure in this file are

- **Domain**—The default domain name. This name is appended to any names that are partially qualified.

- **Search**—This is a search list of domains used to look up names that are not fully qualified. You can specify up to six domain names with a total of 256 characters for this directive.

- **Nameserver**—You can specify up to three DNS servers by IP address with this directive. Note that if you do not specify a nameserver address, the default is the local domain.

For example

```
;This is the /etc/resolv.conf file for local workstations
domain twoinc.com
; Name servers
nameserver 199.45.32.38
nameserver 151.197.0.39
nameserver 216.645.33.219
; search lists
search twoinc.com biznesnet.com
; end of file
```

A client using this file, trying to resolve the name of a host named zira, would first search the domain twoinc.com and then the domain biznesnet.com. The first match found is the one that will be used to resolve the name to an IP address.

To configure a Microsoft Client to use a DNS server, you only need to enter the IP addresses of the DNS servers when you perform the initial client network setup.

Using NSLOOKUP

The NSLOOKUP utility is generally employed by users wanting to find the IP address associated with a name. However, the utility can be used to interrogate the DNS database to find out not only IP addresses, but also for information stored in other records in the database. The utility can be used in either interactive mode, where the user can continue to issue commands, or it can be used in a one-shot non-interactive mode where a single query is executed. The basic syntax for the command is

```
nslookup [[-option ...] [hostname to locate]] - [server]
```

If you omit the last item in this syntax (- server), the local DNS server is queried. However, when you have multiple servers, or if you want to query a server outside your organization, specify it with this parameter.

A simple example of the command is nslookup twoinc.com, which returns the following information:

```
Name:     twoinc.com
Address:  216.65.33.219
```

If you want to retrieve more information about the server, you can use options and specify the information records:

```
nslookup -query=hinfo -timeout=10 www.twoinc.com

twoinc.com
        primary name server = ns1.tentex.com
        responsible mail addr = hostmaster.twoinc.com
        serial   = 1342
        refresh = 3600 (1 hour)
        retry    = 600 (10 mins)
        expire   = 86400 (1 day)
        default TTL = 3600 (1 hour)
```

As you can see, this tool is useful for looking up addresses, but can also be used to query the DNS database and help you debug configuration problems. With this simple query, you can see the serial number of the current database, along with other information stored in the SOA record. The syntax for the options of this command vary depending on your operating system.

Dynamic DNS

Earlier in this chapter, I discussed Microsoft's WINS servers. These NetBIOS name servers can be used to dynamically accept information from clients so that the network administrator does not have to make edits to the database each time a node is added to the network or a workstation is moved to a new location. The Dynamic Host Configuration Protocol (DHCP) has eliminated the necessity of manually configuring each computer host with network information. Microsoft's DNS server can be configured to query the WINS server when it needs to resolve a name it cannot find in its own databases.

This solution does not help if you have a multivendor network with workstations running different operating systems. There are several relevant RFCs that address these problems associated with standard DNS implementations, such as

- **RFC 2136, "Dynamic Updates in the Domain Name System (DNS UPDATE)"**— This RFC describes a method that can be used for dynamic updates to DNS. It provides for an atomic (all-or-nothing) update mechanism that can be used to add, delete, or modify one or more resource records in a zone file.

- **RFC 1995, "Incremental Zone Transfer in DNS"**—Incremental zone transfer means that only portions of the zone database file that have been modified need to be transferred from primary DNS servers to secondary servers. This process conserves network bandwidth and decreases the latency time for changes to be distributed throughout the Internet.

- **RFC 1996, "A Mechanism for Prompt Notification of Zone Changes (DNS NOTIFY)"**—This third piece of the solution enables the primary DNS server to notify the secondary servers that changes have been made to the zone database. Currently, zone transfers can occur only after a refresh interval has passed.

Current offerings for a DNS server that is truly dynamic and the corresponding DHCP server capable of making updates are not widespread at this time. Portions of the technology are implemented here and there. For example, The Internet Software Consortium (ISC), which maintains BIND, has recently released—in March of 1999—version 8.2 of BIND, which supports RFC 2136. You can download documentation or the kit files from their Web site at http://www.isc.org.

At the same site, you will also find a version of DHCP, along with a list of products developed by other developers that are based on or can work with these products.

Cisco had a product called Cisco DNS/DHCP Manager that provided DHCP server functions and DNS functions that were linked so the DHCP server could update the DNS database with IP addresses and name information it dispensed to clients. This product has been replaced with Network Registrar 3.0, which is compliant with RFC 2136 for Dynamic DNS updates. The product also implements RFCs 1995 and 1996, which provide for the Primary DNS server to notify secondary servers about changes to zone information and to allow an incremental zone transfer, rather than causing a replication of the entire file.

With the rapid growth of the Internet and the increasing adoption of TCP/IP as the definitive protocol for business networks, it can be expected that in the next few years, we will see a new generation of products from various vendors that will incorporate these features and interoperate.

Network Information Service (NIS)

As was mentioned earlier, Sun developed a product that was originally called Yellow Pages, but the name was later changed due to a trademark owned by British Telecom. The product was Network Information Service (NIS), a client-server system that allows for the sharing of information on a network that includes not only hostnames and addresses, but other information also, such as password files. The goal of NIS is to reduce administrative overhead problems associated with having multiple copies of files on hosts throughout the network.

NIS is based on a flat name space design and Sun has now released NIS+, which resembles the Domain Name System in its hierarchical structure. NIS+ uses a concept of NIS domains, which might or might not be paired with DNS domains. NIS used a concept called maps for storing data. Maps used a simple keyword/data concept. NIS+ uses a more traditional database format with tables containing multicolumned rows of data.

Summary

Name resolution is an important component in any network, much more so in a large internetwork such as the Internet. Although small networks and business intranets might get by using NetBIOS names and WINS servers, this technology does not scale well enough to work reliably and efficiently on a global scale with millions of users. The Domain Name System is now the de facto Internet name resolution service. Recent developments, such as technology that will enable dynamic DNS servers to exist on the Internet, will most likely revolutionize name registration and resolution in the next few short years.

Part VIII

TROUBLESHOOTING LOGON PROBLEMS

Windows NT Domains

SOME OF THE MAIN TOPICS IN THIS CHAPTER ARE

Workgroups and Domains

Windows NT User Groups: Local Groups, Local Domain Groups, and Global Groups

Managing User Accounts

Passwords and Policies

Strategies to Minimize Logon Problems

CHAPTER 22

The Windows NT domain is a collection of users and resources and is the primary unit of user and resource administration. Administrators in any given domain can control the addition or modification of user accounts in their domain, and can control which resources any user can access, along with the type of access. To begin to understand the logon process under Windows NT, you want to first become cognizant of how users and security information are organized into user groups and domains and how these groups and domains interact.

Workgroups and Domains

In many ways, a domain is similar to a Windows 3.1 workgroup, but with one major exception: The domain has a single, centralized security accounts manager (SAM) database that holds all security information for the domain. In a workgroup, each computer in the network has its own security database, and the user of that computer can set passwords on resources that the computer provides to the network. Whereas a domain provides for centralized administration of the network's resources and users, the workgroup provides a highly decentralized peer-to-peer networking model.

The disadvantages to the workgroup method include not only the decentralized management functions, but also the ways in which this impacts the end user. For example, to access a resource on another computer in a workgroup, the user needs to know the password associated with that share-level resource.

Because each computer or workstation can potentially be managed by different people, you often need to know as many different passwords as you have resources to which you need to connect. Keeping track of multiple passwords usually leads to lax security—you write them all down so you don't forget them.

In a domain, the administrator is in charge of the security policy for the entire domain. Users need only a single username and password to log on to the network and access resources throughout the domain. There are limits, however, to what a single domain can do in a network. As the network grows in size, whether it is in users, resources, or geographical size, using a single security database can have some drawbacks. Specific computers are designated to be domain controllers. These computers are the repositories of the security database, the SAM. This database contains data for four types of security objects, or accounts:

- User accounts
- Computer accounts
- Global group accounts
- Local group accounts

As you can see, in addition to keeping track of usernames, passwords, and other information about the users on the network, the SAM also keeps track of computers that have joined the domain and user groups that have been defined, along with the members of each group. Note that only Windows NT computers are tracked in the database. Users on other platforms, such as Windows 95/98, can log on to a Windows NT domain. Windows NT computers actually join the domain when the administrator creates a computer account for that workstation in the SAM.

The number of accounts that can be accommodated by a single Windows NT 4.0 domain, according to Microsoft figures, is around 40,000. For a larger network, you need more than one domain.

Note

There are actually two places that you can find the SAM for Windows NT. The domain controllers hold copies of the domain database, which is used to validate domain logons and to grant users the capability to access resources in the domain. However, any Windows NT Server or Windows NT Workstation computer that is not a domain controller also has its own local security database, much like a Windows for Workgroups computer. The local user can create individual user accounts on the local computer and can grant access to resources on the computer to these users. However, users who are validated by a computer's local database cannot use this logon to access domain resources. Additionally, when a Windows NT computer joins a domain, the domain administrator's global group is, by default, placed into the local domain administrator's group, giving the domain administrators the capability to control security functions on the local computer.

Of course, it is rare to find a domain that actually has 40,000 user accounts. When a network grows this large, a solution needs to be found that provides a convenient method of managing users and controlling access to network resources.

The solution is to create multiple domains in the network and allow them to interact with each other so that users can access resources anywhere on the network, while still using only a single username and password to log on. In Windows NT, this is done by using a concept called a *trust relationship* between domains.

Inter-Domain Trust Relationships

To support the concept of one username, one password throughout a collection of domains, the trust relationship is used to allow domains to share information contained in the security database. Without a trust relationship, you have to create a new user account in the database of each domain that a user needs to have access to. This is similar to the workgroup model, only on a larger scale, and using domains instead of individual computers.

When a user account is created in a domain, it is assigned a unique identifier, called a *SID*, which stands for *security identification descriptor*. If you create several accounts in different domains for a user with the same logon username and password, the SID is not the same from one domain to another. The user's logon name is ordinary text that is used for the convenience of humans who must remember it. The SID is the actual method that the network uses when identifying a particular user, to identify the domain that holds the user account, and to decipher what access that user is allowed, based on access control lists (ACLs).

Because there should be only one username and password for any user throughout the network, no matter how many domains are created, a method is needed to enable a domain to recognize that a user has already been validated in another domain. If this can be communicated between domains, it becomes possible to simply trust a user if a domain trusts the domain from which the user comes.

A trust relationship is created when an administrator from one domain uses the User Manager for Domains utility to create a specific relationship with another domain. A trust relationship, however, is a one-way street. For example, if domain A has a trust relationship whereby it trusts the users in domain B, the administrator of domain A can grant access to resources in domain A to users who reside in domain B, just as he can for his own users in domain A.

In a Windows NT 4.0 domain, the trust relationships are *non-transitive*. This means if domain A trusts domain B and domain B trusts Domain C, a user in domain A cannot be granted access to domain C, only to the trusted domain B. This has been changed in Windows 2000 to allow *transitive* trusts, where each domain passes its trusted domain access to the trusting domain.

Technical Note

A trust relationship does not automatically give users in one domain access to resources in another domain. Just as users in a domain are granted access to resources by their domain administrators, users from trusted domains must be granted the necessary access rights and privileges in a trusting domain before they can access resources. The trust relationship set up between two domains is merely the prerequisite that enables users to be granted access to resources in another domain.

The trust relationship enables the Windows NT LSA (local security authority) to use *pass-through authentication* to validate a user. When a user from a trusted domain tries to access a resource, the netlogon service contacts the domain in which the user account resides to confirm that the user account is valid. The LSA receives copies of the user's SIDs (the account SID and the SIDs for a global group of which the account is a member). After this pass-through authentication process, the LSA has all the information it needs to evaluate the user against the Access Control List entries that might be present in an ACL for a particular resource.

For users in both domains to have access to resources in both domains, the administrators of the domains have to create two trust relationships.

Creating a Trust Relationship

Trust relationships are created by the domain administrator using the User Manager for Domains utility. To start the utility, click on the Start button, then Programs, Administrative Tools, and finally User Manager for Domains. In Figure 22.1, you can see the utility as it looks when it is first started, showing a list of user accounts in the domain at the top and a list of user groups at the bottom.

To create a trust relationship, the administrator in both domains has to run the utility and enter the other domain's name into the list of domains it trusts or is trusted by. To bring up the dialog box that is used to accomplish this, click on the Policies menu at the top of the utility, and select Trust Relationships (see Figure 22.2).

The administrator of the domain to be trusted needs to run the utility first to add the name of the domain by which it is to be trusted. To do this, click the Add button, which is next to the Trusting Domains list. Another dialog box (see Figure 22.3) is displayed. Here, you enter the name of the domain that is to trust your domain and an optional password.

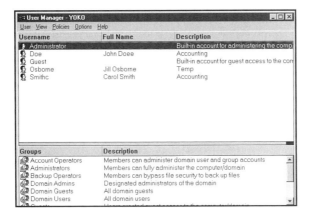

Figure 22.1   The User Manager for Domains is used to create a trust relationship.

Figure 22.2   The Trust Relationships dialog box is simple to use.

Figure 22.3   Enter the name of the domain that is to trust this domain, and enter a password.

The administrator of the domain that is to trust this domain needs to perform the same function, this time selecting the Add button, which is next to the Trusted Domains list. In the Add Trusted Domain dialog box, that administrator puts the name of the domain it will trust and then the same password that was entered by the administrator of the trusted domain.

Although the password is optional, you want to always use one. The password is not used later by domain controllers that are performing pass-through authentication. It is used only to verify both ends of this process of creating the trust relationship. After the trust relationship has been established, the domain controllers use SID information to validate each other from then on.

After the trusting domain has entered the correct password, a message is displayed indicating that the trust relationship was set up. Each administrator then sees the other domain listed in the trusted or trusting section of the Trust Relationships dialog box. If you have a network that has multiple domains and a large number of administrators, it is a good idea from a security viewpoint to regularly check this dialog box to be sure that the trust relationships you expect to exist are there, and that no others have been added. Remember that a trust relationship gives a user with administrative privileges the capability to grant rights and privileges to users outside your domain. This is a very powerful capability.

Again, remember that each trust relationship is unidirectional. If you want both domains to enable users from the other domain to access resources in each domain, you have to repeat the process and create two trust relationships between the two domains.

When it becomes necessary to remove a trust relationship, all you have to do is select a relationship from either the trusted or trusting domain lists in the dialog box, and click the Remove button.

Domain Controllers

The domain controller is a computer that holds a copy of the SAM. Users are authenticated by domain controllers when they log on to the network. In Windows NT, there are two kinds of domain controllers:

- **Primary Domain Controller (PDC)**—This type of domain controller is where the master copy of the SAM resides for the domain. Updates to the SAM can be made only on the PDC, which then propagates the changes to the other domain controllers. Because there can be only one master copy of the domain's SAM, there can be only one PDC in any given domain.

- **Backup Domain Controller (BDC)**—This domain controller holds a copy of the SAM and receives updates to this copy via replication from the PDC. Users can be authenticated by a BDC, but changes to the SAM must be done on the PDC. Because the BDC holds a copy of the SAM, there can be multiple BDCs in the network. BDCs are usually used to offload processing from a busy PDC, provide quick network access to the SAM in network segments that are distanced from the PDC, or to provide for fault-tolerance so that users can still log on to the network when the PDC becomes unavailable. Microsoft recommends at least two BDCs be implemented.

Only a Windows NT Server computer can be used to create a domain controller, and this has to be done during the initial installation of the operating system. Windows NT Servers that are installed as ordinary member servers cannot be upgraded at a later date to become a PDC without a complete reinstallation of the operating system. Windows NT Workstation computers cannot be used as domain controllers in any fashion—their own local SAM enables users to log on to the local workstation but not the network.

All Windows NT computers that participate in a network run a service called the netlogon service. You can see it listed in the Services applet found in the Control Panel. This service is responsible for taking a user's logon request and communicating with a domain controller to process the logon. It is also the entity that handles synchronization between the PDC and BDC copies of the SAM database.

Windows NT Domain Models

The single logon principle that is so important in Microsoft networking is enhanced by enabling domains to trust each other's user base by using trust relationships. However, in a network that contains a large number of domains, it is important to decide on a model to use when establishing trust relationships to make them easy to manage for the particular needs of your environment. Although it is very easy to create trust relationships between every single domain in a large network, that is not the way it is usually done. Instead, four basic models are often used:

- Single domain model
- Master domain model
- Multiple master domain model
- Complete trust domain model

Deciding which domain model to use depends on many factors, but the basic things to consider are the size of the network (in users) and the organization of the business along with management and geographical factors.

The Single Domain Model

For a smaller organization that has a centralized management team for its network, a single domain might be sufficient. In this model, all the user accounts are created in a single domain, along with all the network resources such as file and print services. There are no inter-domain trust relationships to worry about because there is only one domain.

In this model, there is only one PDC, but one or more BDCs are typically created for fault-tolerance purposes. If users are located at different sites geographically, you can use this model and put a BDC at each site to reduce network traffic associated with logons, enabling users to be validated by the local BDC. Having a BDC at each site also enables users to continue working in case the network link between them and the site that has the PDC goes down. As noted earlier, Microsoft recommends at least two BDCs for each domain.

The Master Domain and the Multiple Master Domain Models

In a larger enterprise, it might be desirable to have one central database that contains all the user accounts while maintaining other departmentalized databases that hold security information about resources in the network. In the master domain model, one domain is designated to be the master domain and all user accounts are created in this domain. Additional *resource domains* are then created, which do not have to contain any user accounts at all—other than those used for the local administrators to manage resources. Because of the concept of trust relationships, you don't even have to create accounts for these administrators in their own domains. Using global and local groups, it is possible to give a user account from the master domain the capability to administer another domain by placing that user account in a special Domain Admins user group.

In the resource domains, file and print shares are created and can be managed locally, whereas user accounts can be managed from a central location. In this model, each resource domain has a one-way trust relationship with the master domain, whereby it trusts the users in the master domain, as shown in Figure 22.4.

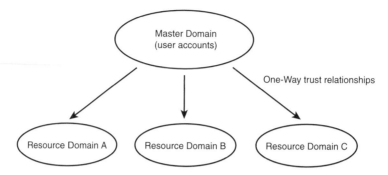

Figure 22.4   Resource domains trust the users validated by the master domain in this model.

This type of domain model is ideal if you need a central place to manage user accounts but want to allow local administrators to take responsibility for managing resources in their areas of the network. In a large company, you might want the personnel or human resources department to be responsible for creating accounts for new employees and deleting accounts when users leave the company. The accounting department can then take charge of managing printers and other resources in their own domain, whereas those in charge of the warehouse can similarly be responsible for granting access to resources in their domain.

The multiple-master domain model is similar to the master domain model, but in this case, there can be more than one master domain. Resource management is still decentralized by enabling resource domain administrators to control local resources, but instead of one master domain to hold all user accounts, there are several. In Figure 22.5, you can see an example of this where users in the United States are managed by one domain, whereas users in the United Kingdom are managed in a separate master domain.

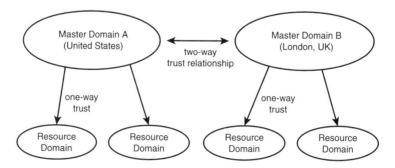

Figure 22.5   In the multiple master domain model there can be more than one master domain to hold user accounts.

This model is the most scalable domain mode because you can just add another master domain if you need to add more users when the existing master domains become highly populated, or when a new geographical area is brought into the company. In fact, if you have a large network that already has more than 40,000 user accounts, and you want some degree of centralized user administration, the multiple master domain model is the best method to use. It provides for local administration of resources, but also enables you to separate users into large administrative groups for management purposes.

In an enterprise that has a global network, this model can be used to allow large divisions of a company to control users located in their area. User account management is still centralized, but into several large groups that are managed by each division. If trust relationships are set up correctly, a user still needs only one logon to be granted access to resources that exist anywhere throughout a worldwide global network.

Another reason you might choose the multiple master domain model over the master domain model is to minimize network replication traffic. Remember that updates to the SAM are made to the database residing on the PDC, and are then sent to BDCs during the replication process. If you have a user base that experiences frequent changes, replication traffic on a global scale can consume valuable network bandwidth. By having several master domains, one for each location, you reduce the bandwidth consumption because replication occurs only within each domain.

The Complete Trust Model

This domain model provides for decentralized user account management and decentralized resource management. Each domain in the network has a two-way trust relationship with every other domain in the network, as shown in Figure 22.6. Administrators can still manage their own local resources but can also manage their own user database. This method requires good communications skills between domain administrators to make sure that users are properly granted access to the resources in other domains.

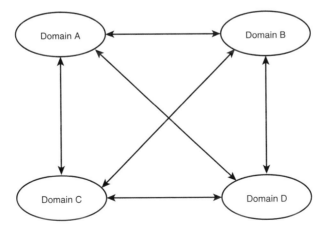

Figure 22.6   The complete trust model provides the highest degree of decentralized management in a large network.

Although this model has the greatest chance of causing confusion when trying to troubleshoot logon or resource access problems, it can be a good method to choose under some circumstances. For example, in the highly competitive business environment of the past decade where growth is achieved by acquisition, this model can be used to quickly join networks when companies merge. This assumes, of course, that both business entities are using a Microsoft Windows NT network.

Windows NT User Groups: Local Groups, Local Domain Groups, and Global Groups

To make assigning access rights and privileges easier to manage, Windows NT enables you to group users together. Rather than spending an inordinate amount of time granting each user the right to access a particular file share, for example, you can simply put multiple users into a user group and grant or revoke the right from the group instead. User groups can be either a local group that exists on a particular computer, or they can be domain-wide local or global groups.

Local groups in a particular server are used to give the local administrator of a member server the capability to control access to local resources. For example, when a member server (a Windows NT Server computer that is not a domain controller) joins a domain, the domain's global group called Domain Admins is placed into the server's local group called Administrators. It is through this mechanism that the domain administrators are granted the capability to administer the local server. Of course, it is also quite possible for the user of the member server to use the server's built-in Administrator account to remove the Domain Admins global group from the local administrators group, and thereby deny the domain administrators of their access to administer resources on the member server.

Local domain groups function in much the same way, but on a domain-wide scale. When a trust relationship is created between two domains, users in one domain do not automatically gain access rights to resources in the trusting domain. Instead, the administrator in the trusting domain needs to grant each user the needed access privilege. Because granting access rights on a user-by-user basis can be quite tedious in a large network, groups and templates can be used for that purpose as well.

Local domain groups can contain users from the domain in which they are created and users or global groups from other trusted domains. Domain administrators can grant or deny access to domain resources by granting or denying access to the local domain groups.

Global user groups can contain only users or groups from a single domain. Global user groups are used to export users to another trusting domain as a single unit. For example, the domain administrator of a trusting domain can place global groups from trusted domains into a local domain group and grant or deny access to domain resources by the local domain group.

Built-In User Groups

To make things easier when you first set up a Windows NT computer, several local and global groups are created by default. If the computer is a Windows NT Server computer operating as a domain controller, you find these domain local groups:

- Administrators
- Backup Operators
- Account Operators
- Guests
- Print Operators
- Replicator
- Server Operators
- Users

The functions of most of these groups are obvious at first glance. The Administrators group is a local group that is granted rights to manage the domain. The Backup Operators group can be used to give users the capability to perform backups, bypassing normal security restrictions for this purpose. The Print Operators group has the necessary privileges to manage printers and print queues for the domain, and so on. The Users local group is used to group users on the particular server, whereas the Domain Users group usually contains all users in the domain. If you look at the membership of the server's Users group, you can see that the Domain Users global group is a member of the group, which is how ordinary domain users are capable of getting limited access rights to the server.

If the server is a domain controller, you also see three built-in global groups:

- Domain Admins
- Domain Guests
- Domain Users

Windows NT Server computers that are operating as a non-domain controller computer—called simply a member server—and Windows NT Workstation computers have the following built-in local groups:

- Administrators
- Backup Operators
- Power Users
- Guests
- Replicator
- Users

Note

The rights associated with built-in user groups are what give them their functionality. For an in-depth discussion of user rights and the functions that can be performed by a member of a built-in user group, see Chapter 26, "Rights and Permissions."

Creating User Groups

These built-in groups make it easy to set up initial groups of users that can perform standard server or network management tasks. For more specific functions, you can create your own groups. To do so, use the User Manager for Domains utility.

First, make a list of the functional groups you want to create, based on the resources or type of access you think each group needs. For example, if your domain supports several different business units, such as an accounting department, a research department, and a warehouse, you might want to create three user groups, one for each of these departments. If one group of users, such as the accounting users, needs to be further subdivided into groups with some having more access to confidential data than others, you can create several user groups for that department instead of a single group.

The important point to remember is that by creating groups, you make the job of granting or revoking access rights easier as resources or users on the network change.

To create a group, select either Create New Local group or Create New Global Group from the User menu in the User Manager for Domains. In Figure 22.7, you can see the dialog box used to create a new local group.

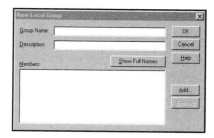

Figure 22.7   To create a new local group, specify the group name and then add members.

After you enter the name of the new group and an optional description, click the Add button to bring up the Add Users and Groups dialog box. This dialog box is used for many different functions in the User Manager for Domains where selecting users is required. In Figure 22.8, you can see that all you have to do is select a username or a group name, and then click the Add button to move that name to the Add Names display at the bottom of the dialog box. You can use the Search button to locate names if the list for your network is very large and you don't want to scroll through the entire list to find the correct name.

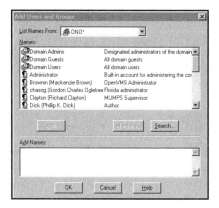

Figure 22.8   Select user or other groups to place into the new local group.

After you have finished selecting users or groups to add to this local group, click the OK button at the bottom. You are returned to the New Local Group dialog box, and the users or group names that were selected now appear in the Members list at the bottom of the dialog box. Click the OK button to dismiss this dialog box when you are finished.

If you need to modify group membership later, all you must do is select the user group from the display on the main window of the User Manager for Domains, and then select Properties from the User menu. Alternatively, you can double-click the group name to bring up the Properties sheet. This display is exactly like the one used when creating the new group, except for its title. You can use the Add and Remove buttons to modify group membership.

Special User Groups

In addition to the local and global built-in groups that were just described, there are several user groups whose membership is not assigned by the administrator. These groups are not seen when looking in the list of user groups in the User Manager for Domains. They are, however, seen when you use other utilities, such as the Windows NT Explorer to grant access to files and directories. These groups are

- **Interactive**—Users who are currently logged on locally to the computer.
- **Network**—Users who are currently logged on to the computer via the network.
- **Everyone**—Just what it says, this means any interactive or network user on the computer.
- **System**—The operating system itself.
- **Creator owner**—The user who creates an object, such as a file or directory.

Managing User Accounts

On Windows NT Server, member servers, and Windows NT Workstation computers, the User Manager utility is used to manage the local SAM. In a domain, the utility is similar but is called the User Manager for Domains. This is the tool that you use for most user account management in Windows NT. To start the User Manager for Domains, select it from the Administrative Tools folder in the Programs folder.

The User menu in this utility can be used to add, delete, or modify user accounts. To modify an existing account, simply double-click the account name, and the properties dialog box appears. You can also highlight the account and select Properties from the User menu.

To add a new user, select New User from the User menu. The New User dialog box (shown in Figure 22.9) appears. You can enter the user's logon username here (up to 20 characters), along with other useful information such as the user's full name and a description of what the account is used for.

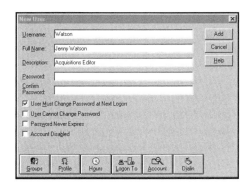

Figure 22.9   Add a new user by specifying a username and other information for the account.

When you enter the password for the user account, you have to enter it twice to confirm what you type because the display only shows asterisks when you type the password. You can select several password options from the check boxes. If you select User Must Change Password at Next Logon, the user is prompted when they first use the account to change the password to a new value known only to them. You can use this same check box on an existing user's properties dialog box when resetting a user password if the user has forgotten it, setting it to a value you can give the user, and still forcing them to change it.

If you select User Cannot Change Password, the user is locked out of this function. This function is useful for service accounts such as for SQL Server because it will preclude anyone from changing the password, which would cause the service to not start.

If you select Password Never Expires, you bypass the password expiration policy you can set for the domain that usually forces the user to change his password to a new value on a periodic basis. Finally, you can use the Account Disabled check box to temporarily disable logons for an account when you do not want to delete the account instead.

After you have finished filling in the information solicited by this dialog box, you can click Add to add the account, or you can use the buttons at the bottom of the dialog box to bring up additional prompts.

Adding a User to a Group

If you select the Groups button from the New User dialog box, you get the Group Memberships dialog box shown in Figure 22.10. When an account is first created it is, by default, a member of the Domain Users local group. You can select other groups from those shown and use the Add button to add the user to the group. You can select a group that the user is already a member of and use the Remove button to remove the user from that group. To specify the primary group to which a user will belong, highlight that group under the Member Of box and click the Set button. When you have finished selecting user groups for this user, click the OK button.

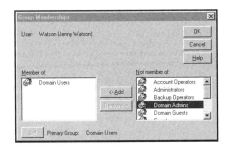

Figure 22.10   The Group Memberships dialog box enables you to control which groups a user belongs to.

User Profiles

You can use the Profiles button to bring up the User Environment Profile dialog box. Here, you can specify a path to the location of the file that contains the user's profile (desktop and environment settings) as well as the name of a logon script that is to be executed each time the user logs on to the domain. In Figure 22.11, you can see that this is also where to specify the path to the user's home directory.

Figure 22.11   The User Environment Profile dialog box enables you to set the user's profile and home directory.

You can also specify drive letters in the Connect box and then specify a path name. This causes the user to be automatically connected to the file shares you specify when the user logs on to the system.

Limiting the Times a User Can Log On

The Hours button brings up the Logon Hours dialog box (see Figure 22.12), where you can select the days and hours that a user account can be used.

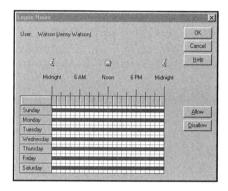

Figure 22.12   Specify the hours an account can be used in this dialog box.

In this display, you can select one-hour time periods by clicking one or more of them, and then using the Allow or Disallow button to specify whether the user can log on during that time period. By default, all the boxes representing hours for all days are filled in with a blue color indicating that the user can log on at that time.

Tip

What happens when a user is already logged on and the time changes to a period where they are disallowed? This depends on the settings you make in the Accounts Policy for the domain. You can allow the user to continue working but not make any new network connections, or you can set the policy to force the user off the server when the time changes to a disallowed period.

Limiting Which Workstations a User Can Log On To

The Logon To button brings up the Logon Workstations dialog box (see Figure 22.13), which you can use to specify up to eight workstations that the user is allowed to log on to using this domain account.

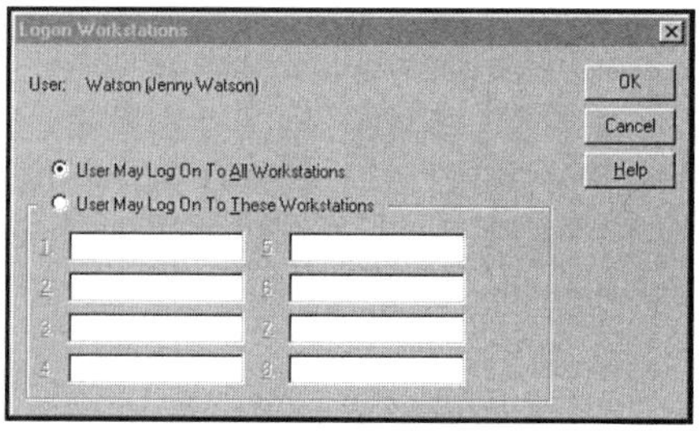

Figure 22.13   The Logon Workstations dialog box can be used to limit the workstations a user can use to log on to the domain.

If you want the user to be capable of logging on by using any workstation in the domain (the default selection), select the appropriate radio button in this dialog box.

This dialog box can be useful in a situation where security is a high priority. For user accounts that have been given advanced rights and are capable of accessing sensitive data, you might want to restrict their use to computers that are in a particular physical location that can be monitored. For example, the payroll process is usually a very sensitive function in any organization. Not only do you want to prevent unauthorized users from modifying information here, but you also want to keep prying eyes out of information that might cause user embarrassment or discomfort. By limiting the payroll applications to specific user logon accounts and by restricting those accounts to selected workstations, you can make the monitoring process easier and more defined.

Account Information

The Account button brings up the Account Information dialog box, shown in Figure 22.14. Here, you can specify that an account will never expire, or you can set a date at which time the account will no longer be capable of being used for a domain logon.

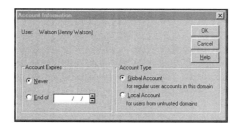

Figure 22.14   The Account Information dialog box can be used to specify the type of account and limit its use.

There are two types of domain accounts, and you can select the type for this account in this dialog box. A global account is the default account for a user in that user's own home domain. This account can be placed into a global group and exported to another domain to be granted access to resources. Local groups are more limited. They are used to provide access for a user who is not a member of a trusted domain. This can be used by a user in another Windows NT domain or by a user from another operating system type. The local account cannot be used to log on locally to a Windows NT computer; it is provided so you can give access via the network. Because the local account is provided so you can give access to your domain to special-case users, you cannot place local accounts into a global group and export them to another domain.

Allowing Dialup Access

If you want the user to be capable of dialing into the network using the remote access service (RAS), click the Dialup button to bring up the Dialin Information dialog box (see Figure 22.15). Here, you can select the call back option, which if enabled means that after a user dials into the network, the server disconnects the phone and then dials the user's computer back. This can be used for security purposes or for cost savings.

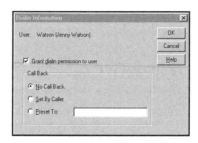

Figure 22.15 The Dialin Information dialog box can be used to control dialup access to the network for this account.

The Call Back options here are

- **No Call Back**—This is the most common form. It enables a user to log in via a modem to begin working, after validation.
- **Set By Caller**—The caller can specify the telephone number that the server is to use to perform the call back function.
- **Preset To**—The administrator can set the telephone number that is to be used for the call back.

If security is not a great issue for this user's account, you can select the No Call Back option. If the user is a mobile user and you want the long-distance charges to be paid by the server's end of the telephone line, use the function to allow the caller to specify the call back number. If security is a very important issue for this account, use the third option so you can specify the number that will always be called back. This prevents users from other locations from using this account to dial into your system and establish a RAS session.

Replication Between Domain Controllers

Modifications to the SAM database are always made on the primary domain controller. On a periodic basis, the PDC checks the database to determine whether any changes have been made. The default value for this time interval is five minutes. When changes to the database are detected, the PDC sends a message to each BDC informing them that it holds changes that need to be applied to their copy of the database. The BDC can then poll the PDC to get the updates. This process is called *directory synchronization*.

To prevent a large number of BDCs from making synchronization requests at the same time, the PDC staggers the messages it sends out to multiple BDCs. By default, the PDC sends the message to only 10 BDCs. When they have finished the synchronization process, the PDC sends the message to the next 10 BDCs that need to be informed.

Full and Partial Synchronization

There are two types of synchronization: full and partial. When a BDC is created during a Windows NT Server installation, one of the first tasks it must perform is to download a copy of the full SAM database. This is an example of *full synchronization*. When complete, the BDC is capable of responding to logon requests from clients.

When changes are made on the PDC, they are not immediately propagated to the domain's BDCs. Instead, a change log file that is 64KB in size is used to buffer the modifications. Each change record is stamped with a serial number and a version number. The change log is a circular file. This means that when it becomes full, it simply wraps back on itself, overwriting the oldest record in the file.

When the PDC sends out notifications that changes exist in the database, it does so only to those BDCs it knows do not have the most recent data. The PDC can do this because it keeps track of the serial number of the most recent records updated to each BDC. This prevents unnecessary replication traffic. When a BDC polls the PDC for the changes it needs, it receives only those changes it has not already gotten during a previous poll, based on the serial number.

A full replication can still occur under this process. For example, a BDC can be taken offline for an extended period of time, or the network link between the BDC and the PDC might be unavailable due to a network problem. Again, using the serial numbers of the records it already has, the BDC can determine whether any changes have been overwritten in the PDC's change log, and can then request a full synchronization so it still has a complete copy of the database.

Logon Failures Related to Synchronization

One common function performed by administrators or help desk personnel is that of adding a new user account or changing the password for an account when the user cannot log on. As simple a matter as this might seem, the role played by backup domain controllers can be an issue when this is done in a Windows NT network.

When a password is changed or an account added, it is done on the master copy of the database that resides on the PDC. Remember that the BDC does not immediately receive updates made on the SAM. If you add a new account or modify a user account, whether it be to change the password or remove a lockout condition, the user who is validated at a remote location by a backup domain controller might not be capable of immediately logging on because the BDC might not be aware of the change.

You can just tell the user to wait and try again, but this is not the kind of response that builds trust with the help desk or the administrator. Instead, Windows NT allows you to force the synchronization process to begin. To do this, invoke the Server Manager, which is found in the Administrative Tools folder. From the Computer menu, select Synchronize Entire Domain. A pop-up dialog box informs you that this might take a few minutes. Click Yes to proceed. The PDC begins to send out messages to the BDS informing them that it is time to synchronize. A message similar to that shown in Figure 22.16 is displayed.

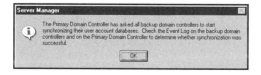

Figure 22.16 This is the dialog box provided by Server Manager when a forced domain synchronization is requested.

After a few minutes, you can check the Event Viewer to find out if the synchronization process has completed. As the message shows, check both the BDC and the PDC for these messages. The Event Viewer utility enables you to connect to another computer to check messages in its log files, so this can be done from one location by the administrator. When synchronization has finished, you can instruct the user to try the new password or account again.

Passwords and Policies

Windows NT gives the administrator the capability to set certain parameters that control passwords and accounts. This is called the account policy for the domain. To view the defaults or to make changes, select Account from the Policies menu in the User Manager for Domains utility. The Account Policy dialog box is displayed (see Figure 22.17).

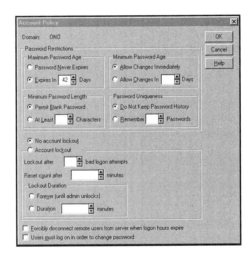

Figure 22.17 The Account Policy dialog box.

As you can see, you have several things to configure. The values you choose for these parameters reflect the degree of security you want to enforce at your sight. At the same time, you need to balance your concerns with the abilities of your users. For example, if you set a large minimum password size and a low value for the number of days it can be used, users might end up writing down passwords just to keep track of them.

You can configure the following parameters:

- **Minimum and maximum password age**—The minimum password age specifies the number of days that must elapse before a user is allowed to change a password. The maximum password age is the number of days that a password can be used, after which the system will force the user to change it. Both of these parameters can be set to a value ranging from 1 to 999 days.

- **Minimum password length**—This is the minimum number of characters that must be used for a password. Too small a value makes it easy for hacker programs to guess a password. Too large a value makes it difficult for users to think up new passwords. This parameter can be set to a value ranging from 1 to 14, or you can permit a blank password (no password). It is hard to imagine a network where you might want to allow, as a policy for every user in the domain, a blank password.

- **Password uniqueness**—The system keeps a "history" list of passwords used by each user and does not enable them to reset their password to one that is still in the list. This prevents users from constantly reusing a few easy-to-remember passwords, which can be bad for security purposes. Set this parameter to a value between 1 and 24. Selecting not to keep a history list is probably not a good idea because many users will take advantage of this, and eventually someone else will find out what their usual password is.

- **Account lockout**—You can set up the system so that a user account is locked out after several failed logon attempts. This can be used to prevent an unauthorized user from trying to guess a password for an account, as is done in the brute-force method by many hacker programs that simply go through a dictionary, trying every word until they crack an account. If you set a value for bad logon attempts, you can also use the Reset Count After field to a time value (in minutes). This field specifies the period of time during which the failed logon attempts are counted. The Lockout Duration fields can be used to permanently lock the account until an administrator intervenes, or to set a time in minutes that the account will be disabled. A good idea is to set a small value for the Lockout After parameter (3–5 is a good choice), while using a long lockout value. Thirty minutes to an hour usually suffices to deter many unauthorized users.

At the bottom of this dialog box, you can see two other check boxes. The Forcibly Disconnect Remote Users check box must be checked for the user to be disconnected from the server when they stay logged on past an authorized time period specified in the Hours button of their account properties dialog box. If the second check box—User Must Log On In Order to Change Password—is checked, users cannot log on after their passwords expire and change them. The administrator has to perform this function instead. If this box is not checked, after a user password expires they can still log on, but only to change the password.

Detecting Failed Logon Attempts

There are many reasons why logon failures can occur. The most common reason is that users forget passwords or type them incorrectly enough times to trigger the account lockout mechanism. Because Windows NT enables you to create a single username and password logon for each user, the problem of multiple passwords is usually not a problem here as it is for some other networks.

The Windows NT Event Viewer utility, found in the Administrative Tools section along with the User Manager for Domains, can be used to check for failed logon attempts. This is the first place you want to look when a user is having problems logging on to the domain or connecting to a resource on a remote server. The user might not be providing the correct password or is trying a username for which there is no account. The Event Viewer keeps three log files: Application, System, and Security. You will find messages relating to logon attempts in the Security log file.

Some of the more common messages related to logon attempts are listed in Table 22.1. You must enable security logging in User Manager to generate these messages.

Table 22.1   Common Logon Errors You Can See Using the Event Viewer

Event ID	Description
528	Successful logon
529	Invalid username or password
530	Violation of logon time restrictions
531	Account is disabled
532	Account expired
533	Logon not allowed on this computer
534	Invalid logon type (network or interactive)
535	Expired password
536	NetLogon service is not running
537	Unexpected error
538	Successful logout
539	Account currently locked out

As you can see, even successful logon and logout events can be tracked. These types of messages can be useful when you are trying to determine who was on the system, perhaps during off hours, when you are trying to troubleshoot security problems. The other messages can be helpful in quickly identifying what the problem is when a user cannot log on to a server or connect to a resource.

The security log file you can examine using the Event Viewer can be configured to track all successful and unsuccessful logon attempts. This includes users who log on locally at the computer, connections made via network access, and logons by special accounts that you set up to run services.

Events such as these are not automatically tracked by Windows NT. You must enable the types of events you want to audit before they can be recorded in the security log file. See Chapter 37, "Auditing and Other Monitoring Measures," for information on how to set up the events to audit for Windows NT computers.

Strategies to Minimize Logon Problems

The best way to solve a problem is to take all necessary measures to ensure that the problem doesn't happen in the first place. Although it is not possible to completely eliminate every source of failed logon problems, you can do a lot to keep your network users happy by taking a few precautions:

- Place a backup domain controller on every physical subnet. If a network link goes down, users can still be validated by the local BDC and continue to work with resources they can still connect to. Any Windows NT Server computer can be created as a BDC, so if you have a server on a subnet that is offering resources and it is not already overloaded, create it as a BDC and allow it to serve two roles.

■ Enforce reasonable password policies. Some operating systems enable you to computer-generate random passwords that are very difficult to remember. If a user cannot remember a password, most of the time they just write it down somewhere, which can compromise security. If you force users to change passwords too frequently, again, they will most likely have a hard time remembering what the recent password is unless they write it down somewhere. If you set the account policy lockout values to low, you will find users get locked out because of simple typing errors, and the help desk will spend a lot of time unlocking these accounts.

■ Keep track of user accounts. You can use a paper method or an electronic one such as a spreadsheet or database. Delete accounts for users who leave the company and create new ones for new employees. Getting rid of the dead wood helps avoid confusion when troubleshooting and helps keep the SAM databases down to a reasonable size.

■ Never use generic accounts in which more than one user logs on under the same username. Although this is a tempting idea because you have fewer user accounts to manage, it can be a security nightmare if something goes wrong and you are unable to use auditing measures to figure out the who, what, and when of the matter. Also, when more than one person is using the same account to log on, it takes only one person with fumbly-fingers to incorrectly type a password a few times and lock an account, preventing others that use the same account from logging on also.

To fully understand how to troubleshoot problems with logons, make yourself knowledgeable about the Windows NT Event Viewer administrative tool. You can find out more about this valuable utility in Chapter 37.

Summary

The logon process in Windows NT is controlled by computers that play the roles of primary and backup domain controllers. These computers hold copies of the security database called the Security Accounts Manager (SAM). Trust relationships between domains in the network enable users to access resources throughout the network without having to enter additional usernames or passwords. To make administration of user rights and privileges easier, users can be placed into administrative units called local and global groups. The administrator can then grant access to resources to these groups instead of just to individual users.

There are four domain models in a Windows NT network. A single domain contains only a single PDC, and all user accounts and shares reside on that domain. A single master domain contains one top-level domain for user accounts and uses resource domains with one-way trusts to manage file and print access. A multiple master domain contains multiple user domains and separate resource domains with one-way trusts to each master domain. The complete trust model has multiple domains, each with two-way trust relationships to all the others.

The Event Viewer administrative tool can be configured to track failed logons and can be used to troubleshoot these problems.

NetWare

23

SOME OF THE MAIN TOPICS IN THIS CHAPTER ARE

NetWare History

The Bindery and Novell Directory Services

NetWare is a networking product that has been around longer than most any other product. While vendors come and go, Novell has continued to upgrade and enhance NetWare, adapting it to new processors, different memory models, and other technologies as the industry grew. Because NetWare has been around for such a long time, it is not easy to lump into one group. From NetWare 2.x through NetWare 5.0, different mechanisms are used to log on to the network or gain access to the services it can provide. For example, NetWare 3.x users log on to each server that holds information they need to access. NetWare 4.x and 5.0 provide NDS, and users can log in via the directory and gain access to resources that reside on servers throughout the network.

In this chapter, you will delve quickly into the background history of NetWare, and then look at the login process that users go through to connect to NetWare servers and services.

NetWare History

NetWare was introduced in the early 1980s as a product called ShareNet. ShareNet enabled PC users to share files and printers on a network. Early NetWare versions were hardware and software dependent, and it wasn't until later that ShareNet became independent of hardware and was completely software driven. Although Novell NetWare is primarily Intel-based, versions of NetWare are available for other platforms.

NetWare 2.x was written for the Intel 80286 processor and was sometimes referred to as NetWare 286. The compilers for NetWare 2.x were written in 16-bit code, thus limiting itself to the memory management of the 286 processor. Because the 286 processor could only address 16 megabytes of RAM, this adversely affected overall performance of all NetWare 286 versions.

NetWare continued to gain in popularity throughout the 1980s and 1990s, adding features such as disk mirroring, support for more advanced processors, and better client shells. Novell introduced *NLMs (NetWare Loadable Modules)* in NetWare 3.0. NLMs are small programs that are loaded to the server's memory when needed and unloaded when they were no longer needed. When they are unloaded, the memory they used is freed up and returned to the memory pool. This was especially useful you had to upgrade an NLM—you just unloaded the module, renamed it or deleted it, and then installed the upgraded NLM.

Tip

Literally thousands of third-party NLMs are available for NetWare. But, before you scramble to introduce a new NLM to your production server, *test it!* Installing your new NLM on a test server that is identical to your production servers can save you tons of headaches, not to mention your job!

Support for the ODI was also a great improvement over the older versions of NetWare. ODI allowed for multiple protocol support over a single network interface card (NIC). In addition to supporting multiple protocols, ODI allowed the NIC to use multiple frame types, which proved valuable in a mixed computer environment. Suppose you had a Production department that had Apple computers with AppleTalk and a Human Resource department that had PCs with IPX/SPX. With ODI in place, the two departments could access the same server.

NetWare 4.x was another substantial upgrade over existing versions of NetWare. NetWare 4.x featured

- Novell Directory Services
- File system improvements
- Network communication improvements
- Client shell improvements

As PC networks came to age, users demanded higher availability, more storage, and an easier interface to the network. NetWare addressed all these by providing a richer set of client utilities and file system features.

If you're familiar with NetWare 3.x file systems, you should be aware of the way Novell organizes volumes into blocks. Files that are larger than the disk block size will need multiple disk blocks to hold the entire file (or part of it). This causes wasted disk space. For example, if you have a block size of 4K on your SYS volume and you have a file that is 6K, you will use two 4K blocks to store the file that uses a total of 8K of disk space. That means 2K of the 8K allocated is wasted.

Disk Block Suballocation optimizes disk storage. Suballocation modifies the disk blocks, allowing you to subdivide a block into smaller units. A 64K block can be divided into (2) 32K units, (4) 16K units, and so on, down to (128) 512-byte units (see Figure 23.1). With the default block size of 64K, a 65K file will be written to one 64K block and one 64K block that has been suballocated into (64) 1K units. The remaining (63) 1K units will be used by other files that need a 1K unit to complete the file write operation.

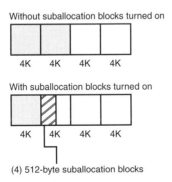

Figure 23.1   Using disk block suballocation allows for more efficient usage of disk storage.

In addition, by using a larger block size, there are fewer entries in the FAT (File Allocation Table), saving disk space as well as decreasing the amount of memory needed to mount volumes. The less memory needed to mount volumes, the faster they will mount.

Tip

Novell recommends using 64K blocks and never letting volume free space go lower than 15–20 percent when suballocation is turned on. This will keep the server from going into aggressive suballocation mode, which can cause disk thrashing.

Other important features include

- **Data migration**—Data migration is the capability to have the operating system automatically move data to another device (tape, hard disk, optical drive, and so on) when a file has reached a specified age. For example, you can set data migration to take place when a file on a volume is one week old. The operating system will move the data to a specified device. The file still appears to be on the volume, but when the file is requested, the file server will search for the file on the device to which it was moved and restore it automatically.

- **File Compression**—After a set period of time, the NetWare operating system can compress files automatically to save disk space.

- **Read-Ahead file access**—Read-Ahead is when the operating system places the next block of data after the requested file into the cache buffers in anticipation that the user will request the next file.

Network administrators also had demands. As networks grew larger, administrators had to work harder to keep up. The administrators were in great need of a manageable network with an intuitive interface, so Novell gave them Novell Directory Services (NDS), which is discussed in the next sections.

The Bindery and Novell Directory Services

The *bindery* is a feature that was part of NetWare's operating systems prior to NetWare 4.x. In NetWare 2.x, the bindery files, NET$BIND.SYS and NET$BVAL.SYS, were located in the SYSTEM directory on the SYS volume. NetWare 3.x made some structure changes to the files and renamed them NET$OBJ.SYS, NET$VAL.SYS, and NET$PROP.SYS.

Bindery files were ASCII flat files that stored information about users, groups, and print queues. Anything that had any kind of security associated to it was stored in the bindery files. Every NetWare server on the network had its own set of bindery files. That meant a user who had permission to access a server had to have an account on that server. The account information was stored in the bindery. Because each server had its own bindery, a user who had access to multiple servers had to authenticate to each one. There was much overhead in this architecture, it was time-consuming to administer, and the users didn't like having to log in to multiple servers.

NetWare Directory Services (NDS)

With NetWare 4.x, the bindery system was replaced by Novell Directory Services (NDS). NDS is a distributed database system that holds all the network's information in a hierarchical tree-like structure. The primary function of the NDS tree is to authenticate users onto the network. The tree is normally broken into portions called *partitions*. The partitions are replicated to other servers on the network to allow for fault tolerance. Should one authenticating server fail or crash, another server with a duplicate partition (replica) can pick up the responsibility to authenticate users and provide access to the network resources.

Note

Directory services are a hot topic in the networking world today. The much delayed Windows 2000 Advanced Server is a vast makeover from its predecessor Windows 4.0. The central feature in Windows 2000, as in NetWare 4.x and NetWare 5.x, is the directory services component. Both systems incorporate technologies that were first defined in the X.500 specifications and later made more usable by the Lightweight Directory Access Protocol (LDAP). To gain a better understanding of the mechanisms underlying directory services, see Appendix E, "Overview of the X.500 and LDAP Protocols."

Along with its authenticating role, the tree holds information about every object on the network (see Figure 23.2). All network resources are objects. An object is everything from a user, a group of users, and servers, to software applications.

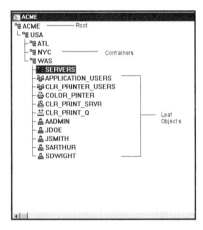

Figure 23.2 The NDS tree contains information about many types of objects on the network.

Every NDS tree starts with a [root], and branches off into containers. A container can hold subordinate container objects and *leaf objects*. A leaf object represents network resources such as printers, users, servers, volumes, and others. Every object has properties associated with it. For example, a user object contains all the information about the user such as first and last name, phone number, and assigned access rights to other objects (see Figure 23.3). The NDS also holds all security information assigned to each object. The Access Control List (ACL) property of an object holds lists of who has access rights (trustees) and what those rights are (rights assignments).

The NDS tree has many tools to administer it, but the most common one is NWAdmin (see Figure 23.4). With NWAdmin, you can create or modify objects in the tree. To maintain the structure of the tree. You would use Novell's Partition Manager.

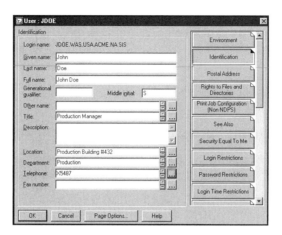

Figure 23.3 Leaf objects in the NDS tree contain information about actual objects, such as users.

Figure 23.4 The NetWare Administrator tool can be used to manage objects in the NDS tree.

When planning the tree structure, plan it from the top down, moving one level at a time. Try to keep the amount of levels to a minimum. A tree with too many levels can lead to poor performance and administrative problems. Normally, the first level, or container, off the root is the organization, and then there is a container for each department. Within every department, you can create containers for each group. However, it is recommended that you create group objects if the groups are small. When departments grow large, you can break the department off into its own tree partition. When you create a partition, the partition is stored and maintained by a server within the partition. When you have more than one server in the partition, NDS will automatically store a replica of the partition's NDS database onto it. This provides fault tolerance for that partition. When a third or fourth server is installed into the partition, it is recommended you create at least one more replica for redundancy.

Context Names

Each object in an NDS tree has an object name. You can have two separate objects with the same name, but the objects have to be in two separate containers. For example, JSMITH can be in the Marketing container and in the Sales container. To identify each user uniquely, use the full *context* name of the object. An object's context is the description of the object's location in the tree. The uniqueness of the name depends on where the object is located in the tree. The users mentioned earlier are unique in their context names listed here:

> *JSMITH.MARKETING.ATL.*
>
> *JSMITH.SALES.NYC.*

Contexts are similar to the file system hierarchy of DOS and UNIX. NetWare keeps track of your current context and uses it as a default when you are trying to access network resources without using the full location.

Another way of identifying an object within the tree is to use *typeful* names. As the name implies, the typeful name specifies the type of object in the context. For example

The typeless name is

> *JSMITH.MARKETING.ATL.ACME.USA*

The typeful name is

> *.CN=JSMITH.OU=MARKETING.OU=ATL.O=ACME.C=USA*

where

- *C* indicates the country
- *O* is the business organization
- *OU* is an organizational unit in the company
- *CN* is the user object's common name

Logging In to the Network

When you log in to the network, the login utility searches for the nearest authenticating server on the network. The authenticating server takes the login request from the workstation and scans its NDS database for the user object. If the user's object is in the replica, the authenticating server grants access to the workstation based on the information in its ACL.

The server also executes any login script associated to the user and the containers that the user is located in. If user JDOE logs in, the script of each container in JDOE's context will be executed. If no login script is present, a default login script will be run. To turn off the default login script, type NO_DEFAULT in the container or profile login script.

A fourth login script can be executed. If the user is associated to a *profile* object in a container, the login script for the profile will execute when the user logs in. A profile login script is normally used when you want to write one login script for a group of users who need a particular drive mapping.

A login script (shown in Figure 23.5) is basically a list of commands that are executed when a user logs in. A login script can use its own commands to map drives or capture network printers. Login scripts can also execute external programs.

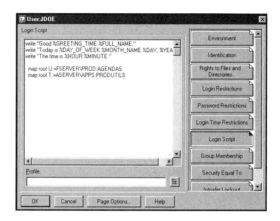

Figure 23.5   The login script is a list of commands that are executed when the user logs into the network.

Login Scripts

There are many commands available to use in login scripts. Using the rich command language that NetWare provides, you can customize the environment that each users sees. By using the INCLUDE command to partition login scripts into several functional units, you can make system management tasks easier by constructing portions of login scripts that can be used by groups of users.

In this section, you will look at some of the more common commands that are used. For a complete reference of login script commands, see Appendix D, "NetWare Login Script Reference."

MAP

To help centrally manage drive mappings, you can use the MAP command in the login script. The MAP command is used exactly like the command-line MAP utility, with an exception. You cannot use the MAP NEXT command, which will automatically assign the next available unused drive letter.

To map a drive letter to a user's home directory on a server, type the following command into the login script:

```
MAP F:=USERS:HOME\%LOGIN_NAME
```

This will assign the drive letter F:\ to the user's home directory on the USERS volume. The %LOGIN_NAME is a variable that a script can use instead of hard coded assignments.

IF...THEN...ELSE

Using the IF commands allows you to execute a command or multiple commands conditionally. The IF command is followed by a condition, the keyword THEN, and then a command or a set of commands to be executed.

For example

```
IF MEMBER OF "MARKETING" THEN MAP H:=USERS:HOME\MRKTNG
```

In this example, if the user who logged in is in a group object named "Marketing", the MAP command will execute and assign the letter "H" to a network drive that is a directory of the HOME directory of the USERS volume.

You can use the keyword "ELSE" if the condition is not met and use END to complete the IF, THEN, ELSE statement.

For example

```
IF MEMBER OF "MARKETING" THEN
    MAP H:=USERS:HOME\MRKTNG
    MAP I:=DATA:SHARED\MRKTNG
ELSE
    MAP H:=USERS:HOME\SALES
    MAP I:=DATA:SHARED\SALES
END
```

INCLUDE

The Include command is a useful command that allows you to include another file within the current login script. The other login script can be a login script for another container or profile or even a text file containing login script commands.

For example, the following line will run the login script associated to the ACME organizational unit:

```
INCLUDE .OU=ACME
```

In most circumstances, you will have groups of users who share common resources, such as those employed in the same department or business unit. It is easier to create a single file that contains all elements common to their login process, and then use the INCLUDE command in each user's individual login script. When you use this technique, changes are easy because you must make changes in only one file instead of many different files.

WRITE

The Write command will display a message to the user as the login script is processed. You can include script variables to show environment information to the user.

For example, the following will display `Greetings, John Smith` when user JSMITH logs in:

```
WRITE "Greetings, %FULL_NAME."
```

You can include other script variables throughout the `WRITE` command, including

MACHINE—Displays the type of machine the user is logging in from.

OS—Displays the operating system type.

OS_VERSION—Displays the version of the operating system, such as WIN95.

GREETING TIME—Displays the time of day: Morning, Afternoon, or Evening.

REM

The `REM` command denotes remarks in the login script. Remarks are comments that the script author uses to describe commands to make it easier for other administrators to decipher the script.

For example

```
REM The following command checks for OS version and executes the
REM appropriate program.
```

You can also use asterisks (*) or semicolons (;) to denote remarks in a login script. The use of comments in any kind of script file, much less one used for login purposes, can greatly enhance readability of the file by those who are not familiar with it. By providing documentation in the file through comments, you can make system administration tasks easier because you do not have to go elsewhere to get an explanation of why the actions taken in the file are being performed.

EXIT

The `Exit` command is used to end the login script either at the end of the login script or inside condition statements.

Troubleshooting Login Scripts

Use the `MAP DISPLAY ON` and `MAP ERRORS ON` when you're trying to debug a login script. With these commands off, you will not see any error information displayed should any of your script commands fail.

Do not execute terminate-and-stay-resident (TSR) programs from your login script. If you desire to execute a TSR, use the @ sign before your command. This will start a separate process outside the login process. If you execute a TSR without the @ sign and the TSR hangs, the login script will hang as well. Also, as long as a login script is open by a user, you cannot edit the login script.

Be careful not to use too many `IF`, `THEN`, and `Else` statements in your login script. This can make it difficult to debug the login script if you run into problems. And always use the keyword `END` at the end of your conditional statements.

Remember the order in which login scripts are executed. The container login script runs first; then the profile login script (if one exists) runs, and then the user login script executes. Each subordinate login script supercedes the login script above it. For example, the user login script overrides the container login script and the profile login script. The profile login script overrides the container login script. If no login script exists, the DEFAULT login script will run. To prevent the DEFAULT login script from executing, you can place the command NO_DEFAULT in the container or profile login script. Also, you cannot edit the DEFAULT login script.

If you want to execute DOS commands from your login script, use the pound sign (#) in front of your command. This creates a child process from your login script process. If you have a pound (#) sign in your login script without a DOS command after it, an error message is displayed.

If you would like to prevent users from executing user login scripts, you can put the EXIT command at the end of the container login script. This will prevent the user login script from executing and is useful if users mistakenly override important system wide settings.

Summary

NetWare networks exist that still run the older NetWare 2.x product, and there are those that are made up entirely of the newest NetWare 5.0 networking software running on IP. Regardless, it is important that the administrator have a good understanding of how each user logs on to a server or NDS to gain access to network resources. A great deal of the environment that the user sees is constructed by the login script, and it is important that the administrator be well versed in the commands that make up these scripts.

UNIX and Linux

CHAPTER 24

SOME OF THE MAIN TOPICS IN THIS CHAPTER ARE

User Administration

The /etc/passwd **File**

Common Logon Problems

Although the UNIX operating system is not as great a success on the user's desktop as the Window platforms, it remains one of the more popular operating systems on which mission-critical applications reside. Many versions of UNIX exist in the world of computing. In addition to the commercial versions of UNIX and freely distributed versions such as FreeBSD, the Linux operating system has made significant inroads in the past few years. Indeed, a large number of Web servers on the Internet are based on Linux platforms, as are many firewall products.

User Administration

Like all major operating systems, UNIX requires that users authenticate themselves before they can use system resources. This is done by using a username and password during the logon process. The administrator is responsible for maintaining the system files that store this information and, unlike Windows NT or Novell's NDS, must keep track of user information in files on each UNIX server in the network.

Administering a large network of UNIX-based machines is made easier by having access to utilities and applications such as the Networking Information Service (NIS). NIS makes it possible to keep changes to important system files, such as the password file, on many different machines. This chapter covers NIS features found in most versions of UNIX and Linux. In addition to administering a network, network administrators also need to pay attention to security; so, this chapter also discusses some security features such as shadowing passwords.

Network Information Service (NIS)

The NIS (also known as the Yellow Pages, or YP, service) allows a networked system to retrieve information stored in databases that exist on a server within the same network. The information stored on the server can consist of user accounts, group information, remote file systems, hosts on the network, and so on. In a very small network, you could get by with storing this information on each local host. However, in a large network setting, this would be rather cumbersome to administer.

NIS provides a way of allowing all nodes on the network to access other systems on the network by authenticating against a NIS database. In an NIS network, there is an NIS master server, and then there are slaves and clients. The NIS master server maintains the database and accepts requests from clients. The NIS slaves have a duplicate database to provide redundancy and reduce the load on the NIS server. Clients are systems on the network that request database information from the NIS server or slaves.

During NIS setup, a utility converts system files into databases called NIS maps. NIS maps are created from files you are used to manipulating to administer your system. Such files are the password file (/etc/passwd) and the groups file (/etc/groups). More databases are created from the following list:

- **/etc/ethers** This file is used to create two NIS maps, ethers.byaddr and ethers.byname. The file is used by RARP, which translates ethernet addresses into IP addresses. This map is normally used when you support diskless workstations on the network.

- **/etc/networks** Produces two NIS maps, networks.byname and networks.byaddr.

- **/etc/services**   Creates one NIS map named `services.byname`. This map reflects port numbers that are assigned to services.

- **/etc/protocols**   This file creates two NIS maps called `protocols.byname` and `protocols.byaddr`. Protocols listed in the `/etc/protocols` file provide the protocol number and any alias for the protocol.

- **/etc/netmasks**   This file contains subnet masks, and an NIS map, `netmasks.byaddr`, is created for it.

- **/etc/hosts**   NIS maps `hosts.byname` and `hosts.byaddr`. These provide an IP address to hostname resolution, and vice versa. When DNS (Domain Name Service) is used, the hosts file is no longer needed to resolve hostnames and IP addresses.

- **/etc/aliases**   Creates NIS maps `mail.aliases` and `mail.byaddr` that define email aliases.

The NIS maps created by all these files are maintained by a centrally located server running the ypserv daemon. This means that workstations no longer need to maintain the preceding files on their workstation as long as they are running the ypbind daemon and are part of the NIS domain. The NIS domain is a totally separate entity from the DNS but they work well together. The NIS domain is more local and DNS is more global. When deciding on an NIS name, it is common to name it the same as your DNS domain name. That way, you avoid confusion when setting up systems.

The NIS maps are stored in a subdirectory of the /var/yp directory of the NIS server. The name of the subdirectory depends on what you name the NIS domain. For example, if you have a DNS domain name of acme.com and decide to name your NIS domain the same, your NIS maps will be stored in the /var/yp/acme.com directory. Normally, the NIS domain name is set during the startup of the machine if the domainname command is entered in one of the startup scripts. If it isn't, you can enter the command from the command line. For example

```
# domainname acme.com
```

This sets your NIS domain to acme.com. Using domainname by itself will display the current NIS domain.

Starting NIS

To get started with NIS, enter ypinit -m at the command line. The ypinit command creates the /var/yp/acme.com directory, reads the files in the /etc directory, and creates the NIS maps. The NIS maps are then saved in the acme.com directory. When the ypinit program is finished, enter the ypserv command to start the NIS server. When the server is up and running, you'll need to start the map transfer daemon. Type ypxfrd at the command line. You could also add the command to the /etc/rc.local file to have it start automatically at startup.

To start the NIS client on the same machine, type ypbind at the command line.

NIS Slaves

NIS slaves hold exact duplicates of NIS maps as the master server. The slave also runs the same ypserv daemon. The only difference between the two servers is that the slave only answers client requests; the slave doesn't make any changes to the NIS maps. Only the master server can update the NIS maps. When the master server makes a change to the maps, it then propagates the changes to all the slave servers in the NIS domain.

Setting Up Slaves

Creating a slave server is similar to creating the master server. First, you set the NIS domain name by typing domainname at the command line. After setting the NIS domain name, enter the following:

```
nisslave# ypinit -s nismaster
```

The -s option specifies you are setting up a slave server followed by the NIS domain master server name. After the slave server is initialized, the master server will transfer all the NIS domain information to the slave. During the setup of the slave server, it does not look at its local /etc files to create the NIS maps. The slave server only has the information that is stored in the maps on the master server.

Deciding when to create a slave server should be done during the initial planning phase of setting up the NIS network. Though growing networks don't exactly grow according to plan, it is possible to add slave servers later. If you add a slave server after the initial setup of the master server, you'll need to add the new slave's hostname to the ypservers map file.

To edit the ypservers map, you'll need to zero out the old information and add the new slave server name. Then you'll need to rebuild the map using the makedbm command. The whole process takes place on the NIS master server.

Type the following at the command line on the NIS master server:

```
nismaster# ypcat -k ypservers > /tmp/ypservers
```

(Edit the /tmp/ypservers with your favorite editor and add the new server name.)

```
nismaster# cd /var/yp
nismaster# /tmp/ypservers ¦ makedbm - /var/yp/NIS domain/ypservers
```

In this example, substitute your actual domain name for NIS domain.

NIS Clients

Starting the NIS client is simple. First, set the NIS domain on the local machine using the domainname command. Then start the ypbind service by entering ypbind at the command line. To have ypbind start every time the machine boots, ensure the ypbind script exists in the /etc/rc.local file and that it is not commented out.

The following is sample boot script to launch ypbind in the correct NIS domain:

```
domainname acme.com
. . .
if [ -d /var/yp ] ; then
  ypbind; echo -n ' ypbind'
fi
```

The *$/etc/passwd$* File

The file /etc/passwd is used by UNIX to store information about each user. This file contains information such as the user's password (in encrypted format) and the user's home directory. It is important that the administrator carefully manage this file to ensure a smooth logon process for users.

During the initial setup of the NIS master server, the ypinit process creates two NIS maps (passwd.byname and passwd.byuid) with the information found in the /etc/passwd file. The local passwd file is still referenced when a user logs in; the login process first tries to authenticate against the local /etc/passwd file. If it is unsuccessful, it authenticates against the NIS mapping on the master server.

The local /etc/passwd file still needs to be kept up to date for individual access to users on the network. The /etc/passwd file has an entry for each user on the system. Every entry in a Linux /etc/passwd file follows this format:

```
username:password:uid:gid:GECOS:homedir:shell
```

The username field contains a unique string of characters that identifies the user. The user uses this name to log in to the system.

The password field contains an encrypted representation of the user's password. If the field contains an asterisk (*), it denotes that the account is disabled. The encrypted password is set by the passwd program when the account is created or when the password is changed. If the field is empty, the user does not need to enter a password to access the system.

The uid (user ID) field contains a numerical identifier supplied by the system to identify the user to processes and file management. The uid and username both identify an existing account.

The gid (group ID) field contains an integer that refers to the user's default group. Valid group numbers are given in /etc/group/. When a process is started, its gid is set to the gid of its parent process. The gid is also referenced when creating new files and directories.

The GECOS (General Electric Comprehensive Operating System) field holds user information that can be retrieved by applications such as finger(1). The field must contain commas if there is more than one entry.

The homedir field contains the directory that the user is positioned in when he or she logs in; this is known as the home directory.

The shell field holds the default shell for the user. If the field is empty, the Bourne shell is normally used by default.

Typical entries in the /etc/passwd file would like this:

```
jdoe:Gfjhjo9Uia$jpo2dYtaGGdsh:223:100:John Doe:/home/jdoe:bash
rsmith:HuiTytsm$ld34tTbd9Saa2:119:110:Rob Smith:/home/rsmith:bash
```

Shadowing Passwords

Shadowing passwords is a method of improving system security by moving the encrypted passwords found in the `/etc/passwd` file to another file (`/etc/shadow`) with more restrictive file access permissions. Although the password in the `/etc/passwd` file is encrypted, it is still susceptible to malicious users who can use computer-based cracking programs to attempt to decipher the password. For this reason, the shadow password file can be used to make it more difficult for an unauthorized person to gain access to the encrypted password.

The shadowing utility doesn't encrypt the password any further than it already is, but it does provide some extra functionality. Some shadowing features include

- Utilities for adding, modifying, and deleting user accounts
- Password aging and expiration
- Account expiration and locking
- Double-length passwords
- Better control over users' passwords
- A configuration file that sets login defaults (`/etc/login.defs`)

With a shadow utility suite installed, the password field in the `/etc/passwd` file is changed to a placeholder of "x." The encrypted password is moved to the `/etc/shadow` file. The `/etc/passwd` file is no longer responsible for authenticating users. The `/etc/shadow` file takes over. The format of each entry line in the shadow file is different than the `/etc/passwd` file. Entries in the `/etc/shadow` file have the following format:

```
username:passwd:last:may:must:warn:expire:disable:reserved
```

The fields in this record are as follows:

- **username**—The user name
- **passwd**—The encoded password
- **last**—Days since Jan. 1, 1970 that the password was last changed
- **may**—Days before password may be changed
- **must**—Days after which password must be changed
- **warn**—Days before password is to expire that user is warned
- **expire**—Days after password expires that account is disabled
- **disable**—Days since Jan. 1, 1970 that account is disabled
- **reserved**—A reserved field

A sample line from `/etc/shadow` might be

```
username:Hj7RydS9a1op:9479:0:10000::::
```

The */etc/group* File

Using groups of users is an easy way of managing access rights to file systems and providing a way for users to share files among each other. Files on the system have user IDs and group IDs associated to them. The user ID identifies the owner, and the group ID identifies which group has rights to the file.

You can create and modify groups by editing the /etc/group file. The format for the file is field entries separated by colons. The exact format is

```
groupname:password:gid:members
```

The `groupname` field is the name of the group. The `password` field is a password assigned to the group to allow others to assign themselves using the `newgrp` command. However, the `password` field is rarely used for administrative purposes. When a password is not used, an asterisk occupies the field. The `gid` field contains a number assigned to identify the group. The same number is in the /etc/passwd file to identify the group the user belongs to. The `members` field lists the members that belong to the group. You could put group names in the `members` field if users need to belong to more than one group.

Common Logon Problems

The most common problem users encounter when logging in to a UNIX system is summed up by the following error message:

```
login incorrect
```

This message doesn't convey a great deal of information to the user, but usually indicates one of the following conditions:

- There is no user account in the /etc/passwd file for this username.
- The password entered by the user is not correct.
- The home directory for the user (as specified in the password file) does not exist.

In the first instance, the administrator might not have gotten around to creating a record for the user in the /etc/passwd file. It is more likely that the user entered the username incorrectly. Remember that in the UNIX operating system usernames and passwords are case-sensitive. For example, if your username is seglerg, entering `Seglerg` or `SEGLERG` will not work.

When choosing passwords, it is a good idea to choose one that is not easy for others to guess. Unfortunately, this sometimes means that it is also easy for a user to forget. Choosing a text string that contains both upper- and lowercase letters, along with numeric and alphabetic characters, is a good idea. When you receive the `login incorrect` error message, check to be sure you are really entering the password as it was originally set up.

In all cases, one of the first things to check is that the Caps Lock key is not on!

If the account is new, it is possible that the user's home directory has not been created or the administrator has not set the correct permissions on the directory to allow the user access to it. Using a script file to create new user accounts can help prevent this problem. Coding all the necessary commands by a script file will prevent the problems caused when an administrator creates a new account in a hurry and forgets a step or two.

Summary

UNIX (and its cousin Linux) requires that the administrator maintain password and other important system files on each UNIX computer system in the network. Using NIS can make the administration of multiple files a simpler task. It is important, however, to ensure that users are adequately trained in the basics of the operating system so that they fully understand the login process and the importance of using the correct login username and password.

Part IX

FILE SHARING

File-Server Protocols

## CHAPTER 25

SOME OF THE MAIN TOPICS IN THIS CHAPTER ARE

Server Message Block (SMB)

NetWare Core Protocol (NCP)

UNIX (NFS)

Microsoft Distributed File System (DFS)

The first thing that comes to mind when you think "network" is probably file and print shares. When a new addition is made to the network for a new business unit or when existing units are shuffled around and users and resources must be regrouped, it is usually the files users access and the printing capacity they will need that will determine where you relocate network pipelines and devices. Chapter 27, "Network Printing Protocols," discusses the protocols used to provide printing services for network clients. This chapter covers the major protocols in use today to provide for the sharing of files. Understanding how a particular protocol functions will better enable you to troubleshoot network problems that prevent users from timely access to file resources. For example, using a LAN analyzer to review network traffic during a troubleshooting session will be of little use unless you know what types of frames you are looking for and understand their function in the file-sharing process.

There are many ways you can share files. You can copy them to a floppy disk or tape cartridge and pass them around the office, although this is not a very efficient method as your volume of data grows and you find yourself trying to keep track of multiple versions of a file.

When TCP/IP was developed, several handy utilities were created to work with the protocol to provide clients some useful functionality. One of these, the *File Transfer Protocol (FTP)*, enables a user to copy a file from a remote computer to his own so that manipulation of the data can be done locally.

FTP doesn't really improve too much on the floppy method, except that the network can probably handle a larger amount of files more quickly. However, because users end up with more than one copy of the file, there is always the potential of creating mismatched versions when trying to coordinate multiple access to a file by making many copies of it. For example, if the user forgets to copy the file back to its original location after making changes, the next user who makes a copy of the file will find herself working on a file that does not contain these changes. Another problem with the copying method is that for very large files the network bandwidth (or lack of it) can become a problem.

Other TCP/IP utilities can be used to remotely access files. For example, you can establish a telnet session to a remote computer and then issue commands locally to manipulate data.

With this method, the user's PC or workstation is used as nothing more than a terminal emulator, and a rather expensive one at that. All applications that are needed to manipulate the data must exist or be installed on the remote computer. This is probably a better method to use than copying from an FTP site or floppy disk when trying to share a single file among many users because it maintains only one copy of the file. However, it is still not a very convenient method for several reasons. If you want to access files on more than one remote system, you need a separate telnet session for each one. This means it is not possible for an application, such as a word processor or database, to access files or remote systems at the same time. When using a telnet client, the user must have a user account set up on each remote system so that the logon can be validated. Obviously, using telnet is not as transparent a process as simply running an application on the user's local system and accessing files in the local file system.

The Network File System (NFS) protocol was developed by Sun Microsystems to make remote file access as simple a process for the user as local file access.

NFS enables a user to access a remote file system while making it appear to be a local file system to the user. There is no need to copy files back and forth from servers. Using NFS, a file system (or a portion of it) residing on a remote system can be made to appear to the client as though it were simply part of the local file system. For a while NFS was found only on UNIX boxes. However, its popularity spread, and you can now find NFS server applications and client applications for most major operating systems. A minor disadvantage to using NFS is that network problems can interfere with file access. However, this is true for any kind of network file sharing protocol.

Microsoft operating systems have long used the *Server Message Block (SMB)* protocol to provide file and printer access to networked clients. This protocol has developed over the years and has been adopted into Windows NT. Whereas NFS is built on top of several other protocols and is used to provide only file-sharing capabilities, SMB is a more basic protocol that can be used across a network to provide network access to files and print sharing to interprocess communication, using named pipes and mailboxes.

In this chapter, you will briefly look at the components that make up the protocols that enable you to share files on a network.

Server Message Block (SMB)

A very common protocol you will find on almost any computer running a Windows operating system, from Windows to Windows for Workgroups to Windows NT, is the Server Message Block protocol. This is a protocol that is used for basic file sharing, printer sharing, and also for a few other network messaging devices, such as named pipes and mail slots. This is a basic client/server protocol that uses request and response messages to accomplish its purpose.

SMB has also been used by many vendors other than Microsoft to provide file and print services, including IBM (OS/2) and Digital Equipment Corporation (now Compaq) in its Pathworks products.

SMB has been around for a while and has been modified to support new functions as PC networks have evolved. Each new version of the protocol is called a *dialect*, and these are listed in Table 25.1. This table shows the dialects in order from the earliest to the latest, and any server implementing a particular dialect must also support interaction with clients of any earlier dialect in this table. This allows for backward compatibility for older clients when parts of the network, such as servers, are upgraded.

Table 25.1   SMB Protocol Dialects

SMB Dialect	Description
PC NETWORK PROGRAM 1.0	The original MSNET SMB protocol, sometimes called the core protocol.
PCLAN1.0	Alternative name for the core protocol.
MICROSOFT NETWORKS 1.03	MS-NET 1.03. Lock&Read and Write&Unlock added to protocol and defined a special version of raw read and raw write.
MICROSOFT NETWORKS 3.0	LANMAN 1.0 protocol for DOS operating system. Same as LANMAN1.0 except that the server must map errors from OS/2 errors to a DOS error.

(continues)

Table 25.1 Continued

SMB Dialect	Description
LANMAN1.0	First complete version of LANMAN 1.0.
LM1.2X002	First complete version of LANMAN 2.0.
DOS LM1.2X002	Same as LM1.2X002 (LANMAN 2.0), except that server maps errors to DOS errors.
DOS LANMAN2.1	DOS LANMAN 2.1 protocol.
LANMAN2.1	OS/2 version of LANMAN 2.1 protocol.
Windows for Workgroups 3.1a	Windows for Workgroups version 1.0 of protocol.
NT LM 0.12	SMB for Windows NT. Added special SMBs for NT.

SMB Message Types

SMB is a message-oriented protocol in which the client makes a request of the server via a message formatted according to a specific SMB message type. The server responds to the client's request using a specific SMB format. There are many different types of messages, which are listed in Table 25.2. Note that not all message types are supported by all clients.

Table 25.2 SMB Message Types

SMB Message	Earliest Dialect
SMB_COM_NEGOTIATE	PC NETWORK PROGRAM 1.0
SMB_COM_CREATE_DIRECTORY	" " " "
SMB_COM_OPEN	" " " "
SMB_COM_CLOSE	" " " "
SMB_COM_DELETE	" " " "
SMB_COM_QUERY_INFORMATION	" " " "
SMB_COM_READ	" " " "
SMB_COM_LOCK_BYTE_RANGE	" " " "
SMB_COM_CREATE_TEMPORARY	" " " "
SMB_COM_CHECK_DIRECTORY	" " " "
SMB_COM_SEEK	" " " "
SMB_COM_TREE_DISCONNECT	" " " "
SMB_COM_QUERY_INFORMATION_DISK	" " " "
SMB_COM_OPEN_PRINT_FILE	" " " "
SMB_COM_CLOSE_PRINT_FILE	" " " "
SMB_COM_DELETE_DIRECTORY	" " " "
SMB_COM_CREATE	" " " "
SMB_COM_FLUSH	" " " "
SMB_COM_RENAME	" " " "
SMB_COM_SET_INFORMATION	" " " "
SMB_COM_WRITE	" " " "
SMB_COM_UNLOCK_BYTE_RANGE	" " " "

SMB Message	Earliest Dialect
SMB_COM_CREATE_NEW	PC NETWORK PROGRAM 1.0
SMB_COM_PROCESS_EXIT	" " " "
SMB_COM_TREE_CONNECT	" " " "
SMB_COM_SEARCH	" " " "
SMB_COM_WRITE_PRINT_FILE	" " " "
SMB_COM_GET_PRINT_QUEUE	" " " "
SMB_COM_LOCK_AND_READ	LANMAN 1.0
SMB_COM_READ_RAW	" "
SMB_COM_WRITE_MPX	" "
SMB_COM_WRITE_COMPLETE	" "
SMB_COM_SET_INFORMATION2	" "
SMB_COM_LOCKING_ANDX	" "
SMB_COM_TRANSACTION_SECONDARY	" "
SMB_COM_IOCTL_SECONDARY	" "
SMB_COM_MOVE	" "
SMB_COM_WRITE_AND_CLOSE	" "
SMB_COM_READ_ANDX	" "
SMB_COM_SESSION_SETUP_ANDX	" "
SMB_COM_FIND	" "
SMB_COM_FIND_CLOSE	" "
SMB_COM_WRITE_AND_UNLOCK	" "
SMB_COM_READ_MPX	" "
SMB_COM_WRITE_RAW	" "
SMB_COM_WRITE_MPX_SECONDARY	" "
SMB_COM_QUERY_INFORMATION2	" "
SMB_COM_TRANSACTION	" "
SMB_COM_IOCTL	" "
SMB_COM_COPY	" "
SMB_COM_ECHO	" "
SMB_COM_OPEN_ANDX	" "
SMB_COM_WRITE_ANDX	" "
SMB_COM_TREE_CONNECT_ANDX	" "
SMB_COM_FIND_UNIQUE	" "
SMB_COM_TRANSACTION2	LM1.2X002
SMB_COM_FIND_CLOSE2	"
SMB_COM_TRANSACTION2_SECONDARY	"
SMB_COM_LOGOFF_ANDX	"
SMB_COM_NT_TRANSACT	NT LM 0.12
SMB_COM_NT_CREATE_ANDX	"
SMB_COM_NT_TRANSACT_SECONDARY	"
SMB_COM_NT_CANCEL	"

From the list in Table 25.2, it is easy to see that SMB has evolved over the years and has a quite specific command set that provides quite detailed functionality while maintaining a simplicity by using a simple message exchange format. Nearly all LAN analyzers have the capability to decode SMB packets, and you can troubleshoot SMB client/server sessions to observe the interaction of the commands shown in this table.

SMB Security Provisions

SMB has the capability of providing for two kinds of security for file sharing:

- Share level
- User level

The most basic level of security that can be used on an SMB network is *share-level* security. This approach offers a disk or directory as an available resource on the network, protecting it with a password. Users who want to access a resource that is protected at the share level need only to know the name of the resource, the server that offers it, and the password for it in order to make a connection. This kind of file sharing is offered by Windows for Workgroup computers and Windows 95/98 computers. In a small LAN where there is not a great need for security among users, it is very simple to set up and maintain a network based on this model.

A superior method that is more likely to be found in the business environment involves making users accountable for accessing resources. A *user-level* security model dictates that each user should log on using a unique identifier, called a *username*, which is associated with a password for the user account. After logging in to the network, users are granted access to resources based on the rights accorded their accounts and the resource protections placed on files or directories. This user-level method enables you to assign different kinds of access based on username and resource.

In the share-level security model, access to a share provides the user with the capability to access any files in the top-level directory of the share and all the files in all the subdirectories that might fall under the top-level directory. In the user-level security model, the administrator can place different access limitations on every directory, subdirectory, and file that exists in the share.

The earliest SMB clients do not have the capability to exchange an account name and password with a server and are thus limited in what they can do in a more modern environment. SMB servers will generally provide some functionality for user-level security. For example, if the client computer's computer name matches an account name that is known to the server and if the password that the client passes as a "share" password matches that of the account, the SMB server can perform a logon for the user and grant access to the resource.

Protocol Negotiation and Session Setup

SMB has a built-in mechanism that is used by the client and server to determine the other's capabilities so that a common protocol version can be established that the two will use for the network connection. The first SMB message that the client sends to the server is one of the SMB_COM_NEGOTIATE type. The client uses this message to send the server a list of the dialects it understands. The server selects the most recent dialect it understands from the client's list and returns a message to it.

The response the server returns depends on the type of client. The information includes the dialect selected and can include additional information, such as buffer sizes, supported access modes, time and date values, and security information. After the client receives this response, it can continue to set up the session by using the SESSION_SETUP_ANDX message type.

If the initial server response indicates that user-level security is being used, this message type can be used to perform a user logon. The client sets a value in the message header called the *UID (user ID)* for the account it wants to use. It also supplies the account name and password to the server by using this message type. If these are validated by the server, the user can continue to use the UID to make subsequent accesses.

Other setup functions that are performed by using SESSION_SETUP_ANDX include the following:

- Set the maximum values for the size of buffers that will be used in the message exchange.
- Set the maximum number of client requests that can be outstanding at the server.
- Set the virtual circuit (VC) number.

If the VC passed to the server is zero and the server has other circuits opened for the client, it will abort them, assuming that the client has rebooted without freeing them first. To properly close a session, the client uses the message type called LOGOFF_ANDX, which causes the server to close all files associated with the user's UID.

Accessing Files

Other SMB message types are used now to traverse the resource directory and to open, read, write, and close files. First, the user must connect to the resource by using the TREE_CONNECT message. The message includes the name of the resource (server and share name) and, for earlier clients that do not perform logons, a share password. The server responds by sending the user a value called the *TID (Tree ID)*, which will be used in SMBs exchanged for this connection.

After the connection has been established, several basic SMB command formats can be used to manipulate files and directories that reside on the share. For example, the CREATE_DIRECTORY message is used to create a new directory in the file share's directory structure. The client passes the pathname for the new directory, and the server creates the directory, provided that the client has the appropriate access rights or permissions. The DELETE_DIRECTORY SMB message can be used to remove a directory, again based on the functions allowed for the username.

Opening and Closing Files

The OPEN message is used by a client to open a file. The path for the file is given, relative to the file share root. The client specifies the access that is desired, such as read, write, or share. If the file is successfully opened, the server returns a *File ID (FID)* to the client, which is used to further access the file using other SMB message types; it is similar to a file handle, which most programmers will recognize.

The server also returns data to the client indicating the actual access that was granted, which is read-only, write-only, or read/write.

The CLOSE message is sent by the client to tell the server to release any locks held on the resource file held by the client. After this message the client can no longer use the FID to access the file, but it must instead open the file again and obtain a new value.

When a client does not know the exact name of a file that it wants to open, the SEARCH message can be used to perform a directory look up. This function enables wildcards to be used, and the server response can include more than one filename that matches the request.

Reading and Writing

The SMB protocol uses the READ and WRITE message types to perform I/O operations on a file for the client. Using the READ request, a client can request that the server return information from the file by specifying a number of bytes and an offset into the file. The server returns the data, indicating the actual number of bytes returned, which can be less than requested if the user tries to read past the end of a file.

The WRITE command updates a file in a similar manner. The client sends in the data that will be written, indicating the number of bytes to write and an offset into the file where the write operation will begin. If the request causes a write past the end of the file, the file is extended to make it larger. The server sends a response telling the client the number of bytes that were written. If the number is less than the requested value, an error has occurred.

To increase read/write performance, the READ_RAW and WRITE_RAW message types can be used to exchange much larger blocks of information between the client and the server. When these are used, the client must have only one request issued to the server. In one send, the server will respond with data that can be up to 65,535 bytes in length. The WRITE command works in the opposite direction, allowing the client to send a large buffer of raw data to the server for a write operation.

Locking Mechanisms

Locking is a means of allowing a particular client exclusive access to a file or a part of a file when it is shared on the network. In SMB the capability to create a lock is called an opportunistic lock, or *oplock* for short. This is better explained by looking at the way in which it works. A client can create a lock on a resource using three different kinds of locks. The first is an *exclusive* lock, in which the client has exclusive access to the data held by the lock. A *batch* oplock is one that is kept open by the server when the client process has already closed the file. A *Level II* oplock is one in which there can be multiple readers of the same file.

The locking process consists of the client requesting the type of lock it wants when it opens the file. The server replies to the client with the type of lock that was granted when it responds to the open request.

A lock serves to give the client the capability to efficiently manage buffer space it uses when accessing a file over the network. For example, if a client has exclusive access to a file and is performing writes to it, it can buffer a lot of the newly written information before having to send it to the server to update the file. This can provide for a reduced number of network packets when updating a file. A client that has an exclusive lock on a file can also buffer read-ahead data to make reading a file much faster.

These locks are called opportunistic locks for a reason. A client can be granted exclusive access to a file if no other client has it opened at the time of the request. What happens when another client needs to read the file? The server notifies the first client that it needs to break the exclusive lock. The client then flushes its buffers so that any data that has not been written to the file is processed. The client then sends an acknowledgement to the server that it recognizes that the exclusive lock has been broken. In Figure 25.1 you can see the interaction between two clients and a server as these messages are exchanged.

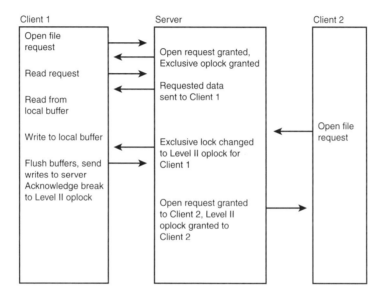

Figure 25.1 Exclusive oplocks are changed to Level II oplocks when a second client wants to open a file.

Batch oplocks are used to reduce the amount of traffic on the network used when some programs require continual reopening of a file to obtain commands, as when a batch command procedure is executed. For example, a batch procedure executed by the command processor usually opens a file, locates the next line to be executed, reads that line, closes the file, and then executes the command. The problem with this is that it does this for each command line in the procedure, resulting in multiple file open/closes that are not really necessary.

This is done by using a batch oplock whereby the client can read the data from its local read-ahead cache instead of reopening the file on the remote server to get each line.

Level II oplocks are new with the NT changes to SMB. This kind of lock provides for more than one client to have a file opened for reading. When a client must read from a file that is opened by another exclusively, the server informs the current client that its exclusive lock has been broken and is now a Level II oplock. No client that has a Level II oplock will buffer data to or from the file. Thus, after the lock has changed to a Level II oplock (and the first client has flushed any data in its buffers), both clients can continue reading the file.

NET Commands

The NET command is the command-line interface that the client can use to access SMB-based file services. This command can be used to make a directory available for sharing, to connect or disconnect a resource, or to view resources available on a server. Clients using operating systems such as Windows 95/98 or Windows NT can also use the Microsoft Windows Explorer application to connect to file resource shares on the network. However, the NET command provides a simple interface that can also be incorporated into command procedures, such as user login script files. You can also use these commands during troubleshooting. For example, you can establish a telnet session with a remote client who is having problems with a file share and execute the NET commands directly.

Because the NET command can be both a useful tool for setting up users to connect to resources and for troubleshooting clients, it is worth looking at the basic functions you can perform using this command.

There are several command parameters you can use with NET. For file sharing, the most basic commands are the following:

- SHARE
- USE
- VIEW

NET SHARE

The NET SHARE command enables you to offer a disk or directory structure for sharing on the network. If used by itself with no other parameters, the command will show you the current shares that are being offered by the workstation or server, in the following example:

```
F:\>net share
Share name    Resource                          Remark
-------------------------------------------------------------------------
IPC$                                            Remote IPC
D$            D:\                               Default share
print$        F:\WINNT\System32\spool\drivers   Printer Drivers
E$            E:\                               Default share
C$            C:\                               Default share
F$            F:\                               Default share
ADMIN$        F:\WINNT                          Remote Admin
documents     d:\
HPLaserJ      LPT1:                    Spooled  HP LaserJet 6L
The command completed successfully.
```

In this example, you can see that SMB is not only used to provide network communications for file sharing, but it is also used to provide shared printing (HPLaserJ LPT1:) and interprocess communications (IPC$).

The basic syntax for sharing is as follows:

```
NET SHARE sharename
```

To make a directory available for sharing, specify the name you want the file share to use on the network and follow it with the path to the directory to be shared:

```
NET SHARE sharename=drive:path
```

You can further configure the share by using the following qualifiers:

- **/Users:***number* or **/UNLIMITED**—You can specify the maximum number of users that are allowed to simultaneously connect to the share.
- **/REMARK:***text*—You can display text to describe the share.
- **/CACHE:**—You can specify manual, automatic, or no.

See the following example:

```
F:\>NET SHARE ACTFIL=D:\ACCTPAY /USERS:5
ACTFIL was shared successfully.
```

This code offers the file share actfil on the network. It will allow up to five concurrent connections to the files contained in the directory D:\ACCTPAY and all subdirectories that fall underneath it.

Deleting a file share on the server is also a simple matter:

```
F:\>NET SHARE ACTFIL /DELETE
ACTFIL was deleted successfully.
```

In this example, you can also specify the pathname that is being shared:

```
F:\>NET SHARE D:\ACCTPAY /DELETE
ACTFIL was deleted successfully.

D:\ACCTPAY was deleted successfully
```

In both of these instances, of course, the actual directory that was offered for sharing is not deleted. Only the file share offering is terminated.

Troubleshooting Using NET VIEW and NET USE

These two commands enable you to view the resources available on the network and to then make connections to them. NET VIEW returns a list of the servers it knows about on the local network. You can use NET VIEW //servername to get a list of services offered by any server in the list, as in the following example:

```
F:\>NET VIEW \\bca-nj-s1
Shared resources at \\bca-nj-s1

Share name  Type          Used as  Comment
-------------------------------------------------------------------------
acct        Disk                   Accounting
cdrom       Disk                   CD Drive on BCANJS1
documents   Disk
dvdrom      Disk                   DVD Drive on BCANJS1
HPLaserJ    Print                  HP LaserJet 6L
Rschlz      Disk                   Restricted
The command completed successfully.
```

It is easy to get confused when trying to troubleshoot problems with users connecting to shared resources. If you are using a Microsoft-based network that provides file sharing via SMB mechanisms, the NET VIEW command can be extremely useful. You can determine from this command whether the remote resource server is even seen in the browsing list by the client computer. If it is, you can display the resources offered. To connect to a resource manually, you can use the NET USE command. When executed by itself with no other command-line parameters, this command displays a list of your current connections.

To make a new connection, the syntax is very basic, though it has variations:

```
NET USE device sharename
```

Here, device can be an actual drive letter (such as D:, E:, and so on) or a device name for a printer (LPT1:), or it can be the wildcard *, in which case the next available drive letter will be chosen automatically when the connection is made. Observe the following example:

```
NET USE X: \\BCANJ1\DOCUMENTS
```

This would attach the drive letter X: to the resource documents on the server BCANJ1. You can also specify a username that can be used to evaluate your access rights to the remote resource:

```
NET USE X: \\BCANJ1\DOCUMENTS /USER:[domainname\]username
```

Here, you would specify a valid username and, if it is a domain account, the name of the Windows NT domain. To delete a connection to a remote resource, use the /DELETE qualifier:

```
NET USE X: /DELETE
```

The NET USE command is most often associated with creating user logon scripts or other batch-oriented procedures that are used to interact with files offered as resources on a network. It can also be a very handy command to remember when performing a new installation or upgrading a user. For example, when installing a new application or troubleshooting a misbehaving one, you can quickly connect to a remote resource to download configuration or driver files.

On Windows NT clients, it is helpful to know that in addition to the shares that you explicitly create to offer on the network, there is also a hidden share for each disk drive on the system, and the name consists of the drive letter followed by the dollar-sign character. If you know an administrator account password on a remote system, you can easily connect to the computer's system disk (or any other drive) by specifying the hidden-share name and an administrator's account name and password. These share names do not show up in an ordinary browse list for all users to see. They can be very handy when you need only to connect to another computer to quickly retrieve a file that can help you on the system you are troubleshooting.

Monitoring and Troubleshooting SMB Communications

You can use the NET STATISTICS command to obtain a quick view about statistics related to the SMB protocol.

Use either WORKSTATION or SERVER as a keyword to indicate which set of statistics you would like to see, as in the following example:

```
F:> NET STATISTICS SERVER

Server Statistics for \\BCA-NJ-S1
Statistics since 7/6/99 10:38 AM
Sessions accepted                 1
Sessions timed-out                0
Sessions errored-out              0

Kilobytes sent                    3
Kilobytes received                3

Mean response time (msec)         0

System errors                     0
Permission violations             0
Password violations               0

Files accessed                    7
Communication devices accessed    0
Print jobs spooled                0

Times buffers exhausted

   Big buffers                    0
   Request buffers                0

The command completed successfully.
```

From this display, you can quickly see whether a server is having problems with a recent password change—password violations will probably be excessive. A high value for permission violations can indicate that an access control list on a file or directory might have recently been changed. The other statistics shown here can also be used for many different troubleshooting scenarios.

The NET command has the capability of showing you a lot of information. For example, in addition to SMB statistics, the NET command can also be used to show the services currently running on an NT computer. Using the NET START command with other parameters on the line displays a list of the services currently running. If you are troubleshooting a client and see, for example, that the Workstation service is not running, you can then use the NET START WORKSTATION command to start it. The NET command enables you to view, start, and stop NT services without having to use the graphical interface, which can be a great help when performing remote diagnosis.

When you upgrade a network or make repairs, it is often useful to send a message to users to let them know what is happening. For example, replacing a network card might require that a server be out of commission for a short period of time. Changing a network cable might disrupt network access for users. You might have established a telnet session with a user's workstation and want to send him a message on the screen to let him know that you are working. You can use the NET SEND command, using the following syntax, to send a message to users:

```
NET SEND {name ¦ * ¦ /DOMAIN[:domainname] ¦ /USERS} message
```

Here, you can see that you can send a message to a single user or use the wildcard * character to send the message to all users. You can use the /DOMAIN:*domainname* variation to send the message to all users in a particular domain, for example. See the following command:

```
NET SEND * I am monitoring your workstation right now. Will call when finished.
```

When logged in to a server, this produced the pop-up message on the terminal of the logged-in user shown in Figure 25.2.

Figure 25.2   The NET SEND command can be used to send a message to users when you are logged in to their workstations.

To carry problem diagnosis any further when using SMB for file sharing, you need to resort to a LAN analyzer of some sort. You can use this to verify that the correct SMB messages are being exchanged between the client and the server. In Figure 25.3, you can see the Microsoft Network Monitor being used for this purpose.

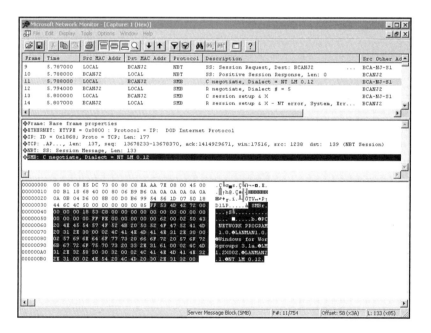

Figure 25.3   Using Microsoft Network Monitor, or a similar LAN analyzer, you can examine the exchange of SMB packets between the client and server.

You can step from one packet to the next to discover where a problem might be occurring. For example, is a password required? Are there problems opening a file? You can watch the sequence of commands that are used to connect to a tree, open a file, and make an attempt to read or write.

Although it would be necessary to have more detailed information about the format of SMB packets to make a detailed diagnosis at this level, it is still very helpful to be able to see the types of messages being exchanged, regardless of whether you can understand every byte in the packet. Viewing the data at this level can be used to troubleshoot most problems with this protocol. You can also use the event-logging capabilities of Windows NT (the Event Viewer) to look for problems. For example, if you have a password failure and have set the server to audit failed resource accesses, the Event Viewer will have a record showing you the failed attempt, and you can quickly resolve the problem by giving the user the correct password or by changing it.

Using the SMB Protocol on Non-Microsoft Clients: Samba

SMB is a protocol that is highly entrenched in the Microsoft world of operating systems and networking products. It makes sense, then, that there would be a way that these workstations and servers could be integrated into a UNIX environment without a lot of difficulty. The answer to this problem is called Samba, which is a set of products that provide for SMB conversations between SMB servers, such as Microsoft Windows operating systems, and those that do not use it natively, such as many different variants of UNIX or Linux systems. In addition, Samba has been ported to a number of other popular operating systems, including OpenVMS.

Samba was originally developed by Andrew Tridgell and is now maintained by him and other developers (the "Samba Team") on the Internet. You can go to the home page for the Samba effort by using the URL

```
www.samba.org
```

From this location, you can view the documentation for Samba and download the most recent version. The software is freely distributed under the GNU public license. The most recent version of Samba (2.0.x) provides the following capabilities:

- The functions of an SMB server to Windows NT clients, LAN Manager clients, and other SMB clients such as Windows 95/98 and others.
- Browsing support by way of an RFC1001/1002-compliant name server. Samba can be configured to be the master browser on the LAN.
- A few utilities (such as an FTP-like SMB client) and other functionality, such as some command-line functions used for administrative functions.

Samba is not a complete replacement for the functionality provided by a Windows NT domain controller, but the aim to be so appears to be the goal. In addition to the basic Samba code distribution, there is also available a separate update called the Samba Domain Controller source code. This adds a lot of functionality related to domains as they are understood under Windows NT. Some things that are not available yet in version 2.0 are the following:

- Trust relationships (between domains)
- Integration of PDC and BDC computers
- Complete print server functionality
- Access Control Lists

These limitations are not really that much to worry about if you have a mixed environment of UNIX and NT servers. You can configure Samba servers on your UNIX boxes to enable high-performance machines to be used as file servers on the NT network. You can still manage the servers using UNIX file administration procedures, and yet to the client computers, the shares appear as if they were being offered by other Windows NT computers.

Troubleshooting a Samba server can be made easier by starting the Samba server software using the -d parameter to specify a debug level (from 1–100), which will cause more output messages, depending on the level you specify. Another good thing to use when you are having problems with a Samba server is to use a LAN analyzer to view the SMB frames to determine whether any problems exist between the SMB client and server that are involved in the communications.

You can also use a LAN analyzer to view the sequence of exchange of SMB messages between server and client. Available as a download from the Samba home page is an extension to the tcp-dump utility, called tcpdump-smb. You can use this to capture smb packets and decode the header information.

NetWare Core Protocol (NCP)

NetWare is composed of several different protocols. *IPX* is a connectionless delivery service that can be used by higher level protocols (such as NCP or SPX) to create a connection-oriented, reliable transport service. Two other important protocols used in NetWare are the *Service Advertising Protocol (SAP)* and the *Routing Information Protocol (RIP)*. It is through SAP that servers announce their presence periodically and through which clients can make requests to locate resources. RIP is used to locate servers on the network.

Another protocol, called *NetWare Core Protocol (NCP)*, is used for communications exchange between a client and a server when file reads, file writes, or other file-related activities are being performed. It provides connection control and defines the methods used to encode requests and replies. NCP is a simple request-response protocol, similar to SMB in that respect. NCP requests are encapsulated in IPX packets. The NCP header information, which follows the IPX header information, consists of five fields. The first indicates the request type, which provides the function of the packet.

The client can make a request using four request types in this field, and the server can use this field to indicate a type of reply:

- Create a service connection (1111).
- General service request (2222).
- General service replies (3333).
- Terminate a service (destroy) connection (5555).
- Request burst-mode transfer (7777).
- Request being processed (9999).

These services can be further qualified by function and subfunction codes contained in the request packet. Other fields in the NCP header include the following:

- Sequence Number field, which is used to track the sequencing information for the connection.

- Connection Number Low field, which is a service connection number that is assigned to the client when it logs on to the server.

- Task Number field, which is a value that identifies the client that is making an NCP request.

- Connection Number High field, which is currently not used and should always have the value of 00 hex.

The header information for the response packet that the server sends back to the client will contain these same fields, but it will also add to additional fields. The first is a Completion Code field, which will be set to 0 if the request was successfully completed or to 1 if an error was encountered in processing the request. The Connection Status field might have values indicating an error condition between the client and server connection.

When the client initiates a connection request with a server, it will create a service connection (1111) request type. The server gives the client a connection number in its response. This connection number is used by the client when it submits its remaining requests. Each time a request is sent on the particular connection, the sequence number is incremented. The response to a request contains the same sequence number, making it easy for the client to match up responses to pending requests.

General Requests and Responses

Most of the exchanges between client and server are usually the result of requests made by the client (type 2222) and the replies sent by the server (type 3333). These requests can be used to search directories or to open, read, and write to files.

The server uses the connection ID number and the sequence number when it sends a reply to a request. The Completion Code field is filled in to indicate success or failure, and other data might follow in the packet that is used to fulfill the request (such as data read from the file).

Burst Mode

NCP provides commands that can be used to read and write blocks of information in files that reside on the network. However, when larger files must be transferred, a special NCP request (Request Type value=7777), using burst mode, allows the server to send a larger, single burst of data to the client at one time—much larger than the amount allowed by the regular read and write requests (up to 64K).

Burst mode capabilities can be found on NetWare 3.0 and later servers.

The actual mechanics of burst mode involve more than just sending larger amounts of data in a single operation. The client first performs testing to determine a value that will be used for the Interpacket Gap Time (IPG) and the size of the data request (the burst windows size). The window size might vary during the history of the connection, based on how successful communications are. When data is lost during a transmission, the client can send a request to the server to transmit only fragments of the original data stream, those that were not correctly received.

An error condition such as this causes the window size to be reduced. As communications continue with no problems, the window size gradually increases.

Request Being Processed Response

When a client does not receive a response to a request after a timeout period, it will send in a duplicate request. If the server is heavily loaded, it might send back a request that has a request type value of 9999, which is the Request Being Processed type. This is an indication to the client that the request has been received, but that the server is just too busy to do anything about at it at the time. This reply does not guarantee the client that the request ever will get answered, however. It only lets the client know that it can reset its timer and wait longer if need be.

When the client's timer expires, it can send another request to the server, which might respond to the request or which might send another message telling the client to wait. This response type is used to help reduce congestion in a busy network by reducing the number of requests transmitted on the network.

Terminating Connections

This request type is used to end a connection between the client and server. The only information needed in this packet, other than the request type (5555), is the sequence number of the request and the connection ID number. The server will respond with a standard response packet (3333) with a completion code of 0 to indicate that the connection has been successfully brought to a close.

UNIX (NFS)

The Network File Systems (NFS) protocol consists of several different protocols that perform specific functions. Sun Microsystems has published the specifications for NFS so that other vendors can easily implement these protocols to allow for remote mounting of file systems independent of the operating system of the computers. RFC 1094 defines the most widely used version of NFS (version 2). RFC 1813 documents version 3, which adds better support for wide area networking. If you think you will be involved in troubleshooting NFS on the network, you should find out which version your NFS software is based on and become familiar with these documents.

NFS is built on routines made up of *remote procedure calls (RPC)*. XDR is used as the data format so that data from different systems can be represented in a common format for interchange. In addition, the *Mount* protocol is used to make the initial connection to a remote file system. Because NFS is built in this layered fashion, and problems can occur at any level, you will need to understand not only how the NFS protocol functions but also RPC, XDR, and the Mount protocol.

Protocol Components: Remote Procedure Call Protocol (RPC)

RPC is a simple client/server protocol application. RPC defines the interaction between a client, which formats a request for execution by the server, and the server, which executes the client's request on the local system. The server performs whatever processing is required and returns the data and control of the procedure to the client. Sun developed RPC for use in NFS, but it has since been employed quite usefully by many other client/server-based products.

The `rpcbind` daemon (a process that runs in the background waiting for requests) runs on both the client and the server and is responsible for implementing RPC protocol exchanges between hosts on the network.

A service is a group of RPC procedures that have been grouped together into programs. A unique number is used to identify each service, which means that more than one service can operate at any given time. An application needing to use a service can use the different programs that make up the service to perform specific actions. For example, when designing an NFS service, one program might be responsible for determining a file's attributes, and another program can be responsible for the actual transfer of data between the client and server computers.

The unique service number is used to identify different network services that run on a particular system and the mapping for this is usually found in the file `/etc/rpc`. The RFC that defines RPC sets forth numbers used for many common services.

The portmapper service (using port 111 for UDP or TCP) manages the port numbers used in TCP/IP communications. Because there can be more than one open connection between a client and server, a *port number* is used to identify each connection.

Don't confuse port numbers with the numbers assigned to services. Service numbers are used to identify a particular RPC service. *Port numbers* identify connections between two computers that use a service.

External Data Representation (XDR)

A common format is used when exchanging data between computer systems that are running different operating systems. Some use ASCII code for text, whereas others use UNICODE. Some use big-endian encoding techniques, whereas others use little-endian, which determines the order in which bytes are used to represent data (left to right or right to left). It is even more complicated when you look at how different computer systems represent numeric data in memory or storage. When using a multiple-byte value to represent a floating point number, for example, you need to know which bits are used for the exponent and which are used for the mantissa.

NFS uses the External Data Representation (XDR) standard for data exchange. The details of XDR are covered in RFC 1014. It is a C-like notation for representing data, not a programming language itself. An item, such as a character or numeric value, is represented in XDR by using 4 bytes (32-bits), with the lower bytes the most significant.

Other encoding features of XDR include the following:

- Signed integers are stored using "twos" complement notation and range in value from –2,147,483,648 to +2,147,483,647.
- Unsigned integers can range from 0 to 4,294,967,295.
- Hyper integers and unsigned hyper integers are 8 bytes in size and can be used to represent larger integers.

- Floating point formats are also defined, and so are the enum type (familiar to C programmers) and a Boolean type.

- Structures, arrays, constants, and many other data types are also defined.

XDR provides an extensible data description format that makes implementing NFS on multiple hardware and software platforms much easier.

The NFS Protocol and Mount Protocol

The NFS protocol is a set of procedures (called *primitives*) that is executed via RPC to allow an action to be performed on a remote computer. NFS is a *stateless* protocol, which means that the server does not have to maintain information about the state of each client. If the server (or the network) fails, the client needs only to repeat the operation. The server doesn't have to rebuild any data tables or other structures to recover the state of a client after a failure.

Note

Certain operations, such as file or record locking, do require a *stateful* protocol of some sort, and many implementations of NFS accomplish this by using another protocol to handle the specific function. NFS itself is composed of a set of procedures that deal only with file access.

The RPC procedures that make up the NFS protocol are the following:

- **Null**—The "do nothing" routine. It is provided in all RPC services and is used for testing and timing operations.
- **Get File Attributes**—Gets the file attributes of a file on a remote system.
- **Set File Attributes**—Sets the file attributes of a file on the remote server.
- **Get File System Root**—No longer used. Instead, the Mount protocol performs this function.
- **Look Up a Filename**—Returns a file handle used to access a file.
- **Read From Symbolic Link**—Returns information about symbolic links to a file on the remote server.
- **Read From File**—Procedure to read data from a file on a remote system.
- **Write to Cache**—Cache feature to be included in version 3 of the protocol.
- **Write to File**—Used to write data to a file on a remote server.
- **Create File**—Creates a file on the remote server.
- **Remove File**—Deletes a file on the remote server.
- **Rename File**—Renames a file on the remote server.
- **Create Link to File**—Creates a hard link (in the same file system) to a file.
- **Create Symbolic Link**—Creates a symbolic link (can be used to link a file across file systems). A symbolic link is a pointer to a file.
- **Create Directory**—Creates a directory on the remote server.
- **Remove Directory**—Deletes an empty directory on the remote server.
- **Read From Directory**—Obtains a list of files from a directory on the server.

■ **Get File System Attributes**—Returns information about the file system on the remote server, such as the total size and available free space.

There is no provision in these procedures to open or close a file. Because NFS is a stateless protocol, it doesn't handle file opens or closes. The Mount protocol performs this function and returns a file handle to NFS. The mountd daemon runs on both the client and server computer and is responsible for maintaining a list of current connections. Most implementations of NFS recover from client crashes by having the client send a message to the NFS server when it boots, telling it to unmount all its previous connections to the client.

When compared to the NFS protocol, the Mount protocol consists of only a very few procedures:

■ **Null**—The do nothing procedure just like the one listed under the NFS protocol.

■ **MNT**—Mounts a file system and returns to the client a file handle and the name of the remote file system.

■ **UNMT**—The opposite of the MNT procedure. It unmounts a file system and removes from its table the reference to it.

■ **UMNTALL**—Similar to the UNMT procedure, but this one unmounts all remote file systems that are being used by the NFS client.

■ **EXPORT**—Displays a list of exported file systems.

■ **DUMP**—Displays a list of file systems on a server that are currently mounted by a client.

Configuring NFS Servers and Clients

The biod daemon runs on the client system and communicates with the remote NFS server. The daemon also processes the data that is transferred between the NFS client and NFS server. The RPC daemon must also be running and either UDP or TCP needs to be running, depending on which your version of NFS uses as a transport. Users can mount a file system offered by an NFS server, provided that they are not prevented from mounting the file system by the server, by using the mount command.

NFS Client Daemons

On the client side of the NFS process, there are actually three daemon processes that are used. The first is biod, which stands for block input/output daemon. This daemon processes the input/output with the NFS server on behalf of the user process that is making requests of the remote file system. If you use NFS heavily on a client, you can improve performance by starting up more than one biod daemon. The syntax used to start the daemon is as follows:

```
/etc/biod [number of daemon processes]
```

This daemon is usually started in the /etc/rc.local startup file. Modify this file if you want to permanently change the number of daemons running on the client system. You can first test by executing the command online to determine how many daemons you need to start and then place the necessary commands in the startup file.

When deciding performance issues, remember that on a heavily loaded client, making a change in one place might result in poorer performance from another part of the system. So, don't assume that you need a lot of extra daemons running unless you can first show that they are needed and do improve performance. Each daemon process is like any other process running on the system, and it uses up system resources, especially memory. Begin by using one or two daemons if you are using a workstation dedicated to one user. For a multiple-user computer, test your performance by increasing the number of daemons until NFS performance is satisfactory (all the time checking, of course, other performance indicators to be sure the overall system impact is justified). Although multiple daemons mean that NFS requests can be processed in parallel, remember that the network itself might be a bottleneck. Additional `biod` daemons will not increase throughput when the network itself is the limiting factor. Also note that the `biod` daemon is a client process. You should not run it on an NFS server unless that server is also a client of another NFS server. In addition to the `biod` daemon, the `lockd` and `statd` daemons also run on the client. For more information on these, see the section "Server-Side Daemons," later in this chapter.

The mount Command

The `mount` command is used to mount a local file system, and you can also use the command to mount a remote NFS file system. The syntax for using `mount` to make available a file system being exported by an NFS server is as follows:

```
mount -F nfs -o options machine:filesystem mountpoint
```

In some versions of UNIX, the syntax for mounting a remote NFS file system is a little different. For example, in SCO UNIX you use a lowercase `f` and an uppercase `NFS`:

```
mount -f NFS -o options machine:filesystem mountpoint
```

In BSD UNIX, there is a command called `mountnfs`, which uses the system call `mount` to perform most of its functions. This version of the `mount` command comes with a lot of additional parameters, including the capability to specify on the `mount` command line whether to use UPD or TCP as the underlying transport mechanism.

The value you supply for `machine:filesystem` should be the hostname of the remote server that is exporting the file system you want to mount for `machine`. Substitute the name of the file system for `filesystem`. The following example will cause the remote file system on host `zira`, called `/usr/projectx/docs`, to be made accessible in the local file system hierarchy at the `/usr/docs` directory:

```
mount -F nfs -o ro zira:usr/projectx/docs /usr/docs
```

This is just as you mount other local file systems into the local hierarchy. Under the `/usr/docs` directory, you can access any other subdirectories that exist on host `zira` under the `/usr/public/docs` directory.

The `-o` parameter can be used to specify options for the `mount` command. In the preceding example, the letters `ro` for the option were used to make the remote file system *read only* by users on the local computer.

Other options that can be used when mounting a remote file system include the following:

- **rw**—Mounts the file system for local read-write access, which is the default.
- **ro**—Mounts the file system for local read-only access.

- **suid**—Allows setuid execution.
- **nosuid**—Disallows setuid execution.
- **timeo=x**—Specifies a timeout value (in tenths of a second). The mount command will fail if it cannot mount the remote file system within this time limit.
- **retry=x**—The mount command will attempt to mount the remote file system x number of times, with each attempt lasting for the length of time specified by the timeo parameter.
- **soft**—Causes an error to be returned if the mount is unsuccessful. Opposite of the hard option.
- **hard**—Causes the mount attempt to continue until it succeeds. Opposite of the soft option.

For more command-line parameters and options, see the man page for the mount command for your particular system.

Caution

A computer can be an NFS server, an NFS client, or perhaps both a server and a client. However, you should not try to mount an exported file system on the same server that is exporting it. This can lead to looping problems, causing unpredictable behavior.

The *mountpoint* is the path to the location in the local file system where the remote NFS file system will appear, and this path must exist before the mount command is issued. Any files existing in the mountpoint directory will no longer be accessible to users after a remote file system is attached to the directory with the mount command, so do not use just any directory. Note that the files are not lost. They reappear when the remote file system is unmounted.

Using the `fstab` File to Mount File Systems at Boot Time

When you have file systems that need to be remounted each time the system reboots, you can use the file /etc/fstab to do this. This file is also used to mount local file systems, so be careful when making edits. The format for a record is as follows:

```
filesystem   directoryname   type   options   frequency   pass
```

The *filesystem* field for a record used to mount a remote file system would include the server hostname and the pathname of the remote file system separated by a colon (*hostname:path*). The second field, *directoryname*, is the path for the mountpoint on the local system, which indicates where the remote system will be mounted and made available for access. The next field, *type*, is used to specify the file system type, which can be any of the following:

- **ufs**—A typical local UNIX file system.
- **mfs**—The memory file system.
- **nfs**—A NFS remote file system.
- **swap**—A disk partition used for swapping by the virtual memory system.
- **msdos**—An MS-DOS compatible file system.
- **cd9660**—A CD-R file system as defined by ISO 9660.
- **procfs**—A *filesystem* structure used to access data about processes.

- **kernfs**—A *filesystem* structure used to access kernel parameters.

The *options* field is used for a comma-delimited list of mounting options (such as rw, ro, and so on). *Frequency* is used in determining when a file system will be "dumped" for backup purposes. This can usually be set to zero for NFS systems mounted on a client because it is usually the NFS server that is responsible for making backups of local data. The last field, *pass*, can also be set to zero most of the time for an NFS file system mounted on a client. This field is used by fsck utility to determine on which pass it is to check this file system.

Caution

The order in which you place entries in this file can be important. For example, do not place a command in this file to mount a remote NFS file system on a mount point unless the file system that contains the local mount has been mounted earlier in the file!

Configuring Server Daemons

For an NFS server, choose a computer that has the hardware capabilities needed to support your network clients. If the NFS server will be used to allow clients to view seldom-used documentation, a less powerful hardware configuration might be all that you need. If the server is going to be used to export a large number of directories, say from a powerful disk storage subsystem, the hardware requirements become much more important. You will have to make capacity judgements concerning the CPU power, disk subsystems, and Network adapter card performance.

Setting up an NFS server is a simple task. Create a list of the directories that are to be exported and place entries for these in the /etc/exports file on the server. At boot time the exportfs program is started and obtains information from this file. The exportfs program uses this data to make exported directories available to clients that make requests.

Server-Side Daemons

The nfsd daemon process handles requests from NFS clients for the server. The nfsd daemon interprets requests and sends them to the I/O system to perform the requests' actual functions. The daemon communicates with the biod daemon on the client, processing requests and returning data to the requestor's daemon.

An NFS server will usually be set up to serve multiple clients. You can set up multiple copies of the nfsd daemon on the server so that the server can handle multiple client requests in a timely manner.

The syntax for the command to start the daemon is as follows:

```
/etc/nfsd [number of nfs daemons to start]
```

For example, to start up five copies of the nsfd daemon at boot time, modify your startup scripts to include the following command:

```
/etc/nfsd 5
```

UNIX systems and the utilities that are closely associated with them are continually being updated or improved. Some new versions include using the concept of threads to make it possible for a daemon to be implemented as a multithreaded process, capable of handling many requests at one time. Digital UNIX 4.0 (now Compaq True64 UNIX) is an operating system that provides a multithreaded NFS server daemon.

Other daemons the NFS server also runs include the `lockd` daemon to handle file locking and the `statd` daemon, which helps coordinate the status of current file locks.

Sharing File Systems: The `exportfs` Command

At system boot time, the `exportfs` program is usually started by the `/sbin/init.d/nfs.server` script file, but this can vary, depending on the particular implementation of UNIX you are using. The `exportfs` program reads the information in the `/etc/exports` configuration file.

The syntax for this command varies, depending on what actions you want to perform:

```
/usr/sbin/exportfs [-auv]
/usr/sbin/exportfs [-uv] [dir ...]
/usr/sbin/exportfs -i [-o options] [-v] [dir ...]
```

Parameters and options you can use with this command are the following:

- **a**—Causes `exportfs` to read the `/etc/exports` file and export all directories for which it finds an entry. When used with the `-u` parameter, it causes all directories to be unexported.

- **i**—Specifies options in the `/etc/exports` file to be associated with each directory to be exported. It is used to tell `exportfs` to ignore the options you placed in this file.

- **u**—Used to stop exporting a directory (or all directories if used with the `-a` option).

- **v**—Tells `exportfs` to operate in "verbose" mode, giving you additional feedback in response to your commands.

The options you can specify after the `-o` qualifier are the same as you use in the `/etc/exports` file (see the following section, "Configuration Files").

To export or un-export (stop sharing) all entries found in the `/etc/exports` file, use the `-a` or `-u` options. This is probably the most often used form because you can specify the other options you need on a per-directory basis in the `/etc/exports` file. This example causes all directories listed in `/etc/exports` to be available for use by remote clients:

```
exportfs -a
```

The following example causes your NFS server to stop sharing all the directories listed for export in the `/etc/exports` file:

```
exportfs -au
```

The second form can be used to export or un-export (stop exporting) a particular directory (or directories) instead of all directories. You specify the directories on the command line. You can use this form if you want to stop sharing a particular directory because of system problems or maintenance, for example. Using the following syntax causes the NFS server to stop sharing the `/etc/user/accounting` directory with remote users:

```
exportfs -u /etc/users/accounting
```

The next form of the command can be used to ignore the options found in the /etc/exports file. Instead, you can supply them (using the -o parameter) on the command line. You will probably use this in special cases because you could just as easily change the options in the /etc/exports file if the change were a permanent one. If, for example, you decided that you wanted to make an exported directory read-only that is currently set to be read-write, you could use the following command:

```
exportfs -o ro /etc/users/purch
```

You can also dismount and mount remote file systems using different options when troubleshooting or when researching the commands you will need when preparing to upgrade a network segment where connections need to change.

If changes are made to the /etc/exports file while the system is running, use the exportfs command (with the -a parameter) to make the changes take effect. To get a list of directories that are currently being exported, you can execute the command with no options, and it will show you a list.

Of course, it is not necessarily a good idea to make changes on-the-fly without keeping track of the connections. When you decide to perform online testing to mount or dismount file systems, be sure that you are not going to impact any users who are currently making productive use of the resources. To make testing more foolproof and to provide a quick back-out procedure, try copying the /etc/exports file to keep a safe starting copy and making changes to the copied file, loading it by using the exportfs -a command. When you determine that something has been done incorrectly, you can simply use the backup copy of the file you have made to restore the status quo.

Configuration Files

To make a file system or a directory in a file system available for export, add the pathnames to the /etc/exports file. The format for an entry in this file is as follows:

```
directory [-option, …]
```

The term *directory* is a pathname for the directory you want to share with other systems. The options that you can include are the following:

- **ro**—This makes the directory available to remote users in a read-only mode. The default is read-write, and remote users will be able to change data in files on your system if you do not specify ro here.

- **rw=*hostnames*—**This specifies a specific host or hosts that you want to have read-write access. If a host is not included in *hostnames*, it will have only read access to the exported file system.

- **anon=*uid*—**Use this parameter to set the *uid* (user ID) that will be used for anonymous users, if allowed.

- **root=*hostnames*—**Users who have root access on a system listed in *hostnames* can gain root access on the exported file system.

- **access=*client*—**A client that can have mount access to this file system.

For example

```
/etc/users/acctpay  -access=acct
/etc/users/docs  -ro
/etc/users/reports/monthend  -rw=ono
```

In this file, the first directory, /etc/user/acctpay, which stores accounts payable files, will be shared with a group called acct—the accounting department. The /docs directory can be accessed by anyone in read-only mode. The /reports/monthend directory can be accessed in read-only mode by most users, but users on the computer whose host name is ono will have read-write access.

Caution

You should give considerable thought to the matter before using NFS to export sensitive or critical data. If the information is subject to cause great harm if it is altered or exposed, you should not treat it lightly and make it available on the network via NFS. NFS is better suited for ordinary user data files and programs, directories, or other resources that are shared by a large number of users. There are not enough security mechanisms in place when using NFS to make it a candidate for a high-security environment.

Automounting File Systems

The Mount protocol takes care of the details of making a connection for the NFS client to the NFS server. This means that it is necessary to use the mount command to make the remote file system available at a mount point in the local file system. To make this process even easier, the automountd daemon has been created. This daemon will listen for NFS requests and will mount a remote file system locally on an as-needed basis. The mounted condition usually persists for a number of minutes (the default is usually five minutes) in order to satisfy any further requests.

As with other daemons, the automountd daemon is started at boot time in the /etc/rc.local file. You can enter it as a command after the system is up and running, if needed. When a client computer tries to access a file that is referenced in an automount map, the automountd daemon checks to see if the file system for that directory is currently mounted. The daemon temporarily mounts the file system so that the user's request can be fulfilled, if needed.

The *automount map* is a file that tells the daemon where the file system to be mounted is located and where it should be mounted in the local file system. Options can also be included for the mount process, for example, to make it read-write or read-only. The automountd daemon mounts a file system under the mountpoint /tmp_mnt. It then creates a symbolic link at the mountpoint the user recognizes to point to this temporary mountpoint.

Mounting File Systems Using the Automount Command

The /etc/rc.local file usually contains the command used to start the automountd daemon. This daemon is responsible for processing NFS mount requests as they are defined in special files called map files.

The syntax for the automount command is as follows:

```
automount [-mnTv] [-D name=value] [-f master-file]
[-M mount-directory] [-tl duration] [-tm interval]
[-tw interval][directory mapname [- mount-options]]
```

The options you can use are the following:

- **m**—Ignores directory-mapname pairs that are listed in the master map file.

- **n**—Dynamic mounts are to be disabled. If a directory is already mounted, the user's request will succeed, but no further file systems will be mounted.

- **T**—Causes the daemon to provide trace information about each request. The output is sent to standard output.

- **v**—Verbose; causes the daemon to send status messages to the console.

- **D** *name=value*—Defines automount environment variables. The text associated with value is assigned to the variable name.

- **f** *master map file name*—Provides the name of the master map file to the automount daemon.

- **M** *mountpoint directory*—Specifies a directory to use for the temporary mount point (one other than /tmp_mnt).

- **tl** *time value*—Specifies how long a file system should stay mounted after the last user request before automount automatically dismounts it. The default is usually five minutes.

- **tm** *time value*—The amount of time (in seconds) that should elapse between attempts to mount a file system (the default is 30 seconds).

- **tw** *time value*—The amount of time (in seconds) between attempts to unmount a file system that has exceeded its cached time. The default is usually one minute.

- **mount_options**—Options to be applied to all the directories listed in the map file. Any options listed in a map file override those listed here on the command line.

Master Maps

The automount daemon uses the master map to obtain a list of maps. The master map also contains mount options for those maps. The master map file is usually named /etc/auto.master. The syntax for the entries in this file is as follows:

```
mount-point map [mount-options]
```

mount-point is the pathname of the local directory for an indirect map specified in the map field. If the map specified in the map column is a direct map, the mount-point is usually /-.

The data listed under the *map* field is used to find the map that contains the actual mountpoints and the locations of the remote file systems. Any data you supply for *mount-options* will be used when mounting directories in the map file associated with it.

Following is an example of a master map file. Lines that begin with # are comments:

```
#mount-point   map                 options
/etc/users     /etc/auto.usr       -ro
/ -            /etc/auto.direct     -rw
```

When the automount daemon determines that access is needed for files found in the `/etc/users` directory, it will look for another map file, named `auto.usr`, to get the reset of the information. The `-ro` options are specified for this entry and will be applied to the file system designated in the `auto.usr` map file.

The argument `/-` is used to specify that a map file it points to, in this case `auto.direct`, is a direct map file or one that contains the mount-points and the remote file system information needed to complete the mounts.

Direct Maps

The remote file systems can be mounted into the local file system, and what the mount-point should be is information you will find in a direct map. The construction of this file is very direct. The syntax for an entry is as follows:

```
key   [mount-options]   location
```

The *key* field is the mount-point to be used for this entry. *mount-options* are the options used with the `mountd` daemon discussed earlier in this chapter. The *location* field should be in the format of *machine:pathname*, where *machine* is the hostname of the remote system that the file system actually resides on and *pathname* is the path to the directory on that file system. You can specify multiple locations to provide for redundancy. The automount daemon will query all locations in this case and take the first one to respond to its requests.

Indirect Maps

In an indirect map file, most fields are the same as in a direct map file, except that the first field (*key*) is not a full pathname. It is a pointer to an entry in the master map file. You can list multiple directories in an indirect map file, and each of these remote file system directories will be mounted under the mount-point designated in the master map file that contains a reference to the indirect map.

Check the man pages on your system to be sure of the syntax for options used in map files because they might vary just like options do for the `mount` command among different UNIX systems.

Troubleshooting NFS Problems

Many of the TCP/IP utilities that are used for troubleshooting can be employed when trying to diagnose and fix problems having to do with NFS. For example, if a remote file system suddenly becomes unavailable, it only makes sense to first determine whether the remote server is still functioning. You can do this quickly by using the `ping` command to establish basic network connectivity. A failure to communicate using this small utility indicates that there is a server problem at the other end or perhaps a network malfunction that is preventing communications with the remote system. When troubleshooting, this tells you that the problem is most likely not one to be found in the NFS subsystem. You can find detailed information about using various TCP/IP utilities for troubleshooting purposes in Chapter 18, "TCP/IP."

The tracert utility can also be used when ping fails to determine how far along the network route the packet is getting on its trip to the remote system. Use this when trying to isolate the particular point of failure in the network.

There is a useful command specific to NFS that can be used to display statistical information about NFS. It is nfsstat. This command will show you statistics about NFS and RPC. The syntax for nfsstat is as follows:

```
nfsstat [-cnrsz] [vmunix.n] [core.n]
```

The options you can use are the following:

- **c**—Shows only client-side information.
- **s**—Shows only server-side information.
- **n**—Shows only statistics for NFS, both client- and server-side.
- **r**—Shows only statistics for RPC, both client- and server-side.
- **z**—Is used to zero out the statistics. You can combine it with other options to zero out statistics referred to by those options (for example, -zc to zero client size information). Write access to /dev/mem is required to zero statistics.
- **core.n**—The name of the system's core image.
- **vmunix.n**—The name of the kernel image.

All statistics are shown if you do not supply any parameters when executing the command. The statistical data that will be displayed depends on the options you choose. For an example of the detailed data you can obtain using this command, see the man page for nfsstat for your particular UNIX or Linux system.

Examining the output from the nfsstat command can be useful on an ongoing basis to help you establish a baseline for performance evaluations you will need to make at a later time when thinking about upgrading. You can easily selectively store data output by this command in a text file or spreadsheet. You can also create a simple script file that can be use to gather statistics using this command on a periodic basis, storing the results in a temporary directory for your later review. For example, the command nfsstat -s will display statistics for the NFS server as follows:

```
# nfsstat -s

Server RPC:
calls       badcalls    nullrecv    badlen
23951       0           0           0

Server NFS:
calls       badcalls
23164       0
null        getattr      setattr      root        lookup       readlink
1   0%      64   0%      0   0%       0   0%      121    0%     0   0%
read        wrcache      write        create      remove       rename
22951 99%   0   0%       0   0%       0   0%      0    0%       0   0%
link        symlink      mkdir        rmdir       readdir      fsstat
0   0%      0   0%       0   0%       0   0%      25   0%       2   0%
```

In this display you can see statistics for the total number of remote procedure calls, along with information about those RPC calls that relate to NFS. In addition to the total number of calls, you can see statistics about the following items for RPC:

- **badcalls**—Number of calls that were rejected by the server.
- **nullrecv**—Number of times that no RPC packet was available when the server was trying to receive.
- **badlen**—Number of packets that were too short.

In addition, some implementations might show additional RPC fields. For the NFS server, many columns of information are displayed, showing you the number of read and writes, along with other useful information. For example, you can examine cache usage (*wrcache*) or determine when other file commands are used to create or remove directories.

If the number of badcalls begins to become significant when compared to the overall number of calls, a problem obviously exists. If the value displayed for badlen is consistently more than a few percent of the overall number of calls, a client might be misconfigured or a network problem might be causing packets to become corrupted. Again, you might see different or additional fields of information in the display, depending on the UNIX and NFS implementation you are using. A careful review of the documentation for your system will give you a good idea of the performance to be expected from your server and the kinds of events to look for.

Microsoft Distributed File System (DFS)

For the Microsoft Windows NT Server platform, you can obtain Microsoft Distributed File System Version 4.1 from Microsoft (www.microsoft.com). The downloadable version can be installed on Microsoft Windows NT Server 4.0 systems and can be used to provide a service to clients similar to that offered by NFS.

Like NFS, DFS employs a tree structure for file systems. A directory that is being imported by a client is attached at a point somewhere in the local file system, where it is then made available to applications as if the directory and its files were local.

Windows 2000 includes DFS as an integral part of the operating system. The interface is written as a snap-in to the Microsoft Management Console (MMC) tool, making administration a simpler process. A wizard prompts you through setting up a DFS root, and from there on out you can add, modify, or remove directory paths from the DFS tree. Paths represented in the DFS tree can come from one or more servers on the network. A tree is not bounded by a single host.

DFS does not add any additional security features to the file system. Instead, the usual rights and permissions that are already in place on the server are used when evaluating a client's access to a file or directory in the DFS tree.

One major difference between NFS and DFS is that DFS is built using SMB messaging techniques for the most part and is not compatible with all NFS servers. If you have a mixed-environment network where most of your data files are offered via NFS on UNIX servers, it would be more economical to acquire PC-based NFS client software than it would be to replace all your existing servers with NT machines.

Summary

To troubleshoot problems related to file sharing on the network, you must have a good understanding of how the underlying protocols function. You also must become familiar with the tools that can be used to provide information about the functioning of the protocol and any network components that it interacts with it. For basic troubleshooting, you can use TCP/IP utilities such as ping and tracert for NFS, for example. For more complex problems you might find yourself using a LAN analyzer to decode the actual messages that are exchanged between the client and server systems. In a larger network it is common to use more than one solution to provide access to files, such as using UNIX servers configured with Samba to provide file services to Microsoft clients, while using NFS to provide a similar service to UNIX clients.

In the next chapter, the access mechanisms used by operating systems to grant or restrict access to both local and network resources is discussed.

Rights and Permissions

CHAPTER 26

Controlling access to system and network resources is important to understand. In a homogeneous network where all file servers and clients are of one particular brand name, keeping track of all file and print shares and which users need access to them can still be difficult. When you begin to mix components to create a more diverse network, you can end up with a requirement that you understand the access restrictions imposed by more than one operating system, and also by the restrictions imposed between them.

In general, two kinds of identifying values are used to decide access. The first is an identifier that uniquely specifies the user who is logged on to the system and the specific rights, as defined by the operating system, that the user possesses. These rights are definitions of the kinds of actions that can be taken on the system by the users.

The next set of values are the permissions that are placed on each resource. Permissions usually are granular, giving permission separately to read, write, execute, or delete a file or directory. Depending on the operating system, the names used for these permissions can vary, and other types of permissions and combinations of these basic types can be found.

The important point to remember when setting up new users or resources, or when troubleshooting existing connections, is that you might need to look at both ends: What rights does the user possess and what access controls (permissions) exist on the resource? Both of these factors determine what users can do on the network. In this chapter we take a quick look at the concepts of rights and permissions in several major operating systems and discuss some of the methods used to solve related problems.

User-Level and Share-Level Resource Permissions

There are two basic means for protecting resources offered on a network. Each method strives to make the protected resource available only to a user who has been authorized to access it. They do so in different ways, however, and grant widely different kinds of access.

Share-level security involves securing connections to a network share point by a password. Users who know the name of the share point and the password can connect to the share point. All subdirectories and files found under the share point are accessible by using only that single password.

User-level security involves linking access controls further down in the file system and does not stop at placing a single password on an entire tree of resources (although you can do it that way if you really want to). Instead, access permissions can be placed on any directory or file in the tree. When a user connects to a resource protected by user-level security mechanisms, the user must first authenticate himself (log on to the server). The user is then granted access rights to each file or directory on the resource, each by the access control restrictions placed on it by inheritance or implicitly.

Obviously, the user level of security permissions provides the administrator a finer granularity of detail when deciding on resource access decisions. By using a logon username to identify the user who is accessing a resource, an audit trail with more specific detail can also be kept for troubleshooting purposes.

Microsoft (Windows 95/98/NT/2000)

Microsoft networks allow for both share-level and user-level permissions on network resources. Windows for Workgroups, the predecessor to Windows 95 and Windows 98, allowed each computer in the workgroup to offer a directory as a file share on the local area network and protect it with a password. This distributed security database meant that a user might need to learn several passwords, depending on the number of share connections that were needed for his workstation.

Windows 95/98 also enable users to create these kinds of user-level shares. These operating systems reside on a file system that is basically mired in technology and goes back many years to the MS-DOS operating system. It is the *FAT*, or file allocation table file system. Newer versions, such as FAT 32, have allowed the FAT method to grow as disk sizes become much larger. However, the amount of information you can store in this kind of file system is limited. It does not lend itself easily to storing security access information for individual files and directories.

Windows NT enables you to format a disk partition using the NTFS file system. When you use this file system for a disk, you can apply user-level security permissions on individual files or directories. For a more secure environment, the NTFS partition is the choice to make. Additionally, the Windows 2000 operating system allows for other features that make NTFS a more secure choice, including the capability to encrypt and decrypt data on-the-fly when storing or retrieving it from disk.

▶▶ To learn more about security in Windows 2000, check out *Special Edition Using Windows 2000 Server*, also published by Que.

Assigning User Rights

Users who are logged on to a Windows NT computer or domain can be granted rights by the administrator of the computer or the domain. Rights granted to an account that resides on an individual Windows NT computer are good only for accessing resources on that computer. Accounts that are created on a domain controller can be used when accessing resources throughout the domain. To grant a right to a user, use the User Manager for Domains utility in the Administrative Tools folder.

The easiest method for granting rights to users in an environment where you have a large user base is to create user groups consisting of users who need the same kind of access, and grant rights and permissions based on these groups. Windows NT enables you to use two basic kinds of groups: *local* and *global*. Local groups can be local to a particular computer or can be domain local groups. Global groups are used to group users from one domain so they can be managed as a unit in another domain where the administrator can place the global group into a local group for administrative purposes. The accepted practice of using groups is to include users in global groups, include global groups in local groups, and then assign resource permissions to the local groups.

Windows NT computers come with several built-in user groups, which vary depending on the role of the computer in the network. These groups are explained in detail in Chapter 22, "Windows NT Domains." What is important to understand here is that although NT enables a large number of specific rights to be identified and assigned to users, you can do it on a group basis rather than an individual one if you want to make user management tasks easier to perform.

Windows NT User Rights and Advanced User Rights

Windows NT divides user rights into User Rights and Advanced User Rights. The advanced group consists of rights that are designed for functions performed by programmers or administrators who might need the capability of performing actions that ordinary users do not. Following is a list of the basic user rights that you can grant to a user or a user group, each with a brief description of the functionality they afford a user:

■ **Manages auditing and security log**—Ability to set up auditing (determine which events are audited) and to manage the security log file using the Event Viewer.

■ **Backup of files and directories**—Users with this right can make backups of disk volumes even if they do not have the correct NTFS access permissions to read the files on the disk.

■ **Restore files and directories**—Similar to the Backup right, this right allows the user to restore files from a backup to a disk for which he or she has no NTFS access.

■ **Log on locally using keyboard and mouse**—Offers the ability to log on locally at a workstation or server.

■ **Change system time**—Grants the ability to change the computer's time and date.

■ **Access this computer from the network**—Offers the ability to log on to the computer from the network. In other words, the ability to make a network connection, such as to access a file share on the computer.

■ **Shut down the system on the computer**—Grants the ability to shut down the system.

■ **Add workstations to a domain**—A user holding this right can add new workstations to the domain database. This right is a built-in capability of the Administrators and Server Operators groups in a domain.

■ **Take ownership of files and other objects**—This right allows the user to take over the ownership of files or directories that are owned by another user.

■ **Force shutdown from a remote system**—Offers the ability to shut down the system remotely from another computer.

■ **Load and change device drivers**—Allows the user to unload device drivers.

In addition to these basic rights, the Advanced User Rights adds to this list other capabilities that are useful for some user tasks, but also provides rights needed by parts of the operating system or certain kinds of programs, such as background services. The following are these additional rights:

■ **Act as part of the operating system**—This right is usually granted to subsystems of the operating system. It allows the holder to act as a secure, trusted part of the operating system.

■ **Bypass traverse checking**—The user holding this right can read through a directory tree, even though he might not have access to all directories in the tree.

■ **Create a pagefile**—Usually a right granted to just the Administrators group. This right allows the user to create additional page files using the System applet in the Control Panel.

- **Create a token object**—This is the right to create a user logon token and is usually not granted to an individual user, but instead only to the local security authority (LSA) on the Windows NT computer.

- **Create permanent shared objects**—This is the right to create special resource structures that are used internally by the operating system. Again, this is not a right generally needed by or granted to users.

- **Debug programs**—This right allows a programmer to do low-level debugging. Helpful for applications developers and administrators.

- **Generate security audits**—This right is needed to create security audit log entries. This is also a right not generally assigned to a user.

- **Increase quotas**—This right offers the ability to increase the quotas for an object in the operating system. Administrator accounts generally have this right granted to them.

- **Increase priority**—Gives the ability to boost the scheduling priority of a process. Administrators and Power Users do not have this right by default.

- **Load and unload device drivers**—Offers the capability to load and unload device drivers.

- **Lock pages in memory**—This right provides the capability to lock pages into physical memory so that they do not get swapped out to the page file during normal virtual memory operations. Useful for a process running a real-time application, but not a right generally given to ordinary users.

- **Log in as a batch job**—The user can run a job using a batch scheduling utility (such as the AT command).

- **Log in as a service**—This right is usually given to accounts that are created to run a program in the background as a service. Services are controlled by using the Services applet in the Control Panel. Use this applet to specify the username for the service. Grant that username this right.

- **Modify firmware environment variables**—Offers the ability to modify system environment variables, which is usually granted to administrators only.

- **Profile single process**—Allows the user to collect information about a process, used for measuring performance. Administrators and power users usually have this right.

- **Profile system performance**—Allows the user to collect information about the system, used for measuring performance. This right is normally used only by administrators.

- **Replace a process level token**—A right that is usually restricted to the operating system, which gives the user the ability to modify a process's security access token.

NTFS Permissions

When a disk partition is formatted using the NTFS file system, you are able to grant permissions that control how directories and files are accessed by users. You can use the Windows Explorer utility to add or change permissions on files and directories, or you can use the command-line utility CACLS. To view or modify the permissions on a file using the Windows Explorer, right-click on the file or directory and select properties. From the File Properties sheet select the Security tab, and from this tab click the Permissions button. In Figure 26.1 you can see the Permissions dialog box for the C:\WINNT4\system32 directory on a Windows NT Server.

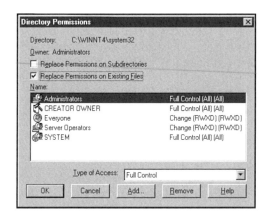

Figure 26.1   Permissions are granted by username or user group.

In this figure, note that the username or user group name is listed in the first column and the access granted to it is listed in the second column. In the second column, you can see there are two ways of representing the access permission. The first is a text string, such as Full Control or Change, which is followed by two other sets of permissions in parentheses. This is showing that there are two ways to look at permissions under Windows NT: There are special permissions and standard permissions.

Near the bottom of this dialog box is the Type of Access menu. In Figure 26.2 this menu is expanded to show the types of access you can grant to users for this directory.

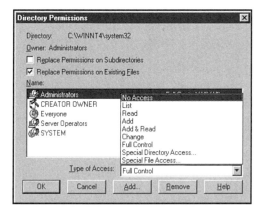

Figure 26.2   Select the type of access to allow for the user or group.

The list of permissions shown in Figure 26.2 includes the familiar terms such as List, Read, Add, and Change. There are also selections for Special Directory Access and Special File Access. You use these two selections when you want to select from the group of permissions known as special permissions.

Standard Permissions and Special Permissions

NTFS provides two different ways to assign permissions to resources. You can use individual permissions that are contained in a group called the *special permissions*, or you can use a smaller group that is made up of combinations of these special permissions, called the *standard permissions* group. The easiest way to explain these is to list the special permissions, and then show which ones make up the standard permissions that most users are used to seeing.

The list of special permissions consists of actions you can take on a resource and describe the finest granularity of control that can be managed:

- **R**—Read permission
- **W**—Write permission
- **X**—Execute permission
- **D**—Delete permission
- **P**—Change permission
- **O**—Take ownership permission

To make it easier to assign permissions, you can use the standard permissions for files, which are defined using the following combinations:

- **Read**—RX
- **Change**—RWXD
- **Full Control**—RWXDPO
- **No Access**

As you can see, using the standard permissions reduces the granularity used to assign permissions, but the grouping of permissions provided by the standard permissions will suffice in most circumstances to grant or deny access to a resource.

The standard permissions that apply to directories are a little different than those that apply to files. When defining this type of permission, two sets of permissions are listed. The first set of permissions applies to the directory itself. The second set of permissions applies to files in the directory, where applicable. The standard permissions for directories are as follows:

- **List**—(RX) (unspecified)
- **Read**—(RX) (RX)
- **Add**—(WX) (unspecified)
- **Add and Read**—(RWX) (RX)
- **Change**—(RWXD) (RWXD)
- **Full Control**—(RWXDPO) (RWXDPO)
- **No Access**

From this list you can see that the List permission implies the read and execute special rights for the directory file. The Read permission also grants read and execute rights to the directory file, and also read and execute are the default inherited permissions for any file created in the directory. The Add and Read right grants read, write, and execute access to the directory, but only read and execute rights to files created in the directory.

You can select from the standard permissions when you are granting or denying access to a resource. If you want to use the more detailed special permissions instead, select Special Directory Access or Special File Access from the Type of Access menu. In Figures 26.3 and 26.4 you can see the dialog boxes for each of these selections.

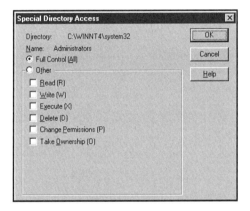

Figure 26.3   The Special Permissions dialog box for directory access.

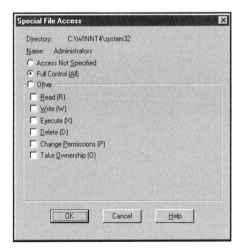

Figure 26.4   Special permissions for file access.

The Special File Access permission selections are used to set the permissions that files created in the directory will inherit by default. Choosing Access Not Specified will prevent the inheritance of permissions for files created in the directory.

Permissions Are Cumulative

When a user is a member of more than one group, the rights they hold are cumulative. In addition, permissions on a resource are also cumulative, with the exception of the no access permission. For example, a user has been granted the Read permission to a directory because of his membership in a group (such as World), but the user is also a member of another group called Accountants. The Accountants user group has been granted the Change permission for the directory. Thus, the user has both the Read and Change permissions when he is evaluated for access to the directory.

The only exception to this rule is the No Access right. This right specifically denies all other access. Thus, if a user is a member of one group that has been granted Full Control over a directory, but is also a member of another group that has been granted the No Access permission for the directory, the user will not be able to access the directory. The No Access permission overrides other access permissions.

The ability to selectively deny access to specific users can be a useful tool when setting up or managing user accounts. It is easier to grant access to everyone in a large user group, and then deny access to a few select individuals who should not be allowed to use the resource. The alternative is to create a more finely tuned user group that eliminates those who do not need access, and then grant the access to this new group. This method, however, increases the number of user groups you must manage, and thus its use becomes less effective the more you use it.

Share-Level Permissions

You can also set share-level permissions under Windows NT and Windows 2000 systems, though they are tied to user accounts. You can do this in several ways. The easiest is to use the Windows Explorer. Right-click on the device or directory that you want to share on the network. Select Properties, and then select the Sharing tab on the Properties sheet for the directory or device. Here you can select the Shared As option and fill in a share name and comment. Then set the maximum number of users that can connect to the share concurrently (see Figure 26.5).

By default, the group Everyone (which literally means everyone logged in to the system either interactively or via the network) is granted access to the new share. You can use the Permissions button to add or remove users and specify the specific access they can have when using the share.

Note that this kind of share-level security is a little different than that found in a workgroup environment, where each share has only a single password that all users must know in order to make a connection. Here you would connect to the share using a valid user account and password for a user who has been granted access to use the share. By using the server or domain security database to allow access by users, it is possible to audit access based on users also.

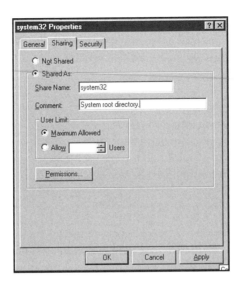

Figure 26.5   To create a share, give it a name and use the Permissions button to grant or deny user access.

If the file share is created for a directory that resides on an NTFS partition, the user's access to information on the file share is governed by both the file share permissions and the NTFS permissions, whichever is more restrictive. It is important to remember that the permissions you set for the share apply only to users who will connect to it via the network. If a user has the right to log on locally to the workstation or server that is offering the file share, the NTFS permissions will be all that apply when the user attempts to access the same files that make up the file share.

You can use the combination of share permissions and NTFS permissions to develop solutions for protecting files based on how your users are organized and how they make access to the shares. For example, it is easy to create more than one share for the same directory and then give each share different access permissions. Using this method, you can group users by the access mode they need and use different file shares to give access to different groups to the same files. At the same time, you can use NTFS permissions to selectively deny access to certain sensitive files or subdirectories in the share so that only a few or no users are allowed to access the files through the file share.

NetWare

When a user logs on to a NetWare 4.x or higher network, a three-level tiered mechanism is at work to decide how access of resources is to be granted. The first level of security is logon security. The user must be authenticated against a user object in the NDS (Novell Directory Service) tree. The second level of security is NDS security, in which access can be controlled by granting or denying the user access to an object or its properties. The third level of security is NetWare file systems security, which involves the permissions on files and directories contained in the NetWare file system.

Four types or categories of rights are used in Novell networking. Versions prior to NetWare 4 used only the first two of these.

- File system directory rights
- File system file rights
- NDS object rights
- NDS property rights

The first two categories are those that you normally would associate with an operating system and its file system. These are rights that control access to directories and files in those directories on the disks that the operating system (or network operating system) is responsible for. The last two categories are used for rights that apply to accessing objects that reside in the NDS database.

Trustees

In NetWare 3.x networks, a user or group of users who have a right granted to them for a file or directory are called a *trustee* of the directory. These rights are sometimes referred to as *trustee assignments*. A trustee assignment includes all the applicable rights, including a No Rights declaration. From NetWare 4.x and higher, other NDS leaf objects and container objects can also be granted a trustee assignment.

Trustee rights can be granted by an administrator using a program such as RIGHTS or FILER. These trustee rights relationships can also be inherited. When discussing how rights are granted in a NetWare environment, remember that when a user or group is made a trustee of a file or directory, they have been granted some kind of access permission right.

File System Directory and File Rights

These permissions are familiar to users of NetWare 3.x servers. File System Directory rights control how a user is able to list the contents of a directory, add to it, or remove entries from it. Table 26.1 lists terms used for the rights and permissions that can be placed on a directory, along with a short description of their functions. The first four entries in this table are pretty obvious.

Table 26.1 NetWare Directory Rights

Right	Description
Read	Grants the trustee the right to read the contents of files existing in the directory.
Write	This right gives the ability to add to or modify the contents of existing files.
Create	The trustee is allowed to create a file or a subdirectory in the directory.
Erase	The right to erase a file or subdirectory from the directory.
Access Control	A user holding this right can grant rights to the directory to other users and can modify the Inherited Rights Filter (IRF).
Modify	This right enables the trustee to rename a file or subdirectory in the directory and change attributes of the file or subdirectory.
File Scan	This right enables the user to list the files that are contained in the directory.
Supervisor	This is the most powerful right, giving the holder all other rights to this directory and its subdirectories.

Creators/owners of files and directories usually have the access control right over files that they create. This means that they can assign permissions to other users on the system who might need to access their files. The user who has Supervisor access can do as much or more than the owner of a file or directory can do. The File Scan right gives the user the ability to scan the directory and see its contents when searching for a file. In Windows NT, remember, this was called the List right, and was made up of two other rights: Read and Execute.

Although different operating systems, including a networking operating system such as NetWare, use different terms and procedures for allowing and restricting access to resources, they all usually work in a similar manner (see Table 26.2).

Table 26.2   NetWare File Rights

Right	Description
Read	This right allows the user to read the contents of a file.
Write	The holder of this right can add to or modify the contents of a file.
Create	This right enables a user of FILER to recover a file after it has been deleted.
Erase	The user holding this right can erase the file.
Access Control	A user holding this right can grant rights to the file to other users and modify the IRF.
Modify	This right enables the trustee to rename a file and change file attributes.
File Scan	A user holding this right can see the file even if the user does not have the file scan right for the directory that contains the file.
Supervisor	This right gives the user all the other rights to the file.

Object and Property Rights

The NDS database is a hierarchical tree structure. Rights in this tree flow from top to bottom, so that an object in the directory can possibly inherit the rights values from all parent objects above it in the tree. Two kinds of rights are associated with NDS: Object rights and Property rights. Object rights define the kinds of actions that a trustee can perform on an object in the NDS tree. These rights do not necessarily give the trustee access to any information stored in the object's properties, just access to the mechanisms used to manipulate objects. Inheritance of rights is discussed later in this chapter.

Property rights define access to the information stored in the properties of an object. These rights apply to the properties of an object and not to the object itself. For example, an administrator may choose to grant users the ability to change certain properties of their own user objects in the directory. This would allow users to change their own telephone number properties, email account properties, and so on, relieving the administrator or another resource of this chore.

Table 26.3 lists the Object rights, and Table 26.4 lists the Property rights, along with descriptions of their use.

Table 26.3   NDS Object Rights

Right	Description
Supervisor	This is the most powerful object right, granting the trustee all rights to the object and its properties. Note that in the case of the other object rights, only the Supervisor right can also grant access to property values.
Browse	This is the right that enables the user to see the object in the NDS tree and search for it based on the base class of the object or the relative distinguished name (RDN) of the object.
Create	This is a right that applies to container objects, and it gives the trustee the right to create a new object in the NDS tree. This right cannot be assigned to leaf objects because, by definition, they cannot contain any other objects. This right can be granted only to container objects and gives the trustee the right to create new objects in the container.
Delete	This is the right to delete an object in the NDS tree. Note that a container object can be deleted only if no other objects are beneath it. If there are, you must first delete any existing objects within the container before you can delete it. The Write right (Property right) for all properties is also needed to delete an object.
Rename	This is the right to change the name (RDN) of an object.

Table 26.4   NDS Property Rights

Right	Description
Add or Delete Self	This right enables you to remove yourself as a value of a property. You cannot use this right to change other property values, however.
Compare	This is the right to make a comparison of a value to the value of a property. This right does not enable you to see the actual value of the property.
Read	This is the right needed to see the value of the property of an object. This right includes the Compare right.
Supervisor	This gives you all rights to the property. This right can, however, be blocked by an Inherited Rights Filter (IRF).
Write	This is the right to add values, change values, or delete values of a property. This right also includes the add or delete self right.

Differences Between NDS and File System Rights

NDS rights are used to assign access capabilities to objects and their properties that are contained in the NDS directory database. File system rights are used to assign access capabilities to directories and files stored in the file system. The first difference you will notice between the two is that the NDS rights consist of two other kinds of rights: Object and Property rights. This concept does not exist in the file system rights.

In NetWare 3.x, the capability to block the inheritance of rights was done using an Inherited Rights Mask (IRM). With NetWare 4.x, the Inherited Rights Filter (IRF) performs this task for both NDS and file system rights.

There is a difference, however, in how inheritance operates for the two kinds of rights. The Supervisor Object and Property right can be blocked in NDS using an IRF. The Supervisor file system right (formerly called the Supervisory right) cannot be blocked using this method. This means that the Supervisor right granted for a directory applies to that directory and all subdirectories and files underneath it.

Finally, trustee assignments in NetWare 3.x could be made only for a user account or a user group. In NetWare 4.x the trustee can be any NDS object, leaf, or container anywhere in the NDS tree. Because the NDS tree is a distributed database, objects located on different servers can be made trustees to files on other servers.

Inheritance of Rights

Inheritance of rights in the NDS tree is the process by which an object acquires some of the rights granted to objects superior to it in the tree. Rights are inherited starting at the top of the tree where objects underneath the [root] object inherit some of the rights granted to [root].

The two methods used to block an object from inheriting rights from a superior object are the inherited rights filter and direct trustee assignments by an administrator. Direct trustee assignments made anywhere in the path from the [root] object to the object in question can change the rights flowing down the tree.

The Inheritance Rights Filter (IRF)

The IRF can be used to stop one or more rights from being acquired in this fashion. The filter is used to block an object from receiving selected kinds of trustee assignments that it would otherwise inherit. When displaying the IRF, you will see a string of characters enclosed in square brackets. Each letter is the first letter of one of the rights that can be inherited by the object or potentially blocked by the filter. The values for directory and file rights can be Read, Write, Create, Erase, Modify, File Scan, and Access Control.

To make modifications to an IRF you can use the utilities RIGHTS, FILER, NetAdmin, or NWADMIN.

Security Equivalence

Security equivalence is another method of granting trustee access rights in NetWare. Using this method, one User object is made equivalent to another object and thus takes on the same trustee assignments. *Security equivalence* is a property of the User object. Trustee rights gained by this equivalence method are in addition to any other rights the User object might possess.

This concept is helpful when it becomes necessary to allow one user to have access to objects in a manner similar to another user. For example, when a user is temporarily out of work and another is brought in to fill in.

Tip

It is not a good idea to grant a user the right to change the Security Equivalent property of his own User object. If the user also has the Write property right to the ACL property of an Admin User object, the user could potentially acquire all the rights associated with the Admin User object.

Effective Rights

When looking at the various means that are used to grant trustee rights to an object in NetWare, it quickly becomes apparent that trying to figure out the actual rights a user possesses can become confusing. The actual rights that a user will end up with are called the *effective rights* to the object. A few simple rules can be used to deduce effective rights:

- If no trustee rights are granted to the directory, the effective rights are computed by a logical AND operation of the parent directory's effective rights and the IRF.

- An explicit assignment of trustee rights to a directory overrides an IRF.

- If the supervisory right is granted to a directory, the trustee will have all rights for all files and subdirectories underneath the directory.

- If the supervisory right is granted to a volume, the trustee will have all rights for all directories and files contained in the volume.

Rights are additive in this computation. Inherited rights are masked by the IRF, and then added to any direct assignments made to the object and any rights acquired by security equivalence. If the access granted from one source is less than that granted by another source, the higher-level right is used.

The Everyone Group and the [Public] Group

In NetWare 3.x a group called Everyone was usually assigned the read and the file scan right to SYS:PUBLIC. This user group allowed the administrator to assign rights to all users in a convenient method. The Everyone group consists of all users on a NetWare 3.x server. In NetWare 4.x and above, there is no Everyone group, by default.

Technical Note

By default, NetWare 4.x does not contain an Everyone group. However, the migration process from NetWare 3.x to NetWare 4.x can cause the Everyone group to be migrated as a user group.

Novell Directory Services (NDS) allows for the creation of user groups. The hierarchical nature of the NDS database enables you to place user objects into container objects. Using this method, you can group together users who share the same level of access permissions, for example, so that you have to modify the permissions only at the container level instead of at the individual user object level. However, a user object (or any object in the NDS tree) can be associated with only one container object. Of course, the container object itself can be encompassed by another container object. But it is not possible to take a single user object and place it into multiple containers at the same time. Instead, you can create a Group object. This kind of object has a property that lists members of the group, which consist of user objects that reside elsewhere in the NDS tree.

The explicit group [Public] exists by default and is made up of all users who have a network connection. This includes users who have not been authenticated by NDS, meaning that you can effectively assign rights to objects in the database for workstations that do not have to use a username/password to connect to the database. This gives you the capability of assigning the browse right to all users by creating a trustee assignment for the [Public] group on the root object in the tree. Sometimes, though, it can be a security problem to let unauthenticated users even see (browse) the database. In this case you would not want to grant this right to [Public], or you might want to consider removing the browse right via an IRF for sections of the tree.

UNIX and Linux

Under UNIX and Linux, users will fall into one of the three following camps:

- User
- Group
- Super User

Every user on a UNIX system must be identified by a username, just as in Windows NT/2000 and NetWare. The user can also belong to one or more groups, one of which is considered to be the user's primary group. User groups provide a method for assigning access permissions to directories and files based on groups of users with similar needs. Finally, there is a special user called a superuser, whose capabilities on the system are superior to ordinary users.

The superuser (or root user) account is all powerful. The root account, as it is usually called, is represented by the user ID (UID) of 0. This UID can access any file on a local file system and access information about any process on the system. Some functions that only the superuser can perform on most UNIX systems include

- Mount or unmount a file system
- Create device special files
- Create user accounts
- Change another user's password
- Change the date or time on the system clock
- Change the owner of files
- Modify the local network interfaces
- Copy all files
- Format drives
- Shut the system down

In Windows NT it was possible to assign a varying number of specific rights to a user or group so that different users could perform functions requiring different degrees of access. In the UNIX environment, the root user account is the one that possesses the super-powers, so to speak, and to perform these functions you must log on as or become the root user.

File permissions are assigned to each file or directory in the following three categories:

- Owner
- Group
- Other

The first category defines permissions that apply to the owner of the file. Group permissions apply to users who are in a group to which the file belongs. The last category is the permissions that will be applied to all other users who try to access the file. The access permissions that can be granted to each of these categories are basic:

- **Read**—This permission enables the user to read the contents of the file. For a directory it allows the user to list the files stored in the directory along with their attributes.

- **Write**—This permission enables the user to change the contents of the file. This right enables a user to add or delete files in a directory.

- **Execute**—For a program file, this right enables the user to execute, or run, the program. For a directory, it enables the user to access the directory.

Viewing File Permissions

The `ls` command can be used to show a listing of files along with information about the permissions applied to the files. There are many command-line parameters you can use with this command, but the simple usage shown here is sufficient to view the ownership and permission information about a file:

```
ls -l /usr/bin/two
dr-xr-xr-x   1 two     biz               0 Jul 12   1999 html
dr-xr-xr-x   1 two     biz               0 Feb 13   1998 invoices
-r-xr-xr-x   1 two     biz            1624 Jun 20   1998 notices.txt
-r-xr-xr-x   1 two     biz            1624 Jun 20   1998 appt.dat
```

The first entry in the directory listing shows a directory file named `html`. You can tell it is a directory because the first character on the line is a `d`. The next file is also a directory, named `invoices`. Both of these directories are owned by the user listed in the third column, `two`. The group the file belongs to is found in the next column and in these examples is `biz` for all entries. The remaining items on each line show the size and date of the file and its name. Note that UNIX is case-sensitive when it comes to filenames; keep this in mind when using the `ls` command with wildcards hoping to locate a file.

In the preceding listing, the first thing you notice on each line is a string of letters separated by dashes. This string contains the access permissions for the entry. It is sometimes called the *permissions array*. This is followed by other information separated into columns. Each line represents either a directory or a file in the current directory. The permissions array can be easily deciphered. The first character indicates whether the file is a directory or a user file (·), and the remaining three groups of letters indicate the access permissions for the file or directory's owner, the file's group, and then a group called other.

Note that the dashes in the permissions array are not separators. Each position in the array is a fixed place that can either contain a permission for the file or directory, or it can represent the absence of the permission using the dash (hyphen) character. In the previous listing this means that the Owner, Group, and World permissions for each of the directories and files listed is Read and Execute (r-x).

Granting permissions to "other" gives the permission to all users on the system. It is important to remember that in UNIX if you grant access via the World permissions fields, denying access by Owner or Group fields will not work. Thus, use the World access permissions on files to set values that you would like to apply to all users. For example, if all users will be allowed to read the file, set the Read permission in the World permissions. Use the Owner and Group fields to grant more restricted access to smaller groups of users.

SUID and SGID File Permissions

In addition to the ordinary permissions that exist to control which users can access a file or directory, two other permissions are used on UNIX and Linux systems to give special privileges to executable files. These are called the Set User ID (SUID) and Set Group ID (SGID) permissions. When an executable image is run that has the SUID permission set on it, the image will take on the permissions that are equivalent to those of the owner of the executable file.

The permissions available to a user can also be acquired from group membership. When an executable image is run, it usually runs under the permissions of the user who executes the file and the permissions available to the group to which the user belongs. When the SGID permission is set on an executable, it will inherit permissions from the group of the owner of the file.

These two permissions can be useful because sometimes it is necessary to run a program that must have more access rights than the user who is executing the program. For example, when a user must change his password he needs the capability to make edits to the password file. Because this file is normally protected against writing by most users, it is the program that changes your password that is capable of getting the necessary permission to modify the file. This is a simple example of a process that occurs at many levels in an operating system. Other programs use permissions elevated above the ordinary user to accomplish such tasks, manage print queues, and allow basic system management tasks.

When used on a directory instead of a file, the SUID permission, when placed in the group field, indicates that all files created in the directory will take on the ownership of the group that owns the directory.

You can tell from a directory listing (using the `ls` command) whether the SUID or SGID permission has been set for a file. In the permissions array the letter "S" will appear in the position normally used to indicate the owner's execute access. If the "s" is lowercase, the execute permission for the owner is not set. If it is an uppercase "S," the execute permission is also set for the owner.

In a directory file, the "s" character will appear in the character position that normally indicates a group's execute access.

Changing File Ownership

When moving files around on the network it is frequently necessary to change their ownership or the access permissions so that a new set of users will be able to gain the appropriate access. For example, when a user leaves a company it is usually customary for someone else to take over managing files and important directories that the user had been responsible for. The two commands that you can use to modify ownership and access for files are the chmod (change permission mode) and chown (change owner) commands.

The chown command is simple. If you are the owner of a file or the superuser, you can use this command to assign a new owner or group to a file. The basic syntax is

```
chown [ -fhR ] owner [ : group ] file ...
```

Here *owner* is the new user or group ID that will be assigned to the file or files represented by *file...* The -f parameter will suppress error reporting. The -h parameter is used to cause an ownership change to be effective on a symbolic link to a file instead of the actual file the link references. Without this parameter the ownership will be changed on the actual file that is referenced by the symbolic link. The -R parameter causes the command to operate recursively, changing the owner ID for files and subdirectories under the current specification.

You can use chown to easily change the ownership of one or more directories when a new user takes responsibility for them. The chmod command can be used by users and administrators to change the access permissions on files or directories.

This command can be used to change access permissions for the owner, group, or others by specifying the rights by either a numeric or character format. The numeric format for the chmod command specifies rights as a numeric value, totaling each right as described in the following list:

- **0**—No Access
- **1**—Execute File (or search a directory)
- **2**—Write
- **4**—Read

Using this format you would change the access permissions on a file in a manner similar to

```
chmod 666 myfile1
chmod 664 myfile2
chmod 640 myfile3
```

Here the filename myfile1 has its access permissions set to read + Write (4 + 2 = 6) for the Owner, Group, and World fields. The file myfile2 is set to Read + Write for the owner and group fields, but is set to only Read (4) for the other or world field. Finally, myfile3 is set to let the owner Read and Write. The group permission is set to Read only and the other field is set to No Access (0).

Using the other syntax format for the chmod command enables you to change the permission fields without having to memorize numerical values. Instead, you use the letters r (read), w (write), and x (execute) to specify the permissions; use the letters u (user), g (group), o (other), or a (all, indicates user, group, and other) to specify the specific user field for which a permission will be modified. For example

```
chmod u+rw myfile1
chmod g+rwx myfile1
chmod o+rw myfile1
```

Here it is easy to see that the user field (user owner, group, or other) is appended to the letter identifying a right (rw, rwx) by the plus sign. This indicates that the right is to be added to the user field indicated for the file `myfile1`. To remove a right using `chmod` use the minus sign:

```
chmod g-x personalfile
chmod o-w specialfile
```

Here the command is used to remove the execute right from group for the file named `personal-file`. For the file named `special file` the owner has used `chmod` to remove his own right to write to the file. This is not done for security purposes, but only because the owner wants to make sure he doesn't alter the contents of the file by mistake. Because he is the owner, he can always set the mode back to write if it becomes necessary.

Assuming Another User's Rights

To perform some important system management tasks on a UNIX or Linux system, only the privileges granted to the root account can be used. Although it would be a simple matter to let multiple system administrators log on to the root account to perform administrative functions, this is not a good idea from the viewpoint of security. If only one account is used, it is difficult to construct an audit trail to determine which administrator performed a specific function.

To get over this limitation, the su command enables you to log on using your normal user account, and then become the root user or another user. The log file `/var/adm/sulog` tracks attempts to become another user using the su command, so an audit trail is kept to help when troubleshooting. You can use the su command by itself to become the root superuser, or you can use it in the form of su *username* to become another user. In all cases you will be prompted for the password for the user account you want to become, unless you are already logged on to the root account.

The power that the password to a root account holds should be seen by how it can be used with this command. As a standard security matter you should regularly review the `/var/adm/sulog` log file to keep track of how the command is being used.

Summary

User rights and access permissions control who can do what on a computer or network. It is important to understand the capabilities you can grant to a user or a group of users. In a network that consists of multiple operating systems, the administrator must be cognizant of the different mechanisms each platform uses to enforce access.

Windows 95/98 only provide basic share permissions and cannot block access to specific files. Windows NT/2000 provide both share permissions, and NTFS provides file-level rights.

NDS is organized in a tree format, providing the capability to assign permissions to an object at any level within the tree. The user will have permissions to any objects below the parent object.

UNIX-based operating systems operate in much the same way as Windows NT/2000 but also provide the capability to assume the rights of another user to perform specific tasks.

When deciding to upgrade to one of these operating systems, it is important to take the time to map out a clear permissions and access strategy for the network. It is much easier to do it from the beginning than to just give everyone access to everything, or restrict access to everything, and then try to assign appropriate permissions as required. Having a clear idea of how permissions are assigned and being used also makes troubleshooting permissions much easier.

Part X

PRINTING

Network Printing Protocols

SOME OF THE MAIN TOPICS IN THIS CHAPTER ARE

Printing Protocols and Printing Languages

TCP/IP Printing

Data Link Control Protocol (DLC)

Internet Printing Protocol

CHAPTER 27

The most basic functions provided by a local area network (LAN) are the file and print services. A computer that has one or more physical printers attached to it and accepts data for printing from other computers is called a *print server*.

When directly connecting a printer to a computer, the parallel port is usually used. This port provides a high-speed connection on a set of wires that is used exclusively by the printer and the computer for this communication path. It is becoming increasingly more common to find printers that are connected directly to the network, just as servers and workstations are.

This chapter is concerned with protocols that are used to communicate with a printer or a print server to exchange data and command information.

Printing Protocols and Printing Languages

There are a lot of different types of printers on the market today. From under $100 ink-jet printers to high-volume color laser printers, you can find something that suits most any need. When evaluating a printer purchase, you will need to understand the protocols that can be used to communicate with the printer and the languages that the printer understands.

A printer language is not the same as a printer protocol. For example PostScript and PCL (Printer Control Language) are languages that describe how a document is to be rendered into the final printed product by the printer. When a printer is directly connected to a printer port on a computer, the printer language is used by the software driver to format the information being sent to the printer.

A network protocol, however, is used to send the formatted job, both data and instructions compiled using the printer language, to the printer. Some very common general network protocols, such as IPX/SPX, can be used to communicate with printers and are described in other sections of this book.

▶▶ For more information on IPX/SPX, see Chapter 19, "IPX/SPX."

In this chapter we will examine a few protocols that are more specific in their use and implementation; that is, they are generally used mostly for the purpose of communicating with a printer.

Several protocols are used for network printing. Some are proprietary protocols that are used only by one computer or network operating system; others, such as lpr/lpd, have been implemented in many environments. Data Link Control (DLC) is an IBM protocol that has been adapted for use on many printers, particularly HP laser printers. This chapter covers the basis of these major protocols, with examples from UNIX, Windows NT, and NetWare systems.

Additionally, you will look at the new kid on the block, Internet Printing Protocol, which is under development by a working committee of the Internet Engineering Task Force.

TCP/IP Printing

TCP/IP was originally developed for the UNIX operating system, of which there are several flavors. Depending on the version of UNIX running on a workstation or server, you will find that printing falls into one of two major types:

- BSD (Berkeley System Distribution) Spooling System
- SVR4 (System V, Release 4) Printing System

The BSD system uses the lpr program and the lpd daemon to send files to printers. The /etc/printcap text file is used to set up characteristics for each printer. The terms *lpr* and *lpd* are short for line printer daemon and line printer remote, respectively.

The SVR4 system uses the *lp* (line printer) program and the *lpsched* daemon (printer scheduler) to print files. Although the SVR4 system is considered to be more sophisticated in that it has several utility commands for managing the system, the BSD system is probably easier to manage in a networked environment.

Note

In this section, we will examine the commands used to set up and administer printing systems on UNIX systems. However, TCP/IP-based printing is not limited to servers running this operating system. Many operating systems, from OpenVMS to Windows NT, can use the lpr/lpd printing protocol and are discussed later in this chapter.

The BSD Spooling System: lpr and lpd

BSD printing uses the lpr and lpd programs. The user sends files to print by using lpr, and the lpd daemon handles the details needed to get the data in the file formatted and sent to the physical output print device.

To set up a printer on a UNIX system that uses lpr/lpd you must do several things. How these functions are accomplished will depend on your particular brand of UNIX and whether the vendor has supplied script files or applications to help automate the process. The following basic things must be done:

- Physically connect the printer to a port on the server computer or, alternatively, configure a network printer with a TCP/IP address so that you can direct print jobs to it.
- Create a special device file that UNIX uses to reference devices if the printer is physically connected to the computer.
- Create entries in the printer configuration file (/etc/printcap) that describe the characteristics of this printer, along with management things such as accounting or log files.
- Create the directories that will be used to store files while they are waiting to print (spooling directory).
- Place commands in the appropriate UNIX startup file (rc file) to start the lpd daemon when the system boots.

To create the special device file, use the command /dev/makedev **port**. The **port** should be the port on the server to which the printer is attached. Typically, the parallel ports are named lpt*n* (that is, lpt1, lpt2, and so on). If the printer is connected to a serial port, the name of the port will probably be in the form of tty*nn* (that is, tty01, tty02, and so on). Be sure to check your system documentation to make sure you have the correct port name. Depending on the system, you might also have to make further adjustments to configure the port, such as setting the speed.

Tip

After you have attached a printer and configured the port, you can use the `lptest` command to send a simple stream of ASCII characters to the port. This will confirm whether you have been successful up to this point. You can also use this command when a printer suddenly stops printing, to test simple connectivity. If the printer had been functioning normally, stops unexpectedly, and `lptest` does not succeed, you might want to check the cabling or fault lights on the printer itself.

To create the spool directory, use the mkdir command. The spooling directory is usually created under the /var/spool/lpd directory. After you create a directory for the printer, use the chmod, chgrp, and chown commands to set the proper ownership and permission mode (for the lpd daemon). For example:

```
# cd /var/spool/lpd
# mkdir laser1
# chmod 775 laser1
# chgrp daemon laser1
# chown daemon laser1
```

The lpr command is used to print files in the BSD system. The syntax for this command is

```
lpr [-parameters][filename...]
```

Everything but the command itself is optional. You can specify one or more files, but if you do not specify a filename, the text to be printed comes from standard input. Depending on how your particular UNIX vendor has implemented the command, you have a lot of options you can choose from:

- **#**—Specifies the number of copies to print.
- **c**—The date files to be printed were created by the cifplot filter.
- **C**—Text following the C (Job Classification) character is printed on the burst page for the print job.
- **d**—Indicates that the data files to be printed contain data created by the tex command (DVI format from Stanford University).
- **f**—Printing FORTRAN files. The first character in each line is interpreted as a FORTRAN carriage control character.
- **g**—The data files to be printed contain data created by a program using the standard plot routines.
- **h**—Suppresses printing the burst page.

- **i**—Indent value. A job is printed with an indent of eight spaces by default. You can change it with this parameter. This value is passed to the UNIX input filter, which does the actual formatting of the data to be printed.

- **J**—Job. Text following the J character will be printed on the burst page for the print job. If this parameter is not used, the name of the first file on the print command line is used on the burst page.

- **l**—Control characters are printed and page breaks suppressed.

- **m**—Send a mail message after the job is printed.

- **n**—The data files to be printed contain data created by the ditroff command.

- **p**—Uses the pr command as the filter to process the print job.

- **P**—Name of the destination printer.

- **r**—Removes the file when spooling (or printing using the -s parameter).

- **s**—Indicates that the file should not be spooled. Instead, a symbolic link is used. This is a good option to use when printing large files or a large number of files, to minimize consumption of disk space.

- **T**—Title. Used with the -p option, which causes the pr command to be used to format the file to be printed. Text specified with this parameter is passed to pr. If blank spaces or special characters are used, the text should be enclosed by single quotes ('').

- **t**—Indicates that the data files to be printed contain binary data created by the troff command.

- **v**—The data file to be printed is in raster image format.

- **w**—Number of columns. This parameter specifies the number of characters on one line of the page (width).

Tip

A *burst page* or *banner page* (sometimes called a *separator page*) refers to a page that is printed at the beginning or end of a print job and is used to separate one user's print job from the next. In a high-volume printing environment these pages make it easier to identify print jobs so that they can be distributed to the appropriate user.

This extensive list of parameters is shown here to make the point that the lpr/lpd printing system is highly configurable from the user's point of view. It might look more complex at first glance than it actually is. For example, the command

```
Lpr -Phplj1 letter01.txt report.txt
```

is all you need to send the files letter01.txt and report.txt to a printer named hplj1. In most circumstances the user will not use a large subset of these parameters, but only a smaller combination that fit his work environment. Many of these have default values. For example, if the printer is not specified by using the -P parameter, the UNIX environment variable PRINTER will be evaluated and used for the destination of the print job.

After the lpr command has determined the printer to which the data will be sent, it scans the /etc/printcap file to get information about the printer, such as the spooling directory path. It then creates several temporary files and notifies the lpd daemon that the file is ready to print.

The lpd Daemon Controls the Printing Process

The `lpr` command creates a data file in the spooling directory associated with the printer and a control file that contains information telling the lpd daemon how the file should be printed. This daemon process usually starts when the system boots by commands found in one of the rc files. However, when troubleshooting printing problems, it is often necessary to kill the lpd daemon process and restart it. The syntax for restarting the daemon is

```
lpd [-l] [-Llogfile] [port#]
```

The `-l` parameter tells the daemon to record valid network requests in a log file. The uppercase parameter `-L` is used to specify the name of the log file. The *port#* parameter is used to specify the Internet port number the daemon will use for process-to-process communications.

When the daemon first starts it reads the `/etc/printcap` file to obtain information about the printers it can use. If any print jobs are outstanding since it was last running, it will begin to print them after it reads the printcap file.

When it needs to actually print a file, the lpd daemon first checks to see if another lpd daemon process is currently processing print jobs for the particular printer. If so, it passes the print job to that daemon. If not, the lpd daemon will create, or *spawn*, a copy of itself for the printer destination and that process will continue to process jobs for the printer. The original lpd daemon starts at boot time then continues to listen for print requests and spawn new copies of itself when needed. A spawned copy of the daemon will continue to run until there are no more files to print on the printer it was invoked to handle.

The lpd daemon and its spawned copies control the printing process but do not perform the mechanics needed to get the data to the printer. Instead, a filter program is run by the lpd daemon and the filter program sends the data to the printer, and optionally does some formatting that is needed to make the data compatible with the specific printer.

Troubleshooting

In a multiuser environment such as UNIX, a locking mechanism can be used to prevent a resource from being used to prevent multiple processes from trying to access the same resource at the same time. When a new lpd daemon is spawned to perform print processing functions, it creates a lock file (by using the UNIX system call **flock**) in the spooling directory. This lock file remains in the directory while this particular lpd daemon processes files to prevent other lpd daemons from being spawned for the particular directory. The lock file is a simple ASCII file that contains the process ID (PID) of the current lpd daemon and the name of the control file for the current print job.

When troubleshooting lpd daemons, you can examine the lock file to determine whether the daemon listed there is still running. In some versions of UNIX, the second line of the lock file also shows the status of the current job as the daemon believes it to be. In some others a file named status is used for this purpose.

The /etc/printcap Configuration File

When you set up printing on a UNIX computer that uses lpr/lpd, you must create the `/etc/printcap` file. It is a good idea to keep a written log on hand listing changes as you make them to this file. That way, when something suddenly goes wrong with a printer that has been working just fine, you can check the log to see whether anyone has recently made a change to the entry in the printcap file for the troublesome printer. This file is not a user-friendly file. In many cases the syntax for each entry will be a few lines, but for complicated setups, editing this file can become confusing if you make changes on only an infrequent basis.

Entries in this file specify the name used for a printer along with two-character symbol/value pairs (*symbol=value*) that define the characteristics for the printer. The printer can have more than one name (aliases), which is separated by a vertical-bar character. For example, an entry for a printer named "laser" could be as simple as this:

```
laser|laser1|lp|lp0|HP Laser Jet Accounting:\
       :d=/var/spool/lpd/laser:\
          :tv01:
```

ne name of the printer (`laser`) followed by several alias names that users printer. The last alias on the first line shows a common technique used by s: Describe the printer and its location. You can also put comments into the by using the pound-sign character (#) as the first character in the line. In this an see that a colon (:) is used to separate the symbol/value pairs from each nly one colon character is needed between each pair, it is customary to put one of a line and one at the end of the line when the entry spans multiple lines. The following itries are equivalent:

```
:sd=/var/spool/lpd/laser1:br#9600:
```

```
:sd=/var/spool/lpd/laser1:\
:br#9600:
```

Note that the backslash character (\) is used to indicate continuation of the entry across multiple lines. Also, some entries in the file do not have a value. For example, some are Boolean entries that have no value associated with them and are activated by their presence in the file.

In these examples, the `sd` symbol is followed by a directory path. This specifies the spooling directory that lpd will use to store files waiting to be printed. Multiple users can send files to the printer using the `lpr` command; copies of the files to be printed are created by the lpd daemon in the spooling directory and remain there until they are printed. After a file has been printed, the lpd daemon deletes the control and data files used for it.

The `lp` symbol is used to indicate the special device file for the printer. In UNIX, device files are used as a link to a physical device. The `makdev` command is used to create the device file just as for any other device attached to the computer. However, in the case of a remote printer, you would use the hostname/queue name on the remote system for this value instead of a device file-name. Entries can be much more complex than this example. Table 27.1 lists the symbols you can use to customize a printer.

Table 27.1   Symbols Used in the */etc/printcap* File

Symbol	Type	Default Value	Description
af	string	NULL	Name of accounting file
br	numeric	no default	Baud rate if lp is a tty
cf	string	NULL	The cifplot data filter
df	string	NULL	The TeX data filter (DVI format)
du	string	no default	Used to specify a nonstandard user ID for the daemon
fc	numeric	0	If lp is a tty, clear flag bits
ff	string	/f	String to send to printer for form feed
fo	Boolean	false	Print a form feed when device is opened
fs	numeric	0	If lp is a tty, set flag bits
gf	string	NULL	Graph data filter (plot format)
hl	Boolean	false	Print the burst header page last
ic	Boolean	false	Driver supports (nonstandard) ioctl to indent on printout
if	string	NULL	Accounting text filter
lf	string	/dev/console	Name of error logging file
lo	string	lock	Name of lock file
lp	string	/dev/lp	Output device
mc	numeric	0	Maximum number of copies allowed
mx	numeric	1000	Maximum file size (in BUFSIZ blocks)—zero means unlimited
nf	string	NULL	The ditroff data filter (device independent troff)
of	string	NULL	Output filtering program
pc	numeric	200	Price per foot or page (in hundredths of cents)
pl	numeric	66	Page length in lines
pw	numeric	132	Page width in characters
px	numeric	0	Page width in pixels (horizontal)
py	numeric	0	Page length in pixels (vertical)
rf	string	NULL	The FORTRAN-style text file filter
rg	string	NULL	Restricted group. Only members of this group are allowed access to the printer
rm	string	NULL	Machine name for remote printer
rp	string	lp	Remote printer name argument
rs	Boolean	false	Restrict remote users to only those who have local accounts
rw	Boolean	false	Open the print device for read/write
sb	Boolean	false	Short (one line) banner
sc	Boolean	false	Suppress multiple copies
sd	string	/usr/spool/lpd	Spooling directory or /var/spool/lpd
sf	Boolean	false	Suppress form feeds
sh	Boolean	false	Suppress printing of burst page header

Symbol	Type	Default Value	Description
st	string	status	Name of status file
tf	string	NULL	Name of troff data filter (cat phototypesetter)
tr	string	NULL	Trailer string to print when queue is emptied (that is, form feeds or escape characters)
vf	string	NULL	Raster image filter
xc	numeric	0	If lp is a tty, clear local mode bits
xs	numeric	0	If lp is a tty, set local mode bits

Following is an example of a more complicated entry:

```
lp¦lp0¦Color Laser: \
      :af=/usr/adm/printer/clp.acct:\
      :br#9600:\
      :lf=/usr/adm/lpterror:\
      :lp=/dev/tty05:\
      :mx#0:\
      :sd=/var/spool/lpd:\
```

This example defines the spooling directory for a printer as well as the log file and accounting file. The mx#0 entry means that there is no maximum size limit for files that can print on this printer.

When specifying a printer device, you can also tell the lpd daemon to use a print queue that resides on another system. For example

```
xprint¦laser2¦Manufacturing printer:\
      :lp=:\
      :rm=mfgunix:\
      :rp=lp:\
      :sd=/var/spool/lpd/xprint:\
      :mx#0:\
```

In this example, the lp symbol is set to null. This indicates that the print device is not on this system. You still must include the lp symbol so that the default value for it will not be substituted by the lpd daemon. The rm symbol is used to indicate the hostname of the remote computer, and the rp symbol is used to define the name of the printer on that system. Also, even though the actual printing is done on the remote computer, you must still specify a spooling directory because files submitted to the queue still need to be temporarily stored before they are copied to the remote system.

Useful Commands: lpq, lprm, and lpc

From the user's perspective, printing is a simple task—just use the lpr command and wait for the paper to come out of the printer. As the administrator you need commands that can help you manage print queues and track usage. The lpq command is used to show information about jobs waiting in the print queue. This command shows you the following information:

- The order of print jobs in the queue
- The name of the user who submitted the job to print
- The job identification number
- The names of files waiting to print
- The size of the print job (in bytes)

For example

```
Rank    Owner      Job  Files        Total Size
active  ogletree   133  prm0d1x      31540 bytes
1st     heywood    141  letter1      3423  bytes
2nd     chasog     216  jandata      98465 bytes
3rd     peter      323  twoinchtml   2342  bytes
4th     menton     122  queulst      55432 bytes
```

You can use the -P parameter to specify the printer just like you can with the lpr command. Similarly, the UNIX environment variable PRINTER will determine the printer to display if you do not specify one. The syntax for the lpq command is

```
lpq [-Pprinter][-1][+[interval]][job#...][username...]
```

The -1 parameter will cause a "long" listing to be displayed. The plus sign (+) can be used by itself or with a numeric value, and will cause the command to continuously display the status until the print queue empties. If you follow the plus sign with a numeric value, it will be used as the number of seconds between each refresh interval.

Use the job ID numbers or the user's username when troubleshooting specific print jobs and you will not have to look through a long listing of all print jobs. The job ID number can also be used by other print queue management commands, so it is common to use lpq to get a job's ID number before executing other commands.

To remove a print job from the queue you can use the lprm command. Its syntax is similar to the lpq command:

```
lprm [-Pprinter][-][job#...][username...]
```

Although any user can remove his or her own files pending in a print queue, only the superuser can remove other user's files. You can specify the job ID number associated with a specific file or specify a username to remove all print jobs currently pending in the queue for that user.

Technical Note

To remove jobs from a print queue, use the **lprm** command to kill the current lpd daemon that is processing files for that queue. It then deletes the necessary files from the print queue and restarts a new daemon process to continue processing the remaining files.

Examining a print queue and removing pending jobs can be useful for troubleshooting simple problems. For more control over the BSD printing system, you can use the `lpc` (line printer control program) command. The syntax for this command is more complicated than that of the `lpq` and `lprm` commands because of the more complex functions it can perform. The syntax for lpc is

```
lpc [command [parameters...]]
```

The commands you can use with lpc are as follows:

- **abort [all ¦ *printer*...]**—Kills the active lpd daemon, and then disables printing for the specified printers. Stops the print job that is currently printing. After this, lpr will not be capable of creating a new lpd daemon for the specified printers. Use this option when you need to quickly disable a printer.

- **clean [all ¦ *printer*...]**—Removes temporary files (including control and data files) from the specified printer's spooling directory when the files do not form a complete print job. Useful for cleaning up a spool directory when something has gone wrong.

- **disable [all ¦ *printer*...]**—Prevents lpr from submitting new print jobs to this print queue. This command turns off printing for the specified queue.

- **down [all ¦ *printer*...] *message*...**—Turns off the print queue and disables printing. "*Message...*" text is entered into the status file for the printer so that lpq can report it.

- **enable [all ¦ *printer*...]**—Enables spooling on the printers so that users can begin to use the `lpr` command to submit print jobs.

- **restart [all ¦ *printer*...]**—When a printer daemon dies unexpectedly, you can use this command to start a new daemon for the queue. The jobs currently existing in the queue will be printed by the new daemon. You should perform this command when the lpq command gives you the no daemon present message.

- **start [all ¦ *printer*...]**—Enables printing and starts a spooling daemon for the printers specified. Changes the owner's execute permission on the lock file in order to accomplish their tasks.

- **status [all ¦ *printer*...]**—Gets the status of printer daemons and queues. Shows whether the queue is enabled or disabled or whether printing is enabled or disabled. Also shows the number of entries in the queue and the status of the printer's lpd daemon.

- **stop [all ¦ *printer*...]**—Stops a spooling daemon and disables printing. The daemon stops after it finishes the current print job. Use the abort command if you want to stop the daemon and kill the current job that is printing.

- **topq *printer* [*job#.. .*][*username*...]**—Entries are printed on a first-in, first-out (FIFO) basis. Use this command to move print jobs to the top of the queue. Specify one or more job numbers as an argument to this command. Specify a username as the argument to move all jobs pending for that user to the top of the queue.

- **up [all ¦ *printer*...]**—Opposite of the down command. Enables all printing and starts a new printer daemon.

- **exit or quit**—Causes the lpc program to exit (when in interactive mode).

- **? [*command*] or help [*command*]**—Displays a short help text for each *command*. If no command is specified after the help command, a list of all commands that the lpc program recognizes will be displayed.

Although the lpc program is usually used by an administrator (superuser), ordinary users can use the restart and status commands.

In the following listing you can see an example of using the lpc command to get the status of a printer named laser1. In this example the queue is enabled and printing. There is only one job in the queue. When you use the command without command-line parameters it prompts you in interactive mode:

```
% /usr/sbin/lpc
lpc> status laser2
laser1:
        printer is on device '/dev/tty03' speed 9600
        queuing is enabled
        printing is enabled
        1 entry in spool area
lpc>quit
```

In this next example the lpd daemon for this queue has exited unexpectedly. Using the lpc command, you can detect this condition and fix the problem:

```
% /usr/sbin/lpc
lpc> status laser2
laser2:
        printer is on device '/dev/tty03' speed 9600        queuing is enabled
        printing is enabled
        7 entries in spool area
        no daemon present
lpc> restart laser2
lpc>quit
```

Examining Printing Statistics

Part of managing a network is gathering statistics. This is done for several reasons. First, historical data is nice to have when you are trying to determine the circumstances leading up to a problem. Second, statistical data can help you plan for enough capacity when you are deciding on expansion or reorganization. Another use for the information is user or department accountability. In environments where costs are charged back to a department, you can use the pac command to gather the data you need.

The syntax for this command is

```
pac [-Pprinter][-cmrs][-pprice][username]
```

As is the custom with other printing commands, the -P parameter allows you to specify a printer. If you do not, the value of PRINTER is used or the system default printer is assumed. The other parameters you can use are

■ c—Sorts the report by cost instead of machine/username.

■ m—Groups charges by username with no regard to the hostname of the computer from which the jobs were submitted.

■ r—Reverses the sort order for the report.

- **s**—Summarizes the accounting data and writes it to a summary file. The summary file is usually in the form of *printer*.acct_sum.

- **p***price*—Allows you to specify the cost per unit (foot or page) for print jobs. The default is two cents per unit.

- **username**—If you supply usernames at the end of the command, only statistics for print jobs for those users will be included in the report.

Tip

You can include the **pac** command in script files to create automated procedures to produce accounting reports. For example, you could use a script file to produce reports by user or department and then email a copy of the report to a responsible person.

The sample report in Listing 27.1 shows the type of information you can get by using the pac command. Realize that the costs for each print job are just simple calculations based on the unit and the cost you supply to the command.

Listing 27.1   Accounting Report Output from the *pac* Command

```
Login              ages/feet    runs    price
atlunix1:harris        14.00    1       $ 0.28
atlunix1:brown          3.00    2       $ 0.06
pluto:ogletree         21.00    3       $ 0.42
```

The SVR4 Printing System

Another major type of UNIX variant is the System V, Version 4 system, and its printing system uses the lp command and lpsched command to print and manage printer queues. Although an /etc/printcap file is also used, it doesn't have to be edited manually. A utility called lpadmin will do this for you.

Using *lp*, *cancel*, and *lpstat*

The lp command is used just as the lpr command. However, the lp command does more than just send files to a printer; it can also be used to modify print jobs. The cancel command is used to remove a job from the print queue. The syntax for the lp command comes in two different forms:

```
lp [-c][-m][-p][-s][-w][-d dest]
    [-f form-name [-d any]][-H special-handling]
    [-n number][-o option][-P page-list]
    [-q priority-level][-S character-set][-d any]]
    [-S print-wheel[-d any]][-t title]
    [-T content-type][-r]][-y mode-list]
    [filename...]

lp -i request-id ... [-c][-m][-p][-s][-w]
    [-d dest][-f form-name[-d any]]
    [-H special-handling][-n number][-o option]
    [-P page-list][-q priority-level]
    [-S character-set[-d any]]]
    [-t title][-T content-type[-r]]
    [-y mode-list]
```

The first version of this command is used to send files to print. The second version is used to modify a print request that is already pending. If you use the second version to modify a job that is already printing, it will stop the job and restart it with the changes you have made.

You can use the following parameters with the `lp` command:

- **c**—A copy of the file to be made before it is printed. The default action is to create a link to the file. If you use the `-c` parameter, you should not delete the file before it is printed. Any changes you make to the file after submitting the print request will not be reflected in the output if you use this parameter to create a copy of the file.

- **d** *dest*—Specifies the destination printer or class for the print job.

- **f** *form-name*—Specifies a form to be mounted on the printer to process the print request. If the printer does not support the form, the request is rejected. Note that if you use the `-d` any parameter with this one, the print request can be sent to any printer that supports the form.

- **H** *special-handling*—Puts the print request on hold or resumes requests that are holding. If you are an LP administrator, it causes the request to be the next one to print. The terms you use for *special-handling* are hold, resume, and immediate, respectively.

- **m**—Sends mail after the print job has finished.

- **n** *number*—The number of copies to print.

- **o** *option*—Specifies printer-dependent options. You can specify more than one option by using the `-o` parameter more than once. You can also include multiple options by enclosing them in quotes; for example, `-o "option1 option2 ..."`.

  Terms you can use for the *option* are

  - **nobanner**—Do not print banner page.

  - **nofilebreak**—Do not insert a form feed character between files when multiple files are printed.

  - **length=**scaled-decimal-number—Specifies the page length. You can specify lines, inches, or centimeters. Length=66 specifies 66 lines per page, while length=11I specifies 11 inches per page, for example.

  - **width=**scaled-decimal-number—Similar to the `length` option. Use this format to specify page width in columns, inches, or centimeters.

  - **lpi=**scaled-decimal-number—Like `length` and `width`, use this to specify line pitch (lines per inch).

  - **cpi=**scaled-decimal-number—Like `length` and `width`, use this to specify characters per inch. You can also use the terms pica (10 characters per inch), elite (12 characters per inch), or compressed to allow the printer to fit as many characters on a line as it can.

  - **stty=**'stty-option-list'—Specifies options for the `stty` command, which is used to set terminal options. Enclose the list with single quotes if it contains blank characters.

- **P** *page-list*—If the filter can handle it, this will cause only the pages specified by *page-list* to be printed. You can specify single pages or a range of pages.

- **p**—Enable notification on completion of the print request.

- **q** *priority-level*—Priority levels range from 0 (highest) to 39 (lowest). This parameter changes the print priority of a print request. Giving a request a lower priority causes it to print before requests with a higher priority.

- **s**—Suppress messages from lp.

- **S** *character-set* **or S** *print-wheel*—Used to select a character set or print wheel to be used on the printer for the request. If the character set or print wheel is not available, the request is rejected.

- **t** *title*—Prints *title* on the banner page. Use quotes around the text if it contains blank spaces.

- **T** *content-type*—Causes the request to be printed on a printer that supports *content-type*, if available, or uses a filter to convert the content to the appropriate type. If you specify -r with this option, a filter will not be used. The request is rejected if no printer for this type is available or a filter cannot be used.

- **w**—Sends a message to the user's terminal after the print request completes. If the user is not currently logged in, a mail message is sent.

- **y** *mode-list*—Use *mode-list* options to print. The allowed values for mode list are locally defined, and the job is rejected if there is no filter to handle the request.

If you must stop a job from printing, you can use the cancel command. The syntax for the cancel command is

```
cancel [request-id...][printer...]
cancel -u login-ID-list [printer...]
```

The first syntax example can be used to remove a specific print job by specifying its ID number. The second example shows how to remove all print jobs for a particular user (or users). If you list multiple users on the command line, enclose the list in quotes and use a space between each ID name. Ordinary users can only cancel print requests that they submitted. Administrators can cancel any print job.

To get the request ID of a print job, you will need to use the lpstat command. This command can be used by ordinary users with no parameters and will return information about only their print jobs. However, the administrator can use this command to see data about the entire printing system. The syntax for lpstat is

```
lpstat [-d] [-r] [-R] [-s] [-t] [-a [list]]
    [-c [list]] [-o [list]]
    [-p [list]] [-P] [-s [list] [-l]]
    [-u [login-ID-list]] [-v [list]]
```

Here, *list* can be a comma-delimited list or a series of items separated by spaces and enclosed in quotes. You can omit a list or use the keyword *all* in most instances to get the status of the requested objects. The following are the parameters for this command:

- **a** *[list]*—Use this to show whether print destinations (printers or printer classes) are accepting print requests.

- **c** *[list]*—Use this to see the name of all classes and members of the class. You can specify specific classes using *list*.

- **d**—This will display the system's default print destination.

- **o** *[list]*—This will display the status of output requests. The *list* value can specify either printers or class names or request IDs.

- **p** *[list]*—This will display the status of printers. Use *list* to specify printer names.

- **r**—This will display the status of the print scheduler daemon (lpsched).

- **s**—Displays summary information about the printing system.

- **t** Displays all the available status information about the printing system.

- **u**[*login-ID-list*]—Displays the status of print requests for the users listed in *login-ID-list*.

- **v**[*list*]—Displays pathnames of the output device files for printers indicated by *list*. For remote printers, this will display the name of the remotesystem.

Administering the System: lpadmin, lpsched, and lpshut

The lpadmin command performs a wide range of functions necessary to setting up a printer on a UNIX system. It will add, remove, or modify printers and will create the necessary text files in the spooling directory for you so you do not have to edit them manually. This command can also be used to set up "alerts" when the printer experiences a fault condition. The syntax for this administrative command is

```
lpadmin -p printer-options
lpadmin -x dest
lpadmin -d [dest]
lpadmin -S print-wheel -A alert-type [-W minutes]
            [-Q requests]
lpadmin -M -f form-name [-a [-o filebreak]
        [-t tray-number]
```

The first syntax example here shows how to add a new printer. You specify on the command line the -p option to specify the printer's name, and then list the printer's characteristics. For example:

```
lpadmin –phplj5 –v/dev/tty03 –mdumb -cpr
```

This command will perform the functions needed to create a printer named hplj5. Following the printer name, the options here indicate that the actual printer device is connected to a serial port that can be accessed through the UNIX device file /dev/tty03. This printer uses a dumb interface (-m option) and is a member of a class of printers named "pr" (the -c option).

Tip

After you set up a printer using **lpadmin** it does not automatically allow users to print. Use the **accept** *printer* command to enable printing.

The man pages for your system will give you a full list of the options you can use on the command line, and they will vary depending on the flavor of UNIX you have. However, the following list shows some of the more useful ones which you will find on most systems:

- A *alert-type* [**-W minutes**]—Set up an alert action that will be invoked when a printer fault occurs. The *alert-type* can be mail (sends an email) or write (puts a message on an administrator's terminal). You can also use quiet to suppress alerts, showfault to execute a fault-handling procedure, or none to remove alerts. You can also specify a shell command to be executed.

- c *class*—Use this to specify a class that the printer will belong to. If *class* does not exist, it will be created. The -r parameter can be used to remove a printer from a specific class.

- D *comment*—The text *comment* will be displayed when the user requests a full description of the printer.

- e *printername*—Copies the interface program used by an existing printer (*printername*) for use with the printer you are creating. Using this option, you can quickly clone entries when adding a printer of a type you already have, or if you are setting up a network that has many printers of the same type, at the same time.

- i *interface*—Specifies the interface program for the printer. See the -e printername option to copy an interface from an existing printer.

- m *model*—Selects the *model* interface program that comes with the lp print service. You cannot use -e or -i with this option.

- s *system-name* [**!*printer-name***]—Used to create a remote printer. A remote printer is a printer that is on another system that you want your users to be able to use as if it were local. The *system-name* should be the name of the computer on which the printer resides and !*printer-name* is the name the printer uses on the remote system. You can use a different printer name on your system than the name on the remote system.

Tip

In this chapter, the UNIX man pages have been referred to several times. These are the help files for the UNIX system and you can consult them when you need help for a particular topic. For example, the command man lpadmin can be used to get the help text for the lpadmin command on the system so you can see a full list of the options supported.

To remove a printer from the lp printing system use the -x command-line parameter:

```
lpadmin -xhplj5
```

This command removes the printer hplj5 from the system. Also, if this is the last printer in its class of printers, the printer class will also be deleted.

In the file /etc/init.d/lp you will find commands that can be used to start the print scheduler daemon at boot time. The syntax, in case you want to change the boot-time command, is

```
lpsched [-nofork][-debug][-nobsd]
```

You can also use this command to restart the daemon if you find it necessary to kill it when troubleshooting printer problems. The lpsched daemon works sort of like the lpr daemon—it creates a new copy of itself to handle print jobs. The original daemon remains free to respond to additional user requests.

Troubleshooting

The -nofork parameter can be used to suppress the creation of a separate daemon process. This is recommended to be used during debugging. You can also use the -debug parameter to put the daemon into *verbose* mode. In this mode more messages are displayed that can be useful when trying to solve printer problems.

The -nobsd parameter can be used to tell lpsched to ignore the BSD spooler's well-known port. If you are also running an lpd daemon on the system and it is using the default port, use this option to change the port used by lpsched.

Tip

Well Known Ports are listed in Appendix B, "TCP and UDP Common Ports." A *port* is used in TCP/IP protocols to specify an endpoint that an application can use along with an IP address so that it can send a message to a specific process on a computer. For example, the FTP protocol uses ports 20 and 21 (usually) and the Telnet daemon uses ports 23 and 24 (usually).

To shut down a printer there are several commands you can use, depending on just what you need to do:

- **lpshut**—This command stops all printers. Jobs that are currently printing will be stopped but will be reprinted in their entirety when the printer is again started, as will other print jobs waiting in the spooler directory. Users can still continue to submit to a printer that has been stopped using this command. Use lpsched when you want to start printers again.

- **reject [-r *reason*] *printer***—This command will stop a printer from printing, but when this command is used it will no longer be possible for users to continue to submit jobs to the printer for later printing. If you want the users to know what is happening with the printer, use the -r command and specify the text you want them to see. If the text contains blank characters (it's more than one word), enclose the text in quotes. To restart the printer use the accept *printer* command.

- **disable[-c ¦ -W] [-r [reason]] printer**—*This command can be used to disable a printer temporarily, while still allowing users to submit jobs to the spooling directory that will print when the queue is restored to service. The -c and -W options are exclusive. Use -c to cancel the job that is currently printing and -W to have the printer stop after the current job finishes. Both of these parameters are ignored if the printer is on a remote system. Again, use -r to specify a text to be displayed to users (when they use the* lpstat -p *command to check the printer's status). Use the* enable printer *command to restart the printer.*

If a printer is going to be out of service for a while and you don't want users to keep submitting jobs, use the reject command. If a printer is going to be taken out of service completely, use the lpadmin command to remove it.

If some major problem is plaguing your entire printing system, use the lpshut command to bring everything to a halt while you investigate the problem.

One last command that might be handy when performing troubleshooting or maintenance duties is the lpmove command. As you are sure to guess, this command can move pending print requests from one printer to another. For example

```
lpmove hplj5 -221 hplj5land -232 laser3
```

In this example, the print job identified by the request ID number 221 will be moved from the hplj5 printer to laser3. The print job identified by the request ID 232 waiting for hplj5land will also be moved to laser3.

Using TCP/IP (*lpr/lpd*) Printing on Windows NT Server

Windows NT Server can use several network protocols to connect to a printer on the network, and then make the printer available via the server to other clients on the network that do not have support for the particular protocol. Among the supported protocols for Windows NT Server are TCP/IP and DLC.

To configure Windows NT Server to use a networked printer using the TCP/IP protocol, you will need to know the IP address of the printer. You can usually find this on a test page or configuration page for the printer. If it has not been configured you will need to consult the manual.

Before you can use the Printer Wizard to install a printer that uses TCP/IP, you must install the Microsoft TCP/IP Printing service. This can be done quickly using the Network applet in the Control Panel. Select the Services tab, click the Add button, and select Microsoft TCP/IP Printing. After the installation procedure has copied the files that it needs from the installation CD, you will have to reboot the server before you can use the service.

After the server has rebooted, use the Printer Wizard to create the printer. Select Add Printer from the Printers folder. The first dialog box will ask if the printer is a local printer (My Computer) or if it is a network printer (Network Printer Server). Here a distinction must be made between how Windows NT uses the terms *printer* and *print device*.

A print device is the actual physical printer that attaches to the computer or to the network via a network adapter card. A printer, under Windows NT, is a logical construct, or object, to which you send print jobs. So, when the Add Printer Wizard asks you if the printer is to be managed by My Computer or Network Printer Server, you should select My Computer. Although the print device is actually going to be accessed by the TCP/IP network protocol, the "printer" object will be managed on the local server.

The next dialog box (see Figure 27.1) will allow you to select the port to which the print device is attached. The usual communication ports (LPT1:, LPT2:, COM 1:, and so on) will be displayed here.

Because the printer will be on the network it will be necessary to create a new type of port. Select the Add Port button. The next dialog box will allow you to select the type of port you want to add; select LPR port.

Troubleshooting

If you neglected to install the Microsoft TCP/IP Printing service, you will not see LPR Port as an option in the dialog box when you try to add a printer port. Go back and add the service, reboot the server, and then you can continue to create the printer. Remember to reapply the latest NT service pack after adding any services.

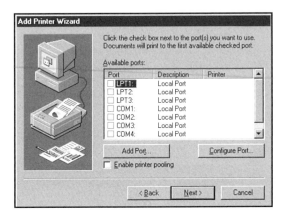

Figure 27.1   The Add Printer Wizard prompts you for the port to which the print device is connected.

The Add Printer Wizard will then prompt you to enter the IP address (or hostname) of the remote printer and the name of the printer or print queue on that remote system. In many cases you will not have to enter a print queue name if you are using a printer that is directly connected to the network. Check the configuration printout for the printer to be sure.

If you are creating a printer that will send jobs to a remote print queue on another system, such as a UNIX or Linux system, you will have to enter the name of the printer or print queue. After you have entered the necessary address and print queue information, click OK, and then click Close when you are returned to the Printer Ports dialog box.

The new printer port will now be displayed in the list of available ports along with LPT1: and the others. Select the new port by clicking the check box next to it, and then click Next.

The Add Printer Wizard will then display a dialog box from which you can select the printer's manufacturer and model so that a print driver can be installed. If your model is not among those displayed and you have a floppy disk that contains the driver, or if you have the driver files on a local or network disk, click the Have Disk button and supply the correct path to the files.

When you have selected the correct model click Next. You will be asked to supply a name for the printer. It is best to use something descriptive that indicates the type of printer and its location if you plan to let other computers connect to the server and send print jobs to it.

The next dialog box asks you if you want to share the printer on the network. If you select to share the printer, you can also designate, from the list displayed, to load additional printer software drivers for other operating systems. This allows you to share the printer with clients that do not have the driver installed on their computers. The raw print job will be sent by the client and formatted locally by the server using the appropriate driver before it is spooled to the network printer. Click the Next button when you have selected to share or not share the printer.

The last dialog box will prompt you to print a test page. You should always do this to test the configuration you have just set up.

Configuring a NetWare Printer for TCP/IP Printing

The printing process under the NetWare architecture separates the printer physical device from the print queue much like Windows NT Server. In the NDS database the administrator defines three objects and configures their properties to make printers available to clients. The *printer object* represents the physical printer itself, which can be attached to a computer or directly to the network with its own network card. The *print queue* is a directory that resides on a NetWare volume and is used to buffer print files until they can be sent to a printer. The *print server* can be either hardware or software and is the component that controls the actual printing process by taking the file from the print queue and delivering it to the physical printer.

To configure a printer object that will be used for a printer that is connected directly to the network, you will have to specify the protocol and the network address for the printer. To do so, use the Configuration button on the Printer object dialog box and, from the Printer type field, you can select one of the following:

- UNIX
- XNP
- AppleTalk

For TCP/IP printing, select UNIX. Then, in the field labeled Network Address Restriction enter the IP address for the printer. You can also use this feature to connect to a printer attached to another server. In that case, enter the IP address for the server. The address you enter will be the only address used to connect to the printer.

The *print server* object should then be created. PSERVER.NLM is NetWare software print server, although you can also use a third-party print server if one is provided by the manufacturer for its printer. The dialog box for the print server object enables you to specify the name that will be used to advertise the printer on the network and the network address of the print server.

The printer, print server, and print queue do not all have to reside on the same network server. Indeed, you can connect the physical printer directly to the network, define the print queue object on a server, and then define the print server object on another server. This flexibility comes at a cost, however. When a client wants to print, the NetWare client software will send the file to the server where the print queue resides. When it is time to print the file, it is sent to the print server, which then sends it to the printer. Obviously, if all three objects are on the same server, or if the print server and print queue are on the same server, less network traffic is generated.

Data Link Control Protocol (DLC)

In a network where the IP address space is beginning to become a scarce resource, there are other methods you can use to connect printers to your servers. For example, the HP Jet Direct card, which can be used to connect many HP printers directly to the network, can communicate with servers on the network using TCP/IP. You can also use the DLC protocol, which does not require you to assign an IP address to the printer's network card.

The Data Link Control (DLC) protocol was developed by IBM primarily for use in connecting to mainframe computers as part of its Systems Network Architecture (SNA) specifications. It is also used today to establish sessions with AS/400 computers. In addition to the HP Jet Direct card, you will find that other vendors also make network cards for printers that can use DLC. For example, the Brother NC-600X and NC-2010h network cards can both be used for this purpose.

Internet Printing Protocol

The newest thing on the horizon for printers has to be the Internet Printing Protocol (IPP). Although most network servers and clients can be configured to use the lpr/lpd or DLC protocols, there are still many other diverse methods used to send print jobs to printers. The driving force of the Internet is making many vendors conscious of the need for more unified standards for basic functions, such as printing, and new protocols are constantly being developed.

Several groups were at work in 1996 to develop a new standard. Novell and Xerox were working on a protocol that was titled Lightweight Document Printing Application (LDPA), IBM was developing the Hypertext Printing Protocol (HTPP), and Microsoft and HP were working on still another new protocol. Finally, a working group was formed under the auspices of the Internet Engineering Task Force to work on a new standard.

The goals of the first efforts of the project are to develop a protocol that defines the user end of the printing process and includes the following capabilities:

- Allow a user to discover the capabilities of a particular printer.
- Allow a user to submit jobs to the printer.
- Allow a user to get the status of the printer or the print job.
- Allow a user to cancel a print job.
- Define a set of directory attributes that will make it easy to find a printer in a directory database.

All these are pretty standard items that will be incorporated into the first version of the standard. Later revisions will include mechanisms to provide for security, such as user or printer authentication, and functions for administrators who manage a printing system. Another goal of the standard will be to define methods to allow IPP to interact with lpr/lpd systems so that it will not be necessary to throw out your entire printing infrastructure and start over again.

Standards

The work of the IPP group so far has been defined by several RFCs:

RFC 2565, "Internet Printing Protocol/1.0: Encoding and Transport"

RFC 2566, "Internet Printing Protocol/1.0: Model and Semantics"

RFC 2567, "Design Goals for an Internet Printing Protocol"

RFC 2568, "Rationale for the Structure of the Model and Protocol for the Internet Printing Protocol"

RFC 2569, "Mapping Between LPD and IPP Protocols"

IPP Object Types

In the first version of this protocol, two basic object types are defined: *printer object* and *print job*. The printer object encompasses the functions that are done by the actual physical printer, such as rendering the printed page, as well as some of the functions that are traditionally performed by the print server, such as spooling the print file and handling scheduling procedures. The functions of the printer object can be implemented in a print server or on the printer itself. The printer object can be used to send output to a single physical printer or to more than one device.

When a user sends a document to a printer, the printer object creates a new object called a print job. The print job object contains the document to be printed and can contain more than one document per job. The printer object manipulates the print job and handles how it is sent to the physical printer.

IPP Operations

The protocol defines several operations that consist of a request and a response. An operation allows the client to communicate with the object. The operations defined in the first version of the protocol that can be used with the printer object are

- Print-Job
- Print-URI
- Validate-Job
- Create-Job
- Get-Printer-Attributes
- Get-Jobs

The operations that can be used with the print job object are defined as

- Send-Document
- Send-URI
- Cancel-Job
- Get-Job-Attributes

Technical Note

The term *URI* used in these operations refers to *uniform resource identifier*, which is described in RFC 2396. URIs are used to unambiguously identify an object. You might be familiar with the term URL, which stands for uniform resource locator, another standardized term that can unambiguously identify a location for a resource. The concept here is similar—a unique identifier is assigned to the print job.

A client submits a document to print by using the Print-Job request. Using this operation, the client "pushes" or sends the text to be printed. A client can also submit a job using the Print-URI operation, in which the client sends only the URI reference for the data to be printed and the printer object "pulls" the data itself. To send multiple documents to be printed, the client uses the Create-Job operation, which is followed by multiple Send-Document or Send-URI operations, which also operate in a push-pull fashion.

The printer object responds to Validate-Job requests from the client, depending on the current state of the printing job (pending, processing, and so on). For example, the printer object may return information to the client that the supplied URI is no longer valid, or it might return error messages to the client.

Other operations are pretty much self-explanatory. The Get-Printer-Attributes and Get-Job-Attributes operations return information about the printer or the print job. The Get-Jobs operation allows the client to get a list of job objects that are being processed by the particular printer object. The Cancel-Job operation is used by the client to remove a job from the printer object, basically stopping a job from printing.

The RFCs also go into detail describing the attributes of each object, some of which are required and some of which are optional. These attributes include information about the job, such as its name, time stamps for different parts of the printing process, and the output device assigned to print the job. Attributes for the printer object include the name of the printer, its location, location of the printer driver, and other information such as the make and model of the printer.

The Future of IPP

The IPP protocol will most likely be widely adopted in a few years. It will solve a lot of problems for both end users and for vendors of printing equipment. Many companies are beginning to use the Internet to create virtual private networks (VPNs) instead of creating WANs using leased lines and other dedicated links. As the Internet continues to weave itself into every nook and cranny of the modern business world, standards such as IPP will generate new types of services. It is easy to foresee a business segment that will take over handling some or all of the aspects of printing for a large organization. Standards like IPP will make implementation of these sorts of services much easier because it will not rely on multiple proprietary protocols and skill sets.

Summary

Some of the most common reasons for networks in the business environment are to provide central printing or file services to clients. For the most part, it is becoming more common for printers to be connected directly to the network rather than attached to a server. For that reason, protocols used to exchange data and control the printing process will become more important. In the next chapter, print servers, both software- and hardware-based, will be examined.

Print Servers

The last chapter discussed several protocols used for networked printing. In this chapter we examine some of the ways in which printers can be deployed on the network and made available to users. When local area networks (LANs) were in their infancy, this function was usually performed by a printer that was attached to a network node. Today it is more common to find printers or hardware-based print servers directly attached to the network. Each method has its advantages and disadvantages, and there are combinations of both that can make the situation even more confusing.

This chapter gives you an overview of the process of setting up printing services for both Windows NT Server and NetWare networks, and takes a look at hardware solutions that allow printers to live on the network as independent hosts.

Printing Under Windows NT

Windows NT Server provides a very flexible printing system that can be used to direct user print jobs to a printer that is directly connected to the server, to print queues on other hosts, or to printers that are directly attached to the network. Setup is performed using a wizard that can be used to create a printer in just a few minutes. Unlike some other operating systems, Windows NT does not use the term *print queue* to refer to the interface between an application and the actual physical printer. Instead, a print queue is simply a collection of documents that are waiting to print.

Printers and Printing Devices

The terminology used by Windows NT to refer to the actual physical printer is *printing device*. The term *printer* is used to refer to a logical construct, or an interface to the print device. The conceptual difference between these two terms is that they do not necessarily imply a one-to-one relationship. In Figure 28.1 you can see that several logical printers can be set up to send print jobs to the same printing device.

Using this kind of setup, it is easy to define several different logical printers for a device, with each printer set up to take advantage of different characteristics of the physical printer. All the logical printers are then pointed to the same output device. For example, you might have one logical printer set up to print in a portrait orientation and then another set up to print in a landscape orientation. Users would be able to send print jobs to the printer that matches the format they desire, without having to select the necessary configuration options themselves. Other possibilities are configuring multiple printers that select different paper trays or print in draft or letter quality format.

Conversely, you can also do the opposite, as shown in Figure 28.2.

This setup is usually called a *printer pool*. In an environment where a high print volume is the norm, setting up a printer pool can provide a much faster throughput for end users who will spend less time waiting for their printouts than if only a single printing device was used. It also eliminates the necessity of having to create and manage multiple logical printers. This situation also makes it easier for you to add additional print devices to the printer pool without having to make users aware. One of the best features of using a printer pool is that it can be used to eliminate the physical print device as a single point of failure. If a printer begins to malfunction, it can be taken offline and print jobs can continue to be rendered into final format by other printers that are members of the printer pool.

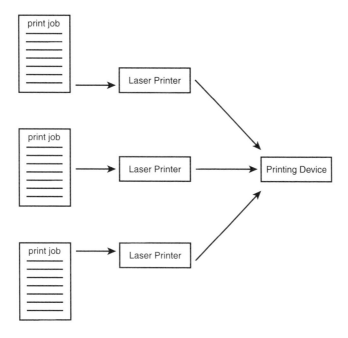

Figure 28.1 In Windows NT, more than one logical printer can send print jobs to a single physical printing device.

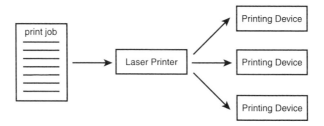

Figure 28.2 A printer pool allows a logical printer to distribute its load over several output devices.

When using printer pools you must keep several things in mind:

- Each output printing device should be of the same type or be set up to emulate the same kind of device, because the printer driver used by the logical printer will be specific to a particular kind of printer.

- When a job is submitted for printing to a printer that uses a printer pool, it is printed on the first available device. As long as there is an available printer, the user's job will not have to wait for another job to finish before it will print.

■ It is a good idea to locate all the printers that are part of the same printer pool in a single location. Users will not be happy if they have to walk all over the office to find out where a print job was completed.

Adding a Printer

To add a new printer, select Add Printer from the Printers folder that you find under My Computer. The Add Printer Wizard will ask you a few simple questions.

Where Will the Printer Be Managed?

This first question can be confusing if you are not familiar with Windows NT printing. The available choices are

■ My Computer
■ Network Printer Server

Technical Note

The wizard is not asking you where the printer will be connected. For example, if you select My Computer, this does not mean that the physical printer device will be connected to the **LPT1:** port on your server. Instead, it means that the printer will be managed on your local server. You will load the necessary drivers for the printer on the local computer and will be responsible for any settings or other management functions for the printer on this computer.

If you select Network Printer Server, the wizard will present you with a dialog box that will enable you to connect to a printer that is already on the network or is being offered by another server. The wizard will then prompt you to load a driver for the printer, unless one is already loaded on the server that hosts the printer. When you connect to a printer using this method, you can send print jobs to the printer but you cannot manage its properties.

Port Selection

If you chose My Computer as the place where the printer will be managed, the next prompt the wizard displays will ask you for the name of the port to which the printer is attached. This can be a local port, such as LPT1:, LPT2:, or even COM1:, and so on. You can select to have the printer set up to send the print job to a file instead. Sending output to a file can be an easy method of capturing the output from an application that doesn't provide such a function.

Technical Note

If you want to create a printer pool, select the check box labeled Enable Printer Pooling, which appears on the Available Ports dialog box. You will then be able to select more than one port for this logical printer.

If you want this logical printer to manage documents that will be sent to a printer elsewhere on the network, select Add Port, and then supply the necessary configuration information that the wizard needs to create a port for the printer. The following kinds of ports are supported under Windows NT 4.0:

- Digital Equipment Corporation Network Port
- Hewlett-Packard Network Port
- Lexmark DLC Network Port
- Lexmark TCP/IP Network Port
- LPR Port

Note

Not all the ports listed here will necessarily be displayed. For the Hewlett-Packard Network Port to appear, you must first install the DLC protocol. For the LPR Port option to appear, you must first install the Microsoft TCP/IP Printing service. Both can be installed by using the Network applet in the Control Panel, after which you will have to reboot the server.

Highlight the port you want to create, and then click the New Port button. Depending on the choice you have made, a dialog box will appear to prompt you for more information for the specific kind of port you want to create. For example, in Figure 28.3 you can see the information that is needed to create a Hewlett-Packard Network Port.

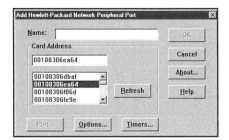

Figure 28.3   Fill in the information needed to create a Hewlett-Packard Network Port.

You will need to fill in the name you want to give the port, and then select from the dialog box the 12-digit LAN (MAC) hardware address that corresponds to the address of the printer. You can get the address for the HP printer by printing a self-test page. Note that if no addresses appear on this dialog box, the printer might be powered off or there might be a network error preventing the server from obtaining it. If you click the Options or Timers button you will be able to further customize this printer port by specifying such things as the logging level that will be performed (information, warning, error) and values for timers associated with the DLC protocol.

In the preceding chapter, the UNIX LPR/LPD printing system is discussed. Windows NT Server can send print jobs to printers that are connected to UNIX systems as well as to networked printers that understand the LPR/LPD printing system. If you choose to create a new port using the LPR protocol, a dialog box (shown in Figure 28.4) enables you to enter the IP address for the printer or the host on which it resides as well as the name of the printer or print queue.

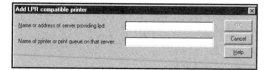

Figure 28.4 For an LPR port you must supply the IP address and the name of the printer or the print queue.

Selecting Printer Drivers

After you complete the dialog box for the port you want to use and return to the main dialog box, click the Next button to bring up a dialog box from which you can specify the manufacturer and type of printer that will be used. This information is used to determine which drivers NT will need to load for this printer. In this dialog box (shown in Figure 28.5) you can also click the Have Disk button if your printer is not listed and if you have a driver from the manufacturer that you can use.

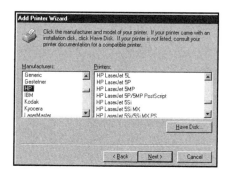

Figure 28.5 The Add Printer Wizard prompts you to select a printer driver. Use the Have Disk button if your printer is not listed.

Giving the Printer a Name

Finally, the wizard will prompt you to enter a name to use for the printer (see Figure 28.6). This is not the name that will be used as the printer share name, it is a descriptive name for the printer. The check boxes at the bottom of this dialog box can be used to set this printer as the default for this server. This does not set the printer as the default for users who connect to it over the network. It sets it as the default printer that will show up when you send print jobs from applications while you are logged in to this server locally.

Sharing the Printer on the Network

The last dialog box you will see is used to allow the printer to be offered as a printer share for network clients. In this dialog box (see Figure 28.7) you must select the Shared check box, and then give the printer a name that will be displayed to users. Note that the Name field will default to the type of printer and the first eight characters in order to be available to clients that have restrictions on the length of resource names, such as MS-DOS clients. You can edit this field and use any name that makes sense to your users. It is usually best to use a name that indicates both the location of the printer as well as the kind of printer.

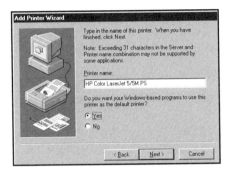

Figure 28.6   Give the printer a name and select Yes if you want it to be your default printer.

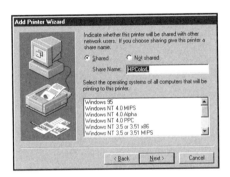

Figure 28.7   Click the Shared check box to offer the printer on the network to clients and to load additional drivers for those clients.

This dialog box can also be used to load additional drivers for clients that will connect to the printer over the network. For example, if you have Windows 95 clients on your network, you should select Windows 95 from the dialog box. When this type of client must send a print job to the printer, Windows NT Server will download the driver to the client so that the print job will be formatted correctly for the printer. If the driver you specify is not already loaded on the system (for another printer, for example), you will be prompted for the location of the driver. When you have finished specifying a share name for the printer and have selected any additional printer drivers you want to load, click the Next button.

The final dialog box asks if you want to print a test page. This is highly recommended because if the test page doesn't print, nothing else is going to print. If the test page does not print, review the selections you have made to be sure they are accurate. Or, there might be a network problem that needs to be looked into.

Print Server Properties, Printer Properties, and Document Properties

Windows NT Server enables you to configure properties for the print server as a whole and configure properties that are specific to each printer that you create. You can also configure default properties that will be applied to documents that are printed on the server.

Print Server Properties

To bring up the properties sheet for the print server, select Properties from the File menu in the Printers folder. There are three tabs on this property sheet:

- **Forms**—Use this tab to define forms that will be available to users who use printers on this server.
- **Ports**—This tab enables you to add, delete, or reconfigure ports and is similar to the dialog box that is presented when you create a printer.
- **Advanced**—This tab enables you to set up logging and notifications for the print server and specify the spooling directory.

Forms are used to define certain properties of the output page that will be printed, including the size of the paper and the margins. Windows NT Server comes with several standard forms already defined, including most standard paper sizes and envelopes. If you have a special form that you have created for your business, such as an invoice format, you can define a new form using the Forms tab.

If you plan to set up several printers but want to get some of the work out of the way beforehand, you can use the Ports tab to create the necessary ports. Then, when you actually get around to creating the printers, you can select the appropriate port rather than create it. This can also be useful in an environment where one administrator is responsible for network functions and another is responsible for printing. The network administrator who is aware of network addresses used by certain devices can create the ports and send a list to the printer administrator who can then create and manage the printers that use the ports.

In Figure 28.8 you can see the Print Server Properties dialog box with the Advanced tab selected.

This tab is an important one to remember for troubleshooting purposes where the more information you have the better chance you will have in solving your problem. You can enable the following notification and logging categories:

- Log Spooler Error Events
- Log Spooler Warning Events
- Log Spooler Information Events
- Beep on Errors of Remote Documents
- Notify When Remote Documents Are Printed

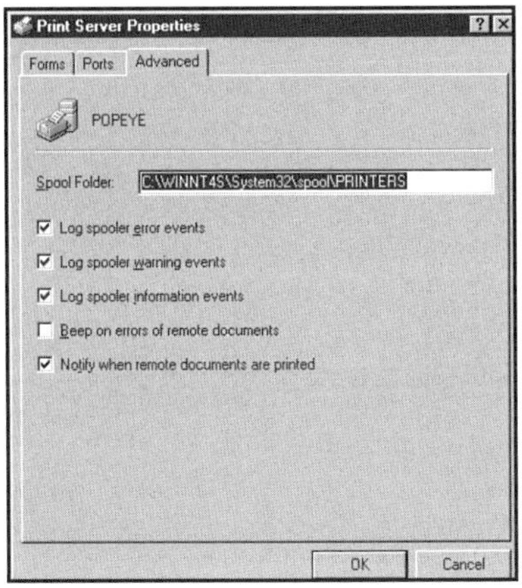

Figure 28.8 The Advanced tab enables you to set logging and notifications for the print server as a whole.

The first options set a logging severity level for events that will be placed into the System Event Log. You can use the Event Viewer administrative tool to examine the logged events. If users are complaining that their print jobs are not being printed, enable all three of these check boxes and, after they have attempted to print, review the records found in the Event Log.

Technical Note

The Event Log is made up of three separate log files: System, Security, and Application. The events you can enable on the Print Server Properties page will show up in the System Event Log. Matters related to printer security, discussed later in this chapter, will show up in the Security Event Log. If applications have been written to use the Windows NT Event Logging service, and if the administrator has enabled the logging of these kinds of events, they may create events in the Application Event Log.

The information that is recorded in the event log will help you determine why the user's jobs are not printing. The third check box, Log Spooler Information Events, can also be used to keep track of the pages printed by individual users. Figure 28.9 shows an example of an informational event that tells you that a document was printed, by whom, and the number of pages that were printed.

It can be tedious to use the graphical interface provided by the Event Viewer to review each and every record. To overcome this obstacle, you can create a comma-delimited file that contains the information found in the file. However, to do this you will need the Dump Event Log (DUMPEL.EXE) utility, which can be found in the Windows NT Server 4.0 Resource Kit.

Another useful thing you can do on this tab of the properties sheet is to change the spooling directory used by the server. If performance is a problem with the server you might want to locate the spooling directory on a disk by itself to speed up access. For a low-volume print server this will probably not be necessary.

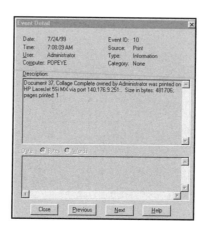

Figure 28.9 The information events you can record in the event log can track printer usage by user.

Printer Properties

You can access the properties page for any printer by using either of the following:

- While in the Printers folder, highlight the printer you want to work with, and from the File menu select Properties.

- While in the Printers folder, double-click the printer you want to work with. A new dialog box will appear. From this dialog box, select Properties from the Printers menu.

The properties page for a printer (see Figure 28.10) is divided into six property sheets that enable you to control a wide variety of properties for each printer on an individual basis:

- General
- Ports
- Scheduling
- Sharing
- Security
- Device Settings

The General tab enables you to modify informational text about the printer that users can view, such as the location of the printer. You can also use this tab to select an existing separator page or create a new separator page. Separator pages can serve two functions. They can be used to print a page before each user's job so that on a high-volume printer used by many users, it will be easy for an operator to separate each print job. Separator pages can also be used to send printer-specific codes to a printer that determines how it prints the document. Windows NT Server comes with three separator pages designed for this purpose:

- **PSCRIPT.SEP**—This separator page changes the printer into PostScript mode. No actual separator page is printed.

- **SYSPRINT.SEP**—This page also switches a printer into PostScript mode but does print a separator page.

- **PCL.SEP**—This page switches the printer into PCL mode (HP's Printer Control Language) and prints a separator page.

Figure 28.10   You can configure properties specific for each printer by using its properties page.

Technical Note

You might not have to use a separator page to cause a printer to change between PostScript and PCL modes. Many newer printers can autosense the kind of print mode the print job requires and make the change automatically. Refer to the documentation that comes with the printer to determine whether you must use a separator page for this purpose.

You can design your own separator pages using escape codes that can be used to include information such as the user's name, print job number, date, and any additional text you would like to have appear on the page.

You can also print a test page from the General tab when troubleshooting the printer. Another useful feature found on this page is the New Driver button, which you can use to load an updated printer driver. This might be necessary when a manufacturer releases a printer driver that is more current than the one found on the Windows NT Server source CDs.

The Ports tab is similar to the ports display that you see when you create a printer or when you view ports using the Print Server properties page. Here, however, you can change the port used by this printer. This is useful when a printer is moved to a new location and a new network connection is required. You will not have to delete and re-create the printer—just go to the Ports tab and select or create the new port after the printer has been moved. Then, go back to the General tab and try to print a test page to see if the port has been successfully created.

The Scheduling tab enables you to set the time of day that a printer is available for use. Generally a printer is available 24 hours per day, but if your circumstances warrant, you can use this tab to change it. Note that users can still send print jobs to a printer outside its available time range.

Their documents will be stored and printed when the appropriate time arrives. It is important to realize, however, that if you choose to allow users to schedule jobs to be printed later, you must also be aware of the disk space that will be used for spooling the documents that must wait. For large files, such as those containing complex graphics, you might need quite a bit of space.

This feature can be used to force certain print jobs, such as lengthy reports, to be delayed until after hours when ordinary users no longer need the printer. For example, you can set up several logical printers, one of which you make available to your normal workday users. A second logical printer can then be set up to allow printing after hours. Applications that produce voluminous print jobs can send their documents to this printer, and users can retrieve their documents the next morning when they come into work.

The Scheduling tab enables you to specify several other configuration options:

- **Spool Print Documents So the Program Finishes Printing Faster**—This allows the application to send a print job quickly because the output is directed to a spooler file instead of directly to the physical printer. Generally, it takes longer to send a job directly to the printer unless it has enough memory to buffer the entire print job.

- **Print Directly to the Printer**—This is the opposite of the previous option and, when used, an application can stall until the printer has finished receiving the entire print job from the user.

- **Hold Mismatched Documents**—This option retains a print job that does not match the current printer settings instead of discarding it. You can then either change the printer or disable this option to cause the document to print.

- **Print Spooled Documents First**—Generally, a spooled print job will begin to print before the document has been completely spooled to a temporary file. This option enables you to specify that jobs which have already been completely written to the spool file will print before those that are still spooling. This setting can override the priority of a spooling print job and allow a completely spooled lower priority job to print first.

- **Keep Documents After They Have Printed**—This setting will cause spooled print jobs to remain in the spool directory after they have printed. This can be useful for troubleshooting print problems. You can look at the original print job and possibly send it to another printer to determine whether the original printer is exhibiting unusual behavior when trying to print.

Normally you will want documents to be spooled before they print so that users notice a faster response time. However, when troubleshooting, you might want to send documents directly to the printer, bypassing the spooling operation. Also, if space becomes a problem on the disk that holds the spooling directory, you can cause jobs to be sent directly to the printer to avoid using additional disk space. Because this option is selectable by printer, you can set up some printers to use the spool directory and others to send jobs directly to the printer.

The Sharing tab enables you to modify the selections you chose when you created the printer and either allow or disallow it to be shared with network users. You can also use this tab to load additional client drivers when new clients are brought into the network or change the share name the printer uses on the network.

The Security tab can be used to set up permissions that control which users or groups can use this printer and to control auditing features for the printer. Users can be denied access to the printer (No Access), allowed to print and manage documents, or be given full control to the printer. Full control allows users to perform the following functions:

- Print
- Change document settings
- Pause or restart the printer
- Delete print jobs
- Change the priority (printing order) of jobs
- Delete the printer
- Change permissions for the printer

Usually only print operators or network administrators should be given full control over a printer. Most users need only the Print permission. This enables users to send print jobs and control their print jobs, but not those of other users.

The Auditing functions found on the Security tab allow you to record events to the Event Log for later review. In Chapter 37, "Auditing and Other Monitoring Measures," you will find a discussion about auditing print events and using the Event Viewer to review the data captured.

The Device Settings tab enables you to configure device-specific values for the printer. This includes information such as tray selection, font cartridges, and so on, depending on the features available for the specific printer type.

Managing Printers

After you create a printer, users can connect to it and use it to print. The administrator, or other users who have the appropriate permissions, can view the status of documents waiting to print and can manage the printer. This is done using the dialog box shown in Figure 28.11, which you will see when you double-click on a printer in the Printers folder.

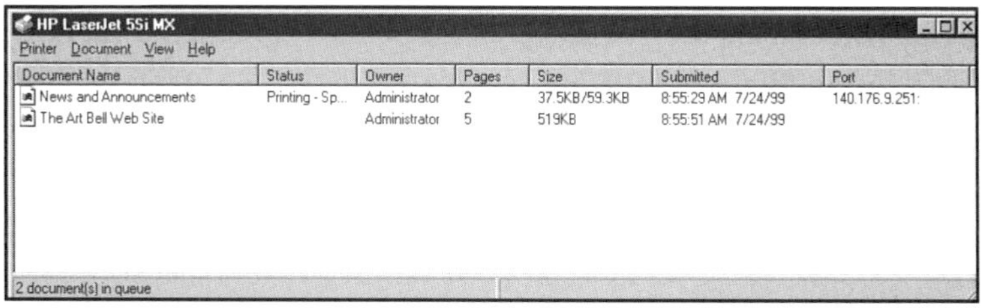

Figure 28.11   You can control a printer from this dialog box.

As you can see, documents that are currently being printed or waiting to print are displayed, showing the title of the document, the user, size of the print job, port the printer uses, and the date and time the job was submitted. Two important menus here can be used to manage the printer or any document. The Printer menu allows you to

- Pause the printer
- Set the printer to be the default on this computer
- Change the defaults for documents sent to this printer
- Change the sharing aspects of the printer
- Remove all documents from the printer
- View or modify properties for the printer

This menu can be useful when you're experiencing problems with a particular printer. You can pause the printer, which stops printing but keeps any documents waiting to print, to fix a minor problem and then resume printing after the trouble has been resolved. You can also remove all documents from the printer. This can be handy when a user or an application has sent numerous documents to a printer by mistake. You can bring up the Properties page for the printer, discussed earlier in this chapter, and modify items as you see fit.

The Documents menu can be used to individually pause, restart, or cancel print jobs. Here you can selectively highlight individual documents waiting to print and then cancel them.

This view of the printer is most often used by print operators who are responsible for managing printer resources on the network.

Printing Under NetWare

Novell Directory Services uses objects in the directory database to represent the functional components of the printing system. Similar to Windows NT, some terms must be defined:

- **Printer**—This is the physical printer, like the printer device under Windows NT.
- **Print Queue**—This is like the logical printer found in Windows NT. Unlike NT, the term *queue* is used. Users send print jobs to a print queue where they are retained until they print.
- **Print Server**—This can be a software print server (such as NetWare's PSERVER.NLM) loaded on a host computer on the network or a physical print server device that is connected to the network.

When the administrator creates a print queue object in the database, a directory that will hold the spooled files is automatically created. The administrator then specifies the print server that will control the queue and the printer (physical device) that will render the print job into a finished document. When configuring a NetWare client, you select a print queue. The user does not have to be bothered with other aspects of the system such as the printer or the print server.

Print queues hold jobs waiting to print. A queue can accept documents even if the printer itself is offline or out of service. The jobs wait in the queue until the printer is restored to service or another printer is assigned to the task. In a manner similar to Windows NT, NetWare print queues can send print jobs to multiple output print devices and multiple print queues can be established to send output to the same printer.

These three entities—the printer, the print server, and the print queue—do not have to reside on the same host computer. However, to reduce network traffic it is a good idea in a high-volume printing environment to locate them on the same server. Or else when a user submits a print job, network bandwidth is used, sending the data to the print queue. Then, more bandwidth is used to send the document from the print queue to the print server, and if the printer is a networked device, additional bandwidth is used to send the document from the print server to the printer.

To create the objects needed for printing in NetWare, you can use either the NetWare Administrator or the PCONSOLE utility. The PCONSOLE utility has an option that provides a quick setup for all three objects and is the recommended route. For more information on how to create objects, see Chapter 23, "NetWare." To use the PCONSOLE utility to set up printing on a server, use the following steps:

1. Log in as an Admin user or a user that has the create, delete, and browse privileges for the container that will hold the printing objects.

2. Run PCONSOLE.

3. From the PCONSOLE menu, select Change Context. Set your context to the container that you want to use for the printing objects.

4. From Available Options, select Print Queues.

5. Press the Insert (Ins) key to create a new object.

6. Enter the name you want to give to the Print Queue object.

7. A dialog box will prompt you for the volume to use for the Print Queue object's spooling directory. Enter an object or use the Insert key to browse for available volumes. When finished, press the Escape key to return to the PCONSOLE menu.

8. Next, create the Printer object. From Available Options, select Printers.

9. Press the Insert key to create a new Printer object.

10. A dialog box will prompt you to enter a name for the Printer object.

11 Select the newly created Printer object from the Printers list.

12 In the Printer Configuration screen that appears, fill in the configuration information specific to the kind of printer the object represents, such as whether it uses a parallel or serial port, address restrictions, and so on.

13 While still in the Printer Configuration screen, select the queue you want to use from the Print Queues Assigned field. When finished, use the F10 key to save the information. Use the Escape key to return to the Available Options menu.

14 Select Print Servers to begin creating the new Print Server object. Press the Insert key to create a new object.

15 A screen will prompt you to enter a name for the new object. The object will be created and you should then select it from the Print Servers list so that it can be configured.

16 Select the Printers option from the Print Server Information list. Press the Insert key.

17 A list of Printer objects will appear. Select the Printer object you just created. You can continue to add other Print Server objects if you like. Press the Escape key until you reach the main menu of the PCONSOLE utility.

You can also use the Quick Setup feature of PCONSOLE. Select Quick Setup from the list of Available Options on the PCONSOLE menu. The Print Services Quick Setup screen will appear and allow you to fill in the fields on this screen.

Tip

You can use the PUPGRADE utility to upgrade NetWare 3.x servers that are already configured as print servers. From the PUPGRADE menu, select Upgrade Print Servers and Printers, and then select the bindery print server you want to upgrade.

Print Queue Object Properties

The print queue object is a logical representation of a print queue. It uses a directory (created as a subdirectory under the /QUEUES directory) on a NetWare volume you select when you create the object to store files waiting to print. The following are significant properties of the print queue object:

- **Volume**—The volume selected to use to hold files that are waiting in the queue to print. Choose a volume that has adequate storage for the typical printing volume on the server.

- **Authorized Print Servers**—A list of print servers that can use this print queue.

- **Printers Servicing Print Queue**—A list of printers to which the print queue can send output.

- **Operators**—The users who are allowed to perform management functions on the queue.

- **Users**—The users who you will allow to send print jobs to the print queue. Instead of listing individual users for this property, it is much easier to use container objects that include users to make administration tasks easier.

- **Print Job List**—A list of print jobs in the queue. It includes such things as a sequence number for each job, a job ID, the current status of the print job, the form used, and the name of the file that is to be printed.

Note that the Printers Servicing Print Queue property is used to link the print queue object to one or more Printer objects.

Printer Object Properties

The Printer object represents an actual physical printer that will accept print jobs from a print queue. The printer can be connected directly to the network, to a workstation, or to a server.

The properties of the Printer object include a name property, which is established when the Printer object is created. In addition, you can assign values to other descriptive properties:

- Other Names
- Description
- Location
- Department
- Organization

More important properties that affect how the queue functions include

- **Print Server**—Shows the Print Server object to which the printer is assigned.

- **Print Queues**—Lists the Print Queue objects that can send print jobs to the printer.

- **Printer Features**—Contains information such as the kind of printer language understood by the printer and the amount of memory installed. This is a useful feature because users can search NDS to find a printer that supports the features they need for a particular job.

- **Printer Type**—Indicates whether the printer is a parallel or serial printer or another kind of printer such as one accessed via AppleTalk or UNIX.

- **Banner Type**—Can be either text or PostScript.

- **Service Interval**—This time interval defines how often the printer checks with the print queue object to see whether there are any jobs to print. The value can range from 1 to 255 seconds, with a default of 5 seconds.

- **Buffer Size in KB**—This property defines the size of the data segment sent to the printer. The value can range from 3KB to 255KB, with a default of 3KB.

- **Network Address Restrictions**—The network address of the printer's network interface or the address of the host computer to which the printer is attached.

- **Service Mode for Forms**—Indicates the policy for changing forms and can be set to Starting Form or Service Mode for Forms. The Starting Form value is the identifying number of a form that the Print Server object expects to be loaded on the printer by default. The Service Mode for Forms is used to indicate whether the form can be changed, and how, or if only the currently mounted form should be used.

- **Notification**—A list of users who will be notified when a problem occurs on the printer, such as a paper-out condition.

The Print Server property and the Print Queues property are used to link the three objects that make up the path from the user to the finished print job.

Print Server Object Properties

The Print Server object represents the print server program (PSERVER.NLM), which runs on a server to control the printing process. The only properties defined when the Print Server object is created are the Name property (common name) and the Advertising Name, which is used to advertise the service using the Service Advertising Protocol (SAP).

The Print Server object, like the Printer object, also enables you to define descriptive properties such as Department and Location. In addition, the Network Address field will display the address on the network of the print server when it is up and running. The Version property shows the version of PSERVER.NLM that is being used by the print server.

Other important properties include

- **Printers**—The Printer objects that the Print Server can use to render a print job into its final output form.

- **Operators**—Users listed in this property can perform management functions for the server. This can include users, groups, and user templates, as well as Organization or Organizational Unit container objects in the NDS tree.

- **Users**—Users who can use this print server. Again, the values here can also be container objects so you do not have to list each user individually. Although users only need to be listed as users for a print queue in order to print, if you list them here also they will be capable of checking the status of the print queue.

- **Password**—Allows you to assign a password to this Print Server object so that it cannot be loaded (via LOAD PSERVER) by unauthorized users.

The properties for a print server are loaded into memory when the module PSERVER.NLM is loaded. If you make changes to the object after it is loaded, they do not take effect until the print server is unloaded and loaded again.

PSERVER.NLM and *NPRINTER.NLM*

On a host that is acting as a print server, the PSERVER.NLM module must be loaded. When it is loaded it will activate any printers defined by Printer objects that are listed in its Printers property. NetWare allows for both local and remote printers. Local printers are attached to the host print server. Remote printers can be serviced by this Print server but reside on other computers. The NPRINTER.NLM module is used to control the printer and will be automatically loaded for each locally attached printer. Because of this, these printers are called *Autoload printers*.

To load the PSERVER module, use the LOAD PSERVER command:

```
LOAD PSERVER <print server object name>
```

The PSERVER.NLM can support up to 256 printers, of which up to five can be connected locally to the server on which PSERVER.NLM is loaded.

The NPRINTER.NLM module must be manually loaded on remote servers (and the program NPRINTER.EXE for remote workstations). When multiple printers are hosted on a single remote server or workstation, NPRINTER must be loaded for each one. The syntax used depends on the computer on which the module will be loaded. For DOS machines, use

```
NPRINTER <name of print server object> <name of printer object>
```

For NetWare servers, use

```
LOAD NPRINTER <name of print server object> <name of printer object>
```

Hardware-Based Print Servers

There is no longer a need to dedicate a network host to act as a print server, either dedicated or otherwise. It is now very cheap to connect a printer directly to the network using a small hardware-based print server device. These devices come in sizes that range from a device that will fit in your hand to larger boxes that look like hubs or routers.

Think about how you will locate printers in relation to users when making purchase plans. How many printers will be located in a single place? For example, if you have a central print room where you keep multiple printers, copiers, and other similar equipment, it might be economical to purchase a more expensive model that supports several printers. If you are placing only one or two printers at strategic locations throughout the enterprise, it might be more economical to buy the small palm-sized devices that can support one or two printers. You should also consider the following:

- **Price**—Especially price per port.
- **Number and kind of printer ports**—You might want to plan for expansion and buy devices that leave an extra port available for future use.
- **Network connection type**—Some models support one connector type, such as RJ-45 or BNC. Some have several types.
- **Management software and supported operating systems**—An often overlooked feature.
- **Upgrade path**—Don't lock yourself in to a print server that can't be upgraded, unless it is inexpensive and will perform the tasks you need for a while to come.

Price might not be an important factor unless you are purchasing a lot of equipment. Take into consideration the number of printer ports that each device makes available. Some devices offer both serial and parallel ports, so be sure to check that the ports are compatible with the kind of printers you have or plan to purchase. Another useful feature for a serial port is the capability to attach a local console terminal for management functions. Although it is preferable to be able to remotely manage the print server from a workstation elsewhere on the network, the ability to attach a local console terminal can be a helpful feature when troubleshooting. Troubleshooting printer problems is common, as most network administrators will tell you.

Check to be sure that all ports on a model that offers multiple ports can be used at once. Hard as it might be to believe, some models offer two ports but only one can be active at any time.

The type of network connection supported by the device is very important. Is it a standard 10Mbps ethernet connection, a 100Mbps connection, or a token-ring adapter?

Technical Note

The Internet Printing Protocol (IPP) is likely to be a major player in the future of network printing. Although the standard drafts for IPP as proposed at this time do not provide a full-featured set of functions that can be used to manage all aspects of the printing process, some print servers do implement some or all the functions as they currently stand. Don't let buzzwords such as IPP determine your decision when trying to select a print server at this time. Wait until the standard has been more completely defined before using it as a major purchase criterion. Instead, if this feature is important for you now, be sure that the print server has the capability to download new firmware when it becomes available from the manufacturer.

Management software is another important factor that should be given careful scrutiny when making a purchasing decision. Some print servers have only basic software that runs on a Windows platform. Newer models have the capability to present Web pages on the network so that you can manage them from any workstation that has a browser loaded on it. The information that the management software provides can vary widely from one product to another. The typical status information includes paper-out conditions and whether the printer is online or offline at the moment. More advanced management packages can tell you whether the toner is low in a laser printer.

Another useful feature for any device on the network, much less a print server, is that it be capable of being updated with new functionality as technology develops. A print server that uses some kind of rewritable memory (for example, flash memory) and can be updated by downloading new software might save you money in the long run because you won't necessarily have to purchase a new device when your needs change.

Summary

Network printing can be easily configured under most operating systems, including Windows NT, NetWare, and UNIX. Printers can be placed strategically throughout the enterprise so that they are conveniently located near the users that make the most use of them. By using printers that have built-in network adapters or by employing hardware-based print servers, it is no longer necessary to dedicate a computer on the network to host printers.

In the next chapter, a technology that can be used to reduce printer usage is examined: email systems. By allowing users to send information to each other at network speeds, email has revolutionized business messaging.

Part XI

TROUBLESHOOTING NETWORK APPLICATIONS

Email Systems

SOME OF THE MAIN TOPICS IN THIS CHAPTER ARE

Common System Types

Third-Party Providers

Typical Problems

Clients

MIME, Smail, and X.400

Free Email Accounts on the Web

Maintaining a Mailing List

CHAPTER 29

One of the most important business uses for networked computers is email. Whether computers are connected over a local area network (LAN), a wide area network (WAN), by modems, or over the world's largest network, the Internet, the capability to reliably send and receive messages and files of all types is critical to modern business productivity.

The many different types of email systems in use around the world and the different standards they follow provide a challenge for email users and support personnel alike. In this chapter, we'll examine the different types of email systems and provide you with the help you need to keep those streams of electronic information flowing freely.

Common System Types

The most common types of email systems are those based on popular computing standards, including the Internet-pioneering UNIX and Linux-based programs, backbones for connecting different email architectures together, the many versions of Microsoft email servers and clients (Exchange and Outlook), and those based on HTML and Web access. Each of these will be examined in this chapter.

UNIX and Linux Sendmail

Sendmail is an MTA (mail transfer agent) that is a standard part of typical UNIX and Linux distributions, including the popular Red Hat Linux and Caldera OpenLinux distributions. Sendmail (shown in Figure 29.1) is responsible for the delivery and reception of email, but not the creation of email messages or attachments. MUA (mail user agent) programs such as Eudora, Pine, mutt, elm, and others are used to create the email messages and attachments.

Note

Sendmail uses SMTP (Simple Mail Transfer Protocol) to deliver mail (see the "POP3/SMTP" section later in this chapter).

The latest release of Sendmail as of this writing is version 8.9.x, available from www.sendmail.org and many other sites. This release features improvements in spam control (spam is unwanted junk mail), insurance against security threats from other email systems, and a new, experimental fax transmission feature. This version also introduced a new default folder location for configuration information: /etc/mail. Sendmail uses a configuration file called /etc/sendmail.cf. This file is normally created when the sendmail service is installed, and is created by running the appropriate .mc (make) files through the M4 macro processor program.

Sendmail is an open source product offered by Sendmail, Inc. (see Figure 29.2). It is also available in commercial versions for Windows NT (Sendmail for NT) and many popular UNIX and Linux releases (Sendmail Pro). For more information about both the open source and commercial versions of sendmail, see the Sendmail, Inc. Web site at www.sendmail.com.

Figure 29.1 The freeware version of Sendmail is supported by extensive technical information available at the www.sendmail.org Web site.

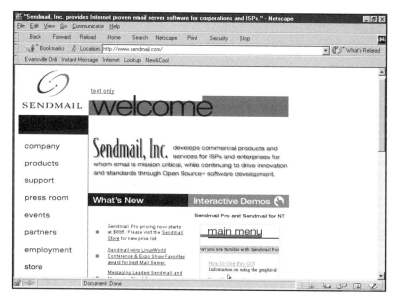

Figure 29.2 Interactive demos of sendmail's commercial products can be viewed at the Sendmail, Inc. Web site.

The sendmail program itself must be compiled before use, as with virtually any UNIX/Linux program. Although the basic compilation process is straightforward, using the sh Build script, the many different versions of UNIX and Linux distributions introduce many subtle changes that can cause problems. Before you build your sendmail, go to http://www.sendmail.org/compiling.html and check out your UNIX or Linux distribution's compilation issues.

Sendmail is widely supported by users across the world, and many patches, enhancements, tips, and tricks are available. A good starting place to help you solve sendmail problems is the www.sendmail.org site's links page. An excellent online reference for using sendmail is http://www.harker.com/sendmail/sendmail-ref.html (see Figure 29.3).

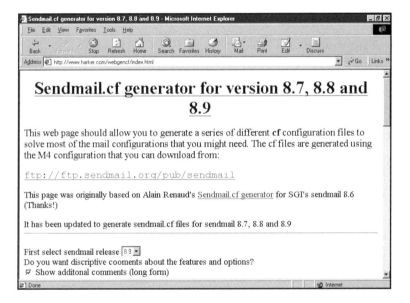

Figure 29.3   Harker Systems's Sendmail online reference features an automatic sendmail configuration generator (seen here), reviews of books about sendmail, technical guides, and much more.

Configuration of Sendmail

Configuration of sendmail can be extremely complex if performed manually. The sendmail.cf generator available online from Harker Systems (www.harker.com) can be used to automate this process for easier and more accurate sendmail setup. It supports recent and current versions of sendmail (version 8.7 and above).

The sendmail configuration must contain at a minimum the user name to receive and send mail, but send can also be configured to handle mail for multiple users and multiple domain names through modification of the sendmail.cf file.

Changing Setup After Sendmail Is Started

Because sendmail is a *daemon* (a process that runs in the background to transfer mail to and from the user's system), it's important to stop the sendmail daemon (process) and back up the old `sendmail.cf` (configuration file) before installing a new one. Then, the sendmail process (daemon) must be restarted.

PMDF

PMDF, from Innosoft (see Figure 29.4), is one of the leading enterprise backbone systems or "Email Interconnects," according to its Web site. PMDF, built for SPARC, OpenVMS, and Digital UNIX servers, provides a single point of control for all types of email traffic, ranging from Internet-bound SMTP to IBM and Digital mainframe and legacy PC email systems (such as cc:Mail, MSMail, and GroupWise), Microsoft Exchange Server, x.400, and Lotus Notes. PMDF and other enterprise backbones act as a message switch between these different systems and can also provide antispam, antivirus, directory and encryption services to all email clients.

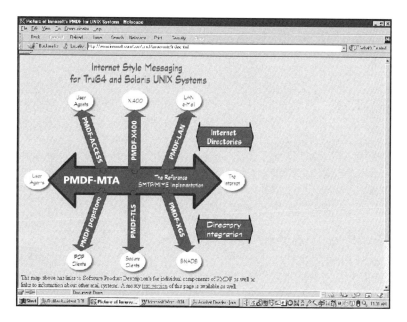

Figure 29.4 PMDF's family of products is designed to connect all major types of email systems together for smooth, controlled interchange of message data.

PMDF's technical support site (`http://www.innosoft.com/iii/tech_support/`) provides solutions for the issues that you might face trying to connect such disparate email systems to each other, including Y2K date calculations for non-Y2K compliant email clients, stopping spam, buffer overruns, and attacks from email viruses such as Melissa.

Because email backbones are used to tie different types of email systems together, the backbone must have both flexibility (to handle different email types) and durability (to resist spam and virus attacks among other threats).

PMDF, like sendmail, requires expertise with UNIX to configure and administer. The latest version of PMDF, which contains many enhancements for system and user security, is v5.2x as of this writing.

Y2K Issues

PMDF uses a variety of methods to handle year-2000 date issues arising from two-digit emails (PMDF itself uses four digits for all dates). One method is to use a *date-pivot* or *date-windowing* technique, which assumes that two-digit year dates from 00–49 are 2000–2049, thus making two-digit year dates from 50–99 1950–1999. Other methods are also used to assure that reliable dates are passed between different email systems.

Controlling Viruses

PMDF can be configured to stop transmission of all Word or Excel attachments containing WordBasic macros because these macros can be used to spread Melissa, Papa, and other macro viruses. This blocking process is done by modifying the conversion channel configuration. The configuration can be modified to block only tell-tale subject lines such as "Important Message From" or by blocking all documents containing macros. Because many documents contain legitimate WordBasic macros, a preferred solution is to incorporate antivirus software (available from McAfee for UNIX and Sophos for OpenVMS) into the backbone's configuration.

Managing Spam

PMDF can be configured to allow both the backbone and individual users connected to a PMDF backbone to take steps to prevent unwanted bulk email (spam) from entering their systems while permitting legitimate users access to email. Recent versions of PMDF contain relay-blocking features (which prevent "hijacking" of the mail servers by spammers), Simple Authentication and Security Layer protocol for authenticating remote email users, address authentication, and other options. Because many advanced security features are version-dependent, upgrading might be necessary to obtain the highest level of protection.

Microsoft Exchange Server

The popularity of various versions of Microsoft Windows as both a client and server has helped fuel the popularity of Microsoft Exchange Server, which is part of the Microsoft BackOffice family of server products.

Note

Various versions of the Microsoft Outlook client (previously the Microsoft Exchange client) are standard features of both Microsoft operating systems and major applications, such as Microsoft Office 2000 (which features Outlook 2000).

Exchange Server is Windows NT-based, allowing companies that have standardized on Windows NT servers to continue to use a familiar operating system environment for their email servers. However, clients can reside on Windows NT, Windows 95 and 98, Windows 3.1, or Macintosh-based systems. Exchange Server (see Figure 29.5) supports the IMAP protocol, allowing your email to remain on the server for access from different PCs. (See the section "IMAP," later in this chapter.)

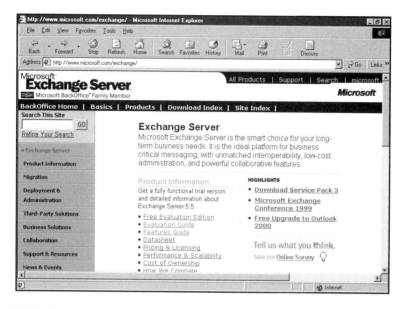

Figure 29.5 You can download an evaluation version of Microsoft Exchange from the BackOffice section of www.microsoft.com.

Because Exchange Server can be used for both internal and Internet email traffic, it has several built-in security features that can allow Exchange Server to "screen out" unwanted email (see Figure 29.6). These options can be enabled by the administrator as desired, and include

- The capability to accept email only from known IP addresses
- The capability to control size of message files (to help prevent "denial of service" attacks)
- The capability to limit "I'm out of the office" vacation messages to internal email only, rather than broadcasting them to the Internet
- Standard 40-bit encryption for traffic

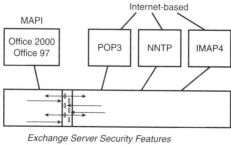

Exchange Server Security Features
Act as a "Screen" to Filter out Email

Figure 29.6 Use the Exchange Server security features listed earlier to create an effective "screen" between MAPI (internal office) email clients and email originating on the Internet.

One nagging concern about Microsoft Exchange Server and its clients is the program's vulnerability to *Trojan Horse* software that uses the mailing lists of users to propagate rapidly across corporate networks. Melissa and CIH were just two of the programs that have exploited weaknesses in Exchange, highlighting the need for countermeasures that should include server-based and workstation-based antivirus software, which guards against email-delivered attacks and a common-sense reminder for users: "Beware of geeks bearing gifts (file attachments)"!

HTML-Based Email Systems

One limitation of many email systems is the need to have a particular email client installed on a single computer, or in the case of networked systems, as part of a "roving user profile." As long as the user has access to a computer with the appropriate client and can access the email server, the messages can come and go.

But what about the user in the field who might be servicing different clients, running through airport terminals to catch flights, or "borrowing" client computers as part of the job? It's both impractical and dangerous to ask that worker to carry around client software to be installed on the computers available on any given day.

What's the solution? Have the user pick up email via an HTML-based client; essentially a Web page with a password-protected login system that can be accessed from any browser with an Internet connection. Many ISPs and email providers offer HTML-based email systems, either as their standard email system or as an alternative to their normal email clients. HTML-based email offers the following benefits:

- Browser-based access from any Web-enabled computer
- Secure email storage on a server with frequent backups
- The capability to read and respond to email without receiving every message in your email box; the message headers appear online

Even if your normal ISP's email system uses a special client, some might offer HTML-based email access as an option (see Figure 29.7). If you will be away from your normal computer but still want access to your email, this is useful. My ISP has used this system for years, and I've read my email everywhere from Maine to Hawaii without needing anything more than a browser and a connection to the Web.

Keeping Your Email Private with HTML-Based Email

If you read any email messages, keep in mind that they are transmitted to the computer you're using. To keep them confidential, be sure to clear disk and memory caches before leaving the browser, and delete any temporary files in the computer's TEMP folder as well.

After you finish using your HTML-based email account, use its Logout option to close your session. Otherwise, another person using the computer after you might be able to use the Back button on the browser to go back into your email folder and read your messages. If your service lacks a "logout" option, close the browser to end the session. See Figure 29.8 for a graphical description of this process.

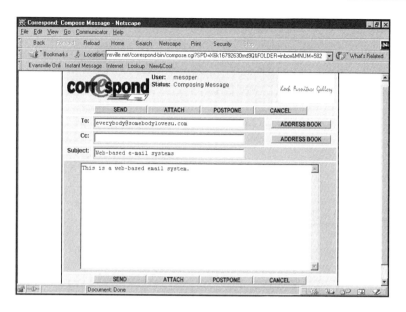

Figure 29.7 HTML-based email systems enable users to check their email through any browser. Although some display the message as plain text (shown here), most allow other types of files to be sent as attachments.

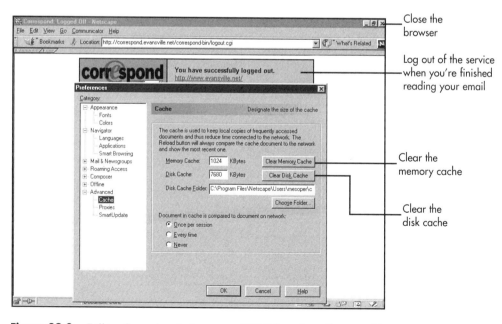

Figure 29.8 Follow these steps to keep your HTML-based email secure (Netscape Communicator 4.6 for Windows 9x is shown here).

Third-Party Providers

Although most email services are provided as part of an ISP account (dial-up or LAN-based), there are situations in which using a separate third-party email provider can be useful:

- Anonymous email providers allow you to protect your privacy when sending or receiving email.

- Email-only providers often offer additional email accounts for far less than the cost of adding them through an ISP (sometimes as little as $1/month or $12/year)

- Email-only accounts can be used to allow minors access to email without the dangers of Web surfing.

- Commercial email accounts allow full use of advanced email features such as file attachments, features that are often missing or present only in a scaled-back form with free email services.

Make sure your account offers at least POP3 access (SMTP access is useful also) and that your email or other personal information isn't sold to the highest bidder.

Although free email accounts might seem like a better deal, paying for email services sets you free from the tradeoffs of advertising and loss of privacy inherent in the "free" email services. (See "Free Email Accounts on the Web," later in this chapter.)

Juno (see Figures 29.9 and 29.10), a leader in free (advertiser-supported) email services, launched Juno Gold ($2.95/month) in the summer of 1999 because of the demand for file attachment services, an option often omitted when choosing free email services (including standard Juno).

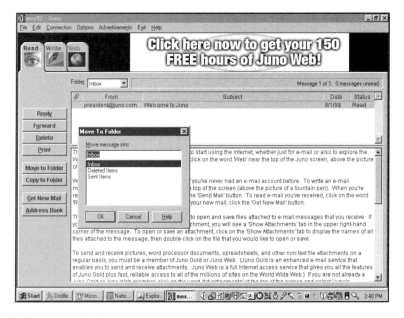

Figure 29.9   One of the leading free email services is advertiser-supported Juno. Click the tabs at the top-left side of the program screen to read email, write (compose) email, or learn about Juno Web.

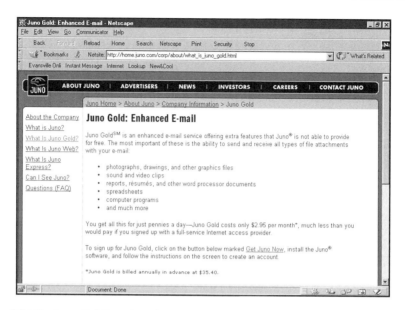

Figure 29.10 Juno Gold's major advantage over its sibling, the free Juno email service, is Juno Gold's capability to send and receive file attachments

Typical Problems

Regardless of your email system (or systems), there are typical problems that every email user must face, including configuration, file attachments, security (against viruses and invasion of privacy), and capacity. This section provides tips that can be used with virtually any email system.

Configuration Issues

To configure your email client successfully, you must know the following information:

- Incoming and outgoing mail server names
- Mail server type (POP3 or IMAP)
- Your email username (not necessarily your Internet username)
- Your email password (not necessarily your Internet password)

An email client cannot access mail servers or send or receive mail unless this information is entered correctly. Figure 29.11 shows a sample email configuration screen.

Other typical options include

- Selecting whether to retain or delete mail from server when deleted from local drive
- Setting up a rule-base for antispam filtering
- Setting up address books
- Setting a limit for the size of messages that will be downloaded automatically to a POP3 client (this keeps attachments on the server until you request them)

Any options that can lead to the loss of legitimate (non-spam) messages should be approached with caution.

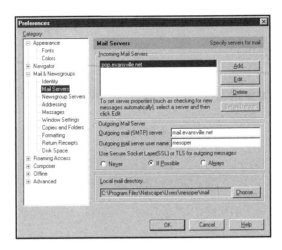

Figure 29.11   A typical email configuration screen (Netscape Messenger) after correct configuration for incoming and outgoing mail servers. Contact your ISP for the correct settings for your email system.

Handling File Attachments

Although any email system can handle simple text messaging, more and more users require the ability to handle file attachments reliably. Whether it's a Zip file full of company data for some after-hours work at the home PC or a video postcard on its way to a faraway family member, file attachments have the potential to provide both exciting content and excruciating headaches for email users.

Unfortunately, file attachments are handled in a variety of ways by the different email clients and systems in use today.

For example, users of Pine (see Figure 29.12) and many other UNIX-based email systems must convert file attachments into ASCII text for incorporation into the message body using a format such as MIME (also known as 64Base) or UUencoding.

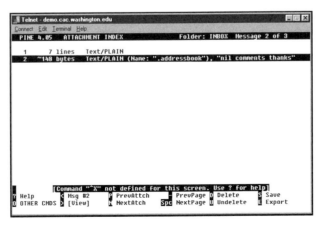

Figure 29.12   The Pine UNIX-based email system uses MIME encoding for file attachments.

Some email systems are designed to automatically encode (convert binary files into 7-bit text) and decode such attachments, while others require the use of external programs to encode and decode text.

UUencoding and UUdecoding

A UUencoded message looks like the example shown in Figure 29.13.

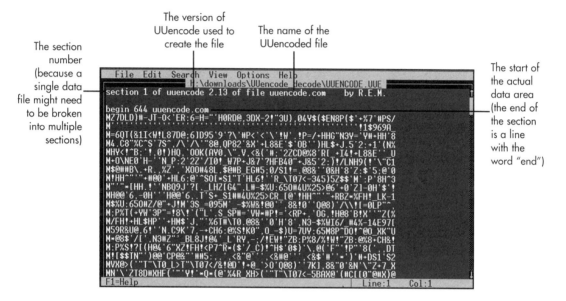

The version of
UUencode used to
create the file

The name of the
UUencoded file

The section
number
(because a
single data
file might need
to be broken
into multiple
sections)

The start of
the actual
data area
(the end of
the section
is a line
with the
word "end")

Figure 29.13   A UUencoded file has these elements.

This looks like gibberish and will stay gibberish unless it can be converted back into its original form. Many of the latest programs designed for zipping and unzipping files can also work with UUencoded files, but if you lack a UUdecoding utility, look for UUdecode.com on the Web. One of many sites offering these and other file utilities is http://www.beaunet.force9.co.uk/IT4IT/support/info.htm.

When a multisection UUencoded file is decoded, you start with the first section, and the UUdecode program finds each section in turn. Because this file would be inserted into the text of an email message, successful UUdecoding requires that the file be edited so that the start and end are as seen in the preceding figure. If the text between the beginning markers and end is damaged, the file cannot successfully be decoded.

Note

UUencode.com is the command-line MS-DOS program used to create UUencoded files.

Base64 MIME Encoding

A newer encoding standard you might also encounter is the Base64 MIME encoding (see Figure 29.14), which can be decoded by the MUNPACK utility created at Carnegie Mellon University.

Figure 29.14   A Base64 MIME-encoded file attachment has these elements.

As with a UUencoded file, a MIME-encoded email message would need to be edited so that the beginning resembles Figure 29.13. Then, the MUNPACK utility can be used to re-create the file. The corresponding MIME-encoding program is MPACK. The UNIX MPACK.TAR (archive) contains MPACK and MUNPACK, which can also be used for UUdecoding.

Netiquette Considerations

Good netiquette suggests that before you send a new online acquaintance a file attachment, send a plain-text message to ask whether they have a preference or any special instructions on how to send them attachments. A second suggestion is to send the message with the attachment to yourself. If you can't open your own attachment, how will anybody else be able to do it?

Compression Utilities

You can avoid other potential problems if you use a compression utility to shrink the size of the file you want to send and combine multiple files into a single archive. This two-pronged strategy allows you to avoid attachment file size and quantity limits imposed by some online services. (For example, AOL allows only a single file, and CompuServe and Microsoft Hotmail have a 1MB limit per attachment.)

Duplicate Messages

Sometimes file attachments simply repeat the contents of the original plain-text message. This happens if a user of Microsoft Internet Explorer or Outlook forgets to turn off the default Rich Text-HTML setting in the email preferences. These options work correctly (sending a single font-enhanced message) only in the Microsoft world. With any other email system, you get the message twice: once as text and once as HTML.

Managing Viruses

In addition to being hard to open because of some email client limitations, file attachments can actually be used to distribute Trojan Horse programs to your system, such as the notorious CIH, Chernobyl, or Melissa. Trojan Horse programs are usually sent as self-extracting EXE files, but DOC files also carry the risk of macro viruses. Use up-to-date antivirus software like that shown in Figure 29.15 for extra protection when opening attachments from people you trust (after all, they might have been fooled into passing along something like PICTURE.EXE!). *Never* open file attachments from unknown people.

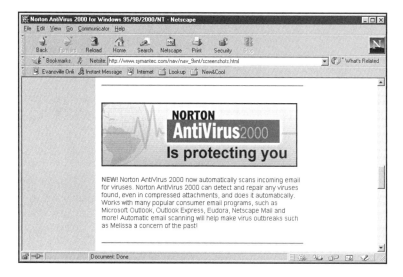

Figure 29.15 Norton AntiVirus 2000 is one of several antivirus programs designed to check attachments and email for virus and Trojan Horse programs such as Melissa or CIH.

Troubleshooting Security Holes

Both Microsoft and Netscape email clients have experienced numerous security holes in their latest releases, several of which revolve around buffer overflows and file attachments. Keep your email clients up-to-date with the latest patches, and watch for security warnings from reliable sources (such as www.bugnet.com, shown in Figure 29.16) or your antivirus software vendor.

Note

A good rule of thumb about file attachments is this: If your receiver doesn't need it, don't send it! Remember, if the file or article you want to attach is available on the Web, send your receiver the URL instead of the file.

Figure 29.16   Use the search and Alert options at http://www.bugnet.com to locate problems with your software. Bugnet offers various types of subscription programs for its bug detection and fix services.

Capacity Problems

Running out of space for your email can be even more catastrophic than an overflowing mailbox. A physical mailbox that's stuffed to the brim can have a note stuck in it to "see the counter" for the rest of your mail, but emailers just get their messages bounced back at them.

To avoid problems, follow these suggestions:

- Find out what the capacity of your email account is (usually measured in megabytes). When you receive messages with file attachments, download them and delete them off the server (but not your local system!) to free up space. Some ISPs will put a surcharge on your account if you exceed the average daily usage levels; this hits the wallet, but it's better than losing messages. See Figure 29.17 for an example of Microsoft's Hotmail client.

- If your email provider limits the number of messages you can store, you'll also want to "clean off" your email server as often as possible.

- If you're in a storage crisis and you have multiple accounts, forward the mail from the account with too many messages to an empty or nearly empty mailbox with adequate capacity. You can then delete the messages from the account, retrieve the ones you really want to keep from the account you used for overflow, and delete the rest.

- Consider using a "known-user–only" rule for some of your accounts if your email filtering program offers this option (or get an add-on that will). This will keep only mail from recipients on a list you define.

Small messages...

...are plain text, but
large messages...

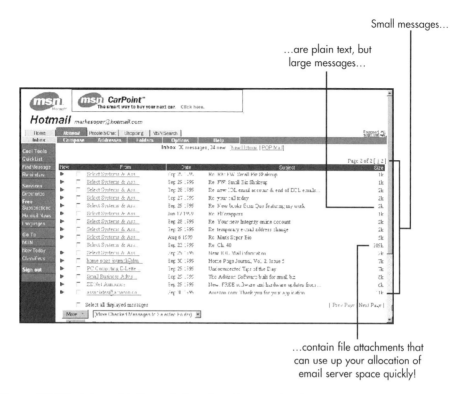

...contain file attachments that
can use up your allocation of
email server space quickly!

Figure 29.17 Microsoft's Hotmail client lists the size of each message.

Controlling Junk Mail

Tired of deleting "get rich quick," "foxy babes," or other offensive, time-wasting, illegal, immoral, or fattening unwanted junk mail from your email box? Take the following steps to stem the tide of cyberjunk:

- Never use your "real" email account for contests.

- Contests and "market surveys" are favorite ways for ejunk-mailers (spammers) to get your email address. It's worth the time to set up a free account (see "Free Email Accounts on the Web," later in this chapter) to be able to enter a "disposable" account you don't check very often if you do enter contests.

- Check your browser configuration. Consider changing your name, organization, email address, and other information stored in your browser's "Identity" screen to help conceal this information. See Figure 29.18 for an example.

- Use an "anonymous" Web-surfing site such as www.anonymizer.com as the starting-off point before you go to any sites that get information from your browser. What kind of information is available about you? For a shocking look, go to privacy.net/anonymizer/ and wait a couple of minutes for your IP address, browser configuration, and lots of other information to show up on your screen—all pulled silently from your system as soon as you arrived! See Figure 29.19 for examples.

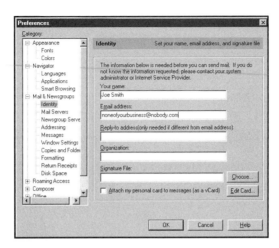

Figure 29.18   Your browser's Identity information can be used to "tell" Web sites you surf who you are. You can omit or alter this information to help protect your privacy.

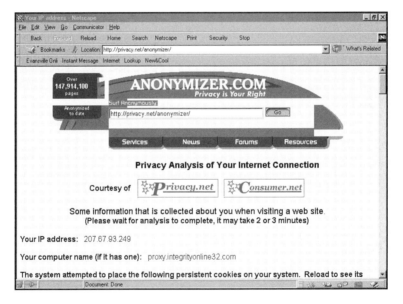

Figure 29.19   A visit to `http://privacy.net/anonymizer` reveals how much your browser "tattles" about you as you surf the Net.

These methods can help keep you from being added to more email listings, but what if you're already getting spammed? Check your email client for spam filtering options and consider using them in conjunction with antispam tools available from many different online sources as shareware or freeware products. See how Microsoft Hotmail handles this in Figure 29.20.

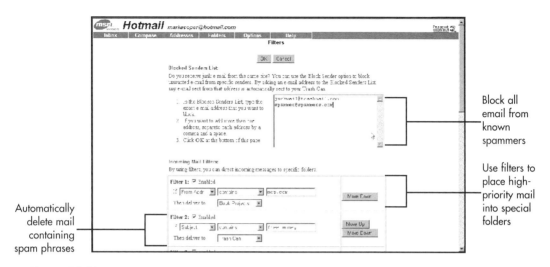

Automatically
delete mail
containing
spam phrases

Block all
email from
known
spammers

Use filters to
place high-
priority mail
into special
folders

Figure 29.20   Many email clients, such as this Microsoft Hotmail client, help you deal with spammers.

One of the biggest problems with junk mail is determining its actual origin. Many spammers will create bogus origin headers, hijack a mail server temporarily, or use other methods to avoid the wrath of fed-up receivers like yourself or the increasing number of ISPs who are ready to administer the "cyberdeath penalty" (loss of service) to those who are caught spamming. Check with your ISP or other email provider for help tracking down repeat spammers. In some cases, you might be able to query WHOIS servers to locate "unreachable" spammers by their domain names. You can find links to U.S. and foreign WHOIS servers, along with a form-based search tool, at `http://www.switch.ch/search/whois.html`.

If an Unsubscribe option is listed in the junk email, try it, but don't be too surprised if it bounces back as undeliverable.

Clients

Although many vendors of email client software exist for different systems, only a few types of email clients exist, distinguished by how email is sent and delivered and where email resides.

MAPI

MAPI (Messaging Application Programming Interface) provides a common library of routines for Microsoft Windows programs. A developer who incorporates MAPI routines into his software makes that software mail-enabled. MAPI isn't an email client as such, but most Windows-based email clients will work with MAPI.

MAPI allows Windows software such as Microsoft Word to create and send an email message by

- Creating the file
- Using File, Send from the pull-down menu
- Opening up the email client to allow the sender to choose address and other options and send the file

MAPI means that sending email is as fast and easy as printing the file; there's no need to save the file first, open the email client, and retrieve the file before sending it. See Figure 29.21 for an example.

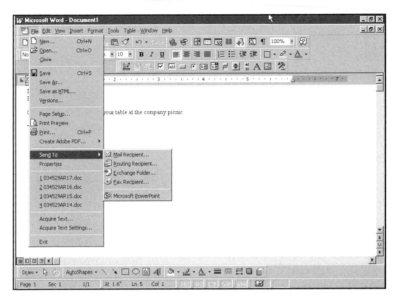

Figure 29.21   When a MAPI server such as Microsoft Outlook is installed, Microsoft Word (a MAPI client) can send the current document as email directly from the File menu.

MAPI "clients" and "servers" are a bit different than normal email clients and servers. Because MAPI "connects" applications with email programs, the application used to create the message (Microsoft Word, Microsoft Excel, and so on) is called the "MAPI client," whereas the email program used to send the message (Microsoft Outlook, Eudora, and so on) is the "MAPI server."

Another benefit of MAPI is that it enables users who are already familiar with the Microsoft Outlook email client to use it with other email systems (such as Lotus cc:Mail) by purchasing MAPI-enabling software to act as the "glue" between the Microsoft Outlook and other email systems. An example of this is Transend's MAPI ConnectorWare for cc:Mail (www.transend.com). No change to the email server is required, as it would be if you wanted to replace another email system with the Microsoft Exchange Server (which uses Outlook as a client).

POP3/SMTP

The Post Office Protocol version 3 (POP3) is the most common incoming email protocol, but not every email client is a POP3 client. Many versions of the Microsoft Exchange client, including the one that's standard with Windows 95, lack this built-in support. However, it can be added (use the Plus! CD-ROM for Windows 95 to add this feature, for example). Having POP3 support in your email client is important for multiplatform email access, unlike the Microsoft Post Office, which supports only Windows-based systems. A POP3 mail server doesn't care what operating system the client is, as long as the client has correctly configured POP3 support. Thus, a POP3 mail server can handle a mixture of Windows, Macintosh, and UNIX/Linux clients.

POP3 authentication can be performed in a variety of ways. The best methods are secure, but in the Microsoft Exchange Server situation in the previous paragraph, this would be possible only for email users in a domain controlled by a Windows NT server that can perform challenge and response authentication. Because not every POP3 client will be in such a situation, Basic Authorization (using clear text) is also an option.

If the POP3 clients allow it, SSL (Secure Socket Layers, the same technique used to make Web-based purchasing more secure) can be used to provide extra security for both types of user authentication.

Note

With most POP3 schemes, mailbox names for a POP3 server must be the same as the usernames, so plan accordingly to avoid problems.

One crucial concern about POP3-based email is its lack of portability. With POP3 clients, the "client" is actually the PC, not the user. This makes roving access a problem for users whose companies use "hoteling," where users might be at a different PC every day, or traveling users (see Figure 29.22).

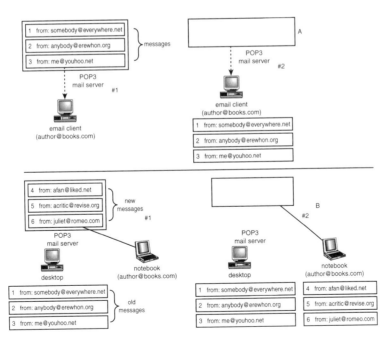

Figure 29.22 POP3 email and portability.

In Figure 29.22, Portion A shows how email is stored on the POP3 email server and then forwarded to the email client. However, if the user goes to another computer to check email (Portion B), the POP3 email server will forward the email to that client system. The result is that the email will be scattered across different computers.

While a traveler with a notebook computer can set up the browser's email reader (such as Netscape Messenger) in the computer as a POP3 client, the email will need to be forwarded by the user to the normal client at the end of the trip, unless there's an option for keeping the mail on the POP3 server (see Figure 29.23). An even bigger issue is that POP3 email is designed to "deliver," or download, all your new mail to you whenever you start your client. On a slow dial-up connection, you might spend many minutes drumming your fingers waiting for new messages to arrive.

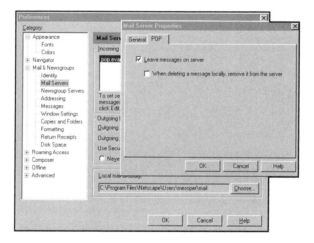

Figure 29.23   Check the configuration options for your POP3 email client to determine if you can retain messages on the server. Other options such as maximum size of messages to be downloaded automatically and length of time to save messages might also be available.

Many add-on freeware and shareware utilities have been designed for POP3 email clients to allow users to read just the message headers rather than download the entire message. These utilities make it easier to delete the junk email with minimal wastage of time.

If you'd prefer an alternative to having bushels of digital mail dumped into your desktop PC every time you check your email, but want to use an email client, take a look at the next option—the IMAP protocol.

IMAP

Unlike POP3, which leaves email filing and organization to the individual user and desktop PC, IMAP keeps the email on the server, allowing filing, sorting, and organization on the server (see Figure 29.24). IMAP also makes it easy for a user working from different PCs to access that email from any connected PC.

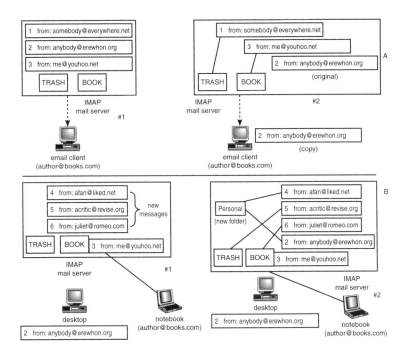

Figure 29.24 An IMAP-based email system.

With an IMAP-based email system, a user can read and file messages on the server (figure A). Message #1 is trashed, message #3 is filed into the BOOK folder, and a copy of message #2 is downloaded but the original stays on the server. If the user accesses the mail server from a different computer (figure B), the original messages (#2–3) are still accessible, as are the new messages (#4–6). A new folder (Personal) is created to store the new message #4 and the old message #2, while message #5 is trashed and message #6 joins message #3 in the BOOK folder.

IMAP support is important for corporate users because it allows standards-based email to have the same power as proprietary standards. Thus, IMAP support has been added to recent versions of Novell GroupWise, Lotus Domino, Lotus Notes, and other formerly "closed" corporate email and messaging systems. IMAP support is also available in recent and current releases of Netscape Navigator (through its Netscape Communicator email client) and Internet Explorer (through its Outlook Express email client).

Disconnected Use in IMAP

To get the full benefits of IMAP, an IMAP email server should support disconnected use, which allows the user to

- Connect to the IMAP server.
- Make a copy of selected messages from any folders desired.
- Disconnect from the IMAP server and work with the messages on the local system.

- Flag messages by status or to be deleted; move messages between folders.

- Compose new messages.

- Reconnect with the IMAP server to send messages and synchronize client- and server-side messages by duplicating the locally made changes on the server. Some popular email systems, such as the version of Microsoft Outlook Express supplied with Internet Explorer 4.0, don't support disconnected operation. Because this is a feature added since the original version of IMAP was introduced, it should be present over time as older IMAP-compliant systems are upgraded.

Discovering IMAP-Enabled Products

For the latest information on IMAP-enabled products from email notifiers to gateways and servers, check out the University of Washington's IMAP Connection web site: http://www.imap.org/.

For users of ISP-based email services, POP3 is still standard. To simulate the "no-download" benefit of IMAP on a POP3-based email system, check for optional HTML-based email support because these systems do retain the mail on the server's folder.

MIME, Smail, and X.400

This section examines several other email protocols and standards: MIME, Smail, and X.400.

The MIME Standard

Earlier in this chapter, we looked at MIME, the Multi-Purpose Internet Mail Extensions, from the standpoint of email attachments. However, there's more to MIME than email. MIME is a standard that applies to virtually any Web-based content, as well as email.

With a Web browser, the MIME header tells the browser the content type, enabling the browser to determine if it can view the content with its own handlers, must use a plug-in, must use a helper program, or must prompt the user to download and install a new plug-in or helper program.

If your browser displays garbage when you click a URL, that URL's MIME content-type might not be known to your system. Normally, this means that you should take one of the following steps:

- If the content is designed to be viewed online, check with the site or the browser vendor for a plug-in (Netscape Communicator) or an ActiveX control (Microsoft Internet Explorer) that will enable you to view the content correctly. If you are using Netscape Navigator, you will need to shut down and restart your browser after downloading and installing the plug-in to register it. Microsoft ActiveX controls allow immediate viewing of content.

- If the content is Java-based (not JavaScript), the developer might not have the Java class libraries loaded on the Web server correctly. Without these library files, the content can't be viewed correctly by anybody. Send the Webmaster an email, but make sure your browser has its Java support enabled.

- As an alternative, try right-clicking on the URL and downloading it to your system with Save Target/Link/Picture As. Use your own system's software to view or edit the file.

As you saw earlier, with email, MIME refers to the process of converting binary data into encoded streams of ASCII text when a file attachment is sent, and converting the encoded ASCII stream back into the original binary file at the receiving end. Most modern email clients are MIME-compatible for sending and receiving attachments. Thus, you seldom need to manually convert a MIME-encoded attachment yourself. However, MIME readers, such as the freeware MUNPACK.EXE or the commercial Dataviz Attachment Opener (www.dataviz.com, shown in Figure 29.25) are helpful to keep around if you occasionally receive "garbage" email attachments.

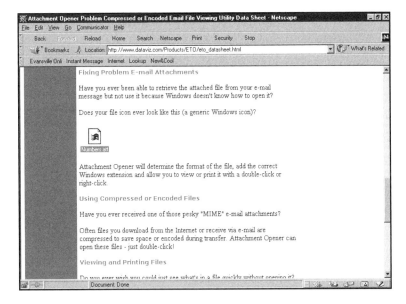

Figure 29.25 Dataviz's Attachment Opener is designed to handle "problem" email attachments, including missing extensions, MIME attachments, UUencoded messages, and others.

UUCP and Smail

Closed UNIX-based email systems are often based on the UUCP (UNIX-to-UNIX Copy Program) protocol. UUCP can also be used to transmit Internet mail between UNIX and other systems via dial-up (modem) and network (TCP/IP) connections. It is a daemon-based program, which means it provides background processing for email transmission. Smail is the mail transport agent (MTA) typically used in these systems, although it is also used by some SMTP sites.

UUCP Variations

UUCP has many variations, and both ends of a UUCP connection must be using the same protocol, sometimes referred to as a UUCP *grade*. The UUCP g protocol was the original version of UUCP and offers many different settings for packet size and window size. It is an 8-bit protocol supporting error-correcting, which makes it a good choice for transmitting binary data and program files and archives as well as plain text over modems. Some other versions of UUCP, including the t and e protocols, don't include error-correcting and should be used over TCP connections (which provide error correcting themselves). Many other UUCP protocols have been developed to support faster transmission or particular modem types, and are not supported in all versions of UUCP.

An excellent online resource for UUCP, written by the creator of UUCP Taylor (Ian Lance Taylor) is available at `http://www.faqs.org/faqs/uucp-internals/index.html`.

Advantages of UUCP

UUCP can be used as part of specialized LAN email to Internet Email solutions to allow the existing email system (such as Novell GroupWise or others) to also be used to send and receive Internet email at a cost far less than an SMTP-based system because it's a dial-up rather than an "always-on" connection. This also allows the network to be more secure against outside intruders than with an always-on connection.

Smail

Smail is supplied as a standard part of some Linux distributions, such as the Debian GNU/Linux distribution (`www.debian.org`). It can be used as a drop-in replacement for the more common sendmail and is designed to be easier to configure, although less powerful. The latest version of Smail, version 3.2, is available from the following site:
`ftp://ftp.uu.net/networking/mail/smail/`.

An excellent (English-language) online source explaining typical configurations of UUCP and Smail as a team is available at `http://www.uni-tuebingen.de/zdv/projekte/linux/books/nag/`.

The X.400 Standard

X.400 is a group of standards for interconnecting different email systems. X.400 was developed by ISO (International Standards Organization) and ITU (International Telecommunications Union); it is a popular standard in Europe and Canada.

Unlike SMTP, X.400 is an official standard with more configuration options. However, the SMTP versus X.400 debate is far from over. An email system that must communicate with non-U.S. clients should support X.400 as well as SMTP standards.

x.400 and Microsoft Exchange Server

X.400 support (called the x.400 Connector) is a standard feature of the Microsoft Exchange Server 5.5 Enterprise Edition but is an extra-cost add-on to the standard version of Exchange Server 5.5. An x.400 Connector license is required for each server requiring x.400 capabilities. If you plan to use Exchange Server 5.5 to relay messages between x.400 and SMTP networks, download and install the Service Pack 3 for Exchange Server 5.5 to obtain the new MTA Mixer feature.

If you need help configuring the x.400 connector, see
`http://www.ntfaq.com/ntfaq/exchange29.html`.

You can learn more about x.400 from the following Web site: `www.alvestrand.no/harald/x400/` (see Figure 29.26).

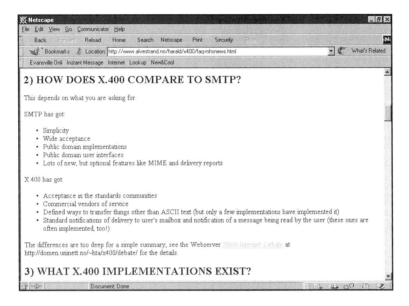

Figure 29.26   Harald T. Alvestrand's x.400 Web site provides comparisons between x.400 and SMTP email standards, as well as a lot of other information on the x.400 standard.

Free Email Accounts on the Web

More and more email users are finding it useful to maintain multiple email addresses: one for corporate business, one for email from family and friends, one for "free" offers, one for a side business... and the list goes on.

Although most ISPs offer the option for multiple email addresses, you might still want to use third-party email providers for more flexibility in addresses or to keep different types of email separate. If you don't need full-featured email services for these additional accounts, why not get your additional addresses free?

The Free Email Providers Guide Web site (`www.fepg.net/`) provides links to all types of free email providers, including those that use proprietary email readers, offer Web-based access, or use POP3 readers (see Figure 29.27).

To make managing multiple accounts easier, this site also lists forwarding services, which allow you to direct all the mail you receive at multiple addresses to a single address for easier reviewing. I have reviewed many email forwarding services for the *PCNovice Guide Series: The Web's Hidden Treasures* issue in an article called "Eliminate Web Confusion," available online from `www.smartcomputing.com`. See the example in Figure 29.28.

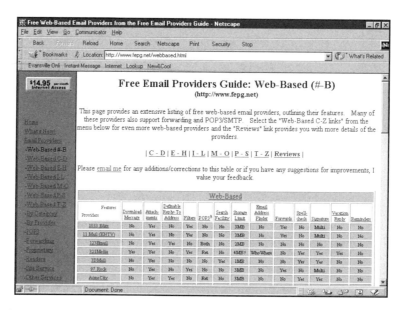

Figure 29.27 The Free Email Providers Guide listing of Web sites provides detailed information about POP3 compatibility, storage limits, forwarding, and other features offered by free email services it lists.

Figure 29.28 A typical free (advertiser-supported) email redirection signup sheet (www.myezmail.com). You select a new email address and enter your regular email address, and email is forwarded from the new address to your regular address.

What's the catch with free email services? Depending on the service, you might need to put up with a barrage of ads, lack the ability to receive or send file attachments, lack defined reply-to addresses, and other limitations. Use the feature comparison tables and glossary available at www.fepg.net for more information.

Note

If you use a forwarded email address for contests and surveys, spammers won't get your real email address. With many email clients, you can set replies to a given address to go straight to the trash or to a special folder. Also, you can keep your personal correspondence from being mixed up with company email by creating separate email addresses for business and personal use.

Maintaining a Mailing List

If the people on your email address list naturally fall into groups (co-workers, friends from civic or religious groups, sports fans, and so on), why not create customized mailing lists to make sharing important news easier? Then, you're just a click away from sending out a mailing to only the people who want to know about the topic in question.

Maintaining Mailing Lists with an Email Client

Even the simplest email systems enable you to maintain a list of addresses, but better systems allow you to create separate lists of correspondents. Depending on the client, you might be able to

- Create group lists, which allows you to send a message to an entire group with a single selection: the annual letter to the "friends and family" group, a reminder about the next workgroup meeting to the "workgroup" group, and so on. The popular Eudora email client calls this feature "nicknames," and when you select a nickname as the recipient for email, the nickname or group name is replaced by the actual recipients when the message is sent.

- Control the types of mail you receive from your mailing list (some email clients, such as Eudora 3.0 and above, allow you to do this). You can automatically accept all sizes of emails from family and friends (specified by name), but limit the size of automatically-downloaded messages from those not on the list.

- Use BCC: (blind carbon copy) to mail to a group of recipients if you don't want the recipients to know who else is getting the message. This option is important for privacy protection, and for keeping recipients of the message from "harvesting" other email addresses for their own purposes.

- Be careful when importing address books from one email application to another. Eudora nicknames don't import properly into Microsoft Outlook and must be re-created manually.

- Selected names from a contacts list in Microsoft Outlook 98 can be converted directly into a customized email list (mimicking a distribution list) by assigning each contact to a Category (or multiple categories) and then grouping the contacts by category. For more information, see the Microsoft Knowledge Base article Q18149.

- Refer to individuals in a group by their aliases (Eudora "nicknames"), whenever possible. This allows the group mailing to work correctly for all members, even if the actual mailing address changes for some members in the group.

Here is an example using classic TV spies; create the individuals first:

Alias/Nickname	Email Address/Members	Actual Name
Secret_Agent	jdrake@dangerman.org	John Drake
Man_from_Uncle	nsolo@uncle.gov	Napoleon Solo
Spies	Secret_Agent, Man_from_Uncle	

Send a mailing to Spies, and Secret_Agent and Man_from_Uncle will receive it at their listed email addresses.

Change the first entry to

```
Secret_Agent    #2@theprisoner.org    John Drake
```

The email address has changed. Send a mailing to Spies, and he'll still get his email.

For more help with creating and customizing Eudora email (including import/export tips), see `http://www.cs.nwu.edu/~beim/eudora/index.html`.

Help for Roving Email Users

One problem with conventional email lists is that they reside on a single computer, requiring a roving user to synchronize them or export/import between systems. If you use multiple computers, you can now use online address books, including group mailing list features, with Netscape's Netcenter Address book.

With even the most sophisticated email client, there's a limit to how much management you can do, especially if there are frequent changes in the members of the mailing list for a particular topic. That's when a mail-list server is useful.

Maintaining a Mail-List Server

If you are a content publisher with a Web site, you can automate the task of distributing information to interested parties by setting up a mail-list server to distribute technical information, allow interaction between members, and attract new users to your site.

Mail-list managers such as the popular freeware Majordomo (`www.greatcircle.com/majordomo/`), L-Soft's LISTSERV (`www.lsoft.com`) and others are designed to automate the adding and deleting of mail list members and provide automatic mailing of selected documents. Majordomo (see Figure 29.29) is a collection of Perl scripts, and is a good choice for programmers who use Perl. It is a so-called "groupware" product, with much free technical support from many Web sites.

Most mail-list managers are UNIX/Linux-based, but mail-list managers such as LISTSERV are also available for Windows NT servers.

With any mail-list manager, you must set up various aliases that will be used to join the list, leave the list, get help, and join a discussion (if the list allows threaded discussions).

Because configuration and management of some mail-list managers is time-consuming and expensive, small organizations that want to use a mailing list should consider mailing-list hosting services such as L-Soft's EASE (Expert Administration and Supervision of Email lists—see Figure 29.30). These services use a sliding price scale to determine costs and are quite reasonable for organizations who use virtual servers and otherwise lack the staff and resources to configure and maintain mailing-list managers and servers.

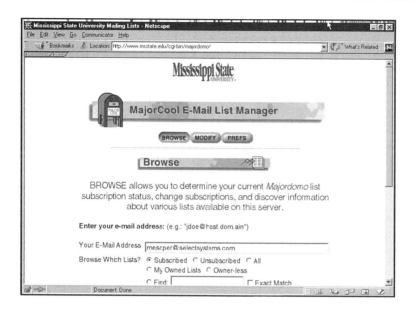

Figure 29.29 Many Web-based interfaces to Majordomo are available, including MajorCool, available from `http://ncrinfo.ncr.com/pub/contrib/unix/MajorCool/`. MajorCool makes it easy for users to join and leave mailing lists.

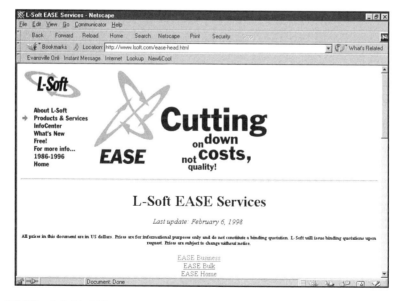

Figure 29.30 L-Soft's EASE service enables you to outsource your mailing-list management needs.

Summary

Email systems enable individuals and groups of users to communicate instantly, and are therefore "mission-critical" applications for any organization.

Email users should be provided with flexible clients capable of handling mail from both internal and external (including Internet) sources, email client software and add-ons able to compress (archive) large files and decipher file attachments from any source, and reliable operation. As networks have replaced the hodge-podge of proprietary network protocols with the single TCP/IP standard of the Internet for all types of networking, email is slowly moving away from closed systems to open access.

The rise of IMAP and Web-based email systems allow roving users to access email from anywhere, but the bulk of business systems still use POP3 servers, making it more difficult to keep track of email when more than one computer is in use.

Maintenance of mailing lists (both for personal and company use) is an important process that can be automated through the use of better email clients and mailing-list programs, allowing email to reach its goal of communicating accurately and quickly with many people at once.

Database Systems

SOME OF THE MAIN TOPICS IN THIS CHAPTER ARE

Open Database Connectivity (ODBC)

Application Programming Interface (API)

Database Software

Client/Server Databases

Other Database Systems

Improving Performance

If you look at the network as the circulatory system of your business computing environment, the databases you employ to manage valuable information can be considered a significant portion of the brain of your environment. Networks enable users to exchange vast quantities of information in the business environment. Databases and the applications based on them are the tools that enable users to manage this information and put it to good use. Choosing a database product that is appropriate for your business should not be a task you take lightly.

This chapter examines some of the more popular database products to help you understand the kinds of problems a database product can solve.

Open Database Connectivity (ODBC)

ODBC (Open Database Connectivity) is a standard protocol for database access that allows applications to connect to an external database. The application that uses ODBC makes a request to the ODBC Driver Manager on the local computer, which selects the appropriate ODBC driver needed to connect to the database. This makes ODBC very flexible, and it can be used to connect to a variety of database types (the *database source*), from the usual database servers, such as Microsoft SQL Server or Oracle, to more common information stores, such as spreadsheets and text files. As long as the application requesting the database access and the database source are both written to be ODBC-compliant, access to external databases can be made almost transparent to a user sitting at the workstation.

ODBC drivers are libraries that are used to implement the functions found within the ODBC API. Database vendors create drivers that are designed to be used with their products. For example, the ODBC driver for Microsoft's SQL Server cannot access data directly from a DB2 or Oracle database.

In most businesses, information is stored in a variety of formats. Yet, to make good use of information, tools are needed to plow through the many different formats used by competing applications and focus on data relevant to the problem at hand.

For example, consider a retail Web site that presents a catalog of products to the end user. The end user is only concerned with selecting a product and, of course, paying for it. The user does not have to understand that behind the scenes, several departments are involved in designing, testing, and marketing the product. Each department might have unique data requirements that are dependent on their function, but it is likely that they also share a large amount of data. The marketing department can produce useful data that predicts sales for the coming months or year. This data can be used by the manufacturing department in forecasting capacity or material requirements. The purchasing department can then use these forecasts to enter into contracts with suppliers so that materials needed to manufacture the product arrive at the appropriate time, which in turn can help lower costs because excessive warehousing costs can be reduced.

If each of these departments were simply islands within the business and could not readily access information managed by other departments, the efficiency with which the product is produced and marketed could suffer. The solution is to either allow for a single common database product, shared by all the departments, or to use a tool such as ODBC so that data can be managed and used from a variety of different sources.

Using the example of a Web-based retailer, the application that creates the Web pages of the catalog users see can draw on information from all parts of the company. If a product is not available, for example, and information from manufacturing forecasts indicate that it will not be available for some time, the application could be coded to not show the particular product to the end user. This is certainly much more efficient than accumulating a large number of back orders and having the customer service department deal with upset or impatient customers.

Application Programming Interface (API)

An application programming interface (API) is a library of routines that can be used by the programmer to quickly add functionality to a program. Routines in APIs can be used to eliminate the chore of creating code to perform functions that are frequently used or are of a complex nature. Creating a window on the user's screen and displaying the results of a report might take hundreds of lines of code. Using a few API calls, which perform the tedious details, is much more efficient.

Just as vendors provide APIs to access operating system functions, ODBC has an API interface that can be used by programmers to manipulate information residing in one or multiple database files. The API for ODBC is used to access the functionality and information of the drivers and to access the data within an ODBC data source.

Database Software

The advantage of using a database to store your information is in the capability of the database software to retrieve that information in various forms and create reports based on that returned information.

Most modern database systems are known as Relational Database Management Systems (RDBMS). An RDBMS stores data in related tables; hence the name relational.

Most database systems provide a relatively user-friendly interface for retrieving the data stored in the files. The user can request this data using a *query*—a question that specifies a set of conditions or a filter for the requested data.

Suppose you have an employee database file that maintains information on your staff, such as

- Employment start date
- Employee number
- Salary rate
- Name
- Address
- Department

Now assume that you are in a company that rewards its employees for years of service with a dinner and special gift. You might need to print off a report for the manager each year so that the correct people are sent the invitations.

With the query capabilities of your RDBMS, you can select only those employees who fit your criteria—for example, all employees who have a start date 10 years less than the current date. Your RDBMS can quickly search your data files and produce the information you request. You can also set up the software to create a preconfigured report and send it via email or print a hard copy to the appropriate person.

Microsoft Access

Microsoft has created Access as its entry into the personal database market. Access presents an easy user interface with a fairly powerful database engine.

You can customize Access databases with the use of forms and the Visual Basic programming language. This provides an almost limitless capability to make Access work the way you do and provide even easier or custom forms for user interaction.

For example, you can create an application within Access. This ability allows the user to open Access and have a default application run on startup. This can reduce the amount of time that a new user would need to spend learning all the aspects of Access. Your custom application provides the entire interface they need to gain access to the underlying data structures.

Another big advantage to using Microsoft Access is that the Visual Basic programming language is incorporated into the product in the form of Visual Basic for Applications (VBA). VBA is a subset of the actual Visual Basic programming language and allows any programmer familiar with it to bring their knowledge to Microsoft Access.

Microsoft also purchased the FoxPro database and has added it to its "visual" library of applications and development tools. Visual FoxPro is included in Microsoft's Visual Studio and poised as an integrated database and development tool.

Lotus Approach

Although primarily a name synonymous with spreadsheets, Lotus has a database application known as Approach. Although not as popular as Microsoft Access, it contains many of the features found in Access and adds some more.

Approach is an easy-to-use relational database system that allows for ease of access to larger ODBC-compliant database systems like Oracle, Notes, and DB2.

Borland/Corel

Paradox is a database that was originally developed by Borland but which was bought by Corel Corporation. It is now sold as a part of Corel's WordPerfect suite and Office 2000 products and is also available as a separate product.

In version 9, Paradox comes in two editions: a regular database application and a developer edition. This new version offers you the ability to learn how to use the product while creating a database with online tutorials.

Paradox provides support for the SQL language and also incorporates a new "Expert" to make formulating SQL queries easy. For those not familiar with SQL, this can be an added bonus because the language has a bit of a learning curve.

Although these database systems are great for storing and retrieving information, when it comes to a networked environment, they have one drawback that comes in the form of multiuser access. Although they can allow multiple users to access the database, they are not really meant for this type of operation. This is where client/server databases come into play.

Client/Server Databases

Database software that takes advantage of the client/server model is ideally suited to a multiuser, networked system. A *client/server* application is split into two components: One component runs on a powerful server computer while the second component runs on the client computer.

In a client/server database, the client makes a request to the database on the server. The server takes the information from the client and uses it to perform a search on the data, and then returns the results to the client. The only thing the client is responsible for is the display of that data. The major processing and searching is done on the server.

Another advantage to this scenario is that the server and the database can handle multiple requests, thereby allowing more than one user to gain access to the data.

In Chapter 32, "Other Client/Server Applications," you will find an overview of some of the more popular database products, such as Microsoft SQL Server and Oracle.

These database applications are enterprise class database servers. They provide a robust set of features and are optimized for multiuser capabilities.

With the recent interest in data warehousing, large database servers and software are entering the limelight. Some vendors are even pushing the e-commerce concept, extolling the benefits of their software and its capability to embrace the idea.

Not only are database applications required to work in a traditional network environment, they are now being used quite extensively to fuel interactive and dynamic Internet Web sites. The benefits of this type of application for a database engine are that a Web administrator does not have to update countless pages on the Web site. By using a database to maintain dynamic data, the Web administrator can link the various pages to the database fields that contain the necessary data. In this way, he needs to update the data in only one place, the database. The Web pages will be updated automatically as a result of the links.

Microsoft SQL Server and Database Architecture

Structured Query Language (SQL) is actually a database concept that is used in most databases. It simply means, as the name suggests, that you use special language syntax to structure a query or question to the database server or software. One of the biggest hurdles in learning database programming with Visual Basic is digesting the SQL language.

Microsoft SQL Server Version 7.0 presents a scalable database platform that integrates well with Microsoft's Office 2000 suite. It is capable of developing large-scale databases in the Terabyte range.

SQL Server stores all its data in databases. These databases are stored as files on the hard drive of the server. The databases created by SQL are arranged into logical components that the user sees and interacts with. Examples of these components are tables, views, and stored procedures.

The actual data is stored in tables within the database. The concept of a table stretches across the SQL and Microsoft Access database architectures.

Within the table, data is broken down into rows and columns. The rows represent one complete record in the database, such as an employee's record. Each column represents an attribute of that record, such as employee ID or phone number.

SQL server contains multiple database files on the server. They are broken down into two discreet groups: system databases and user databases.

Under the system databases, you will find four different databases.

- master
- tempdb
- msdb
- model

The *master* database contains all the configuration information for the SQL system as well as user account information. It also contains information pertaining to all other SQL server databases on the system, along with the location of each of those database files.

The *tempdb* database is responsible for all temporary tables and stored procedures. tempdb is not used just to hold temporary information pertaining to the system databases; it also is used to hold all user databases.

The SQL Server Agent uses the *msdb* database to schedule jobs and alerts. It is also used to record operators.

The *model* database, as the name suggests, is used as a model for all newly created databases on the system.

Any other database created is considered a part of the user database group.

Figure 30.1 shows an example of a SQL server database architecture. In this setup, you can see the four system databases and two user databases that would likely be common within most companies.

Figure 30.2 shows SQL Server 7.0 Enterprise Manager under the Microsoft Management Console. Enterprise Manager is the interface to use when interacting with SQL Server for administrative purposes.

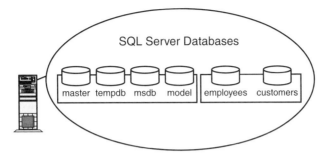

Figure 30.1 The SQL Server database is composed of several files.

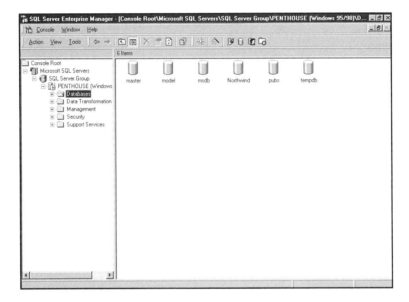

Figure 30.2 SQL Server 7.0 Enterprise Manager is a Microsoft Management Console snap-in that can be used to manage the server.

The addition of wizards in this version makes SQL Server easier to work with by prompting the user through many complex tasks. There is also a Web page interface that is presented to you for working with the database structure after it is created. This can be seen in Figure 30.3, which depicts the SQL Server Web interface.

To gain access to the data stored in a SQL Server database, the client software formulates a request or a query for data based on a set of conditions or filters. This query takes the form of a Transact-SQL statement. Transact-SQL is the language incorporated into database software for the purpose of requesting data.

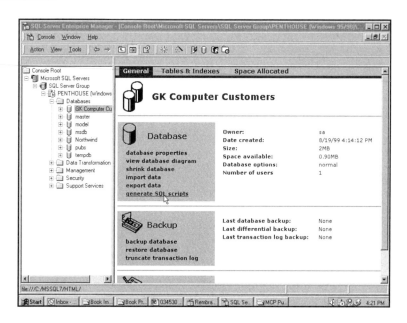

Figure 30.3 You can also use the Web-based interface to manage the server.

For example, let's say that you wanted to find out some information from a customer database that indicates the name and address of those customers who have purchased products costing $500 and up. You might want to send them a thank-you card or an invitation to a special sale. Here is the Transact-SQL statement that would be used:

```
SELECT Name AND Address FROM Customer WHERE Purchase >= 500
```

In this example, you can see several capitalized words. These are known as keywords or reserved words for SQL. They do not have to be capitalized, but it makes for easier reading of SQL statements.

The first word, SELECT, instructs the server to choose from the Name field. The word AND is used to combine another field, which in this case is the Address field. Note that Name and Address are fields in the database.

Next, you must tell the server what table your data resides in. This is what the FROM keyword is for. Your data is coming from the Customer table.

Then you must set the filter or criteria. Tell it to return only those records that have a value of $500 or greater in the Purchase field.

So, there you have a simple SQL statement that is designed to pull information from a SQL-enabled database. Now let's take a look at some database software from other vendors.

Oracle

Oracle has been a strong contender in the database market for some time. The latest version, Oracle8i, is based on features that allow it to be used for Internet applications as an e-business tool. It can be used to power a back-end data store for Web pages and applications deployed over the Internet or an intranet.

Note

Although it is similar in many ways to Microsoft's product, it stands out because of one very important feature: Microsoft SQL Server runs only on Microsoft platforms (Windows NT or Windows 2000), while Oracle has been ported to many different platforms, from Windows NT to UNIX. There is even a version of Oracle that runs on OpenVMS AlphaServers (from Compaq, which recently acquired the original vendor, Digital Equipment Corporation). If scalability is important to you, do not discount this important feature when making decisions about upgrading or replacing your current network database product. Getting stuck with one particular hardware or software platform can leave you vulnerable to the whims of that particular vendor.

Oracle has taken the time and consideration to design database software that can be used to support mission-critical Online Transaction Processing (OLTP) applications as well data warehousing.

Java

Most people have, no doubt, heard of the Java programming language. Oracle realized that Java provides a language that is portable and usable on the Internet and have, as such, incorporated the language into the Oracle8i product.

Oracle has integrated a Java Virtual Machine (Java VM) into its Oracle Data Server. By doing so, they enable developers to write, store, and execute code within the database.

SQLJ

Oracle teamed up with IBM and Sun to develop an open standard for integrating Java with SQL. By doing this, they've allowed SQL to be embedded into Java code and communicate with relational databases.

Oracle WebDB

In order for you to take advantage of the World Wide Web with your Oracle database, Oracle has created WebDB. It uses an HTML interface and browser-based HTML tools to allow you to quickly Web-enable your database. You can use the tool to build, deploy, and monitor your Web application.

Oracle iFS

Another unique feature of Java Virtual Machine Oracle8i is Oracle *i*FS (Oracle Internet File System). This is a Java application that presents itself to the user as if it were a volume on the network.

By using *i*FS, Oracle allows users to access the information through a variety of methods, Windows Explorer, Web browser, or even an email client.

IBM DB2

IBM provides the DB2 database software, a product that has been around and fine-tuned for many years. It is available for the following platforms:

- AS/400
- RISC System/6000
- Windows NT
- Windows 95/98
- OS/2
- AIX, IBM's version of UNIX
- HP-UX, Hewlett-Packard's UNIX variant
- SCO UnixWare
- Linux
- Sequent
- Sun Solaris
- Windows CE and other palm computing environments

As you can see, IBM has ported the DB2 database to a variety of platforms. If you are running an integrated environment, there is clearly a distinct advantage in running DB2.

IBM provides DB2 in a variety of versions as well. These are listed here:

- **Personal Developer's Edition**—This product is available as a development-only tool for a single developer wanting to write applications to access the DB2 database server.
- **Universal Developer's Edition**—This package is designed to allow a developer to write client/server applications for use on the DB2 Universal Database on any of the supported platforms and includes additional tools.
- **Database Personal Edition**—This is a single-user RDBMS for desktop use and mobile and power users. The product incorporates multimedia and replication support along with SDKs and the GUI administration tools.
- **Database Workgroup Edition**—Aimed at the small business or departments within a company, this version provides a multiuser RDBMS with all the features discussed so far. It is available for the OS/2, Windows NT, and Linux platforms.
- **Database Enterprise Edition**—This edition is aimed at providing a database server for large organizations that might want to support data on LANs, WANs, and over the Internet.
- **Database Enterprise Extended Edition**—The extended edition is aimed at systems using massively parallel processors (MPPs) and cluster server environments. This edition is ideal for data warehousing, data mining, or where parallel processing is required.

Sybase

E-business is another of the industry's buzzwords that has risen from combining the traditional with new technology and the Internet. Sybase enters the e-business market with its own database offering as well. Sybase software is available on the following platforms:

- Sun Solaris
- IBM RS6000
- Digital UNIX
- HP UX
- Windows NT

Database Servers

Under the Database Server category, Sybase lists products in the Adaptive Server family.

Adaptive Server IQ is a very high-end tool for data analysis and uses a patented query technology.

Adaptive Server Anywhere is incorporated into SQL Anywhere Studio. This product is designed to provide database service on mobile and embedded systems.

Application Tools

Sybase offers an Enterprise Application Server as a foundation for application development for distributed applications.

They also offer a variety of development tools. PowerBuilder is an enterprise development environment that has support for Web applications. PowerJ allows you to build sophisticated Internet apps with Java and Power++, which is a C++ tool incorporating a RAD environment used to build distributed applications.

As you can see, without going into too much detail, Sybase brings a varied assortment of tools and applications to the database market. To learn more about what they have to offer, I suggest you take a look at the Sybase Web site for more information on products and services.

Informix

Informix is another seasoned player in the database market. Its products can be broken down into three categories:

- Data warehousing
- I.Informix
- Transaction

Data Warehousing Products

Informix has created a suite of applications for the data-warehousing arena named Informix Decision Frontier. It consists of the following products:

- **Informix Dynamic Server**—A powerful database that Informix has optimized for high-volume use
- **MetaCube**—A sophisticated management and analysis tool
- **Seagate Info**—An easy-to-use tool that can be used to produce reports from information stored in a database
- **I-Spy**—A smart tool for monitoring and optimizing Informix databases

If you are creating a data mart, Informix offers the Seagate Info and MetaCube tools but substitutes Informix Red Brick Warehouse (a relational database designed for data marts) and Informix DataStage (a tool for extracting data and loading it into a data warehouse or data mart).

Informix Products

Informix provides products to Web-enable your data as well. Informix Internet Foundation.2000 is a data management platform that enables you to publish your business data to the Web and can function as a back end for Internet-based applications.

Informix i.Reach allows individual users or owners of data to publish that content and maintain it.

Informix i.Sell is a platform for providing an electronic storefront with integrated tools for operating and maintaining the site.

Transaction Products

Online transaction processing (OLTP) is a necessary requirement for database engines publishing to the Web. Informix provides their entry into this arena with Informix Dynamic Server.2000.

This product is a scalable and fast transaction engine that is used by retail giant Wal-Mart and by VISA. This alone is a strong indicator of the reliability and functionality available in this product.

Informix has been in the database market for many years and, like other major players in this ever expanding field, it is keeping up with the advancement of database technology with all the previously listed products.

Other Database Systems

The products covered in this chapter are among the more popular, but many other available database products are either commercially sold or available as shareware.

One example of another commercially sold database product is included in the Microsoft Works package. Works is an integrated software program that is designed for home users to be able to create a simple database without requiring an in-depth knowledge of database architectures.

A quick look at the Linuxberg Web site, `http://www.linuxberg.com`, will reveal a wider range of database software available for the Linux platform. Some of this software is shareware and some is freeware. You will also find database applications for the console and X environments.

Improving Performance

Many factors influence the performance of client/server database systems, but the three most important things to consider are as follows:

■ Network bandwidth usage

■ CPU usage

■ Disk I/O operations

If you are making plans to upgrade hardware on the network, you should closely study your current environment and design your upgrade plan to improve the performance of these key resources.

Network bandwidth is an obvious factor. For clients to interact with the database, an information dialog must be established between the application residing on the user's workstation and the database engine on the server. In the early days of ethernet, the simplest method for improving this data channel involved placing users on the same segment with the server, using devices such as bridges to minimize unnecessary network traffic on each segment. Today you have more options. Switches, for example, can be used to isolate traffic and provide a full-duplex connection for high-end servers or heavy-duty users. Additionally, consider using a server that has multiple network adapter cards, allowing the server to make the best use of its processing power. A fast CPU doesn't improve performance if it must wait on the network.

On the server side, you can use several methods to improve CPU performance. Of course, choosing a server with a faster CPU is important. It might seem that the price you pay for a small increase in performance is high, but when you cost-out that price over the life of the machine and factor in the improvement in database access it can provide, it might not seem that bad after all. For machines that are heavily accessed, consider using a server that has multiple CPUs installed.

Another method you can use to improve CPU performance is clustering. Some clustering products, such as Microsoft's NT clustering, are built on an architecture that concentrates on the failover capabilities that clustering can provide. That is, only one system in the cluster can "own" a disk resource and share it with the network. This does not increase CPU power, but it does provide redundancy that can improve the overall uptime of the system. Higher end products, such as OpenVMS or UNIX clusters, allow multiple systems to share one or more disk volumes in the cluster, and it is this feature you should look for if you have a large client base that must simultaneously access the same database files.

Disk I/O has always been the slowest part of a computer system. In a fast network environment, it can become the limiting factor that prevents other improvements from being used to their fullest. Again, a fast CPU or multiple network cards don't help much if the system sits around waiting for disk I/O to complete. For this reason, you must be keenly aware of the organization of your database from the physical standpoint. For example, which files contain the information that is accessed the most frequently? Do you have several of these "hot files" residing on the same disk?

There are several methods you can use to maximize disk I/O. The first, obviously, is to place hot files on separate disks. In a high-performance environment this might mean dedicating a single disk to a single file. The expense might seem extravagant, but again if it's performance you're after, the price is negligible. In Microsoft's SQL Server, it is recommended that you place the log file on its own disk. Because this file is accessed continuously, recording each change to the database, it must be quickly accessed.

Large files can be a problem. When you put all your data into one file, all I/O requests must wait their turn. Consider this when designing the database at the start. For example, if you have a large customer database and you know it will be accessed heavily, consider putting groups of customers into different files. A common method for doing this is to divide the customer database into groups alphabetically. Records that start with A–C go into one file, D–F into another, and so on. This way, a single file is not hit continuously by every access to the customer database. The load is distributed among many files that reside on different disks.

From the physical level, looking at the disks themselves, consider RAID (Redundant Array of Independent Disks) technology. RAID uses multiple disks that are presented to the operating system as a single unit. Although some operating systems, such as Microsoft's Windows NT Server, can perform RAID functions at the operating system level, this is usually done for purposes of fault-tolerance, not performance, because the CPU itself spends a lot of time running both the server application and the RAID system. Instead, use a hardware-based RAID system in which the controller assumes the responsibility of managing the disk volumes, relieving the CPU of this task.

Which RAID technique should you use? RAID comes in many flavors, some of which are even proprietary to a particular manufacturer. Generally, RAID techniques are classified as RAID levels. RAID level 0 is called *disk striping*. This method uses multiple disks, spreading the I/O across the available disks. Because multiple read/write heads are involved, throughput can be vastly improved. The drawback is that in a RAID 0 array, the failure of a single disk can lead to failure of the entire disk volume.

RAID level 1 is called *disk mirroring*. In this setup, data is written to two disks at the same time. Because the data needs to be coordinated between the two disks, the actual time to write the data can be a little slower than when using a single disk. However, read I/Os can be distributed between the two disks, so reads are generally faster. Mirroring also provides fault tolerance because the failure of one disk will not result in a loss of data. A complete copy is on the remaining disk.

RAID levels 2, 3, and 4 have also been defined but are not used very often. However, RAID level 5 is widely used. In this level, disk striping is also used, just as in level 0, but a parity stripe is also written across the disks, just like data. Because the parity information for a particular block of data is always put on a different disk than the data it is computed from, fault-tolerance is provided as well as the increased I/O from striping. The problem with level 5, though, is that if a disk does fail, the overhead needed to re-create the missing data using the parity information can slow things down.

Perhaps the best of all these is RAID 1+0. Using this technique, you first create several mirror sets and then combine these mirror sets into a stripe set. Using striping greatly improves I/O performance. The disk volumes that compose each member of the stripe set are made fault-tolerant because they are mirror sets. Thus, you get the benefits of both mirroring and striping. The cost can be considerable in a large database environment because you are essentially doubling the number of disks that would be needed for an ordinary stripe set. However, if you want fast I/O performance and you require a high degree of fault-tolerance to give your users maximum uptime for the database, this is the way to go.

One final note on RAID disk systems: many support hot-swappable drives. This means that, if a particular drive fails, you do not have to shut down the system to replace it. Instead, you simply remove the failed drive and plug in the new one. Depending on the vendor, there may be a few configuration commands you need to execute to bring the new drive back into the storage set of which the original drive was a member. This capability can help you provide a non-stop computing environment for your users.

Finally, another method that can be used to improve I/O performance does not involve disks at all. You can use an emulator product that creates an in-memory "disk" volume if you have files that are not very large but are frequently accessed. The time needed to access data that is already in memory is much faster than when accessing from a mechanical device like a disk drive. Here, you also must consider the fact that the CPU will be involved in managing this data, but with a multiple-CPU system this can generally be solved easily.

Summary

This chapter defined ODBC, the technology used to access databases over dissimilar systems. And I explained how they are implemented using an interface that provides a developer or application with functions from an API.

We then took a look at some issues concerning the client/server style of computing. I explained hardware, software, and network issues and gave examples of problems and resolutions for some common issues you might face. We also looked at the database offerings available from the major vendors and Microsoft's SQL Server package and gave you a URL to follow that depicted the scalability features of SQL server.

The discussion of database software continued by looking at the other two major providers: Oracle and IBM. Both vendors' products bring unique and common features for presenting or serving data on various platforms.

Client/server computing has borrowed from the mainframe environment and added its own set of rules as well. You can expect to see technology advancements and changes to this type of computing over the next few years as the dominance of data warehousing and data marts provide companies and organizations with better access to their own and public domain data.

Web Servers

## CHAPTER 31

SOME OF THE MAIN TOPICS IN THIS CHAPTER ARE

Web Server Software—Behind the Scenes

Apache Web Server

Internet Information Server for Windows NT Server 4.0

It's hard to believe that before 1993 there were only about 50 Web servers on the Internet. Today they number in the hundreds of thousands. What started at the European Center for Nuclear Research (CERN) in Geneva in 1989 as a project to link information on the Internet and make it easy to access by research teams, has grown into a technology that is invading business and home computing at an astonishing rate.

Since the Web explosion started, Web servers have played a major role in almost every facet of information delivery. In this chapter, we'll use two popular Web servers, Apache Web Server 1.3.6 and Microsoft's Internet Information Server 4.0, to demonstrate the functions a typical Web server can be expected to perform. We'll also describe some of the common problems associated with operating a Web server on the Internet today.

Web Server Software—Behind the Scenes

Web server software accepts browser requests and retrieves files (normally Web pages) and executes any associated CGI scripts and serves them back to the client. Web pages are created using the Hypertext Markup Language (HTML) and travel across the Internet using the Hypertext Transfer Protocol (HTTP). The Web server runs continuously and listens to a port (usually port 80) on the server machine, and browsers send requests to these ports. Most server software on the market also provides other network service functionality, such as FTP or multimedia services.

The first Web software used a command-line interface; however, as the technology developed, graphics were incorporated. In 1992 the Mosaic browser was developed at the National Center for Supercomputing Applications (NCSA), under the direction of Marc Andreessen. Mosaic was a truly graphical browser. Andreessen went on to help found Netscape and develop the Netscape Navigator browser and, as they say, "the rest is history."

Just as browser software has evolved rapidly these last few years, server software has also grown considerably. New functionality has been added to provide support for new kinds of information, particularly in the multimedia category, and new management tools have been developed. Some server software is even available on the Internet at no cost. Some of the more popular servers on the Internet these days are

- **Apache server**—A freely distributed Web server available at `www.apache.org`. As of this writing, it is estimated that 56 percent of WWW servers are running Apache.

- **Microsoft**—Microsoft's Internet Information Server (IIS) Web server software comes free with its Windows NT operating system.

  The Windows NT Option Pack, available for download, contains components to upgrade it to IIS version 4.0. Microsoft also has a Personal Web server for its Window 9x operating system family downloadable from `www.microsoft.com`.

- **Netscape Enterprise Server**—Netscape's version of its Web server. Netscape and Sun have recently begun an alliance. You can find information about Netscape servers at `www.iplanet.com`.

- **CERN Web Server**—A Web server created and maintained by the World Wide Web Consortium. CERN is freely available from `www.w3.org`.

The Apache Web server has been ported to many different computer system platforms, whereas Internet Information Server is platform specific: Windows NT. In the remainder of this chapter, the installation of both Apache and IIS is covered.

Apache Web Server

One of the first Web servers was httpd 1.3 from NCSA (National Center for Supercomputing Applications). The Apache group was a number of people that had written "patches" for the Web server and eventually took over the project and created the name: "Apache" or "A patchy" Web server.

From the beginning, the Apache group took great pride in developing a stable Web server with performance taking second chair. Still, performance of Apache Web server is quite satisfactory. The Apache Group also maintained focus on configurability. As of this writing, more than 50 percent of all Internet Web sites are sitting on top of Apache.

Where to Obtain Apache

Apache is available for free from www.apache.org and is available for the following operating systems:

- OpenVMS and Digital UNIX
- Linux (most popular)
- Solaris
- Windows (Win32)
- HPUX
- FreeBSD
- Irix
- NetBSD
- Sinix
- SunOS
- AIX
- AUX
- Others

Win32 Installation

The current version of Apache, 1.3, has been tested to work only on Windows NT 4.0 and the binary installer will work only on Intel processors. Apache will run on Windows 95/98 but they haven't undergone the same testing as Windows NT 4.0. Prior to installing Apache, you should install the TCP/IP protocol stack and have a valid IP address.

Note

From the Apache Web site, download the latest release. You will have the option to choose a precompiled version (the .exe extension) or a binary version. Select the executable version unless you plan on customizing your server.

When you run the installer, it will prompt you to enter the directory you would like to install Apache Web server in to (see Figure 31.1). The default path is usually fine.

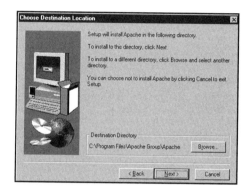

Figure 31.1 Apache 1.3 Installer enables you to select directories.

If you have a prior version of Apache in the default conf directory, the installer will not write over any existing files. The installer will install a corresponding file with an extension of .default. When the installation is complete, you should consider checking the newer conf files to update your older ones.

Choosing Typical from the Installation Type dialog box will install everything but the source code. If you choose Minimal, only the bare minimum will be installed—documentation and source code will not be installed. If you have the space, I recommend selecting Typical.

After the installation is complete, you have the option of starting the Web server as an NT service or as an application. Using the service is recommended if you plan to use Apache as a dedicated Web server. If your intention is to use Apache infrequently, you can start Apache by double-clicking Start Apache console app. This will open a console window and Apache will start within it. This is the only way to run Apache under Windows 95/98. To stop the Apache HTTP daemon, double-click the Shutdown Apache console app.

With NT 4.0, you can choose Install Apache as Service, and Apache will start and be available automatically when NT boots. To easily control the Apache service, you can go to the Services application from within the Control Panel. An alternative way to start and stop the Apache service is to type NET START APACHE and NET STOP APACHE at a command prompt. Also, if you prefer the command line, Table 31.1 shows some other useful Apache commands.

Table 31.1   Apache Commands

Desired Result	Typed Command
To install Apache as service	`apache -I -n service name`
To remove Apache service	`apache - -n service name`
To start apache as a service	`apache -n service name -k start`
To restart apache	`apache -n service name -k restart`
To shut down apache	`apache -n service name -k shutdown`

Note

The default *service name* is Apache unless one is specified.

When Apache is started, it will be listening to port 80 by default. You can change this port in the configuration files. To verify Apache has started, launch your Web browser and type the URL `http://LocalHost/`. The default page should be displayed. If you do not get the default page, look in the `error.log` in the `logs` directory to check for any messages the server may have written. If you are not connected to a network with a Domain Name Service, type `http://127.0.0.1/` in the URL address bar.

Apache Win32 Configuration

Apache enables you to configure many different aspects of the server's operation. To customize your Apache Web server, you will need to edit the configuration files located in the `conf` directory. The default directory for HTML documents to be served by Apache is in the `C:\Program Files\Apache Group\Apache\htdocs\` directory. If you prefer a different directory, open `httpd.conf` in the `conf` directory and scroll down to the `DocumentRoot` directive and change the path to your preferred path. Other important things you can manage using the configuration file include

- The default HTML document to be served in any directory is `index.html`. If you prefer `home.html` or anything else to be the default page in the directory, you will need to modify the `DirectoryIndex` directive.

- Modifying the `ScriptAlias` directive to set the directory to where you want to have your server scripts run from. You will also have to modify the directory tags below the `ScriptAlias` directive to reflect the change you made to the `ScriptAlias` directive.

- The default setting for `ThreadsPerChild` directive is 50. This is the maximum number of connections that Apache will handle at one time. If you expect high utilization, set this number higher.

When you make any changes, you need to restart the Web server. The simplest way is to send a restart signal to the server via the command line. Refer to Table 31.1 for the appropriate command.

Within the `conf` directory, you will see the `access.conf` and the `srm.conf` files. By default, these files are empty. They used to supplement the `httpd.conf` configuration file and are processed during the startup of Apache. If you would like to use these files, you would have to uncomment the `ResourceConfig` and `AccessConfig` directives.

Upgrading Notes

If you are upgrading from a previous version of Apache, you should not have to change anything for Apache to run properly. When Apache is upgraded, all your previous configuration files are preserved and Apache should start without a hitch. It is a good idea, however, to review the newer configuration documentation to learn of any new directives that may be of use to you.

The files that are served to clients by the server software are standard HTML documents. This means that you can easily migrate from another Web server by making sure to maintain the identical directory structure while you move the data over. An easy way to do this would be to back up the server or drive volume to tape and restore just the directory structure to your default HTML directory. However, you should also consider file system incompatibilities. If you're just moving to another machine with the same operating system, you shouldn't have any difficulties.

Troubleshooting Apache Web Server

Unfortunately, because the Apache Web server is a collaborative *open source* effort, there is not one company that is responsible for providing support for the project. However, because Apache is used widely throughout the Internet, there are newsgroups and Web sites devoted to it that can be used to glean troubleshooting information. Nonetheless, just as Linux (also an open source free product) has been adopted by some commercial companies, so has Apache. Thus, for a fee you can obtain support for some configurations.

In addition to the documentation provided on the `Apache.org` Web site, you should periodically review the Frequently Asked Questions (FAQs) for Apache, which is located at `www.apache.org/docs/misc/faq.html`. This evolving document can be used to research common problems that other users have encountered with installing or operating the server.

You can also find the *bug database* for Apache at this site. Here you can review problems reported by other users, any resolution that has been applied, and you can also post your own bug reports for the rest of the community to review.

Checking the Error Log File

One of the first places you can go to when you suspect problems with the server is the error log file, which, by default, is `/usr/local/apache/logs/error_log`. If you do not find it here, check the `conf` configuration file to see whether the ErrorLog directive was used to change the location of the file.

Subscribing to the Email Mailing List

To keep up-to-date with events and problem reporting for the Apache Web server, you can subscribe to the email mailing list for the organization. You can send email to `new-httpd@apache.org` or join the mailing list by visiting the Web site `www.apache.org`.

Internet Information Server for Windows NT Server 4.0

Microsoft's Internet Information Server (IIS) does exactly what every other Web server does; it serves HTML documents. However, Microsoft's Web server offers a Web platform that rivals all others in the industry. By today's standards, just serving Web documents isn't enough. Microsoft puts together a package that comes complete with

- **Internet Information Server (IIS)**—Microsoft's HTTP and Web application server.
- **Transaction Server**—A transaction processing system that processes Web application requests with external applications.
- **Index Server**—A supporting application that indexes the contents and properties of documents on the server on which it resides.
- **Certificate Server**—Manages the issuance, revocation, and renewal of *digital certificates*. Digital certificates are used for public-key cryptography applications such as server and client authentication under the Secure Sockets Layer (SSL).
- **Data Access Components**—Consists of ActiveX Data Objects(ADO), Remote Data Service, and the Microsoft OLE DB provider for ODBC (Open Database Connectivity).
- **Site Server Express**—A smaller version of Microsoft's site server. It includes site analysis and publishing tools.

Microsoft also includes a Management Console application to administer your Web server. You can administer your Web server from any workstation with a Web browser installed. To manage your IIS Web server via a Web browser, the workstation must be in front of any proxy server if you want to use Microsoft's Challenge/Response authentication mechanism.

Installing Microsoft Internet Server (IIS)

Microsoft's Internet Server (IIS) is included with Windows NT 4.0. Version 3.0, however, has been upgraded since the initial release of NT 4.0. The IIS 4.0 server software can be obtained from www.microsoft.com by downloading the Windows NT 4.0 Option Pack. The option pack contains other software, and the download for all the components can take quite some time. You can choose to download only the IIS components if you do not need the functions provided by the other applications.

Before Installing Microsoft Internet Information Server 4.0, you will have to install Service Pack 3 onto your NT Server and Internet Explorer 4.01. If you installed Service Pack 4 for Windows NT, you will get a dialog box that *says* `Windows NT 4.0 SP4 or greater has been detected on your machine. We haven't tested this product on SP4. Do you wish to proceed?` If you do not want to proceed but still would like to have MS Internet Information Server, you can do so with IIS version 3.0 on a Windows NT Server with Service Pack 3 installed. The NetLogon and Computer Browser services must be running. If these services are not running, you will receive an error message that says `Cannot detect OS type`, and the installation will fail.

The Option Pack uses an installer program to install components. You need to simply double-click on the installer and keep the default settings for the directories.

You will be prompted to select the type of install you prefer. If you have the space, choose custom and select the options you would like to have installed.

The next screen will show you the default directories for

- **WWW Service**—This directory is where you will start your HTML directory structure. When you finish the installation and go to your site with a Web browser, the homepage.htm in this directory will be displayed.

- **FTP Service**—FTP access starts at the directory listed in this field and will be the area you have access to when you FTP into your server.

- **Application Installation Point**—This is where the applications associated with IIS 4.0 will be installed.

If you want to change these settings, you can do so now or wait until the installation is complete and change the default directories with the Microsoft Management Console.

If you select to Install Microsoft's Transaction Server, you will be prompted to select a directory to install it in. The default directory is normally fine.

The next screen asks whether you would like to administer the Transaction Server remotely. If so, you need to create an Administrator account and enter a desired password.

If you selected to install Microsoft's Index Server, the next screen will let you choose where your default index directory will be.

The next setup screen tells you where your SMTP (Simple Mail Transport Protocol) will create the mail queue, mailbox, and badmail directories. You can change this if you want.

When the installation is complete, you will be prompted to restart your machine.

Configuring IIS 4.0

After you have installed IIS, you will be able to serve HTML documents immediately. To customize and manage IIS, you use the Microsoft Management Console (MMC).

Start the MMC by clicking on the Internet Services Manager from your Start menu. The application will be under the Windows NT 4.0 Option Pack folder unless you chose to place it elsewhere during the installation or upgrade. You can select either the Management Console application or the HTML version. The HTML version is somewhat slower but provides the same functionality as the Management Console. The HTML Console is useful for administering your Web site remotely. Figure 31.2 shows the MMC version of the IIS MMC snap-in. In this figure, you can see that the console allows you to manage applications using a common interface.

The first toolbar at the top of the console (the MMC toolbar) lists menus that can be used to manage the MMC application itself. For example, you would use this toolbar if you wanted to load another snap-in to manage another application. The second toolbar, which begins with the Action menu, is the Snap-in toolbar; it contains menus that can be used to manage objects that appear in the MMC's two panes which fall under the toolbars. In the pane on the left, you can see the objects that can be managed, the first of which is IIS. In Figure 31.2, this object has been expanded to show the IIS server Popeye—the Web sites that reside on that server appear in the right pane.

The MMC toolbar ——

The Snap-In toolbar ——

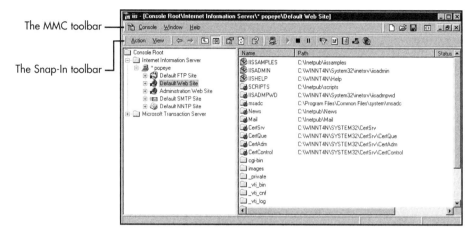

Figure 31.2   The Microsoft Management Console.

Managing Defaults for a Web Site

To manage an object, highlight it, and then click on the Action menu to display its options. For example, for the Default Web Site object shown in Figure 31.2, the possible actions include such options as starting, stopping, or pausing the object. You can also use this menu to create a new object of this type. Another important option available here is the Properties option, which allows you to configure specific properties of the object. Figure 31.3 displays a properties page.

Figure 31.3   The properties page of a Web site can be used to manage many aspects of the site.

The properties page of the Web site object is divided into categories as shown by the tabs on the page. Properties you define here will apply to child objects you create under this object, unless you change the default by modifying the properties page of the child object. The property sheets available for the Web site object include

- **Web Site**—Use this property sheet to manage basic information about the Web site, such as its description, IP address and port, and the number of users that can connect to the server. You can also enable and manage error logging for the site on this tab.

- **Operators**—This property sheet allows you to specify users or user groups that will be granted operator access to the Web site.

- **Performance**—You can use this property sheet to tune the server according to the estimated number of hits you expect to receive on a daily basis and to enable bandwidth throttling (to limit the network bandwidth used by this Web site). This tab is also used to enable HTTP Keep-Alive messages.

- **ISAPI Filters**—This property sheet allows you to install ISAPI filters and determine the order in which they are executed on the Web site.

- **Home Directory**—Here you can specify the home directory for the Web site, which can be on the local machine, another computer, or a redirection to a URL. If the directory is local to the server, you can also control access permissions here. This page also allows you to configure a default application for the Web site.

- **Documents**—Use this property sheet to enable a default document for the Web site and to specify its name.

- **Directory Security**—This property sheet is where you can configure anonymous access, use the Key Manager to receive an SSL certificate for the Web site, and to grant or deny access according to the requestor's IP address or domain name.

- **HTTP Headers**—Information specific to HTTP headers is managed on this property sheet, including parameters such as content expiration, content rating, and MIME mapping.

- **Custom Errors**—This property sheet allows you to customize the error messages associated with specific events that clients will see.

You can use the Action menu to create multiple Web sites that can reside on the same server. By managing the properties of each Web site you create, you can maintain multiple Web sites on the same server, each with different configurations.

Managing Web Site Objects

Under each Web site that you create, you can create objects that are used on the Web site, such as the default page which is presented to clients. To manage an object, highlight it, and then choose an option from the Action menu. Remember that the options available from this menu will depend on the object selected. The most useful selection, again, is Properties, which you can use to manage specific aspects of the object. In Figure 31.4, you can see the properties page for the default object (`default.asp`).

As you can see, some of the property sheets, such as Custom Errors, allow you to manage properties for this object, which are also established, as defaults, for the Web site as a whole. If this object needs to have a different value for a property than the default for the Web site, you can change it here.

Figure 31.4 The properties page for the default object for the Web site.

For example, you can use the File property sheet to specify the file that is used for this default page. You can specify whether the file is local to the server on another networked computer or is a redirection to a URL; this is similar to specifying the Web site object property. You can also manage access permissions for the file, if it is local.

For each page you create for the Web site, you can modify properties using MMC. You can exercise overall control or attend to the basics for each object by arranging the Web site in a hierarchical fashion and defining defaults for the Web site. You can do all this and still manage child objects individually.

Troubleshooting IIS 4.0

IIS 4.0 is a complex product. It provides far more than a simple HTTP Web server, which makes it difficult to troubleshoot at times. However, the operating system provides an error-logging facility, and you can access information about application event errors, security events, and system events by using the Event Viewer tool found in the Administrative Tools folder. This is probably the first place to start when trying to determine the cause of a problem with IIS.

IIS Error Logs

IIS 4.0 enables you to manage error logs by using the properties page for a Web site. You can choose from three formats for the log files that are kept:

- WC3 extended log file format
- NCSA common log file format
- ODBC logging

The first two are compatible with many applications you will find available that can be used to analyze Web site usage and other data. The ODBC option allows you to send the log file information to an SQL database so that you can easily manipulate the information to produce reports on a regular basis or to quickly drill down to specific information when troubleshooting.

The default directory for log files is `%WinDir%\System32\LogFiles`, but you can change this on the properties page if you want to locate the log files elsewhere.

You should regularly review the log files that Windows NT keeps until you become familiar with the ordinary informational messages that may appear. When looking for problems with IIS, be sure to check all three log files. IIS works tightly with the operating system.

For example, suppose you have just set up a new Web site and, after copying the site's content to the proper directories, clients receive error messages denying access when they try to go to your Web site. You look in the properties pages for the particular documents that they are failing with and find that there are no restrictions that should be keeping them out. A quick check in the Event Viewer, however, reveals that the files you copied to the document directories for your site have NTFS permissions that restrict access more so than the IIS restrictions. You can now quickly resolve the problem by changing the NTFS permissions for the affected files.

IIS Exception Monitor

Another tool that Microsoft has developed is the IIS Exception Monitor. You can download this application from Microsoft's Web site. The Exception Monitor is an advanced tool that can be used in many ways, from analyzing the log files to monitoring and collecting data while the server runs. If you are experiencing frequent problems with IIS, downloading and using the Exception Monitor would be a good idea. The tool begins with a wizard that you can use to walk through the process.

Summary

A technology that started out as a tool to provide research teams with quick access to information has grown into what will perhaps be seen as one of the most significant advancements in communications made during the 20th century. For a business to survive in the next few years, it will most likely have to concentrate on creating a Web presence, both to entice new customers and to hold on to existing customers.

There are many WWW server products on the market from which you can choose. Some are simple applications that can be used to create and present simple Web pages for ordinary users. More advance products, such as the Apache and Microsoft Web servers discussed in this chapter, can be used to create robust Web sites for business.

Other Client/Server Applications

CHAPTER 32

Chapter 30, "Database Systems," examined several of the more popular database products and issues dealing with performance and troubleshooting for client/server databases. This chapter looks into some other client/server applications that are in widespread use today. Client/server applications are not limited to just database access. For example, Microsoft's System Management Server (SMS) is a collection of tools that can help automate and simplify many mundane tasks that the network administrator usually performs manually. Other client/server products, such as SAP3, can be used to model the business environment to create distributed applications.

This chapter examines a few of the more popular client/server packages in use today, as well as relatively new technologies such as thin-client computing.

SAP R/3

SAP R/3 is made up of a group of sophisticated modules that can be used to implement standard business processes. These modules are available to developers through an API known as the Business Application Programming Interface (BAPI). By using BAPI, developers can work with a familiar object-oriented approach to SAP.

SAP R/3 consists of the following components:

- **SAP R/3 Financials**—This integrated suite of application components enables you to handle accounting, investment management, and enterprise controlling.

- **SAP R/3 Logistics**—Under this title, you'll find modules for sales and distribution, materials management, plant maintenance, and quality management.

- **SAP R/3 Human Resources**—You will find all your human resource needs here with payroll, time management, reporting capabilities, and more.

SAP R/3 Financials

SAP's Financials components are fully compliant with the accounting industry's GAAP and IAS standards. They also offer support for the EURO. The following modules are included in the Financials group of components:

- General Ledger
- Accounts Receivable
- Accounts Payable
- Fixed Asset Accounting
- Legal Consolidation

Also included are modules that deal with investment management and treasury management.

SAP provides an easy way for you to deploy the system on your network by using *Accelerated*SAP. This process allows a rapid deployment of your SAP system that gets you up and running in a minimal amount of time. *Accelerated*SAP uses a roadmap approach to implementation. The following steps are outlined in the roadmap:

1. **Project preparation**—During the project preparation phase, you gather your resources and key personnel to ensure a smooth implementation by getting everyone on board.

2. **Business blueprint**—In the business blueprint phase, you document the requirements of your business according to its practices and rules. The blueprint created is used as a visual guideline to help keep you on track.

3. **Realization**—In the realization phase, you use the blueprint as a model to configure the SAP system.

4. **Final preparation**—In the final preparation phase, you test and train staff members on the system.

5. **Go live and support**—In the go live and support phase, the SAP system is brought into production use in the business.

Tuxedo

The Tuxedo product provides a framework for developing distributed applications. Tuxedo helps simplify the process of developing these applications by hiding some of the complexities normally involved in a large-scale application development project.

The following are some of the programming methods supported by Tuxedo:

- Remote procedure calls (RPCs)
- Connection-oriented processing
- Reliable queuing
- Event queuing

Tuxedo uses a domain model to ease the administration of the distributed application. In this way, each business segment or collection of applications can be administered separately. In Tuxedo, the domain is capable of operating across different departments—even those spanning the globe—and can even be distributed among different companies.

Gateways are used to allow communication between multiple domains, and the BEA Connect gateway can be used to provide connectivity between Tuxedo and other transaction-processing gateways.

Programming Tuxedo

By using familiar programming tools such as C++ and COBOL, you develop your application by using the component method. You write each process as a separate component that is run in the Tuxedo environment.

Tuxedo uses the three-tier development architecture for application development by separating the processes into the User, Business, and Data Layers. Tuxedo provides the central point of location for your business objects.

PowerBuilder

PowerBuilder is a tool for developing client/server and distributed computing applications. It is designed to run on and develop for multiple platforms. If you are developing an application that needs access to a database, PowerBuilder provides support for ODBC, JDBC, and direct database connectivity.

PowerBuilder applications are built on objects, which are listed in Table 32.1.

Table 32.1   PowerBuilder Objects

Object	Purpose
Application	This is actually an entry point into the application
Window	The user interface
Data Window	Retrieves data from a data source
Menu	Commands selectable by the user
Global Function	Performs generic processing
Query	SQL statements for retrieving data
Structure	Group of related variables
User object	Control or set of controls
Library	Stores PowerBuilder objects
Project	The package used for application distribution

Application Object

As mentioned in Table 32.1, the Application object is the entry point into the application. This object defines the application behavior, such as the fonts used and any startup or shutdown functionality of the application.

Window Objects

As the user interface, the Window object is one of the most important objects for design considerations. This is the object that the users of your application interact with. The Window object is identical to any Windows application: It contains properties dealing with its appearance and has controls and events.

Data Window Object

The Data Window object is used to retrieve data from the data source. You can design your data window with the functionality needed to modify the data. You can also apply formatting to this window by using various text fields and pictures that are tied or linked to certain fields within the database.

Menus

Like most applications, menus provide a means of interaction to the user. By placing the commands and functions on menus, you give the user a much easier method of determining the functionality and capabilities of your application.

Global Functions

You can use two types of functions under PowerBuilder: Global and Object-Level. As you can likely determine from the name, a Global function does not pertain specifically to an object or component within the application. Instead, it is used for general-purpose procedures that must be accessed by all portions of the application.

In contrast, an Object-Level function is designed to work with or on a specific object.

Queries

You use queries to retrieve data from the data source. The most common way of doing this is by formulating SQL statements. SQL statements are based on a set of keywords and structures that provide the necessary instructions to a database for retrieving a specific set of data from the database. The following is an example of a SQL query:

```
SELECT * FROM Customers WHERE Sales = "Tires"
```

By issuing this request to the database, you are saying "Show me all records in the Customers table that have the term Tires in the Sales table."

Of course, this is only a simple SQL statement. They can become quite complex, based on the requirements or data you might have stored.

Structures

The Structure object borrows its name and functionality from a C language component. C programmers are familiar with what is known as a STRUCT, which is short for structure. They both mean the same thing.

Essentially, a *structure* is related information grouped into one component and referenced by a single name. An example would be a structure with the name Employee. You can group related information such as ID, Pay Rate, Department, and so on under the Employee structure.

User Objects

User objects can be controls set up to have the same functionality. In this way, if you are using the same feature over and over again, you can define a user object based on that feature. This enables you to use that feature or object over and over again.

Libraries

Libraries under PowerBuilder are stored as PBL files. These libraries contain components such as menus, windows, and other objects. Your application can access these objects by referencing and using the libraries.

Projects

A project is the collection of files, components, and libraries that your application uses to perform its tasks. When you are designing and building your application, you are using a project file. Your projects can be used to create executable applications, dynamic link libraries (DLLs), or other components such as Java classes.

PowerBuilder's Environment

PowerBuilder uses the term *Painter* to describe the tool used to create a user interface. When you create a window, you use the Window Painter.

After you create the window, you are free to add the necessary controls that the user will interact with. You can use text boxes for entering and displaying textual data, and you can use command buttons to allow the user to execute procedures or functions.

PowerBuilder is a complex development tool that requires its own tutorials and manuals to describe its functionality and use. The goal here is simply to introduce the tool. For more information about PowerBuilder, visit the Sybase Web site at

```
http://www.powersite.com/products/powerbuilder
```

Microsoft Transaction Server (MTS)

Microsoft Transaction Server (MTS) is Microsoft's entry into the transaction processing arena. It is used by developers to create and deploy scalable, high-performance applications for use on intranets, the Internet, and enterprise computing platforms.

MTS is responsible for monitoring the components that are running in an application. It helps to ensure that processes don't fail.

At its root, MTS keeps an eye on all the changes made to the data in a database. After all changes are made successfully, MTS allows the transaction to update the database. Until this time, all transactions or modifications can be rolled back to their original state, preventing data corruption.

Take a look at a bank's ATM machine for a good example of why you want to implement this. Suppose you are in the process of withdrawing a substantial amount of money from your account. You have entered your PIN number, chosen the withdrawal option, and selected the account, and your hand is poised at the cash drawer waiting for the money to slide out. Suddenly, there is a power failure, the ATM machine halts, and you find yourself without the cash you expected. What has happened to your money? Was it deducted from your account? Hopefully not, because you never actually received it. How can you prove to the bank that you were in the middle of the transaction? Your receipt didn't even print.

This is where the benefit of a transaction processing system comes into play and how MTS can help you ensure the integrity of your data. The bank transaction never completed successfully, so the original records maintained in the database were never actually updated. All transactions took place within a temporary environment.

MTS is capable of working with components in an enterprise-networking environment or over the Internet.

The MTS architecture is made up of the following elements:

- **ActiveX components**—Transaction Server application components are in-process DLL servers. They are ActiveX controls, so they can be developed by any language or tool that supports ActiveX technology, such as Visual Basic, Visual C++, and Visual J++.

- **Transaction Server Executive**—This is actually a DLL that provides the runtime services for the components. The Executive runs transparently in the background and manages process threads, which perform the actual processing chores for the application.

- **Resource managers (RMs)**—Server applications use resource managers to maintain items such as pending orders and inventory. SQL Server is an example of a resource manager.

- **Resource dispensers**—Manage the nondurable state of the data. The ODBC Resource Dispenser manages pools of database connections. The Shared Property Manager is used to provide synchronized access to variables, such as a hit counter for a Web page or cached data.

- **Distribution Transaction Coordinator (DTC)**—Provides coordination of transactions across multiple resource managers. DTC uses a two-phase commit protocol to ensure the outcome of the transaction and to make it consistent across all resource managers.

- **Transaction Server Explorer**—A GUI-based administration tool.

Microsoft Systems Management Server (SMS)

What is SMS? Better yet, what could you use SMS for? If you are reading this book, you are obviously interested in either setting up a network or looking to expand the network you already have. In today's business place, managing users, applications, workstations, and other components that make up the network can be a complicated task. SMS is not a tool for developing client/server applications. Instead, it is a client/server tool that can be used to help automate many of the tasks the busy network administrator performs, from distributing new applications to inventorying existing applications and hardware components.

SMS can assist you with the following functions:

- Central management of hardware and software
- Centralized software distribution
- Management of shared applications
- Conducting network protocol analyzing
- Remote troubleshooting
- Remote control of PCs

Central Management of Hardware and Software

This part of SMS is a great time-saving feature. It enables administrators to find out what software packages are installed throughout the organization. SMS can also query workstations on the network to get information on things such as the amount of free space on disk drives and types of hardware components installed. This relieves the administrator of the manual task of visiting each machine in person to create a listing of the components.

Centralized Software Distribution

This feature makes upgrading software over the network a snap. It also reduces the cost of upgrading software by enabling the administrator to perform the upgrades from the network rather than making a trip to each workstation. Instead, packages are created that perform the installation automatically.

Management of Shared Applications

This enables you to maintain control over shared applications on servers. It also enables you to run these applications from anywhere on the network.

Conducting Network Protocol Analyzing

By utilizing this feature, you can watch the network and determine where any bottlenecks exist. This time-saving tool helps increase productivity by enabling you to make the necessary changes to the network to prevent and correct these bottlenecks.

Remote Troubleshooting

By using the hardware and software inventory database created by SMS, you can troubleshoot network and application problems much more easily.

Remote Control of PCs

If you need to perform troubleshooting at the PC level, SMS enables you to take control of the mouse and keyboard on Windows and MS-DOS PCs. This not only has advantages for troubleshooting but also enables you to offer some training for users by taking control of their keyboard and mouse and showing them the procedures or steps necessary to perform an action.

SMS provides support for the following operating systems and networks:

- Windows NT Server
- Novell NetWare
- Microsoft LAN Manager
- PATHWORKS by Digital Equipment Corporation (now owned by Compaq Computer Corporation)

SMS is capable of functioning over TCP/IP, SNA, X.25, ISDN, and Asynchronous WAN protocols. It also supports the following client operating systems:

- MS-DOS version 5.0 and later
- Microsoft Windows 3.1 and later
- Microsoft Windows for Workgroups 3.11

- Microsoft Windows NT version 3.1 and later
- IBM OS/2 versions 1.x and 2.x
- Apple Macintosh System 7

Deploying Applications Using SMS

What types of applications can you deploy with SMS? Essentially, you can distribute commercial applications (if you have the necessary licensing), custom applications, and data files. You can perform tasks such as data or file backups and run antivirus software. The client computer must be listed in the SMS database before it can be the target of the SMS software.

You use the SMS Server Installer, an add-on pack, to create a distribution package. You can use this tool to ensure that each desktop is consistent. The Server Manager Installer has four main features:

- Software installation recording
- Software removal
- Software upgrading
- Script editor

Software Installation Recording

Also known as repackaging, this feature enables the administrator to create a base installation on one computer as a reference and then duplicate the installation on other computers.

Software Removal

Software removal is known as a rollback feature. Using this feature completely removes an application, including all files and registry entries. It replaces the original registry keys as they were before the installation.

Note that this feature can be used only to remove applications that were installed with the SMS Server Installer.

Software Upgrading

This feature enables the administrator to upgrade existing applications by adding files or patching files to create an updated application.

Script Editor

As you can guess from the name, the Script Editor is used to create or edit installation scripts.

Remote Control and Diagnostics

The remote control and diagnostics capabilities of SMS are a powerful feature. Table 32.2 lists the diagnostic utilities to give you an idea of their capabilities.

Table 32.2   SMS Diagnostic Utilities

Utility	Operating System	Description
CMOS Info	MS-DOS and Windows	Displays the client's CMOS info relevant at start-up.
Device Drivers	MS-DOS and Windows	Used to determine which drivers are loaded.
Interrupt Vectors	MS-DOS and Windows	Used to determine the IRQs being used by hardware devices and to see whether there are any conflicts.
DOS Memory	MS-DOS and Windows	Shows applications that are loaded in upper and lower memory. Also used to check the amount of free memory available.
Ping	MS-DOS and Windows	Used to verify connectivity between the client and server. Note that this is not the same as the TCP/IP PING utility.
Windows Memory	Windows	Displays memory allocation on the client and is used to determine the cause of out-of-memory errors.
Windows Modules	Windows	Displays all loaded modules on the client, including drivers and DLLs.
Windows Tasks	Windows	Shows all open tasks that appear in the task list.
Windows Classes	Windows	Determines the Windows classes currently in use.
Global Heap	Windows	Displays all the free memory available to applications.
GDI Heap	Windows	Displays the memory available for the graphical device interface (GDI).
OS Version	Windows NT	Displays the version, installation date, and build number of the OS.
Services	Windows NT	Displays installed services and their status (running or stopped).
DMA/Memory	Windows NT	Lists information on DMA memory for ports and channels.
Hardware	Windows NT	Displays BIOS and CPU information.
Devices	Windows NT	Lists the channel, port, and IRQ information for installed devices.
Network	Windows NT	Lists protocols, settings, and statistics of the network.
Drivers	Windows NT	Displays device drivers and their statuses.
I/O Port Status	Windows NT	Lists interrupt and port information.

As you can see, SMS is quite an extensive package and offers more features and functionality than can be described in one section or even one chapter. It can be a very valuable management tool in a large network environment. However, the benefits do not come without a cost. Because of its complexity and the many functions that can be performed using SMS, an administrator might need considerable training in its use.

Programming for Client/Server Systems

Developers who want to program for the client/server environment must be aware of the constant and rapid changes that are part of it. A client/server programming model can be broken down into services. You might have heard the terms two-tier, three-tier, or *n*-tier. The most common of these, found in the client/server environment, is the three-tier model, which places services into three levels (tiers):

- User Services
- Business Services
- Data Services

By using this approach to developing for the client/server network, you can break your development tasks down into groups. Each group of developers would be responsible for writing the code that pertains to its service.

User Services

This is the actual interface with which a user interacts. User Services are normally set up as an actual executable program. This program would reside on the client, the user's workstation.

To design an effective application at this level, you must take a few things into consideration. The first and foremost consideration is how the users perform their tasks under the current system. By ensuring that your application mimics as closely as possible this environment, you can reduce the learning curve and prevent or reduce any productivity lost due to retraining or users not understanding the interface.

If the present methods are paper based, you should use any forms as a basis for your electronic representation. This provides the user with a familiar interface.

Business Services

Business Services are also known as "middle-tier" services. This is the layer that responds to the user requests from the User Services Layer. This layer will execute business tasks by using a set of guidelines that are normally set up as formal procedures or business rules.

This layer communicates directly with the database server. In doing so, it means that the user does not need to access the database server and be familiar with its syntax or rules of operation.

You will find that the Business Services Layer is dynamic. There will often be requirements for changing the business rules or methods used within these services.

As a result of the dynamic nature of this layer, a components approach to development will save time in the long run. By implementing your services as components or ActiveX controls, you are allowing yourself the ability to incorporate changes into these services without affecting the interface at the user level.

If you are familiar with ActiveX controls, you will understand the concept with ease. If you are new to this technology or are just embracing it, I'll explain how it makes life easier for a developer.

Earlier forms of programming dealt with incorporating the entire functionality into the whole application. When a change in the way the application was used required changes in the actual application, the developer had to rewrite the sections of the code that pertained to the specific function needing change as well as the user interface or its methods of accessing these functions.

By developing dynamic portions of your application using the ActiveX or component scheme, you can prevent a lot of changes later. When you access the functions that are exported by an ActiveX control or component, you don't need to concern yourself or other programmers with details on how the functions are implemented or handled within the component. You just need to know how to call these functions.

In this way, when changes to the functionality are needed, you simply make the changes within the component. The access methods don't change.

Data Services

This is where the actual data is maintained and updated. The Data Services are also responsible for dealing with the Business Services and satisfying the requests for data. You will find these services residing on the server where the database is located.

Although these three services form the basis for communication with the client/server application, note that each of these services should be capable of communicating with each other. There is no requirement for information to flow from user to business to data and back again. A User Service component can and should be able to communicate with the Data Services if it needs to, effectively bypassing the Business Services.

Distributed Processing Techniques

To implement distributed processing, you must be aware of the requirements that arise from this type of computing. The following list of requirements provide for a good client/server development environment:

- Maintainability
- Location independence
- Application management
- Resource usage
- Legacy support

Maintainability

When using a distributed application, the whole process is typically used for a long time due to the time and money invested. For this reason, your application should be capable of being updated easily as required. During the use of the application, you will often find new ways to do the same task, or perhaps some of the procedures change.

By building your application on reusable components, you provide that maintainability. As a procedure or business rule changes, you can easily adapt by making the necessary amendments to the required components only. The user interface or data will not necessarily need to be updated.

Location Independence

When designing your distributed solution, an area that you should pay close attention to is allowing your components to operate independent of their physical location.

The separation of your User, Business, and Data Services should be logically based and not physical. In this way, you can take advantage of hardware investments by being able to place the Business Services on either the server or client machine. Another possibility might be to move a component to its own hardware platform, allowing optimized performance.

If this is your goal, you want to make sure that the separation should have little or no impact on the remaining components.

Application Management

You must put into place the ability to maintain the system. This includes enabling certain users to check the status of applications.

Resource Usage

This can be a Catch-22. You must ensure that your application takes advantage of the available resources, but you don't want to choke a system and prevent the ability to expand and add users later. You can prevent this from happening by providing a scalable solution.

Legacy Support

When designing your solution, you might have to take into consideration any existing systems that are in place. Your organization might not want to throw out its existing hardware and replace it with new PCs just to support a new application. Consider the slowest or oldest clients that will be accessing the system and design the user services application accordingly.

If you have an environment in which all the existing systems are old, you might need to look at placing the business services on the server or a dedicated platform.

By using the tools and applications discussed thus far in this chapter, you can resolve these issues and create a truly distributed application that takes advantage of existing and new resources, provides a gentle learning curve to the users, and maintains the integrity of the data.

Distributed processing is a huge undertaking, and I certainly don't pretend to have all the answers. Each organization will have its own set of rules or requirements, which should be used as the groundwork or foundation for the design.

Take a look at some case studies to gain a better understanding of how others have implemented their solutions. They might not be the same needs as yours, but they can still provide a good insight to the process.

Another good source of information is Distributed Computing Online. Visit its Web site: http://www.distributedcomputing.com.

Troubleshooting Client/Server Applications

To troubleshoot a client/sever application, you must determine which particular aspect is causing the suspected problem. You effectively break it down into three groups:

- Client software
- Connectivity
- Database

Client Software

This is actually one area in which troubleshooting should be a major factor simply because most user interfaces, as mentioned earlier, are complete executable applications unto themselves. For this reason, their internal functionality will never change unless the original developer rewrites the code to optimize performance or fix any bugs. If this is the case, then troubleshooting is essentially done by the developer or by the developer and a test user.

Looking at the Business Services side of things, you can again make assumptions that the components have been tested. When they have been implemented and are working, you will not see a change in the functionality here, either.

Connectivity

This is the area in which most of your problems are likely to occur. You can run into physical connection problems, protocol issues, and bandwidth problems.

The first indication that there might be network or connectivity issues will come from the users telling you that they are receiving a message indicating that they cannot connect to the server. If you run into this type of scenario, you can take several steps to resolve the problems:

1. Verify that there is a physical connection. You will need to look at the network cabling to ensure that it is intact and is actually plugged in to the client machine and the hub. You might also need to use cable testers to verify that the cable is good.

2. Verify that the server is online. This might sound like a simple step, but all too often, connectivity issues arise from the fact that the server was not running. A good example of this is a situation in which an administrator using a Windows NT machine has the Recovery Options set to not reboot the server during a crash. In this case, the server displays the "blue screen of death" (BSOD) and does not allow any connections to the server.

3. If you are running on a TCP/IP network, you can use utilities such as PING and Traceroute to verify the connections.

Troubleshooting network connectivity problems should be done at several levels: from the higher-level protocols used on the network (such as TCP/IP) to the low-level hardware itself (such as cables and network adapters). Chapter 2, "Tools," can give you a good start toward learning about tools that can be used to troubleshoot network cabling, as well as utilities such as SNMP and RMON that can be used to gather information about many different aspects of network operations. Chapter 4, "Network Interface Cards," can assist you in diagnosing problems with workstation or server NICs. Chapter 18, "TCP/IP," Chapter 19, "IPX/SPX," and Chapter 20, "NetBIOS and NetBEUI," can be helpful in solving problems associated with higher-level protocols.

Database

You can run into some problems with your application on the database end as well. Make sure you implement good database administration techniques and perform regular backups. Chapter 30, "Database Systems," discusses several things that can be helpful in diagnosing problems or performance issues involving database products. It also discusses proactive techniques, such as using a fault-tolerant RAID disk subsystem to help minimize downtime caused by failed components.

Because of the large and complex nature of distributed computing, you will no doubt encounter problems sooner rather than later. By maintaining good records, network diagrams, and documentation of the processes and flow of information, you can narrow down the search to the specific areas causing the problem.

Using "Thin" Clients

What are thin clients? Some consider them to be the network computer (NC). The NC is heavily promoted by Oracle and Sun and relies a lot on Java. In reality, a *thin client* is really a computer that does not contain a large amount of computing power, but instead relies on a server to do most of the processing. An example of this is Windows NT Terminal Server Edition.

A thin client merely acts as a terminal, and each keystroke and mouse click is sent over the network to the server where it is interpreted and processed. The server merely sends any requested data, including the screen refresh instructions, back over the network to the client.

When you set up this type of scenario using a fast server and a fast client, you can see that the main bottleneck will be the network itself. If you intend to use multiple thin clients, ensure that the network bandwidth is sufficient to support the data exchanges that take place in this kind of computing environment.

One of the biggest advantages that thin clients bring to an organization is reduced cost of ownership because of the lower initial costs for hardware when compared with purchasing a PC. Another advantage is reduced support requirements. Your support staff can concentrate most of their troubleshooting efforts on the server rather than on the simple client.

Thin client computing also increases the costs of equipment for servers because it requires larger, faster, and more powerful hardware. Some organizations feel that is an even trade-off in the savings on the client side.

Two major players in the software aspect of thin computing are Microsoft and Citrix. Microsoft provides a thin client OS in its Windows CE operating system. Microsoft also provides server-side support with the introduction of Terminal Server. Citrix brings its Metaframe software to market for this type of environment as well. The technology behind Terminal Server is actually licensed from Citrix Systems. For a thin client to access Terminal Server, it must use the CE OS or go through the Citrix Metaframe gateway.

Network Computing Devices (NCD) has released a thin client designed to take advantage of Terminal Server. Its model 200 runs on a RISC processor and the Windows CE OS, whereas the 300 model uses an Intel processor and CE. ThinPATH software and ThinPATH Windows Based Terminals (WBTs) are available for the Windows NT Terminal Server environment. They also provide software and terminals for the X Window environment on the UNIX platform as well as Java-based NCs.

In addition to network bandwidth problems, one other caveat to thin client computing should come to mind almost immediately: Relying on a central server means that it becomes a single point of failure. If the server fails, or if a network problem prevents clients from accessing the server, the thin clients are out of business until the problem is solved. This situation can also occur using regular workstation clients accessing a database server. However, in that case the users of a PC or workstation can still perform other tasks that are not dependent on the database server. The thin client relies on the central server for everything but its input and display capabilities and cannot operate without the server.

For this reason, it might not be wise to use thin clients for mission-critical applications. Also, servers for these clients should be constructed to minimize downtime, using such techniques as clustering and fault-tolerant disk subsystems (RAID).

Whether thin-client computing will become a major player in networks remains to be seen. At this time, the technology can help reduce costs by enabling you to use older hardware platforms that would be impractical or too expensive to upgrade for today's operating systems or applications. However, as it becomes possible to pack more and more into today's silicon real estate, there might come a time when stamping out a new client computer is so inexpensive that they will be cheaper to replace than today's models, effectively rendering a thin client a relic of the past.

Summary

The client/server computing model has been around for quite some time and has been successfully used to create a large number of distributed network applications. This is not limited to just database access products. Indeed, although Microsoft's SMS uses the SQL server, it goes beyond database processing and helps the network administrator manage and deploy users, hardware, and applications. Products such as SAP3 can be valuable tools for managing many different areas of the enterprise. Twenty years ago, PCs were mostly standalone machines that were used to automate many of the jobs a typical user performed at his or her desk, such as word processing. Today, the networked environment is the preferred method of business computing, and client/server applications that use resources throughout the network are more the norm.

The next two chapters examine some of the technologies used to access or tie together network components.

Part XII

TROUBLESHOOTING INTERNET CONNECTIONS

Dial-Up Connections

SOME OF THE MAIN TOPICS IN THIS CHAPTER ARE

PPP/SLIP

Windows 95/98 and Windows NT Dial-Up Networking

Server-Side Connections

Linux Dial-Up Connections

ISDN

ADSL

Cable Modems

Using Modem Pools

General Troubleshooting Tips

CHAPTER 33

PPP/SLIP

Anyone who uses a modem to connect to the Internet can access any resource available on the World Wide Web because of the SLIP and PPP protocols. Simply put, these protocols transform your standalone PC into an Internet workstation for the duration of your telephone call. You can surf the Web with a browser, use FTP to maintain a Web site, access newsgroups, and perform any other Internet task because PPP/SLIP allows your machine to mimic the behavior of a computer that connects to the Internet via a network.

The original version, SLIP (Serial Line Internet Protocol), became popular despite many flaws (a lack of support for protocols other than TCP/IP, differences in implementation, and the requirement that both ends be preconfigured). This made SLIP suitable for fixed-location workstations (your home computer dialing in from the same number every time), but not suitable for roving use, either from different shared machines or from a notebook computer. The addition of PPP (Point-to-Point Protocol) provides for dynamic allocation of IP addresses, authentication of the user, and other features that have made it easier to manage the explosive growth of Internet users. Imagine if every computer that you'd ever want to use on the Internet required its own, exclusive, IP address! The widespread use of Dynamic Host Control Protocol (DHCP) for IP address allocations makes this unnecessary.

Logon Script Files

If your dial-up connection is preconfigured by an Internet service provider (ISP), you might never need to look at a logon script file. However, some services might require you to create a logon script file or to modify a predefined one if you change usernames or passwords. Typically, if you are using Windows 95, 98, or NT 4, you will not need to create a text-based logon script. With other operating systems, you might need to. However, regardless of whether you need to create a logon script manually, any dial-up networking logon has the same basic elements:

- The telephone number you call
- Username
- Password
- IP configuration information (IP address, server type)
- Other network configuration information (other protocols and settings)

Whereas a Linux-based system might require the user to create a script from scratch using a text editor (a good example of such a script is available at `http://www.clug.org/minutes/ppptalk.html`), the Dial-Up Networking wizard used with Windows 9x creates a logon script from menu configuration options, as you will see in detail in the following text.

This information must be supplied, either as part of a network logon script or manually by the user, depending on the connection type or the security needs of the user. If multiple users will share a single machine, it would be better to set up the logon to ask for the username and password each time.

Analyzing Log Files

Most dial-up systems enable logging of dial-up sessions. These log files can be useful for troubleshooting. For example, the Linux pppd program saves all warnings and error messages to the syslog facility. Normally, this information is discarded, but it can be saved for analysis. Create a file called /etc/syslog.conf, and make sure it contains the following line:

```
daemon.*     /tmp/ppp-log
```

This will transfer these messages to the ppp-log file stored in the /tmp folder. This redirection command should be removed after things are working correctly because the file is appended with each new dial-up session.

A Windows 9x log file for a PPP session can be created by adjusting the properties for the Dial-Up Adapter in the Network section of the Control Panel. Select Properties, Advanced, and change the option for Record a Log File to Yes. The PPPLOG.TXT file is stored in the \Windows folder and records activity for all your dial-up connections.

PPPLOG.TXT Examples

The following section lists a few examples from PPPLOG.TXT. For more details about interpreting the contents of this file, see Microsoft Support document #Q156435, available from www.microsoft.com/support. Because each dial-up networking session appends its results to PPPLOG.TXT, you should periodically delete this file or disable its creation to avoid creating a very large file.

In PPPLOG.TXT, the following abbreviations are used for the major network protocols:

- **NBFCP**—NetBEUI
- **IPCP**—TCP/IP
- **IPX/CP**—Novell IPX

If DUN is being used to set up a NetBEUI-only connection (NBFCP), the PPPLOG.TXT file will indicate that the IP Control Protocol (IPCP) and IPX Protocol (IPXCP) are being skipped:

```
FSA : Adding Control Protocol 803f (NBFCP) to control protocol chain.

FSA : Protocol disabled by user — skipping control protocol 8021 (IPCP).

FSA : Protocol disabled by user — skipping control protocol 802b (IPXCP).
```

If all three protocols are listed as disabled by user, the connection will fail. At least one of these three protocols must be bound to the dial-up adapter.

If DUN is being used to set up a connection to an ISP, the PPPLOG.TXT file will indicate the following:

```
IPCP : Layer started.

IPCP : IP address is 0.
```

Later in the `PPPLOG.TXT` file, you'll see references to changes in IP address and often DNS entries. This information is listed in hexadecimal number format rather than the more "friendly" decimal numbers used to enter these numbers into the TCP/IP configuration screen:

```
IPCP : Received and accepted IP address of d0cae50b.
```

Other abbreviations found in `PPPLOG.TXT` include the following:

- **LCP (Link Control Protocol)**—Used to establish the operational parameters for link-layer control of the connection, user authentication (see next section) and the shutdown of the connection

- **FSA (Finite State Automation)**—Controls the process of adding or skipping the control protocols required by the connection

- **CHAP (Challenge-Handshake Authentication Protocol)**—A more secure authentication method than PAP

- **PAP (Password Authentication Protocol)**

- **ND (no description)**—The Shiva-PAP (SPAP), used with Shiva network devices only

The end of the `PPPLOG.TXT` records statistics about the connection. A large number of CRC or other errors indicates a possible problem with line noise or poor-quality telephone or serial cables. Because lower-speed connections often result from noisy lines, create and view `MODEMLOG.TXT` (see the following section) for more information about the modem-hardware part of your dial-up session.

Using *MODEMLOG.TXT*

An additional log file that will be useful to Windows users of dial-up networking is the `MODEMLOG.TXT` file, also stored in the default Windows folder. This file is created by selecting Record a Log File in the Advanced Configuration Settings for the modem in use. Use `MODEMLOG.TXT` to verify which modem type is in use, what initialization strings it uses, what `.INF` file it uses, what telephone number it uses, and the connection speeds and compression types the connection uses. Because both `MODEMLOG.TXT` and `PPPLOG.TXT` date and timestamp each line of their logs, you can correlate the files if necessary to troubleshoot a connection problem.

The beginning of a typical `MODEMLOG. TXT` is shown here.

```
08-19-1999 14:24:27.02 - Cardinal-336 Internal #2 in use.
08-19-1999 14:24:27.02 - Modem type: Cardinal-336 Internal
08-19-1999 14:24:27.02 - Modem inf path: CARDIN~1.INF
08-19-1999 14:24:27.02 - Modem inf section: MVPV34I
08-19-1999 14:24:27.24 - 115200,N,8,1
08-19-1999 14:24:27.47 - 115200,N,8,1
08-19-1999 14:24:27.48 - Initializing modem.
08-19-1999 14:24:27.48 - Send: AT<cr>
08-19-1999 14:24:27.48 - Recv: <cr><lf>OK<cr><lf>
08-19-1999 14:24:27.48 - Interpreted response: Ok
08-19-1999 14:24:27.48 - Send: AT &F &C1  S95=47 W2 S0=0<cr>
08-19-1999 14:24:27.49 - Recv: <cr><lf>OK<cr><lf>
08-19-1999 14:24:27.49 - Interpreted response: Ok
08-19-1999 14:24:27.49 - Send: ATS7=60S30=0L0M1\N4%C3&K3B0N1X4<cr>
```

```
08-19-1999  14:24:27.49  - Recv: ATS7=60S30=0L0M1\N4%C3&K3B0N1X4<cr>
08-19-1999  14:24:27.50  - Recv: <cr><lf>OK<cr><lf>
08-19-1999  14:24:27.50  - Interpreted response: Ok
08-19-1999  14:24:27.50  - Dialing.
```

Authentication Schemes

All dial-up connections that use passwords (and all of them should) use some form of authentication to verify that a user is who she claims to be. The two major types of authentication schemes commonly used are PAP (Password Authentication Protocol) and CHAP (Challenge-Response Authentication Protocol). How do they differ?

A server that uses PAP issues a one-time request for the username and password, and that information is passed in a clear-text, unencrypted fashion. A server that uses CHAP, on the other hand, will request the username and password at 10-minute intervals throughout the connection process. The information is transmitted in an encrypted form for additional security. Systems can be configured to handle both CHAP and PAP authentication, but CHAP, because of its improved security, is the preferred authentication method.

Shiva products use S-PAP as their default authentication protocol, but they can be configured to use CHAP and PAP as additional authentication protocols.

As you have previously seen, PPPLOG.TXT and other log files of dial-up networking sessions can be viewed to determine which authentication scheme is being used.

Windows 95/98 and Windows NT Dial-Up Networking

The dial-up networking features in Windows 95/98 and Windows NT provide an easier, graphical method for creating both the modem and network configurations needed to connect with another computer via modem. Rather than creating or modifying a script, the connection is built using wizards in a step-by-step manner.

Configuring the Server

The Dial-Up Networking Server feature in Windows 95/98 and Windows NT is used to enable remote users to dial in and access a single computer or a network through the single computer used as the Dial-Up Networking Server.

The Dial-Up Networking Server is not a standard part of Windows 95's dial-up networking. Instead, it must be installed from the Microsoft Plus! CD-ROM, which must be purchased separately for users of "retail" Windows 95 and some OEM versions. Some OEM versions of Windows 95 OSR 2.x might include a Plus folder, which contains the same programs found on the Plus! CD-ROM.

The DUN Server is installed through the standard Windows 9x installation procedure: Open SETUP.EXE on the CD-ROM or in the \Plus folder, enter the CD-ROM Key number, and select either the Typical or Custom installation. Because the Typical installation will install some products that are now obsolete (such as IE version 3.x), I recommend selecting the Custom install and choosing only the Dial-Up Networking Client. The 320KB program installs in just a few moments and requires that you restart the system because it installs new shared files.

After the DUN Server software is installed, open the DUN folder (select Start, Programs, Accessories, Dial-Up Networking). If you have more than one modem installed, select the tab for the modem you want to use. Open the Connections menu item. Dial-Up Server should now appear on this menu. Specify whether you want caller access (the default is no, so you should select Yes to allow the server to accept calls).

Controlling Access

After you select Allow Caller Access, you will have two options, depending on whether your system offers user-level access (such as on a Novell NetWare or Windows NT Server/Windows 2000 network) or share-level access (such as on a Windows-based peer-to-peer network without dedicated servers).

If you have user-level access, you will see a list of users. Select the users you want to have access via a dial-up connection. Click Add after you select each one, and click OK when you finish. You can also use the Remove button to highlight users who should no longer have dial-up access via this server.

If you have share-level access, click Change Password to enter or change a password (which should be done periodically). After entering a new password, click OK to return to the server configuration screen. You will need to distribute the password to only those users who should have access to this system.

If the password is lost, you must delete the password file from MS-DOS. Start the computer in MS-DOS mode, go to the default \Windows folder, and delete the RNA.PWL file to remove password protection for the Dial-Up Network Server (the name comes from Remote Network Access). Then restart Windows and create a new password for the DUN Server as previously explained.

Selecting a Server Type

Click Server Type to change the server type used to provide DUN Server access (see Figure 33.1). The default (also called Default) will try to use both PPP and Remote Access Service (a type of NetBEUI access over an asynchronous connection). To use only PPP, select PPP; to use only RAS, select Windows for Workgroups and Windows NT 3.1. The choice depends in part on what types of client systems will be accessing your DUN server. If only Windows 9x, NT Server, or Internet clients will be accessing your DUN server, use the PPP option.

After you complete these options, a user with the correct telephone number who has the correct password or is on the authorized user list can dial in to the DUN Server computer and access its resources or the network's resources.

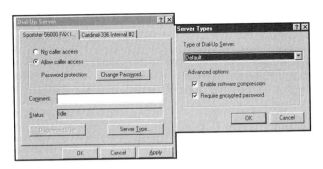

Figure 33.1 The Dial-Up Networking Server also allows you to select which modem to use for access if you have multiple modems installed. The Server Type button allows you to choose which server type to use, depending on your clients.

Configuring Windows 95/98 Clients

The DUN folder is also used to configure Windows 9x clients. Open the folder (select Start, Programs, Accessories, Dial-Up Networking) and select the Make a New Connection icon, which starts a simple wizard to help you set up your connection (see Figure 33.2). If you want to take advantage of the Multilink feature, which allows you to use multiple modems to create a single high-speed connection, see the section "Analog Modems and M-PPP," later in this chapter.

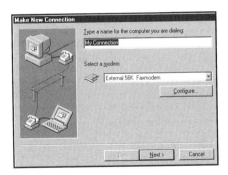

Figure 33.2 To make a new connection with Windows 9x Dial-Up Networking, you must first enter a name for the connection and select an installed modem.

Enter a name for the computer you'll be connecting with. This does not need to be its IP address or the "official" name of the computer on a network. Instead, just use a simple descriptive name, such as AOL Connection or Host Computer.

Select the modem you want to use for the new connection if you have more than one modem installed.

Next, click the Configure button and make sure that the following options are set correctly.

The following settings are under the General property sheet:

- Make sure the modem is set to the correct port (if it's external, you can change this value).

- Adjust the speaker volume as desired. For internal modems, you might want to use a higher volume; for external modems, a lower volume. It's comforting to many users (including this author) to hear the modem clearly negotiate the connection.

- As shown in Figure 33.3, adjust the maximum connection speed (I recommend 57,600bps for a 28.8Kbps or 33.6Kbps modem, and 115,200bps for a 56Kbps modem). This will enable the modem to use compression techniques when possible. Do not select the Only Connect at This Speed option.

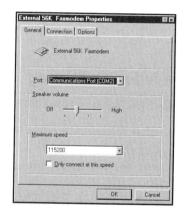

Figure 33.3 Because the modem is a 56Kbps modem, selecting the maximum speed of 115,200bps allows the modem to use data compression if possible.

Click the Connection tab to set the following options (see Figure 33.4):

- Set data bits, parity, and stop bits according to the host's requirements. If you are using dial-up networking to call into a mainframe computer, you might need to adjust the default values for data bits, parity, and stop bits. Otherwise, the default values of eight data bits, no parity, and one stop bit will be correct for most connections.

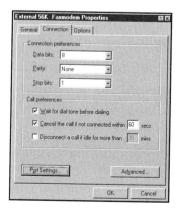

Figure 33.4 The Connection properties sheet also provides the gateway to adjusting the FIFO buffers (Port Settings), error control, and flow control (Advanced).

■ Under Call Preferences, you can specify whether to wait for a dial tone, how long to try a call before quitting, and how long an idle call should run before it's disconnected. Normally, the default values need not be changed.

Verify that port settings are correct; click the Port Settings button to see the current settings for the FIFO buffers used on 16550-series serial ports (see Figure 33.5). The default settings are 14 for receive buffers and 16 for transmit buffers. The settings should be altered only if there are receive or transmit problems and the correction for such problems is to reduce the values as needed. Click OK when you finish with port settings.

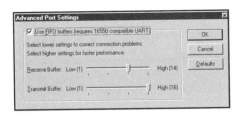

Figure 33.5 Adjust the number of FIFO buffers only if you are using 16550-series or better UARTs in your serial ports and need to improve transmit or receive reliability. You can verify the UART type through the Modems icon in the Control Panel.

Click Advanced Settings if you need to change the default for any of the following (see Figure 33.6):

■ Checking Error Control enables the modem's built-in error control features, if present. Use this option unless you have problems connecting. If so, disable it.

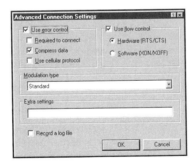

Figure 33.6 The Advanced properties sheet settings seldom need to be adjusted in normal circumstances, but users who need to troubleshoot a modem connection will find them useful.

■ Select Required to Connect to improve the reliability of connections over very noisy phone lines.

■ Select Use Compression to enable the modem to compress data being sent. Disable this feature if you have problems connecting or if you are sending precompressed data (such as ZIP files, GIF or JPG graphics, or self-extracting EXE archive files).

■ Select Use Cellular Protocols if you are making a connection using a cellular telephone with your modem.

- Select Use Flow Control - Hardware for external modems that use the CTS/RTS wires; otherwise, and for internal modems, select Use Flow Control - Software.

- The Modulation Type setting should be left at Standard unless you are trying to connect with a modem using a nonstandard modulation such as Bell or HST. In such cases, select Non-standard.

- The Extra Settings box should be left blank unless you need to insert a special initialization string (modem commands) that will be sent to the modem before dialing. Do not insert the AT prefix—Windows 9x will do this for you during the initialization of the modem.

- For troubleshooting, you can enable Record a Log File, which will create a file called MODEMLOG.TXT in the default \Windows folder.

- Click OK when done.

You can click the Options tab if you need to adjust the default settings for any of the following options (see Figure 33.7):

- Connection Control—You can bring up a terminal window before or after dialing to enable you to log on to a service. The default is to leave both boxes blank.

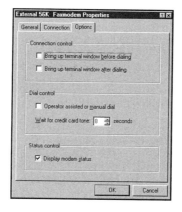

Figure 33.7 Use the Options properties sheet to make it easier to control your modem connection and dialing options.

- If you're working from a hotel room and need to use a calling card, you can select Operator Assisted or Manual Dial and select a time period to wait for a credit-card tone. These options can be tricky to use and might require that you have your telephone cabled in-line with your modem.

- The default Display Modem Status is recommended, to enable you to see connection information during the duration of your call.

Next, enter the telephone number and area code for the computer you'll be calling (see Figure 33.8). Click Next to continue.

At the final screen, click Finish to complete your connection. In reality, your connection isn't ready to go unless you verify the correct TCP/IP settings.

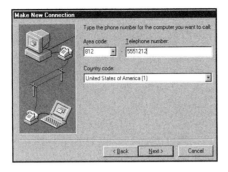

Figure 33.8   Enter the phone number and area code only when prompted. You add call-waiting and other prefixes elsewhere.

Viewing and Changing TCP/IP Settings for Windows 95/98

To verify that your TCP/IP settings are correct, make sure you have the correct settings information from your ISP or network administrator. To check or change them, open the Dial-Up Networking folder and right-click the appropriate connection icon. Depending on the version of DUN that you're using, you'll see at least a General and a Server Types tab. With Windows 95 DUN 1.3 and with Windows 98, you'll also see a Scripting and a Multilink tab.

Click the Server Types tab. The default setting for the Dial-Up server type is PPP, which is correct for TCP/IP connections (see Figure 33.9). However, note that TCP/IP, NetBEUI, and IPX/SPX protocols can all be carried by PPP. If you don't plan to use your PPP connection for anything other than Internet traffic, disable NetBEUI and IPX/SPX, because enabling these protocols could be a security risk if the computer you use to call from is networked.

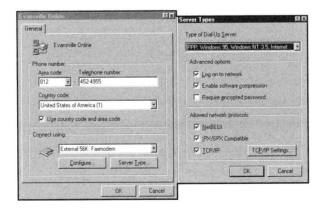

Figure 33.9   A PPP connection can carry all three of the major networking protocols, but you should select only the protocols you actually need for this connection. For a connection to the Internet, select only TCP/IP.

Click the TCP/IP Settings button. The defaults are Server Assigned IP Address, Server Assigned Name Server, Use IP Header Compression, and Use Default Gateway on Remote Network.

You can enter an assigned IP Address and/or an assigned primary and secondary DNS server and WINS server if necessary (see Figure 33.10). For example, an ISP might use a setup such as the following for its dial-up clients:

Server Assigned IP Address (enabled by default)

Primary DNS: 208.202.226.13

Secondary DNS: 204.120.16.222

Primary WINS: 0.0.0.0

Secondary WINS: 0.0.0.0

Use IP Header Compression (enabled by default)

Use Default Gateway on Remote Network (enabled by default)

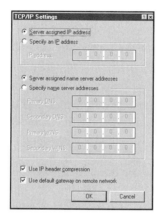

Figure 33.10   Replace the default values shown here with the appropriate values assigned by your ISP or network manager.

Because incorrect settings for TCP/IP addresses will prevent you from logging on, I recommend that you write down or screen-capture your TCP/IP and other properties for all your dial-up and other network settings. It's too easy to delete or change these settings—and a real pain in the neck to get them working again in the event of problems. Even if your TCP/IP settings are established for you by a setup program supplied by your ISP, you should still document them.

To start a dial-up session, open the session's icon. You'll be prompted for password and username, if required.

Configuring a Windows NT 4.0 Client Using the Dial-Up Networking Wizard

The Windows NT 4 DUN client has many differences in configuration from the Windows 9x DUN client. Also, there are two ways to create a Dial-Up Networking client; by using the default "wizard" supplied with Windows NT 4 or a non-Wizard method (see the following steps).

The fastest way to start the creation process is to open My Computer and open the Dial-Up Networking icon listed next to the drives and other objects on the system (see Figure 33.11).

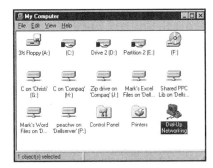

Figure 33.11 You can access Dial-Up Networking through the Programs-Accessories menu, but the Dial-Up Networking icon in My Computer is faster. Open it to create a new client or dial with an existing client entry.

If you haven't created a phone book entry before, you're prompted to click OK to add an entry. If you have existing phone book entries, you see a screen that lists the last phone book entry you used. Click the New button to create the new entry (see Figure 33.12).

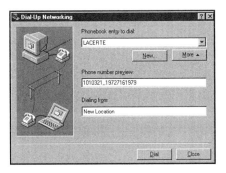

Figure 33.12 Click the New button to create a new client entry if you have existing phone book entries.

The first screen you'll see prompts you to provide a connection name similar to the way you'd enter the name in Make a New Connection with Windows 9x (see Figure 33.13). If you click on I Know All About Phonebook Entries, you'll go to the tabbed interface listed in the next section. Click Next to continue through each screen when completed.

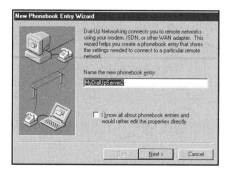

Figure 33.13   After you enter the connection name, you can continue with the wizard by clicking Next or enter the properties directly by choosing the option box.

The next screen is called Server and requires that you enable or disable each of the following options as appropriate for the server you'll be calling (see Figure 33.14):

■ Select I Am Calling the Internet if you're creating an Internet connection for use with an ISP account.

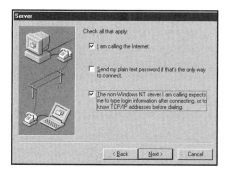

Figure 33.14   On the Server screen, choose the options needed based on what your server administrator recommends.

■ Select Send My Plain Text Password if the server can't understand an encrypted password.

■ Select The Non Windows-NT Server Expects...Login Information or...TCP/IP Addresses... if you will need to log in manually or supply a TCP/IP address.

Get the correct answers to these questions from your server administrator. You can select more than one of these options.

On the Phone Number screen, enter the telephone number for the server (see Figure 33.15). Click the Alternates box and enter any additional numbers that will work if the regular number is unavailable (see Figure 33.16). Check the Use Telephony Dialing Properties box if you have configured the system to add a 9,, for outside lines or *70,, to disable call waiting and want this added automatically to your number.

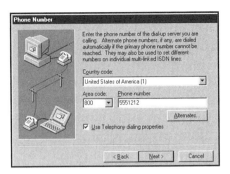

Figure 33.15 Enter the preferred number for the connection on the main Phone Number screen.

Figure 33.16 If you click the Alternates button, you can enter additional numbers and choose to have an alternative number become the first number to try if it connects first.

On the Serial Line Protocol screen, select PPP (Point-to-Point Protocol) to enable both TCP/IP and other protocols to work during your connection (see Figure 33.17). Use SLIP only if directed by the server administrator.

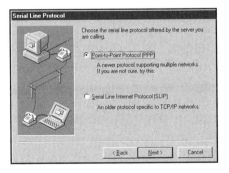

Figure 33.17 PPP is the preferred connection type to use on the Serial Line Protocol screen.

On the Logon Script screen, you can specify whether you need a logon script, you want a terminal window for manual entry of username, password, and options, or you want to use a generic or specialized script to automate the logon process (see Figure 33.18).

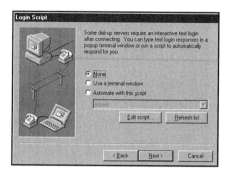

Figure 33.18 Although most PPP Internet connections don't use scripts, other types of dial-up connections do. Choose the Edit Script button to create or change a script by using Notepad.

On the IP Address window, enter `0.0.0.0` if the server will automatically assign you an IP address when you connect, or enter the specific IP address assigned to the system (see Figure 33.19).

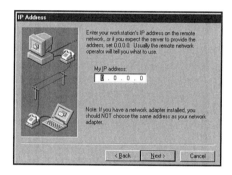

Figure 33.19 Depending on the server you are calling, you may enter specific addresses into this screen (IP Address) or the next screen (Name Server Address), or use 0.0.0.0 for both.

On the Name Server Address window, enter the Domain Name System server address or WINS server address if your server requires these, or enter `0.0.0.0` if not needed.

On the last screen, click Finish to save the session. The session is added to your existing phone book or a new phone book is created if this is your first entry.

Modifying an Existing NT 4 Dial-Up Networking Client or Creating a New One Without Using the DUN Wizard

If you open an existing NT 4 phone book, you can modify an existing entry by selecting More or create a new one by selecting New. If you have disabled the DUN Wizard in the User Preferences, you can create your connection with the same tabbed interface used to edit an existing entry.

Although the process of creating a connection without using the DUN Wizard is more involved, using this method gives you access to more options than the wizard does. The screens listed here are the same screens you'll see if you edit an existing entry.

Click the Basic properties sheet and enter a server name in the Entry Name box, similar to the way you'd enter the name in Make a New Connection with Windows 9x (see Figure 33.20). Also enter the telephone number for the server here. Click the Alternates button and enter any additional numbers that will work if the regular number is unavailable. Check the Use Telephony Dialing Properties box if you have configured the system to add a 9, for outside lines or *70, to disable call waiting and want this added automatically to your number. Select the Dial Using option to select the modem you want to use for your connection. You can configure the modem with the Configure button if desired. The modem is configured in a fashion similar to that seen with Windows 95 earlier.

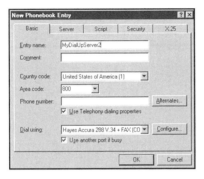

Figure 33.20   The Basic screen also provides options for configuring the modem to be used as well as telephone number and dialing options.

Click the Server tab to select the correct server type (see Figure 33.21). Different options are available depending on which server type you choose.

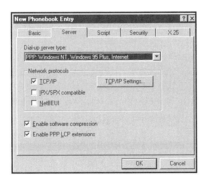

Figure 33.21   The protocols available to you depend on the server type you select. The PPP server is the most flexible server type available in Windows Dial-Up Networking.

If you choose PPP, you can enable or disable any combination of TCP/IP, NetBEUI, and IPX/SPX protocols. You can disable the Enable PPP LCP Extensions to disable the use of advanced PPP features such as Time-Remaining and Identification packets and requesting callback.

If you select the SLIP server type, you can use only the TCP/IP protocol.

If you choose the Windows NT3.1/Windows for Workgroups server type, you can use only NetBEUI.

From either the PPP or SLIP options, click the TCP/IP Settings button to enter the appropriate TCP/IP settings for your connection.

Enter the IP address, DNS and WINS primary and secondary name server addresses, and other items as needed (see Figure 33.22).

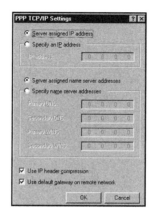

Figure 33.22 The TCP/IP settings for a PPP connection are shown here. An SLIP connection uses a similar properties sheet that also enables you to specify the frame size.

As shown in Figure 33.23, click the Script tab to select options for terminal window, modem, or COM port parameters (choose the Before Dialing button), and scripts (usually needed only for SLIP connections). You can use the Edit Script button to run Notepad to create or edit a script. NT 4 supports its own scripting language (see the file Switch.INF for examples) or the easier scripting language used in Windows 95.

Click the Security tab to select the type of authentication used by the server you're calling (see Figure 33.24). You can also use the Unsave Password option on this screen to change or delete a password previously saved with this connection.

The X.25 screen enables you to choose from proprietary networks used by some servers, including the CompuServe network.

Click OK to save your new phone book entry or to save changes to an existing entry.

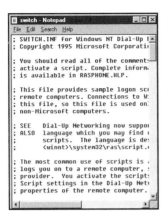

Figure 33.23   Selecting the Edit Script button from the Script tab starts Notepad. If you don't select a script file to edit, Notepad loads the `Switch.INF` file, which is an annotated script template.

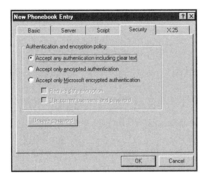

Figure 33.24   You'll use this screen frequently to unsave your password and allow a new one to be stored if your server is set to require new passwords at frequent intervals.

Additional Configuration Options

Select More after you have created a phone book entry to change the following options:

- Edit the current entry
- Clone the entry to create a new entry by cloning an old one and modifying it
- Delete the current entry
- Create a shortcut to an entry you use frequently

Select Monitor Status to display a call monitor that displays detailed information about the current call (see Figure 33.25).

Other options include Operator Assist or Manual dialing, User Preferences to enable or disable the New Phonebook Entry Wizard, Autodialing, Callback, Phonebook options, and Logon Preferences. Logon Preferences are similar, but apply to all users of the system and must be set up by the administrator of the system.

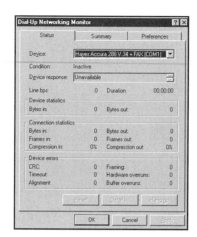

Figure 33.25 The Monitor Status screen at rest. During a connection, the monitor will display real-time statistics, including error rates. Use this feature to help determine line quality.

Multilink Connections

Multilink connections enable multiple data channels to be joined, or *bonded*, together to create a single high-speed data connection. This capability has been used for years with ISDN connections to put two 64Kbps "B" channels together for a single 128Kbps connection. The ISDN version of multilink communications allows the bond to be broken temporarily to allow one of the "B" channels to handle a voice or fax call while the second "B" channel continues to handle data transmission. When the voice or fax call is over, the second "B" channel joins the first to re-establish the full 128Kbps rate.

Analog Modems and M-PPP

To improve beyond the 53Kbps (maximum allowable) speed of a single high-speed analog modem, Windows 98 is designed to use multilink bonding (also called multichannel aggregation). This feature can also be used with conventional analog modems, including the 56Kbps models. A new version of PPP is included as part of the support for multilink connections: Multilink Point-to-Point Protocol (also called M-PPP or MP, depending on the vendor).

Windows 95 requires the Dial-Up Networking version 1.3 Update to use multilink bonding.

Windows NT 4.0 is also designed to use multilink bonding, typically referred to as Remote Access Service (RAS) Multilink.

M-PPP also requires the following:

- An Internet service provider (ISP) that supports Multilink Point-to-Point Protocol (M-PPP).

  The charge for M-PPP service is usually at least 50 percent more than for a normal dial-up account or might require the purchase of a separate dial-up account for each modem used.

- Two or more modems. (They do not need to be the same speed or even the same type.)

Although M-PPP support can be used to "recycle" existing 33.6Kbps, 56Kbps, or even older modems, the easiest way to work with M-PPP might be to purchase new modems designed to handle this feature. Diamond Multimedia's SupraSonic II is an M-PPP ready modem and has two modems built in to a single board. Diamond's Shotgun software, which is also available with other Supra single-modem models, enables the user to switch a line to voice use on demand and then return the line to data transmission in a fashion similar to what can be done with dual ISDN "B" channels.

Configuring Multilink Services for Windows 95/98

First, make sure that the modems you want to use have been correctly installed and are working. You can check the modems by opening the Control Panel and selecting the Modems icon and the Diagnostics icon. Select each modem and click the More Info button. The modem should respond in a few seconds with configuration information.

Next, open the Dial-Up Networking folder and create a new connection as detailed earlier or clone the single-modem connection you are already using to contact your remote server.

Right-click the connection icon and select Properties. The fourth tab is Multilink. Click that tab, and then select Use Additional Devices (see Figure 33.26). Use the Add button to select the modem you want to use in conjunction with the original modem. Because both the original modem and additional modems are listed, make sure you are choosing the second modem. Make sure the correct telephone number for the remote server is entered in the Phone Number box. Click OK when finished.

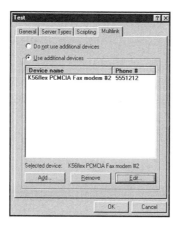

Figure 33.26   The Multilink option enables you to join multiple modems into a single logical unit for high-speed Internet access with compatible ISPs.

Configuring Multilink Services for Windows NT 4.0

Make sure that the modems you want to use have been correctly installed and are working. Both the original modem and the additional modem must be installed through the Network icon in the Control Panel. Select the Services setting, Remote Access Services option, and Properties.

From here, click Modem if you must install a different model of modem or Clone if your second modem is identical to the first model. You might need to restart your system after you install the new modem before you can continue.

Open Dial-Up Networking and click New to create a new phone book entry. Enter a name such as Multilink for the computer name. Click Next to continue and choose the correct type of server from the next dialog. Click Next to continue.

Select the modem you want to use as the primary one on the Modem or Adapter screen and click Next to continue. Then enter the telephone number for the remote server, and click Next.

Click Finish to complete the phone book entry, which must then be modified to enable multilink connections. Edit the entry by selecting the new phone book entry and selecting More (see Figure 33.27). Select Edit Entry and Modem Properties to display the Edit Phonebook Entry window.

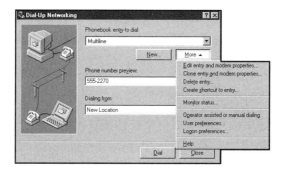

Figure 33.27 Use the More button to make changes to any existing phone book entry.

As shown in Figure 33.28, select the Basic tab, open the Dial Using option, and choose Multiple Lines (listed after the modems you have installed on your system).

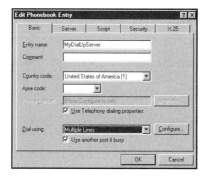

Figure 33.28 Choose Multiple Lines to access the additional modems you have on the system, so you can choose one or more to add to your connection.

Click Configure, and put a check mark next to the modem that isn't selected already (see Figure 33.29). This will allow your system to use both the original modem (showing as selected) and the one you just chose to make the connection.

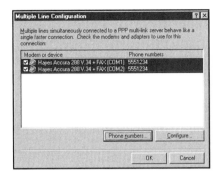

Figure 33.29   Select the modems you want to use for the Multiline connection, and make sure the correct phone number is listed for each one.

Click Phone Numbers and enter the same telephone number you used for the first modem for the new modem selection. Click Add. Click OK to close the Phone Numbers dialog, and then click OK to close the Multiple Line Configuration dialog.

When you click OK to close the Edit Phonebook Entry dialog, your changes are complete. When you use this entry, both modems will dial, and you should have much faster download and upload speeds.

Linux Dial-Up Connections

Linux, the most popular operating system for Web servers, is also becoming popular as a dial-up client.

A Linux dial-up connection can be created in one of two ways: by using a shell script that uses the pppd and chat commands to set up the system and make the connection, or by using the pppd and chat commands interactively.

Requirements for PPP Support in Linux

In either case, the following must be present on your machine. Your Linux kernel must have PPP support enabled, and you must get and install the pppd (Point-to-Point Protocol Daemon) program. (A *daemon* is a program that runs tasks in the background.)

To determine whether your Linux kernel has PPP support, enter the following command:

```
cat /proc/net/dev
```

You should see a reference to the ppp0 device listed if your system has PPP support included in its Linux kernel. You can also use dmesg, More to view boot messages, which should also list PPP support during the startup process. If you do not see references to PPP support, rebuild your kernel, and during the make config step, answer Yes when asked if you want PPP (Point-to-Point Protocol) support.

pppd and *chat*

The Linux pppd program is used to create the PPP connection, whereas the chat program is used to send the password and username information to the remote server and to invoke a menu. Both pppd and chat must be installed on your Linux system.

You can verify the version of pppd you have with the following command:

```
/usr/sbin/pppd -v
```

The version, if present, will be displayed. Note the version number because some ISPs support only certain versions of pppd.

Other Files to Edit

Depending on the requirements of your remote server, you will need to create or edit some or all of the following files:

- **A file to enable DNS support**—This file will contain the names of domains and name servers:

    ```
    /etc/resolv.conf
    ```

- **A dial-up script**—This script makes the connection with the remote computer and contains the telephone number, username, and password values. This should not be world-readable—others shouldn't be able to read this sensitive information.

- **A ppp-on script**—This script supplies the correct IP addresses for the remote server and your system, indicates what serial port is used for the connection, and starts the pppd and chat programs.

- **A ppp-off script**—This script drops the PPP connection.

You will also need to create a ppp folder to store configuration information (if it doesn't exist already) by using the following command:

```
mkdir /etc/ppp
```

Some ISPs provide logon scripts that combine the features in the preceding list.

As an alternative to a script, some ISPs recommend the use of pppd and chat in simple commands like the following:

```
pppd connect 'chat -v "" ATDT5559062 CONNECT "" ' /dev/modem 38400

debug crtscts defaultroute modem +ua ~/.ppp_login
```

In the example using pppd and chat, the user must create a password file called .ppp_login, and this file must contain the username and password, separated by a new line.

You must make sure that your modem is working correctly, regardless of your connection type. After your modem is installed, in Red Hat Linux, use this command to add a modem entry to your /dev folder:

```
ln -s /dev/cuaX /dev/modem
```

Log on as root to add the files listed here to your system if required.

Some dial-up connections require that you add an options file to your system's /etc/ppp/ folder, with settings for hardware flow control, IP address lines, and other information. An example of this file is listed as follows:

```
# /etc/ppp/options (NO PAP/CHAP)
#
# Prevent pppd from forking into the background
-detach
# If you are using a STATIC IP number, edit the 0.0.0.0 part of the
# following line to your static IP number.
0.0.0.0:
#
# use the modem control lines
modem
# use uucp style locks to ensure exclusive access to the serial device
lock
# use hardware flow control
crtscts
# create a default route for this connection in the routing table
defaultroute
# do NOT set up any "escaped" control sequences
asyncmap 0
# use a maximum transmission packet size of 552 bytes
mtu 552
# use a maximum receive packet size of 552 bytes
mru 552
#
#-------END OF SAMPLE /etc/ppp/options (no PAP/CHAP)
```

You might also need a resolv.conf file in your /etc folder to provide name-resolution server IP addresses:

```
search erewhonnet.com
nameserver 100.117.1.1
nameserver 100.117.1.11
```

Procedures for dialing in to a remote server vary a great deal, and the previous examples are intended as guidelines for what might be necessary. Your ISP should provide you with specific recommendations for your scripts or preconfigured scripts for you to use.

ISDN

ISDN (Integrated Services Digital Network) is expensive and has incredibly complicated and confusing pricing, but it provides proven, high-speed digital access for many users across the country. Whereas cable modem and DSL services offer the promise of faster-than-analog dial-up access "someday," ISDN users have it today.

ISDN Versus POTS

ISDN is different than POTS (Plain Old Telephone Service) in a variety of ways, as Table 33.1 indicates.

Table 33.1   ISDN and POTS Feature Comparison

Feature	ISDN	POTS
Line sharing among multiple devices	Yes	No
High-speed upload as well as download speed	Yes	No
Maximum download speed	128Kbps (dual-channel) 64Kbps (single-channel)	53Kbps (due to current FCC regulations; requires 56Kbps modem and appropriate line conditions)
Maximum upload speed	128Kbps (dual-channel) 64Kbps (single-channel)	33.6Kbps or less, depending on modem design
Simultaneous data and voice, data and fax, or voice and fax connections	Yes	No
Unlimited service for a fixed price	Some areas	Yes

The only advantage that POTS has over ISDN is that you don't pay any more for it in most parts of the country, regardless of whether you use it for 10 minutes a month or 100 hours a month. ISDN pricing is affected by many factors, including single-channel or dual-channel connection, distance from the central office, and monthly usage.

There are two types of ISDN channels: Bearer (B-channel), used for voice, fax, and data, running at 64Kbps in both directions per channel; and Delta (D channel), used for control. The D channel runs at either 16Kbps or 64Kbps, depending on your service type.

PRI and BRI

Two basic types of ISDN service are available:

- **Primary Rate Interface (PRI)** is oriented toward business use. A typical use for this (more expensive) form of ISDN is connecting an office PBX (Private Branch Exchange) to the telephone company's central office. In North America and Japan, the PRI service consists of 23 B channels and one 64Kbps D channel for a total of 1,536Kbps, running over a standard T1 interface. The European standard for PRI service is slightly different, using 30 B channels and a single 64Kbps D channel, resulting in a total of 1,984Kbps, corresponding to the E1 telecommunications standard. Multiple PRI connections can be supported with a single D channel by the use of Non-Facility Associated Signaling (NFAS).

- **Basic Rate Interface (BRI)** has a limit of two B channels, but each BRI line can actually support eight different ISDN devices, each with a unique ISDN number, allowing computers, fax machines, and telephones to "share" the connection. The D channel provides the "multiple call signaling" feature, which routes calls and provides "on-hold" features to make this possible.

Terminal Adapters (TA) and ISDN Routers

Because ISDN is a digital, not an analog, connection, regular analog modems aren't used. Instead, you use a specialized device that is properly called a "terminal adapter" but is often referred to—incorrectly—as an "ISDN modem."

Terminal adapters can be purchased in any of the following connection types:

- Internal interface card
- External (serial port)
- External (USB port)

Terminal adapters are specialized, high-speed serial devices whose throughput can easily exceed the 115,200bps allowed by typical 16550-based serial ports. Thus, if you want the convenience and easy replacement (in case of failure) of an external terminal adapter, you should consider the new USB-port versions (which require Windows 98) or purchase a high-speed serial port card (based on the 16650 or 16750 UART chips) and connect the external serial-port terminal adapter to it.

Note

Although the last version of Windows 95 (referred to as Windows 95C or OSR2.5) has limited support for USB, many USB devices won't work with it. Use Windows 98 to enjoy fewer USB woes.

Another advantage of external terminal adapters is their support for multiple analog devices (telephone and fax) as well as your computer.

ISDN terminal adapters with IP routing features, such as 3Com's Office Connect ISDN LAN Modem, provide additional flexibility, allowing more than one PC in an office to use the high-speed ISDN connection for simultaneous Internet access.

With these devices, you install a standard Ethernet NIC into your system and connect to the device containing the router. These devices also provide analog phone ports, and thus combine the features of an ISDN terminal adapter, an ethernet hub, and an IP router into a single device.

Multiprotocol routers that support ISDN digital and (optionally) analog telephone/fax devices can be used to route both IP and other protocols such as Novell IPX.

Getting Local Service

ISDN access is provided by your local telephone company, which is responsible for pricing and installation. Some makers of ISDN terminal adapters, such as 3Com, will work with your local telephone company to make sure that your ISDN installation is performed correctly. An incorrect ISDN installation can prevent you from enjoying advanced ISDN features such as dual-channel data transmission.

Many local telephone companies offer ISDN pricing and configuration information on their Web sites. Contact the local telephone company for rates in your area.

ADSL

Digital Subscriber Line service (also called xDSL, with the "x" standing for two different versions of DSL) is slowly becoming an alternative to ISDN for both business and home users who need high-speed Internet access. The most popular of the many versions of DSL is ADSL. The "A" stands for Asymmetric, meaning that the download speed is faster than the upload speed. Because ADSL can be provided by the local telephone company without expensive rewiring (it runs over the POTS copper wire most people use) or even a service call, and because it allows simultaneous voice and data transmissions, ADSL holds out the promise of being a "poor-man's ISDN," with potential speeds much higher and monthly costs much lower. Although adoption of ADSL has been slow, more and more cities are expected to have it available in 2000 and beyond.

Cable Modems

Cable modems (again, a misnomer) use the bidirectional TV cable to gear Internet traffic to your home or office. A standard 10Mbps Ethernet card is used to connect your computer to the cable modem. A cable modem represents an always-on Internet connection and doesn't require a dial-up session. Instead, the network interface card's properties are set for the appropriate TCP/IP settings.

Limited installation of cable modems service is happening in medium- to large-sized markets around the country, and it appears that the major rivals for the reasonably priced, high-speed successor to analog 56Kbps modems will be either ADSL or cable modems.

One major concern for cable modem users that is not one with ADSL is the issue of security. Cable modem users share a common bandwidth; thus, it is possible for other users on the same connection to see your system and the information on it. Make sure that the cable modem provider has adequate security provisions for you to use to protect the privacy of your system. This is especially important because Microsoft Windows 98 Second Edition has built-in Internet connection-sharing that works with cable modems and some other types of connections. If your ISP doesn't provide some sort of firewall or other security option, your neighbors could see what's on your system—or on your family's network.

Using Modem Pools

When you dial in to an ISP, a bank, or another commercial remote server, you use a single number, but there are many modems at the other end. When multiple modems are configured to answer a single dial-up number, the result is a *modem pool*.

For a dial-up client, accessing a modem pool is no different from dialing a computer with a single modem. You use a single dial-up number, and the modem pool uses the next available modem to answer your call and make your connection. However, there are some factors to keep in mind to help you use modem pools effectively.

First, know what the call duration standard is. Because a modem pool represents a finite resource (it contains only a certain number of modems), but the potential users are much more in number, most modem pools are designed to disconnect callers after a predetermined length of time.

Check with technical support for this value, and keep it in mind before you start a long download. With Windows dial-up clients, check the status box onscreen to see how long you've been connected.

Second, know what the technical standards are for the modem pool you're connecting with. If you're using an older 33.6Kbps or 28.8Kbps modem, you can connect equally well with a modem pool that supports only this speed or a faster one. However, if you have a 56Kbps modem, you must know which standard your modem supports and what the modem pool supports.

The final official standard for 56Kbps (limited to 53Kbps by current FCC regulations) is the ITU V.90 standard. Some ISPs have already converted all their modem pools to this standard, which means that users of the older, proprietary Rockwell-chipset K56flex and Lucent-chipset x2 modems must upgrade their modems to V.90 or be able to connect at only 33.6Kbps maximum. If your ISP still supports K56flex or x2, you can continue to use your non-V.90 modem at its top speed by using the appropriate dial-up number for the K56flex or x2 modem pool (see Figure 33.30). Because the support for non-V.90 56Kbps modems is likely to vanish at some point, you should check with your modem vendor for a downloadable firmware upgrade to V.90, a chip swap, or a trade-in.

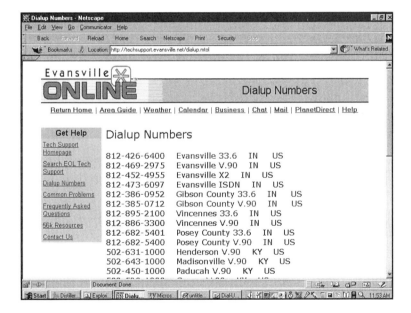

Figure 33.30 This regional ISP still offers an x2-specific dial-up number but only for customers in a single city. This ISP, like most, has switched virtually all its 56Kbps modems to the V.90 standard. This ISP's V.90 modem pool also supports K56flex modems.

General Troubleshooting Tips

The following troubleshooting tips will work with any operating system and any modem or dial-up connection type.

Disable Call Waiting

The number one "killer" of a dial-up connection, other than being disconnected by the remote server because you've been on too long, is failing to disable the popular call-waiting feature before you make your connection. Because call waiting interrupts your current call to prompt you to switch to the incoming call and answer it, failing to disable this feature will cause your connection to fail as soon as anyone tries to call you.

Disabling call waiting is simple. Just add `*70,,` to the beginning of the dial-up number you use, whether it's a local or long distance call. This can be placed directly before the number in the phone number entry for a Dial-Up Networking icon or telephone book entry, in the default properties for all calls, or in a dial-up script for use with a Linux system.

If your ISP's number is 555-1234, for example, enter the number as `*70,,555-1234`. The `*70` is the code that actually disables call waiting. Each comma after `*70` results in a two-second pause, which allows slow telephone switches to have enough time to get ready for the actual telephone number.

Note

`*70` is the most common code to use to disable call waiting, but check with your local telephone company if you have problems. Some local telephone companies might use a different code (such as 70#) or might require you to add "Call waiting disable" service to your account.

Check Logon Scripts

Whether you actually write a logon script with a text editor (as you must for many Linux dial-up sessions) or enter the properties for a Dial-Up Networking icon (as with Windows), make sure you have provided the correct information. You must specify, somewhere in the dial-up process, all the following information:

- The telephone number (including area code and prefixes)
- The modem and/or serial port that will make the call
- The TCP/IP properties for your system
- The TCP/IP and server properties for the remote system
- Your username
- Your password

Errors in any of this information will cause your logon process to fail. If you've cloned an existing dial-up networking connection or edited a script for Linux use that was provided by your ISP, double-check your new version against the original. Watch for incorrect telephone numbers in either case and for spelling errors and typos in the Linux script.

Check TCP/IP Settings

Because dial-up connections to the Internet use TCP/IP, having these settings correct is vital to the success of your connection. If you use Windows 9x or NT, make sure that you adjust the

TCP/IP properties for each dial-up connection, not for the Dial-Up Networking Adapter found in the Networks icon. This isn't a physical card, but merely a sort of placeholder for attaching modem support and properties.

As you've already seen, this might require changes to the IP address, DNS (domain name service) entries, and WINS (Windows Internet Naming Service) entries for each different dial-up connection. An easy way to document this information is to use the print-screen key to capture each screen containing this information to the Windows clipboard. Paste them one by one into Windows Paint, and save the resulting files.

Make sure the server type is specified correctly. Some ISPs with roots in older proprietary online services use nonstandard versions of PPP instead of the Microsoft standard. "Classic" CompuServe, although it now uses dial-up networking, still uses its own nonstandard CISPPP protocol instead of normal PPP. Forget to specify it, and your connection dies without a decent online explanation.

Get Rid of Previous Installations

Windows dial-up networking can be difficult to get working if you've had problems with installations. Sometimes, the best way to solve the problem is to delete an old installation before you try a new one.

If you decide to "nuke" your current DUN installation, make sure you've recorded IP, DNS, WINS, dial-up telephone numbers, server type, username, password, and other information necessary to re-create your connection. You can then delete the particular dial-up networking connection icon and rebuild it.

If you continue to have problems, you might want to delete all support for dial-up networking and reinstall it from either the Windows CD-ROM or from an updated download. To delete it, open the Network icon in the Control Panel, select the Dial-Up Adapter, and then select Remove. You'll need to restart Windows to finish the removal process. Then, you can reinstall Dial-Up Networking. This remove and reload process is also useful if you suspect a problem with the modem drivers themselves.

Troubleshooting Checklist

Use the following troubleshooting checklist to help resolve problems with dial-up connections:

- Check the telephone line and jack with an ordinary handset. If your phone can't get a dial-tone, neither can your modem.
- Make sure you are using the line connector and not the phone connector on the back of an internal or external modem for the telephone cable to the wall jack. The phone connector enables you to daisy-chain a telephone to the same wire as your modem.
- Make sure an external modem, ISDN terminal adapter, or other dialup/remote access device is turned on and properly attached. Test the cable for correct wiring (especially for serial modem cables) and proper continuity of wiring.
- Check for IRQ conflicts between internal modems and existing COM ports. Because COM 1 and COM 3 normally share IRQ 4 and COM 2 and COM 4 normally share IRQ 3, adding an

internal modem on COM 3 to a system that already has COM 1 and COM 2 on board will usually result in problems. The most common symptom is a "dead" mouse attached to COM 1. The easiest solution is to disable the computer's COM 2 port (usually in the BIOS) and to set the internal modem to use COM 2.

■ Make sure that PCMCIA/PC Card modems are properly detected and enabled in your notebook computer. It's easy to install them without pushing them in far enough to be detected. Open the PCMCIA/PC Card control panel to verify proper modem operation.

■ As shown in Figure 33.31, use the Windows 9x Modem Diagnostics features to test the modem (internal or external). You can access this from the Modems icon in the Control Panel.

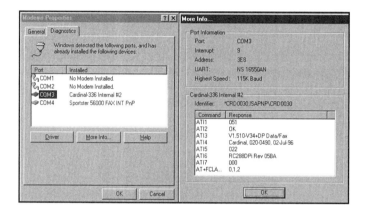

Figure 33.31   A correctly installed modem should respond with messages similar to those shown here when you use the Diagnostics property sheet. The Diagnostics information also lists the UART type.

■ With older versions of Windows or with Linux, open a terminal program and send the modem AT commands. ATDT555-1212, for example, will cause the modem to dial the number listed with tones. If the modem fails diagnostics or won't respond to terminal commands, make sure the correct serial port has been specified.

■ Check the modem initialization string (for Linux) and the correct modem driver (for Windows—this file contains the initialization string). This information is given in the modem's instruction manual. The initialization string sets the modem's S-registers for proper operation, and it must sometimes be modified for special purposes. If you use an incorrect initialization string, the modem can't work because the instructions are incorrect.

■ Check the other software settings listed earlier against the latest ISP-specific information.

Dedicated
Connections

The last chapter went over some of the solutions you can use to allow remote users to gain access to your LAN. Using dial-up connections, whether they are ordinary telephone lines or faster ISDN connections, can satisfy many business requirements for ordinary users. However, if your applications require larger amounts of bandwidth to communicate with remote users, such as a branch office, you might find that a dedicated connection—one that is available continuously—is a better choice. This can be done using a dedicated leased line connection or newer packet switching network technologies can ride on top of digital connections offered by the local exchange carrier.

Leased Lines

Leased lines have been used by businesses for many years to establish point-to-point dedicated connections. Connecting the telephone system from a branch office to the main office, for example, can be more cost-effective by purchasing a leased line from the telephone company and paying a flat fee for its use rather than using the normal long-distance network. Using leased lines to connect computer networks is a logical step up from their use with telephone voice systems.

Leased lines provide a fixed bandwidth for a fixed cost. The leased line might consist of a physical line that traverses the entire length of the connection from end to end, or it might be comprised of connections at both ends to the local exchange carrier, with the two exchanges connected by some other technology. The basics of a leased line, however, remain in that it provides a permanent circuit between two points that you own and do not have to share with others.

Because of their point-to-point topology, no call setup is required at either end. The connection exists and you can use it whenever you need to. The physical lines are also specially conditioned by the carrier to minimize errors as compared to an ordinary connection to the local exchange.

The first type of leased line was based on analog technology, just as the voice telephone network, and often used modems at each end of the connection. Digital leased lines now provide connections of up to 56K and use devices called *channel service unit (CSU)* and *data service unit (DSU)*, which are also used on other digital lines such as T1 and fractional T1 services. It is common to find both a CSU and DSU implemented in the same device, and sometimes in combination with a router.

The CSU is used to provide the basic functions needed to transmit data across the line. In addition, the following are other basic functions provided by the CSU:

- **An electrical barrier**—The CSU protects the T1 (or other line) and the user equipment from damage that can be caused by unexpected electrical interference, such as a lightning strike.

- **Keep-alive signal**—The CSU transmits a signal on the line that is used to keep the connection up.

- **Loopback capabilities**—The telephone company can perform diagnostics on the line using loopback facilities provided by the CSU.

- **Statistical information**—Depending on the vendor and model, the CSU can provide statistical information useful to the network administrator. Some units have SNMP capabilities.

The DSU works with the CSU but provides other functions. The DSU is responsible for translating between the data format used on the line, such as the time-division multiplexed (TDM) DSX frames that are used on a T1 line and the serial data format used on the local network. A DSU usually has RS-232C or RS-449 connectors that can be used to connect to data terminal equipment (DTE), which then provides the actual physical connection to the LAN (see Figure 34.1). Each end of the line requires similar equipment.

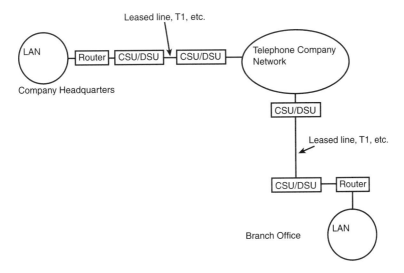

Figure 34.1   The CSU/DSU provides the connection to a leased line or other high-speed service from the local provider.

Other functions that the DSU can perform include

- Timing functions for user ports
- Error correction
- Handshaking across the line

Usually you will find that the CSU and DSU are combined into one device. It is also typical to see these functions incorporated directly into a router. Using a router, instead of another device such as a bridge, to make this connection can reduce the traffic that travels between the two LANs joined by the connection by passing only packets across the connection that are destined for the network on the other end.

Analog leased lines are not as common as they once were. Much of the PSTN has been converted to digital lines and the service a digital line provides is much better than an analog line. One of the disadvantages of a leased line is that it cannot be modified to give you a larger bandwidth. If you need additional capacity on the line, you must add another line or perhaps move up to another technology such as T1.

The T-Carrier System

Leased lines can usually give you a bandwidth of up to 56K. For larger bandwidth you will need to get a larger data pipe, and this is where the T-carrier or, if you are in Europe, the E-carrier, system comes into play. The T-carrier system was developed in the early 1960s by the Bell Telephone System in the U.S. and was used to provide digital transmission of voice communications. The first kind of service offered was the T1, which can provide a transmission rate of up to 1.544Mbps. If you need more bandwidth than can be provided by a T1 line, you can contract for a higher level of service, such as a T3 line, which provides a 44.736Mbps connection. The range of transmission rates and number of channels for each kind of T-carrier service are listed in Table 34.1.

Table 34.1 T-Carrier Services in the North American Digital Hierarchy

Designation	Channels	Transmission Rate
FT-1 / 1	1	64Kbps
T1	24	1.544Mbps
T2	96	6.312Mbps
T3	672	44.736Mbps
T4	4032	274.186Mbps

The T-carrier system is an all-digital transmission system. For voice systems that use a T1 line the signal is sampled at a rate of 8,000 times per second, and the result is stored in 8 bits, or 1 byte. The T1 provides 24 separate channels that can be used to send voice or data from one place to another, using two pairs of wires. Each of the 24 channels can transmit at a rate of 64Kps.

Note

The European equivalent of the T1 line is called the E-1. Although the two use the same kind of technologies for transmission, the E-1 provides 30 channels and a total bandwidth of 2.045Mbps.

Time division multiplexing (TDM), which allows each channel only a very small amount of time to transmit (5.2 milliseconds), is used to combine all 24 channels into one signal. With each channel transmitting at 64Kbps, the total bandwidth on a T1 line is 64Kbps × 24, or 1.536Mbps. The difference between the 1.536Mbps and the full bandwidth of the T1 pipe (1.544Mbps) is due to the overhead used for managing connections (8Kbps).

Fractional T1

In many cases, the full bandwidth provided by a T1 line is more than the end user requires. Yet, a slower 56K leased line might not provide enough bandwidth. To handle this situation the communications provider can allow several users to use the full T1 bandwidth by allocating each user one or more of the 24 channels that T1 provides. This is called Fractional T1.

Diagnosing Problems with T-Carrier Services

When purchasing a T1 or T3 service, the local provider will have to check out the actual physical line and provide "conditioning" to make sure that it can transmit data at the expected rate with minimal errors. Bridge taps and load coils that are normally found on voice grade lines cannot be used and can cause the electrical pulses to be slightly out of shape and, therefore, unrecognizable to devices on each end of the line. Inadequate grounding of the copper cables or physically defective cables are another source of problems.

The loopback capabilities provided by the CSU/DSU unit are used by the provider to check the signal quality on the line. One of the simplest methods for checking the line is the use of a bit error rate tester (BERT), discussed in Chapter 2, "Tools." This provides a simple test to determine whether specific bit patterns transmitted by the test equipment can be received back with no distortions. BERT is usually the first test performed and is used to qualify the line as functional after the physical cables have been installed.

When a T1 line is installed it is usually checked to be sure that all circuits are correctly terminated, which includes checking the user's equipment such as the CSU/DSU. Signal loss can indicate that the connection is broken somewhere along the line, too weak a signal is being transmitted, or perhaps there is a faulty connector.

One problem that can occur is called *timing jitter*. As defined by the ITU-T, timing jitter is "short-term variations of the significant instants of a digital signal from their ideal positions in time." The signal that is transmitted is a wave form, and when viewed on an instrument such as an oscilloscope, you can see the rising and falling edges of the wave. If the wave form is slightly out of sync with the clocking mechanism, the signal might be interpreted by the receiving equipment incorrectly. All T1 circuits have a very small degree of jitter, caused mainly by multiplexers or devices along the line that are used to regenerate the signal. It can also be caused by electrical or atmospheric noise (as in the case of microwave transmissions).

Testing the line by using BERT or other instruments that depend on knowing the bit patterns that will be transmitted is called out-of-service testing. Obviously, this can be used only before the customer takes over the line for its use. In-service testing, sometimes referred to as quality of service (QoS) testing cannot make measurements based on expected bit patterns because the data transmitted by the customer can be roughly assumed to be random. Instead, tests performed when the line is already in service involve checking for things such as framing errors, parity errors, or checksum errors, depending on the kind of traffic carried by the line.

ATM

Asynchronous Transfer Mode (ATM) was developed by AT&T Bell Labs (today called Telcordia, a part of SAIC) during the 1980s. It is a connection-oriented technology, much like the public telephone system, in which a connection is established between two points before the actual data exchange can begin. It can be used in both LAN and WAN environments. One of the factors that influenced the design of ATM is that many different kinds of traffic are being carried on electronic networks today. The public telephone network was originally designed to carry voice communications along with other services such as telex. Today, electronic networks are used to transmit data, voice, and video, and to provide connections for other kinds of multimedia applications.

Attempting to design a one-size-fits-all network and provide for new kinds of traffic in the future, ATM uses a fixed packet size. The packet size that ATM uses to transmit data is only 53 bytes (48 bytes for the payload and a 5-byte header) and is a fixed packet size. When referring to a packet of data in ATM networks the term *cell* is usually used. The advantage to using a fixed-length cell as opposed to a variable-length packet such as that used by frame relay is that hardware devices that are designed to switch network traffic can usually be designed to operate at higher speeds when switching fixed-length packets of information.

ATM **Connections**

Connections created between end points in the ATM network can be either permanent virtual connections (PVCs) or switched virtual connections (SVCs). Each switch in the ATM network keeps track of connections using routing tables, and decisions are made based on the information in the 5-byte header. Because the switch does not have to make any decisions based on the service data contained in the cell's payload section, hardware-based switches can quickly route and transport cells to their destinations.

ATM provides two kinds of transport connections: *virtual channels* and *virtual paths*. A virtual channel is used for an individual connection through the network. The *virtual channel identifier (VCI)* is used to identify cells in this connection. A virtual path is made up of multiple virtual channels that all share a common path through the network; it is identified in the cell header by a *virtual path identifier (VPI)*. By grouping together connections using VPIs, management and controlling functions must be performed only once for a group of individual connections, making the network operate in a more efficient manner.

Before any data can be exchanged, the virtual connection path must be determined. Similar to the mechanism used in the telephone network, the path through the network from switch to switch is predetermined before any data exchange takes place. When determining the path that the connection will use, the quality of service for the traffic is taken into consideration to ensure that a path will be created that can provide the bandwidth needed by the service. Policing of traffic is done to ensure that a particular connection does not abuse the network by making use of resources that it is not entitled to.

ATM **Service Categories**

While early implementations of ATM use the technique of reserving a specified, fixed amount of bandwidth for a connection in advance, these service categories allow for several different levels of service that can be matched to the needs of different types of traffic. Each level of service defines the network behavior of a different kind of network traffic that can be used to specify the quality of service required for certain kinds of applications. For example, some network applications require precise timing and cannot tolerate excessive delays or reductions in bandwidth. Other applications tend to make bursty requests where bandwidth requirements vary widely in just a short time.

The following service categories are presently defined by the ATM Forum:

- Constant Bit Rate (CBR)
- Real-Time Variable Bit Rate (rt-VBR)
- Non–Real-Time Variable Bit Rate (nrt-VBR)
- Available Bit Rate (ABR)
- Unspecified Bit Rate (UBR)

The CBR category is based on providing a constant maximum bandwidth allocation for the connection for time-sensitive applications. The application does not have to always use the maximum bandwidth, but it will be available if needed for this level of service. This service category is suitable for use by real-time applications, voice and video applications, videoconferencing, and other applications of a similar sort.

The rt-VBR service category is also meant to provide a high level of service for time-sensitive applications that do not always generally maintain a constant bit rate but are still time-sensitive applications.

The nrt-VBR service category is similar to the rt-VBR category in that the expected traffic will be bursty in nature, but here the nature of the communications does not have tight constraints on delay factors. Both VBR categories can be useful for applications such as voice, when compression techniques are used, and possibly transaction-based applications, such as reservation systems or for communicating frame relay traffic.

The ABR category is intended for applications that might increase or decrease their traffic level depending on network conditions. In other words, they can be satisfied by using whatever bandwidth is available. Connections of this type can specify a minimum required bandwidth level but can then use more bandwidth as the network can make it available. Typical uses for this kind of service are LAN connections, such as distributed files services.

The UBR service category represents a "best effort" connection and is intended for applications that really don't care about bandwidth or quality of service. This bottom-of-the-barrel kind of service is useful for applications that have traffic which needs to get from one place to another but is in no hurry, for example, file transfers that can be done in a batch mode and do not have users sitting at the keyboard waiting for completion. Messaging services, such as email, also might find this service level sufficient.

LAN Emulation (LANE)

Using ATM in a local area network (LAN) can help reduce congestion if the network consists of multiple kinds of traffic, such as one that supports workstations and file servers along with multimedia applications. Using ATM as a backbone, you can interface it with your normal ethernet or token-ring segments. The ATM Forum has published specifications for LANE to help define the approach to be taken for this.

Standards are still being defined for LANE and it is not yet a technology that should be adopted by those who are expecting a long-term solution now. During the next few years, though, as this technology is subjected to further standardization and equipment manufacturers produce devices that work well with each other, LANE can be expected to become a popular technology.

Interconnections

ATM can be used for WAN connections and to connect workstations and file servers in LANs. Generally, however, it works best as a WAN connection to transport different kinds of traffic. For example, if you have a frame relay connection that you use to connect your network to a branch office, it is quite possible that the actual wide area connection that your vendor uses is made up of ATM switches, while they provide you a frame relay interface at each end.

X.25 and Frame Relay

The X.25 protocol defines an interface into a packet-switched network and does not make any assumptions about the method used to carry the actual data from one place to another. X.25 was developed to allow connection to various public networks such as CompuServe and Tymnet, and provides for speeds of up to 56K. Frame relay is similar to X.25 except that it uses digital connections instead of the analog connections that X.25 was designed for.

Frame relay is similar to ATM in that it is a packet-switched technology. However, ATM uses a fixed size for its cells, while frame relay packets are variable (such as ethernet).

Frame relay can operate at much higher speeds (up to 1.544Mbps) than X.25. This is accomplished because of the digital nature of frame relay, which is usually offered on a T1 or fractional T1 line. The digital nature of the line allows fewer errors than the analog system, and frame relay can operate faster than other technologies because it does not perform any actual error correction. When a frame error is detected, the frame is dropped. It is up to the end points to detect, via some higher level protocol, that an error has occurred.

Technical Note

Some vendors of frame relay services offer much faster capabilities, up to 45Mbps, using T3 lines.

Another important factor that makes frame relay attractive is that because it is a packet-switched technology, you only have to pay for the bandwidth that you expect to use. Instead of paying for the full cost of a T1 line between two geographically distant offices, you can use frame relay services. The carrier mixes traffic from various sources and transmits it over the line, so that frame relay represents a shared medium technology. The downside is that it is always possible that the bandwidth you need might not be available. Just as you sometimes get a circuit busy message when you try to place a telephone call during a peak holiday time period, the same thing can happen if traffic from multiple users of a carrier's frame relay service must transfer large amounts of data at the same time.

For this reason, when you decide to purchase frame relay services, you will get a guarantee of the amount of available bandwidth that the carrier expects to be capable of providing. This is called the *committed information rate*, or *CIR*. You might indeed be able to get higher throughput rates than that guaranteed by the CIR, but there is always the possibility that occasionally you might not achieve rates that are guaranteed by the CIR. It is important to monitor your usage in a high traffic environment to be sure you are getting what you pay for.

Another feature that frame relay provides, which can make it a better choice than dedicated point-to-point lines, is that it can reduce the number of physical connections you need at a site. For example, if you have multiple branch offices, you could use a dedicated T1 (or Fractional T1) line to connect each office to the main headquarters. Or, you could use frame relay, which can use only a single physical connection at the main office, to move the traffic across that connection (see Figure 34.2).

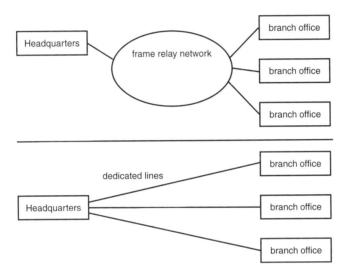

Figure 34.2   Using frame relay can reduce the number of physical connections required when compared to dedicated lines.

You might encounter the following problems when using frame relay:

- **Bandwidth utilization**—As you grow you might find that the amount of bandwidth you purchased is inadequate for your needs.

- **Bursting**—When you try to send a large burst of traffic that is in excess of the contracted rate, the switch might simply discard packets it receives that are above the allowable rate, forcing retransmissions and increased response times.

- **Network congestion**—Although the vendor might give you a guarantee of the available bandwidth (the CIR), when many customers use the network at the same time, network congestion can result.

The Frame Relay Forum is an organization that was formed to promote the use of frame relay technology and help create standards for the technology. You can visit its Web site:

    www.frforum.com

One of the things that the forum has done is to define several metrics that can be used to determine the quality of service in a frame relay network. These metrics, which can be found in the forum's FRF.13 Service Level Definitions Implementation Agreement are

- **Frame Transfer Delay**—The time required to transfer a frame through the network.

- **Frame Delivery Ratio**—This is the ratio of frames received (frames delivered) to the number of frames sent (frames offered), in one direction across a single virtual connection.

- **Data Delivery Ratio**—Similar to the frame delivery ratio, but measuring the ration of payload octets received to those sent.

- **Service Availability**—Outages resulting from faults in the network (called Fault Outage) as well as those beyond the control of the network, including scheduled maintenance (called Excluded Outage).

When reviewing the Service Level Agreement (SLA) that your frame relay provider offers, use these metrics to assist you in understanding what kind of commitment the vendor is making. With these metrics the vendor might further qualify them based on the CIR as opposed to bursts allowed by the agreement. For example, it would be unreasonable to expect to receive the same kind of delivery ratio for bursts of high volume traffic that you receive for traffic that flows through the network at the rate guaranteed by the CIR.

When you review the SLA, be sure you understand how each metric will be measured. Does the vendor use statistics provided by its own switch (and will they allow you access to these statistics?), or does it use an RMON probe or SNMP MIB to define the metrics? What portion of the connection is to be measured for metrics agreed upon? End-to-end or switch to switch?

Summary

You are presented with many choices when connecting a LAN to a WAN. The choice of using a dedicated connection such as a T1 or Fractional T1 line or implementing a cost-effective packet switched solution will depend on the quality of service that is needed to support your applications. It is no longer necessary to purchase a fixed amount of pipe that matches the maximum traffic level you will need only at peak periods. By using packet-switched network solutions, you can pay for only that which you need and at the same time leave room for growth in the future. When making purchasing decisions for packet-switched networks, you should be sure to have all factors relating to service quality spelled out in detail on the service agreement and understand the terms used in the agreement.

Part XIII

IMPROVING NETWORK SECURITY

Basic Security Measures

CHAPTER 35

Keeping a network secure is a time-consuming process that requires a lot of attention to detail. Similar to troubleshooting faulty equipment, tracking down security breaches and finding their cause requires tools made for the job and someone trained to use them. In this chapter, you will examine security from two different angles: first, preventative measures that can be used to help stop problems from occurring in the first place, and then tools and techniques to discover these kinds of problems.

Policies and Procedures

In order to have security practices that make sense, you must first define, for yourself and the users of the network resources, a security policy that spells out exactly what can and cannot be done on the network. Intruders who might penetrate the network and compromise data or programs do so in many ways. One of those is to exploit "friendly users" who are on the network. A good security policy that is enforced can go a long way toward keeping naive users from disclosing information to those who might do harm to your network.

At the same time, you should also establish procedures that are to be followed for routine tasks that are performed on a periodic basis, such as backups, restores, creating user accounts, and so on. When a task is described by a procedure that must be followed, there is less of a chance that something out of the ordinary will be done that can compromise security.

Depending on your site, there are several documents you can use to make users aware of the policies in use for computer and network security. Typically, the human resources department is responsible for having new employees review documents and sign them to show that they have read and understood them. Documents you might find useful for your site are

- Network Connection Policy
- Acceptable Use Statement
- Usage Guidelines
- Escalation Procedures

Network Connection Policy

This type of document should define the type of system that can be connected to the network. It should set forth the security requirements, such as operating system features to be used and a person responsible for approving new devices. The use of security programs, such as virus monitoring software, if required, should be included. Any procedures that must be used to obtain a computer account, along with the types of rights and privileges that can be granted to an account, should also be documented here as well as what network addresses can be used and how they are controlled. Finally, you should explicitly set forth in this document that no connections are to be made to the network without following the procedures in this document and without notifications made to the proper persons.

Acceptable Use Statement and Usage Guidelines

A computer is a very flexible device. It can be used for many things beyond the tasks that are needed by the ordinary worker during a normal workday. Although some might be concerned with the time that can be lost due to a user accessing a computer for non–work-related tasks, there are far more important factors to consider.

One of the most important things you should include in an acceptable use statement is the fact that all computer programs are to be supplied by the company and that unauthorized programs, such as those brought from home, are not to be used on the computer or network. Software piracy is not a victimless crime, as many people seem to think. Pirated software represents lost profits for the software developer, and can even be damaging, such as if it contains a virus added during the copying process. Piracy is a crime that is punishable by stiff fines and jail sentences. It is important that you make sure that users understand this and that you protect your company from possible litigation by showing that you have made an effort to prevent unauthorized programs from being placed on computers at the site.

Piracy is only one half of the issue when it comes to unauthorized programs. Computer viruses can easily make their way from one computer to another via floppy disk or by downloading from the Internet. Unfortunately, it is usually only after more than one system has become infected that a virus is found or reported. If all software that is used on the company network is first examined, approved, and distributed by a central source, you will have better control over this problem.

Of course, you should also state that users cannot make copies of software or data that is owned by the company and take it home or otherwise use it in an unauthorized manner.

In this statement, point out to users that they are required to report any suspicious activity or misuse of network resources. They should be made responsible also for taking necessary measures for protecting data and programs within their scope. This includes not leaving workstations logged on when they are away from them for extended periods of time, not leaving reports or other output containing sensitive information lying around, and so on. If you do not put it in a policy statement, users might not realize that this can be a problem.

If dial-up access is granted to users, they should certainly be made to understand that they cannot give information used for this access to anyone else, either inside or outside the company. Many times it has been shown that hackers penetrated a network not through repetitive password cracking techniques, but because a user left a password lying around or used one which was so obvious that it could not be considered secure.

The things you can put into an acceptable use policy are extensive. You must examine the specific types of resources you are trying to protect and think up ways to include them in the statement. Some other issues you might want to consider addressing are

- Harassment of other users, especially sexual harassment. For example, if this is done via email, the company can be sued as promoting a hostile work environment.
- Removal of hardware from the premises without written authorization.

- Using company email for personal uses. This is more of a personnel policy than for security, though it would also cover someone emailing sensitive data outside the company.

- Bringing hardware into the premises without authorization, such as laptop computers or network analyzers. This hardware could be used to try to hack into a network server or to copy sensitive data and carry it off the premises.

- Attempting to access data not relevant to the user's job, sometimes referred to as "probing" the network. This can include someone trying to access payroll data or production figures, for example.

Employees

Any document that outlines guidelines for using the network should point out to employees that they are to behave ethically on the network. Help desk personnel, for example, often must access data owned by another person when helping them with a problem. Disclosing information to a third party that is obtained during this type of work is unethical. Administrators and operations personnel often have elevated rights and privileges on the workstations and servers that are distributed throughout the network. They should be made to understand that these privileges include a responsibility to professionally carry out their work without causing problems.

Vendors and Outside Connections

Another area often overlooked is when outside persons are allowed to access the network. If you have contractors who are brought in to do work that cannot be done by in-house persons, be sure that you have a usage guidelines document for them to review and sign. It should specifically include the fact that information on the network is of a proprietary nature and cannot be disclosed to any outside party or to any employee in the company who does not need to know it.

Additionally, the policy document should state that the contractor cannot even discuss with others the type of information to which they have access. A little information can go a long way when given to the wrong person.

When hardware repair must be done it is usually done by a third-party maintenance organization or perhaps by the vendor who manufacturers the equipment. Diagnosing some problems might require that the repairman have access to a logon account. If you maintain a user account just for this purpose, be sure that it is one that can be enabled and disabled so that it is available only when it is needed. For example, the OpenVMS operating system has, by default, a FIELD account that is meant to be used by field service when they need access to the computer. This account is disabled when it is created and must be enabled by the administrator before it can be used. Because OpenVMS is a widely used operating system, a lot of hackers are aware of this account and also know that many times you will set an easy password for it. Don't make the mistake of leaving this kind of back door open to your network. Disable or remove accounts such as these when they are not needed.

Escalation Procedures

Having a plan of action that should be followed in response to a specific event is a good idea. There should be a specific person or persons in the company who are designated to be responsible for and investigate matters relating to security. A document that sets forth the procedures to be followed for specific security violations will also show users that security is important for the network and that actions will be taken.

A document covering escalation procedure should indicate the kinds of things that are considered a security breach. These can include the following:

- Theft of hardware or software
- Password discovery or disclosure
- Improper disposal of media, including tapes, floppy disks, and printed reports
- Sharing of logon accounts
- Probing the network to look where one is not authorized
- Interfering with another user's data or account
- Suspected network break-in from outside sources
- Computer viruses
- Physical access violations

Some of these probably seem very obvious when you look at them. To think that you will know how to handle these kinds of problems without a written procedure, though, is a little naive. For example, it is common for users to allow others to use their accounts. It's a lot simpler to let another employee use your workstation when theirs is out of service than it is to get the appropriate permissions from upper-level management. However, often when you give someone a password to use on one occasion, it also gets used on another.

When you suspect that the network has been infiltrated from an outside source, what do you do? Shut down the routers? Change all the passwords? Think about this ahead of time and write down a list of steps to follow. These should include methods used to determine the source of the break-in as well as procedures to be followed to punish the intruder and reassert ownership of any pilfered information. For example, if information that is confidential has been compromised, what steps do you take to notify the person to which the information relates? Are there legal matters you must be aware of that pertain to the data that resides on your network?

Perhaps one of the hardest things a manager must do is fire an employee. When someone leaves the company voluntarily and is on friendly terms with management, deactivating the user's account and making sure that all access doors are closed is a simple matter. When an unfriendly termination happens, though, you must have in place steps to follow to make sure you are aware of all access methods that were available to the unfriendly employee. In the case of an employee who is terminated for actions that caused deliberate damage to the network, how do you determine whether any other "time bombs" have been planted? What steps do you take to isolate the resources that were available to this employee until further analysis can be done? Do you need to change passwords on accounts other than the user's?

As you can see, network security has far-reaching implications. Knowing what to do in the event of a specific security event will make things easier for you when they happen.

Drafting Your Own Security Policy

When writing a security policy, you should first perform an inventory of the resources you want to protect. Identify the users who must access each resource and determine where the most likely place a threat to the resource might come from. With this information, you can then begin to construct a security policy that users will have to follow.

The security policy should not be simply a verbal agreement. It should be an actual written document; and to remind users about the importance of security, you might want to post copies of it around the office so they will see it on a regular basis.

A good security policy will be composed of several elements, including the following:

- **Risk assessment**—What are you trying to protect and from whom? Identify your network assets and possible sources of problems.

- **Responsibilities**—Describe who in the company is responsible for handling specific matters relating to security. This can include who is authorized to approve a new user account to who will conduct investigations into security breaches.

- **Proper use of network resources**—State in the policy that users are not to misuse information, use the network for personal uses, or intentionally cause damage to the network or information that resides on it.

- **Legal ramifications**—Be sure to get advice from the proper sources about any legal matters that apply to the information you store or generate on your network. Include statements to this effect in the security policy documents.

- **Procedures to remedy security problems**—State what procedures will be followed when a security event occurs and what actions will be taken against those who perpetrate them.

Request For Comments (RFC) 1244 ("Site Security Handbook") is a good document to read before designing a security policy. This RFC gives a list of resources that are found in most networks that are vulnerable to potential security threats. You can find a list of the current and proposed RFCs at `http://www.rfc-editor.org/isi.html`. These resources include the following groups:

- **Hardware**—This includes workstations and servers, printers, disk drives, network wiring, and disk drives. This also includes internetworking devices such as bridges, routers, and switches.

- **Software**—Every piece of software that you run on any computer in the network is a potential security problem. This includes programs purchased from outside vendors and software created in-house by your own programming staff. Operating systems frequently must be patched as new "bugs" are discovered that give an intruder an easy way to infiltrate.

- **Data**—The most important asset on your network is probably the data that is generated or used by your business. You can replace software programs and operating systems. When important data, such as customer lists, sales information, or proprietary trade secrets is compromised, it can have a significant impact on business.

- **People**—Users, operators, and anyone else who interacts with your network or any device attached to it are a potential security risk.

- **Paperwork**—Often overlooked by many, this is a very valuable resource to hackers. Passwords are written down. Reports are generated that have confidential information contained in them. Often this resource is simply thrown in a dumpster when it is no longer needed. A better approach is to shred or otherwise make it unusable before getting rid of it.

A good security policy that is understood by users will go a long way toward preventing some of the problems that you can potentially encounter. Make it a regular event to review the policy with users on a periodic basis, such as at quarterly meetings, and be sure that they understand the responsibilities that go along with having access to the company network.

Physical Security Measures

Preventing unauthorized access to resources means that you must first prevent unauthorized access to the physical components that make up the network. This includes user workstations, servers, network cables and devices, and so on. After the network connection leaves your physical area, such as when you connect to an outside Internet provider, you lose control over the physical aspects of the network. At that point you must rely on other techniques, such as encryption or tunneling, to maintain security. However, the equipment over which you have control should be closely monitored to ensure that no one is tampering with anything in a manner that might serve to defeat the security policy in effect at your site.

Lock the Door

As silly as it might seem, the simple door lock is an often overlooked security device. You wouldn't leave your front door at home unlocked all the time, would you? The servers in your network that hold valuable or sensitive data should not be sitting out on a desktop or in an unlocked room where anyone can access them. Routers, hubs, switches, and other devices should be similarly protected. Wiring closets and computer rooms should have a lock on them or be protected by some sort of monitoring on a 24-hour basis. If you have a round-the-clock operations staff, you might not need to lock the computer room. But, if that staff consists of only one person during any particular time period, get a lock for the door!

Backup media, such as tapes or writable CDs, should be treated the same as live data. Don't back up a server or your own personal workstation and leave the tape cartridge lying on the desk or in an unlocked drawer.

Uninterruptible Power Supply (UPS)

Keeping data secure can mean keeping it out of the hands of those who are not permitted to view it. It can also mean keeping the data safe from corruption. As more and more business-critical information is being committed to electronic form, it is important to take steps to be sure that it is not unintentionally compromised. A good UPS will pay for itself the first time you have to spend days reconstructing a database or reinstalling programs that become unusable because of a power outage or other problem of this sort.

Most computer operating systems have features that will work with a UPS so that the UPS can perform an orderly shutdown when it detects that power has been lost. If you are using a battery-backup UPS that has only a limited supply of power, an orderly shutdown can save a lot of problems when compared to a system crash.

Dispose of Hardware and Media in a Secure Manner

When you upgrade your network and bring in new workstations or servers, it is generous to give employees or an organization such as a school your old equipment if it is still usable. However, you should establish and follow a policy that dictates that all hard disks are to be erased and, when appropriate, a legal copy of the operating system reinstalled on it. If you leave important information on a computer you give away, don't be surprised when you see it again.

There is also the legal aspect to this. If you give away an old computer system, do you have the legal right to keep the software packages and install them on a new system? Probably not, unless you have a site license or other license that allows you to do so. For that reason, do not give away a computer that has applications installed on it unless you intend to give away the software packages also.

Disposing of used floppy disks, backup tapes, and tape cartridges also pose a potential security threat. It is better to destroy these information carriers than to give them away without being absolutely sure that you have rid them of any information. A bulk magnetic eraser can be a good security tool to use before disposing of this kind of stuff.

The Two Sides of Security

Locking the computer room door is a preventative measure that is intended to keep out those who have no business being there. Preventative measures should be taken for software access mechanisms also. However, no matter how good you are at putting into place the access control mechanisms to protect resources, there is always going to be someone who will try, and possibly succeed, in breaking through. For this reason, you also must be able to keep audit trails of events on the network so you can determine whether someone is trying to break your security, or if indeed they have done so.

Before the Fact: Controlling Access

Controlling access to the network is done by several common mechanisms, including the following:

- User accounts and passwords
- Physical identifiers
- Resource protections

In many operating systems the concept of a *resource owner* is important in this scheme. For example, OpenVMS and Windows NT keep track of the user who creates a resource, such as a file. That owner is able to change the protections applied to the file and can grant others the permissions needed to use the file.

Identifying Users

In a homogeneous network where only one user account and password is required for access to permitted resources throughout the network, system management is not usually a complicated matter. Windows NT allows for the creation of areas of control called *domains* that operate as security boundaries. Users in a domain can be granted access to resources on any computers—either servers or workstations—that the network administrator wants to give them. In addition, trust relationships can be established between domains when administrators cooperate, making it possible for the user to still use only one username and password to connect to resources throughout the network.

Novell NetWare provides this functionality by giving the user a logon to the network that is controlled by the Novell Directory Services. Each user is represented in the directory by a User object, the properties of which specify information about passwords and connections.

The UNIX operating system does not use the concept of a domain. Instead, each UNIX host maintains a password file that stores information about each user, including an encrypted password. In order to access resources on other network hosts, the UNIX user must either log on when accessing the computer or use a proxy mechanism. TCP/IP utilities such as FTP and Telnet send user passwords across the network in clear-text format (non-encrypted) and are easy targets for interception.

The UNIX remote utilities, usually called r-commands because they all start with the letter R, are used to perform ordinary network functions such as copying or printing files or logging in to a remote system. This is useful in the network environment where a user performs functions on many different machines. These utilities are not necessarily good when looked at from a security standpoint, however. Although the user must have a valid user account on the remote hosts on which these commands execute, the user does not have to provide the password.

Technical Note

Although most Telnet applications still use clear-text passwords for authentication purposes, some use encrypted authentication. If security is of a great concern on your network, be sure to examine the documentation closely before using these utilities on any node in the network. This also applies to other TCP/IP utilities such as the r-commands and FTP.

Instead, an entry in the /etc/hosts.equiv file or the .rhosts file on a remote computer is what determines access. The remote machine trusts the computer on which the user executes an r-command if it can find an entry in either of these files for it. Each entry in the /etc/hosts.equiv file contains a hostname and username to identify users and the hosts that are allowed to execute these commands without providing a password. The assumption is that if you have logged in to the remote host, you have already been authenticated. The .rhosts file works in a similar manner, but resides in a user's home directory. The remote users entered in this file can perform functions based on the account associated with that user.

Although this sounds a lot like NT's trust mechanism, it is not. It is easy to impersonate a remote node and gain entry into a UNIX system by using the r-commands.

Note

More specific information about user logon accounts can be found in Chapter 22, "Windows NT Domains," Chapter 23, "NetWare," and Chapter 24, "UNIX and Linux."

Resource Protections

After a user has been authenticated by the operating system, the next step is for a check to be done to see whether the resource has any access controls placed on it. Typically an operating system will grant access to a resource, such as a file, by granting users the right to

- Read the file
- Write to the file
- Execute the file
- Take ownership of the file
- Delete the file

These concepts can also be extended to resources such as printers, modems, and so on. When granting these rights, most operating systems also allow you to specify which rights are applied to users or groups of users. For example, Windows NT enables you to group users together into local or global groups. When you set the access controls on a file, you can specify the access rights by group. Using this method, one group of ordinary users might be able to read a file while a group of users that manages the file might be granted read and write access as well as delete access to the file. To prevent programs from being run by unauthorized users, the execute right can be granted or denied to a user or a group of users.

Tip

Windows NT enables you to format a hard disk using the NTFS file system or the standard FAT system that is compatible with DOS and other operating systems, such as Windows 95/98. If you want to provide access controls on individual files and directories under Windows NT, you must format your disk partitions using NTFS. The access rights that you can assign to files and directories have no effect on FAT partitions. Also, Windows 2000 adds a new feature to Windows NT that enables you to encrypt individual files on disk. The encryption is done on-the-fly as a file is written or read, so for a high-security environment, this might be a good option to use.

For more information on user rights and permissions and how they are implemented by different operating systems, see Chapter 26, "Rights and Permissions."

After the Fact: Auditing Usage

In Chapter 37, "Auditing and Other Monitoring Measures," you will find an in-depth discussion about the tools you can use to keep track of resource usage, both attempted and successful attempts. Organizing users into groups and assigning permissions to the groups for network resources is not enough. You must also audit the usage of these network resources to help identify access and security problems.

There are several reasons for this. A large user base combined with multiple servers that hold valuable resources makes it difficult at times for an administrator who is not familiar with the information resources provided by a specific server to understand the permissions needed. For example, a new user in the accounting department might need access to accounts receivable files and accounts payable files, or they might need access to one or the other. A manager in that department would probably be the likely person to make the decision about what files the user should be able to access.

However, if the user is placed into a group, which is generally done to make administration easier, compromises sometimes happen and the user might be granted access via the group to resources that they do not need to access.

Another reason is that sometimes mistakes are made. No one is perfect, and no system for allocating resources is going to get it right 100 percent of the time. When users are granted the ability to read a file, you can be sure, if the data contained in it is interesting enough, that they will do so. Indeed, even if a user does not have appropriate access rights to a file, some will try to get at interesting information anyway.

For these kinds of reasons, a good operating system will provide auditing controls that will enable you to look back after a security breach to try and determine who did what and where they did it. UNIX (and its variants such as Linux), Windows NT, and Novell all provide features that enable you to record both successful and failed attempts to access resources. They all do it in different ways, so if you have multiple operating systems on the network, it will be important that you understand each of them so that you can best use these capabilities.

Passwords

It might not seem like an important thing to mention at this point, but you must enforce a policy that makes users choose good passwords. And when you do that, you must decide what makes a good password for your environment. Simply put, a good password is one that is hard to guess. When you consider that a standard password cracking technique used by hackers is to try every word in a dictionary, you can begin to understand that luck doesn't have a lot to do with penetrating a network. It comes mostly from lax security.

Enforce Good Passwords

When deciding on how passwords are to be constructed, there are a few guidelines you can follow:

- **Use more than one word**—Multiple words "glued" together make a pattern of characters that is much harder for a simple password cracking program to guess. Don't use words that naturally go together. For example, Atlantabraves is not a good choice. Atlantabarbie is a better choice.

- **Use non-alphabetic characters somewhere in the password**—This can be numeric characters or punctuation characters, provided the operating system you use will permit them.

- **In UNIX, passwords are case-sensitive**—If you use characters in a password using both upper- and lowercase characters you can confound the guessing mechanism.

- **Don't make passwords too difficult to memorize**—The last thing you want is to have frustrated users writing down passwords so they will be able to remember them.

- **Use password history restrictions if the operating system permits it**—This means that the operating system keeps track of a limited number of passwords that the user has previously used and will not allow them to be reused within a certain time frame. A common practice is to change your password when forced to do so, and then to change it back to a value that you like and can easily remember.

Make sure that you do not create user accounts and assign them a password that never gets changed by the user. Most operating systems will allow you to set a password to be expired on its first use so that when a new user logs in the first time they are required to change their password.

Sometimes it is important to have a password that makes no sense whatsoever. In a highly secure environment, this can make sense—you want something that is hard to guess. However, remember that when something is difficult to remember it usually gets written down somewhere, which can defeat the purpose of a password altogether. UNIX has a command, `passwd`, that can be used to computer-generate a password for a user. For example, the command

```
Paswwd username
```

will display a list of potential passwords that are generally difficult to guess. The user can select a password from this list if he or she is having a difficult time thinking of one.

Password Policies

No user account, including one used by an administrator, should ever be allowed to keep the same password for an extended period of time. A good idea for passwords is to require that they be changed every 30–60 days, depending on the level of security you need at your site. You should also enforce a minimum length for passwords. Most operating systems will allow you to specify this value so that users cannot change their password to one that is shorter than the required size.

On Windows NT computers, you can do this by using the User Manager for Domains utility and selecting Account from the Policies menu. The dialog box that pops up will allow you to set the minimum password length along with other domain policies related to user accounts.

On UNIX systems, you can set the password minimum length by specifying it in a field in the file `/etc/default/passwd`.

On Novell NetWare servers, you can enforce a minimum password length by modifying the object properties of the template object used to create a user account or by modifying the properties of an individual user object for a particular user.

Depending on the particular operating system, you can enforce other restrictions on passwords or user accounts to enhance security on the network. Some of the capabilities you might find include the following:

- **Password expirations**—A password should not be used indefinitely.
- **Password history lists**—This feature prevents a password from being reused within a specified time period.
- **Account lockouts**—When a hacker is trying to use the brute-force method to guess a password for an account, you should be able to lock the account out automatically after a specified number of attempts within a specific time frame.

Password Grabbers

About the oldest trick known to those who would want to break into another user's account is the use of a program that imitates the operating system's own logon procedure. This kind of program generally is executed by someone who logs on using their own account on another's workstation. They then run a program that does nothing but wait until the unsuspecting user tries to log on. The program prompts for a username and password, mimicking the operating system in every respect. However, instead of logging on the user to the system, which the program is unable to do, it stores the password in a file and generates a phony error message.

If the user is not too concerned about security, he will probably never know that he has been fooled. He might think he has entered his password incorrectly and try again. The second time it will succeed because the operating system is prompting him this time. The password grabber program has already done its job, and it disappears.

The user who began this fraud then retrieves the file, thus getting the password, and can freely log on as that user, which causes many problems when it comes to tracking down the real person who is abusing security. Because the hacker is now using someone else's username and password, he or she is difficult to catch.

Technical Note

This subterfuge is one of the reasons why Windows NT uses the key sequence of Ctrl+Alt+Delete to begin the logon process. It is generally difficult to write a program that mimics the Windows NT logon screen because the Ctrl+Alt+Delete combination of keystrokes is trapped by a processor interrupt and, unless the system has been grossly compromised, any program attempting to pass as the logon screen will fail.

However, this does not mean that NT is completely immune to this kind of attack. It is easy to write a program that runs under DOS. If the workstation can be booted using a floppy drive, it is easy to run a program that looks and acts like Windows NT's logon screen. After capturing the password, such a program, which cannot return to NT because it is not running, can mimic the "blue screen of death" or reboot the computer.

System Daemons and Services

Windows NT Server has background processes that perform many functions called *services*. UNIX systems also have background processes that work in a similar manner and are called *daemons*. Regardless of what you call them, these processes, which are called *background* because they do not require interaction with the keyboard, but instead execute on the computer waiting to perform some function, can introduce security problems when they are not needed.

You should become familiar with the background processes on any servers in your network and disable those that are not needed. For example, on UNIX systems, many background daemons are associated with the TCP/IP suite of protocols. Some systems might need all these, whereas some might need just a few or none of them. Table 35.1 lists some of the daemons you might want to look at to determine whether they are needed. If not, disable them.

Table 35.1   TCP/IP Services That Might Not be Needed on All Systems

Service Name	Description
uucp	UNIX-to-UNIX copy
finger	Provides information about users
tftp	Trivial file transfer protocol
talk	Allows text communications between users on the network
bootp	Provides network information to clients
systat	Gives current system information
netstat	Gives current network information such as current connections
rusersd	Shows logged on users
rexd	Remote execution utility

It could be that you do not need these services, or it could be that they must be configured properly to prevent their misuse. You should read the documentation that comes with your UNIX or Linux system to determine the capabilities that these daemons provide, and disable them on systems that do not need them. For more information on using UNIX-based systems, including Linux, check out Que Corporation's *Special Edition Using Linux, Fifth Edition*, and Sams Publishing's *UNIX Unleashed, System Administrator's Edition*.

For example, TFTP is a stripped-down version of FTP. It is compact and can usually be easily implemented in an EPROM. For this reason, it is useful in some devices that must download operating software from a host. However, note that unlike FTP, TFTP has no access control mechanisms. This means that a username and password are not used. Because there is no authentication, this can be a real security problem if it is not configured properly hso that it can only be used for its intended purpose.

On Windows NT you can use two programs that are provided with the Resource Kits to install or run almost any executable program or batch file as a service. These are INSTRV.EXE, which can be used to install an executable, and SRVANY.EXE, which can be used to make other kinds of files into services. On a server that has many users logging in frequently, you might want to make it a regular part of your routine maintenance to review the services running on the machines and disable or remove those that are not installed by the initial operating system installation or those that did not come from products you have applied to the system.

To do this you will need to keep an inventory of what runs on each server, but this kind of inventory information can be useful for other purposes too, such as when you need to reinstall a server that has been destroyed by a catastrophic failure.

Removing the Deadwood

Every operating system comes with default options installed that you might not be aware of unless you have carefully read the documentation. For example, default user accounts can be created when you install the OS or later install a product. For example, the GUEST account in Windows NT is installed by default. You should always disable or remove this account. The ADMINISTRATOR account is also a vulnerable target because it is present on all Windows NT Server computers. You cannot delete this account, but you can rename it so that the hacker's job is more difficult.

Regularly review the user accounts that exist on the network. Use the auditing features provided to determine when an account has not been in use for a long period of time and, if you can find no reason for its existence, disable it. Maybe someone in another department did not notify you when a user was terminated. Maybe an account was created for an expected new employee or contractor who later changed his or her mind and did not come on board. New accounts such as these are typically created with a simple password and can leave gaping security holes in your network.

Old programs and files that are no longer needed, or the use of which you are not sure, are also easy targets to cause security problems. As a rule of thumb, if it's not needed, back it up to tape and delete it. If users find that something they need is missing, they will tell you.

When installing a new application product for a user, be sure you know the capabilities of the application. Don't install unneeded optional features that will not normally be used. Read the documentation!

Delegating Authority

In a network of any size other than a simple workgroup, it is usually necessary to delegate authority to other administrators or middle-level management personnel. When you find that you must create accounts that have privileges to perform administrative functions, do not give carte blanche access to every account. Keep track of the exact functions for which an account will be used and grant only the access rights and permissions needed.

For example, if an operator will be performing backup functions on a server, they do not need to have full rights and privileges on the server. Under Windows NT you can place the user's account into the Backup Operators user group to give them the capabilities they need, without compromising all files on the system. If you have users who must be able to add or modify user accounts, check the operating system documentation and give them access to only the resources and data files they need.

User Accounts

Generic accounts might seem like a good idea at first, but they provide nothing in the way of auditing. If you let one or more users share the root account on a UNIX system or the ADMINIS-TRATOR account on an NT computer, you will have no way of determining who did what when something goes wrong. Indeed, because you can grant the same capabilities to any new account you can create, why not do so?

Give each user who requires elevated capabilities his or her own account and grant the necessary privileges to the account. This way you can track each user to make sure they do not abuse their account or use it in a way that you do not expect.

When you have more than one user using the same account, there is also the likelihood that the password will be compromised, and someone who is not authorized to use the account will do so.

Application Servers, Print Servers, and Web Servers

One particularly common error that you can make is to put all your eggs in one basket. Instead of using one server to provide print services, file services, or Web services, many administrators use one server to provide all three. This is not necessarily a good idea.

Specialized servers can limit the damage that can be done by intruders and can also make it easier to delegate authority so that a particular administrator can concentrate on a limited set of functions for a certain server. Web servers are particularly prone to attempts by hackers to intrude onto your network. New applications and technologies are being developed and deployed all the time, and the newer they are the more likely they will have bugs or other loopholes that make them more risky than other applications that run on the network.

Placing sensitive data files on a Web server because it is convenient to use the machine's resources is not a good idea if it is also being used as a Web server. Make it more difficult to get at these files by dedicating a file server computer to them instead.

Delegating servers is almost like delegating authority to users. When you divide resources and partition them into manageable groups, you make it less likely that an attack on one object will result in damage to all.

Denial of service attacks are very common on networks now. This kind of attack can be done by a malicious person who takes advantage of a known weakness in a protocol or an implementation of a particular service. One common mistake that administrators make when setting up an FTP site is to place it on an ordinary server.

For example, you might want to have an FTP server that enables customers to log on to your system and download information, patches, or other files. You might also want to be able to let them upload files or messages to your site. If you are going to allow anonymous FTP access, be absolutely sure that the service is configured so that it can access only a dedicated disk or set of disks. Do not allow anonymous access to an FTP service that writes to a system disk or a data disk that is important in your network. It is easy for an outsider to fill up the disk with meaningless data, causing a system to lock up or crash, depending on the operating system. If an important data disk becomes full, it can cause an extended period of downtime, putting employees out of work for hours while you try to determine the cause and then remedy it!

Computer Viruses

This is a hot topic on the Internet as well as the news media. Barely a year passes that some new virus is discovered that has found a new way to infiltrate networks, workstations, and home computers. Viruses are nothing more than programs that are capable of reproducing themselves. They do not have to be destructive, but most are.

Viruses come in many types. The National Computer Security Association and other security organizations categorize them into groups based on how they operate and how they are implemented. Some of these types include

- **Boot sector virus**—A virus of this type infects the master boot record of the computer. It overwrites the boot code and replaces it with its own infected version. The Michelangelo virus is an example. These types of viruses are easily spread by floppy disk.

- **File virus**—A virus of this type infects an executable program on the disk. Instead of replacing the boot code, this kind of virus replaces or attaches to a program that exists on your hard drive. When the program is executed, the virus does its damage.

- **Stealth virus**—This kind of virus is particularly hard to detect; it makes a specific effort to make itself invisible to the operating system or virus detection software. For example, it can alter the size of a file but hide this fact from the operating system.

- **Macro virus**—This is a rather new kind of virus that uses the macro programming capabilities that are being increasingly incorporated into to word-processing and spreadsheet applications. Open the file and the virus executes.

- **Polymorphic virus**—This virus is particularly difficult to locate. Many virus detection programs look for a specific signature to identify a particular virus. This kind of virus has built-in code that causes it to mutate itself when it copies, so it might not look the same the next time you see it.

The stealth virus is a particularly horrible creature. It can fight back or even alter some virus detection programs that you think are protecting your system. One key method used to locate this kind of virus, if you suspect it, is to completely remove your current virus protection and detection software, and then perform a new install of the latest version. If the installation procedure complains, you might still have a problem.

Other Destructive Programs

In addition to viruses, you must be aware of other types of destructive programs that can wreak havoc on a computer or network. Trojan horse programs are not necessarily considered to be a virus, but can be just as destructive. This kind of program masquerades as another program. Sometimes it performs functions that seem perfectly normal for what the user expects. It also, however, performs other functions that you do not expect. For example, a Trojan horse program can collect information from your workstation in the background and send the information to another computer on the network or, possibly, over the Internet.

Bombs are programs that are usually left behind by an unfriendly employee who wants to do harm. These bomb programs will usually "explode" and cause their damage after a set period of time or when an event occurs on the system. This is a good reason to archive a terminated user's programs and data files off to backup media unless they are needed and investigate any common files that the user had access too. About the best protection you can offer yourself from this kind of program is to keep regular full and incremental backups of all important system data so that in a catastrophic failure you can restore your systems.

How Infections Occur

The most common ways that a virus finds its way onto your system are through

- **Floppy disk**—This is why your computer security policy documentation should explicitly instruct users that they cannot bring in files from outside the company and load them onto their networked computer.

- **Email**—Several years ago a large portion of the Internet was brought to its knees by a virus that took advantage of known limitations that existed in mailer software.

- **Bulletin boards**—Although the Internet has pretty much replaced the popularity of these dial-up services, they do still exist, and if a user has a modem attached to a workstation, this can still be an avenue into your network.

- **Data files**—It used to be unthinkable that you could catch a computer virus by loading a data file onto your computer. With the more complex object-oriented types of data that exist today, this is no longer true. Witness the many viruses recently that exploit technology found in word-processing or spreadsheet documents. The macro coding capabilities of these kinds of documents is all that is needed by a crafty coder to construct a virus.

How do you know that your system has been infected? Without an up-to-date virus program, it is almost impossible to tell until it is too late and damage has been done. However, some of the things you should look out for include

- Unusual error messages
- Missing files for which there is no explanation
- Files that have increased or decreased in size dramatically
- The system is operating slower for no apparent reason

Preventative Measures You Can Take

Establish educational programs that make your users aware of your computer and network policies and tolerate no infractions lightly. If you find a user has brought in a floppy disk from home, treat it as a major problem. A floppy disk that appears to be blank can indeed still contain a hidden virus that can infect your computer.

Review all bulletins that are issued by Internet authorities about current virus infections.

When obtaining software from a vendor, you might want to consider setting up an isolated system or network of computers in a lab to perform tests before you release the software application to the network. It is a lot easier to cope with an isolated incident than to have to go troubleshooting the whole network.

If your network has no need for devices such as floppy disk drives, remove them. There are also programs you can obtain that will render floppy drives unavailable to users.

Obtain a good virus package—there are many on the market—and subscribe to the vendor's update program. Virus protection software is not an application you purchase once every few years. For example, Norton Antivirus software enables you to download code that can recognize new viruses as they are discovered, by using their live update method over the Internet.

Most antivirus software will function in several ways. The most obvious function is to allow you to scan your system any time you want to look for potential infections. Another important feature is scheduling, or the ability to run on a periodic basis without the user requesting the scan. Finally, a really nice feature is one that automatically intercepts data coming into your computer by disk, network, or email, and performs a scan of the data or program to help keep you from inadvertently infecting the computer.

Sources of Information About Viruses

There are several good places you can go on the Internet to gain knowledge about viruses so that you can keep up to date on the issues that surround them.

- **www.icsa.net**—This is the home page for the ICSA, Inc., formerly the National Computer Security Association (NCSA). This site provides information about computer viruses, firewalls, and other matters related to security.

- **www.antivirus.com**—Trend Micro offers antivirus software for multiple operating system platforms and also provides a lot of information about viruses.

- **www.symantec.com**—Symantec Corporation makes antivirus software and offers information about its software. This is the company that makes Norton Antivirus software.

- **www.macafee.com**—Macafee is another major antivirus software producer.

Summary

Security is more than just assigning a user an account name and enforcing good password rules. Security can be involved at all levels of network planning and execution. Physical access as well as network access both bring important considerations to the table.

You must be able to have some degree of trust over the users who use the network. You do not have to trust them completely, however, so be sure to use every available auditing tool at your disposal and periodically review the data gathered by these tools so you can feel comfortable about the status of your network systems, data, and other resources.

In the next chapter another important security measure is discussed. If you are going to connect your network to the Internet or to other wide area networks that are out of your control, you will definitely want to use firewall technology to further insulate yourself from those who might do harm to your network.

Firewalls

SOME OF THE MAIN TOPICS IN THIS CHAPTER ARE

What Is a Firewall?

Packet Filters

Proxy Servers

Hybrids

How Do You Know the Firewall Is Secure?

CHAPTER 36

You must be on the Internet if you want your business to remain competitive during the next decade. In just a few years it will be unthinkable that a major corporation or business does not have a network address that customers can use to access literature, place orders, or receive support. Could your business survive without a telephone number? The convenience to the customer and the opportunity to increase business will be so great that the Internet will transform the way many business transactions are done in a very short time.

Yet, there are serious problems that you must consider when deciding how to make your appearance on this new frontier. Can you use your existing corporate network and just install a gateway to connect yourself to the global network? Or, should you depend on some third party that specializes in creating Internet sites? In the long run you will probably end up having some sort of connection between your corporate network and the Internet, if only to allow the exchange of email and other business transactions.

The first measure of defense you must know about when connecting to the Internet is what a firewall is and what it can do to protect you. This chapter discusses the different technologies used to construct firewalls.

What Is a Firewall?

A *firewall* is a device that stands between your network and the Internet and acts as a gatekeeper, allowing in trusted friends and keeping out known or suspected enemies. A firewall is a device, such as a router, workstation, or dedicated hardware device, that has software capable of making the decisions needed to monitor the flow of data to and from inside the corporate network to the outside world. There are several kinds of firewalls, and they can be classified into the following categories:

- Packet filter
- Proxy servers
- Stateful inspection
- Hybrids

Although there are many different vendors offering firewall products, the technology used is so diverse that it is difficult to make direct comparisons between products. The best you can do is carefully review each product and ask a lot of questions before deciding whether it will offer the protection you need for your network. Remember also that even though new security holes are always popping up for firewall products, networks, and computer operating systems, many times a security breach occurs due to misconfiguration of the product.

Look for the following things when evaluating firewall products:

- Security (of course)
- Performance
- Support
- Price
- Manageability

Caution

A firewall protects you only at the point where your network connects to an outside network. One of the most common mistakes administrators make is assuming that the network is secure and overlooking the modems that sit on many desktops throughout the enterprise. Even if a modem is used only for dial-out purposes, you still run risks of virus infections and other security problems when users dial out to other sites and download programs or data to their workstations, which are connected to the network. Worse yet, modems used for dial-in purposes, such as remote access for users, present an easy entry point for those who would do harm.

The most important aspect of the firewall is the security it will afford your network. You should be sure to question the vendor about the specific methods that are used in the product and whether there have been any evaluations of the product by outside sources.

If you use the Internet connection only for the exchange of moderate amounts of email and an occasional Web browsing session, performance might not be a significant factor in your choice. However, if you expect heavy demand on the Internet connection, from within or without, check to be sure that the product you acquire can handle the load. Packet filter firewalls will provide a higher degree of performance; the trade-off is that they do not protect you as well as a proxy server might if it is configured properly. Because a proxy server is responsible for closer examination of each packet and can be configured to perform other tasks, it will be inherently slower than a packet filter.

Support is a critical item to consider. When purchasing an expensive firewall, many vendors will include onsite assistance in configuring and setting up the firewall. Additional support, including consulting and hotline help desk services, is important because the Internet is in a state of rapid growth, and what works today might not be sufficient tomorrow. Unless you have a highly skilled technical staff that is capable of making decisions about firewall techniques and implementing them, support from the vendor should be a major consideration.

Again, because a firewall is not something you simply configure and then forget, the management interface will be important. You should look for a product that provides easy access to configuration options so that you can review them and modify them as needed. Reporting capabilities should be easy to understand so that you can review data and statistics audited by the firewall. Another important aspect of the management interface is the capability to notify you when something appears to be targeting your network with not-so-good intentions. Alarms that appear onscreen are fine, if you have a round-the-clock operations staff that will be monitoring the screen. The best products provide email or paging for specific events for which you can set a trigger.

Finally, in many cases remote management can be a plus, if it is implemented correctly. Any remote management capability should include a secure authentication technique. What good is the firewall if you use a clear-text password when logging in to it remotely? You should proceed under the pretense that someone is always watching what you do on the network.

Price should not be the most relevant factor in your decision. There are firewall products you can download off the Internet and use free. Some firewalls sell for a few hundred dollars, and some range up into the tens of thousands of dollars. The more expensive the firewall is, though, is no indication of its safety or capabilities. As a matter of fact, some of the free firewalls you can get from the Internet are actually quite good. One of the things that the Linux platform excels at is implementing firewall technology. Its robust speed and low overhead make it a good choice for this type of chore. However, no matter on what product you decide, be sure that you have the skills and know-how to properly configure and operate it.

What Will You Expect from a Firewall?

A firewall is not a single application or hardware device that you can buy at the local computer store and plug your network into to get blanket protection from all the possible evils that lurk on the Internet. A common mistake that is often made is to assume that a firewall will do more than it can because of its name. In the building trade, a firewall that is used to protect individual units in an apartment complex or condominium is designed according to rules laid down by the local authorities. In the networking trade, no authorities exist to specify what a product must do to carry the label "firewall."

As a matter of fact, several kinds of applications and devices can be classified as firewalls. Do you need a packet filter? Do you need a device that can perform "stateful inspection"? Before you answer these questions, you first should decide what you are trying to protect and what methods you are currently using.

What Do You Want to Protect?

For example, if you have highly confidential information, such as patient records or financial information about customers, you should definitely get some good legal advice on your responsibility about keeping this information from the general public. Keeping important information on a dedicated server that cannot be accessed by ordinary users on your network is the first thing to do. However, assuming an off-the-shelf firewall application will protect you from outside penetration is being a bit simplistic.

First you should decide what your vulnerabilities are and examine your current network. Look at how sensitive data is protected now and look at the means used to access it. Then factor in how your current safeguards will enable you to keep the data secure.

Some information is usually available to everyone in the network. For example, an employee home page that contains information about processes and procedures, such as how to request a vacation or get a purchase order approved, will not usually be considered a high priority security item. Other information, such as information you keep about your customers, is not only important to your bottom line, if you want to keep the customer happy, but also might be confidential, such as a doctor's records about patients. This kind of information should receive your utmost attention when trying to decide how it can be accessed after you connect to the Internet. It might be generally available to a large number of employees, depending on your business, or it might be sequestered by operating system protections so that only a single department can use this kind of data.

Of course, if you perform your payroll in-house, you are probably already aware of how sensitive this kind of information is. It must be protected from prying eyes both inside your network and from those that try to intrude from outside.

Levels of Security

Because there are different kinds of information on networks today that need various levels of security, you should carefully structure your network to handle the way information is accessed.

One connection to the Internet, through a firewall, can serve to protect you. However, with one connection and one firewall, you must make sure that the firewall is the most restrictive you need to protect the most sensitive data that you have. One firewall to protect the entire network is one point of failure. One mistake, and the whole network can be vulnerable.

Another drawback is that many users will resent extremely restrictive access mechanisms and will, if allowed, circumvent them.

One method is to segment the internal network and use firewalls not only to keep intruders from outside the company from getting access, but also to keep out those internally who might do mischief. Also, by creating different levels of security, you can act to prevent a single security breach that causes extensive damage.

Instead of using a single network, you might want to consider creating several smaller networks and using firewall technology to connect them. For example, in-house data that never needs to be accessed from external sources can reside on one network, while another network can host machines that provide WWW, ftp, and other services to your external clients. The firewall that connects this network to the Internet would not have to be as restrictive as the one that joins the two networks at your site.

If you have data that is so confidential that its compromise could do severe harm, you should place it on a computer that does not have a connection to the Internet. Remember that there is no way to guarantee that a computer cannot be hacked via a network, short of pulling the plug.

Tip

Remember that firewalls can operate in both directions. Although the first thing that probably jumps into your head when you think about a firewall is that it will keep out unwanted packets, the reverse can also be true. For example, you might want to connect your network to the Internet to allow email or ftp access to and from customers and your employees. You might not want your employees to access Web pages, however, and you can block their outgoing requests to prevent this type of access.

Packet Filters

This type of firewall provides the most basic functions of a firewall and can be implemented with a simple router. A packet filter examines every packet that passes through it and will either forward or drop a packet according to a set of rules established by the administrator. Almost every router being manufactured today will allow you to restrict traffic flowing inward or outward based on the contents of the TCP/IP packet header.

A firewall of this type can be configured to block traffic by creating filters for the following:

- **IP addresses**—Both source and destination addresses. You can specify individual addresses or ranges of addresses.
- **Protocols**—Such as UDP or TCP.
- **Port Numbers**—Used to identify connections between applications. You can usually specify a range of port numbers, or use filters that allow you to say "greater than" or "less than" a port number.
- **Direction**—Inbound or outbound.

For example, you might want to allow some users to use telnet (port 23) or ftp (ports 20 and 21) to connect to servers outside the corporate network while denying this ability to others. You can do this by setting up rules in the packet filter and specifying both a host address and a port number. In Appendix B, "TCP and UDP Common Ports," you will find a list of the port numbers used by TCP and UDP.

This type of firewall has several advantages over others:

- It is usually inexpensive. If you use a router to connect to external sources, you already have the hardware—you just need to configure it.
- It is fast because it does only minimal processing on the header information and does not make decisions based on multiple packets.
- It is flexible. It is easy, though some would say cumbersome, to configure as many address inclusions or exclusions as you like.

However, there are also several disadvantages to using a packet filter firewall:

- **Packet filters perform no authentication functions**—A packet is a packet no matter "who" the sender is. The address is the only thing that matters.
- **There are usually no auditing features**—You will most likely not even know that attempts were made to break in to the network and, if the router does provide some kind of statistical information, you will not be able to determine from where the attack came.
- **Packet filters operate at the network level**—They are not very effective at stopping sophisticated attacks that are directed at higher-level protocols, such as TCP/IP.
- **Internal network information is not kept from outside prying eyes**—Using ordinary utilities, such as tracert and ping, mischievous persons can gain knowledge about your network unless you specifically block this protocol (ICMP).

A good approach for configuring the rules to use on a packet filter is to first deny all traffic. Then, selectively enable only those addresses or services that are essential to your business. If you try to do this in reverse—allowing all traffic and then denying specific items—you might leave out something that did not seem important at the time you did the configuration, or a new twist on an old technology might creep up and surprise you later on.

IP Address Spoofing

One of the common methods used by hackers to gain access is to attempt to fool your network into thinking that they are part of it. To do this, they construct packets which have a source address that looks like it came from within your network. To prevent this type of access, be sure to deny any external traffic that contains an address that is in use on your network. Using the Cisco IOS software, you can use access lists to do this.

An *access list* is just a sequence of statements that are used to permit or deny packets from passing through the router's interfaces. You can design access lists to screen selected IP addresses or a range of addresses. This is called an *area* or *network* access filter. You can also use a service filter to screen network traffic based on the protocol used (such as UDP or SMTP).

Intrusion Detection (Stateful Inspection)

A *stateful inspection* device operates similarly to a packet-filtering firewall in that it also examines the source and destination addresses of every packet that passes its way. However, a packet filter is never aware of the context of any communication. Each packet that passes through it is treated on an individual basis. A firewall that employs stateful inspection techniques attempts to keep track of requests and responses to be sure that they match.

This type of firewall will maintain tables of information about current connections so it can determine whether incoming packets are unsolicited or are in response to a request that was made by a user on the internal network. Another name sometimes used for this type of firewall is *dynamic packet filter*.

When a connection terminates, the firewall will remove the reference from its internal table so that an external source cannot use it to gain entry again.

Proxy Servers

The data and applications that live on the machines in your network are not the only thing you must guard from outside mischief. The identity of the workstations, servers, and other devices should also be closely guarded. A proxy server can perform this function by managing connections to and from the outside world.

Impersonating the End User: Network Address Translation (NAT)

When an application that lives on your network must make a connection to a resource on the Internet, a proxy server will set up a connection to the resource and impersonate the application in dealing with the resource. For example, a user wanting to access a Web page on the Internet using a browser sends a request to the resource that includes the address of his workstation. The proxy server substitutes its address for the user's when it forwards the request. When the Web page data is returned from the outside resource to the proxy server, it then places the address of the user's workstation in the packet and sends it on to the end user.

This type of service is also referred to as *Network Address Translation* (*NAT*). You can see an example of this in Figure 36.1. A user on your network wants to retrieve a Web page, so a request packet is created containing the address of the sending workstation (the end user) and the address of the Web server that hosts the Web page.

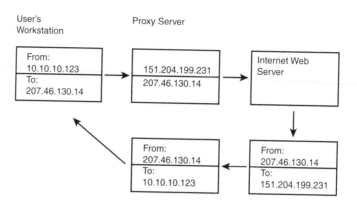

Figure 36.1   A proxy server impersonates the end user when communicating with resources outside the local network.

When the proxy server sees the packet, it repackages it and substitutes an address that will get the packet back to it. The proxy server sends the packet out onto the WWW without revealing the address of the user's actual workstation on the corporate network.

When the Web server receives the request for the Web page it does not know, or doesn't need to know, the request is forwarded by a proxy server. The proxy server creates a series of packets that carries the requested information back to the requestor and sends them back out on the Internet. When the data arrives at the proxy server, it again repackages the data and this time substitutes the real address of the end user so that the data can be delivered on the internal network.

Increasing the Address Space

Proxy servers can serve a purpose that is not directly related to security matters. When you have a limited amount of addresses that are valid on the Internet, what do you do when you find you have more workstations than addresses? A simple thing to do is use any range of addresses you like on the internal network, and use a proxy server to connect to the outside world. If you use an address space that was not assigned to you on the Internet, you will have a problem: You can send packets out but you will most likely never receive a response back. Instead, the real owner of the address would receive the data and be quite confused.

However, using a proxy server to substitute a valid address for the convenient one you use on the internal network will allow you to have a virtually unlimited amount of addresses to choose from when assigning addresses to your end users.

Application-Level Gateways

Proxy servers that function as firewalls are sometimes referred to as *application-level gateways*. Although a firewall based on packet filtering doesn't have any knowledge of the upper-level protocol being used, a proxy server does need to know—that is, it is application-specific. You don't just plug into a proxy server and start working. Instead, it must be configured for each application for which it will perform the proxy functions.

Most off-the-shelf firewall products come with proxy applications for commonly used network applications, such as

- Telnet
- FTP
- X Window
- HTTP
- Mail (POP and SMTP)
- News (NNTP)

An example of an application gateway is a dual-homed host that runs the proxy software. In this setup a computer has two network cards, each attached to a different network. Proxy software runs on the host and mediates between the two, deciding what traffic it will allow to flow between the two networks. You can set up a UNIX or Windows NT Server computer to perform this kind of function. In Figure 36.2 you can see a small network that uses a router to connect to the Internet.

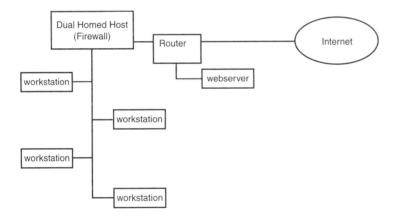

Figure 36.2 A dual-homed host is used to connect the local network to the Internet.

However, the network is not directly connected to the router. Instead, a computer has been designated for this purpose. The dual-homed host has two network cards—one talks to the router and the other participates in the local network. The router can be configured to perform filtering functions, while the dual-homed host can supply the proxy functions for any services you want to allow between your network and the Internet. When this host is configured with maximum security measures to provide a defense from external sources, it is sometimes referred to as a *bastion host* or a *screened host architecture*.

As an added advantage, another computer is used to host the company's Web pages so that Internet users can access them without penetrating the interior company network.

You can carry this concept further by using multiple routers to connect to the Internet. In Figure 36.3 you can see a setup similar to the one just described, but there are two routers between the innermost network clients and the Internet.

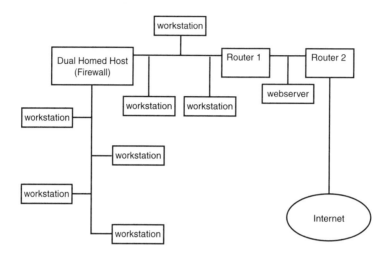

Figure 36.3   Use multiple firewalls to segment users into restrictive and less restrictive networks.

The dual-homed host connects the most secure clients to the first router. Between the dual-homed host and the first router are other computers that do not need the same level of restrictions imposed by the proxy server. Once again, the Web server sits on the network at a point closest to the Internet and is thus subject to fewer restrictions than the other computers on this network.

You can take this concept further by adding additional proxy servers or packet filters. The point is to understand that you are not limited to one solution for all the users on your network. The most restrictive environment required to protect ultra-sensitive data might not allow users who do not need this level of protection to perform their jobs easily.

Advantages and Disadvantages of a Proxy Server

As with every type of firewall, there are good and bad things you can say about proxy servers. Their capability to hide the identity of workstations on your network is a definite plus. They are usually highly customizable, and most come with a graphical interface to make the management chores a little more understandable than those that use a command-line set of cryptic instructions.

One thing that packet filters usually excel at when compared to proxy servers is speed. Filtering a packet is not much more complicated than any other task a router does. It already must look at the information contained in the header so that it can make routing decisions. Checking a table of addresses to determine which ones are allowed and which are not isn't much different from checking the routing table to decide where to forward a packet.

Note

Some advanced firewalls that provide proxy functions can be configured to support authentication and time-of-day controls. If you have a very secure environment and need to control who gains access, and want to limit the time of access, look for these features in the documentation before you acquire a firewall.

Proxy servers are applications that are implemented in software and are limited by the platform on which they run. In many stress tests done in recent years (you can check the magazines yourself), proxy servers will perform just fine on a 10Mbps network, such as 10Base-T. But when you connect them to a high-speed network such as 100Base-T or to T1 lines, their performance degrades rapidly. That is not to say that there are proxy servers that cannot keep up to these speeds. It's just that, to find one that does, you will have to incur a much larger expense for both the hardware and software components.

Hybrids

No one type of firewall that has been discussed can meet the needs of every situation. As mentioned earlier in this chapter, it is often a good idea to have several levels of defense against attack from outside your network. It is easy to segment your network so that it does not appear as one entity to the Internet. You can create several subnetworks, isolate them within your network using internal firewalls, and then enclose the collection of subnetworks with firewall protection from outside intruders.

You can also use more than one firewall between your network and the outside world. In the previous example of a dual-homed host, this was done because the host served as a proxy firewall that was connected to a router that performed packet filtering.

Most of the quality firewall products on the market today are not distinctly packet filters, proxy servers, or stateful inspection machines. Many are hybrids that incorporate the functions of all these firewall technologies, though by different degrees depending on the implementation. As long as you understand the concepts of the functions a firewall performs, you will be in a better position to make an informed choice of what will work best for your environment.

How Do You Know the Firewall Is Secure?

The problem with security is that the environment, either internal or external, is always changing. As soon as a bug in an operating system or network application is found and exploited by mischievous persons, someone comes out with a fix. As soon as the fix is applied, something else crops up. When you set up a firewall to protect yourself from those who might do harm to your network, you must perform tests to be sure that it does what you think it does.

The problem with testing, though, is that you already know what you are looking for when you create and execute the test. It's what you don't know that can cause problems. To keep on top of things, you should continue to monitor the data collected by any auditing or logging functions the firewall provides to make sure it is working as you expect. Look for attempts to breach the firewall and watch for unusual activity. You might find that you can stop an attack before it succeeds. Using other tools, such as tracert, you might be able to locate the perpetrator and handle the matter using legal means.

There are no RFCs to define what a firewall must do or how it should do it. There are several organizations on the Internet, however, that you can contact to get information about current firewall and security software.

Summary

Choosing a firewall strategy to shield your network from unwanted intrusions should be done with great care. Firewalls can be composed of packet filters, proxy servers, stateful inspection engines, or hybrids of all these technologies. You can find firewall solutions that range from the very low cost (or even free) to those that are prohibitively expensive. However, the amount of money you spend will not necessarily be a factor in the amount of protection you receive. It is important to understand what it is you are trying to secure and what the firewall is doing when it is used to protect your network.

Auditing and Other Monitoring Measures

SOME OF THE MAIN TOPICS IN THIS CHAPTER ARE

UNIX and Linux Systems

Windows NT Systems

Novell Security

So, What Is This SATAN Utility?

## CHAPTER 37

Security for an individual computer system or for the network as a whole requires a two-pronged approach. First you must try to ensure that all applications and data are secured against unauthorized use. This can mean anything from setting up and enforcing a good password policy to using the access mechanisms (such as rights or privileges) provided by the operating system or network software to secure resources. However, no matter how good you are at this before-the-fact approach to preventing security breaches, it is almost impossible, short of taking a system off the network and locking it in a room with a guard outside, to ever be absolutely sure that a breach will not occur.

The second approach you can take to securing the network is to use all practical auditing features to record access to resources and set up a policy for reviewing the data gathered on a regular basis.

Almost every operating system (with the notable exception of MS-DOS) that is in use in a business environment today and which is connected to a network has the capability to set up auditing for selected resources. You can keep track of file accesses, user logons, and other information that will help you with the who-where-what information you need when you believe a security problem exists. The methods of auditing and the tools used to exploit this data will depend on the network or computer operating system. Because most networks are hybrids that have multiple operating systems, it is a good idea to have someone in each environment who is intimately familiar with the peculiarities of each system.

UNIX and Linux Systems

Although UNIX was originally developed to be a programmer's operating system and not a business production system, it has been enhanced over the years to include several utilities that can track resource usage. The files discussed here can vary from one UNIX system to the next, but in general most systems will have these available for the system administrator's use. The syslog utility covers the widest area of system resources because you can configure it to record messages from many different system utilities, and you can also decide how the utility will notify you of events as they happen. Other files, such as /etc/utmp and /usr/adm/wtmp, keep track of who is currently logged on to the system and who has logged on to the system.

Linux systems use many of the same files as UNIX. Understanding each utility or log file and the type of information you can derive from it will enable you to set up a good auditing policy for your systems.

Using syslog

The syslog utility can be used to set up logging for many components that make up the UNIX operating system. By using this utility, you can set up message logging so that messages from a wide variety of programs can be managed from a central location. To enable syslog logging, you will need to edit a configuration file called /etc/syslog.conf and enter a record that contains a selector for each type of message you want to be logged by the facility as well as an action that the daemon should take for this type of message.

The syslog daemon (syslogd) is usually started when the system boots by placing commands in one of the rc files. The syntax for starting the daemon is

```
/etc/syslog [-mN] [-ffilename] [-d]
```

The `-f` option can be used to specify a configuration file other than the standard `/etc/syslog.conf` file. The `-m` option sets a "mark" interval for placing timestamps into the file. The `-d` option turns on debugging mode.

The `syslog.conf` File

This file stores the information the syslog daemon uses to decide which messages to accept (source and severity) and what to do with them (log file, notify user, and so on). You can use any ASCII text editor to configure this file. Each line should be composed of two components:

- **The selector**—This part of the record is composed of two pieces of information separated by a period. The first part of the selector is the name of the system facility from which the message will originate. The second part of the selector is the severity of the message. You can place multiple selectors on one line if you separate them by a semicolon.

- **Action**—This tells the daemon what to do when it receives a message that matches the selector criteria.

Table 37.1 lists the facility names you can use when composing the selector portion of the record.

Table 37.1   Facility Names Used in the *syslog* Configuration File

Name	Description
user	Generated by user applications
kern	Kernel messages
mail	Mail system messages
daemon	System daemons
auth	Authorization file (for example, login)
lpr	Line printer spooler system
news	USENET
uucp	UUCP (not currently implemented)
cron	cron and at utilities
local0-7	Reserved for local use
mark	Timestamp messages
*	All the above except for mark

Table 37.2 lists the severity levels you can use as the second component for the selector.

Table 37.2 Severity Levels Used in the *syslog.conf* File

Severity Level	Description
emerg	Panic condition. Something usually broadcast to all users.
alert	A condition that needs immediate attention.
crit	Warnings about critical situations.
err	Other errors not warranting **emerg**, **alert** or **crit**.
warning	Warning messages.
notice	Situations that require attention, but not as important as a warning or other error. Not necessarily an error condition.
info	Informational messages.
debug	Messages generated by programs running a debug mode.
none	Suppresses messages for this entry.

To create a selector, select one of the facilities listed in Table 37.1 and combine it with one of the error conditions listed in Table 37.2. For example

```
kernel.info
mail.notice
lpr.crit
```

To create the rest of the record, specify an action to take. The action portion of the record is separated from the selector portion by a space character. The syslog daemon can write the message to a logging file, send it to another computer, send it to one or more usernames, or do all these things.

For example, because kernel events are usually very important and must be looked at immediately, you might want to send them to the computer's console device. To do this, use the following entry:

```
kern.* /dev/console
```

The asterisk tells syslog to log all message types generated by the kernel, and the /dev/console part of the record specifies the console device.

If the message will be something that is important, but not so critical that it needs immediate attention, you can send it to a user. The following example sends all messages from the mail facility (at a severity level of info or above) to the mail administrator named Johnson:

```
mail.info johnson
```

For security reasons you might want to send important logging messages to another host. In a large network you can dedicate a single host computer to this function and use other security measures to make the computer inaccessible to ordinary users. To send messages relating to kernel events and authorization events to another computer, for example, use the following:

```
kern.*;ath.* @yoko.ono.com
```

Some message types are more useful for reviewing at a later date to evaluate the overall functioning of the system. Using log files for these kinds of messages is a good idea. To send messages to a log file, specify it in the action field:

```
mail.info;lpr.info;news.* /var/adm/messages
```

Tip

When sending messages to a log file, you can send them all to the same file as shown in the previous example (/var/adm/messages). However, to make administering the logged messages easier, you might want to create several log files and group similar message types together. This way you do not have to search through a large file that might contain a large number of entries to find just a few records that are of interest. By using separate log files you can also make it easier to write script files that can be used to automate the process of searching for important messages.

When sending syslog messages to files, don't forget to review the log files on a periodic basis. Depending on the severity level you set for each facility, these files can grow to be quite large over a short period of time. To make administration more efficient, decide on a policy for reviewing, archiving, and deleting log files on a regular basis.

System Log Files

UNIX systems have many log files that are not related to the syslog utility which you can review for security purposes. For example, user logins are recorded in a file as are usages of the switch user (su) command. When you are new to a system, you should review the documentation to make sure you are aware of all the logging facilities that exist on the computer, where the files are located, and what maintenance procedures are needed.

Some of the more useful files are as follows:

- **/usr/adm/wtmp**—This file keeps track of all logins, showing the username, terminal, and connect time. System shutdowns (but not system crashes, of course) are also listed in this file. Use the last command or the ac command to view entries in this log file.

- **/etc/utmp**—This file is similar to the /usr/adm/wtmp file, in that it stores information about users logging in to the system. However, this file only shows information about users that are actually logged on to the system currently and is not a historical file.

- **/var/adm/sulog**—This log file is an important one and should be looked at often. It records the usage of the su command.

- **/var/adm/aculog**—This file records usage of dial-out utilities, such as tip or cu.

- **/var/log/cron**—Actions taken by the cron utility are recorded here. This utility is used to schedule events for execution on the system. By reviewing this file you can determine whether unauthorized users are running procedures they should not or if programs or files are being run during off-hours when they are not likely to be noticed.

- **/var/adm/lpd-errs**—This file is used to record messages having to do with the lpr/lpd spooling system. Although not really of a great concern from a security point of view, it can be a potential tool to use when looking for security breaches.

- **/var/adm/acct**—This is the process accounting file. Use the sa or lastcomm command to view the contents of this file.

Windows NT Systems

Windows NT also uses the two-pronged method for security by enabling you to secure resources and then audit resource usage and access. To secure the system, you can use

- User rights and permissions
- NTFS file and directory access control lists (ACLs)
- Passwords, groups, and interdomain trust relationships

To audit the system, you can configure the events that you want to track, and then use the system's Event Viewer to examine the data collected by the system auditing software.

Setting Up Events to Audit

To set up categories of events to be audited, run the User Manager for Domains utility and select Audit from the Policies menu. Remember, by default Windows NT does not have auditing enabled. In Figure 37.1 you can see the Audit Policy dialog box enables you to select which event category to audit and whether to audit success or failures associated with each category.

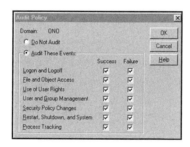

Figure 37.1   Use the Audit Policy dialog box in the User Manager for Domains to configure events to audit.

If you do not want to audit any events, select the Do Not Audit radio button. Or, select Audit These Events and click the Success and/or Failure options for each category. You can set up auditing for the following types of events:

- **Logon and Logoff**—Track users logging on to the system. This also tracks network logons from remote systems.
- **File and Object Access**—This category includes file and directory access and sending jobs to printers. It requires you to further define the events for the file, directory, or printer that will be audited.
- **Use of User Rights**—Records when a user uses rights you grant to them when you set up their account with the User Manager for Domains.
- **User and Group Management**—Tracks changes to group accounts. Creating, deleting, and renaming user groups is done in this category, as are changes to passwords.
- **Security Policy Changes**—This category keeps track of changes to user rights and audit or trust relationships.

- **Restart, Shutdown, and System**—Tracks when the system is shut down or restarted, and other events that relate to system security. This category also includes changes to the security event log on the system.
- **Process Tracking**—Records voluminous information about user processes, including when programs are executed, object accesses, and program exits.

In most cases, you will not want to select success and failure for every category in this list. For example, the data collected when you select Process Tracking can create a large event log file very quickly. You should probably turn on this event logging mechanism only when you have a definite suspicion about a particular user's activities, and then review and purge the log on a regular basis. Another category that can generate a lot of log file data is the Use of User Rights category.

Other categories such as users' logins can be useful and do not take a lot of space in the log files. The data collected for files and object accesses will depend on the specific events you select to audit for them.

File and Directory Events

If you have selected to audit this event category, you will need to use the Windows NT Explorer application to set the specific types of events to audit. To set up auditing on a directory or file, highlight it, and then right-click and select Properties. Alternatively, you can highlight the file or directory and select Properties from the File menu.

When the Properties sheet is displayed, select the Security tab and then the Auditing button; you should see a display that looks like Figure 37.2.

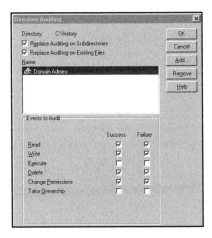

Figure 37.2   Use the Auditing button on the Security tab on the file or directory's property sheet to set up events to audit.

You can audit the following event types:

- Read
- Write

- Execute
- Delete
- Change Permission
- Take Ownership

However, because these will be audited by user or group, you should first select the Add button to add a user or group of users. The Add Users and Groups dialog box (shown in Figure 37.3) displays the current list of user groups. You can use the Show Members button to display the individual users in each group. Select users or groups by highlighting them and using the Add button.

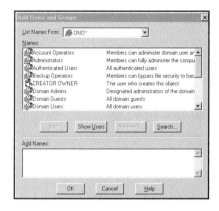

Figure 37.3   The Add Users and Groups dialog box enables you to select which users to audit.

You can continue to select users and groups and when finished, click the OK button. After you return to previous the screen, you can highlight each user or group and select the events to audit for that file or directory on a per-user basis. You can also use the Remove button to remove the auditing configuration for a particular user or group.

For any event, you can select Success or Failure. For example, if you selected Success for the Read event type, every time an audited user was able to read this file, a record would be generated in the event log. If you selected Failure, each time an audited user tries to read the file, but does not have the correct access permissions, a record would be created in the event log file.

Printer Events

You select events to audit for printers in much the same way that you do for files and directories. However, instead of using the Windows NT Explorer you use the properties sheet for the particular printer. You can get to the properties sheet by right-clicking the icon for a printer in the Printers folder. You can add or remove users using the same type of dialog box. The events you can audit for printers, however, are different:

- Print
- Full Control

- Delete
- Change Permissions
- Take Ownership

Using the Event Viewer

The Event Viewer is a utility found in the Administrative Tools folder that can be used to display events from three different log files:

- System
- Security
- Application

The System log file records certain system events, and the Application log file records events generated by many different applications. The Security log file is used to track events you have set up for auditing purposes. To start the event viewer, select Start, Programs, Administrative Tools, Event Viewer. Figure 37.4 shows the Event Viewer with the Security log file selected.

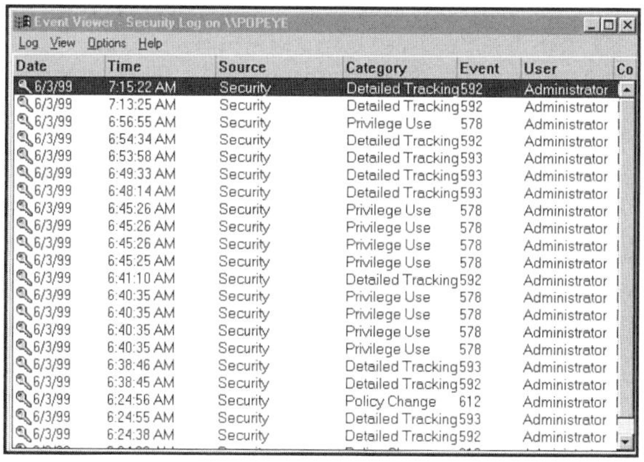

Figure 37.4 The Security log file can be viewed using the Event Viewer.

If the Event Viewer starts up with another log file displayed, such as the Application log file, use the Log menu and select Security to change to the correct display.

This view shows the list of events currently in the log file. To get the detailed record for any event double-click it. The Event Viewer does not have a reporting capability like the AUDITCON utility in NetWare. However, you can select Save As from the Log menu and save the data to either an ASCII text file or a comma-delimited file and use another utility, such as a spreadsheet, to perform further filtering or analysis on the data.

You can also change the log file settings by choosing Log Settings from the Log menu. This allows you to set the maximum size the log can grow to and cycle around and overwrite older events when the file is full. From the Log menu you can also select to clear all the events in the log file, at which time you will be prompted to save the current file in a backup file. This is something you should do on a regular basis; archive the previous log files for a period of time consistent with the security policy in force at your site.

Novell Security

Novell has been one of the most popular network operating systems for many years. Early versions were limited in their capability to keep track of events but this has changed with NetWare 4.x. The most useful tool is the AUDITCON tool, which can be used to configure and audit a wide range of system events.

SYSCON and AUDITCON

The SYSCON utility that was used in NetWare 3.x was limited in the type of information it could provide to the administrator. It was basically limited to statistical information such as the number of blocks read/written and the services the server provided. In NetWare 4.x, the AUDITCON utility provides an advanced tool that is superior to SYSCON in two ways:

- The information is more granular. File system events, such as access and modifications to individual files or directories, can be tracked. Events are also audited for NDS objects.

- The auditing role has been separated from the administrator's role, providing the ability for an employee other than the administrator to act as the network auditor.

Both of these are significant advances. The first makes the information gathered more than just statistical. You can now track access and the type of access to individual files or objects. The second can be used to ensure that the network administrator, usually an all-powerful person who can do anything on the network, will also be held accountable for his or her actions. Network security is not compromised by the auditor, however, because this person does not have to be granted administrator-like rights to objects such as the SYS:SYSTEM directory. The administrator and the auditor's functions are separated.

Technical Note

The administrator does have some control over the auditor: The administrator must set up the auditor so that he can perform his functions. After an auditor has been assigned and the account is set up, the auditor can change his or her password, thereby keeping the administrator locked out of the auditing functions. This approach allows the administrator and the auditor to balance each other. The auditor can track the administrator's actions and the administrator can always change the person designated to be the auditor.

After the administrator has enabled auditing on volumes or containers and designated the auditor, the auditor can then use the AUDITCON utility to check the system. Using AUDITCON the auditor can modify which events are audited on which resources and can produce reports showing auditing information.

Auditable Events

The precise granularity of things you can audit is what makes AUDITCON a powerful tool. The person who has been set up as the auditor has access to the following:

- **Audit by event**—This includes file-related events such as open, read, write, and create files or directories. These can be audited for all users (global) or on a per-user basis. You can also audit printer queue events (QMS), server events (such as when it is brought down or restarted), and user events (such as user logins and logouts or the creation or deletion of user objects).

- **File or directory events**—You can select files or directories for which all access will be audited.

- **User**—You can select individual users for which auditable events will be recorded.

Auditing Files

The auditing software stores its data in several places:

- **NET$AUDT.DAT**—This file can be found at the root of every volume that has auditing enabled. It is always flagged as an open file to prevent anyone other than the auditor from accessing it directly. This file stores binary information in a binary format only for the volume on which it resides.

- **NDS Database**—Auditing for events for the directory (NDS) is stored in the NDS Database.

- **AUD$HIST.DAT**—This file is used to keep track of actions taken by the auditors. After all, someone has to watch the watcher! When more than one auditor is assigned to the network, each should have a separate user account so that this file can be used to track the actions taken by each auditor, giving still more checks and balance to the system.

- **NET$AUDT.CFG**—This file contains audit file configuration information and is found at the root of the volume that is being audited. Using the AUDITCON utility, you can change the configuration information stored here, such as the maximum size the audit file can grow to, whether to allow more than one auditor to access the audit file at the same time, and whether dual-level passwords are used, among other things. The dual-level password requires an additional auditor password to be used when changing configuration information.

Technical Note

No system, of course, is perfect. It is easy for the auditor to clear the **AUD$HIST.DAT** file when he has performed some action that was not allowed. However, the new file created after the old one is cleared will record that fact. Thus, although you might not be able to find out what was done, you can still find out that something suspicious is going on.

Using AUDITCON to Enable Auditing

An Admin user can enable auditing on a volume by running the AUDITCON utility. From the main menu select the Enable Volume Auditing option and enter the password for that volume. If an old audit data file exists on the volume, it will be replaced by the new file.

After this has been done the administrator should give the volume password to the auditor, who should run AUDITCON and change it to a new value that the administrator does not know. Note that if the password is forgotten, it will be necessary to delete and re-create the volume if you want to change the password. You cannot recover it if you forget what it is. Also, without the correct password you can disable auditing on the volume!

To change the audit password the auditor should run the AUDITCON utility and select Audit Files Maintenance. From the next menu, select Auditing Configuration, and then Change Audit Password. When prompted, enter the new password.

Producing Reports

Reports are produced to translate the binary auditing data into a format readable by humans. These reports can be produced by selecting Auditing Reports from the AUDITCON main menu. For security purposes you should never leave these reports in a directory that can be easily accessed by other users. Instead, view or print the report text files and then delete them. You can always rerun the report later if you need to obtain another copy.

When producing an audit report you can select events by date and time and by event, and you can also select to include or exclude selected files, directories, or users. This filtering capability makes it easy to get right to the important data when you are troubleshooting a security breach. If you are simply performing a regular review of the system, you can select all data and spend hours pouring through it, but a large volume of data will most likely make it easy to miss an important event. In other words, when performing an analysis of the data, it's best to have a target objective of files or events, or possibly users, on whom you need to keep an eye.

So, What Is This SATAN Utility?

It has often been said the best person to consult about security a house so that it cannot be burglarized is the burglar himself. Along this line of thinking comes a utility known as SATAN— Security Analysis Tool for Auditing Networks. This application is an extensible utility that can be used to attempt to compromise your network's security so that you can close holes that more knowledgeable hackers might try to use. The original authors of SATAN (Farmer and Venema) wrote a paper titled "Improving the Security of Your Site by Breaking Into It." It describes the functionality of SATAN perfectly.

This utility is written mostly in C and has an HTML interface. It is not something that will easily be used by someone who is not familiar with the network or the systems it is comprised of. However, for an advanced technical person, SATAN can be an extremely useful tool.

SATAN is a configurable utility that can be set to do a light or heavy scan. It will perform a variety of checks to determine what is running on the target system. It can check TCP and UDP ports for vulnerability and utilities such as FTP or NFS. The extent to which you can use it to probe your system for security holes is quite large.

The utility can be downloaded for no charge from several sites on the Internet:

```
ftp.mcs.anl.gov/pub/security/satan-1.1.1.tar.Z

ftp.nenet.dk/pub/security/tools/satan/satan-1.1.1.tar.Z

ftp.acsu.buffalo.edu/pub/security/satan-1.1.1.tar.Z
```

After you finish the download you will have to read the documentation—configuration can be quite complicated—and use your system's C compiler to compile the source code.

Summary

Every computer system on a network should have some form of auditing enabled, depending on the use to which the system is put. A network is vulnerable from many different perspectives, sometimes from the least suspected client or server. Although you might feel secure having used all available techniques to block access to network resources from unauthorized access, auditing tools are a necessary component of system security.

Each system has its own set of tools for auditing. You should become familiar with those for each kind of operating system (or network operating system) in use on your network. Regularly review the data generated from these tools so that an intrusion or other security breach can be detected in a time frame that will allow you to minimize the damage that might be done.

Encryption

SOME OF THE MAIN TOPICS IN THIS CHAPTER ARE

Computers and Privacy

Symmetric Encryption

Asymmetric Encryption

Pretty Good Privacy (PGP)

CHAPTER 38

Encryption is the process of performing some function on a set of data that attempts to render it into a format that makes it unreadable or unusable by anyone but the intended recipient. In order to read something that has been encrypted, a secret key is used. Some cryptographic methods use the same key for encrypting and decrypting information, while others use separate dissimilar keys for these functions. This chapter provides a quick overview of a few of the most popular encryption technologies and shows how they can be applied to networks to help keep programs and data secure or to prevent unauthorized persons from gaining access.

Computers and Privacy

When computers were standalone systems that were easily controlled by a central administrative group, the problems with keeping data out of the hands of those who did not need to see it were already a difficult chore. Usernames and passwords were designed to keep unwanted persons off of systems and to allow different people to be granted different capabilities on the system if they did log on. File and resource protections enforced by operating systems made it simple to keep most prying eyes out of sensitive files, but where there's a will there's usually a way, and even these techniques could fail at times.

Passwords are easy to obtain if security is not considered a high priority in your environment. Just go up to a user and ask them what their password is. More often than not if you ask this of someone who you know and pretend to have an urgent problem, you will get a password. This is just another reason why a security policy at any business is not going to work unless you continually remind users that it is important and that there are consequences.

When computers are networked, or internetworked as is the case with the Internet, the problems associated with keeping important information private are compounded many times over because there are many more access points to the information. Each computer on the network becomes a potential security risk to all the information on the network, not just to the information on that single computer.

To solve this problem you must employ techniques that can render pilfered information unusable. Cryptographic techniques are the answer to this problem.

Encryption can be used to solve two major problems that creep up when you connect to a wide area network (WAN), such as the Internet, and need to exchange data:

- Data privacy
- Authentication

The first item in this list is the one you probably think about most often when you hear of encryption techniques. Data files, documents, and other important information is encrypted before being copied or emailed to a remote site. At the remote site, only those who possess the "key" can unlock the file to garner the information contained inside.

The second item in this list, though, is equally important. The network connection exposes the username/password technique to potential snoopers who can listen in on the network communications to steal this kind of information. When authentication is done across a network to allow access to resources that do not live on the user's own computer, encryption techniques can be used to help protect from this kind of password hijacking so that users and resources can be kept secure.

Two major types of encryption techniques are in use today. The first is *symmetric encryption*, in which the same secret key is used by both the sender and the receiver of the information. The same key is used to encrypt a file and decrypt it. The second technique is called *asymmetric encryption*. This technique uses one key to encrypt the data and a different key to decrypt it.

Symmetric Encryption

The most popular form of symmetric encryption is the Data Encryption Standard, or DES. This technology was developed by IBM during the 1970s. It was adopted as a federal standard in 1976. DES is thought by most to be an extremely secure system. It is used across networks by many businesses, such as banks, to transfer information across great distances.

Technical Note

DES is currently in use by the federal government and the military. However, it is already believed that DES is not as secure as it once was. High-power computers can process much more information in a much shorter time than they could 20 years ago. At this time a new standard, called Advanced Encryption Standard (AES), is being developed by the National Institute of Standards and Technology (NIST) to replace DES.

The problem with using only a single key to perform both ends of the encryption is that both parties to the secret information must know the secret key. If you send the secret key across the same communications pathway that you send the encrypted data, your data is immediately subject to be compromised. Thus, when using cryptographic techniques that depend on a single key, provisions must be made for transferring the key from the sender to the recipient.

Asymmetric Encryption

Asymmetric encryption is often referred to as *public key* encryption. It is called public key encryption because you can publish your public key so that anyone who wants to send a secret message to you can encrypt the data. Only your matching secret key, which does not have to be given to anyone else, can be used to unlock the encrypted data. Even the original public key that was used to encrypt the data cannot be used to unlock the encrypted file. This technique overcomes the major limitation imposed by symmetric encryption: A key that can unlock the encrypted data is never made public. There is no need to find a way to securely transmit a key to the other person with whom you want to exchange messages.

Using this method, it is easy to freely distribute the public key half of your key pair. Anyone who can get a copy of your public key can send messages to you that are safely encrypted and theoretically readable only by you. When you receive an encrypted message, you can use your secret key to get the message that was sent. However, another problem quickly becomes apparent. How can you be sure that the person sending the message is really who they say they are?

Digital signatures solve this problem. The person who uses your public key to send an encrypted message can use their own *secret key* to sign the message. You can then use that person's public key to verify that the message most likely did originate from that person (see Figure 38.1).

In both of these examples—encrypting a message and then signing it with a digital signature—each person's secret key is never made public; only the public key is disclosed.

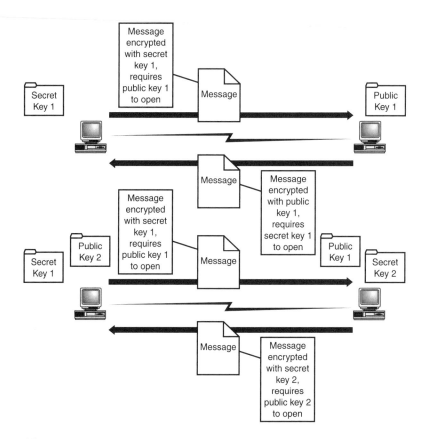

Figure 38.1 Public key encryption provides security for sent messages and can use digital signatures to verify responses.

Pretty Good Privacy (PGP)

Phillip Zimmerman created Pretty Good Privacy (PGP) using public key encryption techniques. It is the most popular form of encryption used on the Internet, mainly because you can obtain a free copy and more importantly because it works extremely well. PGP is available for many different computing platforms, including UNIX and Windows operating systems, and it enables users all over the world to send encrypted messages and use digital signatures to protect their messages.

PGP is a public key encryption system based on patented technology called RSA public key encryption. The name RSA is taken from the initials of the developers of the technology: Rivest, Shamir, and Adelmen. Because PGP is based on technology that is patented, you must purchase it if you want to use it commercially. However, you can obtain a free copy for nonprofit personal use from Network Associates at the following URL:

```
http://www.nai.com/default_pgp.asp
```

At this site you will find PGP in two forms: source code and executable. For Windows, DOS, and Macintosh platforms, you can download the executable form and install it on your workstation. For UNIX, you might want to download the source code format and compile it on your local system (see the following section, "Installing PGP on UNIX Systems"). In addition, PGP is available in a GUI or command-line format, depending on the operating system. PGP is available from Network Associates as freeware for the following platforms:

- Windows NT, Windows 95 and 98 (executable, GUI, or command-line form)
- Macintosh (executable and source code, GUI)
- Linux (executable, command-line form)
- Solaris (executable, command-line form)
- DOS or UNIX (source code, command-line form)

Installing PGP on UNIX Systems

Installing PGP on a UNIX system consists of compiling the source code and placing it in a directory. You can then configure PGP for your personal use by creating your public/private key pair.

After you unpack the `.tar` file, read the text file called `setup.doc`. This file contains the instructions for compiling PGP on the different UNIX or Linux variants that exist. The GNU CC compiler is assumed by the documentation but is not required. After you compile the source code, you will need to create a directory for PGP. To simplify its operation you should also define an environment variable `PGPPATH` to point to this directory. For example:

```
#mkdir .pgp
#setenv PGPPATH /user/ogletree/.pgp
```

Next, you should generate the public/private key pair that you will use. Use the `-k` option with the `pgp` command to create the key pair:

```
# pgp -kg
```

After you enter this command, PGP will prompt you for additional information:

- **Key size**—Use a large key size if you want to make it more difficult to break the encrypted data. PGP will prompt you to enter 1 (512 bits), 2 (768 bits) or 3 (1024 bits), or any number other than 1 through 3 to specify a specific key size.
- **Key user ID**—Here you should enter a name that will be used to refer to the key. The common method of naming keys is to use your name followed by your email address enclosed in angle brackets. For example, `Terry W. Ogletree <ogletree@twoinc.com>`.
- **Pass phrase**—Just as a password is used in the login process when you first log in to the computer, a pass phrase is used by PGP to help generate the key pair. The term *phrase* is used because rather than using a single word as you would with a password, a longer phrase is used to make the key more secure. The text you enter for the pass phrase will not be echoed to the screen so PGP will prompt you to reenter it to confirm that you have indeed typed what you think you have.
- **Random typing**—PGP will ask you to start typing, randomly. The text you enter does not matter. Instead, PGP is using the timing of your keystrokes to generate a series of random numbers that will be used to help create the key pair. When you hear a "beep" sound, PGP is finished timing your keystrokes and you can stop.

Note

The pass phrase is an important element of PGP. You will need the pass phrase to access your secret key. So, remember it! When deciding on a phrase to use, make sure it is something that is not hard for you to remember, yet not so common that others who know you will easily guess it. Of course, as with passwords, don't write down your pass phrase.

PGP will then generate the key pair. It might take some time, depending on the size of the key you have requested. A series of dots will be generated onscreen so that you know the program is still working.

Key Rings

PGP uses a file called a *key ring* to store the keys it generates for you and to store the public keys that you receive from other people. Although you can easily store your key ring on your computer's local hard disk, you can guarantee yourself additional security by using a floppy disk instead. The advantage to this method is that you can always physically lock up the floppy disk so that no one else can get to it. No matter how secure you might think your computer's hard disk is, it still stands a chance of being hacked if the computer is connected to a network.

Although obtaining the key ring file will not give a malicious user immediate access to your keys (they will need to know your pass phrase for quick access), you should still protect the key ring file. A persistent hacker can use other techniques to attempt to decipher your secret key.

The key ring is contained in a file named keys.asc. This file is what you use to store keys that you receive from other people. You can also use a *public key server* to obtain public keys. A network of public key servers exists on the Internet to store public keys of those who want them to be available to the general public. To make your key available in this manner, you "publish" your key. This is a simple matter of extracting it to a file and sending it to the key server network by using the ADD command. When you have published your key in this way you don't have to worry about sending the key to other public key servers. They communicate among themselves and replicate the information to other servers. Thus, when you want to send an encrypted message to someone, you must look up their public key on a key server if you do not have it already on your key ring.

For more information about PGP public key servers and the commands used to access them, send an email with the text "help" in the subject line to pgp-public-keys@keys.pgp.net.

PGP Commands

Although there are many commands that you can use with PGP, it is most likely that many users will need to use only a small subset of them.

To extract your public key so that you can give it to others (or publish it on a public server), type the following:

```
#pgp -kx userid keyfile [key ring]
```

In this command line, userid is the name that you gave the key when you first created it. The value for keyfile is the name of the output file that will be created containing your public key.

This is the file you will give to others who want to send you messages. The value for *key ring* is optional and is used if you have more than one key ring file.

When you receive a public key from another person, you can add it to your key ring as follows:

```
#pgp -ka filename
```

In this command, *filename* is the name of the file that contains the person's public key.

To view the contents of your key ring, type the following:

```
#pgp -kvv
```

This command displays information about the keys you have. For housekeeping purposes you might want to remove a key that you no longer need. Use the following command to remove keys from the file:

```
# pgp -kr
```

Of course, the command you will probably use most often is the command that allows you to encrypt a file. To do this, first create the message you want to send as an ASCII text file, word processor document, or other graphics or data file. Then use the -e parameter to encrypt it:

```
#pgp -e messagefile userid
```

In this example, *messagefile* is the file you want to encrypt and *userid* is the user ID for the public key of the user who will be the recipient of the message. The output file from the encryption command will be a binary file. However, some email programs or other programs do not like using binary files. For this reason, PGP can create a file that is called *ASCII Armor*, which is the same binary file encoded in ASCII characters:

```
#pgp -ea messagefile userid
```

PGP Digital Signature

Remember that encrypting a file solves only part of the problem of secure communication. To be truly secure, the recipient must be able to confirm that you are the actual sender of the file. To produce this confirmation, attach a digital signature to the message using your own secret key:

```
#pgp -sea messagefile userid
```

Here your pass phrase comes into play. Because you are attempting to use your secret key, PGP will prompt you to enter your pass phrase to unlock the secret key. Protect that pass phrase!

Reading PGP Encrypted Messages

All you must do to read a message that was encrypted by PGP using your public key is to issue the following command:

```
#pgp filename
```

filename is the name of the file you want to read. Just as when you use your secret key to digitally sign a message, PGP will again ask you to enter your pass phrase to unlock the secret key. After PGP decrypts the message it will attempt to verify the digital signature, if one was attached to the file. For this purpose, it will search your key ring for the public key of the sender and use it to verify the signature.

Installing PGP on Windows NT

Installing the freeware version of PGP on a Windows NT computer (or Windows 95/98) is a simple task of running the setup program. There is no need for a C compiler to create the executable images as might be the case with a UNIX or Linux variant. The setup procedure works in the same manner that you will find with most applications, with dialog boxes that display the copyright and licensing information, along with a description of new features.

Next, a dialog box will solicit your name and company name and another will allow you to select the directory that will be used for the installation. Figure 38.2 shows the Select Components dialog box. Here you must decide which features you want to install.

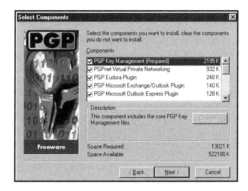

Figure 38.2   Select only the components you will need to use.

The following components will be available in this dialog box for you to choose from:

- **PGP Key Management**—This is a required component and is used to manage the keys; it is similar to the key ring file that was used in the UNIX version.

- **PGPnet Virtual Private Networking**—You can use PGP to create a VPN for secure communications on your network.

- **PGP Eudora Plugin**—If you use the Eudora mail program, this plug-in should be selected.

- **PGP Microsoft Exchange/Outlook Plugin**—If you use either the Microsoft Exchange mail client or Microsoft's Outlook, select this component.

- **PGP Microsoft Outlook Express Plugin**—This plug-in is for use with Microsoft's Outlook Express, a slimmer version of Outlook.

- **PGP Command Line**—This provides you with commands that can be used at the command prompt (sometimes called the MS-DOS box). If you are used to using the UNIX version, you might be more comfortable with this component.

- **PGP User's Guide**—It is recommended that you select this component and read it to become proficient in the many uses that you can make of PGP.

Of these components, perhaps the most important are those that are used as "plug-ins" for the mail clients. They will add PGP items to menus in the selected client so that you can directly invoke PGP for your email messages without having to create a separate file and go through the process of using PGP for encryption or decryption.

After you click the Next button, the setup procedure will copy the necessary files for the components you selected to their target directories. If you elected to use the PGPnet Virtual Private Network component, you will be prompted to indicate which network adapter to use, as shown in Figure 38.3.

Figure 38.3   If you have more than one network adapter installed, PGP will prompt for which one to use for VPN.

Next you will be asked if you already have an existing key ring that you want to use. If you have a previous version of PGP installed, or if you have a key ring file from another workstation that you want to use, you can let the setup program read the information in this file. Finally, setup will ask you to reboot your computer before the new PGP applications can be used.

Configuring PGP for Windows NT

After you reboot, the first thing you must do is to generate a key pair that you can use to encrypt your messages. To begin, select Start, then Programs, PGP, and then PGPkeys. From the main window (see Figure 38.4) select New Key from the Keys menu.

This will launch the Key Generation Wizard. The first dialog box is informational only and describes the functions that the wizard will perform. Click Next to get to a dialog box where you are prompted to enter your full name and email address.

You do not actually have to use your real name or address here. The purpose of the information is to make your public key recognizable by others you will give it to. Additionally, if you are using a plug-in for a mail client, the plug-in will be capable of automatically looking up the appropriate key if the email address matches. If you are producing a key that will be used by a business for multiple users, you should enter text here that will make the key easy to identify if it does not match an email address.

The next dialog box asks you to decide which kind of key type you want to use (see Figure 38.5). Older versions of PGP use a method known as RSA. The newer PGP versions (from 5.0 and higher) use Diffie-Hellman/DSS.

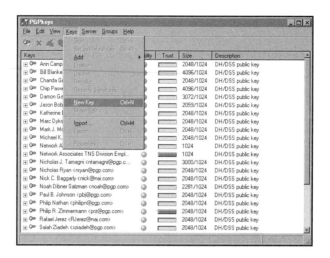

Figure 38.4 To create a new key pair, select New Key from the Keys menu.

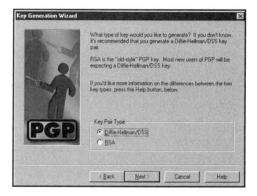

Figure 38.5 Select RSA only if you are going to correspond with others who use an older version of PGP.

You can always generate two key pairs, one for each of the key types, if you correspond with many people and need to use both kinds.

Next you will be asked to specify the size of the key to be generated. The longer the key size, the more difficult it will be to crack your messages. However, depending on the kind of computer you are using, it might take longer to generate the key and encrypt or decrypt messages when you use it.

Next you are asked to specify a date that the key pair will expire, or to indicate that it will never expire.

Most likely you will select here to create a key that will never expire. However, if you have a special need to use a key for only a short period of time, you can create one with an expiration date. This can be handy to use for a special project, for example, where the time frame of its use is known in advance and you want to make sure it cannot be used to create new encrypted messages after that time.

To protect your secret key you will have to enter a pass phrase that will be used each time you access it. In the next dialog box (see Figure 38.6) you should type in the pass phrase you select (it will not be echoed on the screen), and then enter the same phrase in the Confirmation portion of the dialog box.

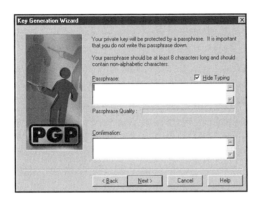

Figure 38.6   The pass phrase is used to access your secret key.

Remember that the pass phrase works like a password. It should not be a common phrase that other people know you are fond of. It should contain more than one word, and punctuation characters and spaces will make it harder to guess. You should not write down this phrase because anyone who can figure out your pass phrase will be able to use your secret key as if they were you. You should also make the phrase something that you will be able to remember. If you forget the pass phrase, there is no way it can be recovered and you will lose access to your secret key (and any encrypted messages that use this key pair).

PGP will now create the new key pair. It might take a few minutes, depending on the speed of your computer and the size of the keys to be generated. When finished, it will ask if you want to automatically send your public key to a public key server on the Internet. If you choose not to, you can do this at a later time. The last dialog box will prompt you to make a backup of your key ring, preferably to a disk drive other than your main drive on your computer. A floppy disk is a good place to store this information, and it should be physically secured if you use this method.

Using PGP with Windows NT

After you have created your key pair , you can use PGP. If you selected an email plug-in during setup you will find that your mail client now has been PGP-enabled. For example, in Microsoft Outlook Express the Tools menu will now have an entry for PGP.

If you want to use PGP at the Command Prompt, you can use the following commands:

- **pgp -kg**—Use this command to generate a new key pair. See the section "Installing PGP on UNIX Systems," earlier in this chapter, for help on using this command.

- **pgp -e** *filename userid*—Encrypt the file specified by *filename* using the key for *userid*.
- **pgp -s** *filename* [*-u your_userid*]—Signs a text file using your secret key.
- **pgp -es** *filename userid* [*-u your_userid*]—This can be used to encrypt the file, and then sign it using your secret key.
- **pgp** *encrypted_file* [*outputfile*]—Use this command to decrypt an encrypted file.

If you want to create an encrypted file that is based on ASCII text instead of a binary file (*ASCII Armor*), add the -a parameter to your command. This is useful when you have an email client that does not reliably transfer binary files.

Summary

As more business matters become dependent on networks that include components that are beyond your control, such as a WAN or the Internet, you will find that you will need to take precautions to protect your data. Authentication, by using digital signatures, will also become more important as more and more information passes through public networks. Encryption by any method will be an important feature of networking during the next few years. PGP is a product that you can use for your personal use for no charge. It is also available to purchase for commercial use.

Part XIV

UPGRADING HARDWARE

Preparing to Upgrade

CHAPTER 39

This chapter discusses some things you should consider when deciding when an upgrade is needed for the network, and some of the steps that should be taken to accomplish the task.

The first place to start is to determine the need and then set goals. Next, create a plan to guide the process. After this has been done, carefully investigate to help ensure that the upgrade plan will succeed. The following basic steps will be covered in this chapter:

- **Evaluating**—Understanding the current environment.
- **Determining needs**—Why are you upgrading?
- **Setting goals**—What will the upgrade accomplish?
- **Budgeting**—Determine what financial resources are available and set a budget.
- **Planning**—Creating a detailed plan for the upgrade.
- **Testing**—Evaluate components of the upgrade in a laboratory or pilot project environment.
- **Training**—Will users need to be trained on any new applications or features?
- **Backing-out and recovering**—Coping with the unexpected.
- **Deploying**—Implementing the upgrade plan.
- **Post implementation review**—Did the plan work as expected? Are the results what was expected, possibly more?

The Evaluation Process

A data network in a business is much like a nerve system in a living organism. When the business grows, the network usually must grow also to keep up with new users and newer functions. When a business suffers and shrinks, the costs associated with a larger network must be reevaluated to determine whether they are still feasible under a smaller business organization. A network rarely goes unchanged year after year. A top network professional must be aware of trends in the overall business so that he or she can make good judgments when it comes to making new purchases or commitments.

Before you begin to write an upgrade plan for part or all of a network, you first must have determined that there is a need for an upgrade. There are several reasons as to why a network needs to be upgraded:

- **User complaints**—When top-performing users complain, their managers usually do their best to make them happy.
- **New technology has been adopted**—Sometimes the upgrade can be application driven. A new kind of hardware or software needed by a business unit demands a network with higher performance capabilities or different features.
- **Business mergers and expansions**—After figuring out a way to join two networks when companies merge, a long-range plan must be developed to make the network work best for the new business entity. This can include performance enhancements, adoption of standards, and elimination of duplicated components.
- **Business is good, let's spend money**—This is not an uncommon motive for making a new system or network purchase. Sometimes when economic times are going well for a business it's also a good time to make long-range plans and upgrade part of the infrastructure.

The first of these reasons, user complaints, probably will never go away. No matter how fast the network or how powerful the machine, there will always be someone who wants more. Usually a good network administrator has a good overview of the people or departments that are major consumers of network resources and are able to filter out realistic complaints. So, when deciding when and if you need to perform some kind of overhauling of the network, you should carefully research your current network's capacity and compare it to the business needs currently loading the network. Sometimes a simple overview of the network can reveal that all you must do to satisfy one or two small bottlenecks is reconfigure part of the network. Usually a reconfiguration will be cheaper and easier to implement than a major upgrade.

When capacity problems cannot be solved by reconfiguring the network, it might be time to look at other media to handle the network traffic. Chapter 3, "Testing Cables," gives you a good overview of the specifications and capabilities of this most basic part of the network. Other chapters, including Chapter 9, "Ethernet Topology Restrictions," Chapter 10, "FDDI," and Chapter 11, "Monitoring Wireless," contain useful information that can help you make decisions about how to lay out an ethernet network. For token-ring users, Chapter 14, "Token-Passing Technology," gives a good refresher course into the mechanics of token-ring network operations. Chapter 15, "Token-Ring Topology Restrictions," Chapter 16, "Design Rules," and Chapter 17, "Monitoring Token-Ring Utilization," can help you make decisions about how to implement a network upgrade.

Adopting new technology usually entails additional tasks such as training users and administrative personnel in the use or management of new products. For example, a major paradigm shift such as migrating an all-Novell network to Windows NT networking (or vice versa) would have to entail months of training for network administrative personnel. Presently, it appears that TCP/IP is becoming a network standard supported by the large majority of networking vendors. NetWare administrators who have been comfortable with the IPX/SPX protocols will most likely be learning the ins and outs of TCP/IP when upgrading to NetWare 5.x.

If you are considering a change in computer or network operating systems, become familiar with the underlying protocols that will be used. Chapter 18, "TCP/IP," and Chapter 19, "IPX/SPX," cover the two most popular network protocols, while other chapters such as Chapter 21, "Name Resolution," and Chapter 26, "Rights and Permissions," can help you better understand how to control access to network resources. One area of new technology that most businesses are quickly adopting is the Internet. Chapter 31, "Web Servers," Chapter 33, "Dialup Connections," and Chapter 34, "Dedicated Connections," cover some of the basics you must know before jumping into the Internet arena. Along this same line, you might want to review Chapter 35, "Basic Security Measures," and Chapter 36, "Firewalls," before you decide to connect your network to a wide area network or the global Internet.

Determining Needs

One of the simplest methods of finding out what is needed on the network is to ask the users. Although this technique might not give you the most accurate results, it will at least give you an idea of what the user community expects from the network, and you can use this information to guide you when making long-range goals. Conducting a simple written survey can bring light to factors that administrative and support personnel might not be aware of.

Similar to surveying end users is soliciting suggestions from support staff who encounter user problems on a daily basis. Logs of support calls can be a valuable source of information.

However, the most basic way to determine overall capacity needs is to establish baseline data for your network components and then make comparisons on a regular basis with the production network. By keeping data that reflects the baseline mode of operation, you will have empirical data that can be used to make projections about future use. By regularly benchmarking your systems and keeping track of the data, you can also become aware of capacity problems that begin to creep up before your projections or expectations.

Other factors that can be reviewed to determine if changes are merited include the following:

- **Maintenance costs**—The network might be functioning nicely with equipment that is several years old. However, the maintenance costs associated with older equipment might be justification for upgrading to newer, more reliable equipment.

- **Existing contracts**—Leased equipment can usually be purchased or returned to the lessor at the end of the lease period. Contracts that are about to expire should be examined and taken into consideration when deciding whether to keep the existing equipment or upgrade.

- **Network traffic**—Regular monitoring of network traffic to locate bottlenecks or congested areas can be helpful. Recognizing that some problems are intermittent, base your decisions on not just the fact that a problem exists, but instead make a rational decision on whether the physical network really must be modified. Is it possible that user work habits or procedures can be changed so that problems that occur only at peak hours or on specific days do not lead you to spending too much on a small problem that can be better solved by other methods?

Supporting Legacy Applications

There comes a time in every application's life when it really should just die and go away. However, when you consider the costs associated with replacing a legacy software application with one that is state of the art, sometimes what you find might lead you to listen to users who like their software and keep the application around a few years longer.

The following are some hidden costs that you might overlook at first glance:

- Ongoing maintenance or support costs
- Employee support costs
- Infrastructure overhead costs

Maintenance and support costs can be hidden in part of the budget for the department that an application or hardware platform supports. When multiple suppliers are involved, you will usually find multiple contracts, some of which even overlap each other. Another problem with ongoing support costs is that manufacturers tend to raise these costs when products become outdated to help encourage users to adopt newer ones.

The number of employees you dedicate to a particular part of the network is an important cost. If you have a large staff that is used for mostly maintaining an old application, consider the costs associated with them, from salary to overhead, and decide if it might be better spent training them on newer technology and replacing the legacy system.

Overhead costs associated with building costs, utilities, and other costs related to the space taken up by network equipment must be considered. Older minicomputer and mainframe computers required a strictly controlled environment, usually provided by a "computer room." Now it is feasible to place departmental servers in locations throughout a building or the company; a special computer room, with its attendant expenses for air conditioning and fire-prevention equipment, might be a cost you no longer have to bear.

Legacy applications are usually either loved or hated by their users. Some people think with the mindset "But we've always done it that way" and do not want to change for fear of the unknown and love of the familiar. Other users who are used to better technology might hate a legacy application. The point to remember here is that it does not always matter what the user thinks about the application. What is most important to the business's bottom line is the costs associated with it compared with the benefits the company receives.

Determining Resources

If you already have a good inventory of the network, you are ahead in the planning game. Keeping an up-to-date listing of network components, including hardware and software, along with other pertinent information such as network addresses, serial numbers, manufacturer's help line numbers, and so on, is a task that, when done on a regular basis, will yield great results down the line.

Without a good network map document, you won't necessarily be sure that you're not violating some of the topology rules for your network. Remember that the ethernet 5-4-3 rule states that there can be no more than five cable segments, connected by four repeaters, and only three of the five cable segments can be used for workstations instead of for linking purposes, between any two nodes on the LAN. For token-ring networks, a similar set of rules applies, though it can vary depending on the particular vendor's equipment. The important point to remember here is that even a simple addition to a network can cause problems throughout the entire network if it violates some physical boundary such as those proscribed by a particular technology.

Before beginning to plan an expansion or the addition of new equipment, review documentation for that which you already possess. You might have some devices that do not need to be replaced. For example, if you already have network adapter cards that are 10Mbps/100Mbps, you would not need to add the cost of new cards to an upgrade plan when going from a 10Base-T network to a 100Base-T network.

Items that you should be sure to inventory include the following:

- Workstations and servers
- Network adapters
- Hubs, routers, and switches
- Test equipment
- Workgroup and end user software applications
- Mechanisms used to exchange data with contacts outside the company
- Management and control applications, such as SNMP, DHCP, DNS, NIS, and so on

When determining your resources, don't forget people. People are a resource. A major project of any kind should always have an identified set of team players that will be responsible for the project. A clearly defined project team will identify the person responsible for each aspect, such as purchasing, infrastructure, systems, and documentation. This will greatly improve communication during the length of the project because a point of contact is identified for specific areas.

A project leader should be designated to be the focal point for both the project team and for others in the company who need to get information about the project or its progress. Each project team member should have a clearly defined role and area of responsibility. The area of responsibility is a very important one. As in any social interaction, overlapping duties can generate personal resentment between people working on the same project. When a clear, defined set of job responsibilities and duties is spelled out in writing, you have a better chance of achieving harmony among the team members.

A project team will work best when it is dedicated to the project. Giving users multiple roles to fill in their job can lead to confusion, unexpected priorities, and degradation in the progress of the overall project. Although the current support staff might be knowledgeable in the network and its quirks, bringing in additional help, by using experienced contract workers, for example, might help keep the project focused on its goals and the time frame associated with them.

The Planning Process

Planning is the process of deciding what actions will be needed to accomplish a goal. This necessarily implies that the plan will describe the specific goals to be achieved and the benefits that will come from them. However, the steps that will be required in a plan will be dictated not only by the goals that are to be accomplished. You must also take into consideration how a network upgrade will affect users (down time), what established corporate standards must be followed (or possibly reexamined), and what criteria can be used to measure the progress or success of the plan.

The planning process should include input from both technical personnel and end users. After reviewing user requests and deciding which issues will be addressed, goals can be established and written documentation can be produced that details the plan, its goals, and how they are to be achieved.

Documenting Your Plan

Planning is essential in a complex environment to ensure that a project will be successful. Planning can encompass more than one document. For example, there can be a detailed plan that contains check lists for tasks that need to be accomplished, along with time-frame assumptions and resource requirements. For top-level department heads, an executive overview can serve to garner support for the project without forcing them to get bogged down in details they do not understand.

Whatever planning you undertake must be put into the form of a written document. Plans should be carefully reviewed by persons representative of the areas that will be affected in order to solicit their feedback and ensure their cooperation. However, as with most things in life, even a good plan is likely to undergo changes during its execution. It is important to create a process that can be used to evaluate changes and incorporate them into the plan in an orderly manner. Put the process in writing along with the other details of the plan. If you have it in writing, it becomes much more difficult for a disagreeable person to protest when deadlines must be met and resources are limited. An orderly change process can always include a method for recording potential change ideas so that a decision can be postponed to a later date.

Examining Corporate Standards

Before beginning to write any kind of plan that will be used for a major upgrade project, be sure to review the current corporate standards. When PCs first began to proliferate in the work environment during the 1980s, one of the biggest headaches for information technology departments was the haphazard acquisition of computers and software that left administrators in a position of having to support multiple applications that performed the same function. A company should have one standard word processor that is used throughout the company, or at least throughout any major division of the business.

Most applications today that perform ordinary tasks, such as spreadsheets, word processing, and database functions, also come with tools that enable you to interchange data with other vendors' products. Although this might seem to alleviate the problem of using multiple products for the same purpose, there is another factor to consider: end user support. Even if data can be easily exchanged, the extra expense of having to support more than one application for a single function is an ongoing cost that doesn't go away.

When developing the plan, first examine the current standards. Then, taking into consideration the future expansion of the network, capabilities of products currently in use and the direction certain technologies seem to be taking, develop a revised list of standards and sell it to the organization.

Of course, there will always be exceptions. For example, the corporate standard might require that the Oracle database application be used throughout the company. However, a specific vertical market application used in a research lab might work only with another database product. In cases where there isn't a wide variety of vendors to choose from, you might be forced to accept a deviation from the standard here and there. However, be sure to document these exceptions and do what you can to keep them to a minimum.

Setting Goals

Any good plan will have a clearly defined set of goals to provide some kind of benefit to the business. Although an overall view of the project's goals can be used to help sell the idea to upper-level management, the goals that should be included in a detailed project plan must be more specific. The following are two important reasons why you should have a defined set of goals:

- If defined with enough detail, goals can give you something to gauge progress of the upgrade project.
- Goals can keep you on track, preventing you from getting side-tracked by other ideas that will inevitably come up during the project.

After you come up with a written list of the goals that will serve to guide the project, prioritize the list. It might be that further down the line you find that some goals might not be easily attainable because of unforeseen factors. When initially developing a list of project objectives, your staff might be over-enthusiastic, and you can find yourself with a large shopping list that attempts to solve every problem and please every department. Set realistic priorities based on the benefit each goal is expected to provide, and then remove items from the list that provide little benefit or do not address an immediate need.

Scheduling Downtime

Users should not be expected to understand what goes on behind the scenes in the complicated area of networked computer systems. They may only know that they can or cannot get their job functions performed in a timely manner because "the network is down." By planning ahead and letting everyone know when resources will be unavailable, you will find that users are more likely to cooperate.

Milestones and Criteria

Based on the goals that the project is expected to achieve, build into your plan the procedures that will be used to measure success. Select items from your list of objectives that represent major changes to the network and define the metrics that will be used to determine whether the goal has been met.

For example, a goal can consist of achieving a reduction in network utilization for overloaded segments. Monitoring utilization using a LAN analyzer can be done before and after the upgrade to obtain factual information that can be used to establish the success of this upgrade. Other metrics might include items such as network response times, user satisfaction, or new functionality. In an environment where high availability and reliability are a concern, measurements showing the percentage of uptime or downtime can be used to determine whether efforts involving redundant hardware and software configurations have succeeded.

To come up with a list of items you can use to judge the outcome of a network upgrade plan, you must have a coherent plan that has well-defined goals. If you find that you are having trouble deciding which benefits you will gain from the upgrade and cannot devise a list of metrics to be measured, it is possible that you haven't fully thought through what you are trying to accomplish. In that case, it is time to reexamine your thought process, decide definite goals, and rewrite the plan.

Back-Out Procedures

Nobody is perfect, and no plan can ever be precise enough that you can bet your life that everything will go as expected. Whenever possible, for any major modification that you intend to make to the network, you should also have a plan that can be used to restore the network to its previous state. Having good documentation about the network that is up-to-date can be useful for troubleshooting, but when you have scheduled downtime with users and are under a deadline to finish a task or a project, it is more useful to have a definite set of procedures to follow if problems arise that prevent the execution of a task or tasks in the project plan.

The Testing Process

The complexity of networking technology today makes it important that you test new equipment and software before committing it to production use. You might find that devices do not function as you expected when deployed using the planned configuration. New operating systems or applications might run slower than the vendor leads you to believe. Management software might be cumbersome and difficult for users to understand. In the end, if end users are not satisfied and cannot perform their jobs efficiently using the tools you provide, it is likely that they will find someone else who can.

Testing involves examining the functions of individual components and the interaction between components when they are used in an environment that simulates production usage.

Evaluating Competing Products

Careful selection of new equipment or software up front can save time and money after the upgrade is finished. Evaluate competing products carefully so that you can select those which will best meet the goals of your upgrade plan. When looking at different vendors' products, try before you buy. For a large hardware purchase, many vendors will loan equipment for a trial period so that you can make a better determination as to its suitability to satisfy your needs. Almost all major software applications can now be obtained from a vendor in a "demo" or "evaluation" copy so that you can test their features.

When it comes to evaluating end user software applications, involve the users with testing the evaluation copies and use their feedback in making purchasing decisions.

Another very important factor to consider is the vendor itself. You might find a great product that looks like it will work miracles for your network. However, if the vendor is not reliable, what will you do when you encounter problems later on? Things to think about when choosing vendors include

- **Responsiveness**—Do you get through to the help you need when you call the vendor, or do you have to play telephone-tag in order to get answers?
- **Availability**—Does the vendor actually have a good stock of products, or will you be subjected to back orders that can take days or weeks? When you have to replace a part due to malfunction, can your network wait until the part arrives?
- **Service**—Does the vendor provide service for the product? Is on-site service available or do you have to return the item to the vendor for repair?
- **Training**—Does the vendor provide training for the product? Is the training of good quality?
- **Price**—This factor usually comes into play when a product is a commodity item. For specialized products or applications, price might not be as important as the other items listed here.

The Pilot Project

Every good plan should include a pilot project. This involves taking a small part of the network, such as a network-friendly department, and implementing part or all the project modifications in that localized area. Not only will it help you determine whether you have made the right choices for new hardware or software, it will also help you further refine the installation procedures that will be used to execute the rest of the plan.

If it is not possible to do this in a "live" environment, create a test lab where you can simulate the production environment or network. Use script files to automate processing and perform stress testing on the new components or applications to see if they really perform as you expect.

Sometimes new is not always better. In a recent project on which I worked, a major upgrade to a database product was planned for months. Less than one day after the final implementation, the help desk was swamped with user complaints about the slowness of the system. It took long hours to locate the problem, which was buried in a customized script file that took advantage of quirks in the previous system.

Don't let this happen to you! Evaluate! Test! Test again! And, of course, involve the end users when it is feasible because it is very likely they will know more about how the application or product is used.

The results of a pilot project or a test lab setup can be used to refine and modify the plan and make it more likely to succeed.

Deployment

After you have evaluated and reevaluated, tested and retested, and are sure that your plan is a sound one, implement the plan to upgrade the network. Depending on the scope of the upgrade the deployment stage can be done all at once, or it can be done in a migration process over time. Adding additional segments to a network for new offices or to replace older cables can be a simple matter that can be done over a weekend. Migrating a large network to a faster topology might require that you deploy only small segments at a time to ensure that disruptions for users are minimized.

Deployment Team Personnel

The personnel that will be employed to perform upgrade functions should be well trained far in advance of the actual deployment stage. Each person should be knowledgeable in the area of expertise for the functions they will perform. To aid the upgrade team it is a good idea to have specific written task lists that describe what is to be done. For example, a recent network upgrade in which I participated required that network adapter cards be replaced in a large number of workstations. The process involved the physical actions required to remove the old card and replace it with the new card.

After the card replacement, however, there were still additional chores to do. For example, each card had to be configured with the correct drivers so that the operating system would be capable of using it. Each workstation had to be tested for connectivity to ensure that the card was correctly configured to work with the network. The task list for this was written in detail describing each step the team member needed to perform, and included a check-off box for each step. Why a check-off box? Well, if you have to take the time to check off each step, you are less likely to forget one. When a person is performing the same actions over and over, moving from workstation to workstation, the odds are likely that mistakes will be made.

It is also a good idea to designate one or more persons to be a resource focal point that team members can use when problems arise. If one person is aware of the problems that are occurring, it is easy to implement a fix throughout the project so the same problem doesn't have to be solved over and over.

Keeping Users Informed

Network users should be kept up-to-date about the progress of the upgrade. At the beginning of the deployment stage, present the users with an overview of what will be happening and how it will affect their work. As specific tasks are ready to be done, let the users who will be immediately affected know shortly before you begin. For example, if you plan to replace workstations throughout the enterprise, create a list of replacement candidates each week and notify the affected users via a memo or an email so that they will be reminded. For a long project, it is easy for users to forget what you told them weeks or months earlier.

Along this same vein, it is a good idea to get some kind of response from a user when you have made changes to their workstation. For example, having a user test the system for a day or so and then "sign off" on the work lets them know that (for them) the process is complete; this is known as user acceptance testing.

Tracking Progress

Use the metrics that you designed to measure the progress you make as you implement the plan. It is important to keep track of the progress so that you can coordinate your people, resources, and the delivery of additional equipment or outside services. If you find that you are falling behind in one area, it can cause you to reschedule tasks in other related areas. A close watch on progress is necessary so that you can quickly detect when something is not going as expected and begin to come up with an alternative method for getting things done.

The mechanisms you can use to track implementation of the plan might include a spreadsheet, a diary-like text file, check lists, and so on. To present information to upper-level management, you might find that weekly or monthly summary reports help to keep their support. If you find yourself in a position where you need to report on progress to high-level managers, graphical displays, such as graphs or charts, can help get your point across.

Post-Mortem

When a major project comes to a close, it is a good idea to compile a short report that details the project, from the evaluation and planning stages all the way through to the deployment and user acceptance stage. This historical document can serve in the future when it comes time again to take on another project of a similar scope. It can also be presented to management to make them aware of the scope of what has been accomplished. This visibility can be very beneficial to a network administrator's career!

User Training

The topic of training can cover a large territory. Users should be trained to acquire the necessary skills needed for new applications or new ways of doing ordinary tasks when the network changes. Training can be done by in-house personnel who have the skills and also have the time to devote to the process. For large projects it might be more economical to employ outside resources for training users. Additionally, there are a wide variety of training resources you can make available to your users for most popular applications. These include training videos, computer-based training (CBT) applications, programs presented by user groups, and so on.

Training should not be delayed until the end of the project or to the point where the user is directly affected. Instead, consider setting up a training lab, similar to the test lab you used when planning the upgrade. Make users aware of the resources at their disposal and begin training before major changes are made so that the users will be better able to cope with the new environment. Users who are trained in advance for a new application or procedure are less likely to cause a strain on the upgrade team's resources while the upgrade is proceeding.

Other Considerations for Upgrading

Undertaking a major upgrade to a network is not a task to be taken lightly. As with any large undertaking, it is best to try to accomplish your main goals with the least amount of excess baggage. With a large number of users, it is easy to become overwhelmed with a large number of suggestions or requests when the user community finds out that major changes are being planned. However, for each additional task you add to your plan, you also add to the probability that something will go wrong. So, after deciding on the basic goals, try to stick to only the tasks that will be needed to achieve them; do not get sidetracked by unimportant issues that can be best settled at a later date.

However, you should consider this time to be an opportunity that can be used to incorporate new technologies or functionality into the network that otherwise would require additional down time for the network. For example, if you are about to begin upgrading user workstations throughout a department or enterprise and you have been considering adopting DHCP, what better time to do so than now? If you are already going to put the user out of work for a short amount of time, and the workstation is off the network, this kind of situation is ideal for bringing in a new administrative tool such as DHCP.

Housekeeping is another function that can fit nicely into an upgrade plan. Out with the old and in with the new, so to speak. Old programs that never quite went away can be removed during an upgrade process. An upgrade can be a good time to set a deadline for users who have not yet abandoned older applications that can be better performed by newer applications.

Summary

In this chapter, you looked at the process of planning a network upgrade. Before you begin to start a major upgrade, you need to evaluate the network as it currently stands and then come up with a clear definition of the goals an upgrade will be expected to achieve. To define goals you will need to determine what needs to change, and why, and then perform testing to be sure that the solutions you come up with will solve the problems you expect.

Other factors that need close attention include training users and network administrators on new equipment or procedures so that the network will continue to operate smoothly after the upgrade. It is also important that the planning process produce a written document which details the actual steps that will be taken, as well as procedures that can be used to back out when unexpected problems arise.

In most of the remaining chapters of this book, you will examine some of the processes involved in performing upgrades from one hardware or software architecture to another. In the last few chapters, you will look at hybrid networks that incorporate multiple operating systems.

10Mbps to 1000Mbps Ethernet

SOME OF THE MAIN TOPICS IN THIS CHAPTER ARE

The Existing Cable Plant

Upgrading to Gigabit Ethernet

Most existing Ethernet installations are either the obsolescent 10Mbps 10Base-T or the newer 100Mbps 100Base-T Fast Ethernet type. With the rise of Gigabit Ethernet and the never-ending demand for more speed and higher capacities, many network users are wondering if their existing Ethernet installations can, or should, be upgraded to this fastest-yet Ethernet standard. This chapter explores the issues you'll need to deal with if you move to Gigabit Ethernet, including cable types, standards, and alternatives to making the move to Gigabit Ethernet right away.

The Existing Cable Plant

Depending on the existing cable plant, the conversion from 10Mbps Ethernet to faster versions can be extremely simple or more complicated. This is because of the different standards that exist for unshielded twisted-pair cabling. Standard 10Base-T Ethernet can use Category 5 cable, but the older Category 3 cable, which resembles standard telephone cabling except for the use of the larger RJ-45 connector instead of the RJ-11 telephone connector, is often found in older Ethernet installations that use UTP cabling. The most popular, faster versions of Ethernet require higher quality cable that meets Category 5 standards.

Why is cabling the most critical factor in changing from 10Base-T Ethernet to faster versions? There are several reasons. First, cabling is the most difficult item to change in the entire network hardware configuration because it is very often located inside walls and ceilings and because the costs of laying cable (either on initial installation or when re-cabled) continues to be one of the most expensive parts of any network. Second, most network cards today are dual-speed, capable of running at either 10Mbps or 100Mbps (also called Fast Ethernet). Third, replacement of hubs, switches, and network cards is relatively simple.

Determining If Your Existing Ethernet Cable Can Handle 100Mbps or Faster Speeds

Here are the general rules that you can use to determine if your existing ethernet cable can carry Fast Ethernet or Gigabit Ethernet traffic:

- If your existing network cable is Category 5 or better, and if it uses no connectors or uses Category 5-rated connectors, it is capable of handling faster traffic. Obviously, the existence of Category 3-only rated connectors (which are used to convert two short cables into a single longer cable) will limit that cable segment's rated speed to only 10Mbps.

- If you are using Category 3 cabling, you might still be able to use the form of Fast Ethernet that can use all four wire pairs found in Category 3 cabling—100BaseT4—although this type of ethernet isn't common and can't be used for Gigabit Ethernet. Some Category 3 cabling uses only two of the wire pairs for data and uses the other two for voice. Category 3 cabling used in this fashion cannot run faster than 100Mbps.

With most new network installations using Category 5 cabling, it will be relatively easy to move from 10Base-T to 100Base-TX–type Fast Ethernet. To move to so-called Gigabit Ethernet, the presence of Category 5 cabling is only one of the factors required. To be certain of the cable plant's capability to handle any type of ethernet standard, use cable testers (see "Common Wiring Practices and Connections That Can Cause Gigabit Ethernet Problems," later in this chapter) to certify the cable for the standard you are trying to meet.

Table 40.1 lists the cabling types that can be used for different ethernet standards that use UTP cabling, and Figure 40.1 compares Category 5 cables using two or four twisted pairs.

Table 40.1   UTP Cabling and Ethernet Standards

Cable Type	Wire Pairs Used	Standards
Category 3	2 pairs	10Base-T
Category 3	4 pairs	100Base-T4
Category 5	2 pairs	10Base-T, 100Base-TX
Category 5	4 pairs	10Base-T, 100Base-TX, 1000Base-T

As you can see from the table, Category 5 cabling, with all four wire pairs available, is capable of handling all UTP Ethernet standards from 10Mbps through so-called Gigabit Ethernet speeds. Specifically, the Category 5 cabling should be certified to correspond to TIA/EIA-568-A (1995) standards in North America and ISO 11801 internationally.

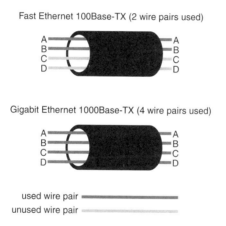

Figure 40.1   Gigabit Ethernet uses all four wire pairs in Category 5 UTP, unlike the most common form of Fast Ethernet, which uses only two wire pairs.

What Makes Gigabit Ethernet Over UTP Possible

Gigabit Ethernet is already available for high-performance servers running multi-mode or single-mode fiber-optic cables (see "Standards for Gigabit Ethernet Over Wire and Fiber" later in this chapter), but it is also possible to run it over conventional UTP cable.

Gigabit Ethernet is made possible over ordinary Category 5 twisted-pair cabling by transmitting scrambled data in a "spread-spectrum," allowing the entire bandwidth to be used efficiently and minimizing crosstalk between wire pairs. Because randomly scrambled data can't be reconstructed, the actual scrambling is done using a pseudo-random value obtained from the network's linear feedback shift register (LFSR), allowing it to be reconstructed accurately by the receiver.

To keep the data from being corrupted by the extremely fast data transfer rate, Gigabit Ethernet uses a special type of block coding called *convolutional coding*. The encoding process used to turn the data into blocks is called Trellis encoding because the mathematical pattern used to trace the coding process looks like a trellis when diagrammed.

At the receiving end, the Trellis-encoded data is decoded by a process called Viterbi decoding. Viterbi decoding is capable of correcting transmission errors, not merely detecting them as with less-capable decoders used with slower networks.

Another important element making Gigabit Ethernet possible is the use of all four wire pairs rather than the two wire pairs used in most slower forms of twisted-pair Ethernet. The use of all four wire pairs means that the data transmission rate per channel (wire pair) is only 250Mbps. Gigabit Ethernet uses full-duplex data transfer in a switched environment, meaning that there is a direct logical connection between the transmitter and the receiver of data, eliminating the collision detection/retransmission slow-downs of older ethernet standards. The speed of Gigabit Ethernet would not be possible without these changes.

Because the output of Gigabit Ethernet is similar to 100Base-TX signaling, dual-speed Fast/Gigabit Ethernet implementations are possible, similar to the 10Base-T/100Base-TX configurations that are common.

Common Wiring and Connection Practices That Can Cause Gigabit Ethernet Problems

According to the Gigabit Ethernet Alliance, less than 10% of existing Category 5 cabling is improperly installed, meaning that it doesn't meet the 568-A standards (and isn't suitable for Fast Ethernet, let alone Gigabit Ethernet!). However, the problem isn't the cable itself, but lies in several common wiring and connection practices, including the use of

- Substandard connectors between wire segments
- Cross-connects
- Substandard patch cords
- Substandard wall connectors
- Substandard interconnects
- Excessive bundling of network cable for pulling

Use of devices and methods like these will cause several types of interference, including alien crosstalk, Equal-Level Far-End Crosstalk (ELFEXT), and return loss.

Alien crosstalk refers to the interference caused by adjacent cables that have been bundled together to allow them to be pulled as a unit during installation. Although the level of interference caused by alien crosstalk isn't usually significant for standard Ethernet, it is more troubling for Fast Ethernet users and a significant issue for implementing Gigabit Ethernet over Category 5 cabling.

The problem of alien crosstalk is especially significant for the commonly used 25-pair UTP backbone cable, which is not supported for Gigabit Ethernet usage. This type of cable simply has too many wire pairs near each other to escape major interference problems.

Equal-Level Far-End Crosstalk (ELFEXT) is electrical noise at the far end from the transmitter.

Return loss is a measure of the energy reflected back by wire impedance mismatches.

These problems can be resolved by taking the following steps:

1. Use connection products rated as meeting the proposed Cat5e (enhanced Category 5) standard, which provides standards for ELFEXT and return loss that surpass the minimum requirements for a 1000Base-TX wiring installation.

2. Replace patch cords with cords constructed from patch cable that meets the Enhanced Category 5 specification.

3. Replace cross-connects with interconnects.

4. Remove transition point connectors.

5. Replace the work area outlets and interconnects with products that meet the Enhanced Category 5 specification.

For more information about the Enhanced Category 5 specification and its use to meet Gigabit Ethernet standards, see the white paper *Gigabit Ethernet Over Copper*, available online at `http://www.gigabit-ethernet.org/technology/whitepapers/gige_0399/copper_2.html`.

Existing Category 5 cabling that meets the existing TIA/EIA-568-A standard must be recertified for use as Gigabit Ethernet cable, and new installations must be designed to minimize alien crosstalk and other problems as listed above.

Existing and new Category 5 networks can be tested for suitability for use with Gigabit Ethernet. Among other, you can obtain cable testers from

- Datacom/Textron (`www.datacomtech.com`) LANcat System 6 with C5e Performance Module (see Figure 40.2)
- Fluke's (`www.fluke.com/nettools/`) DSP4000
- Hewlett-Packard/Scope's (`www.scope.com`) Wirescope 155
- Microtest's (`www.microtest.com`) OmniScanner
- Wavetek's (`www.wavetek.com`) LT8155

Testing for Gigabit Ethernet applications should meet the standards specified in ANSI/TIA/EIA TSB 67 and 1000BASE-T (IEEE802.3ab) or, when published, ANSI/TIA/EIA TSB 95.

Standards for Gigabit Ethernet Over Wire and Fiber

Gigabit Ethernet, which runs at speeds 10 times faster than Fast Ethernet and 100 times faster than 10Base-T, can be run over several different types of connections. In addition to the 1000Base-TX standard discussed in the earlier section titled "Common Wiring and Connection Practices That Can Cause Gigabit Ethernet Problems," several other standards apply to wiring closet, fiber optic, and other specialized uses:

- 1000Base-CX is the Gigabit Ethernet standard for short-distance cables used in a switching closet or computer room as a jumper.
- 1000Base-SX is the Gigabit Ethernet standard for multimode fiber-optic cable, rated for distances of up to 550 meters.
- 1000Base-LX is the Gigabit Ethernet standard for the more expensive single-mode fiber-optic cable, rated for distances up to 5,000 meters.

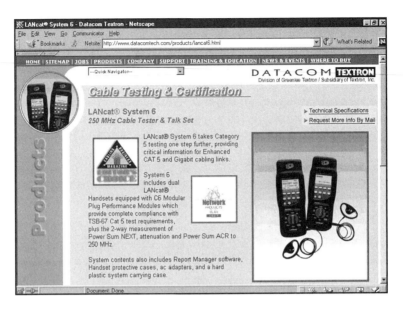

Figure 40.2 Datacom Textron's LANcat System 6 unit is one of several cable testers that can be used to qualify Category 5 cable as either Fast Ethernet or Gigabit Ethernet-capable.

For more details about these standards, see the following Web site: www.gigabit-ethernet.org. This site (see Figure 40.3) also offers links to Gigabit Ethernet products, technical papers, and presentations.

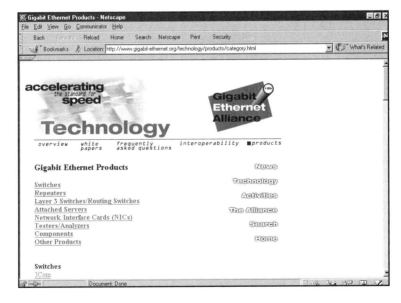

Figure 40.3 The Gigabit Ethernet Alliance Web Site provides a wide range of theoretical, practical, and product information about the fastest form of Ethernet.

Upgrading to Gigabit Ethernet

There are several situations in which the superior performance of Gigabit Ethernet can be useful (see Figure 40.4). Table 40.2 lists some of these situations and what components would need to be replaced.

Table 40.2   Typical Situations for Upgrading to Gigabit Ethernet

Situation	Items to Replace or Upgrade
Upgrade switch to server links	Switch and server NICs
Upgrade switch to switch links	Switches at each end of link
Upgrade backbone with routers and switches	Backbone switches and routers; workgroup switches and routers
Upgrade FDDI backbone with switch	FDDI concentrator

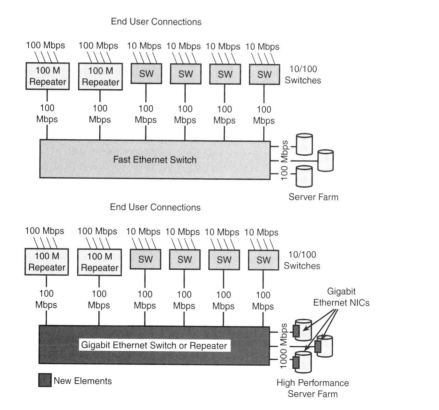

Figure 40.4   File servers can handle more traffic when converted to Gigabit Ethernet NICs, and the use of a multispeed switch means that they can be upgraded to Gigabit Ethernet without requiring the workstations, workgroup switches, or repeaters to be upgraded.

Note that in most cases just listed, there's no need to replace NICs (Network Interface Cards) in servers. The changes to switches and routers might require just an upgrade instead of replacement, depending on the product design. This makes the upgrade to Gigabit Ethernet easier than one might anticipate, because the best place to use Gigabit Ethernet is in the highest traffic areas of your network; those closest to (or at) your servers.

Speeding Up Fast Ethernet as an Alternative to Gigabit Ethernet

Although Gigabit Ethernet is increasingly common for servers, the problems listed earlier with qualifying existing Category 5 cable plants as Gigabit Ethernet-ready, and the cost of replacing existing Fast Ethernet network hardware (switches, hubs, routers, and NICs) with their Gigabit Ethernet counterparts offer several reasons to look at alternatives for speeding up Fast Ethernet networks. One very popular way to do this is to use multiple NICs in a server.

Using multiple NICs in a single server can be useful for improving performance of a single network (or multiple networks interconnected through multispeed switches or routers). The traditional approach has been to add a second NIC to the server, and then subdivide the network into two subnetworks and reconfigure them. With the near-ubiquitous use of the TCP/IP protocol and IP addresses, this means a lot of reconfiguration work is necessary and might need to be repeated with each additional NIC added to the server.

An alternative is to use server NICs that are designed to provide load balancing, which treats multiple server NICs as a single logical unit with a single IP address. Load balancing distributes the network load at any given time equally among the server adapters. Assuming a fast enough server with enough cache RAM to handle the traffic, your network will continue to operate quickly. Load-balancing NICs usually also feature fail-safe features that reroute network traffic around a failed connection. Load-balancing server NICs can be added to an existing Fast Ethernet network without requiring the expense of recertifying the existing cable plant or replacing switches that would be necessary in a change to Gigabit Ethernet.

For networks that are already upgraded to Gigabit Ethernet, the same load-balancing and fail-safe features are also available on Gigabit Ethernet server NICs.

Summary

Ethernet-based networks are becoming faster and faster with the widespread adoption of Fast Ethernet and the development of Gigabit Ethernet standards and products. Carefully evaluate your existing wiring plant and need for Gigabit Ethernet products before making the investment. Keep in mind that a Fast Ethernet network that meets enhanced Cat5 (Cat5e) standards can enable you to migrate to Gigabit Ethernet with minimal problems in the future. Gigabit Ethernet is best used for very high-traffic, high-bandwidth situations and can be used between switches and routers, as well as directly to a server or group of servers ("server farm").

A Fast Ethernet network can also be enhnced through the use of load-balancing and fault-tolerant NICs to meet many network needs at a lower cost than Gigabit Ethernet.

10Base-2 to 10Base-T

SOME OF THE MAIN TOPICS IN THIS CHAPTER ARE

Hardware Factors

Other Possibilities

CHAPTER 41

Although 10Base-T using Category 5 cabling is now the most popular method for installing a local area network, there are still a large number of existing networks that were created using 10Base-2 technology using thin coaxial cable. Although both operate at the same speed of 10Mbps, there can be advantages to upgrading from 10Base-2 to newer standards, though if you have only a very small network that you don't expect to grow for several years, and if you have no other reason to upgrade from 10Base-2, then you shouldn't.

If, however, your business is growing and the network is expected to play a key role in that growth, you will find that upgrading to newer standards such as 10Base-T, or possibly even Fast Ethernet or a mixture of both, will probably make your job easier in the long run. Although going to 100Base-T directly from 10Base-2 can be much more expensive in terms of hubs and network cards, the cost should be considered against the added speed.

In addition to upgrading to 10Base-T, incorporating newer network devices such as switches and intelligent hubs, which are now common items in the workplace, will most likely improve the performance of the network.

Hardware Factors

10Base-2 and 10Base-T have more differences than the type of cables they use. Although both of them use the same signaling technique (CSMA/CD), their topologies are different: 10Base-2 uses a bus topology and 10Base-T uses a star topology. The distances that can be covered by cable segments are also different. The network adapters transmit signals at different speeds. When preparing for an upgrade, check your network inventory to determine which parts of the hardware you will have to upgrade in addition to the cabling.

▶▶ For more information on cabling requirements, see Chapter 3, "Testing Cables."

▶▶ For more information on Network Interface Cards (NICs), see Chapter 4, "Network Interface Cards."

The major considerations that need to be researched when upgrading from 10Base-2 to 10base-T are as follows:

- **Network cables**—The fundamental difference between 10Base-2 and 10Base-T is the move from coaxial cable to twisted-pair wiring.

- **Network topology**—You will be going from a linear bus topology to a star topology. The distances covered by 10Base-T are shorter than those allowed using 10Base-2.

- **Network adapters**—Older network adapters might have only a BNC connector on them. You will need cards that provide an RJ-45 jack for 10Base-T.

- **Connectors**—The connectors you will use on the twisted-pair cables will be RJ-45 instead of BNC connectors.

- **Hubs and other devices**—While the 10Base-2 network allowed you to use multiport repeaters, no central wiring device was actually required. Because 10Base-T uses a star configuration, a hub is required to link the segments together.

Network Cables

This should be the simplest decision you have to make. Although it is possible to continue to use existing Category 3 wiring to construct a 10Base-T network, if you are going to install a 10Base-T network to replace a 10Base-2 network based on coaxial cables, Category 5 is the only twisted-pair solution you should consider installing. Why? Further down the road you will most likely be upgrading again, to Fast Ethernet or Gigabit Ethernet. Both of these technologies will require Category 5 cables or higher.

The amount of cable you will need may work out to be a lot more than you used for the 10Base-2 network. Remember that a bus topology, which is used by thinnet (coaxial) networks like 10Base-2, can daisy chain one workstation to another on a linear bus. Each end of the bus is terminated by a 50-ohm terminator and there is no central point where wiring can be concentrated. When using 10Base-T each workstation is connected to a central hub by its own cable, which is not shared by any other workstation.

Because you will be stringing cable from a central location to each workstation, you will need to have a place you can use as a wiring closet to store the hub and any other interconnecting equipment used to join the LAN to a larger network. Of course, if you are upgrading a small office LAN that stands alone, you can use an inexpensive off-the-shelf hub from your local computer store and place it out of the way.

Another thing to consider when planning the cable layout is that the distances you can cover using 10Base-T are much less than those covered by 10Base-2. In Figure 41.1 you can see a situation in which several workstations are connected on a bus that totals 225 meters in length. This kind of layout can be found in large buildings, such as a factory. Obviously, replacing this cable with a single hub to connect all workstations is not an option.

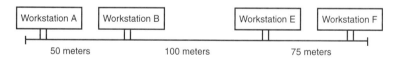

Figure 41.1 Replacing a single coaxial segment with one hub might not be feasible.

Instead, you will have to use multiple hubs to connect workstations that reside on existing segments that are longer than the distances allowed by 10Base-T rules (see Figure 41.2).

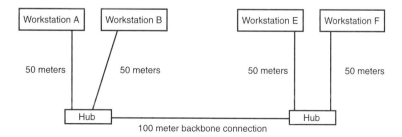

Figure 41.2 Multiple hubs can be used to replace a single segment when distance is a factor.

Although thinnet cable is not an ideal choice to linking workstations to a network, it can be economically used as a backbone, as shown in Figure 41.2, when speeds above 10Mbps are not required.

Network Adapter Cards

If you had the foresight to purchase the kind of network adapter cards called combo cards, which have connectors compatible with both BNC connectors and RJ-45 connectors, this is one piece of hardware you will not necessarily have to replace. The minimum requirement for the NIC is that it has a place you can plug in the RJ-45 jack to connect the adapter to a hub.

If you plan to incorporate switches into the network and want servers to use full-duplex connections, however, you might need to purchase network adapters that support the full-duplex standard.

If you are going to have to upgrade a large number of workstations to newer NICs, think about the future when you make a purchase. If your budget is limited and all the bandwidth you need for the next few years is 10Mbps, then you can purchase adapter cards for about $30 each—usually less when they are on sale or purchased in quantities. The added expense for a card that supports features you do not yet need (such as Fast Ethernet) might not justify the price of getting more expensive equipment.

However, if you are concerned primarily with network performance, you should look at a more costly solution. As mentioned earlier, you can use a switch to create a full-duplex connection to a high-end server in a 10Base-T network. If you have multiple servers that need to be connected in this manner, don't skimp on the expense of a few network cards that will be important performance components in your network.

Similar to the combo cards that come with two different kinds of adapters, most cards being manufactured now have the capability of operating at either 10Mbps or 100Mbps, and many have an autosensing feature that allows them to detect the speed of the network to which they are attached. If you foresee that you will be continuing the upgrade from 10Base-2 to 10Base-T onto the much faster 100Base-T network, plan ahead and buy the 10/100 cards now.

Connectors

Although you are probably aware that you will have to use a different kind of connector for 10Base-T than you do for 10Base-2, you should pay attention to the details when ordering connectors (if you plan to make cables yourself) or when ordering ready-made cables that have the connectors attached. When upgrading to twisted-pair wiring you should use Category 5 cabling instead of a less capable variety such as Category 3. This will enable you to use the cabling when you decide it is time to install 100Mbps segments on part or all of the network.

Connectors, like cables, can exhibit different performance characteristics depending on how they are manufactured. Be sure that the RJ-45 connectors you choose are compliant with the specifications for Category 5 cables. Inferior connectors can cause a lot of trouble later (such as noise or near-end cross-talk), causing you to spend a lot of time troubleshooting.

Bridges, Hubs, and Routers

To extend the length of a LAN based on 10Base-2 technology, the standard technique is to attach multiple segments with a *bridge* or a multiport *repeater*. A repeater works similar to a hub, making one large broadcast domain out of the various cable segments that are connected to it. A bridge connects two segments together but is capable of learning MAC addresses and, therefore, reducing traffic by passing frames on to segments only if their destination is not on the local segment on which they originate.

▶▶ For more information on bridges and how they operate, see Chapter 5, "Bridges, Routers, Switches, and Repeaters."

You can use bridges on a 10Base-T network for the same purposes you use them in 10Base-2: They can group like-users on local segments, reduce traffic on individual segments, and extend the length of the LAN. They can also perform other functions related to performance, such as discarding packets with errors and reducing noise. The newer Layer 3 switch technology accomplishes much of the same function, reducing traffic between segments and between specific ports on the switch. However, switches can be much more expensive than bridges. If you are using a multiport repeater, replacing it with a more functional hub will seem logical. However, remember that the topology rules for 10Base-2 and 10Base-T networks specify different maximum cable segment lengths, so you might have to relocate wiring closets or make other accommodations if your current distances are too long:

- Maximum segment length for 10Base-2: 185 meters
- Maximum segment length for 10Base-T: 100 meters
- Maximum number of devices on a 10Base-2 segment: 30
- Maximum number of devices on a 10Base-T segment: 2

Also, in anything but a small network you will need to use more than one hub to connect user workstations to the network. If you are planning ahead for a future migration to 100Mbps networking, you will find that a multitude of hubs operate at both 10Mbps and 100Mbps. Look at the cost difference and decide whether making an investment in a 10/100Mbps hub will save you money in the future.

If your existing network already uses a router to connect to a larger network, check to be sure that it will accept RJ-45 connectors. Most routers made today accept cables terminated with several different kinds of connectors, so this will probably not be a problem. However, you should check the capabilities of the routers being used when making an upgrade plan.

Other Possibilities

This chapter covers the basic components that you will need to change out when converting a network from 10Base-2 to 10Base-T. However, in addition to the cables, connectors, network adapters, and other devices, a change such as this may warrant further research into the larger network to which you are connected. In many cases the local LAN is, in reality, part of a much larger network. When you have frequently accessed resources outside the local LAN, you need to consider the big picture when you make decisions about the LAN.

For example, do you need to replace the equipment that has been used to connect to the larger network? Are you currently using a bridge that can be replaced by a switch to improve performance? Do you have multiple small LANs than can now be merged into a single larger LAN connected by multiple hubs?

In several chapters that follow you can examine the possibilities offered by incorporating other network devices, such as routers and switches, into your network.

Summary

If you need to upgrade your LAN from using 10Base-2 to 10Base-T components, first make an inventory of the items you have and a map of the network as you expect it will be. You will need to be aware of the different rules for creating the 10Base-T star topology compared to the 10Base-2 bus topology. Most especially, you will need a central place to locate a hub, and you will most likely use a larger amount of cabling than you did in the older network. When purchasing new equipment, such as network adapters, consider your plans for the near future. If you foresee another upgrade to 100Base-T or other technologies, purchasing equipment that can be used both now and in the future might save you time and money.

The next few chapters consider several other upgrade situations. These include things such as migrating from one operating system to another and moving from Token Ring to Ethernet.

Token Ring to Ethernet

CHAPTER 42

Token-ring networks have been around for about the same length of time as ethernet. These two network technologies both accomplish the same thing in that they allow devices on the network to exchange data in an orderly fashion. The methods they employ, however, are fundamentally different. Because of the different methods used to mediate access to the network, the hardware used for token-ring and ethernet networks is not generally interchangeable. That is, you cannot simply pick up a workstation that is configured on an ethernet network and move it to a token-ring network without some hardware changes.

Why Ethernet?

When planning a major network upgrade on an installed token-ring network, why would ethernet ever enter into the planning process? There are bridges and routers that work just fine with token ring and allow you to create large LANs and WANs, so how would an administrator justify making a fundamental shift in technology to an ethernet-based network?

Although each technology has its proponents, installations of ethernet far outnumber those of token ring. The volume of ethernet sites brings with it a larger number of vendors who manufacture equipment. This volume usually results in lower prices and more innovative products. If you are planning to add a few departmental LANs to a large network, the cost of new equipment might not be that great when compared to replacing network adapters, and possibly the wiring infrastructure, for an entire network. But if you can see in your immediate future a large increase in your network, it might pay to sit down and look hard at the figures to make sure you can justify the costs of staying with token-ring hardware.

Token-ring networks have been around for about 20 years. When the technology was first developed, PCs were not as important a business tool as they are today. The main rationale for hooking a PC to a corporate network in the early days was to provide access to larger computer systems, such as mainframe and mini-computer systems. In that kind of scenario most of the data flow was within a small workgroup of computers with only a small percentage of network traffic from PCs traveling over a backbone to a larger WAN. In today's client/server atmosphere, where intensive traffic loads can be generated by applications such as multimedia or Web servers, this might not be the case. Token-ring does not adapt to heavy internetworking traffic without experiencing problems with congestion as well as ethernet does.

Some might argue that token ring has built-in mechanisms for handling heavy traffic loads because its basic frame structure includes bits set aside for prioritization. However, in reality, not many manufacturers have implemented priority-based schemes using these bits. Although there have been some technological improvements in token ring over the years, they are a far cry from the changes that have been made to ethernet standards. For example, the IEEE 802.1p standard, which was ratified recently, provides for a filtering process that allows multicast traffic to be forwarded only to end nodes on the network that make the request. The IEEE 802.1p Class of Service specification allows for eight priority levels of network traffic. When this standard is widely implemented (which it most likely will be in a very short time), it will be possible to provide a high level of performance for applications such as voice-over IP and other applications that generate large volumes of network traffic.

To sum it up, the following are some of the factors you might want to consider when deciding on a major upgrade to a token-ring network:

- The cost of the hardware portion—both now and in the future. Can you be sure that there will be a sufficient number of vendors producing token-ring devices in the future to keep prices in a reasonable range? Will there be enough vendors involved to promote the development of new and innovative additions to the technology?

- Will you be able to continue to find technicians that are proficient in token-ring technology or will you find yourself spending additional funds training new employees?

- Will you be forced to find some kind of interoperability solution in the near future if your business merges with another that already has a large installed base of ethernet equipment?

Phasing Ethernet into the Token-Ring Network

If you've decided that you are going to have to embrace the ethernet network in your token-ring shop, the next step is to decide on a plan for making the change. The most disruptive method would be to go ahead full force and swap out all the hardware at one time and hope for the best. Depending on your circumstances, that might be the only choice you have. The issue that will make this decision is whether you can segment your network into functional components where you can identify which end stations need to communicate with other stations. Why? Because of the fundamental differences between ethernet and token ring, it can be very difficult in many cases to make the two work together.

There are translational bridges and other internetworking devices that you can use to connect token-ring LANs to an ethernet LAN or a backbone joining the two. It is not terribly complicated to use a backbone to provide a high-speed transport to both kinds of networks. ATM, for example, can be used to carry both kinds of traffic. But without some kind of translation capability to account for the difference in frame formats, a network of this sort can be limited to allowing token-ring stations to talk only to token-ring stations and ethernet nodes to talk only to ethernet nodes.

Differences That Make Translation Difficult

There are several reasons why it is not an easy task to make a perfect translation device that can allow token-ring and ethernet nodes to communicate with each other. These are

- Canonical versus non-canonical bit ordering
- Embedded MAC addresses
- Frame size
- Notification of delivery (token-ring status bits)
- Token-ring routing (RIF) information
- Cabling requirements (ethernet requires Cat. 5)

Bits and Frames

The most basic difference between these two networking technologies lies at the very beginning of the network transport process: They interpret the ordering of bits for addressing purposes in the opposite direction. That is, although they both use a 6-byte MAC address to uniquely identify a network adapter on a LAN, ethernet considers the first bit in the serial stream to be the low-order bit (the canonical method), whereas token ring considers the first bit to be the high-order bit (the non-canonical method).

This problem can be easily addressed with a hardware device, such as a bridge or router, which reorders the addressing bits depending on what kind of network is attached to the port on which the frame is to be sent. However, there are cases, such as in the Address Resolution Protocol (ARP), where MAC addresses ride in portions of a frame in addition to the addressing fields. Designing a hardware device that can determine all the cases where this is possible is a daunting task. And, when such an attempt is made, latency factors will enter the picture because the device will be forced to read much more of the frame than just the header fields that contain the source and destination fields.

Frame size is another important factor. Ethernet networks use a frame size that can be up to approximately 1,500 bytes, whereas token ring uses a frame size that can be a lot bigger, possibly up to 17.8KB on a 16Mbps token-ring LAN. If the higher level protocol that is being transported on the LAN does not allow for fragmenting packets (as TCP/IP does), it will be necessary to force the entire network to use the lowest common denominator of ethernet's 1,500 byte frame.

Notification of Delivery

Token ring uses three bits in its frame to notify the sender what happened to the frame after it was sent out onto the ring. The *Address Recognized* bit is set when a station recognizes that it is the intended destination of the frame. The *Frame Copied* bit is set if the destination station is capable of copying the frame from the wire into an internal buffer. The *Error bit* is used to indicate that some kind of error was encountered in the frame somewhere along its travels. Using the information signaled by these status bits, the sending station can determine whether it must retransmit the frame.

Ethernet doesn't worry about such things. It provides a "best effort" delivery system and depends on the higher-level protocol whose traffic it is transporting to decide whether the frame is capable of successfully navigating the network to its destination.

When designing a translational device, you must know how these bits are to be handled when a token-ring frame is sent out onto an ethernet network where there are no built-in mechanisms for storing this kind of information. There are differences in how these bits are handled from vendor to vendor, and you must be aware of how their devices handle this situation. For example, some set the Frame Copied bit when the frame is received at the device, but not the Address Recognized bit, while others set both bits before sending the frame back onto the ring. When the frame makes its way back to the sending station, you must know it will interpret these bits. Because the translational device is not the final destination of the frame, the higher-level protocol must be capable of coping with this.

Routing Information

Token ring uses *source-routing bridges* (SRB), whereas ethernet uses *transparent bridges*. In the source-routing algorithm, an "explorer" frame is sent out through the network to discover a path to the destination computer. When more than one path exists in the network, the frame is duplicated and is capable of traveling more than one path. As the explorer frame travels from bridge to bridge to its destination, it compiles a list of addressing information that details the route it has taken. This information is stored in the *Routing Information Field* (RIF). When it reaches its destination, it can use this routing information to travel back to the sending station. The sending station can then decide from the multiple frames that come back to it which route it wants to use to communicate with the destination station.

There is no concept like this in an ethernet network. Transparent bridges don't perform this "routing" function like SRB devices do. They simply keep a table of MAC addresses as they learn which segment a device is on and try to send frames out only on the port on which the destination MAC address is known to exist.

A translational device can sometimes be made to work by caching the information in the RIF before it translates the packet from token-ring to ethernet format. When a frame with a unicast address returns, the translation bridge can check its cache and reconstruct the token-ring frame from the data stored there before outputting it on the token-ring network.

However you look at it, trying to create a gateway between these two fundamentally different kinds of networks is not an easy task. If you must gradually phase ethernet equipment into an existing token-ring network, you might have to deal with the incompatibilities and incur the expense of translational devices that might solve all the problems. If you can localize your users and their servers into units that can be swapped out all at once, the process will be much easier to implement).

Replacing All Token-Ring Equipment

In a small LAN, the prospect of having to swap out all the token-ring hardware and replace it with ethernet equipment can be a feasible idea. If you carefully plan the implementation around the users' work schedules, you can minimize disruptions on the network. Before beginning you should inventory the existing equipment to see what, if any of it, can be retained, and what will need to be replaced.

Hubs, Switches, and Routers

Some of the newer routers and switches that have come onto the market in the last few years have the capability to operate with either ethernet or token-ring networks. If you are contemplating a changeover in the near future, this should be a consideration when making any current purchases. It might be less expensive to purchase a device of this sort now, even it if it is more expensive than a simpler model, when you compare it to the cost of completely replacing it in a year or two.

If you have been using a gradual-phased approach, the router or switch that is currently operating as a translation device might easily be reconfigured to work just fine in an all-ethernet network. Read the documentation for each device to determine what steps need to be taken.

If you cannot find the information readily available in the documentation that came with the equipment, check with the manufacturer. Many times a simple download of a new version of the device's firmware can solve this kind of problem.

Network Cabling and Connectors

Most new installations of network cabling are of the Category 5 twisted-pair type. This cable is capable of supporting ordinary Token Ring 4 or 16Mb networks as well as ethernet networks running at speeds from 10Mbps to 100Mbps with no problems. You will need to consult your network map to be sure that any existing cabling infrastructure for the LAN does not violate any of the distance or nodes-per-segment rules that apply to ethernet. If the existing cables have been installed for quite some time and are of a grade not equal to Category 5, you should probably go ahead and replace them.

The connectors used for token ring and ethernet might be different on your network. Ethernet networks based on 10Base-T or 100Base-T typically use an RJ-45 connector. Although this kind of connector can also be used on a token-ring network, the wires used and the pins to which they are attached on each end will be different from the pinout used on ethernet networks. You will need time to make the actual physical wire-to-pin changes as well test the cable to be sure the connectors have been properly installed and will function with a minimum of errors on the new network.

Network Adapter Cards

Token-ring and ethernet network adapter cards are basically different and are not compatible. Token-ring NICs usually cost much more than ethernet cards because token-ring NICs take on more responsibility for managing transmission of data on the local LAN than ethernet cards do. When making a change over, it will be necessary to acquire a new card for each end-user workstation as well as for any servers on the network.

Network Conversion Scenario

Let's now go through an example of converting a LAN from token ring to ethernet. In this example, there are two network segments connected via a router (see Figure 42.1).

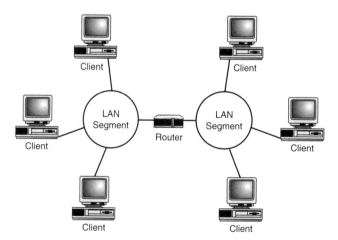

Figure 42.1   Two network segments connected via a router.

The following steps detail the process of converting to ethernet:

1. Develop a project plan. This plan should lay out the order in which the network will be converted. Are both segments going to be switched over all at once or is each segment going to be done separately? What are the personnel requirements? How long is it going to take to install and configure the hardware?

2. Identify infrastructure hardware. This can include cabling (must be Category 5), router network adapters, or a new router if necessary. Are you going to switch to 10Base-T or 100Base-T? This can impact the router configuration also because older routers might not have a 100Base-T adapter available.

3. Configure the clients. This includes testing the new network adapters on all hardware configurations. For example, if the network card you want to use works only on IRQ 9, you would need to verify that all configurations have this IRQ available.

Every conversion is different, so it is important to make sure that all these areas are considered to ensure that the process goes smoothly. Larger network segments that cannot be done all at once will provide more of a challenge because you will need to temporarily separate the segment into two separate LANs, which means having the capability to have different cabling sections and an additional adapter in the router.

Summary

Changing your network from token ring to ethernet can be a difficult task in a large network environment and requires a lot of planning. In a small office LAN, you can easily swap out all the necessary components in a day or so, transparent to the users. In a large environment, it might be necessary to carefully segment the network into domains that contain most of the resources users need so that you can change over one segment at a time. Depending on your needs, translational bridges or routers can be employed to make the change over a period of time, but might involve some problems that you must cope with because the technologies are fundamentally different to begin with. Because of the unclear future of token-ring networking devices and the rapidly advancing ethernet technologies, such as Fast Ethernet and Gigabyte Ethernet, it is most likely that in the near future you will have to make the change. Planning in advance can make the change much less painful.

Bridges to Routers/Switches

SOME OF THE MAIN TOPICS IN THIS CHAPTER ARE

Growing Beyond a Small LAN

From Bridges to Routers

From Bridges to Switches

There are many kinds of network devices that you can use to expand a local area network (LAN) or to connect it to a wide area network (WAN). These range from simple repeaters to devices with more intelligence such as bridges, routers, and switches.

As a small LAN grows it is a simple matter to use bridges to segment a few small workgroups. You can use bridges to isolate local traffic among groups of users and thus cut down on the overall traffic on the LAN. However, there are limits, depending on the kind of network (for example, ARCnet, ethernet, or token ring), for how many bridges (repeaters) you can use in a LAN. In addition to their usefulness in solving network traffic congestion problems, you can use routers or switches to solve two other important problems: expanding the LAN beyond the size that bridges will allow and connecting the LAN to a larger WAN.

This chapter discusses these two possibilities, along with information you need to consider when bringing routers or switches into your LAN.

Growing Beyond a Small LAN

Chapter 5, "Bridges, Routers, Switches, and Repeaters," covers the basic devices used to interconnect network segments. Each of these devices builds on the one previous to it, so that together they span a continuum of functionality that you can use to solve problems with the LAN or WAN.

To quickly summarize:

- **Repeaters** are simple devices that just connect network segments (usually two segments). They repeat all traffic and thus do nothing to help segment network traffic patterns. Repeaters are used to expand a LAN when it grows beyond the limitations imposed by a single network segment.

- **Bridges** are similar to repeaters except that they apply a little intelligence to the packet forwarding process: bridges learn MAC addresses of devices on each segment when they make an initial transmission. From then on a bridge will not pass traffic to another segment if it knows the recipient is on the segment local to the transmission. Bridges are helpful for expanding a LAN and can be used to organize nodes to lower overall bandwidth consumption.

- **Routers** work like bridges in that they are selective about which packets get forwarded on which ports. However, while bridges operate at the layer 2 of the OSI reference model (the Data Link Layer) and only look at the flat namespace provided by the MAC addresses, routers operate at layer 3 (the Network Layer) and make decisions based on the addressing scheme provided by a higher level networking protocol. Bridges are typically used to create larger networks. Connecting the LAN to a larger WAN can be done using a router.

- **Switches** are the newest technology for connecting network segments. Switches operate like bridges in that they keep track of which network node is located on each port by remembering MAC addresses. When retransmitting an incoming packet, the switch will only send it out on a port that will get it to its destination, provided it has already learned the destination's MAC address. While bridges usually have only two ports, switches are like hubs and contain many ports. Some switches will allow for full-duplex operation, thus effectively doubling the available network bandwidth for a single node connected on a segment.

From this summary you can see that it's easy to use repeaters or bridges to grow the small LAN, but when it becomes necessary to expand beyond certain limits, or when it becomes necessary to make a connection to a larger LAN, you need to incorporate routers or switches. Growth is not the only reason you might want to use a router or switch, however. These devices can also be used in a small LAN. For example, a small LAN that is experiencing network traffic congestion may find relief by replacing the hubs in the LAN with switches to cut down on the overall network traffic. Routers may be used in a campus LAN to allow network administrators to logically group network segments using the addressing scheme provided by TCP/IP, for example.

Segmenting the Network

You might need to segment users on the network for many different reasons. These include

- **Topology limitations**—You need to add more nodes to the network but the expansion will break distance limitations or maximum nodes-per-segment rules.
- **Networking protocol limitations**—Address space is fragmented and you need to connect segments that have different network addresses.
- **Network bandwidth limitations**—As when a few high performance servers or workstations consume too much of the segment's available bandwidth.
- **Security reasons**—An ethernet adapter set to promiscuous mode can intercept all packets that are sent out on a particular segment, for example. You need to place a few high security workstations on their own segment, yet allow some kind of connection to the reset of the network.
- **Geographically distant connections**—It's best to segment each geographic location to ensure that unnecessary traffic isn't being sent across the remote connection and wasting valuable bandwidth.

Depending on which combination of these reasons apply to your situation, a router or switch may be the solution you need to segment the network.

Connecting Remote Locations

When a business expands geographically you will find that using bridges to connect remote locations is not a feasible solution. There are so many different technologies that you can choose from today, from simple dedicated lines to ATM and frame relay, to connect geographically distant locations. For these kinds of connections you will find it necessary to incorporate routers or switches.

When to Use a Router

Routers are similar to bridges only in the fact that they can both be used to connect multiple network segments. While bridges make all their decisions based on the MAC address of a particular network packet, routers access the addressing information provided by a higher level protocol to decide how to best forward a packet. Using the OSI reference model you can see that the bridge operates at layer 2, the Data Link Layer, while routers usually operate at layer 3, the Network Layer. With bridges, the address space is flat: It is simply the MAC addresses associated with nodes on each segment, each one unique. For protocols operating at the Network Layer, the address space becomes more complicated, because there must be a mechanism for identifying the network as well as the individual node.

When to Use a Switch

Switches are one of the fastest growing categories of network equipment. They can act as a wiring concentrator for a LAN just as a hub does, but they can also make available a much larger bandwidth to clients because they selectively forward traffic from one port to another based on the destination address of each packet. When you use a switch with only one node attached to each port, you are in effect creating a collection of broadcast domains that consist of only two network nodes: the switch and the client node connected to the port. For network adapters and switches that support full-duplex operation, the effective bandwidth is doubled for each client.

From Bridges to Routers

Routers are inherently slower than bridges when it comes to forwarding network packets. This is because a router needs to read further into each packet to get Network Layer addressing information while a bridge merely looks at a fixed location for the MAC address. This means that routers are not plug-and-play types of devices. Hubs, bridges, and switches can be set up in a short amount of time and usually require little or no configuration. Routers require that the network administrator configure networking information for each port that is used. The command set available to configure a router is quite large, because it is a very flexible device and can be confusing for a novice.

The kinds of information you will need to configure a new router are

- A list of the network protocols you will be using the router for.
- The routing protocol that you will use for each network protocol.
- Information about the address space used on each segment the router will connect.

Network Protocol Issues

In many networks more than one network protocol is used on the same medium. In order to do their job, routers need configuration information about each protocol for each port. For example, since each port on the router connects to a different network segment, each port must have a unique network address that it can use to communicate on the segment. If you plan to restrict some segments for security or other reasons, you will need to create a set of access control lists for each port, which indicate which packets are allowed through.

When using a router to connect to a larger WAN, you will probably be faced with having to configure a port on the router that uses a WAN protocol, such as frame relay, in addition to protocols you are already familiar with on your network. With a WAN connection you will have to coordinate your activities with other system administrators to ensure that the router is configured with the correct information for the larger network.

Network Addressing Issues

Because the router makes decisions based on a higher level networking protocol, such as TCP/IP, you will have to take into consideration your current address space when you decide to introduce a router into the network. If you are adding new segments to the LAN and have the freedom to choose a new network address, this can be an easy task. If you are going to take an existing LAN and use a router to separate it into more manageable segments, you have two possible choices. You can use your original network address for one segment and create new networks on the remaining segments, or, you can use subnetting, as described in Chapter 18, "TCP/IP," to divide your current address space into smaller subnetworks.

Regardless, you will have to then reconfigure each client with new addressing information. If you are using DHCP, the process is made simpler because you can make the changes at a central location and have clients request the new information after the changes have been made.

If you are going to use a router to connect your LAN to a larger corporate network, you may not have to make any addressing changes on your network, depending on the company's overall network plan. You will still have to configure the ports, however. If you are going to connect the LAN to the Internet, using a router configured as a firewall might be something to consider. For more information on using a router for this purpose, see Chapter 36, "Firewalls."

Other Router Management Issues

Routers are very much like smart PCs that have been customized to perform the routing function efficiently. They have CPUs, memory, and I/O ports just like an ordinary PC. They also have an operating system, which is subject to periodic updates by the manufacturer. So, in addition to learning how to configure the router, you will also need to become familiar with other commands used for such functions as saving a copy of the system image to a server for backup purposes or commands used to perform troubleshooting testing.

Managing a network that uses routers can seem at first a difficult task. However, by allowing you to organize your network according to the hierarchical network address spaces used by upper-level network protocols, the initial configuration problems will be worth the effort.

Using a Router to Segment the Network

Like bridges, routers can be used to isolate traffic between network segments. Unlike bridges, routers further reduce network bandwidth usage because they do not pass broadcast messages from one segment to another unless programmed to do so. A router also does not have to take time to learn which nodes are connected to each segment. The information it needs is configured in advance, such as when the administrator assigns protocols and addresses to each port. Routing protocols also use various methods to update each other about network topology as it changes.

One very important reason why routers are used to help organize a network into segments is that routers will allow you to connect many more end nodes together. While bridges are limited to a few thousand nodes, depending on the topology used, routers can allow the LAN to be connected to an infinitely larger WAN, such as the Internet.

The internal processing that routers must perform basically makes them slower than bridges, which only need to examine a small amount of data in the packet header. Although this performance difference will not be noticed on network segments with only moderate traffic usage, you may find that you need to place routers only at strategic locations throughout the network, retaining bridges for some segments. This will depend on the usage patterns that can be monitored for each segment and the cost of the links used to connect different segments.

Connecting to a Larger WAN

When connecting the LAN to a WAN a router is still the best solution to use in most cases. When connecting to the Internet, for example, you cannot use a bridge or a repeater. The Internet is composed of a hierarchical TCP/IP address space and a router is needed to participate in this hierarchy. Or, you may plan to use a dedicated line of some sort to connect to a larger corporate network. In this case, placing a router between your LAN and the WAN hardware, such as an ATM switch connection, will help reduce the traffic that crosses the expensive dedicated connection by keeping local traffic confined to the local network segments.

Although you will certainly have to configure the ports that connect the local LAN and the WAN interface, you might have to reconfigure addressing information on clients. For example, if you are already using a valid TCP/IP network address, possibly a subnet of the corporate network address space, you will only need to configure routers.

If your business has just been acquired by a larger concern, however, you may find that your LAN has been assigned a new subnet by the larger corporation and you may possibly have to plan for downtime for end users if you cannot make the client configuration changes outside of normal business hours.

From Bridges to Switches

Switches can be useful for solving network problems related to traffic congestion and network segmentation. For example, they can be used as replacements for hubs at the LAN level. In Figure 43.1, you can see a small LAN that uses two hubs. The three servers for this network share a common broadcast domain with all the other users on the network.

When this LAN was first installed there was more than adequate bandwidth available and users were satisfied with the response time. Over time, however, each of the servers was replaced with a more powerful model and some of the end users' workstations were replaced with high-performance machines and new database software that relies on information stored on the servers.

Network traffic has increased considerably, users are dissatisfied, and the network administrator must take action. Since the main problem is the traffic exchanged between the servers and the high-performance end user workstations, a switch can be a simple solution. There are two simple solutions you can devise using switches. In Figure 43.2, you can see that both of the 8 port hubs have been replaced with a single 16-port switch.

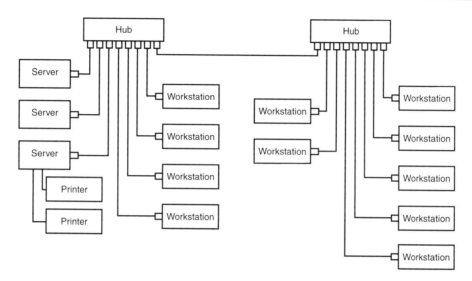

Figure 43.1 Hubs do nothing to limit network traffic on the LAN.

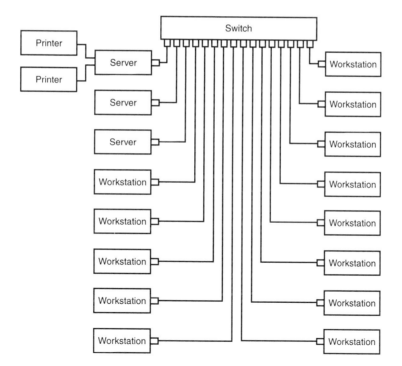

Figure 43.2 A switch can be used to isolate high bandwidth network nodes.

This layout will give each node that is connected to the switch a full 10Mbps network connection (or 100Mbps, depending on your hardware). Each connection is a broadcast domain with only two end nodes: the connected workstation or server and the switch. In this solution, the server nodes were equipped with full-duplex network adapters, effectively doubling their available network bandwidth. Provided the switch is capable of handling the traffic load, individual users on the workstations who only moderately use the network should notice a better response time through the switch, as compared to a hub connection.

The servers and high-performance workstations should also notice better performance, yet their network traffic is no longer broadcast on the segments of the other moderate users, effectively isolating this traffic.

Figure 43.3 shows another solution. Here a hub is used for the workstations that make only moderate usage of the network.

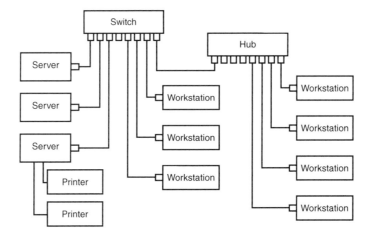

Figure 43.3   Traffic on the hub is not hampered by traffic generated by the other high-performance servers and workstations.

Here the three servers that are responsible for much of the bandwidth usage have been placed each on a separate port on the switch. Again, full-duplex network adapters were installed to further increase the available bandwidth to each server. The three high-performance workstations were also placed on separate switch ports so that their network usage does not directly interfere with other nodes. A hub was retained for connecting moderate network users. Since these nodes do not generate a lot of network communications, placing them on a hub connected to the switch should allow them fast communications among themselves while still allowing access to the other servers and workstations.

Summary

Bridges will allow you to expand a small LAN to its limits, as determined by the network topology. Routers and switches can be used to connect the LAN to a larger network or segment it into smaller subnetworks that can be more easily managed. Like bridges, switches usually require no configuration to get them up and running. Just plug your segments into the ports and start operating. Routers, however, operate based on the network address space provided by the network protocols, and require that the administrator understand the protocols used on the network so that ports on the router can be configured accordingly. In addition to these devices, you will find modern hybrids, with some vendors' products performing the functions of both a router and a switch. The device you chose will depend on the topology and traffic patterns of your current network as well as what you want them to become.

Part XV

NETWORK OPERATING SYSTEMS

Migrating from ARCnet to Ethernet

SOME OF THE MAIN TOPICS IN THIS CHAPTER ARE

ARCnet Overview

Upgrading to Ethernet

Of the networking technologies still widely in use today, ARCnet (Attached Resource Computer Network) is the oldest. It was created at Datapoint Corporation in the 1970s and is a token-passing system similar in some ways to token ring. For small networks, ARCnet is a reliable technology that is easy to configure. However, also like token ring, ARCnet equipment is produced by only a small number of manufacturers when compared to ethernet. Along with its slow network speed (2.5Mbps), this makes it a prime candidate for an upgrade to newer technology.

In this chapter, you will first quickly review the makeup of an ARCnet LAN, and then look at options for migrating to ethernet.

ARCnet Overview

Because it is a token-passing system, ARCnet is a deterministic network technology—the nodes sequentially communicate and are provided equal access (similar to the later token-ring topology)—which is useful in situations where a predictable throughput is required. It became a very popular technology during the early 1980s when ethernet was still quite expensive. It is most likely to be found in older departmental LANs or in an industrial manufacturing plant or other similar settings. It operates at a rate of 2.5Mbps and can be used to create a LAN of up to 255 computers.

Although development had begun before the OSI reference model was defined, ARCnet provided functions along the same lines as those defined in the Physical and Data Link Layers of the reference model. The logical topology of the network is always a token bus, although it can be physically arranged as a bus, star, or a topology, which is a combination of the two. ARCnet uses a token bus logical topology because no matter which physical topology is used, the token frame is passed around in a sequential manner from one node to the next so that all nodes get an equal chance to access the network media. Each node on the LAN is manually configured with an address of 1-255. The 8-bit address length is the limiting factor in this node addressing restriction.

Hubs and Network Wiring

The ARCnet network can be wired using twisted-pair cables, coaxial cables, or fiber-optic cables. For UTP, Category 3 or above should be used. Coaxial cables should be RG11U, RG-59U, or RG-62. The distances between network nodes depends on the type of wiring used and whether active or passive hubs are used as wiring concentrators.

Active hubs provide the longest distance capabilities for the ARCnet network. The active hub acts much like an ethernet hub and is usually manufactured in 8 to 16 port units. An active hub takes the incoming signal and amplifies it before sending it back out on the other ports. Some active hubs perform other tasks, such as segmenting a port that exhibits errors so that other segments are unaffected. Passive hubs usually have only four ports and do no signal amplification. Instead they act as a signal-splitter taking the incoming signal and dividing it among other three ports. The primary function of a passive hub in a larger LAN is to join individual workstations to an active hub. Unused ports on a passive hub should usually be terminated. Unused ports on active hubs, depending on the manufacturer, may or may not need to be terminated.

Bus Topology

The simplest network topology that can be used for ARCnet is a bus using coaxial cables with BNC T-connectors. Up to eight nodes can be connected to any bus segment in a daisy-chain made up using the T-connectors. The total length of the segment is limited to 300 meters (1,000 ft.). As you can see in Figure 44.1, an active hub can be used to join multiple segments to create a larger LAN. A passive hub cannot be used to connect individual segments based on a bus topology. They can only be used to connect individual workstations.

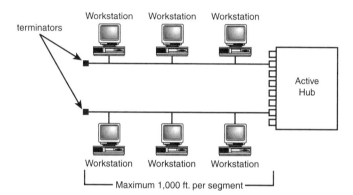

Figure 44.1   An active hub can be used to join together multiple coaxial segments.

You can also create a bus topology using UTP cables. The UTP ARCnet adapter will have two connectors, usually RJ11 or RJ45. Stations are daisy-chained from one node to the next using both connectors. In some cases, the last node on each end of the bus will need to have a terminator inserted into the last connector. Some cards provide an auto-termination feature. When using UTP you can have up to 10 nodes on one segment, with any repeater counting toward that limit. Each node on the bus must be separated by a *minimum* of about 6 feet. The segment can be up to 400 feet (120 meters).

Star Topology

By using hubs you can create a physical star topology. By cascading hubs, you can create a tree structure of multiple stars. Figure 44.2 shows a small network that uses both active and passive hubs and also has workstations that connect directly to an active hub.

Note

You can use active hubs to reach the maximum distance of 6,000 meters. When a large LAN is constructed in this manner, remember that no loops can exist in the physical topology, and the total number of network nodes is limited to 255 because of the 8-byte address used.

Network Interface Cards (NICs)

Because ARCnet has been around for so long, there are a lot of different network cards still in use today. ARCnet cards are not interchangeable with ethernet cards so in the event of an upgrade you will have to incur the cost of new NICs for each node on the network. There are two main categories of cards used in ARCnet networks:

- Bus NIC (high-impedance driver)
- Star NIC (low-impedance driver)

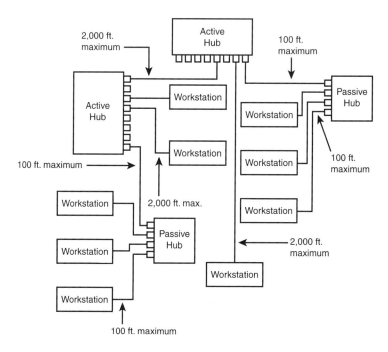

Figure 44.2   The star topology can be extended using additional hubs.

As their names imply, they are differentiated in that the Bus NIC should be used on a bus topology and the Star NIC should be used on a star topology. Some newer cards may provide both options.

When deciding on Ethernet NICs, be sure to plan for the immediate future. While you can purchase very inexpensive Ethernet NICs for under $30, which work fine in a 10Base-T (10Mbps) network, you may opt for cards that work at both 10Mbps and 100Mbps if you think that you will be needing the increased network bandwidth any time soon. The difference in the price will not be that great for the two cards and will most certainly be less than the expense of purchasing new cards in a few years, the additional user downtime, and the labor needed to make the replacements.

Interoperability of New and Old Equipment

In some cases, it is possible during a migration to replace components of the network by sections so that older and newer equipment interoperates during the migration. This kind of network upgrade plan usually can be used to minimize the impact on end users. When upgrading from

ARCnet to ethernet, however, this is not likely to be possible. Just as token ring and ethernet have basic differences in the protocols used for communicating on the wire, you will find the same differences, more or less, exist when trying to connect ARCnet to ethernet. While there are vendors that can provide bridges or other gateway devices for joining token ring to ethernet with some success, you won't find the same completely true for ARCnet. And, if you do locate a suitable device, it is likely to be expensive and not a good investment for a short-term migration project.

Upgrading to Ethernet

From the discussion of ARCnet technology so far in this chapter, you can probably safely assume that any conversion to ethernet is going to require replacing network adapter cards, hubs, and most likely network cables also. In other words, just about everything except for the workstations and servers.

For the upgrade, you will have many choices to make, all of which will depend on your current network layout and the functionality you expect from the new network.

You should ask yourself the following questions when determining which choice to make:

- Do you need the higher bandwidth provided by 100Base-T or will a 10Mbps network suffice?
- Which current cabling is in use?
- While Category 5 is the standard installation type today, will you want to create some network links using fiber to cover longer distances or provide a higher bandwidth?

Network Cables

If you have used Category 3 or better cables, you may be able to reuse some of the cables, but this is not likely. To do so you would need to modify the connectors to use the appropriate cable pairs and pin-out specifications for 10Base-T. Also, ethernet does not support daisy-chaining using twisted-pair wiring. Small segments of cable that are currently used to daisy-chain workstations over a small distance are probably not worth recycling because of labor costs and the current low prices for new cables. Because stringing cables throughout a building is one of the more expensive items in a network upgrade, it would be wise to use Category 5 or better cables when you upgrade. To cover distances that ARCnet allows, you might need to use coaxial or fiber cables for some links.

Choosing Ethernet Solutions

ARCnet was usually used to create small LANs. There are a few manufacturers that sold bridges that could be used to connect the 255-node LANs into larger configurations. The majority of ARCnet LANs operate at the standard 2.5Mbps rate. Other versions, such as ARCnet Plus, can be used at up to 20Mbps. To decide which ethernet technology you want to use, examine the current layout and identify important nodes and the bandwidth you think they will need. Try to locate bottlenecks that occur in the current topology, if any.

The following are questions to ask yourself:

- Which servers are used by the majority of nodes in the LAN?
- Which servers get the heaviest usage in terms of network bandwidth?
- Are there any groups of users and servers that can be segmented?
- If this upgrade is the result of merging with another network, what kind of interconnection will be made?
- What are the distances to be covered?

ARCnet provides a physical LAN that uses a token to allow access to the network medium. Since there is no prioritization built into the protocols used, each packet that is sent out on the wire will have to be processed by every other node in the LAN. Conversion to a simple ethernet broadcast domain seems to be a simple task. However, you should look closely at the distances between hubs and between hubs and workstations. Group users that are in close proximity to each other when deciding on the placement of ethernet hubs. Because ARCnet allows for up to 2,000 feet between active devices, make decisions on what kind of technology you will use to bridge distances greater than ordinary 10Base-T will make possible.

Although a switch might not be an immediate need, you might want to make the investment now if you plan to increase the workload provided by servers on the network or if you plan to add any high-performance workstations to the new network that require additional bandwidth.

Ethernet offers many different solutions to help build networks that range from 10Mbps to giga-bit speeds. What you use will depend on the current needs of the network, projected usage for the next few years, and the distances to be covered.

Lay Out the New Network

In a small network, such as an office setting where there are from two to a few dozen computers, a simple solution is to replace the current ARCnet hubs with one or more ethernet hubs. Run new cables to the workstations and equip each workstation with a new ethernet network adapter card. This kind of a swap-out can be done easily over a weekend without causing downtime for network users.

When the LAN is of a larger size, however, you may need to sit down and think about how users make use of network resources before you decide on a migration plan. For example, ARCnet allows you to place a workstation up to 2,000 feet from an active hub. Ethernet's 10Base-T allows a maximum distance of only 328 feet. If your network actually has multiple workstations that are using cables that extend the maximum distance allowed by ARCnet, you will not be able to per-form a simple swap-out and replace ARCnet hubs with ethernet hubs. Instead, you will have to look at the geography of your building and decide on locations for hubs that can be used to stay within the 10Base-T limit of 328 feet. The end result is that you will probably use more hubs than you do on the present ARCnet network.

Figure 44.3 shows an ARCnet LAN that uses two active hubs and one passive hub. On the first active hub, you can see there are five workstations that are all placed the maximum distance from the hub—2,000 feet. The passive hub, however, cannot be farther than 100 feet from the active hub, and the workstations connected to it are also bound by this limit.

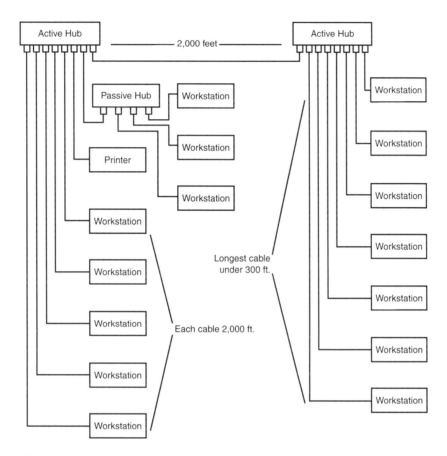

Figure 44.3 ARCnet allows the LAN to span distances of up to 2,000 feet between hubs.

The second active hub in this layout has workstations that are distanced from it no more than 300 feet, which is within the ethernet 10BaseT limit of 328 feet. It is a simple matter here to replace this second active hub with a 10Base-T hub, and then replace the cables that connect the workstations to the hub and the network adapters in each workstation.

The first active hub, however, poses a problem because it has workstations that are beyond the distance limitation imposed by 10Base-T. Here a solution might be to replace the active hub and the passive hub with a 10Base-T hub, and then connect the printer (and the workstations attached to the passive hub) to the new 10Base-T hub. From here you can run an additional link to another hub that is situated closer to the other workstations, placing it in a location that allows it to reach the additional workstations without breaching the 328 foot limit (see Figure 44.4).

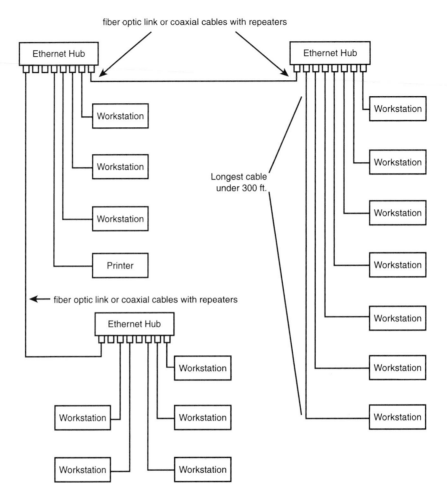

Figure 44.4   Use additional hubs to group workstations that are beyond the maximum allowable distance for 10Base-T.

To connect these three hubs together you will need to use a fiber-optic link, or perhaps coaxial cable with repeaters to span the distance. When you are looking at hubs to purchase, make sure that they have the correct ports that you will need to connect both 10Base-T and coaxial or fiber. A cheap 5 or 10 port hub that you can purchase for under $100 will probably not be suitable for this kind of application.

The purpose of this simple example is to show that in addition to swapping out the networking equipment when you upgrade to ethernet, you will have to pay close attention to the current ARCnet topology. Whether you plan to use bridges (repeaters), 100Base-T or some other ethernet technology, pay close attention to the limits imposed and compare them with the current layout of user workstations and servers. You will probably find that additional hubs will be needed when the ARCnet network is stretched to its limit.

Solving Performance Problems

Another consideration for the upgrade path is what kind of interconnecting devices (hubs and switches) you must use. In a very small network, one or more 10Base-T hubs will probably suffice and be an easy upgrade. ARCnet is not known for having a large bandwidth (2.5Mbps for the standard ARCnet), so it may appear that you will not have to worry about bandwidth problems. Even if the ARCnet bandwidth usage is becoming saturated (at about 65 percent of the total possible 2.5Mbps), a simple 10Mbps ethernet LAN handling the same amount of nodes will probably show some improvement.

But, as always, you should be looking to the future. For example, it is typical that when upgrading an old LAN you will be upgrading not just the physical infrastructure, but also the end user applications that are used on the network. While a simple word-processing program that was marketed 10 years ago may not require a lot of network bandwidth to run from a server, the newer models will seem gigantic in comparison. If end user workstations are also being replaced, you might find it easier to install a copy of the application on each workstation, assuming it will have much more hard disk storage space than its predecessor. If you plan to continue serving applications from an application server, you might find it necessary to use ethernet switches and possibly a higher bandwidth technology than 10Mbps ethernet.

Connecting servers that will need a large amount of bandwidth to a switch, in full-duplex mode, can be used to help in this kind of situation. Whether you need to use a switch port for each user workstation or whether a hub will be sufficient depends on the current user work habits along with a projection of network usage you expect after you upgrade applications.

Summary

ARCnet is perhaps the oldest networking technology you will encounter that is still in use today. It was suitable for small LANs, and is considered easy to install and reliable by its users. However, with its limitations, such as the 255 user limit, it is not a technology you would be likely to employ to solve today's problems. Instead, if you work with this kind of network, you should be laying out a plan to upgrade to ethernet instead. This will give you more flexibility for future expansion of your LAN and better options for interconnecting with other networks to create wide area networks.

Migrating from Novell NetWare to Windows NT 4.0

SOME OF THE MAIN TOPICS IN THIS CHAPTER ARE

- Protocols
- Services for NetWare
- Migration Tool for NetWare
- User Options
- File Options
- Logon Scripts
- Trial Migration
- Start Migration
- Folder and File Restrictions
- File Shares
- Printer Shares
- Applications
- Conversion Tools
- Retraining

CHAPTER 45

You must consider the following items when you make the decision to migrate from Novell NetWare to NT 4.0:

- User accounts
- Login scripts
- File and print shares
- Applications
- Conversion tools
- Retraining

The way you approach retraining will determine whether you are going to do a complete migration or integrate NT into your existing NetWare environment and gradually migrate while training your users. If you have invested heavily in the NetWare network, you might need to perform a gradual migration because your employees and network administrators have all been trained to use the NetWare environment. In terms of dollars and cents, this likely has cost the company a considerable amount over the years.

A gradual migration to the Windows NT network environment allows you to utilize your existing hardware and software, which gives you the opportunity to train only those needed at the onset of the installation.

First, let's take a look at the resources that are available for providing interoperability between NetWare and NT 4.0.

Protocols

NetWare networks operate primarily on the IPX/SPX set of protocols, although in versions 3.11 and later TCP/IP has been added as a supported protocol known as NetWare TCP/IP.

Microsoft provides the NWLink protocol, which is a NetWare IPX/SPX compatible transport. This protocol comes with both the Server and Workstation versions of NT and allows both operating systems to connect to NetWare servers. You may also use NWLink as the only protocol on an NT network.

Services for NetWare

Microsoft has also made available three services for NetWare.

- Client Services for NetWare (CSNW)
- Gateway Services for NetWare (GSNW)
- File and Print Services for NetWare (FPNW)

Each of these services provides different functionality for accessing NetWare or NT resources; they are all discussed here.

Client Services for NetWare (CSNW)

To provide an easier migration path to Windows NT from NetWare, you can use the Client Services for NetWare utility. CSNW is a 32-bit native Windows NT service and device driver.

CSNW comes with the Workstation version of NT. It is used to allow direct connection from Windows NT Workstation to file and print services on a NetWare 2.x or later server.

For NetWare 4.x servers, CSNW provides support for Novell Directory Services (NDS) only if bindery emulation is enabled on the NetWare server. There is also built-in support for login scripts. Although this support is there, you will need the Windows NT Resource Kit to fully implement NetWare scripts on the NT Workstation.

CSNW relies on the NWLink IPX/SPX protocol for communication with NetWare servers, which means the protocol must be installed before installing CSNW. You can install them both at the same time if you do so during the initial setup of NT Workstation.

CSNW also provides support for the following protocols:

- **Large Internet Protocol**—Used by routed connections to negotiate the packet size
- **NetWare Core Protocol**—Provides file- and print-level access that can be compared to Server Message Blocks (SMBs)
- **Burst Mode**—Used for large data transfers by providing sliding window enhancements

After installing CSNW and rebooting the computer, you are asked for your preferred server during the login phase. The NetWare servers that are present on the network are listed. This server is the one that will be used to validate the NT logon.

If at any time the server you have listed as the preferred server is removed from the network or taken down, you can use the CSNW Control Panel applet to change the preferred server.

Gateway Services for NetWare (GSNW)

Windows NT Server provides GSNW to enable the server to connect to NetWare servers. Although it provides the same basic connection to a NetWare server that CSNW provides for Workstation, GSNW has a few more features and capabilities.

The main reason for using GSNW is to allow the NT server to act as a gateway to the NetWare servers from Microsoft client software that does not have CSNW installed.

One of the biggest advantages to using the GSNW service on an NT server is that it prevents the need to purchase NetWare client access licenses. This is possible because you must create only one user account on the NetWare server for the Windows NT Server acting as the NetWare gateway. Your Microsoft clients such as Windows 3.x, Windows 9x, and NT can now access the NetWare network using that one account.

It also makes life a little easier for your users because you can create network shares on the NT server that map to the various NetWare shares. Your users can then transparently use these shares without having to navigate the NDS structure themselves.

GSNW is a Windows NT Network Service; therefore, it is installed through the Network applet in Control Panel. You must create an account on the NetWare server and then a group account on the NT server called NTGATEWAY for both.

File and Print Services for NetWare

Although CSNW and GSNW are available with the Windows NT operating system, FSNW must be purchased separately. By installing this software, your NT server can provide file and print services to NetWare computers.

As far as the NetWare clients are concerned, they are connecting to a NetWare server and they need no additional software to make this connection. Although these services are available for allowing NetWare and NT to coexist, the recommended approach by both OS vendors is a complete migration from one platform to the other. (Chapter 47, "Migrating from Windows NT 4.0 to NetWare," covers the requirements and procedures for migrating from NT to NetWare.)

The simplest way to migrate your users and resources to NT is through the use of the Migration tool for NetWare, which is discussed next.

Migration Tool for NetWare

Microsoft Windows NT 3.51 and 4.0 contain the Migration tool for NetWare (NWConv.exe). It is also included with the FPNW add-on package discussed earlier. This tool lets you transfer NetWare user accounts and file resources from a NetWare volume to a Windows NT computer.

Note

There are two important issues to keep in mind when using the Migration tool. You must have GSNW installed on the NT computer and the accounts and resources can only be migrated to a domain controller on the NT network.

Microsoft recommends performing the migration in a two-step process.

1. Migrate user accounts

2. Migrate file resources

A more detailed description of the migration process follows the steps that appear here:

1. Click Start, Run.

2. In the Run dialog box, type in nwconv and click OK. (Or click Start, Programs, Administrative Tools (Common), and then choose Migration tool for NetWare.)

3. Select the NetWare and NT servers that the migration will be performed on.

4. If you must add more than one server, do so by clicking Add.

5. Click the Start Migration button.

Your user accounts will be migrated to your NT server.

This is the quick and dirty method. You will of course need to be a little more concerned with some issues prior to, during, and after the migration process.

Some of the issues you will come across are the fact that login scripts cannot be migrated. These must re-created on the Windows NT Server computer, and some will require the use of utilities supplied in the Windows NT Resource Kit.

NetWare passwords also cannot be migrated, so you must either present a new one during the migration process or specify none.

You can also run into situations in which accounts being migrated will conflict with existing accounts relating to usernames.

The Detailed Approach

To start the Migration tool under NT 4.0, click Start, select Programs, Administrative Tools (Common), and then choose the Migration tool for NetWare. You will be presented with the Select Servers for Migration dialog box as displayed in Figure 45.1.

Figure 45.1 Select servers for migration.

You have two options for entering the server names: You can type in the names if you know them or you can click the buttons with the ellipses … on them to search for the servers. After you have entered the server names and clicked OK, you are presented with the Migration Tool for NetWare dialog box, as illustrated in Figure 45.2.

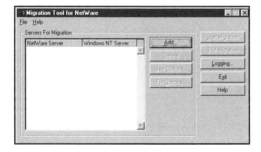

Figure 45.2 The Migration Tool for NetWare dialog box.

From this dialog box, you can choose to add more servers to migrate from or to, as well as delete any multiple or unneeded servers. You will of course require at least one NetWare server and one NT server.

Notice that along with the Add and Delete buttons, there are seven others:

- User Options
- File Options
- Start Migration
- Trial Migration
- Logging

- Exit
- Help

The User and File Option buttons are both important for the same reasons. For the purposes of migration, there are concerns regarding the transfer of user accounts and file and print shares between the two operating systems.

When you are transferring user accounts, you might run into a situation in which one or more accounts being transferred already exists. This can cause an obvious conflict, which is discussed in the section "Username Conflicts," later in this chapter.

Note

You must be logged in to the NetWare server as Supervisor to select the server. You must also be a member of the Administrators group under NT to transfer data to that server.

User Options

By clicking the User Options button, you are presented with the User and Group Options dialog box shown in Figure 45.3.

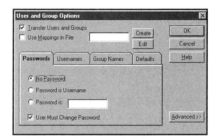

Figure 45.3 The User and Group Options dialog box.

Under the User Options settings, you are given the opportunity to set options for the following considerations:

- Password Options
- Username Conflicts
- Group Name Conflicts
- Account Restrictions
- Administrative Rights
- Mapping Accounts

Each of these considerations can be seen on the appropriate tabs of the dialog box.

Password Options

NetWare is the same as any other OS in that it stores the user passwords in encrypted form. This makes it extremely difficult to steal them. Unfortunately, it also means that the Migration tool cannot read them either. You will need to set the passwords yourself. You can do this in one of four ways by using the options available on the Passwords tab:

- **Assign a null password to the accounts**—By doing this, users will be able to log on to the NT server without specifying a password.

- **Use the username as the password**—This allows users to log in using the username as their password.

- **Use one password for all transferred accounts**—You give each user this password to log in with.

- **Use a mapping file**—This option means that you must create the mapping file and specify each user account with a new password. The Migration tool reads this file and sets the passwords accordingly.

There is a default setting requiring the users to change their password at the first log in. This should be left as is if you are using one of the first three methods listed earlier.

Username Conflicts

During the migration process, if an account exists on the NT server that has the same username as one being transferred, by default, that account is not transferred. You can find out if this happened during the migration by examining the `Error.log` file.

If you would like better control over this portion, you can choose one of the following options:

- **Transfer no account information**—This option is useful for transferring accounts from multiple NetWare servers that might contain duplicate usernames.

- **Overwrite existing accounts**—This option will completely overwrite the existing NT account including password and restrictions.

- **Create a new account**—This option will create a new account on the NT server but it will add a prefix to the username to preserve the existing account.

Recall that you can use the mapping file to gain better control over the migration process.

Group Name Conflicts

If a group name already exists on the NT server, the migration process will merely add the users to this group. If this default option is not satisfactory, you have two choices:

- **Record the information in the Error.log file**—This will still add the users to the group but offers a means to review what has happened.

- **Add a prefix to the group name**—By adding a prefix, you will actually create a new group on the NT server and the users will be added to this group.

Account Restrictions

Account restrictions are normally transferred during the migration process. You can choose not to transfer these restrictions and have the existing domain restrictions apply.

Here is a list of the NetWare restrictions that are affected:

- Require Password
- Minimum Password Length
- Require Password Change
- Password Reuse
- Intruder Lockout

Administrative Rights

To ensure the security of the NT domain, any user or group accounts on the NetWare server that have Supervisor rights lose those privileges during the migration. This is the default setting.

You can transfer them to the Administrators group if you so desire.

Mapping Accounts

Recall that you can use a mapping file to set the necessary passwords and options required for the migration. This file can be created in two ways: manually before you start migration or by using the Migration tool to create it setting migration options. Using the Migration tool is the easiest way.

By choosing Create in the User and Group Options dialog box of the Migration tool, you create a mapping file. Once the file has been created, you are prompted to edit it. You can do so at this time or you can reserve the changes for later. It is an ASCII text file, so you can use NotePad to edit the file. This is where you can specify a new username or password for an existing account.

A mapping file consists of two sections: Users and Groups. Each user or group exists on one line of the file:

```
[users]

gobrien, gobrien, next34$$n
brubble, mnewname, ret34HJK

[groups]

Accounting, ACCT
Admin, Office
```

The users section contains two usernames. The first user, gobrien, will be transferred using the same username with a password of next34$$n. This password is not in encrypted form.

Next, we are going to give brubble a new username and password.

The next section, groups, will transfer the Accounting group to the NT server with the new name of ACCT and the Admin group to the Office group.

If you used the Migration tool to create this file and there are users or group entries that you do not want to transfer, remove the names from the file.

File Options

When you click the File Options button, you are presented with the File Options dialog box, as shown in Figure 45.4.

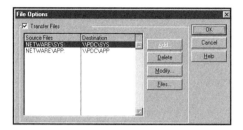

Figure 45.4   The File Options dialog box.

The following are options related to transferring files and folders:

- Selecting Volumes to Transfer
- Specifying Destination Shares
- Selecting Folders and Files to Transfer
- Transferring Hidden and System Files

Selecting Volumes to Transfer

By leaving this at the default setting, all NetWare volumes will be transferred. You can choose not to use the default, in which case you must manually select the volumes that you want to transfer.

Specifying Destination Shares

During the migration process, each NetWare volume that is transferred creates a new shared folder on the NT server with the same name as it had on the NetWare server.

You can specify a new folder name or the name of an existing shared folder as the new destination.

Selecting Folders and Files to Transfer

All files are transferred by default with the exception of files located in the following NetWare administrative volumes.

- \SYSTEM
- \LOGIN
- \MAIL
- \ETC

Transferring Hidden and System Files

You must manually select the hidden and system files that you want to transfer because they do not get transferred by default. There is an option to transfer all system and hidden files as well.

Logon Scripts

NetWare users have logon scripts that are run each time they log on to the system to connect to shared folders or run programs. Windows NT does not use logon scripts by default, but you can incorporate the NetWare logon scripts into the NT process. For these scripts to function, you must have FPNW installed on the NT server.

Trial Migration

Notice on the Migration Tool dialog box that there is a button labeled Trial Migration. This is a safe and recommended option to perform before you do the actual migration.

Reviewing the Log Files

When you click this button, the Migration tool will run a trial migration and track all events during the process. It creates a set of log files that detail what would have taken place during an actual migration with the current settings. To see these log files, you use the logview.exe utility. With this utility, you can view and print the log files.

The following is a list of the files created along with a brief description of each:

- **Logfile.log**—This file contains user, group, and file information.
- **Summary.log**—This is an overview of which servers were migrated and also includes the number of users, groups, and files that were migrated.
- **Error.log**—As you might expect, this file shows any errors that occurred such as files or users that could not be transferred or other errors relating to the process.

By performing a trial migration first, you can view the log files and correct any problems that might otherwise prevent a smooth migration.

Start Migration

After you have confirmed that all settings will provide an error-free migration, click the Start Migration button and watch as your NetWare system is migrated to your new NT server.

The remaining three buttons on the dialog box are used to enable logging, to get help on the Migration tool, and to exit the Migration tool.

Although the Migration Tool for NetWare should provide you with a relatively easy way to perform the migration, you also must be aware of the differences between the NetWare and NT concepts regarding user restrictions and file and directory permissions. By understanding these differences, you will be able to troubleshoot any migration problems that might pop up after you make the switch over.

The account restrictions, when compared between NetWare and NT, are broken down into two groups. Table 45.1 is a comparison of these restrictions when the NT server is not running FPNW and Table 45.2 shows the additional restrictions when you are running FPNW.

Table 45.1   Account Restrictions Without FPNW

NetWare Restrictions	NT Equivalent
Expiration Date	Expiration Date
Account Disabled	Account Disabled
Limit Concurrent Connections	No Equivalent
Require Password	Permit Blank Password
Minimum Password Length	Minimum Password Length
Force Periodic Password Changes	Password Never Expires
Days Between Force Changes	Maximum Password Age
Grace Logins	None
Allow User to Change Password	User Cannot Change Password
Require Unique Passwords	Password Uniqueness
Station Restrictions	None
Time Restrictions	Logon Hours
Intruder Detection/Lockout	Account Lockout
User Disk Volume Restrictions	None

Table 45.2   Additional Restrictions with FPNW Installed

NetWare Restrictions	NT Equivalent
Limit Concurrent Connections	Limit Concurrent Connections
Grace logins	Grace logins
Station Restrictions	Station Restrictions
Login Scripts	Login Scripts

As you can see, by adding the FPNW software to a Windows NT Server, you can include functionality and support for security issues that are not a part of the NT software.

A few differences must be mentioned here as well in regards to some of the account restrictions:

- The Expiration Date restriction is supported by both operating systems. It is implemented a little differently though.

- Windows NT will use the last day that the account is valid. NetWare uses the first day that the account is expired.

- During the migration, if any NetWare accounts expire later than January 1, 2000, they will automatically be given a new expiration date of February 6, 2006. Any other expiration dates are not affected.

- The Limit Concurrent Connections, as stated, will only be available on an NT server running FPNW. This does not mean that NT will now support this feature for non-NetWare clients though.

- NetWare uses a minimum password length of five characters. Windows NT defaults to a minimum length of six. Password changes are required by default every 40 days on NetWare. Windows NT uses 42 days for this setting.

■ NetWare requires a user to use eight different passwords before them to use one that existed before. Windows NT defaults to five but you can select between 1–8.

Another difference between the two is that NetWare sets its time restrictions in half-hour blocks and NT uses full hours. NetWare will allow a user or intruder to make seven login attempts before locking out the account. Windows NT sets this value at five.

Folder and File Restrictions

We will now do a comparison of the rights that are assigned to files and folders on each of the operating systems. It is best to look at these side by side so we will display them in tables. Table 45.3 lists the folder rights.

Table 45.3   Folder Rights

Novell NetWare	Microsoft Windows NT
Supervisory (S)	Full Control (All)
Read (R)	(RX) (RX)
Write (W)	(RWXD) (RWXD)
Create	Not Supported
Erase	(RWXD)(RWXD)
Modify (M)	(RWXD)(RWXD)
File Scan (F)	Not Supported
Access Control (A)	(P)

As you can see from Table 45.3, Windows NT does not support the Create or File Scan rights for folders. During the migration process, these rights will not be transferred.

Table 45.4 shows a side-by-side comparison of file rights as they pertain to NetWare and Windows NT. You can reference this table when making decisions about rights assigned to files transferred to Windows NT.

Table 45.4   File Rights

Novell NetWare	Microsoft Windows NT
Supervisory (S)	All
Read (R)	RX
Write (W)	RWXD
Erase	RWXD
Modify (M)	RWXD
File Scan (R)	Not Supported
Access Control (A)	P

Along with the directory and file rights, it is also important to note a comparison between the way each OS treats file attributes. Table 45.5 shows a side-by-side comparison of file attributes.

Table 45.5   File Attributes

Novell NetWare	Microsoft Windows NT
Read Only (Ro)	Read Only (R)
Archive Needed (A)	Archive (A)
System (SY)	System (S)
Hidden (H)	Hidden (H)
Read Write (Rw)	None, any file that does not have the (R) attribute can be written to

File Shares

If you have moved from NetWare to NT 4.0 and have all the user accounts and files transferred over, you have the fight all but won. You now must take a look at something that the Migration tool will not do for you. What if you must create new file shares on the NT server? How do you do it? Let's take a look at that now.

Windows NT Server supports the sharing of files and folders under either the FAT or the NTFS file systems. There is one exception to this: FAT volumes do not support security at the file level. If you are using the FAT file system, which is not recommended for an NT installation, you will have to share a folder with the correct permissions and place the files into that folder. We will look at file and folder permissions from an NTFS perspective.

The first thing you must do to share a file is to share the folder that the file resides in. You do this by right-clicking on the folder name in the Explorer window and choosing the Sharing option from the pop-up menu. You will be presented with the Directory Permissions dialog box as shown in Figure 45.5.

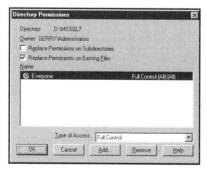

Figure 45.5 The Directory Permissions dialog box.

From this dialog box you can see the directory or folder name, who owns it, and two option boxes that allow you to replace permissions on subdirectories and existing files. These two options allow you give any existing files or subdirectories the same permissions as those for this folder.

Next you will see a list box that contains or will contain the names of users or groups that you want to assign permissions to for this folder.

By choosing the Add button, you are given a list of available groups and users on the system. You can choose from this list and each one will be added to the Name list on the Directory Permissions dialog box. The Add Users and Groups dialog that pops up when you click the Add button is displayed in Figure 45.6.

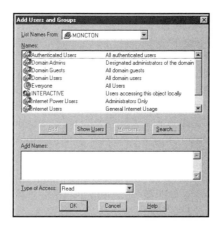

Figure 45.6   The Add Users and Groups dialog box.

By default, this dialog box displays users and groups from the local domain. You can choose another domain or server by clicking the drop-down arrow next to the List Names From drop-down box.

After the users and groups have been added to the Permissions dialog, you can go about setting the individual permission for each. Simply select the users or groups that you want, and then under the Type of Access drop-down box, choose the type of access you want.

You can use the same procedure for setting permissions on files. The same dialog boxes are displayed with the exception being that the File Permissions dialog box will say File Permissions in the title bar and the permissions will differ somewhat.

Order of Precedence for Permissions

To effectively implement file and directory permissions, you need a good understanding of how they interact when compared by user and group. The reason for this is simple. You might have a user assigned to one or more groups. Each of these groups, or even the individual user, might have different permissions assigned to a file or directory resource; so, you must understand the order of precedence in this case.

Here is an example case. You have two groups in your network named ADMIN and Engineering. Each group has access to its own files but share some other files for administrative purposes. A file called timesheets.xls is a spreadsheet file that the Engineering department uses to enter the amount of time spent on projects. The Administration office requires access to this file so that it can read the information into the payroll system. The Engineering group has full control over this file because it might need to delete erroneous entries. The ADMIN group only has Read access because it shouldn't be allowed to modify the information.

Fred is a member of the ADMIN and Engineering groups, and the effective permissions for him are a combination of the two permissions assigned to each group. In this case, he would have Full Control and Read access. However, this is rather superfluous as Full Control contains the Read access anyway. The only exception to this rule is the No Access permission. If this is assigned, it will take precedence over any other permission.

Conflicting File and Directory Permissions

There is another issue to watch out for as well. File and Directory permissions can conflict. A directory might have Read permission but a file within the directory might have Full Control permission assigned to the same user. The solution to this problem is that File permission override Directory permissions. Therefore, the user who has Full Control permission on the file can still access and modify the file, even though he or she only has Read access to the folder.

Note

The user cannot change the directory or any other files within it. He or she can only change the file with the correct permissions.

Take Ownership Permission

Another permission that hasn't been mentioned thus far is the Take Ownership permission. Under normal circumstances, members of the Administrators group can take ownership of files, directories, and other resources such as printers. For example, say you are the administrator of the network. You have an employee who has been let go for some reason. All his or her duties are to be assigned to another staff member. To complete some unfinished projects, the user needs access to the original employee's files. You, as the administrator, can help the user by taking ownership of the files needed and assigning ownership to the new user.

Printer Shares

Sharing a printer is just as easy as sharing a file or folder. There are a few considerations regarding printers that don't affect files.

When you install a printer under Windows NT, it asks you if you want to share the printer with other network users. There is not much sense in placing a printer on the network if you aren't going to make it available to the other users. When you choose to share the printer, NT asks you for the operating systems that will be sharing the printer. This is so that Windows NT can install and make available the necessary printer drivers for your client computers.

This has a distinct advantage when it comes to upgrading printer drivers. If a manufacturer makes a new printer driver available, you would have to manually install that driver on each client computer if you were not sharing the printer on an NT computer. By providing a shared printer, all the administrator needs to do is to install the updated driver onto the NT server computer. When a client requests to print a document, Windows NT will download the new driver to the client at that time.

Applications

Applications under Windows NT fall into two basic categories: Administrative Applications and User Applications.

Administrative Applications

Under this category you will find programs such as

- User Manager for Domains
- Event Viewer
- DHCP Manager
- Server Manager

Although there are more applications under this category, these are the most commonly used and will be described here. Check the online help or Books Online for more information on the other available applications.

User Manager for Domains

This is the program that NT uses to administer the users and groups on the network. You access this utility by clicking on Start and choosing Programs, Administrative Tools (Common). Figure 45.7 shows the User Manager for Domains window.

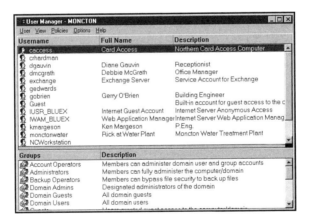

Figure 45.7   The User Manager for Domains window.

Notice that this is a two-paned window that displays the users in the upper pane and the groups in the lower pane. The User Manager for Domains program lets you add and delete users and groups on the local domain and any other domain that you have established a trust relationship with.

You have complete control over a user's account here and can set such things as log on hour restrictions, whether the user can dial in to the server for remote access, and even change the user's password.

Note

You cannot see the user's existing password as the password box displays only asterisks (*). To change the password, you must highlight and replace the entire entry in the password field.

Event Viewer

The Event Viewer is a utility that is a great troubleshooting tool. This is essentially a log of activities that has occurred on the system. The Event Viewer window is shown in Figure 45.8.

The Info icon indicates that the following event entry is not critical and is information only.

The Warning icon indicates a critical error. Usually the event will not prevent the server from operating but needs to be looked at.

The Stop icon indicates an error that a service or device did not start correctly.

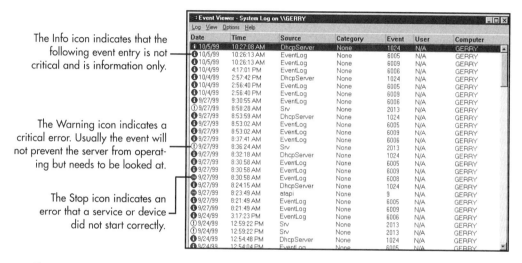

Figure 45.8 The Event Viewer window.

As you can see from Figure 45.8, the Event Viewer displays the following information in columns:

- **Date**—Displays the date that the event took place
- **Time**—Displays the time the event took place
- **Source**—Indicates which particular service or application caused the event
- **Category**—Lists a category, if one exists
- **Event**—Gives you an ID number for the event
- **User**—If applicable, you will see a username here; an example of this would be a user sending a document to the printer
- **Computer**—Lists the particular server in the domain that the event occurred on

Also notice that there are icons next to the Date field. These icons are shown below with an explanation.

The Event Viewer is capable of displaying information taken from the following logs.

- **System log**—Reports errors that are caused by services and devices pertaining to the operating system.

- **Security log**—This log needs to have auditing enabled in the System Policy section of User Manager. You can view user and system activities that pertain to permissions on resources.

- **Application log**—This log keeps track of application errors. Even though NT can run some DOS and 16-bit Windows applications, this log can only maintain information on 32-bit Windows applications.

DHCP Manager

Windows NT is capable of using the TCP/IP protocol along with the NetBEUI and NWLink protocols. TCP/IP presents a challenge when it comes to accessing computers. Each computer on a TCP/IP network must have an IP address. This is how the network forwards files and requests to the correct computer.

DHCP (Dynamic Host Configuration Protocol) allows IP addresses to be assigned on an as needed basis. Prior to DHCP, administrators had to assign each host computer with its own IP address. This can turn out to be time-consuming on large networks. By using DHCP, the administrator can set up a pool of IP addresses and have the client computers request one when they log on to the network. The DHCP Manger window is displayed in Figure 45.9.

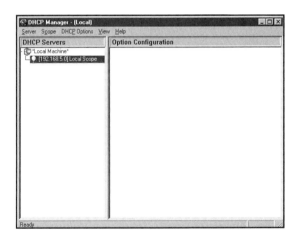

Figure 45.9 The DHCP Manager window.

To use DHCP, follow these steps:

1. Start DHCP Manager from the Administrative Tools program group.

2. Click the server name listed in the left pane.

3. Click the Scope Option and choose Create Scope. The Create Scope dialog appears, as illustrated in Figure 45.10.

4. Fill in the appropriate start and end addresses, the subnet mask, and any IP addresses in the range that you do not want to be assigned.

5. Choose the lease duration options and provide a name and comment to describe the scope.

When you click OK, you will be presented with a dialog box that tells you the scope is not activated and asks you if you would like to activate it. Choose Yes.

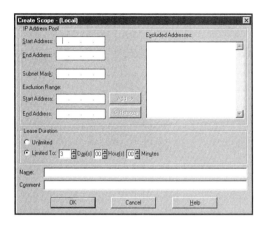

Figure 45.10   The Create Scope dialog box.

You now have DHCP configured and any client that requests an IP from this server will be offered one within the range that you specified.

Server Manager

Server Manager is a utility that is used to view the computers on the network and if they are Windows NT Workstation or Server computers, the ability to administer them as well. The Server Manger is shown in Figure 45.11

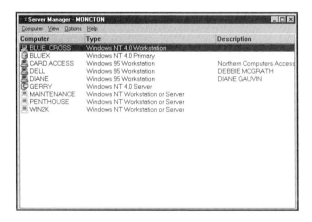

Figure 45.11   The Server Manager.

If you have computers or servers that have been removed from the network, you can remove the computer account here.

Server Manager is also used to perform directory replication among Windows NT computers on the network.

You access the Server Manger program by clicking the Start button, choosing Administrative Tools (Common), and then Server Manager.

User Applications

Under this category, you will find applications that do not pertain to the administration of the computer or network. There are a considerable number of these applications available and we will only list some of them here for you.

- Office suites such as Microsoft Office, Corel WordPerfect Office, and Lotus SmartSuite. These suites of application provide word processors, spreadsheet programs, database programs, and some even provide presentation programs
- CAD and CAM applications used for computer-aided design and manufacturing
- Antivirus utilities
- Desktop publishing software

To go into every application that is included with or available for NT would take quite some time. Microsoft includes the standard NotePad and WordPad text editors as well as multimedia applications like the CD player.

You will also find your favorite Solitaire game along with Minesweeper and Hearts.

Obviously, a book on networks does not cover this topic. There are some very good books available on Windows NT Server that concentrate on the applications and utilities included with the OS. These are your best source for the proper usage of these programs.

Conversion Tools

At this point in time, Microsoft's Migration tool is the only conversion tool that is available. As Windows NT gains more market share, you might see third-party developers provide more migration tools for making the switch from NetWare to NT.

Retraining

The amount of retraining involved depends entirely on the way you set your network. For instance, if you merely incorporate NT into your existing NetWare environment, install the FPNW service on the NT computer and don't change out your clients, the only training needed is for the administrators.

If you decide to replace your NetWare network and switch completely over to NT, not only will you have to provide training for the administrators, but you will need to retrain the end users. This retraining is necessary as each client computer will need to have Windows client software installed. This can create a loss in productivity if it is done all at once. This is one reason that you should look at integrating NT into the NetWare environment and gradually phase out the NetWare system over time.

Summary

You now have a good comparison between the user and file restrictions for a NetWare and NT environment. You also have a good understanding of these differences and similarities to help you when you migrate these resources manually.

Migrating from Novell NetWare to Windows NT is not a complicated task thanks to the efforts that Microsoft put into the Migration Tool for NetWare. You still must understand the differences and similarities between the two operating systems to effectively migrate all your users and shares.

NetWare has been the preferred and most-used network operating system for a few years now but Microsoft is making serious strides in overtaking Novell's market share. As a result, Novell has had to make some changes and enhancements to its product. The main push has been in the area of Internet and intranet connectivity.

The two operating systems can coexist in the same network and provide file and print sharing resources as well as application serving to each other. This makes the migration a little easier on your administrators and users by making the switch gradual.

UNIX to Windows NT 4.0

With all the hype about Windows NT, UNIX administrators are finding themselves faced with a new challenge and a few questions. "Should I make the switch to NT?" "Should I integrate NT into the existing network?" Sometimes, the administrator doesn't get the opportunity to answer these questions before management makes the decision.

If you find yourself faced with the situation of having to move to NT or integrate it into your existing UNIX network, this chapter can help. The topics covered here include

- Migrating user accounts
- Creating login scripts
- Creating file and print shares on Windows NT 4.0 servers
- Applications
- Microsoft DNS Server
- Microsoft's conversion tools
- Third-party conversion tools

Each issue is important to consider when making the move because each operating system implements each of these differently or with enough difference that they can create problems.

We are not going to attempt to make you a Microsoft Certified Systems Engineer (MCSE). Microsoft and other third-party companies provide self-paced training and classroom courses that will help you achieve the certification. Our purpose is to help those who find themselves with a brand new Windows NT computer sitting on their desk with a note that says, "Hook it up."

How do you make the move from UNIX to a Windows NT environment? Windows NT has so many differences from UNIX that most UNIX administrators find it hard to adapt. UNIX has long been a command-line driven OS, albeit the X Window system has added GUI capabilities to it. Most UNIX gurus, however, still use the command line for most administrative tasks.

Windows NT 4.0 provides a graphical user interface (GUI) as the means for user interaction, however, command-line options and programs under NT that can be run from the command line. Windows NT provides a command-line window for this purpose that looks a lot like Windows 95's DOS prompt. NT of course, does not use or have DOS in the operating system.

So how do you move from UNIX to NT? Well, you have to take it one step at a time. The first and foremost issue concerning an administrator is users, user accounts, and permissions. UNIX and NT store this information differently.

Migrating User Accounts

UNIX stores user account information in text files (`/etc/passwd` for users and `/etc/groups` for groups). Within these text files resides information regarding the user's home directory, the shell they use, their initial environment, and their user ID (UID) and group ID (GID). Windows NT places user accounts in a central database. This database is known as the *Security Accounts Manager* database, (SAM). In a Windows NT Domain, the SAM is stored on the Primary Domain Controller.

Let's first look at the login processes for each operating system, and then we will do a side-by-side comparison of the user rights and permissions between the two. This will help you determine the correct permissions to add when creating the user accounts on a Windows NT machine.

Logging On to the System

To gain a better understanding of this process, let's look at what happens when a user logs on to each system.

UNIX Login

In UNIX, a user logs in to the system by entering a login name and password. UNIX compares the name and password to its /etc/passwd file. This information is compared with the /etc/group file to determine which groups the user belongs to. The user is then granted access to the appropriate resources.

Windows NT Logon

In NT, there are two different logons available. Logging on to a Windows NT computer and logging on to a Windows NT domain. Note that Windows NT uses the phrase *log on* rather than *log in*. Let's look at logging on to a Windows NT computer first.

While a user logs on, access to any user mode applications is halted or suspended to prevent any user or application from stealing a user's password during the logon phase.

Logging On to an NT Computer

All users must log on to the Windows NT computer to gain access to the resources that it provides. The Windows NT logon process requires a unique username and password combination to authenticate the user.

The logon process for a local computer differs from that of a domain logon. The differences are described here.

Winlogon will request a username and password. Winlogon is the logon banner that is displayed when NT starts in the GUI interface. This username and password are then sent to the Local Security Authority (LSA), which resides in the security subsystem on the NT computer.

1. The LSA will send a query to the SAM, which will check to see if the username and password are authorized.

2. The SAM will check this information against its directory database.

3. If the username and password are authorized, the LSA will create an access token that contains the rights assigned to that username password combination. This access token is then passed back to the Winlogon process.

4. Winlogon will create a new process for the user and attaches the token to it. (Normally, the first process created is Explorer.exe. This is not Internet Explorer but the Windows NT Explorer that controls access to drives and system functions.)

Logging On to an NT Domain

To log on to a Windows NT Domain, the process must add a few more steps. The complete process is outlined here.

1. Winlogon requests a username and password as before and sends them to the LSA.

2. The security subsystem will pass this request on to the Net Logon service on that client.

3. This Net Logon service will send the request on to the domain controller's Net Logon service.

4. From here, it is passed to the domain controller's SAM for authentication.

5. The SAM will query its database.

6. The domain controller's SAM will pass the results back to its Net Logon service.

7. The domain's Net Logon service passes this on to the Net Logon service on the client computer.

8. The client's Net Logon service will relay this to its LSA.

9. Provided that access has been granted, an access token is created by the LSA and passed on to the Winlogon process.

10. Winlogon will call the Win32 subsystem. This subsystem is responsible for attaching the access token to the new process.

It is with this access token that NT can determine what the user has access to.

So, as can be seen here, there is a little more going on behind the scenes when you log on to a Windows NT Domain.

User Accounts

To understand the complexities involved in migrating user accounts, you must look at the similarities and differences between the way each OS handles its accounts. As mentioned, UNIX user accounts are stored in text files; Windows NT uses a central database known as the SAM. However, this is not the only difference between the two.

UNIX Accounts

In UNIX, a user account can have any of three kinds of permissions. These are read, write, and execute. UNIX accounts define access through three different designations as well. Access can be defined by owner, group, or world/other. These access permissions are indicated in the long list of a file listing. They are specified by w, r, or x and set up in three groups of three. A sample file listing follows:

```
-rwxrw-r--    gobrien    admin    512    09 aug 99 08:09 admin.txt
```

You can see the permission for this file in the left column. The first space contains a dash (-) that indicates this is a file. If it were a directory, there would be a d in that space. The next set of letters indicates the permissions that are assigned to the owner of this file. The three letters indicate r for Read, w for Write, and x for Execute. The next group of letters is used for the group access permissions. This file has the admin group assigned to it and it offers the Read and Write permissions but no Execute. Any space with the dash indicates no selection.

The last three letters are for the world/other group. This allows Read access only for anyone not belonging to a specific group.

You can then see the remaining information in the other columns that indicate the owner, the group, the file size, creation date/time, and the filename.

Windows NT Accounts

Windows NT differs somewhat in the way it provides access to files and printers. Windows NT uses an analogy called *sharing*. Sharing is the concept of permitting access to files, folders (directories), and other devices such as modems or printers. Windows NT must use NTFS to provide file-level security. These permissions are set in the Properties dialog box under Security for the Resource. Figure 46.1 shows the file permissions dialog box where user access rights are granted.

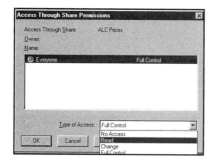

Figure 46.1   The File Permissions dialog showing the available permissions that can be assigned to this resource.

Windows NT can assign any of the following permissions to a shared resource:

- **No Access**—No access is granted to the resource
- **Change**—Allows viewing the file, running the file if it is an application, changing data in the file, or deleting the file altogether
- **Read Access**—Allows viewing the file and running it if it is an application
- **Full Control**—Allows all that Change Access allows plus it allows changing permissions on the file and taking ownership of it

We will go into the procedures to set these permissions in the "Creating File and Print Shares on Windows NT 4.0 Servers" section, later in this chapter.

Note

Windows NT administrators use the User Manager or User Manager for Domains applet to create and maintain user accounts.

As you can see, you cannot simply migrate UNIX user accounts to a Windows NT computer with any amount of ease. So, let's get into the process of how to create user accounts on Windows NT. The examples used here will show creating user accounts on an NT Primary Domain Controller.

Table 46.1 shows how each attribute of the permissions assigned to files for user access differ between the two operating systems. Using this table will make the migration of the user accounts easier.

Table 46.1   Comparison of Permissions

Attribute	UNIX	Windows NT
User Tools	Security Accounts Manager	User Manager for Domains
Auditing	syslog	Event Viewer and System Log
User divisions	Owner, Group, Other	Owner, Group, Everyone
File Reading	r	Read
File Writing	w	Write
Execute a file	x	Execute
Delete a file	rw	Delete
Change a file	rw	Change
Ownership of a file	chown	Take Ownership
No Access	—	No Access
All permissions	rwx	Full Control

Tip

Microsoft recommends that when you are assigning permissions to users, it is better to assign the user to a group, and then assign permissions to the group. This process seems like a long way around things at first, but in the end, such as a domain with hundreds of users, it is easier to assign permissions to one group than to have to assign the same permission to 100 users.

Creating an NT User Account

To create a user account in NT, you must use the User Manager for Domains application. You can find User Manager by choosing Start, Programs, Administrative Tools (Common), and User Manager for Domains. Figure 46.2 shows the User Manager for Domains.

Notice in the User Manager window there are three columns in the upper pane: Username, Full Name, and Description. Username is what the user will log on with. The Full Name is for entering the user's full name, and the optional Description can be used by the administrator to enter some descriptive text for identification purposes or other things like "This user forgets his password weekly."

In the lower pane, you will see two columns: Groups and Description. The Groups column lists the available groups that users and permissions can be assigned to. You can also create your own groups here if you want. We'll see that in the "Assigning Users to Groups" section a little later in this chapter.

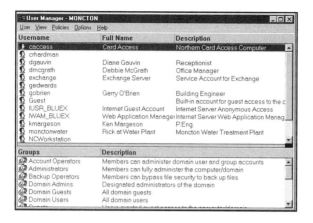

Figure 46.2 The User Manager for Domains window is where you add, remove, or edit the users on your Windows NT 4.0 Server computer.

If you click the User menu in the menu bar above the User pane, the drop-down User menu shown in Figure 46.3 will appear.

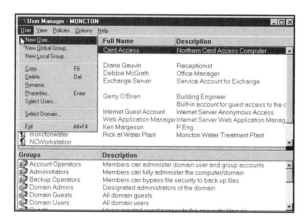

Figure 46.3 The User menu enables the administrator to create, delete, and edit user accounts as well as copy accounts and administer users on other domains.

Let's look briefly at each option:

- New User creates a new user account. This allows the creation of a completely new user with no group assignments other than Domain Users.

- New Global Group allows you to create a new group that will be used throughout the domain. Global groups can have permission assigned that allow access to domain resources.

- New Local Group allows for the creation of a new group local to that particular computer.

The next group of options allows for modification of existing accounts and groups:

- **Copy**—Use this option if you have a set of permissions and groups assigned to a user already and you need to add one or more users with the same permissions. This is a short-cut that copies all but the username, full name, description, and password from a previous user. This can save valuable time by making it unnecessary for the administrator to re-enter all the group and permission assignments. He or she only needs to add the pertinent information.

- **Delete**—By first selecting a user or group from the appropriate pane, you can remove them by choosing the Delete option. This removes all information regarding the user including the user security identifier. If you need to add that user again, you will have to re-create the entire account again.

Tip

If you are in an environment where you need to remove a user's access for a certain period of time, or you may have students coming and going every year that need the same access levels, it is better to disable the account and the re-enable it as needed. This way, you won't need to re-create the accounts again.

- **Rename**—This option allows you to change the person's username. When they log on the next time, they will have to use the new username. This comes in handy if you have a lot of temporary positions. Instead of deleting the accounts, rename them and tell the new user to change the password when they log on. The account still holds all its access permissions.

- **Properties**—In the Properties dialog box, you can view and change all the user properties except for the username. Figure 46.4 depicts the User Properties window. As you can see by the picture, the username is not available to be selected, as it presents no text box around the Username.

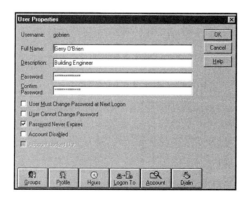

Figure 46.4 The User Properties Window is where you enter user-specific information such as name, password, and account restrictions.

- **Select Users**—This option gives you the opportunity to select users by group. This is useful for changing the properties of multiple users at one time or for deleting a group of users.

- **Select Domain**—This option is used for administering users and groups on another domain. You must have Domain Trust Relationships set up for this to work. Trust Relationships deal with NT Server in an enterprise environment, and that is not discussed here.

■ **User, New User**—The New User dialog box comes into view ready to accept our information as shown in Figure 46.5. Use the Tab key to navigate the fields in this dialog.

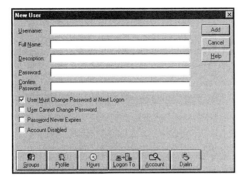

Figure 46.5 The New User dialog box is where you enter the user-specific information pertaining to user accounts.

Next you will see four option check boxes:

■ **User Must Change Password at Next Logon**—To have the user change the password when they next log on, leave that option checked. You would do this during a new user creation and any time you have to change the user's password.

Tip

When you enter a user's password, it appears as asterisks for security reasons. After a user changes their password, not even the administrator can see what that password is. To fix a forgotten password, the administrator must change it completely, give the new temporary password to the user, and have them log back on and change to another password again.

■ **User Cannot Change Password**—If you don't want the user changing the password—say, for example, they keep changing it and can't remember it—select this option. It prevents the user from changing the password at all.

■ **Password Never Expires**—This option tells NT that this user's password will not expire after a certain amount of time. You can set all passwords to expire after a set amount of time to enforce password changes.

■ **Account Disabled** Use this option when you want to prevent access to the account. This could be due to a manager being on vacation or a summer student's position being vacant for the winter months.

Note

There is another option check box, the Account Locked Out check box, that is not visible in this window but you will see it when a user or intruder has made the maximum amount of incorrect logon attempts using this account. This option indicates that the account is locked out. If you have a user tell you that they were told their account is locked out, you will know that they, or someone else, tried unsuccessfully to log on using a bad account and password. You will have to clear the check box to restore the account.

Assigning Users to Groups

Now that you have entered all that information, you need to look at the buttons along the bottom of the dialog box:

- **Groups**—Pressing this button will allow you to assign the user to groups within the local computer or domain. Figure 46.6 is a picture of the Group Memberships dialog. Note the Domain Users group in the Member of List. All users are automatically made a member of this group and cannot be removed because it is a primary group.

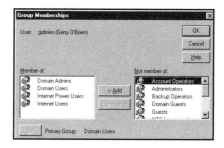

Figure 46.6   The Group Memberships dialog box enables you to assign users to groups.

- **Profile**—User profiles are used when you want to restrict access to certain areas of the computer and operating system or provide a user with a consistent look and feel regardless of which NT workstation in the domain they log on to. You must provide the path to the user profile as well the logon script name if applicable.

Figure 46.7 displays the User Environment Profile dialog, which is displayed when you click the Profile button.

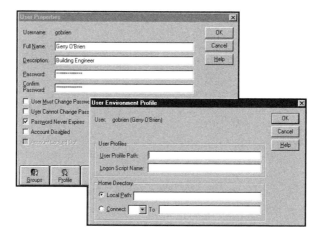

Figure 46.7   You enter information relating to user profiles such as home directories or login scripts in the User Environment Profile dialog.

Notice that there is an option to provide a user local path for a home directory. This will be the same as the UNIX user's home directory that they are connected to after logon. Or, you can specify a network drive to map to when they user logs on by selecting the Connect option, choosing a drive letter, and typing in the share name such as *servername**share*.

■ **Hours**—This option allows you to set the allowable hours or time frame that a user can log on to the system. This can be used to restrict users from accessing company resources outside of office hours or as a security measure to prevent unauthorized access to your system after hours through remote access (RAS). Blue indicates log on allowed and white indicates log on not allowed.

Figure 46.8 shows the current log on hours for this user in the Logon Hours dialog box.

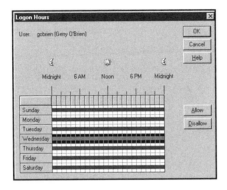

Figure 46.8 The Logon Hours dialog offers you a chance to set the time that a user will be allowed to log on to the system.

■ **Logon To**—This option allows users access to all workstations on the network or only those workstations that you select. Figure 46.9 shows the Logon Workstations dialog with access granted to all workstations.

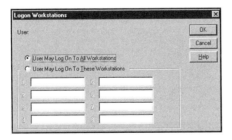

Figure 46.9 Use the Logon Workstations dialog to restrict logon to certain workstations on the network or to allow the user to log on to any workstation.

■ **Account**—This option allows you to set account information, such as Expiry Date, and the type of account, such as Global or Local.

■ **Dial In**—This option grants users the right to dial in to your computer or network using Remote Access Service (RAS). By checking off the Grant Dial-in Permission to User check box, shown in Figure 46.10, you are allowing that user to dial in to the server or network over a phone line. They must use their normal username and password to log on.

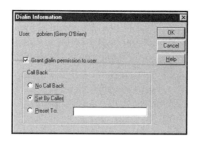

Figure 46.10 The Dialin Information dialog controls how your dial-in security is configured for users who connect over a Remote Access Server (RAS).

■ **Call Back**—These options can help to increase security by having the server hang up after a successful log in and call the user back either at a caller set phone number or a preset number.

By setting the callback to a preset number, you can prevent unauthorized access by ensuring that the caller is actually at their home number. This prevents users from dialing in from a hotel if they are on the road, however. Use the Set By Caller option for that.

After you set all the user's options, click Add. If you've finished adding all the users you want, click the Close button to end the session. Now you know the differences between UNIX and NT user accounts and how to migrate those accounts to an NT network and assign permissions to them. Microsoft now has an add-on for UNIX interoperability but, unfortunately, it'll cost you about $149 U.S. We will look at this add-on later in this chapter.

Login Scripts

Windows NT can process login scripts when the user logs on to the system. Login scripts on NT are used to connect to drive mappings automatically at login, to run applications or batch files, and to configure the system. The script file can be in the form of a batch file (`.bat` or `.cmd`), or it can be an executable program. NT must be told where the script file is located by using the Login Script Path. This is the path that was specified in the User Manager for that user.

Tip

If you are running a Windows NT Workstation computer, the script path cannot be changed from its default of `%systemroot% \System32\Repl\Import\Scripts`). This directory is shared as the netlogon share and is executed from the domain controller that authenticated the user.

The `%systemroot%` variable mentioned above is a place holder that is used to specify the directory in which Windows NT is installed. This directory is WINNT by default.

You should maintain a master copy of each login script on one Windows NT Server. This will allow for easy replication of the script to multiple servers in an NT Domain. This is necessary because most domains will have multiple servers performing logon requests—one PDC but multiple BDCs).

One of the main reasons that a login script is used in an NT environment is to provide for a consistent layout as seen by your network clients. Problems can arise when users have drive mappings that don't match. They might need to locate a file that two users are working on—one user has the folder mapped as drive M while the other has the same folder mapped on his workstation as drive Q. This login script is critical if OLE (object linking and embedding) is being used in the document because embedded links are path specific. If one user opens a file created by a second user and that file makes use of OLE, the embedded object will not be present because the drive mappings do not match and the document can't locate the embedded object.

Note

OLE is a Microsoft term for a technology that was developed to allow the sharing of information between dissimilar applications. An example would be embedding a chart from a spreadsheet program into a word-processing document.

Creating Login Scripts

To create a login script, you can use a simple text editor and save it as a batch file with a `.bat` extension or `.cmd` extension. You can list each command in turn in the batch file and it will be processed one line at a time.

Here is a quick example of a script file that will set the clock on the user's workstation to the same time as that of the server; we will map the user's home directory and then start an application.

```
@echo off
net time \\Donut /set /yes
net use h: /home
call ..calc.exe
```

The first line, `@echo off`, turns off the echoing of the script file to the screen. If you omit this line, the script file will be displayed, as it executes, on the screen. This could be helpful to prevent users from seeing what is going on during the login process.

Line two uses the `net time` command to connect to the server with the name `Donut` and retrieve the time from its clock. It then uses that time to synchronize its own clock to the server's.

Line three maps the drive letter `H` to the user's home directory that was specified in the user's profile.

The last line causes the calculator program to run. This can of course be any valid application file.

So essentially, a login script file is a series of NT commands that you want to run whenever the user logs on.

Creating File and Print Shares on Windows NT 4.0 Servers

For client computers and other servers on an NT network to access files and printers on an NT Server, they must first be shared. Each resource that is to be made available to other computers must be shared.

File Shares

Windows NT 4.0 supports two file systems for use on a hard drive: FAT16 and NTFS. FAT is the file system that has been around for years. It is compatible with DOS, Windows 3.x, Windows 9x, NT, OS/2, and UNIX/Linux. It can be read and written to by all these operating systems. Windows NT and Windows 9x have enhanced the original FAT file system and it now supports long filenames. DOS and earlier versions of Windows suffered from an 8.3 filename convention. With FAT16 and FAT32, it now supports long filenames (up to 255 characters including the path).

Windows NT 4.0 can use FAT16 but not FAT32. Windows 2000 will be capable of reading FAT32 when it is released. One issue that will be present in a Windows 2000 and Windows NT 4.0 dual boot scenario is that Windows 2000 makes some changes to the NTFS file system and requires you to install Service Pack 4 or later to allow NT 4.0 to dual boot with Windows 2000.

It is recommended that if you want maximum security over file sharing on Windows NT, you need to format your hard drive using NTFS (NT File System). Real original, eh? FAT partitions only support passwords on folders. You cannot implement file-level security, which is one of the many advantages that NTFS has over FAT.

File Access Permissions

You might recall that each file can have certain permissions assigned to it:

- **No Access** prevents users from viewing or modifying the file at all. It is not the same as a hidden attribute that prevents a file from showing up in a directory listing.

- **Read Access** allows a user to view the file's contents and, if it is an application, the user can run that application. The user cannot delete the file or modify it in any way.

- **Change Permission** grants the user the Read Access permissions, and the user can modify the file and delete it as well.

- **Full Control** gives the user all the previously mentioned permissions, plus it allows the user to change the permissions on the file and take ownership of it.

File Ownership

Much the same as in UNIX, the creator of the file is the owner of the file and, by default, he or she has full control over that file and may assign permissions to it.

An administrator can take ownership of files and printers to change permissions or to assign ownership to another user. You would need to do this if an employee no longer works for the company and another employee needs to take over his or her duties. The co-worker would need access to his or her files. The administrator would take ownership of them and then assign ownership to the co-worker.

Sharing Files

So, how do you share these files and then assign permissions to them? Let's walk through the process of sharing first. Fire up Windows NT Explorer (shown in Figure 46.11) and have a look at the files on the hard drive.

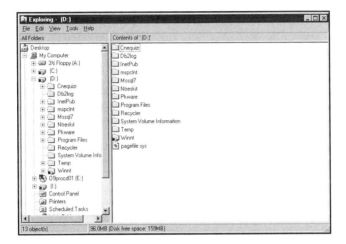

Figure 46.11   The Windows NT Explorer is the tool you would use to navigate the directory and file structure of the hard drive or network drives.

In the left pane, you will see a list of drives and directories that are present on the computer. You will also see a Printers folder, Control Panel folder, and Scheduled Tasks. We don't need to concern ourselves with these at this time, just the drives and directories.

Tip

Since the introduction of Windows 95, Microsoft has renamed "directories" to "folders." The idea behind this was to make it easier for the average user to identify a directory. Windows NT version 4.0 adopted this analogy at the same time it took on the Windows 95 interface. The two terms are used interchangeably in this book.

In the right pane, you will see the subfolders and files that exist on the drives. Take note of the Winnt folder at the bottom of the subfolders on drive D. It has a hand and arm underneath. This is a visual indication that this directory, or folder, is being shared.

It is important to note that the FAT file system and NTFS differ in the way they can apply sharing. NT on a FAT volume can only apply sharing permissions to folders, not files. When you share a folder, you share the entire contents of that folder. NTFS allows you to set up sharing on individual files within a folder.

To share a folder under Windows NT using the FAT file system, you can access the folder using Windows NT Explorer or from the correct drive icon under My Computer. Right-click the folder to bring up the context menu and choose the sharing option.

The one little trick to keep in mind here is you must share the folder before you can share any files in it. On NTFS, only the folder is shared. Until you apply a share to the files within the folder, the files are not available as shared. What I have done to give you some practice on sharing is to open the Winnt folder by clicking on the plus sign next to it and choosing the Config subfolder.

Access the context-sensitive menu by right-clicking the Config folder icon. You should see its pop-up menu. If you attempt to share a file that is in a non-shared folder, you will not see the Sharing option on this menu.

The menu choice you want is Sharing. Click this menu item to display the Config Properties dialog shown in Figure 46.12.

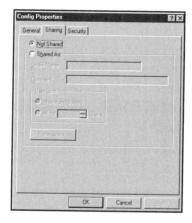

Figure 46.12   The Config Properties dialog shows you the available settings for this folder pertaining to attributes such as hidden or read only as well as the sharing and security information.

This is the same dialog box that comes up when you choose Properties, but by using the Sharing menu option, it selects the correct tab automatically. This makes life easy for those of us who don't like too many mouse clicks.

You are concerned with the Sharing tab. Note that by default, NT does not share any other folder except the Winnt folder. This is because it needs to be shared as the netlogon share.

To provide sharing permissions on this folder, you need to click the Shared As radio button. When you do so, the other text boxes become available to enter the appropriate information.

Until you choose the Shared As radio button, you cannot enter information into the text boxes because they are grayed out. This indicates that if no sharing is enabled, the information is not required and should not be entered.

Enter a name for the share that is descriptive and will serve to tell users what it is. Or you can simply give it a drive letter for a share name and use the Comment field to enter a description.

Under the User Limit, you can set Maximum Allowed or set your own limit.

By clicking on the Permissions button, Windows NT displays the Access Through Share Permissions dialog box. By default, NT places the Everyone group in the Name list with Full Control. Click the Remove button and the Everyone group is removed from the list.

To add a user or group, click Add. The Add Users and Groups dialog box is displayed. From the list of groups displayed, select the group or groups that you want to have access to the share. You can do this by clicking on the group and choosing Add or by double-clicking the group name.

If you want to add specific users instead of a group, select the Show Users button. At first, it doesn't appear as though anything has changed, but if you scroll the Names list, you will now see that all users are listed from which you can select.

After you have added the users or groups, be sure the set the access permissions using the Type of Access combo box at the bottom of the Add Users and Groups window. Click OK to close the window and apply the changes. You should now see your users/groups in the list of names for that share. Click OK to close the Access Through Share Permissions window. Click OK to close the Share properties dialog and that's it. You have just created your first share.

Creating Printer Shares

To allow other users on the network to print from a network printer, it must be shared. By sharing a printer, you make it available to users for printing and administrative purposes. Obviously, you do not want every user to have the ability to administer the printers on your network, so you must set the access permissions accordingly. You will see how to do this shortly.

You can share a printer in one of two ways:

- During install
- After the printer is installed

Sharing a Printer During Installation

When you first set up a new printer on the server or workstation, you are given the option to share the printer after choosing and installing the drivers. Initially NT defaults do not share the printer and you must select the Shared radio button.

Windows NT lists the available operating systems that it will allow you to provide printer sharing for. These include Windows 95, (Windows 98 is included as well), and also NT 4.0 in the MIPS, Alpha, and PPC versions. The list also includes NT 3.1, 3.5, and 3.51.

To share the printer with Windows 95, you will need the manufacturer's CD or disks with the printer's drivers. NT does not supply the necessary drivers itself for Windows 95. When a Windows 95 client first connects to the server to send a print job, the driver will be loaded into the client's RAM.

After you select a share name and operating system to share with, your printer will appear in the Printers dialog box with the little hand to indicate that it is being shared.

Sharing an Already Installed Printer

If you have a printer already installed on the NT computer, you can share it by right-clicking on the icon for the printer in the Printer's window. Figure 46.13 shows the Printer's window. Note that yours may differ from this picture depending on the version of Internet Explorer installed on your system.

Figure 46.13   The Printers window enables you to add, remove, share, and edit the printers that are connected to this computer.

When you right-click on the icon, you will be presented with a pop-up menu. Select the Sharing menu option to bring up the printer properties. The Sharing tab is already selected for you with the name of the printer, the Not Shared and Shared radio buttons, the Share Name text box, and the available operating systems with which NT will share the printer.

There is a difference between this properties page and the sharing page displayed when installing the printer. To set permissions for the printer with this method, you must select the Security tab of the Printer Properties dialog box. There you will find a window displaying the Permissions, Auditing, and Ownership options. As with files, you can set the access permissions to users or groups and audit the printer and take ownership of it.

Auditing Printer Users

Auditing provides you with the ability to watch how users interact with the printer. The available auditing options are for the success or failure of the following events:

- Print
- Full Control
- Delete
- Change Permissions
- Take Ownership

After you have all the necessary permissions and auditing settings to your liking, close the dialog boxes to start sharing the printer.

When printers are shared on an NT server, client computers query the server to see if they have the updated driver already installed. What this means for the network administrator is that he or she does not have to update each client's printer drivers separately. All he or she needs to do is install the updated driver on the server and the next time the client sends a print job to the server, the new driver is automatically downloaded to the client.

Applications

How do UNIX and NT applications compare? Actually, both operating systems have some applications in common while each have some very distinct and different applications. We can break down the applications into categories to make them easier to discuss.

- Utilities
- Word processing
- Databases
- Spreadsheet
- Graphics
- Email
- Usenet news
- Network applications

Utilities

UNIX and NT share some common goals in relation to managing the OS and the network. UNIX administrators are familiar with the command line and the various commands to accomplish their tasks. NT brings some command-line utilities as well as graphical-based tools. See Table 46.2 for a comparison of familiar UNIX and NT utilities and commands.

Table 46.2   UNIX and Windows NT Commands Compared

UNIX	Windows NT	Description
AT	AT, WinAt	AT is identical in both operating systems but if you have the Resource Kit for NT, Cory Gill has supplied a command scheduler that presents a graphical interface to the **AT** command.
CAT	Type	Both command-line utilities will display a file onscreen.
CD	CD	Used to change the current directory.
CHGRP	User Manager or NET GROUP	In UNIX, it is used to change the ownership of a file. The NT utilities are used for changing the group that is associated with the file.
CHMOD	ATTRIB, file properties	UNIX uses this for changing a file's permissions and its mode. NT uses the attributes of a file to set permissions. They can be changed from the command line or by using the Properties dialog box.
CHOWN	Take Ownership	Changes the ownership of a file. NT uses the security dialog box rather than a command line.

(continues)

Table 46.2   **Continued**

UNIX	Windows NT	Description
CLEAR	CLS	Clears the screen. Under NT is used only in a command-line window.
CMP, COMM	FC	Compares differences in files.
CP	Copy	Used to copy files from one location to another.
CRON	Command Scheduler	Used for scheduling programs to run at specified intervals.
DATE	DATE, TIME	Used to change the date and time of the system.
DF, DU	Disk Administrator	Used to check free space on a drive.
ECHO	ECHO	Used to send arguments or batch file output to the console.
ED, VI	Edit	Simple ASCII file editors.
ENV	SET	Displays environment variables.
GREP, EGREP, FGREP	Find	Used to locate files. You cannot use regular expressions in NT's Find.
Kill	Task Manager	Used to kill or end a running application or process.
LN	Short Cuts	Both create a pointer or link to an existing file.
LP, LPR	Print	Sends a print job to the printer.
LS	DIR	Displays a directory listing.
MKDIR	MKDIR	Makes a new directory.
MORE	MORE	Used for viewing a file one screen at a time.
MV	MOVE	Moves a file from one directory to another
PASSWD	Ctl+Alt+Del or User	Changes a user's Manager for Domains password.
PS	Task Manager	Displays running processes or applications.
RM	DEL, DELTREE	Used to remove files and directories.
SH	CMD	Calls a command interpreter.
WALL, WRITE	Net send	Sends a message to users.

Word-Processing Applications

Most of the UNIX world is rather comfortable using two familiar word-processing applications. Actually, both can be considered more text editor than word processing because neither is capable of fancy fonts or formatting.

The first editor, vi, has no menu or graphical interface. The user must know the commands and navigation keys to move around in the document and edit it. After a user gains a level of comfort with the program, vi can prove to be a very quick-and-dirty word processor, letting you churn out simple text documents with ease.

Windows NT Word Processing Applications

Microsoft includes two word processing applications with the operating system. The first one, Notepad, is really a text editor. It does not support formatting or typefaces with fancy fonts.

Notepad offers the capability to cut, copy, and paste the text within the window and also provides a search and replace capability.

The second word-processing program provided with NT is WordPad. WordPad can actually be classified a word processor because it provides formatting capabilities not available in Notepad.

WordPad also provides a ruler for indicating text location, margins, and tabs on the document. Additionally, it contains a small status bar at the bottom, which allows users to know when they have the Caps Lock and Num Lock keys turned on.

There are of course third-party word-processing applications from vendors such Microsoft Word, Lotus Ami Pro, and Corel WordPerfect. All these packages offer considerable functionality with the newer versions incorporating HTML publishing capabilities.

Database Applications

Both operating systems have a fair bit of available database software applications.

Windows NT 4.0 is capable of running any 32-bit Windows database application that allows you to run programs such as Microsoft's Access, Lotus Corporation's Approach, or Borland's (now Corel's) Paradox.

These database programs are designed more to be used on a standalone computer or network workstation and are more adept at single user environments. You can also use them for a front end to a server database such as SQL server.

If you need a multiuser network database package, you can look into Microsoft's SQL server. Oracle has a version of its database software for Windows NT as well, or you can look to IBM for its database implementation of DB2.

Spreadsheets

It seems that the big three business software producers are dominant in most of the important software categories, and spreadsheets are no exception.

Microsoft makes its Excel program available both as a separate application and within its Microsoft Office suite of applications. Excel was a latecomer to the spreadsheet market but has surpassed most of the others in features and usability.

Lotus Corporation is the one that most people think of when they hear the term spreadsheet. Although it wasn't the first spreadsheet software available—VisiCalc holds that title—Lotus 1-2-3 is by far the most familiar and recognizable spreadsheet software program.

Borland entered the spreadsheet arena with Quattro Pro. This version actually started the multi-page spreadsheet trend that most products use now.

Since that time, Borland has sold the software to Corel, which now offers it as a separate product or in its Office suite of applications.

Graphics

Graphics software programs at one time were the domain of Apple Computers. However, with the popularity of the Windows platform, including NT, most vendors now offer their Apple versions in a Windows flavor as well.

Adobe is, of course, one of the most recognizable names in graphics software. They provide programs such as PhotoShop for image creation and editing. They also offer PageMaker, which is a desktop publishing application.

Jasc Software is a company best known for its shareware product called PaintShop Pro. Jasc now offers a full retail version of this graphic editing program with many advanced features.

Email Applications

Both platforms offer a variety of email applications that can be used on the local network or over the Internet. UNIX email applications for the most part are character-based, command-line style programs but some are based on the X Window graphical environment.

Windows NT utilizes GUI-based email applications from Microsoft and Lotus most notably.

UNIX

Email applications for UNIX include sendmail, mail, elm, and Pine. Sendmail is an application found in UNIX and Linux environments for sending email. It has a reputation for being difficult to configure.

The application known as mail is used quite extensively for internal mail on the UNIX network but can also be used to send SMTP mail. It is a command-line application that allows you to compose a message at the time of sending or send a previously prepared message.

The elm and Pine mail programs use a full-screen character-based approach to email. Although they are still not graphical in nature, these two programs make the process of composing and sending email messages easier by providing the user with menu or keyboard shortcuts on the screen.

Windows NT

Windows NT offers the capability to run many different types of email programs. Microsoft's own Exchange Server is tightly integrated with NT and interoperates with User Manager for Domains to provide integration with user accounts and mailboxes. Exchange Server comes with various mail connectors that allow it to share mail with systems such as

- Other Exchange Servers
- Microsoft Mail
- Lotus cc:Mail
- X.25
- Internet

As you can see, Exchange Server provides ample opportunity for integrating mixed mail systems. To fully explain the inner workings of Exchange Server requires an entire book unto its own, so I won't go into it here.

Windows NT can also use email client applications. Some of the more popular ones are Microsoft Mail, Internet Mail, Microsoft Outlook, Outlook Express, cc:Mail, and Netscape Mail. Each of these client applications can operate fully under NT Server or NT Workstation. They can connect to and use the Microsoft Exchange Server as well as Internet mail systems.

Usenet News

One of the more popular ways to exchange information on the Internet, besides email, is through Usenet News. Information is categorized and broken up into topics known as newsgroups. These newsgroups follow a hierarchy in how they are organized.

You will find that some categories are self-explanatory, such as comp, which deals with computer-related issues, or sci.engr, which deals with engineering and scientific details. For topics that don't fit under specific categories, the alt heading serves as the top-level and stands for alternative.

UNIX users have been using Rn for news reading. Rn is a command-line application. It is customizable to a degree by the use of command-line options for starting the program.

Another popular Usenet news program is Tin. Tin is a full-screen newsreader that is actually a clone of elm. It is relatively easy to use and has onscreen menu key choices to help you with the program.

As with all things Windows, NT offers the user graphical-based tools for reading newsgroups. For those who are a Microsoft shop, you will be using programs such as Microsoft News or Outlook Express.

Microsoft News was one of the first applications that Microsoft distributed with Internet Explorer. It has a simple interface and is equally easy to use.

The latest application, Outlook Express, is actually an email and newsgroup application rolled into one. You start a separate instance for each but they are collectively known as Outlook Express.

With Outlook Express, you are given the opportunity to see the entire list of groups available on the news server and can choose from that list. You then receive a visual indication as to which groups you are subscribed to.

Outlook Express also supports the use of HTML in reading and posting usenet articles. If you are sending articles with HTML in them, be aware that not all newsreader applications can read the HTML, and some users will see only garbage in the message.

Network Applications

When I refer to network applications, I am talking about the wealth of programs and utilities that provide administrators with troubleshooting and monitoring tools. More and more applications are being developed for both operating systems. Some are just a rehash of existing applications and some are brand new and designed to solve problems that were normally done with paper and pen. It is impossible to go into every type of application, let alone the entire library that is available. That would take a couple more books, which would never be capable of being up-to-date because of the rapid changes in application development.

UNIX is built on the TCP/IP set of protocol suites. Windows NT includes a comprehensive set of TCP/IP utilities as well. The following TCP/IP applications are common to UNIX and NT:

- Telnet
- PING
- FTP
- DNS

Each of these applications is discussed in the following sections.

Telnet

Telnet is a program that is used by both NT and UNIX to allow a user to control or log in to a remote computer. Telnet provides you with a terminal session on the remote computer. An example of this in the UNIX world would be an administrator who needs to make modifications to user accounts on the server. Rather than going to the server itself, he can telnet into the server from his workstation and perform the tasks without leaving his desk.

Windows NT uses telnet mostly for connecting to mainframe and UNIX systems because terminal sessions on NT computers are not used that much at all. One task that I use it for is to log in to the mail server and rectify problems with users' mailboxes. Our mail server uses Exchange Server, which is not a UNIX application but that still supports telnet sessions with a special set of commands.

To use telnet, you must have an active network connection or dial-up connection that provides a path to the server you want to log in to. The command is

```
telnet server.domain.com [port]
```

The port option is not required on all systems but is needed if you plan to control a specific application. For example, if you need to telnet to a mailserver, the port must be set at 110. This tells the remote system that the telnet session should connect to the mail port.

Not all systems will allow telnet access for security reasons. Proxy servers and firewalls can filter these requests and prevent them from getting through.

PING

Windows NT uses the PING utility for the same reasons as UNIX users: to verify the existence and connection to a remote host. The command for PING is listed here:

```
PING 207.134.23.45
```

The remote system will respond if it is online and available. NT will send four 64-byte packets by default. A variety of command-line options are available for PING as well. These are

- **-t**—Pings the specified computer until it is interrupted.
- **-a**—Resolves addresses to computer names.
- **-n** *count*—Specifies the number of packets to send.
- **-l** *length*—Sends the ECHO packets containing the amount of data specified by *length*. The default is 64 bytes and the maximum is 8192.
- **-f**—Sends a flag to indicate that the packet should not be fragmented by gateways on the route.
- **-i** *ttl*—Sets the Time To Live.
- **-v** *tos*—Sets the Type Of Service.
- **-r** *count*—Records the route of the outgoing and returning packet. It records this in the Record Route field. The range for *count* is 1–9.
- **-s** *count*—Specifies the time stamp for the number of hops specified by count.
- **-j** *computer-list*—Causes the packets to be routed using a list of computers specified in computer list. They can be separated by intermediate gateways. The maximum number allowed by IP is 9 intermediaries.
- **-k** *computer-list*—Routes via the computer-list as well but consecutive computers cannot be separated by intermediate gateways.
- **-w** *timeout*—Specifies a timeout interval in milliseconds.
- *destination-list*—Specifies multiple computers to ping.

FTP

Windows NT includes a command-line FTP program for accessing remote FTP servers. The FTP application uses many of the same commands as its UNIX counterpart. To function as an FTP server, Windows NT requires the installation of Internet Information Server (IIS).

IIS is managed using the Internet Service Manager (ISM), which is a graphical interface to the features and functions of the FTP, Gopher, and World Wide Web Publishing services on NT.

Figure 46.14 shows IIS as a snap-in to the Microsoft Management Console (MMC). You can see the Default Web site, which is rather empty at this time. All permissions and restrictions can be accessed and controlled from this point.

For FTP purposes, it can provide a directory listing identical to that of a UNIX FTP server or in MS-DOS format. If set to display a UNIX style command, a remote user would not that it is an NT server as the commands are identical as well. This feature is less of a concern now because most users have GUI-based FTP clients on their machines that issue the commands in the background and display directory listings differently than the command-line–driven applications.

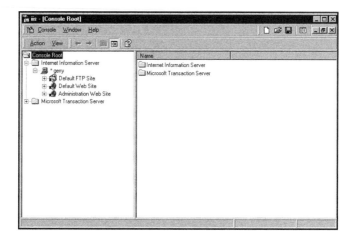

Figure 46.14   Internet Information Server is an application that Windows NT uses to publish Web documents on the Internet and is now a snap-in for the Microsoft Management Console.

DNS

The Domain Name System (DNS) runs as a service on an NT computer. It is tightly integrated with NT's WINS service, both of which are discussed here.

Microsoft DNS Server

The UNIX network relies heavily on TCP/IP and IP addressing. Windows NT uses Windows Internet Name System (WINS) and DNS to resolve hostnames to IP addresses. WINS provides IP addresses for NetBIOS names for use over TCP/IP. DNS under NT provides the IP address to hostname mapping that is used on TCP/IP networks.

The version of DNS that comes with NT 4.0 is fully compliant with RFCs 1033, 1034, 1035, 1101, 1123, 1183, and 1536. It goes beyond these features by providing dynamic mapping through the use of WINS and provides a graphical interface for administration. It incorporates wizards that ease the creation of zones and allows users to administer remote DNS servers. It does not allow you to administer servers that are not NT DNS servers.

Microsoft DNS supports a boot file upon installation that is provided to ease the migration from BIND-based DNS servers.

Installing DNS

DNS is not installed by default when NT is first set up on a computer. If DNS is not present, it can be installed from the Network applet in Control Panel. DNS runs as a service so it is available under the Services tab. Click the Add button and select DNS from the available list of services.

When DNS is installed, you need to configure it to provide the necessary mappings. DNS will start automatically when NT reboots. Although you install DNS through the Network applet in Control Panel, it warrants its own administrative tool and resides on the Start menu, under Administrative Tools (Common).

Select DNS Manager from the list. The DNS Manager is displayed in Figure 46.15.

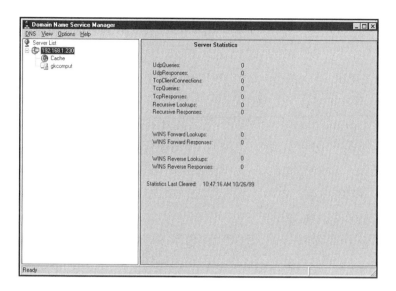

Figure 46.15 DNS Manager is the interface that you use to set up your domain name server information.

Adding a Server

DNS does not contain any servers until you add one to the DNS Manager. Only then can you create zones.

1. Click the DNS menu and choose New Server.

2. Enter the name for the server and click OK.

3. Now that you have a server name entered, you need to create zones. By right-clicking on the server name, you will be given a pop-up; select New Zone.

4. You will be presented with a dialog box asking if you are creating a primary zone or a secondary zone. Select the appropriate option.

5. You next need to enter a name for the zone and a file. The file option is used to determine what filename the zone is stored under. Once all the information is entered, the zone is added to the hierarchy. Follow the same procedure to add any additional zones.

By right-clicking on the new zone, you can choose from the available menu options to add new hosts, new domains, or new records, or you can delete the zone.

Although there are far more details and options available with DNS, the graphical DNS Manager along with the wizards provide an easy-to-use interface for configuring DNS on Microsoft Windows NT. By entering the IP address of your DNS server into the configuration properties of you clients, your clients can connect to and use the name resolution on your NT Server.

Microsoft's Conversion Tools

Microsoft provides the Microsoft Windows NT Services for UNIX Add-On pack to ease the integration of NT computers into UNIX environments. This add-on provides features in three basic categories:

- File services
- Connectivity services
- Usability services

File Services

These include an NFS client and NFS server support. This allows NT computers to gain access to UNIX file systems and allows UNIX computers access to the Windows NT file system.

Connectivity Services

Provides a telnet server, an improved telnet client, and also includes a daemon for password synchronization. This permits UNIX and NT to use a single point of password management.

Usability Services

Provides a limited subset of utilities and a Korn shell. This can help ease the migration process because it provides a familiar interface to UNIX users.

Although it is not really a migration tool, the Add-On pack can be used to ease the migration by allowing the NT and UNIX environments to coexist while the administrators make the transition.

More information can be found regarding the Add-On pack on Microsoft's Web site at `http://www.microsoft.com/NTServer/nts/techdetails/compares/sfuwp.asp`. This link will take you to a page where you can download a white paper describing the SFU Add-On pack.

Third-Party Conversion Tools

Companies such as DataFocus and Softway provide commands and utilities for the migration process as well as header files and libraries for application developers.

DataFocus provides such applications as

- **NuTCracker**—A comprehensive UNIX development and runtime environment for Windows
- **MKS Toolkit Select**—A set of UNIX utilities for Windows that includes an X Server
- **MKS Toolkit**—UNIX utilities

Information on these tools can be found at the DataFocus Web site at
`http://www.datafocus.com/products`.

Softway provides various software products that provide a UNIX environment for NT. These include Workstation and Workstation Lite, Server and Server Lite, and Software Development Kits (SDKs).

The products provide shells, utilities, and Window Managers. A listing can be found at `http://www.interix.com/products/matrix.html`.

As Windows NT becomes more mainstream and starts to take over more of the UNIX share of networking, the demand for migration tools will drive a market to create more tools. Until that time, the your best ally in the migration race is to understand the similarities and differences between the two operating systems. Armed with this knowledge, the transition can be a bit smoother.

Summary

Migrating a network or computer system from UNIX to Windows NT Server 4.0 requires some thought and careful planning. By knowing the similarities and differences between the two operating systems and the environments in which they work, you can make the transition smoother.

UNIX has long been an operating system that was more prevalent on mainframe and mini computers but is also used on a considerable number of personal computers and smaller servers as well.

Microsoft's Windows NT 4.0 is fast becoming the network operating system of choice for local area networks and client/server computing environments. It is taking over from UNIX and Novell's NetWare.

Each OS has equivalent applications that help you perform administrative functions for the computer and network. Each OS also has a multitude of third-party applications that enable you to perform daily computing chores.

Armed with the information presented here, you can make informed decisions about your migration from UNIX to Windows NT Server 4.0.

Migrating from Windows NT 4.0 to NetWare

SOME OF THE MAIN TOPICS IN THIS CHAPTER ARE

Adding Users in NetWare

Login Scripts

Creating Print and File Shares on NetWare

Applications

Moving from Windows NT to the NetWare environment is almost a reverse procedure of migrating from NetWare to NT, which was covered in Chapter 45, "Migrating from Novell NetWare to Windows NT 4.0." There are a few things that make this a little different though.

Note

We won't cover how to install NetWare. The documentation that comes with NetWare fully explains how to install and configure the product. We will assume that you have the OS installed and running and that you are going to convert your user accounts, file and print resources, and applications to the NetWare platform.

To transfer your NT user accounts to a NetWare environment, you must understand how the two operating systems handle these accounts and their permissions or restrictions. Chapter 45 contains various tables comparing these issues, and they are reproduced here for your convenience.

Tables 47.1 and 47.2 show how the restrictions placed on user accounts compare when the NT server is not running FPNW and then shows the changes when it is running FPNW. Windows NT uses the FPNW add-on pack to provide file and print services to NetWare clients without requiring any special software or configuration on the client itself.

Table 47.1 Account Restrictions Without FPNW

NetWare Restrictions	Windows NT Equivalent
Expiration Date	Expiration Date
Account Disabled	Account Disabled
Limit Concurrent Connections	No Equivalent
Require Password	Permit Blank Password
Minimum Password Length	Minimum Password Length
Force Periodic Password Changes	Password Never Expires
Days Between Force Changes	Maximum Password Age
Grace Logins	None
Allow User to Change Password	User Cannot Change Password
Require Unique Passwords	Password Uniqueness
Station Restrictions	None
Time Restrictions	Logon Hours
Intruder Detection/Lockout	Account Lockout
User Disk Volume Restrictions	None

Table 47.2 Account Restrictions with FPNW

NetWare Restrictions	Windows NT Equivalent
Limit Concurrent Connections	Limit Concurrent Connections
Grace Logins	Grace Logins
Station Restrictions	Station Restrictions
Login Scripts	Login Scripts

Table 47.3 shows how the folder or directory rights compare.

Table 47.3   Folder Rights

Novell NetWare	Microsoft Windows NT
Supervisory (S)	Full Control (All)
Read (R)	(RX) (RX)
Write (W)	(RWXD) (RWXD)
Create	Not Supported
Erase	(RWXD)(RWXD)
Modify (M)	(RWXD)(RWXD)
File Scan (F)	Not Supported
Access Control (A)	(P)

Much the same as the directories, files have access restrictions as well. These are displayed in Table 47.4.

Table 47.4   File Rights

Novell NetWare	Microsoft Windows NT
Supervisory (S)	All
Read (R)	RX
Write (W)	RWXD
Erase	RWXD
Modify (M)	RWXD
File Scan (R)	Not Supported
Access Control (A)	P

Although not a requirement for user account purposes, I have included Table 47.5 so that you can become familiar with the various file attributes that each OS uses.

Table 47.5   File Attributes

Novell NetWare	Microsoft Windows NT
Read Only (Ro)	Read Only (R)
Archive Needed (A)	Archive (A)
System (SY)	System (S)
Hidden (H)	Hidden (H)
Read Write (Rw)	None, any file that does not have the (R) attribute can be written to

As you can see, most of the NT and NetWare restrictions have a comparable opposite in the other OS, although they might have a different name or letter designation.

In this chapter, you are going to look at migrating to the Novell NetWare 4.11 product, which is the most popular version.

Adding Users in NetWare

Coming from an NT environment, you are used to dealing with computers in a domain. NetWare structures its network using NetWare Directory Services (NDS). NDS provides several advantages for your network over what was previously available in earlier versions of NetWare. For example, NDS provides for a single login as well as a single point of administration for the entire network. Novell has also made available NDS for NT that allows for easier integration of NT into a NetWare NDS network.

Under NDS, you deal with objects. This means that users are considered as user objects. One of the first considerations in migrating to NetWare is the creation of user accounts so that your network users can gain access to the necessary resources. Novell provides six objects that help you manage users:

- **Organization object**—Enables you to assign login scripts to users as well as any defaults for users. You can also assign trustee rights to users with this object. This applies to the whole organization.

- **Organizational unit object**—Provides the same functionality as the Organization object but is based on objects in an organizational unit (OU).

- **Group object**—Provides a way to manage a group that can contain multiple users. This makes for easier administration when users share common requirements and can be grouped together.

- **Profile object**—This can be used to provide common functionality for groups of users including login scripts.

- **Organizational role object**—You can use this object to set up a position within the organization that may have only one or two members and who may change often. An example would be a president or chairperson in an organization that only sits for a specified term. This means that you assign the rights to a position rather than to an individual.

- **USER_TEMPLATE**—This allows for a default set of rights that can be applied to all new accounts. You then need only to add any user-specific information. This is a time-saving feature because you don't have to re-create the same information over and over.

Using Groups

One of the easiest ways to deal with users on NetWare is to use the same concept found on NT networks' groups. You can reduce your administrative requirements by assigning trustee rights to a group, and then assigning a user to that group. This prevents the necessity of assigning these rights to individual users, which can be time-consuming in a large network with many users.

Creating Leaf Objects

To create user accounts on a NetWare server, you need to create what is known as a *leaf object*. The term leaf is used as a result of Novell calling the NDS structure a *directory tree*. Although you can create different types of leaf objects, we will concentrate on the user and group leaf objects for the purpose of this discussion.

Before you can actually create a new user or leaf object, you must understand the rules governing the naming of these objects.

- The name must be unique within its branch.
- The name can be up to 64 characters in length.
- Some special characters are allowed but if you are in an environment that mixes earlier versions on NetWare, they will not be capable of reading the object names.
- Object names are not case-sensitive but they are preserved for display purposes.
- Names can include spaces and underscores. Underscores are stored as spaces so that the name John_Jacobson and John Jacobson are the same.

Two methods are available for creating leaf objects: NetWare Administrator and NETADMIN.

Creating Leaf Objects with NetWare Administrator

To create leaf objects with NetWare Administrator, follow these steps:

1. Double-click the NetWare Administrator icon.

2. Choose the appropriate object to create the leaf object in (see Figure 47.1, which displays NetWare Administrator showing the available leaf objects).

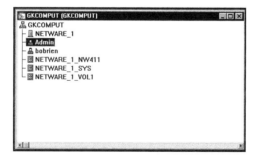

Figure 47.1 A tree of leaf objects.

3. Choose Create from the Object menu.

4. Select the object class from the New Object dialog.

5. Choose OK, and then choose Create.

Creating Leaf Objects Using NETADMIN

To use the NETADMIN utility, must have a computer running DOS 3.3 or later. To create leaf objects with NETADMIN, follow these steps:

1. At the DOS prompt type NETADMIN, and press Enter.

2. From the NETADMIN Options menu choose Manage Objects (see Figure 47.2).

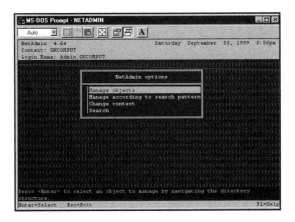

Figure 47.2 From the NETADMIN Options menu you can choose to manage objects, manage according to search pattern, change context, or search for objects.

3. Select the container that will hold the new leaf object.

4. Press Insert.

5. You will be presented with the Select an Object Class screen. From this screen, select the object class that you want to create.

6. Fill in the information as requested and press Enter.

7. You are now given the option to create another leaf object. Select No if you are finished.

8. To edit the object, press F10.

9. From the Actions menu, choose an option and add any necessary information.

10. Press the Esc key until you are at the NETADMIN Options menu to exit.

So there you have the procedure required to enter user accounts, or user leaf objects as they are classed under NetWare 4.11. Ensure that you compare the necessary account restrictions in the tables shown earlier to assign the correct permissions to your new users.

Login Scripts

Windows NT uses profiles for customizing the logon procedures for users on an NT network. These profiles determine user interface options as well as provide a means for automatic drive mappings. Novell NetWare uses login scripts for the same purpose. Here are some of the procedures that login scripts support:

■ Mapping network drives

■ Displaying messages

■ Setting user environment variables

■ Executing programs

These scripts work identically for DOS, Windows, and OS/2 clients.

Login scripts are processed by the LOGIN utility that runs the correct script for the user currently logging in to the system. There are four types of login scripts available:

- **Container**—These scripts are responsible for setting up common environment variables among all users within the container. This is the first script that is run by the LOGIN utility.

- **Profile**—This is used to set up the environment for several users instead of all. These users can be a part of a group.

- **User**—Used to set up the environment for a single user. This script is responsible for settings such as printers and mail directories. Each user can have only one user login script.

- **Default**—This script is the one that is used if a user does not have one set up already. This script is a part of the LOGIN.EXE binary file and is not editable.

To reduce the amount of work required to maintain and create login scripts, it is recommended that you take into consideration all common requirements for your users, such as printers, and incorporate these settings into the profile login script. In this way, all you need to be concerned with in a user login script are settings that relate specifically to the user and nobody else.

It is also important to note that when a user logs in to the system, up to three scripts can be executed. The last script to execute, which will be either the user script or the default script, will override any previous environment variables set by the other scripts.

Login scripts are contained within or are properties of objects. Table 47.6 shows this relationship.

Table 47.6   Objects and Their Login Scripts

Object	Type of Script
Organization	Container login
Organizational unit	Container login
Profile	Profile login
User	User profile

Creating Login Scripts

You use the NetWare Administrator or NETADMIN utility to create the login scripts. Each type of login script uses the same syntax and commands. The only difference is where they are placed within the object structure, as indicated by Table 47.6. We will use the NetWare Administrator utility to create the script. You can check the documentation for the procedures required to create the scripts using the NETADMIN utility.

Using NetWare Administrator to Create Login Scripts

Ensure that the object exists that you are going to assign the script to then follow these steps:

1. Double-click the NetWare Administrator icon.

2. Select the object that you are creating the script for. You can do this by using the browser.

3. From the Object menu, select Details.

4. Choose the Login Script page.

5. Enter the login script commands and information into the text box (see Figure 47.3). (*Note:* For a complete list of the available commands, see the "Login Script Commands and Variables" section in the documentation.)

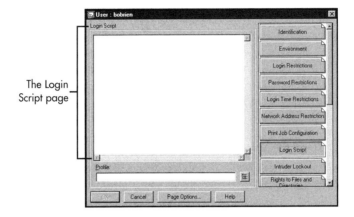

Figure 47.3 The Login Script Page allows scripted commands to be entered into the large text box titled Login Script.

6. Choose OK. This will save the logon script and exit the Details dialog. (*Note:* If you are creating a Profile script, continue with step 7; otherwise, you are finished.)

7. Select the user object that the profile will be assigned to using the browser.

8. From the Object menu, select Details.

9. Choose the Login Script page.

10. In the Default Profile field, enter the name of the profile object (see Figure 47.4).

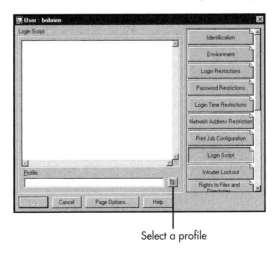

Select a profile

Figure 47.4 The same page as that used for the Login Scripts but you choose the Profile Explorer button on the bottom of this page to locate and choose a profile.

11. Choose OK to save the profile object name and close the Details dialog box.

12. Proceed to add the User object as a trustee of the Profile object.

13. Select the Profile object by using the browser.

14. From the Object menu, choose the Trustees of This Object option.

15. Select Add Trustee.

16. Enter the complete name of the user object that will be using this profile object.

17. Check the Browse and Read rights, and then choose OK (see Figure 47.5).

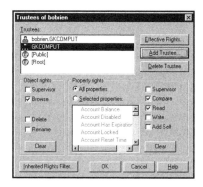

Figure 47.5   This window lists Browse and Read Rights information for the selected object.

Using NETADMIN to Create Login Scripts

To create a login script using NETADMIN, you must satisfy the following criteria:

- A computer with DOS 3.3 or later and the NETADMIN utility
- The existence of an object that will contain the script
- Write property rights for the object that will contain the script

When you are sure that you meet the criteria, start **NETADMIN** from the DOS prompt by typing **NETADMIN** and pressing Enter. Follow the steps outlined here:

1. From the NETADMIN Options menu, choose Manage Objects.

2. Select the object that will contain the script, and press F10.

3. Select View or Edit Properties of This Object.

4. Select Login Script. If the login script is empty, you will be prompted to copy a script from another object. You can do so by choosing Yes or you can create one from scratch by choosing No.

5. Enter the necessary script commands and information into the script text box.

6. Press F10 to save the script, and the process is complete.

Creating Print and File Shares on NetWare

In this section you will look at making file and printer resources available on the network. The first topic discusses sharing printers.

Creating Print Shares

To offer your network users the capability to print to a common printer, you must share the printers on your network. NetWare offers various utilities for creating and modifying your shared print resources. These are listed and explained in Table 47.7.

Table 47.7   NetWare Printer Utilities

Utility	Purpose
NetWare Administrator	A graphical-based tool used to create, modify, and delete printers and print queues.
NetWare User Tools	Another GUI-based tool that allows users to set up printing, set printer options, and connect to and disconnect from print queues.
CAPTURE	This is a command-line utility that allows the user to redirect output to a printer or file.
NPRINT	A command-line utility that prints files from outside an application.
PSC	You can use this tool from the command line to monitor the status of and control the printer.
PCONSOLE	A menu option that is used to create and modify print queues, print servers, and printers.
NPRINTER	Another menu option that loads the NetWare port driver.
NETUSER	When you choose this menu option, you can capture output to the network printer as well as send and modify print jobs.
PRINTCON	Used for creating and modifying print job configurations. It helps to simplify the use of CAPTURE of NPRINTER.
PRINTDEF	Defines printer forms for CAPTURE and NPRINT and defines print devices in a database.
PSERVER	Loads the print server software and controls print jobs.
PUPGRADE	Used for upgrading from NetWare 3 to version 4.

To have users share you, network printers, the NetWare Print Services requires three things:

■ Printer server object
■ Printer object
■ Print queue

The NetWare Administrator offers a "Quick Setup" to aid you in setting up printer shares. Follow the steps outlined here to configure your printer share using this method:

1. Install the printer.

2. Ensure that you are logged in as ADMIN.

3. Run the NetWare Administrator from a Windows workstation.

4. Select the Print Services Quick Setup option from the Tools menu.

5. Type a name in the Print Server Name text box.

6. Type a name for the printer object in the Printer Name text box.

7. Select a printer type from the Printer Type options.

8. Complete the dialog by choosing the printer type from those presented in the list (see Figure 47.6).

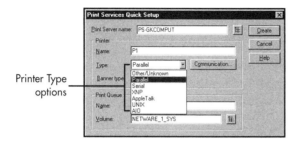

Printer Type options

Figure 47.6 The Printer Type options field lists the available printer interface types.

9. Give the Print Queue object a name in the Print Queue Name text box.

10. In the Print Queue Volume text box, type a name for the print queue volume. (You can optionally browse for a volume and choose one that way.)

11. Choose Create.

Now you must perform some additional tasks to complete the configuration of the printer. These are broken down into three tasks:

1. Load PSERVER.NLM at the NetWare Server Console by typing LOAD PSERVER. You can also place the command in the autoexec.ncf file.

2. From a DOS workstation that has a printer attached, load the port driver by entering the following command and options: NPRINTER <printservername> <printernumber>.

3. Using a Windows workstation, ensure that the NetWare client software is running, and then double-click the NPTWIN95.EXE icon to load the port driver. You will find this located in the SYS\PUBLIC\WIN95 folder on the server.

Your network client should now be capable of sending print jobs to the printer over the network. You can reference the documentation to find out about customization details relating to the printers.

Creating File Shares

Files are located within the NetWare hierarchy known as the *file system*. The servers contain one or more volumes. These volumes get further divided into directories and then subdirectories and finally files.

When dealing with NetWare paths and DOS clients, you must keep one thing in mind. DOS only allows the use of 127 characters in the complete path. NetWare allows 255 characters. After you get past the volume portion of the file structure, NetWare stores files in the same directory\ subdirectory\file scheme that is used by NT. You navigate through the hierarchy to get to the file or directory you want.

Most NetWare volumes divide their structure into operating system and application directories. In this way, users can be given access only to the application directory structure and need never see or interact with the operating system directories and files.

When you create file shares, you are setting the security of the file by allowing or denying access to the file. You use the RIGHTS command to view or modify the rights assigned to files and directories. The command syntax is listed here:

```
RIGHTS path [[+/-] rights] [/options] [/? ¦ /VER]
```

The path variable is used to indicate the path to the file or directory to which you want to add or remove rights.

The +/- is used to add (+) or remove (-) rights.

The variable rights is used to indicate the directory or file rights as outlined in Tables 47.3 and 47.4 earlier in this chapter.

The /option variable is used to set options taken from a list of available options as indicated in Table 47.8.

Table 47.8   RIGHTS Options

Option	Purpose
/C	Scroll continuously through the output
/F	Used to view the Inherited Rights Filter (IRF)
/I	Used to view the inherited rights and to see where they came from
/NAME=*username*	By placing a valid username here, you can view or modify the rights for that user or group
/S	Used to view subdirectories
/T	View trustee assignments

You can view the online help regarding rights by using the /? switch in the command line.

The last switch /VER is used to see what version the utility is.

The following is an example command line that sets the read and write permissions on a file for the user mblanc:

```
RIGHTS + R W /NAME=mblanc
```

You can view more information regarding file security in the Concepts guide under Trustee and Security.

Applications

NetWare classifies applications into three categories:

- **Network Aware**—These applications can run on a network but do not use any special network features.

- **Network Enabled**—Applications that run on the network but rely on services such as authentication, messaging, or print management.

- **Network Integrated**—These applications are designed specifically for a network environment. They take advantage of network features, such as storage.

It is a good idea to ensure that any software applications you are planning to purchase are certified to work with NetWare. Novell offers the NetWare compatible symbols to assure end users that a software product has been tested and approved for use on NetWare networks. If you want to ensure compatibility, always look for the Novell YES symbol on the manufacturers' products.

Novell recommends that you create application directories. This strategy can help you perform load balancing and provide protection for your application directories.

Although a variety of applications and utilities is a part of the NetWare system, other third-party vendors provide productivity applications for your users that are designed to work in a networked environment.

The following is a small list of available applications for the NetWare environment. It is by no means complete and offers only a glimpse of what is available.

Corel WordPerfect Suite

Corel Corporation has made its WordPerfect Suite 2000 application available for the NetWare platform. Version 2000 Professional comes with the following software packages:

- Corel WordPerfect 9 for word-processing tasks
- Quattro Pro 9 spreadsheet application
- Corel Presentations 9 for onscreen and overhead presentations
- CorelCENTRAL 9 personal information management
- Trellix 2 for desktop Web publishing
- Dragon Naturally Speaking for voice recognition
- Corel Print Office for small business publishing such as business cards, brochures, and newsletters
- Paradox 9 database application
- NetPerfect automated Web publishing
- Visual Basic for Applications for customization

Word-Processing Software

The following is a list of word-processing software that has been tested and approved to work with NetWare:

- Microsoft Word
- Software Bridge v5.1, which is a document conversion program

Backup Software

Seagate provides a version of its Backup Exec software for use on the NetWare environment. It also provides another backup application known as Palindrome Backup Director.

Aside from these software vendors mentioned here, numerous other third-party applications are available. Check with your favorite vendor to verify a tested and approved NetWare version.

Summary

Although Windows NT 4.0 and NetWare are both network operating systems, each OS has distinct differences from the other. You will have to decide which one will provide the networking and resource sharing capabilities that are needed. You are the best judge of the requirements that are needed in your organization.

If you have decided to migrate from Windows NT to NetWare, this chapter provides the necessary basis for performing that migration. The information presented here will help you gain a better understanding of the differences and similarities of the two operating systems.

As you can see, NetWare has the support of major software vendors in the industry mostly because it has been around for quite some time. You might find this reassuring in your decision to migrate.

Migrating from Windows NT 4.0 to Windows 2000

CHAPTER 48

SOME OF THE MAIN TOPICS IN THIS CHAPTER ARE

The Active Directory

What Active Directory Delivers

What Is a Domain Tree? What Is a Forest?

The Active Directory and Dynamic DNS

Active Directory Service Interfaces (ADSI)

Preparing to Upgrade to Windows 2000

Implementing a Migration to the Active Directory

Ever since the release of Windows NT Server 4.0, there has been discussion in the computer press about the features that would be included in the next version of Windows NT. Many features that were promised for version 4.0, but later dropped before the final release, were talked about; but perhaps the most widely discussed change to the Windows NT platform concerns the technologies that encompass what is generally referred to as *Active Directory Services*. Microsoft has told network administrators that directory services exist in version 4.0. But trying to call the flat-file–based Security Accounts Manager (SAM) database a true enterprise-capable directory service is quite a stretch.

When migrating from Windows NT 4.0 to Windows 2000, it is important that you first understand what the Active Directory is and how it is integrated so tightly into other parts of the operating system. This chapter points out the differences between the Windows NT 4.0 domain network paradigm and the new Active Directory.

The Active Directory

The only information that is stored in the SAM is user and computer account and security information, such as trust relationships. Information about printers, file shares, and other resources are scattered here and there in separate databases and are managed by separate utilities. Administering network resources using multiple utilities with disjointed interfaces can become quite a nightmare in a large network.

The Directory and the Directory Service

The first thing you will need to understand about the Active Directory is that it is composed of a database and many different programs that can be used to operate on the database. The term *directory* is used to describe the underlying database that holds all the information managed by the directory service. The actual information store, the directory, is housed in a Microsoft Exchange Server database engine store.

The term *directory service* refers to the programs that manage the database and allow users and programs to access its data in a meaningful way. If you look under the Administrative Tools folder you will note that there is a tool called Directory Management, which you can use to view or modify information in the directory. But there are other tools here also, such as the Domain Tree Management tool and the Active Directory Sites and Services Manager tool. In addition to the tools that you use to interface with the directory to perform management functions, there are other applications and services that do background processing, such as replication and security.

The directory service consists of the programs and application programming interfaces (Active Directory Services Interface—ASDI and the C LDAP API) that can be used to manage or query the database by users and administrators. The directory service offers the network a *namespace* that can be used to locate objects throughout the network by querying with the object's name or one of its attributes.

The Directory System Agent (DSA) provides the service responsible for performing actual queries and updates to the database. Because applications and APIs make requests to the DSA in a defined fashion, the functions they perform are separated from the actual underlying format of data storage.

Interesting Objects

The Active Directory in Windows 2000 provides the capability to query a large database that can be used to locate any object, or information about any object, stored in the directory database. To understand how important the Active Directory will be in Windows 2000, you must first understand the kinds of data that will be stored in the objects that the directory organizes.

What kind of data should be a candidate for management by a directory service is not easily answered. Here the definition of a directory service gets kind of fuzzy.

The most common comparison made is of directory services to the white and yellow pages of the traditional phone directory. White pages are specific queries where the input is a person's name and the output is their telephone number. Yellow pages have a more general "browsing" capability, with more general input about a subject or concept. This results in a specific output selected by the user from the information found. The Active Directory provides the best of both. You can search for specific objects whose names you are familiar with, or you can browse for objects by using the data available by the many attributes that objects can possess. For example, you can easily locate a user object if you know the user's name. This is sort of like using the white pages of the telephone book.

However, suppose you are a very mobile employee. You have just walked into the Atlanta office and you must print a document. You quickly search the directory to find an object that is a printer, located in the Atlanta branch on the third floor, and that supports color printing. This situation shows that directory services can also be used in a manner similar to the telephone book's yellow pages service.

However, almost everyone agrees that the information stored in the directory should be interesting or of some practical use.

The first directory that comes to mind when you think of early computer systems is the file system directory. The organization of data files and programs into a structure of directories and subdirectories became more important as the size of the available storage grew. When networking PCs became a necessity, the ability to organize users and secure data from inappropriate access led to the concept of logging in to the computer or network, just as had been done with multiuser, mini, and mainframe computers for many years. This necessitated another database (read *directory*) to keep track of users and security information.

For network administrators and users alike, there is a great need today to be able to quickly locate resources that, in a modern distributed computing environment, can be anywhere from the computer setting on the user's desk to a file server halfway around the world. So, when deciding what kinds of information to store in a directory service database, the needs of both the users and the administrators of the system must be taken into consideration.

What Active Directory Delivers

The target that Microsoft has been aiming at for several years is the development of its "next generation" of directory services, which are supposed to include the following:

- **A single logon for the entire network.** This was present, more or less, in previous versions of Windows.

- **A hierarchical structure** that organizes objects and tasks into a logical format so that you can quickly and easily locate the information you need. The X.500 hierarchical format has been adopted in the Active Directory for Windows 2000.

- **An extendable format** so that the directory can encompass new objects as operating systems and management functions continue to evolve. This means that the schema of the directory should be easy to modify.

- **Fault tolerance and a distributed database** so that you don't need to create numerous domains with primary domain controllers to receive updates and backup domain controllers to "hold the fort" when a PDC isn't available.

- **Scalability** so that management tasks can be centralized or distributed as your needs dictate.

- **Programmability**, which allows application developers and script writers an easy method of interfacing with the database.

- **Manageable security mechanisms**, from the small desktop system to the world-wide enterprise network that consists of millions of users.

But one of the most important features that large enterprises would like to see is a *standards-based implementation* so that you do not get locked into a single vendor for all your software needs. Migration tools, both to and from the directory database, are needed until the standards' issues settle down and products from different vendors work together as seamlessly as they do in the telephone network.

The question, then, is whether Windows 2000 will deliver a directory service that has all these features. The rest of this chapter discusses the methods that will be used to provide the features listed earlier.

From X.500 and DAP to the Lightweight Directory Access Protocol

When you think of standards does the name International Standards Organization (ISO) come to mind? Probably, because it has been involved in efforts for many years to help make the interchange of data between computers less of a proprietary chore and more of a free flow of information. The ISO along with the International Telecommunications Union (ITU) developed the X.500 group of standards to promulgate a global white pages directory service. Under the umbrella of X.500 there are many standards, which include naming conventions and networking protocols (OSI—the Open Systems Interconnection Protocol).

However, the OSI networking protocol never did take off as expected, though parts of it were implemented by some vendors. Digital Equipment Corporation (recently absorbed by Compaq Computer Corporation) tried for years to get OSI standards adopted by evolving its own proprietary networking protocol—DECnet—into an OSI-compliant protocol and by releasing an operating system (OSF) that was based on OSI standards. But, while all this discussion of standards was going on in committees and protocols were being discussed, debated, and refined, the Internet took off. And as everyone now knows, it is TCP/IP that glues the Internet together, not OSI.

It was not just the lack of interest in OSI network protocols that stifled the acceptance of X.500 proposals. Several other important factors were involved, such as the overhead associated with implementing many of the X.500 protocols. While X.500 does a good job defining a protocol, it does not attempt to define standard programming interfaces. (APIs make it easy for different vendors to write applications that implement the protocols.)

Another reason you won't find X.500 implemented in many places is its complicated naming scheme. The hierarchical organization of the directory, which can be seen in its naming format, is a good idea, but the long-winded name is not. For example, which of the following would you rather try to remember when sending someone an email message, the X.500 format or the RFC 822 name?

- X.500

  ```
  CN=John Doe,OU=Accounting,OU=Florida,O=mydomain,C=US
  ```

- RFC 822

  ```
  John.doe@domain.com
  ```

The X.500 name in this example reveals the organization structure of the directory, whereas the RFC 822 name does not. But every user shouldn't have to be fully cognizant of the directory structure in order to use it. If you want to send John Doe a message via email, you should not have to know that he works in the accounting department (organizational unit=accounting) and that he is in the company's Florida branch division (organizational unit=Florida). You shouldn't have to specify that he is in the United States because you have already indicated that he is in Florida! And, because you can have additional organizational units (OU=) in the directory, John Doe's address could actually have been much longer.

Directory services should make things easier, not more difficult. Microsoft Active Directory Services uses the hierarchical organization as spelled out by the X.500 protocols, but adapts the Windows NT domain system, by using DNS as a locator service, to the structure. In addition to the standard container types such as OU for organizational unit, Active Directory has a DC, or *domain component* container object, defined in the schema that can be used to house domains in the directory. By incorporating the domain into the directory rather than simply discarding it, Microsoft has made it easier for users of Windows NT 4.0 to make the migration to Windows 2000. Domains can be imported into the directory when migrating existing Windows NT networks.

The overhead associated with other X.500 recommendations needs also to be overcome. There were four "wire" (or communication) protocols defined:

- Directory Access Protocol (DAP)
- Directory System Protocol (DSP)
- Directory Information Shadowing Protocol (DISP)
- Directory Operational Binding Management Protocol (DOP)

These protocols were developed during a time in which PCs did not have sufficient computing power to host such complex protocols and still be capable of performing adequately as a desktop workstation.

To reduce the overhead associated with the X.500 directory structure, a new set of Request For Comments (RFCs) have been developed to define the Lightweight Directory Access Protocol (LDAP). LDAP is the protocol that Microsoft has chosen to implement in its Active Directory Services. While there have been several products available that use the features defined in LDAP v 2.0, Active Directory Services has been designed to be compatible with both version 2.0 and the newer proposed standard, LDAP v 3.0. A quick review of LDAP and X.500 can be found in Appendix F, "Overview of the X.500 and LDAP Protocols."

Note

Version 2.0 of the Lightweight Directory Access Protocol (LDAP) is defined by RFC 1777.

Version 3.0 of the Lightweight Directory Access (LDAP) Protocol is currently a proposed standard and has been adopted by most LDAP implementations. This LDAP version is defined by RFC 2251, "Lightweight Access Directory Protocol V 3," by Wahl, Howes, and Kille.

By using a standard that is being implemented by many other vendors, including Netscape and Novell, the Active Directory will be capable of exchanging data and queries with other directory service implementations; thus, you won't get stuck in yet another proprietary solution. Of course, this all depends on how Microsoft and other vendors choose to interpret and implement LDAP features as they are standardized and refined.

What Is the Schema?

If you are familiar with databases that are manipulated using the Structured Query Language (SQL), you may already understand what a schema is. Put simply, it is the definition of the types of things, or objects, that you can store in the directory structure. The directory contains many different types of objects, such as user accounts, printers, and computer accounts. Each object is made up of attributes that contain the specific data for the object. The schema is the definition of these objects, their attributes, and the classes to which they belong.

In some directory implementations the schema is stored as an ordinary ASCII text file. Each time the software that runs the directory is booted up the schema file is read into memory. One of the drawbacks of using this method is that if you want to make changes to the schema, you usually have to edit the text file and then reload it into the application. The Active Directory avoids this problem by defining the schema in the directory. You can manipulate the schema just as you do other objects in the directory.

Specifically, the Active Directory schema is made up of four types of objects that are used to define the schema.

- **Schema container object**—Each directory instance has at least one schema container object, which is a direct child of the directory root. The schema container holds the other objects, which describe the object classes and attributes of the directory.

- **Class container object**—This container object holds the object classes that define what kind of objects can be stored in the directory. Class objects reference property objects that store the actual properties, or attributes, of an object class.

- **Property object**—This type of object is used by the schema to define a particular attribute or property of the object. It references the syntax object.

■ **Syntax object**—This object describes a particular syntax that is applied to one or more properties defined by property objects.

Objects and Attributes

For the most part, an *object* is nothing more than a collection of specific attributes that hold the data the object represents. For example, an object that represents a user account contains attributes that hold information about the particular user. When you create user accounts in the Active Directory, you supply the same information that you did when you created user accounts using the User Manager for Domains in previous Windows versions. However, when viewing the property pages for a user account in the directory, you see that you can add much more information than was possible before. In Figure 48.1 you can see that there are eight tabs on the properties page for John Doe.

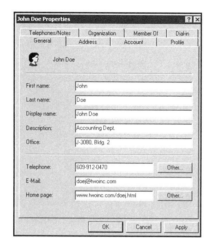

Figure 48.1   The Properties page for the Active Directory User object.

If you select each tab and look at the different fields, you can see that the user object now contains a wealth of information that can be quickly accessed by searching the directory, including the following:

■ **Who Is This User?**—The user's full name, logon name, and a description of the user. The user's title, department, company, manager, and reporting information.

■ **Address**—The office in which the user can be found, the user's address.

■ **Telephone**—Phone numbers, fax numbers, pagers, mobile phone, IP phone, email addresses, and home page URLs.

■ **Logon**—Which servers the user can logon to, during which hours, password information, and expiration and account information. The user's profile, logon path, and home directory.

■ **Dial-In**—Can this user log on via remote access? From where? Callback options and addressing information.

■ **Groups**—User groups to which this user belongs.

The main benefit of having this information available in the directory may not become apparent at first. Most of this information could have been found in the old User Manager utility, the Remote Access Administration utility, or in the Human Resources department. But now it can all be centrally located in a global, searchable directory. With the proper rights and authority, the administrator or user can search the directory for any of the attributes associated with users. And because the Active Directory schema can be extended, you can add additional attributes that contain information specific to your business.

For example, instead of being limited to queries such as "Show me everything about user John Doe," you can now execute queries such as "Show me all users that work in the Accounting department in Florida." or, "Show me all users who work in the Accounting department in Florida that are in the Administrators group and have dial-in access."

But the directory doesn't just contain information about users. It holds information about many different resource types in the network. An object that represents a printer resource might contain the name of the printer, the type of hardware associated with it, and its location. With directory services you do not have to even know the name of a printer. You can execute a query such as "Show me all printers located on the third floor of the Accounting department in the Florida office", and then pick the printer you want to use, based on the information returned from the query.

Another kind of object that can be found in the Active Directory is a container object. In the discussion of X.500 names in the previous section you will remember the term "organizational unit," or OU as it is represented in the X.500 naming scheme. An organizational unit is an object in the directory that holds, or contains, other objects. For example, in the Active Directory a domain is a container object. It holds other objects, some of which are container objects also, such as the Users object. The Users object holds the actual individual user accounts. It is in these instances of the User object that the attributes will be found which define each user on the system.

Attributes are the fine-grained details of the data stored in an object. Each attribute for an object holds a specific kind of data, and thus has a certain syntax associated with it. An attribute that is used to hold a person's name would have a syntax that requires a text string. The syntax would define a minimum and maximum length for the string. An attribute that represents a numeric value would have a syntax that specifies the minimum and maximum value of the number that can be stored in the object.

When a new class of objects is defined, you have the capability of creating two particular types of attributes: *required* or *optional*. If an attribute is of the required type, each object you create of the particular object class must have some value defined for the required attribute. However, there may be other attributes you want to define for the User object class which not all users would share. For example, you might want to keep a list of the names of the user's spouse and children. However, not all users will necessarily have a spouse or offspring, so this kind of attribute would be optional.

Standard Objects in the Directory

The Active Directory comes with two sets of standard objects: *container* and *leaf*.

Container objects hold other objects in the directory. Leaf objects are the endpoints in a directory tree that reference specific attributes about a directory entry. The standard container objects that you are most likely to encounter during day-to-day system management chores are

- Namespaces
- Country
- Locality
- Organization
- Organizational Unit
- Domain
- Computer

Standard leaf objects that are provided are

- User
- Group
- Alias
- Service
- Print Queue
- Print Device
- Print Job
- File Service
- File Share
- Session
- Resource

These built-in object classes give most of the functionality a small network will need when using the Active Directory to manage users, computers, and resources. If you need the capability of storing more or different types of information objects, you can modify the schema by using the Active Directory Schema Manager snap-in.

In addition to these typical objects that you will use to manage the directory and user and network resources, the directory contains hundreds of other objects that are used for many of the applications that interact with it. In Figure 48.2 you can see, using the Active Directory Schema Manager snap-in MMC tool, that the list of object classes in the directory is quite large.

Naming Objects in the Directory

There are two types of names that can be used to identify an object in the directory. The first is called the *distinguished name* (DN) and the second is the *relative distinguished name* (RDN). The relative distinguished name is just a value of a particular attribute of the object. For example, for user objects the RDN is the common name (CN) of the object. So, for the user object that holds account information for user John Doe, the RDN for the object would be John Doe. In the Active Directory there can be more than one John Doe, so there needs to be a method for telling them apart. The distinguished name is that method.

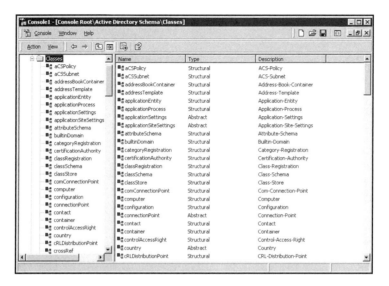

Figure 48.2 The list of object classes in the Active Directory is quite large.

A distinguished name consists of the RDN of the object, plus all the RDNs of every object of which it is an ancestor. Referring back to the X.500 address format, it quickly becomes apparent that the DN of an object not only uniquely identifies the object in the directory, but also reveals its location in the hierarchy.

The example given earlier showing how X.500 defines an object name shows the structure of a distinguished name:

```
CN=John Doe,OU=Accounting,OU=Florida,O=mydomain,C=US
```

Here the RDN of the user object is the common name John Doe. But the object John Doe is located in the container object named Accounting, which is located in the container object called Florida, which is located in the container object called mydomain, and so on. Although there can be more than one John Doe object in the directory, there can be only one object with the RDN of John Doe that is located in the Accounting department in Florida for this domain in the United States. If another John Doe comes to work in that department, he will have to use a different name! There is an easier way around this, of course. When assigning usernames to employees, many companies already use a combination of letters rather than an employee's full name. For example, John Doe might be assigned a username of doej, using the last name plus the first letter of the first name. If another John Doe is hired, a variation on this can be performed by assigning the new employee the username doej2.

However, another distinct John Doe might work in the Manufacturing department in the same organization. For example

```
CN=John Doe,OU=Manufacturing,OU=Florida,O=mydomain,C=US
```

is a perfectly legal distinguished name and can reside in the same directory database as the first John Doe.

Modifying the Schema

The schema in the Active Directory is stored in the directory. The schema comes preconfigured with the types of objects that you need to set up the Windows 2000 server and manage a network of computers. However, the Active Directory is flexible and extensible in that you can modify the existing objects to use new attributes, or you can create new object classes that contain information of almost any kind.

The directory should not be thought of as simply a glorified user database. You can create objects that are used by application programs. Sharing information between different applications can become much easier if the same configuration database is being used. Rather than having a conversion utility of some sort to transfer information between different applications, they can now be written, using the application programming interfaces provided for the Active Directory, to store that information in the directory database.

You can add objects or attributes to store data in the directory that is shared by different applications so that you do not need duplicate databases scattered around that get out-of-synch with constant updating. Extending the schema to include additional employee information, such as vacation schedules, sick time, and pay rates, can allow payroll applications to share the same data with other employee management software. The Accounting department and the Legal department can always be sure they are working with the same set of data if there are no duplicates lying around that can become unsynchronized because of an application failure or user error.

The MMC snap-in that you use to examine or modify the schema is called the Active Directory Schema Manager. Unlike other MMC snap-in tools, such as the Directory Management or the Computer Management snap-ins, this one is not found under the Administrative Tools option in the Start menu. The reasoning behind that is simple: Tools that are used to add or modify user or computer accounts will probably be used frequently by the network administrator. Making changes to the schema will probably be performed only on rare occasions, such as when a new object or attribute is needed by the development of a new directory-aware application.

To start the Active Directory Schema Manager, click Start, Run. The program to run is MMC. When the Microsoft Management Console application appears, use the Console button, and then Add/Remove Snap-in. Select to Add a snap-in and, from the list that is presented, select Active Directory Schema Manager.

In Figure 48.2 earlier in this chapter you saw the extensive list of objects in the schema. In Figure 48.3 you see the snap-in with the attributes category highlighted instead.

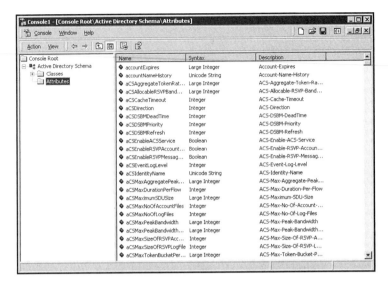

Figure 48.3 The schema is composed of objects and attributes.

When you are using the schema manager snap-in, you can view the details about a particular object or attribute by double-clicking on it or by right-clicking and selecting Properties from the pop-up menu. For example, Figure 48.4 shows the Properties sheet for the User object class. This is the object type that is used to store user accounts in the Active Directory.

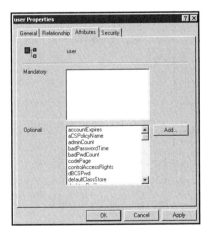

Figure 48.4 The Properties sheet shows which attributes are mandatory and which are optional.

In Figure 48.4 you can see that for each object you can have attributes that are either optional or required. All objects in the directory of a particular class must each have values for all the attributes required by the object class. The optional attributes may be used if you need them.

In Figure 48.3 you saw a list of the attributes that are defined in the directory. When you modify or create a new object in the schema, you can select from these attributes or create a new attribute. Note that each attribute has a particular syntax associated with it, which defines the type of data that the attribute can hold. Figure 48.5 shows the dialog box associated with creating a new attribute for the directory.

Figure 48.5   It's easy to add new attributes using the Schema Manager.

Caution

Modifying the schema is not a task that should be delegated to an uninformed employee. It is easy to add new objects and attributes whenever you want. However, if you are not intimately familiar with the directory you may find that over time you have added superfluous duplicate entries. If the same information can be stored in more than one attribute, it makes searching the directory much more difficult because you must know all the duplicates to search.

Removing an object or attribute from the directory is not something that should be done casually. If your organization creates internal application programs that are written to use ADSI to interface with the directory, you should be sure to implement a program that tracks changes to the schema so that you can always quickly ascertain the uses of a particular customized object or attribute.

What Is a Domain Tree? What Is a Forest?

The active directory gives you one single enterprise-wide namespace. This namespace is used for user accounts, resource objects, application configuration information, and so on. What you decide to store in the directory, beyond the default objects set up by the installation process, is up to you. The namespace can be global, provided you organize your domains into a domain tree.

A domain tree is nothing more than a method of organizing the domains in your enterprise into a structure so that they all share a common directory schema and a *contiguous* namespace. While a domain tree is a structure formed by a collection of domains, a forest is a collection of domain trees. The namespace in the forest does not have to be contiguous, as it does in the tree, so a forest can be used to link together disparate domain trees in the organization so that trust relationships can still be used to allow a single user logon in the network.

To understand what a domain tree or a forest is, you must know what it is replacing in the Windows NT networking scheme.

Domain Models—May They Rest in Peace!

In previous versions of Windows NT, the domain was used to group users and resources together with a common security policy to simplify administrative tasks. In large organizations, a single domain was not sufficient to hold all the users and resources and was not an efficient method of administering user rights and privileges or resource protections. Because of this, multiple domains were created and linked together in what is termed a *trust relationship*. This trust relationship allowed users from one domain to be granted access rights to resources in another trusting domain.

A trust relationship could be a one-way or a two-way relationship. In a one-way trust relationship one domain would trust the users that had been authenticated by another domain. The administrator in the trusting domain could grant users (or groups of users) from the trusted domain access rights in the local trusting domain. In a two-way trust relationship, users of the relationship existed in both directions. The trust relationship is not transitive. That is, if domain A has a trust relationship that allows its users to be assigned rights in domain B, and if domain B has a trust relationship that allows its users to be assigned rights to resources in domain C, user in domain A cannot be granted rights in domain C by use of these trust relationships. That would require that domain A establish a separate trust relationship with domain C.

The way domains were organized into user or resource domains and how the trust relationships were set up led to the development of several domain models that could be used, depending on the size of your enterprise and the methods used to administer them. These were the single domain, multiple domain, master domain, and multiple-master domain models.

Because the domain was essentially the boundary for the security accounts manager (SAM) database, you had two basic choices. You could put all your user accounts into a single master domain, and then grant them access rights to objects in resource domains, or you could put users into separate domains, depending on your organization, and maintain a complicated set of trust relationships and administrative policies.

The headache associated with managing multiple trust relationships and moving users to and from when reorganizations occurred is one of the major drawbacks of the SAM-based domain models.

The Directory Is Partitioned by Domain

When you install Windows NT Server and create a new domain, you are given several choices concerning how the domain will relate to an Active Directory tree. You can create a new forest or become part of an existing forest and create a new tree, making this new domain the first domain in the new tree. Or, you can make the new domain a child domain in a domain tree that already exists in the forest.

Each domain in the domain tree is a security boundary in the Active Directory, just as it is in previous versions of Windows NT. However, you no longer have to create one- or two-way trust relationships between domains in order for users to be granted access rights and privileges in other domains that are in the same domain tree.

When a Windows 2000 domain joins a domain tree, a *two-way transitive trust relationship*, based on the Kerberos security authentication method, is automatically established between the child domain and its parent domain in the tree. Because the trust relationship is *transitive*, there is no need to manually configure additional trust relationships with other domains that exist in the domain tree. This means that once your domain is created and joined to a domain tree, your users can be granted access rights to resources in any other domain in the tree without the need to further create a complicated set of trust relationships with other domains.

Note

The MIT Kerberos (version 5) authentication method is defined in RFC 1510, "The Kerberos Network Authentication Service (V5)," by Kohl and Neuman.

Each domain in the tree holds the portion of the active directory database that represents the objects found in that domain. However, the namespace is contiguous throughout the tree. Each domain controller in the domain holds a complete replica of the directory for that domain. And, to help reduce network traffic and administrative overhead, you can create additional replicas of the domain's portion of the directory and place it close to users in other domains that make frequent access of the resources in your domain.

A Domain Is Still a Domain

The domain in Windows 2000 is still a security boundary, just like it was in previous Windows NT implementations. Domain administrators can still take command and exert their authority over all users and resources in the domain. From that perspective, nothing has changed.

However, the management of your relationships with other domains is now much easier. The two-way transitive trust relationships are set up automatically, so you don't have to coordinate managing this with other administrators throughout the network. If you upgrade from a previous version of Windows NT, all your groups and users are migrated into the Active Directory under your same domain. You can manage them as you always have, though, there are new tools (MMC) that are used.

Trees and Forests

As discussed earlier in this section, a domain tree is a collection of domains that have a contiguous namespace, while trees in a forest can have a non-contiguous namespace. By contiguous namespace I mean that the object in each child domain in the tree has the name of its parent domains prefixed to its distinguished name. This also means that the names used to identify each child domain will have the names of the parents prefixed. In Figure 48.6 you can see an example of a domain tree. The domain tree starts at the top and flows down the tree, rather than from the bottom up.

In this domain tree the most-senior parent in the tree is the acme.com domain. Beneath that are three child domains, nj.acme.com, ny.acme.com, and tx.acme.com. Under the New York child domain you can see a sales domain (sales.ny.acme.com) and another domain called export.ny.acme.com. This tree could be further expanded by adding additional child domains to any of the domains in the tree. The way you construct the fully-qualified domain name for a domain positions it in the tree structure.

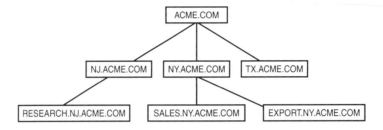

Figure 48.6 A domain tree is a contiguous namespace.

In the best of all possible worlds, each enterprise would have exactly one domain tree and one large contiguous namespace. However, in this rapid paced business world nothing remains the same for long, including business organizational units. Corporate mergers and acquisitions, for example, can bring in large numbers of users and resources that must be incorporated quickly into the network structure. In this situation, it may not be possible to easily include the acquired assets into the naming structure.

But you can still join two disparate domain trees together. You can't put them into the same tree because the naming for all objects would not be contiguous. You can, however, join domain trees into a structure called a forest.

A forest is like a domain tree, but the namespace does not have to be contiguous throughout the forest. The directory schema is still common for all domains, and you can establish trust relationships between the trees. Users can still use a single logon to access resources in domains that reside in different domain trees (see Figure 48.7).

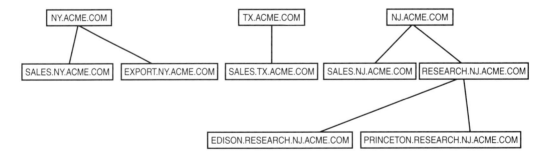

Figure 48.7 Domain trees with disjointed namespaces can exist in a forest.

The Active Directory and Dynamic DNS

DNS, or the Domain Name Service, is the most widely-used address/name translation service in the world and is used on the Internet. This service was created many years ago when the first DARPA network, the predecessor of today's Internet, experienced rapid growing pains and needed a distributed naming service that could be used to locate the address of any server in the network.

The Backbone of the Internet and the Active Directory

The Internet has grown so large in the past five years that without a distributed naming service it would be almost impossible to keep track of all nodes in the network, much less the services they offer. DNS has evolved to contain many different types of records that can be used to translate names to addresses. These include not only names of servers or workstations on the Net, but also services, such as World Wide Web, email, and others.

Dynamic DNS

Administering a large number of , computers in a network can be quite a chore. Moving a computer from one network subnet to another used to require that the administrator manually reconfigure the DNS servers in the enterprise so that they could accurately translate the computer's name to its correct address. With the advent of mobile computing and the proliferation of laptops that are here today, gone tomorrow, reconfiguring network addresses can become a full-time job on a large network.

The Dynamic Host Configuration Protocol (DHCP) solves part of this problem by allowing a computer to request a network address, along with other configuration information, when it boots into the network. However, this doesn't completely solve the problems that arise as the result of mobile computing. After the client computer has obtained network address and configuration information, how does it communicate that information to other computers so that they can locate it on the network?

In early versions of Windows NT the Windows Internet Naming Service (WINS) is the answer to this problem. After a computer boots it can contact a WINS server, which acts very much like a dynamic DNS server. It accepts registrations from clients and stores or updates their information so that other computers can query the database to find the client's network address.

In Windows 2000 you can still usethe WINS service, which might be helpful for downstream clients if you have a mixed network of Windows 2000 and Windows NT 4.0 computers. However, Windows 2000 comes with an updated version of Microsoft's DNS, which includes the capability to dynamically update the DNS database.

Note

Dynamic Updates to the DNS database is defined in RFC 2136. This RFC defines the UPDATE opcode and a format to be used as the update message, along with procedures that can be used to implement dynamic DNS.

How the Active Directory Uses DNS

The active directory uses DNS to keep track of domain controllers. DNS is used as a locator service as well as a name/address translation service. Remember that the active directory provides a service to its users via the LDAP protocol. Services can be recorded in DNS via Service Resource Records (SRV RRs), and this is how the active directory uses DNS.

Note

SRV Service Resource Records are defined by RFC 2052, "A DNS RR for specifying the location of services (DNS SRV)," by Gulbrandsen and Vixie.

An SRV RR record consists of data in the format of

```
<service name>.<protocol>.<domain>
```

Because the active directory uses LDAP, a resource record for this service would look like this:

```
LDAP.TCP.biznesnet.com
```

Because the DNS that is provided with Windows 2000 is a dynamic DNS, there is no associated administrative work when you add domain controllers to your network. Each domain controller automatically contacts a DNS server and provides it with the necessary information to register its name, address, and the services it offers. Each domain controller also checks back at frequent intervals to make sure that the information is accurate and will make changes to the DNS information as changes are made on the server.

One thing to note about the use of DNS as a locator service is that you do not have to use Microsoft's own DNS server in order to have an Active Directory enabled network. The DNS product that you use, however, must support SRV records because this is how domain controllers advertise themselves to the network. The DNS you use does not have to use dynamic DNS functions, however. This just makes the DNS administrator's life a lot easier in a rapidly changing environment.

Using Sites to Manage Large Enterprises

If you are familiar with the concept of a site, as used by Microsoft Exchange, you are going to have to change that idea in your mind when you start to deal with the new site concept that is used by Windows 2000 networking. In Microsoft Exchange, a site is composed of servers which all share a common namespace.

But in Windows 2000, a site is nothing more than a collection of well-connected computers that exist on an IP subnet, and which usually are located close to each other geographically. The grouping of computers into sites is done to make replication fast and efficient. It is not a concept that relates to managing or administering users, resources, or network security. Two important things to remember about a site, as used by Windows 2000 are

■ A domain can have computers in more than one site.

■ A site can contain computers from more than one domain.

Windows 2000 uses only domain controllers to hold the Active Directory database. There is no longer a primary domain controller that controls writing or modifying directory information and backup domain controllers that provide a read-only service to users and computers. In Windows 2000 all domain controllers can receive updates to the database and the changes are then replicated to all other domain controllers that participate in the directory tree.

The Knowledge Consistency Checker service is run on every domain controller and it is this service that establishes connections with other domain controllers within the site to make sure that directory replication can occur. Although the administrator can manually configure connections, the consistency checker will automatically establish new connections when it determines that there is a hole in the replication topology within a site.

The administrative tool that is used to control how servers participate in directory replication is the Active Directory Sites and Services Manager. This MMC snap-in allows you to

- Add new sites and subnets, and associate a site name with a subnet
- Show all the sites that exist throughout the enterprise
- Show all the servers that are contained in each site
- Create and display the links between servers and the links between sites, including the protocols that are used for replication
- Show the timing values used to schedule replication
- Manage subnets

Note

Sites are represented in the Active Directory database and are defined by the site object. Although all computers in the directory have a computer object, domain controllers also have a server object. This server object is a child object of the site object that represents the site the domain controller is assigned to.

Directory Replication

Although LDAP v 3.0 is a proposed Internet standard, there is not (yet) an agreed upon method for replicating data between directory servers. For the Windows 2000 implementation of directory services, Microsoft is using a proprietary method called multimaster replication.

In previous versions of Windows NT, primary domain controllers were responsible for updates to the directory database (the old SAM). Additions or modifications to the database were made on the PDC and at regular intervals replicated to backup domain controllers throughout the network. The most obvious disadvantage this system has is that without a PDC, no changes can be made to the database. When a PDC becomes unavailable, because of its own failure or possible network failure, users can still log on because they can be authenticated by a BDC. However, if you have a large enterprise, perhaps a global one, it is almost necessary to have a PDC at every geographical site where frequent changes occur or an extremely good network infrastructure.

In Windows 2000, any domain controller can receive updates or additions to the active directory database. These changes are propagated to other domain controllers based on *update sequence numbers (USNs)*. The USN is a 64-bit number used by the active directory to determine which updates are the most recent. In addition to the server's USN, each property (or attribute) in the database has its own property version number. These two numbers are used by multimaster replication to ensure that updates are correctly applied throughout the enterprise.

Because all replicas of the directory database can be written to, it is possible that a change can be made before a previous change has been fully replicated throughout the enterprise. Some directory databases use time stamps to determine which update is the most recent. This method requires that every server be tightly synchronized with all other servers with respect to the correct time. Windows 2000 does provide a time service that can be used to synchronize servers, but, with one exception: The time stamp is not the method used to determine which is the correct update to apply to a directory update message.

Each server in network has its own USN, which it advances when it makes an update to the directory. Each server also stores a table of USNs—the highest USN it has received during previous replications from each server in the network. When replication starts, a server requests from other servers only those changes that have a higher USN than the one it has stored for each server during previous replication sessions. This minimizes the amount of information that needs to be exchanged between servers during the replication procedure. Because each server knows exactly which changes it has received from every other server in the network, replication between servers is efficient.

This method also allows a server to recover quickly when it crashes or some other failure, such as a network failure, occurs. All it has to do is to request updates that are greater than the USN it has stored for the other servers in the network. This means that a full replication between servers is not necessary in the event of a catastrophe.

Property Version Numbers come into play when a specific attribute is modified on more than one replica of the database within a short period of time, before the replication service can update the change on all nodes. Remember that with the active directory's distributed nature, each domain controller holds a writable copy of the directory database. Property version numbers are only incremented on the server on which the change is actually made. It is not incremented on a server that is receiving it as an update.

The only time a time stamp is used during multimaster replication is when a collision occurs. This happens when a server receives an update message from another server, and although the property version numbers are the same, the contents of the attribute are not. In this case, and only in this case, the time stamp on the update is used. If the update message has a time stamp later than the value stored with the property, the update is applied to the data, otherwise it is discarded.

Summarizing the Directory Data Using the Global Catalog

The active directory is scalable to millions of objects. The directory is partitioned, into domains, because it would be very difficult to store a complete copy of the entire directory database on a single server. Of course, with the advances being made in CPU speed and storage capabilities, this may be possible in the future, but for the time being it is not practical.

One of the assumptions behind the partitioning of the directory is the fact that most queries that are made to the directory are for local information. Users generally want to locate a printer or another resource that is near them. Occasionally it may be desirable to locate a printer that resides in a different geographical location, but for the most part queries are for local resources.

To satisfy a query for information that cannot be found in the local portion of the active directory, it is necessary to query every other partition of the directory until the information is found.

This too can be an impractical method. In a large enterprise, moderate use of this type of query, whereby the entire database is searched, could cause significant network and CPU resource consumption.

The *global catalog* is the answer that Microsoft has implemented to solve this problem. The global catalog is a subset of the entire directory. It holds entries for every object that exists in all partitions of the directory, but it contains only selected attributes for each object. If your query cannot be satisfied by querying the global catalog, the query will have to be resolved by searching a portion of or possibly the entire directory database.

Active Directory Service Interfaces (ADSI)

To make it easy to directory-enable any application, Microsoft has provided Active Directory Services Interface. ADSI is a collection of several interfaces that can be used to access the Active Directory from within executable application programs. Programmers might want to use ADSI instead of the LDAP C API because ADSI makes it possible to write an application that can access directory services from multiple providers. If the directory service provider has designed their directory service product to be compliant with at least version 2.0 of LDAP, ADSI should be capable of providing an interface into the directory.

In addition to providing access to Microsoft directory products (such as Exchange Server 5.5), ADSI has also been tested by Microsoft against

- Netscape Directory Server 1.0
- University of Michigan's SLAPD Server
- Novell's LDAP-enabled NDS product

ADSI provides an interface that allows all the functionality of the LDAP C API, but does so in a manner that is easier to understand and write to. Another reason for using ADSI in application development is that ADSI can be used by many higher level programming languages, including Microsoft Visual BASIC, Perl, Rexx, and C or C++.

Internet

You can try before you buy with ADSI—Microsoft has a online version of the *Active Directory Programmers Guide*. You can view sections of the guide online or download the Word document. Go to the MSDN Web site and use the SEARCH capability to find it:

```
http://msdn.microsoft.com/developer/default.htm
```

ADSI uses the Component Object Model (COM) interface to allow programmers to access and manipulate the underlying directory objects found in multiple directory services. A program written using ADSI should function correctly with any directory service for which ADSI has a provider interface.

Directory-Aware Application Programming

ADSI is one of the features of Microsoft's development of Active Directory Services that may benefit large enterprises the greatest. If the Active Directory were limited to specific types of objects or attributes that could be stored in the directory, and if only programs supplied by Microsoft were able to access and manipulate the directory store, there wouldn't be much to say about Active Directory beyond it being a major improvement in the administration of NT servers and clients.

However, if properly employed, using ADSI to incorporate application program configuration information into the directory database along with other types of data, can produce real cost benefits in a large network. For example

- Many applications use similar configuration information that is duplicated in each application's specific configuration data file (or, possibly registry entries). Information about computers and locales can be stored in the directory, along with other configuration information, and shared by many applications.

- Shared information that is already stored in the directory can be shared by ADSI-aware applications. User information is already stored in user objects in the Active Directory. By extending this object and adding attributes, you can create a customized user object that can be used by applications unique to your environment. Eliminating redundant resources of information can also help to ensure a greater accuracy in your database because data needs to be updated only once in a single location.

- Applications that depend on central configuration databases found on servers in the network can benefit from reduced downtime. If a server that contains configuration data files goes offline, clients must wait for the server to return to working order. If the clients use the Active Directory, replicas of the directory can be configured so that the loss of a server is no longer a point of failure.

- Applications can "publish" themselves in the Active Directory, listing the services that they can give to clients and the information needed to use the service. In a volatile network in which users move frequently, reconfiguring applications can be simplified by having the application programmed to locate the information it needs for the new locale.

The types of applications that can benefit by using the Active Directory are many. Human Resource departments and Security departments can share a common user database resource by storing information in the directory. System management products can be written to access the information already contained in directory user and computer objects.

Preparing to Upgrade to Windows 2000

Fortunately, when you upgrade your network to Windows 2000, you don't have to jump in and do it all at once. The Windows 2000 Active Directory is backward-compatible with previous Windows NT Server domain controllers. You can choose to upgrade only a few servers at a time while you test the waters on the migration to Windows 2000.

In the past, domains were used to group resources and users into manageable units for administrative control. The Active Directory provides for enhanced security mechanisms, such as the capability to delegate security administration, and a new method of grouping users and resources—the Organizational Unit (OU). These two features can make it easy to reduce the number of domains you have in an existing network as you migrate to a network that will eventually be totally managed using the Active Directory.

Several things must be considered when you are deciding on how to arrange your domains for the migration. These include

- **Existing namespaces**—Do you already have registered Internet domain names in use at your company? Do you have more than one namespace, that is, `acme.com` and `acme-mfg.com`? The Active Directory uses DNS style names rather than NetBIOS style names to name domains.

- **Number of users in the network**—Although the Active Directory is scalable to many millions of objects, hardware capacity and network bandwidth will still limit the numbers of objects any particular domain can handle efficiently.

- **Structure of the organization**—Many existing Windows NT networks make use of domains to model the business' organization structure. In the Active Directory the OU can perform this function.

- **Geographical separation**—If you have a large enterprise with many users separated into distinct geographical sites, you may use either multiple domains to accommodate them or choose to use Active Directory *sites* and a single domain.

Now Its Just Domain Controllers and Member Servers

When you create a domain controller using Windows 2000 Server, you no longer have to do so during the installation of the operating system. And, to make things even easier, you no longer have to create primary and backup domain controllers. In Windows 2000 networking there is no distinction made as to primary or backup domain controllers. Instead, each domain controller in a domain (and there can be as many as you need) holds a complete copy of the domain's partition of the Active Directory. Updates can be made at any domain controller and updates are propagated using multimaster replication to all other domain controllers in the domain.

Remember that in the Active Directory domain names are expressed as DNS style names. That is, instead of naming a domain `acme`, for example, it is now named `acme.com`, which is a DNS style name. When you create a tree of domains in the Active Directory, you must use a hierarchical DNS naming scheme so that you maintain a contiguous namespace.

Each domain in the tree is a subdomain of the top-most domain. The domain tree provides a two-way transitive trust relationship between all domains that exist in the tree. Inheritance of security rights flows downward from the top of the tree, so you can assign users administrative access rights and permissions at a single point in the tree, and therefore grant them the same rights for child objects further down the tree.

When you have a network that is composed of disparate namespaces you can create separate trees and group them into a forest. A forest, as you will recall, is a collection of domain trees. In this type of organization each individual domain tree represents a contiguous namespace, but other disjointed namespaces are in the network. A domain forest is used in a similar manner to a domain tree, in that users can still be granted access rights in domains that are contained in other domain trees. The main difference between a domain tree and a forest is the disjointed namespaces.

Replication of Directory Information

Active Directory domain controllers replicate, via multimaster replication techniques, all changes to the domain's portion of the directory database to all other domain controllers in the domain. Domain controllers for other domains in the domain tree do not receive these replication updates because they are responsible only for the portion of the directory database that concerns objects in their respective domains.

However, all domain controllers in a particular domain tree do receive replication updates that concern the *metadata,* which defines the domain tree. For example, when a new domain joins a domain tree, or when a domain is detached from one part of the tree and reattached at another part, this information is replicated to other domain controllers in the domain tree.

Model the Directory Structure After Your Business Organization

The main points to consider when grouping users and resources is how you want to administer them and what this will do to impact the network traffic associated with logon authentication and directory information replication.

Do you want to create a network that allows centralized or decentralized control? In Windows NT domains were used to allow you to group users and resources into convenient, manageable units that share a common security policy. With the X.500 naming hierarchy adopted by the Active Directory, you might find that you can now get by with fewer domains, while using other methods, such as OUs, to make administration more flexible.

Having a single domain and using OUs to divide users and resources for administrative control purposes is a good idea if the network is connected by high-speed links. If your network is widely dispersed throughout the world, you should, of course, take into consideration the replication traffic that will occur when changes are made to the database. If frequent changes to the database occur, you might want to consider using separate domains to house users and resources in different locations so that only the domain tree metadata becomes the object of replication.

For example, suppose a manufacturer has just decided to upgrade all its business sites to Windows 2000 and use the Active Directory to manage resources. The sales office is located in New York and two manufacturing sites are located in Dallas. The user base at the Dallas site has a much higher turnover rate than that for the New York site. Because users at each site mainly access only resources local to their site, it makes sense to use two domains, one for each geographical site. Using two domains also keeps replication traffic between the sites to a minimum because the frequent changeover of users at the Dallas site do not need to be replicated to the New York site.

Later, the company decides to open another manufacturing plant in San Antonio. A high-speed leased line is installed between the Dallas and San Antonio sites because both plants will be sharing a lot of information between them. The Dallas domain is expanded to include the San Antonio users. However, a separate OU is used for each of these sites so users can be managed easily by local managers for each site. Because both of these OUs reside in the same domain, controlling user access to domain resources is a simple task, no matter which site the user is located in.

Domains Are Just a Part of the Namespace

A domain in the Active Directory is basically a partition of the namespace. The namespace consists of all domains in the domain tree of which the domain is a member. In the Active Directory, each domain controller in the domain holds a complete replica of that domain's partition of the directory database. Each domain is responsible for holding directory information about users, resources, and other objects defined in the domain. The global catalog allows users in other domains in the domain tree the ability to quickly locate resources that are entered in other partitions, or domains, of the tree.

Note

You are not stuck with your initial decision when you set up a domain tree or forest. The Active Directory uses a unique number, the Globally Unique Identifier (GUID), to identify each domain in the network. Because this identifier is used throughout the network to uniquely identify the domain, the directory allows you to add, delete, or change domain names easily as your organization or network changes. Because each domain can be easily identified by its GUID, you can make changes to the shape of the domain tree or forest by moving domains around and reattaching them at different points to match your current needs.

Another important characteristic of a domain is the domain security policy. You define certain characteristics of the security policy, such as the password history and account lockout values, on a domain-by-domain basis. You cannot assign different account lockout values, for example, on an OU basis.

Organizational Units Allow for Delegation of Control

OUs are container objects in the Active Directory. A container object is an object that can hold other objects in the directory. An OU can hold other organizational units and container objects, as well as leaf objects in the directory. Leaf objects are the endpoints in the tree structure of the directory, such a users, or printers, applications, and other resources.

Tip

In the Active Directory you can use the OU to subdivide portions of the directory; by doing so you can reduce the number of domains that you need.

In Windows NT you use the domain to group together users and resources so that they can be managed as a unit. Within a domain you can grant certain users the rights to perform system management and administrative tasks, such as creating user accounts or adding computers to the domain. However, this administrative control is domain-wide. For example, if you grant a user account the right to modify user accounts, that user can modify any user account in the domain.

OUs allow you to further subdivide a domain and grant these same user rights based on the OU instead of the entire domain. This finer granularity of control can make it possible for you to get by with fewer domains in situations where you have a large number of user groupings you want to use for administrative control purposes. Instead of creating a domain for the Accounting department, the Human Resources department, and the Manufacturing department, you can instead create one domain, and then assign administrative privileges by OUs to allow each department to control its own resources.

Migration Considerations: Centralized Versus Decentralized Management

When planning the domain layout for your organization, you should consider the type of management control (centralized versus decentralized), security policies, and the network infrastructure. Although it is generally a good idea to create a larger number of domains when you want to decentralize administrative functions, remember that in the Active Directory you can use the OU to accomplish much the same thing.

When deciding whether to use many or fewer domains as the basis for dividing resources and users, consider what happens on the domain level. Each domain controller in a domain holds a complete copy of the domain's portion of the directory database. Replication between domain controllers happens only within a domain. That is, when you add a new user, file, or print resource, the information is replicated via multimaster replication to all other domain controllers in the domain. The information is *not* replicated outside of the domain to domain controllers in other domains. Thus, by using a larger number of domains for geographically dispersed networks, you can reduce replication traffic.

Security policy is also implemented on a domain basis. If different departments in your business have widely varying security requirements, you may need to use the domain as a tool for organizing users and resources. You cannot define different password history values or set a security policy of how strong a password needs to be based on the OU.

Delegation of Administrative Rights Reduces the Need for Multiple Domains

In Windows NT, you will remember that there are several built-in domain groups that can be used to grant administrative rights to users. These included the all-powerful Domain Admins group, whose members can perform all administrative functions in the domain, down to the Account Operators or Backup Operators groups. Although having these built-in user groups made it easy to grant specific users only a portion of the administrative rights that are possible in a domain, the drawback is that these rights exist throughout the domain. For example, if a user is a member of the Account Operators group, the user can potentially modify any user account in the domain (other than the Administrator accounts).

The Active Directory provides for a finer granularity in the delegation of administrative rights, down to the level of the organizational unit. Because user accounts are not stored in the registry-based SAM anymore, but instead are objects in the directory database, you can grant or deny administrative privileges on specific portions of the directory tree.

Two important concepts to understand about administrative privileges in the Active Directory are

- Per-property access rights
- Inheritance of access rights

Each object in the Active Directory can have an ACL attached to it, which defines who is allowed to perform specific functions on the object. This access can be defined down to the property level. This means that you can grant a specific user the ability to manage all aspects of user account management for a particular container object (OU), or the ability to modify selected properties of user objects within the container, such as the users' passwords or default directories.

Each object in the directory is made up of specific attributes, called properties. Each property is a single type of information about the object. You can grant or deny administrative privileges on each and every property of a particular object type. To make things even easier, you can also grant or deny administrative privileges on groups of properties. The *property set* attribute of the schema defines groups of properties that can be administered together. If the default definitions of this attribute do not meet your needs, you can modify the schema.

Inheritance of access rights is another concept that makes delegating administrative authority more convenient. If you think of the Active Directory as a hierarchical structure, organized in a tree fashion, you can pick a particular point in the tree and grant access rights to a user from that point. The administrative rights flow down the tree to include other container objects and finally down to the end leaf objects of the tree. When a new child object is created in the directory tree, the access rights that apply to the container object that holds the child object are included with the default access rights created on the child object.

This method of inheritance allows for faster authentication time when the operating system needs to determine access rights. It is not necessary to trace back up the hierarchy through all parent objects to determine the access rights of a particular child object. The child object contains all the information that is required to perform an access right check.

Implementing a Migration to the Active Directory

As with any major network upgrade project, you should be sure to carefully plan ahead. Develop a written master plan and schedule for the migration, and review it on a frequent basis. Some of the items to consider in a migration plan include

- **Back-Out procedures**—For any big changes you make on a particular server, be sure that you plan a method to back out the change if it does not function as you expect. *Always* maintain up-to-date backups of key systems that can be used to make a full restoration without seriously impacting the user base.

- **Alternative plans**—Sometimes there is more than one way to effect a solution to a problem. If you can make note of more than one method of accomplishing a particular task, such as the ability to schedule users or resources for the project, the flexibility will allow you to adapt to changes in the project schedule.

- **Assign users and resources carefully**—When you make decisions about which personnel are going to be used to execute portions of the project plan, be sure to keep in mind the existing workload of the person and how participating in the upgrade migration plan will affect their job. Again, it is a good idea to have a "backup" person or backup resource that you can use if unforeseen events limit their capabilities.

- **A well-defined team structure**—There should be a migration team that has a designated leader and assigned duties and areas of responsibility for each member. Nothing makes executing a migration plan more difficult than personality conflicts that can arise from the nonspecific assigning of duties to team members.

Upgrade the Primary Domain Controller First

When you decide to upgrade your network to a Windows 2000 Active Directory-based network you will need to plan the order in which servers and workstations will be upgraded. The Active Directory-based Windows 2000 domain controller is backward-compatible with Windows NT 4.0 domain controllers, so upgrading the PDC will be transparent to the users. Any backup domain controllers in the domain will see the new Active Directory domain controller as if it were a PDC in the domain. That is, once you upgrade a server to be a Windows 2000 Active Directory domain controller, you will not be able, in the same domain, to promote a BDC to become a PDC. The new Active Directory domain controller provides this capability as far as Windows NT 4.0 BDCs are concerned.

Note

Although you cannot promote a Windows NT 4.0 type of BDC to become a PDC when a Windows 2000 Active Directory domain controller has been incorporated into the domain and is online and functioning, you can perform the promotion if the Windows 2000 Active Directory domain controller goes offline. Remember that the down-level NT 4.0 domain controllers see the new Active Directory domain controller just like an NT 4.0 PDC.

Upgrade the Domain's PDC, and Then Any BDCs

When you upgrade the PDC to become an Active Directory domain controller, you are prompted to either join an existing domain tree or create a new domain tree. If this is the first Active Directory domain controller in the network, you will have to create a new domain tree. The operation is a simple, painless one—there is no complicated setup or configuration required to create a domain tree.

After you have created the first Active Directory domain controller from the domain's PDC, you will have a mixed network environment that can still function normally from the user's standpoint. That is, users can still authenticate using the BDCs that remain in the domain. However, because the BDCs do not yet recognize the Active Directory database, but instead see it as a PDC, you still will be unable to create new security principals, such as user accounts, on them. You will have to do so on the new Active Directory domain controller just as you did when it was a PDC.

The new Active Directory domain controller will use the single-master replication method to inform any existing BDCs of changes to the security database. After you promote one or more BDCs to become Active Directory domain controllers in the domain, you can update the security database on any of those new domain controllers because they are all equal peers in the network. Multimaster replication will be used only between the new Active Directory domain controllers.

After you have finally converted all your BDCs to be Active Directory domain controllers and have made the switch to the Windows 2000 Active Directory, from that point on only multimaster replication will occur. This implies that you will no longer be able to add Windows NT Server 4.0 domain controllers to the domain. If you are uncertain about the migration, leave at least one Windows NT 4.0 BDC in the domain and operate in a mixed environment until you are sure that the change over is working like you expect, and you have no need to downgrade back to a Windows NT 4.0-based network.

Tip

You should always keep a "door open" when implementing new technology. When you make the final decision to go with the Active Directory and forego the Windows NT PDC/BDC networking method, keeping an old BDC around may be a lifesaver if something goes wrong. To provide this open door using a BDC you do not have to keep the old BDC online in the new network. Instead, before you make the final switch, take a BDC offline. That is, turn it off or disconnect it from the network. Keep it around for a few months until you are absolutely sure you do not need to downgrade out of the Active Directory. If some disastrous event occurs that forces you to back out of the upgrade, the BDC will not contain any changes that are made after it is taken offline, but it will be a good place to start when trying to recover your old network.

After you have made the switch and all domain controllers are based on the Active Directory, all clients, including those down-level non-Windows 2000 clients, will be capable of taking advantage of the transitive trust relationship that is created between all domains in the domain tree. This is because the trust relationship is created between domain controllers, which perform authentication functions, not by the individual workstations or other clients in the network. This means that you can proceed to upgrade all your BDCs to Windows 2000 Active Directory domain controllers and then, as you find time to schedule the downtime required, you can upgrade client machines at a leisurely pace.

Finally, Update User Workstations to Windows 2000

After you have created at least one Active Directory domain controller, you can upgrade a Windows NT Workstation computer to Windows 2000. Or, you can wait until you have upgraded all remaining BDCs in the domain before you begin to migrate user workstation computers.

If you operate in a mixed network environment, the client workstations that have been upgraded to Windows 2000 (or Windows 98 or Windows 95 clients that have the appropriate Active Directory client software installed) will be capable of using the new features provided by the Active Directory. This includes the capability to query the database to locate resources throughout the domain tree. These clients will then use DNS as their locator service, while any remaining clients that are not Active Directory-aware will still use NetBIOS names.

Other Domains Can Join the Existing Tree

In a multi-domain network, you will first create a domain tree using one of the domain controllers in an existing domain, or you may even create a new domain from a fresh install to serve as the first domain in a new domain tree.

When you later decide to upgrade other domains in your network to use the Active Directory you can still create a new domain tree, or you can choose to join the existing domain tree. Again, the operation is simple. To join an existing domain tree you need only to supply the name of the parent domain where you will attach the new domain to the tree.

Several things occur when you join an existing tree:

- The domain's current SAM database is migrated to the Active Directory database.
- The Kerberos software is installed and is then used to create a two-way trust relationship with the parent domain that the domain has been attached to in the tree structure.
- A domain controller in the parent domain supplies configuration information, such as the Active Directory schema, to the child domain and then informs other domain controllers about the addition of the new child domain.

The Master Domain Goes First

In the master domain model, all user accounts reside in the master domain and resources are created in separate resource domains. When you upgrade a network that is based on a single domain there is not much choice: First upgrade the PDC, and then upgrade the domain's BDCs.

In the master domain model type of network you should choose to upgrade the master domain first, and then upgrade the resource domains. At the completion of the basic upgrade, you use the Active Directory Installation Wizard (see Figure 48.8) to install the Active Directory.

Figure 48.8 The Installation Wizard guides you through the process.

The next few dialog boxes will prompt you to create a new domain tree or create a child domain in an existing tree (see Figure 48.9). If you choose to create a new domain tree, you are prompted to create a new forest or create the domain in an existing forest (see Figure 48.10). Because this is the first server being upgraded to Windows 2000, you should create a new forest.

The wizard will then prompt you for the domain name that you will use. You will have to specify it as a fully-qualified DNS name, however. In our example the domain is named ono. The company has a registered DNS Internet name of twoinc.com. The fully-qualified domain name for this domain then will be ono.twoinc.com (see Figure 48.11).

The wizard will then ask you where you want to create the files that will serve as the database for the directory and for a device to store the log file for the directory. If your domain is large, you should specify a different device for each of these to improve performance.

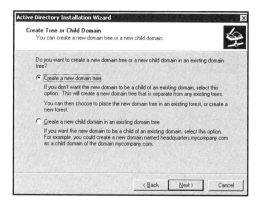

Figure 48.9   If this is the first controller to be upgraded, you create a new domain tree.

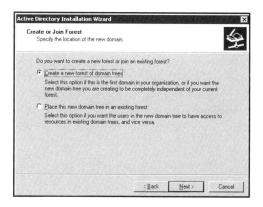

Figure 48.10   Create a new forest for the first domain.

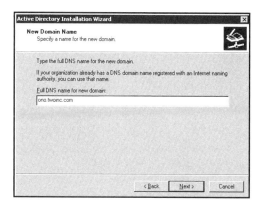

Figure 48.11   Use a fully-qualified DNS name when prompted by the wizard.

If you are not yet using a DNS server in the domain, the wizard will prompt you to install Microsoft's DNS Server. After this prompt you are allowed to view the setup information that you have provided to the wizard and confirm it. If you elect to continue, the wizard continues the process and creates the files and structures for the active directory on your new Windows 2000 domain controller and adds information to the server's registry. As a last step, the wizard will add shortcuts to several tools that you can use to manage the directory and prompt you to restart the computer.

After upgrading the first server, you should experiment with it to get used to the new tools and review your plans for the other servers in the domain. When you are sure that you want to proceed, upgrading backup domain controllers is done in the same way except that you do not create a new domain for the BDCs. When upgrading servers in other domains that you want to place into the same domain tree, you can choose to create a child domain and construct the fully-qualified domain name according to where you want to place the domain in the tree.

Summary

Upgrading from Windows NT 4.0 to Windows 2000 is a time-consuming process, with most of the time spent deciding on the appropriate structure you will use when implementing the Active Directory. You should first examine the domain model you are using in your current network and decide if you need to keep the same domains for the upgrade or if you can use the Active Directory's capability to organize users and computers into other containers to reduce the number of domains you will have to manage.

The actual process of upgrading servers and workstations is not complicated. Indeed it is not much different than upgrading from Windows NT 3.51 to Windows NT 4.0. The Installation Wizard for the Active Directory simplifies the installation after you have upgraded the computer. You can proceed on the upgrade path at your own pace, because Windows NT 2000 will operate with Windows NT 4.0 domain controllers in a mixed environment.

Integrating NT 4.0 to Linux

SOME OF THE MAIN TOPICS IN THIS CHAPTER ARE

Converting User Accounts

File and Print Shares

Printers

Applications

DNS

Hardware Considerations

Third-Party Conversion Tools

CHAPTER 49

With the recent press coverage and industry buzz about Linux, you might be faced with the need to add to, integrate, or replace your existing Windows NT servers with a computer running Linux. This chapter won't go into what Linux is here because it has been covered in previous chapters.

Many of these topics will show some of the previous chapter's ideas in reverse. Linux is, after all, a UNIX clone and contains the same concepts as well as many of the same applications and procedures.

It is important to note here as well that Linux comes in many flavors from many vendors and it is not possible to cover every vendor's methods. As a base point, all references will be made to Red Hat versions 5.2 and 6.0, one of the most popular releases of Linux.

Converting User Accounts

As mentioned in the previous chapter, there are no automatic conversion tools for user accounts from UNIX to NT. Likewise, going from NT to Linux presents the same challenge. The only available method at present is manual labor.

I have often read of requests on various newsgroups for utilities or batch files that could automate the process of configuring users. Perhaps someday someone will write such an application, but until then, this is the only way.

Permissions

A quick rundown of the user's permissions available under Windows NT will serve as a refresher and prevent you from having to flip back and forth through chapters.

Under NT, a user can be assigned the following permissions:

- **No Access**—The user cannot view or modify the file.
- **Read Access**—The user can view the file and, if the file is an executable, the user can run the file (Linux offers the rx permission flags).
- **Change Access**—The user has all Read permissions plus the ability to modify and delete the file (Linux must use rwx).
- **Full Control**—All the previous permissions plus Take Ownership. (For full control, you use rwx. For ownership, you use the chown command.)

A more in-depth discussion of the rights and permissions for both Windows NT and UNIX systems can be found in Chapter 26, "Rights and Permissions."

Groups

Windows NT users belong to groups. You assign users to groups with User Manager for Domains. Groups are an important part of Linux user accounts as well. If you are placing a Linux server into your organization, you will likely need to familiarize yourself with groups. However, if Linux is to be installed on your home PC or in a single-user environment, groups are not that important.

You assign permissions to files based the user's ID (UID) as well as the group ID (GID). Linux assigns users to groups by adding the username to the /etc/group file. You will learn how to do this when you add a user later in this chapter.

Working with Linux Users

If you are a systems administrator on a Linux system, one of your primary responsibilities will be to manage user accounts. Even if you are not an administrator, you should be familiar with user accounts and groups. (You must be logged in as root to create user accounts.)

At home, for example, you might not want to let your wife or younger brother use the system at all. In this case, you need to know how to lock down the computer.

Managing user accounts involves creating and deleting the accounts, assigning groups, setting permissions, and creating and assigning home directories. To add a user to a Linux system, you can use one of two methods. Manually add the user information to the /etc/passwd file, or automatically add the information by issuing the adduser or useradd command. The following is the syntax for adduser:

```
./adduser fflintstone
```

As noted before, different versions of Linux are available, and each one implements the adduser or useradd command a little differently. For example, Red Hat requires you to type only this preceding command, and it performs the rest of the account creation automatically. Another version of Linux, known as Slackware, prompts you for more information than just the username. You must provide it with a password at the same time.

User Account Format and Location

When Linux creates the user account, it actually places an entry in the /etc/passwd file. The entry takes the following form:

```
login_name:encrypted_password:user_ID:group_ID:user_
➥information:login_directory:login_shell
```

Note

If you plan to use the following procedures to manually edit the /etc/passwd file, ensure that you make a copy of the file first. If this file gets corrupted, you will not be able to log in.

To manually add a user, you should fully understand the fields in the entry. Table 49.1 describes them for you.

Table 49.1   Fields Used by the /etc/passwd File

Field	Description
login_name	The username that is used to log in to the system.
encrypted_passwd	The user's password in encrypted form. You cannot enter this manually. An example follows this table.

(continues)

Table 49.1   Continued

Field	Description
user_ID	A sequential number that identifies the user.
group_ID	The initial group ID for users when they log in.
user_information	Usually the user's full name.
login_directory	The user's initial login directory, normally the home directory.
login_shell	The user's initial shell.

As mentioned, the `adduser` or `useradd` commands create user accounts for you automatically. When you type the `./adduser fflintstone` command, Linux creates an entry in the `/etc/passwd` file, gives the user an ID, assigns the user to the default group ID, lists the home directory as `/home/username`, and assigns the default shell. The only information you must add is the user's full name and password.

To create a password for the user, enter the following command:

```
passwd username
```

In our example, as the user you would type `passwd fflintstone` and press Enter. You will be prompted for the password. While you type in the password, nothing is displayed onscreen as a precaution against someone looking over your shoulder. You will then be prompted to confirm your password by typing it again.

Tip

A good, secure password should contain a combination of upper- and lowercase characters and numbers. This makes it much harder to guess. If you use a simple password such as "test," Linux will complain and tell you that it is not a good password. It does not prevent you from using it, though.

Linux will create an encrypted version of the password and store it in the correct place in the file.

User Information

The user information field normally contains the user's full name but can include other bits of information as well, such as office and home phone numbers. If you are feeling adventuresome, you can make modifications to the `adduser` shell script to have the command ask for this information during the account creation.

If you don't like to play with the script files, you can simply use the *Change Finger* (`chfn`) command to enter this information later. The syntax for this command is

```
Chfn <username>
```

Adding a User Manually

You will now look at how to add a user to the system manually. The steps involved should be performed in the following order:

1. Add the user to the /etc/passwd file.

2. Create the home directory.

3. Assign ownership permissions.

4. Copy .profile settings.

Add the User

Using a text editor that will save in true ASCII format, you edit the /etc/passwd file to add a user manually. You will need to add the information to the end of the file on a new line by itself. Each user is entered on its own line. Add Mr. Flintstone manually to see how it works. (This should be all on one line.)

```
fflintstone::120:100:Fred Flintstone:/home/fflintstone:/bin/sh
```

Now look at this entry and see what you have done. Notice that each field is separated by a colon (:). The first field, fflintstone, is the login name. Next, notice two colons. You must skip the password field here because it is stored encrypted and you cannot enter an encrypted password in this way. The colon is still needed to separate the fields even though the password field is blank.

The next field entry, 120, is the user ID. User IDs should be sequential in numerical order. This would indicate that there are previous users in the file.

The next field indicates a group ID of 100. You can, of course, enter the ID of any existing group that you want the user to belong to.

The next field is the user information field that displays the user's full name.

The user's home directory is listed next. (The directory does not exist yet and must be created.)

The last field indicates the shell that will be used by this account. This particular shell is the Bourne shell. (Although you have specified the Bourne shell as the default startup shell, the user can change to another shell later.)

Before you proceed any further, you must assign the password. This can be a simple password for now so the user can log in later and change it to a secure password of his choosing. Type passwd fflintstone.

You will be prompted for a new password entry and to confirm it. Most administrators use either *password* or the username as the initial password. You will then need to give this to the user so he can log in for the first time and change it.

Create the Home Directory

Now that the user entry is created and it has a password, you must create the user's home directory so he has a place to store his personal files when logged in to the system.

To create a directory for fflintstone, type the following command:

```
mkdir /home/fflintstone
```

Mr. Flintstone now has his very own directory in which to store files.

Assign Ownership

For users to have full control over their home directory, you must assign ownership of the directory to them. The command you will use for this is

```
chown fflintstone /home/fflintstone
```

Assigning a User to a Group

To manually add a user to a group, you first must understand the structure of the `/etc/group` file. You should also be aware of some default groups and understand why normal users should not be assigned membership to them.

Before you make any modification to this file, print it or review it in your ASCII editor (such as vi or EMACS, discussed later in this chapter) to become familiar with the way entries are made and also to learn what default groups are available on your system. The default groups that you should not assign regular users to appear in Listing 49.1.

Listing 49.1   Default Groups

```
root
sys
daemon
kmem
tty
```

By assigning users to these groups, you are giving them *root* access. With *root*, they can gain access to areas of the system best left to administrators and power users who really understand the Linux system. If you are not involved in an office environment where users need to be categorized into groups, you should simply make all users members of the *users* group.

Take a look at an entry in the `groups` file to see what makes up the fields. The group you'll deal with mainly is the *users* group, so take that as an example.

```
users::100:gobrien,brubble
```

Note that there are four fields in this entry, each separated by a colon as in the `/etc/passwd` file. The first field contains the group name—in this case, `users`.

The second field is for the group password. In this entry it is empty. Normally, groups are not assigned passwords, but that doesn't mean you can't assign one if you want. If there is a password entered in a group, the user must type that in when requesting to join the group.

Next you see the number `100`. This field is for the group ID number. The number is used by the operating system itself. Group ID numbers should be assigned in sequential order, just as in the `/etc/passwd` file.

The last field contains the names of the users that are members of the group, separated by commas.

If you need to add a group to the file, simply place the group on a line by itself with the correct fields in place and add your users.

Copying Profiles

Now that you have the user account created, you must set up the configuration for the user's shell. The easiest way to do this is to copy over another user's `.profile` file to the new user's home directory. Then, using the `chown` command, you can assign ownership to the user so he can perform customization on it.

Before turning it over completely to the new user, ensure that there are no user-specific configurations in the file, such as home directory listings.

Adding users is only half the battle. What if you need to remove a user? Well, that process is a little easier. Here's how to do it.

Removing Users

As with adding users, you can remove users automatically or manually. Use the commands `deluser` or `userdel` to delete user accounts automatically. Either command will ask you for the username to remove.

To remove a user manually, simply delete her entry in the `/etc/passwd` file. You can then remove her home directory, her mail spool file, and any jobs that she might have scheduled using `cron` or `at`.

A new user has now been added to the system and configured. This is the first step you should take after installing Linux so that you can set up a user account for yourself for everyday tasks. It is not recommended to run as root on a regular basis. Any configuration mistakes could render the system unbootable.

If you must perform administrative tasks while logged in as another user, you can use the super user (su) account. Simply type `su` at the command line and enter the root password. You are now logged in as administrator and can perform administrative duties. Remember to log back out by typing `exit`.

File and Print Shares

Linux handles files a little differently than does Windows NT. There are some similarities, however, most of which derive from the fact that DOS actually borrowed some concepts from UNIX. Let's look at the Linux file system.

Linux File Types

Files under Linux share some of the same restrictions that you find under NT. They can be up to 256 characters in length, although most versions of UNIX allow 14. They consist of alphanumeric characters and do not allow the use of special characters reserved by the shell, such as

```
! @ # $ % ^ & * ( ) [ ] { } ' - \ / | ; < > `
```

Linux, unlike Windows NT, does not allow the use of spaces in filenames. Most users will insert an underscore in the filename in place of the space, such as

```
file_name_with_no_spaces
```

It is also important to note that Linux considers directories to be files as well. There is a distinction between the two, but directory names follow the same naming convention as that for files.

Note

Linux does not use drive letters for disk drives like NT does. To Linux, everything is a file. For example, Linux considers the CD-ROM as **/mnt/cdrom**, which is derived from the **/dev/cdrom** device entry. To access the drives on a Linux system, you use the **mount** command to mount the drive.

You will find that Linux contains four types of files:

- Ordinary files
- Directory files
- Links
- Special files

Ordinary Files

Just as you might expect, ordinary files are those that you work with on a daily basis, such as text files, shell scripts, and even executable files. You can use the file to have Linux tell you what the file contains. Some examples might be ascii text, binary, or symbolic link.

Directory Files

Directory files contain names of files and subdirectories. This is where Linux stores the information about what files exist in what directories. You can use several commands to view the contents of a directory under Linux:

- `dir`
- `ls`
- `vdir`

Each command will give a slightly different file listing. The most common command to use is the `ls` command. When you issue the `ls` command, you are not seeing the directory listing as it exists on the disk, you are just viewing the contents of the directory file.

Links

A link is not actually a file but a directory entry. This entry is a pointer to an existing file's inode. Links aren't required to share files, so this book doesn't cover them any further.

Special Files

As mentioned earlier, Linux treats everything as a file, including disks, printers, and displays. These all constitute special files. For example, a terminal that a user is working on would be classified as `/dev/tty01`. Although it is an actual keyboard and monitor (and might also be a complete workstation), Linux treats it is as a file for the purpose of input and output.

Inodes

When Windows NT formats a disk, it creates a table that contains information about the location of files on the disk. As files are added, removed, copied, and moved, this table gets updated to reflect that information. Linux uses what is known as an *inode table*. Each file has an *inode* assigned to it, which is a unique number. The inode contains all the information about the file, including its location on the disk.

The root directory, or `/`, has an inode of 1.

File Permissions

To successfully set up file and print shares on a Linux system, you need a complete understanding of the available permissions. Linux provides three permissions for files:

- **r**—Indicates read access. When a file has read access assigned, the user or group can only view the file. They cannot modify it or delete it.
- **w**—Indicates write access. Write access grants the user the right to view, modify, and delete the file.
- **x**—Indicates execute access. Execute permission enables the user to execute the file, meaning that the user can run the file like a program.

The way in which the permissions are assigned is very important. First, they are always assigned in the order of `rwx`. However, this doesn't mean that you must assign read permission before you can assign write permission. For example

```
-rw-r--r-- brubble users 512 Aug 8 15:38 bfile
```

From this example, you can determine quite a bit about this file. Going from left to right, let's look at each section in turn.

The first character you see is a hyphen. This simply indicates that you are dealing with a file. If this character were the letter d, you would be looking at a directory.

The rest of the first section is now actually three groups of three characters. If all were filled in, they would look like `rwxrwxrwx`.

Here is how Linux determines permissions for user and groups. The first set of three characters sets the permissions assigned to the owner of the file. The owner of this file has `rw` for permissions. The x permission is not there because the file is not an executable. In the next three characters you see r and two hyphens. This indicates that the group assigned to this file has read-only permissions.

The last three characters are the permissions assigned to everyone else not included in the group section. They also have only read permission.

To recap, the group of characters for permissions lists in order, is

- Directory
- User
- Group
- Everyone

After the permissions, Linux lists the user or owner of the file. Next is the group assigned to the file, the file's size indicated in bytes, the date and time of creation, and finally, the filename.

Permissions are sometimes given using numbers as well. File permissions are assigned using these numbers, so you must familiarize yourself with how this is done.

The numbers are given as a three-digit code; for example, 662. Numbers are arranged in the same order as the permission groups are arranged. For example, the first number depicts the user's permissions, the second is for the group, and the third is for everyone else. Table 49.2 shows you how these numbers are derived.

Table 49.2   Numeric Values for Permissions

Permission	Value
Read r	4
Write w	2
Execute x	1

By reproducing this code,

```
-rw-r--r-- brubble users 512 Aug 8 15:38 bfile
```

you can see how the permissions would be assigned using the numbering system. The command chmod is used to set or change a file's permissions. The command to set these permissions would be

```
chmod 644 bfile
```

As you can see, the user has read and write permission, so adding the values for read and write gives us the number 6. Because the group permission is read-only, its value is 4 and the other permissions are 4 also because they are read-only.

So, you simply take the assigned permissions per section, add the values from the table, and arrive at the correct number for the permission assignment.

```
chmod Options
```

The chmod command, as mentioned, is used to set the file permissions. You have already seen one method for setting the file permissions using the number scheme. chmod offers another way to assign permissions, known as *relative permissions*. This method enables you to assign permissions based on these options:

- **a**—All users and groups
- **g**—The owner's group
- **o**— Others
- **u**—For just the user

There are also three methods used to assign these rights:

- **+**—Adds the mode
- **-**—Removes the mode
- **=**—Sets the mode absolutely

Here are some examples to illustrate the use of the chmod relative permissions use:

```
chmod a=rw bfile
```

This command issues the read and write permissions to all users.

```
Chmod u+rwx bfile
```

This shows how you would add the read, write, and execute permissions to the file for the user only.

Printers

Printing under Linux might not be exactly what you anticipate. Part of the reason for this is because Linux might not fully support all your printer's functionality. Linux must send your output to a file first so the user can resume work without having the print job tying up the operation.

Linux sends your print job to a print spooler much the same as NT does. Windows NT refers to printers as print devices. Linux calls them spooled devices.

Note

Spool finds its roots in the mainframe computer days. It is an acronym that stands for Simultaneous Peripheral Operation OffLine.

Linux is a multitasking operating system that allows multiple processes to operate at apparently the same time. By using this built-in capability, Linux processes print jobs in the background. It does this by spooling all print jobs to a queue.

All print jobs are placed in this queue and are printed in the order they were received. Printing is performed in the background by the printing daemon. It is the job of the printing daemon to monitor the print queue for any new jobs, and then despool or send the data to the physical printer. The physical printer is the device that actually puts the ink on the paper. In comparison, NT calls this a print device.

There are actually five programs that Linux and UNIX use for printing:

- **lpr**—This is a command that places a print job in the queue. lpr is located in the /usr/sbin directory.

- **lpd**—This is the printer daemon and must be running for any printing to take place. This daemon should be started during system startup. You can find the options for the lpd daemon in its man page.

- **lpq**—This command is used to display the contents of the spool directory. This is useful for determining the ID of the print jobs in the event you want to cancel or remove a job from the queue.

- **lprm**—This command is used to remove print jobs from the queue. It can remove only those that have not started printing yet. One way to remove all unprinted jobs from the queue is to log in as root and issue the lpq command.

- **lpc**—This is used to check the status of the printer or printers. You can also control the printer in certain ways using this command. If you want to disable a printer, you could issue the lpc down *<printer>* command. The optional *<printer>* would be the name of the print device that you want to control.

All print devices are listed in /etc/printcap. This is a text file that can be viewed and edited using a text editor such as vi. To prevent accidental erasure or modification of this file, you should assign ownership only to root. The permissions should read -rw-r--r--.

Here is an example of the printcap file from my Linux installation:

```
#
# Please don't edit this file directly unless you know what you are doing
# Be warned that the control-panel printtool requires a very strict format!
# Look at the printcap(5) man page for more info.
#
# This file can be edited with the printtool in the control-panel.

##PRINTTOOL3## LOCAL bjc600 360x360 letter {} BJC600 8 0
lp:\
    :sd=/var/spool/lpd/lp:\
    :mx#0:\
    :sh:\
    :lp=/dev/lp0:\
    :if=/var/spool/lpd/lp/filter:
```

I can guarantee that the first time I looked at the file, I had no intention of modifying it all. As a matter of fact, as the instructions suggest, using the control panel under X Window (a graphical user interface popular on many UNIX systems), you can install and configure printers without any hassles at all.

Without going into too much detail regarding the file, let's look at the fields in the preceding file.

The line containing ##PRINTTOOL3## tells you what model of printer is installed.

The next line, lp:\, starts a section listing necessary information for printing to the device:

- **:sd**—Indicates where the spool directory is located for this printer
- **:mx**—Indicates the largest allowable print job size

- **:sh**—A Boolean value that indicates whether to suppress headers
- **:lp**—Indicates what device to print to
- **:if**—Indicates an input filter name

Other fields are available as well. Check the man page (manual pages, or the UNIX equivalent of a "help" system for online users) for more information.

To enable users to print without requiring them to specify the -P<*printername*> command each time, you can set up a printer environment variable for each user. You can set up this variable in the login script of each user or enter it into the default login script. If the shell is bash, you can add a line such as

```
export PRINTER=<printername>
```

Any time you make changes to or add a printer, you must either restart the system or shut down and restart the printer daemon.

One last issue of concern is sharing printers with any existing Windows NT clients. To provide for connectivity between Windows and Linux, you must implement Samba. Samba is based on the server message block (SMB) protocol for file and printer sharing. Samba is configured through the smb.conf configuration file. The printer section from a typical smb.conf file is shown in the following code:

```
[printers]
    comment = All Printers
    path = /var/spool/samba
    browseable = no
# Set public = yes to allow user 'guest account' to print
    guest ok = no
    writable = no
    printable = yes
```

This configuration is the default entry for printers in the smb.conf file and provides printing capability for all users.

Applications

Although Windows NT provides some applications with the operating system, most are not very robust or are used mostly for administrative tasks. Some of these include

- **NotePad**—A text editor
- **User Manager for Domain**—For managing users
- **Internet Information Server**—For FTP and Web publishing
- **Calculator**—For simple and scientific math calculations
- **Control Panel**—Contains many applets for system configuration

Linux, however, provides quite a few applications with the operating system. Although most are a part of the functionality of the OS, a fair portion of third-party applications are available. Most applications fall under a few distinct groups:

- Word processing
- Spreadsheet
- Database
- Computer-aided design (CAD)
- Productivity
- Utilities
- Communications
- Network
- File management
- Development

Some applications don't conform to these specific groups, such as office suites that encompass some or all of these groups, but these are the main categories for the most common applications. Note as well that when looking for applications to use on the Linux platform, these applications are often classified as console applications or X11 applications. Console applications run at the command line, whereas X11 applications are designed to work under X Window.

Word Processing

NT has a benefit of being a widely supported operating system in terms of commercial software vendors developing applications for it. Linux is starting to develop a considerable following in this arena as well with the announced support of such software giants as IBM and Corel.

Emacs and vi are two of the most popular text editors that have been around for quite some time on UNIX systems and have made their way into the Linux world as well. Although each provides text-editing capabilities, they function differently.

vi

To start vi, simply type its name at the command line and press Enter. This method starts vi with a blank file. You can create a new file at this time by entering it as an option to the `vi` command. You can also open an existing ASCII file in this manner. Your screen clears and vi presents you with a tilde (~) character on the left side of the screen for each line, such as this:

```
-
~
~
~
~
~
```

The number of lines that are displayed depends on your terminal settings. The very bottom line is used as a status indicator that enables you to enter commands and see which of the two modes, command mode or text-entry mode, is enabled.

When vi first starts, it is in command mode. To enter text into the editor, you must type either `a` or `i`. The importance of these two commands comes into play if you are editing an existing file.

- **a**—Appends text after the cursor's position
- **i**—Inserts text in front of the cursor

When you are in text-entry mode, you can enter and edit text.

vi contains several commands that are used to move about the file, edit text, and save files. All these can be found in the help for vi and will not be reproduced here to save space.

Emacs

Another popular text editor is Emacs. Unlike vi, anything you type in Emacs is entered as text in the buffer. You access the various commands using the Ctrl key plus a command letter or the Esc key. Emacs commands are also available in the online help.

Other Editors

The latest release of Red Hat Linux offers a nice graphical-based editor for the X Window system under Gnome called gnotepad. Personally, I enjoy using this editor more than the others, partly because of its easy-to-use interface.

Some large software companies have pledged support of the Linux system, and one of the first to make good on this promise was Corel. It has published a Web site on the Internet at http://linux.corel.com. Along with its support intentions, Corel has made available for download a free personal edition of WordPerfect 8.0, its flagship word processor.

Spreadsheets

Under the XFree86 system, Linux has a spreadsheet program known as xspread. This is a public domain application that provides an interface similar to the earlier versions Lotus 1-2-3. The following are some of the features xspread provides:

- File encryption
- Justification capabilities for labels in cells
- Insertion and deletion of rows and columns
- Naming of ranges
- Mathematical and logical operators
- Graphs
- Menus (mouse-selectable)
- Absolute and Relative references

Many more features are provided. As with many Linux applications, you can include a filename in the command line to start the program and open the file simultaneously.

You can also find some other spreadsheet applications on the Internet, such as

- Abacus
- Abs

- Siag
- Wingz

All offer various functionality with scripting capabilities and macros.

Database

Database applications are becoming very popular with companies trying to maintain larger amounts of data for the purpose of analysis. Windows NT has some very full-featured database applications available, such as

- Microsoft Access
- Microsoft SQL Server
- Sybase
- Oracle
- Quattro Pro

Although Red Hat Linux does not come with a database application, many are available.

Altera SQL server, available from `http://www.altera.gr//`, provides a multiuser RDMS that supports ODBC. This can offer great benefits to an environment switching from NT because any in-house developers using C++ or Visual Basic can still write applications as front ends to it using the ODBC architecture.

If you are looking for a small personal database rather than a full-blown enterprise application, you might want to look at Gaby, `http://gaby.netpedia.net/`. This database uses Gnome for a GUI.

Most of the other application categories previously listed have various shareware and freeware products available as well, but some of the more common ones you should take a closer look at include network and administration applications.

Because we've already covered the use of user management programs under Linux, let's look at some of the networking tools available.

File Transfer

One of the areas that Linux excels at, in terms of applications, is in the TCP/IP arena. Linux, like UNIX, is built on the TCP/IP suite of protocols for a network architecture. Likewise, you can expect to see native TCP/IP tools and utilities.

Built into the OS is the capability to be both an FTP server and a client. Whereas with Windows NT you must install a separate package to upload files to the Internet, Linux needs only some configuration. During Linux installation, you are asked if you would like your computer to be an FTP server. By choosing yes, the install routine builds the functionality into the OS.

Another popular utility is Telnet. By using this program, you can remotely connect to and run applications on another computer. This is useful for monitoring and controlling computers from one central workstation.

Windows NT includes a Telnet client as well, but it requires an add-on or other third-party software to allow it to function as a Telnet server. Linux provides Telnet server functionality as a part of the OS.

Microsoft provides Internet Information Server for the purposes of providing FTP, Gopher, and World Wide Web server capabilities to Windows NT.

The most popular server for providing Web capabilities to Linux is Apache. Apache comes in two different forms for use in Linux. In one form, you can compile it from the source files, making any changes that you require up front, or you can obtain the already compiled binaries, usually on the CD, to start with an already compiled version.

Apache is configured using three different files:

- `http.conf`
- `srm.conf`
- `access.conf`

Configuring a Web server using Apache could easily take two or more chapters. A good start toward setting this functionality up on your computer is to read the WWW HOWTO, written by Wayne Leister. This can be found in the `/usr/doc/HOWTO` directory or on various Linux Web sites.

Although you have learned some of the available applications for Linux here, the total list comprises an extensive array. There are programs that provide network management capabilities, communication programs for modem communications, and, of course, many C and C++ source code compilers.

Most distributions of Linux come with applications on CD when you buy their "boxed sets." You will find many demo applications and full-fledged programs on these CDs. If you are still not satisfied with those or don't see the application that you need, fire up your Web browser and visit

`http://www.linuxberg.com`

DNS

Windows NT uses the Domain Name Service Manager application to configure and manage its DNS services. Linux relies, as usual, on configuration files, as listed here:

- `/etc/host.conf`—Responsible for local resolver libraries. It tells the resolver what services are being used and in what order they appear.
- `/etc/resolv.conf`—Tells the resolver what name servers to use for resolving host names.
- `named.boot`—Provides configuration information for the *named* daemon. *named* is pronounced as "name d."
- `named.hosts`—Holds information relating to your local domain.
- `named.rev`—As you can guess from the name, this file provides reverse name mapping.
- `named.ca`—A cache file for the named daemon.

To set up a DNS server, you need to configure the resolver and the named daemon.

Configuring the Resolver

Configure the resolver libraries by editing the `/etc/host.conf` and `resolv.conf` files.

The `host.conf` File

The resolver looks to the `host.conf` file to determine the services to use and the order in which to use them. This file has five options:

- **order**—Specifies the order in which the different resolution mechanisms are searched.

- **alert**—Deals with attempts at spoofing an IP address. Uses `on` or `off` as its arguments.

- **nospoof**—Comes into play when reverse resolution is used. This aids in preventing IP spoofing. You use `nospoof on` to enable this option.

- **trim**—By giving this option a domain name as an argument, it removes that portion before it performs a lookup on the name in `/etc/hosts`.

- **Multi**—This uses `on` or `off` as arguments. You use this option when hosts are allowed to have more than one IP.

Here is an example of a `host.conf` file:

```
order bind hosts
multi off
nospoof on
alert on
```

In this example, the resolver will use DNS to look up the host name first. If this fails, it will fall back to the hosts file.

Next, you see that multiple IPs for a single host are disabled. You have turned on nospoof, which means that the resolver will use reverse name lookup to verify the IP.

Finally, you have turned on the alert to indicate whether an IP spoof is attempted.

Although this file is just a plain vanilla file, you can enter comments in the file to document the settings for easy recognition. Simply precede the comments with a # character.

The `resolv.conf` File

The purpose of this file is to tell the DNS server which name servers to use for name resolution and to specify the order in which to contact them. Three configuration options are available for this file:

- **Domain**—This option is used to specify the domain name of the host on which it is installed.

- **Nameserver**—You enter the IP addresses of up to three name servers to be used. They will be contacted in the order listed. *Note:* You must enter an IP address here; do not enter a name because DNS will not be able to resolve it.

- **Search**—If you do not specify a domain name as a part of the query, DNS will try searching using a list of domains specified here.

An example `resolv.conf` file is shown in the following code:

```
domain gkcomput.com
nameserver 198.164.30.2
nameserver 198.164.4.2
```

As you can see here, the local domain is listed as gkcomput.com. It's not a big domain, and hardly anybody ever visits it.

Next are listed two name server IP addresses. DNS will use the 198.164.30.2 first; if that server is down, it will try the next one in the list.

Again, you can provide comments in this file by preceding them with the # character.

The Named Daemon

To provide the DNS server under Linux, you must have the named daemon running. Normally this daemon starts at system boot. The named daemon gets its configuration information from the named.boot, named.hosts, and named.rev files. These files are located in the /etc directory as well.

The named.boot File

This is actually the first file read by the named daemon when it starts. It is not a big file in size but it is in importance. It contains information that points to the other configuration files. These options can be used in the file:

- **Directory**—This tells the daemon where to find the zone files for the DNS.
- **Primary**—This option declares the named daemon to be authoritative for the domain. The domain and filename are arguments for this option.
- **Secondary**—This indicates that named should act as a secondary server in the domain. Arguments for this option include a domain name, a filename, and a list of addresses.
- **Cache**—Using a domain name and filename for arguments, this option specifies caching information.
- **Forwarders**—This uses name servers as arguments for resolving addresses if the local name server can't resolve an address from its local information.
- **Slave**—This option makes the local server a slave server. In this case, it will forward requests on to one of the servers listed in the forwarders option.

Here is a sample named.boot file:

```
; named.boot file for gkcomput.com
; this file should be located in the /etc directory
directory /var/named
;
;
cache . named.ca
;
primary gkcomput.com named.hosts
```

As can be seen from this file, comments are preceded by the semicolon (;). You can also use the semicolon to place whitespace within the file to make it easier to read.

The first line that does anything useful is the directory line. This tells `named.boot` where to find its working files. Next you see the cache line indicating that the root sever information is found in the file named `.ca`. Finally, you see the primary line indicating that this server is the authority for my domain, `gkcomput.com`.

The `named.hosts` File

This file contains information about your hosts and zone of authority. This is the file that was listed in the `named.boot` file on the primary line. It does not have to be called `named.hosts`. Although you can give it a name of your choosing, I think that the default name sums up the purpose of the file.

Here is a sample `named.hosts` file and an explanation of the fields:

```
@                  IN      SOA      ns.gkcomput.com. hostmaster.gkcomput.com. (
                                    1          ; Serial
                                    8H         ; Refresh
                                    2H         ; Retry
                                    1W         ; Expire
                                    1D)        ; Minimum TTL
                           NS       ns.gkcomput.com.
          1                PTR      localhost.
          mailhost   IN   A    192.168.5.26
```

The first line starts with the @ character. This simply indicates the current domain. This is followed by the letters IN and SOA. IN means that you are using IP addresses, and SOA tells you that this a Start of Authority record.

Immediately following that you see the name server name and the email contact name for this domain.

In parentheses, you will see the serial number given, a refresh rate of 8 hours, 2-hour retries, a 1-week expiration, and minimum time to live of 1 day.

The next line contains the NS code. This indicates the name sever resource record.

A line with the code PTR follows this and simply tells you that the first host in the subnet is named `localhost`.

Finally, the last line indicates the IP address for the mail server on the domain.

The `named.rev` File

This file is required only for reverse name lookup and mapping IP addresses to host names. Here is an example of this file:

```
@                  IN      SOA      ns.gkcomput.com. hostmaster.gkcomput.com. (
                                    1          ; Serial
                                    8H         ; Refresh
                                    2H         ; Retry
                                    1W         ; Expire
                                    1D)        ; Minimum TTL
                    IN     NS       ns.gkcomput.com.
          1         IN     PTR      mailhost.gkcomput.com
```

As you can see, the file is similar to the `named.hosts` file. The main difference can be seen on the last line. This last line tells named to map the IP address of 192.168.5.26 to the host name of `mailhost.gkcomput.com`. This IP address was given in the `named.hosts` file.

The `named.ca` File

Finally, you come to the last file, named.ca. As you might be able to guess from the name, this file will hold the cache information. Entries in this file are given the names and IP addresses of the root servers in various domains. To obtain up-to-date information for this file, you can use the `nslookup` utility.

DNS is a very complex subject and differs a bit on each OS. I have only covered the very basics of it here. You should familiarize yourself with the particular functions of DNS on your distribution of Linux. One way to aid in setting up DNS is to use the DNS HOWTO. Linux uses the HOWTO documents to describe the process of installing and configuring the various components and services of the OS. You can find other HOWTO documents relating to programming in Assembler, setting up SCSI devices, using CD recorders, and in many other procedures.

Most distributions come with the HOWTO library on the CD and are usually installed during the OS install. I recommend that you read the latest HOWTO on DNS located at

```
http://www.redhat.com/mirrors/LDP/HOWTO/DNS-HOWTO-4.html
```

Hardware Considerations

Microsoft maintains a Hardware Compatibility List (HCL) on its Windows NT Web site. The purpose of this HCL is to inform users of the NT OS what hardware components have been tested and verified to work under the OS.

Red Hat maintains an HCL as well, and you can review the known hardware that has or is being used on Red Hat Linux here:

```
http://www.redhat.com/corp/support/hardware/index.html
```

Although each distribution can have different hardware support, most versions of Linux have drivers or support for the most common hardware on the market today.

Let's take a look at some of the generic concerns.

Motherboards

Manufacturer-specific boards might or might not be supported, and the best source of information is likely the manufacturer's Web site. Linux is making quite a sonic boom in the industry, and most major players are providing information relating to Linux compatibility with their products.

Linux supports all the major bus architectures, ISA, VLB, EISA, and PCI. If you are using an IBM PS/2 or other MCA-based mainboard, it is best to check with the specific Linux kernel that you will be using.

CPUs

Linux is compatible with all major CPU types ranging from the Intel 386SX all the way up to and including the Pentium II. It is also compatible with AMD's K5 and K6 processors, although the earlier K6 CPUs caused some problems. There was a workaround discovered that required the internal cache to be disabled in the system BIOS.

Memory

Linux recognizes and can use DRAM, EDO, and SDRAM. Although most kernels recognize only 64MB of RAM, you can force the kernel to see any extra by adding a line to your LILO configuration stating the memory size.

As an example, if you had 96MB of RAM, you would add a line such as this:

```
append="mem=96M"
```

Don't try to fool Linux into thinking that you have more RAM than is actually installed because it can generate unexpected system crashes.

Video Cards

Most video cards work with Linux right out of the box. The one thing to keep in mind here is that just because your video card works with Linux does not mean it works with X Windows. The best source of information for which video cards are supported is the documentation included with your release of Linux.

Hard Drive Controllers

Linux is capable of working with the older MFM and RLL controllers as well as IDE. Linux also supports the newer Enhanced IDE interface as well as allowing up to four hard drives on two controllers.

Here is a brief list of some supported E-IDE controllers:

■ CMD-640 (support for buggy interfaces in kernel 2.2)
■ DTC 2278D
■ FGI/Holtek HT-6560B VLB (support for secondary interface in kernel 2.2)
■ RZ1000 (support for buggy interfaces in kernel 2.2)
■ Triton I (82371FB) (with busmaster DMA)
■ Triton II (82371SB) (with busmaster DMA)

Linux also supports Tekram and ARCO RAID controllers.

SCSI Controllers

SCSI interfaces present some problems with Linux based on the drivers used. For example, I use a flat-bed scanner that comes with its own SCSI controller. The controller is manufactured by DTC but is actually designed to work with the scanner that I have and the Windows architecture. Red Hat Linux 5.2 and 6.0 will not recognize it.

As is the case with video cards, the hardware compatibility list that accompanies your distribution is the best place to look for compatibility. Ensure that you know the correct model of your SCSI adapter as well.

If you check some of the Web sites, there are workarounds for problems like mine by using a somewhat compatible driver, but these resolutions are like printer drivers. If you are not using the driver written for the hardware, you will likely lose some functionality.

I/O Controllers

Linux offers support for standard I/O controllers for parallel, serial, and game ports. It supports 8250 to 16550A UARTS for serial communications.

Network Cards

Linux provides support for network adapters running on all common network architectures, including

- Ethernet
- Token Ring
- ISDN
- Frame Relay

For a complete list, consult the documentation for your distribution.

Sound Cards

Most of the drivers for sound cards can be found at

```
http://www.opensound.com/oss.html
```

You will find that the major manufacturers of sound cards and chips are supported under Linux. Some of these include

- Creative Sound Blaster
- Ensoniq
- Cards based on the Crystal chipsets
- Yamaha
- Turtle Beach

Tape Drives

If you are coming over from NT, you are likely concerned with the capability to perform backups using tape devices. Linux supports SCSI tape drives. If your SCSI adapter is listed, then the tape drive should work. Be sure to see the SCSI HOWTO for proper configuration.

Linux is also compatible with QIC-20 drives and the Ditto internal drive by Omega.

CD-ROM Drives and Recorders

Once again, there is support for SCSI drives if your adapter is supported. Most IDE and EIDE (ATAPI) drives are supported from manufacturers such as

- Mitsumi
- Sony
- Toshiba
- Panasonic

You will find that CD burners from the major manufacturers are supported as well, such as HP, Plextor, Mitsumi, and Yamaha. There are also a variety of CD recording software titles available.

Mouse Devices

Here is list of compatible mouse devices for the Linux OS:

- Microsoft serial, PS/2, and bus mice
- Logitech serial mouse devices
- Logitech bus mouse
- Microsoft Intellimouse

Some touchpads can work as well, provided they use a supported mouse driver.

Modems

All the standard internal and external modems should work fine under Linux, with the exception of WinModem models.

Another issue to be concerned with is if you have a modem that is upgraded via a Flash program for updating the EEPROM on the modem. Most of these utilities are designed to work under DOS or Windows and might not function correctly under Linux. Read the manufacturer's literature.

Printers

Although not every printer on the market has a driver available for Linux, most work under the OS. I use a Canon BJC-4100 for my home printer and Red Hat supplies a driver that works for the BJC-600 and BJC-4000 models. Although this driver is not written specifically for the 4100 model, I still get good printing results from using it.

Most manufacturers are starting to provide Linux drivers, so this should not pose any problems in the near future. If you are using a Linux application that prints using PostScript, you can obtain an emulator for your printer if it doesn't support this. You can find the emulator, known as GhostScript, at: `ftp://ftp.cs.wisc.edu/pub/ghost/aladdin/`.

Scanners

Linux offers support for a wide range of scanners, including the following:

- Epson GT 6000
- HP Scanjets
- Logitech Scanman scanners
- Mustek
- UMAX

Scanner support is offered through the Scanner Access Now Easy (SANE) package. For more information on this, follow this URL: `http://www.mostang.com/sane/`.

Other Devices

There is support for several other devices, such as digital cameras, joysticks, and touch screens. As with any other hardware item, it is best to check the HCL that accompanies the distribution you are planning to use. This way, you can avoid future hassles and concerns before you even install the OS.

Third-Party Conversion Tools

Oh, to have the ease of converting from one operating system to another at the push of a mouse button. This is the dream of many systems or network administrators. Imagine just simply installing an OS, selecting a migrate from button, and having all the work done for you. Although this dream might become reality some day, at the present time, there exists no automatic method that completely migrates an NT system to a Linux system.

Even though you must convert your user accounts and file and print shares manually, there are methods available to port your application to the Linux platform. If you have in-house developers who write custom applications for you in the C++ language, they can port those applications to the Linux platform. ANSI C++ follows a set of guidelines across platforms that allows for a relatively easy conversion path. Unfortunately, you can't simply recompile an existing source code project under Linux. Each platform has different characteristics and code needs to be optimized for the OS.

Summary

This chapter gives you the information to get started on the track to migrating from a Windows NT environment to Linux. Although not 100 percent complete in everything you need to know about the Linux OS, it serves as a good starting point in transferring user accounts and shares.

Linux is a UNIX clone, and therefore brings with it all the complexities of that operating system. There are various excellent books on the market that describe Linux in depth. One of my favorites is *Special Edition Using Linux, Fourth Edition,* published by Que.

Integrating NetWare to Linux

SOME OF THE MAIN TOPICS IN THIS CHAPTER ARE

Why Migrate to Linux?

Key Differences Between Linux and NetWare

Moving User Accounts

Networking

Applications

Third-Party Tools

Although it might not be obvious why anyone would want to move from a NetWare-based network to one based on Linux, there are some situations in which this can be considered a good idea. The two systems are very different from each other, so considering such a migration requires diligent planning. While Linux has not yet progressed to the stage where it can really compete with other operating systems for the desktop, it does have a good track record when used as a network server, Web server, or a firewall. In this chapter, we look at some of the key differences between Linux and NetWare and discuss a few scenarios in which a partial or total migration might be done.

Why Migrate to Linux?

Many established users of any popular operating system will always find it a mystery when trying to decide why management has decreed that a new system or platform will be used. The old "we've always done it this way" attitude seems to invade a comfortable corporate life in a very short time. The truth of the matter is that not only are the times changing, but technology is changing even faster; if you don't keep up, you may not survive in the business world.

NetWare has been around for many years, and other than ARCnet is perhaps the oldest PC networking technology that is still in existence on a wide scale. It has been deployed in large networks that span great geographical distances as well as in small departmental LANs. In the case of the larger dispersed network, where most users depend on their workstation for word processing and other typical office applications, it would not make a great deal of sense to plan a quick migration to Linux. This is mainly because of the lack of applications that run on the platform.

A good scenario for a conversion is a small LAN. For example, consider a small company that originally created a small LAN to link several Intel-based Web servers that used a Windows operating system. Business has grown and it's time to upgrade. The choices are more powerful Intel-based systems running a windows variant or Linux boxes. In this case Linux has the edge. However, the existing LAN uses NetWare to exchange information between servers, so a switch to Linux will require some new networking skills.

Another reason why you might consider changing to Linux if you have a small LAN is that it's basically free. You can buy inexpensive versions from the many vendors, such as Caldera or Red Hat, that have sprung up to cater to the Linux community, or you can download a version from a Web site and compile it yourself. If you have an experienced UNIX staff at your site, Linux will be much cheaper to implement than NetWare. Without the experienced staff, however, it may become more expensive when it comes to support.

Key Differences Between Linux and NetWare

The most obvious difference that should come to mind when looking at NetWare and Linux is that Linux is a computer operating system and NetWare is a network operating system. NetWare can be run on many different platforms, usually ones having their roots in MS-DOS or Windows of some kind. Yet, no matter which platform you use NetWare on, it basically only provides support for network resource sharing. Authentication services are provided, as are mechanisms for granting or denying access to data held on computers that NetWare is hosted on. However, the underlying operating system can also be used to enforce access permissions and user authentication.

File Sharing

NetWare excels at providing file servers on the network. Either the bindery based NetWare 3.x or the newer NDS versions can be used to exercise a great deal of control over file and directory access for one or more servers on the network. Using NDS you can distribute files throughout the network on multiple servers. Clients can be authenticated by bindery-based servers, or NDS, and access resources they need.

When using Linux you will find that there are no "file shares" and no directory services. Instead, you will have to substitute NFS, the Network File System, which was originally developed by Sun. Access permissions can be controlled using the standard mechanisms provided by Linux. You can set up NFS so that users must log on to each server in order to mount the exported file system, or you can hide the authentication process from users by using proxy-like mechanisms built into most NFS implementations.

Printer Sharing

NetWare is capable of providing support for many different kinds of printing technologies and protocols, including the lpr/lpd protocols used by Linux. When changing the network over to Linux servers, you will have to reconfigure not only servers that provide the gateway to a printer, but also clients so that they can connect to the correct server that hosts the printer they need. Alternatively, for printers or print servers that have a direct network connection, you can configure clients to use that network address.

User Authentication

If the NetWare version you currently employ uses bindery-based authentication services, you will be familiar with having to log on to each server when you need to access a resource. Similarly, Linux uses a `passwrd` file that resides on each system and users need to have an entry in this file that can be used when they log on to the server. Linux does not natively support a directory service, such as NDS, so providing a single logon for the network will not be something you get out of the box.

Moving User Accounts

To establish user accounts on the Linux server you will have to manually configure them yourself. There are no widely available utilities or tools that you can use to perform this function. In Chapter 24, "UNIX and Linux," the typical UNIX/Linux `passwrd` file is discussed and can be used as a reference for the kind of information you will need to create user accounts on a Linux system. If you only need to create a few user accounts, for just system administrators, for example, the process will be a simple one. If you are going to create a large number of accounts, for client workstations possibly, you will probably find it necessary to produce a report from the NetWare system and use this to make the entries or create a script file that can be used for this purpose.

NetWare, particularly the 4.x and higher versions that support NetWare Directory Services, keeps track of a lot more information for a user account than is done on a Linux system. Because of this, and the simplicity of the passwrd file, you won't have to do a lot of work to create new user accounts. However, you may find that the trade-off is that you need to examine security (file permissions, for example) and other aspects of your Linux system to ensure that your users are afforded the same access.

Networking

The TCP/IP protocol is the standard that is used on the Internet. It has become increasingly more popular for use in all kinds of networks in just the last few years. For example, early versions of Windows NT would install the IPX/SPX protocol by default. Starting with Windows NT 4.0 the default is TCP/IP.

However, you do not need to replace your NetWare servers with Linux systems in order to use TCP/IP as your network protocol. NetWare 5.0 supports IP. You would only need to upgrade your network to the new version of NetWare to get access to this important protocol.

Applications

Unfortunately, if you have a large investment in application software that was written (or compiled) for a Windows platform, you will need to invest additional funds to purchase new versions of your existing software or for new software. If you have internally developed applications for which you have the source code, you may only need to make minor changes and recompile the source code on the new Linux system.

The popularity of Linux continues to grow and many vendors have started to think about producing Linux versions of their products. You won't find Microsoft Office there yet, but you will find competing products. Provided that you can use the file conversion capabilities that come with most products of this sort, you might find that changing to a new product is not that painful, short of a little user training.

Third-Party Tools

Linux is an open source product that is supported by many individuals on the Internet, along with several new start-up companies that have began to produce additional utilities and products for the Linux community. In particular, Caldera has produced NetWare for Linux, which can be installed on its version of Linux, as well as those from Red Hat Linux 5.1 and possibly other variants. While the product should probably not be used as a substitute for NetWare in a large environment, it is quite suitable for providing NetWare services to a few clients in a LAN. You might also make use of it when performing a migration to Linux when you have a few clients that need to continue using NetWare for some period of time. You can move your files and printers to Linux servers, configure NetWare for Linux, and then allow those few clients to make use of it.

NetWare for Linux provides

- Novell Directory Services (NDS)
- NetWare File Services
- NetWare Print Services
- NetWare Client support
- NetWare User Account Security and Authentication

The installation can be performed on a Caldera Linux system quickly using a setup file or manually on other Linux systems. To update the Caldera version, you need only to change your directory to the installation CD and enter the command:

```
./update.NWS4L
```

When the procedure finishes, you will need to reboot. Other commands that are useful include

- `nwserverstatus`—Shows status information about the Linux NetWare server.
- `/etc/rc.d/init.d/netware start`—Use this to start the NetWare server.
- `/etc/rc.d/init.d/netware stop`—Use this to stop the NetWare server.

You can also install the Caldera NetWare for Linux client on Linux systems. This allows Linux clients to connect to the Linux server that runs the NetWare services or to an actual NetWare server. In this way, both ordinary NetWare clients and Linux clients can share the same information. Some useful commands for the client include

- `nwlogon <netware user name>`—Log on to NetWare if using NDS. You can also log on to a particular context using the nwlogon command, and connect to a specific NDS tree.
- `nwlogin -s <server> -b -u <NetWare username>`—This form of the command is used to log on to the server when using the bindery instead of NDS.
- `nwlogout -s <server>`—This will log you off the particular server.
- `nwlogout -t <tree>`—This will log you off a particular NDS tree.
- `nwwhoami`—This will display status information about your process, showing the NDS trees you have connected to, the username used, and so on.
- `nwprint <filename>`—This command allows the client to submit files to print.

Accessing files on a NetWare-enabled Linux server is done in the same manner as for other files in the Linux file system. The NetWare files will appear under the /NetWare/bindery directory (if using bindery services) or the /NetWare/NDS directory (when using NDS).

Summary

Although it is not practical yet to convert a large network from NetWare to Linux, under some circumstances it is a doable proposition. The differences between the two systems require that the administrator understand how NetWare and Linux each provide file, print, and other services to clients. Software from Caldera can be used on many versions of Linux to allow you to continue to provide NetWare services to Linux and other clients.

Part XVI

HYBRID NETWORKS

Integrating NetWare with Windows NT

SOME OF THE MAIN TOPICS IN THIS CHAPTER ARE

Microsoft Client Tools

NetWare Utilities

Often, the choices we face are not answered by simple solutions. Previous chapters have examined some of the issues involved with migrating from NetWare to Windows NT, and vice versa, but it is not always the case that a conversion from one to the other will be the best or most cost-effective solution. A simple example is when a business merger or acquisition occurs. If one of the partners to the transaction is a small organization, a conversion of their network to the technologies used by the larger partner might be in order.

However, it is more often the case that you will find it necessary to integrate multiple operating systems and networking technologies so that both can be used throughout the enterprise. This chapter discusses the tools offered by Microsoft and Novell that can be used to allow clients and servers from both companies to communicate and share resources in a network.

Microsoft Client Tools

Microsoft provides four basic tools that can be used to allow NetWare and Microsoft clients to access servers that reside in both environments. These tools are

- **File and Print Services for NetWare (FPNW)**—This tool enables clients using NetWare (in bindery mode) to connect to file and print services offered by Windows NT server computers. To the NetWare client the service appears to be offered by a NetWare server.

- **Gateway Services for NetWare (GSNW)**—This tool enables a Microsoft network client to access file and print shares offered by NetWare servers. The services are provided to the Microsoft clients through a gateway Windows NT server computer that is used to communicate with the NetWare servers.

- **Directory Service Manager for NetWare (DSMN)**—You can use this tool to provide a single logon service to NetWare users on the network who still log on to servers that use the bindery.

- **Client Services for NetWare**—This tool provides a more direct method for a Microsoft client. It allows the client to directly connect to a service offered by a NetWare server.

Note

Another tool that Microsoft provides that is used to assist in integrating NetWare and Microsoft environments is the Migration Tool for NetWare. This utility will enable you to propagate information about NetWare user accounts to a Windows NT server, along with other information such as file permissions and logon scripts. However, this chapter focuses on implementing a mixed network, not a migration. For more information on the Migration Tool for NetWare, see Chapter 45, "Migrating from Novell NetWare to Windows NT 4.0."

Whether you use one or more of these tools will depend on the degree of integration that is needed in the network. For example, if you have a small NetWare LAN whose users have no need to access NT servers, yet you have NT clients that occasionally need to retrieve information from the NetWare LAN, installing the gateway on an NT server might be all that you require. It is inexpensive (free, because it comes with the Windows NT server operating system), simple to configure, and easy to use.

File and Print Services for NetWare (FPNW)

This product is not included with the Windows NT server or Workstation operating systems and must be purchased separately. It is used to allow NetWare clients to access resources on a Windows NT server computer as if they were offered on the network by a NetWare server. FPNW can be used as an intermediate step toward converting your NetWare clients to an NT-only network, or it can be used when you must run both at the same time. For existing NetWare networks, FPNW can help you to seamlessly integrate Windows NT servers into the network without having to install or modify client software. In addition, Windows NT clients can also access the same server and the same files and printers that are made available to NetWare clients.

When FPNW is installed on the Windows NT server several of the administrative utilities, such as the User Manager for Domains and the Server Manager, are updated to include new functionality. You can create user accounts on an NT domain for NetWare users, or you can use the Migration tool for NetWare to copy existing NetWare user account information to a Windows NT server. When a NetWare client has an account in a Windows NT domain, the client can be given access to resources in other trusting domains just like ordinary Windows NT clients.

Technical Note

FPNW can be used to give NetWare 2.x, 3.x, and 4.x clients access to Windows NT Resources in bindery emulation mode. It does not provide functionality to interface with Novell Directory Services.

In addition to providing network file services for NetWare and Microsoft clients, FPNW also enables you to share printers that are connected locally to the NT server computer and those directly connected to the network.

Comparison of Windows NT and NetWare File Permission Rights

In Chapter 26, "Rights and Permissions," the ability to restrict user access to files, directories, and volumes was discussed for both NetWare and Windows NT users. When using FPNW, trustee rights for directories for NetWare clients can be mapped to those used on Windows NT systems, as shown in Table 51.1. Table 51.2 shows the same thing in reverse—how FPNW will translate NT permissions for directories to NetWare directory rights.

Table 51.1   Mapping NetWare Trustee Rights to Windows NT Permissions in FPNW for Directories

NetWare Directory Rights	Windows NT Directory Permissions
Read (R)	Read (RX) (RX)
Write (W)	Write (W) (W)
Create (C)	Write (W) (W)
Erase (E)	Delete (D) (D)
Modify (M)	Write (W) (W)
File Scan (F)	Read (R) (R)
Access Control (A)	Change Permissions (PO) (PO)

Table 51.2   Mapping Windows NT Permissions to NetWare Trustee Rights in FPNW for Directories

Windows NT Directory Permissions	NetWare Directory Rights
List (RX) (not specified)	Read, File (RF)
Read (RX) (RX)	Red, File (RF)
Add (WX) (not specified)	Write, Create, Modify (WCM)
Add and Read (RWX) (RX)	Read, Write, Create Modify, File Scan (RWCMF)
Change (RWXD) (RWXD)	Read, Write, Create Modify, File Scan (RWCMF)
Full Control (All) (All)	Supervisor (S)

For files, Table 51.3 shows the mapping that is done by FPNW from NetWare to Windows NT; Table 51.4 shows the mapping that is done from NetWare to Windows NT. Note that Windows NT server uses directory permissions for granting the Create and File Scan equivalent rights that NetWare uses as file rights.

Table 51.3   Mapping NetWare File Trustee Rights to Windows NT Server File Permissions

NetWare File Rights	Windows NT File Permissions
Supervisor (S)	Full Control (All)
Read (R)	Read (R)
Access Control (A)	Change Permissions (PO)
Create (C)	Write (W)
Erase (E)	Delete (D)
Modify (M)	Write (W) (W)
Write (W)	Write (W)

Table 51.4   Mapping Windows NT Server File Permissions to NetWare File Trustee Rights

Windows NT File Permissions	NetWare File Rights
Read (RX)	Read, File (RF)
Change (RWXD)	Read, Write, Create Modify, File Scan (RWCMF)
Full Control (All)	Supervisor (S)

In addition to having to translate between the rights and permissions used on each system, FPNW also translates between the different kinds of file attributes that both systems use at the file level. Table 51.5 shows the translation mapping that FPNW performs.

Table 51.5 Mapping File Attributes Between Windows NT and NetWare

NetWare File Attributes	Windows NT File Attributes
Read Only (RO)	Read Only (R)
Delete Inhibit (D)	Read Only (R), or remove user permissions to delete the file
Rename Inhibit	Assigned at the directory level by removing the user's permission to write to the directory
Archive Needed (A)	Archive (A)
System (Sy)	System (S)
Hidden (H)	Hidden (H)
Execute Only (X)	Execute (E)
Read Audit (Ra)	Audit Read, Audit Execute
Write Audit (Wa)	Audit Write, Audit Delete

However, FNPW does not provide support for the NetWare attributes:

- Don't Compress
- File Migrated
- File Compressed
- Immediate Compress
- Can't Compress
- Purge
- Index FAT Entries
- Transactional Tracking
- File Migrated

The attribute Shareable can be set only on a per-server or global basis when using FPNW. It cannot be set on an individual file.

You should carefully examine how security is currently enforced for clients on the existing NetWare network before beginning to decide how to offer file shares from a Windows NT server. Understanding the mapping between the two systems can prevent unexpected access violations or errors from compromising security on the network.

Installing FPNW

FPNW is installed as a service on a Windows NT server computer. As with other network services, this is done using the Network applet in the Control Panel. During the installation of the service you will be prompted to enter a disk drive and directory that will be used for the location of the SYSVOL directory, which will be used as the NetWare compatible SYS: volume. To enforce security rights and permissions on the volume, you must use a drive that is formatted with the NTFS file system. It is possible to use a drive that is formatted using FAT, but all security will then be enforced at a share level and not on the basis of individual files or directories.

The installation process will also ask that you enter a name that will be used by NetWare users to connect to the server. This name must be unique on the network and you should enter it in all uppercase letters. Next you will enter a supervisor's password.

FPNW can be installed on any Windows NT server computer. If you are installing the service on a domain controller, a special account called the FPNW Service Account will be created and you will have to also supply a password for this account. If you install the service on other domain controllers, be sure to use the same password.

When you have finished entering this information, reboot the server and the service will start.

If you examine the drive that you used to host the SYSVOL directory, you will find that the installation has created several subdirectories under this directory:

- **\LOGIN**—This directory holds the utilities that NetWare clients use to log in to the NT server.

- **\MAIL**—User subdirectories will be created here and may contain login scripts for users.

- **\PUBLIC**—The following utilities are found here: attach, capture, endcap, login, logout, map, setpass, and slist.

- **\SYSTEM**—Files used to support printing will be found here.

Gateway Services for NetWare (GSNW)

Microsoft employs two methods to allow its networking clients to connect to services offered by a NetWare server. Client Services for NetWare allows each client to make connections directly to NetWare servers, as if they were ordinary NetWare clients. This method has advantages in that only the Microsoft client and the NetWare server are involved in processing the exchange of data. However, in a network where the interaction between Microsoft clients and NetWare servers will not be large, and a large assortment of clients might need to make the connection at one time or another, a better solution might be the Gateway Services for NetWare (GSNW) product.

Technical Note

Gateway Services for NetWare uses Microsoft's implementation of IPX/SPX, called NWLink, to communicate with NetWare servers. You must install NWLink before you will be able to use GSNW.

When using GSNW, a Windows NT server computer acts as a link between Microsoft clients and the NetWare server. Microsoft clients continue to use the Server Message block (SMB) protocols to access network resources, with the gateway server performing the bridging function to the NetWare servers that use the NetWare Core Protocol (NCP) for file and print functions.

The gateway server does this by redirecting a drive to the NetWare volume. It then offers the drive as a share to Microsoft clients. You can treat this share just like any other share offered by the server, when it comes to management utilities.

Another feature that GSNW provides is the capability for the Windows NT server that is hosting the gateway software to make direct connections to NetWare services just as workstations do when using the Client Services for NetWare product. A local user on the server can elect to connect to NetWare resources without offering them to other clients via the gateway.

Installing and Configuring GSNW

You install GSNW by installing a network service using the Network applet in the Windows NT Control Panel. On the Services tab (see Figure 51.1), click the Add button to see the Select Network Service dialog box, showing a list of the services that you can add (see Figure 51.2).

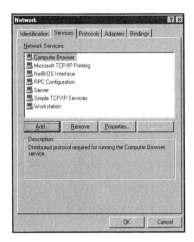

Figure 51.1   Use the Services tab of the Control Panel's Network applet to install GSNW.

Figure 51.2   Select the service from the list shown.

After the files have been copied you must reboot the server and reapply the latest service pack. When this has been done you will find that there is now an icon in the Control Panel labeled GSNW, which can be used to configure the service. Additionally, when the server is first rebooted after installing the gateway service, you will be prompted (as shown in Figure 51.3) to enter either

- A default NDS tree and context
- A preferred NetWare server

Figure 51.3   Enter the information that will be used to authenticate the server to the NetWare network.

You must choose one or the other. You can have either a default NDS tree and context or you can elect to use a preferred server. The preferred server should be selected if your network does not use NDS. In this case you will be authenticated by that server when accessing resources on NetWare. If you do use NDS you can select to use a default NDS tree and set the context. Using this method will still allow you to connect to NetWare servers that use bindery security instead of NDS.

Note

If you plan to use the gateway NT server to access both NDS resources and NetWare servers that run in bindery mode, you should use a bindery account instead of an NDS tree and context. If you plan to use only NDS resources, you can use an NDS account. If you use a bindery account, it will be capable of using bindery emulation to connect to NDS resources.

After you have installed the software and have entered the authentication information needed to access services on the NetWare network, you must do several things to make NetWare resources available to your Microsoft clients. First, you must make sure that there is a user account on the NetWare network that has the needed access rights to the resources for which you want to create a gateway. On the NetWare side there must also be a group named Ntgateway that has the needed rights for the resources. The NetWare user account that you will use must be a member of this group.

To create a gateway

- **Enable gateways on the server that is running the GSNW software.** This must be done only once to establish the gateway.
- **Activate each file or print resource gateway.** This must be done for each resource you want to offer to Microsoft clients.

To enable a gateway, use the GSNW applet that is now found in the Control Panel (see Figure 51.4). Use the Gateway button to bring up the Configure Gateway dialog box (see Figure 51.5).

In the Configure Gateway dialog box you will again have to enter a method and the information required to access the resources you need on a NetWare server. This is in addition to the account that you supplied when the Windows NT server was first rebooted after the gateway service was installed. That first logon information is used to enable the Windows NT server to log on as a user to the NetWare account. The second account will be used here to actually access the needed resource.

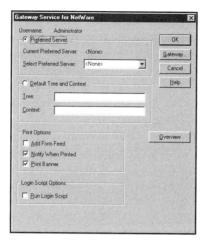

Figure 51.4   The GSNW applet in the Control Panel enables you to configure the gateway service.

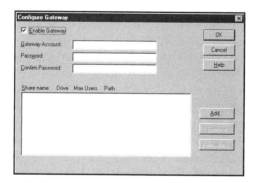

Figure 51.5   Use the Gateway button on the GSNW dialog box to bring up the Configure Gateway dialog box.

After you supply a gateway account and password (and type the password in again in the confirm box), use the Add button to add a NetWare file share resource that you want to add to the gateway. In Figure 51.6 you can see the dialog box that enables you to add a resource.

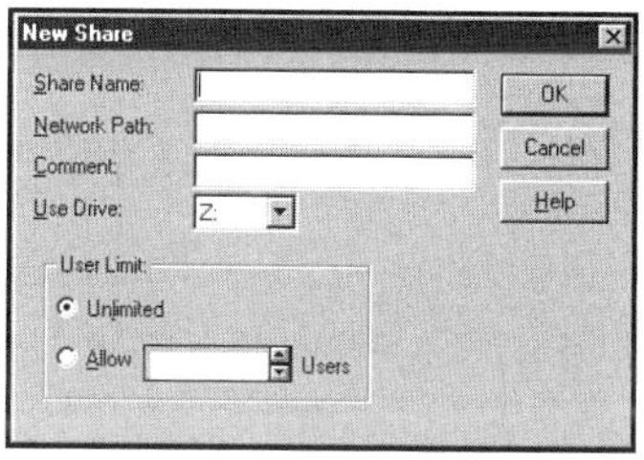

Figure 51.6   Enter the path to the NetWare resource and select the drive letter that will be used on the Windows NT server.

You can also place comments in the appropriate field and elect to limit the number of simultaneous users that can connect to the share when it is offered to Microsoft clients via the gateway.

Setting up a printer that will allow Microsoft clients to send documents to NetWare printers or print queues via the gateway is performed in a manner similar to setting up other printers in Windows NT. The difference is that you must correctly specify the port for the printer. To make a NetWare printer available through the gateway, follow these steps:

1. Click Start, Settings, Printers.

2. From the Add Printer Wizard dialog box that appears, select My Computer. Do not select Network Printer Server.

3. The next dialog box shows available printer ports on the server. Click the Add Port button.

4. Depending on the network protocols and services installed on the computer, you will then be shown a list of printer ports that can be added. Select Local Port from this list and click the New Port button.

5. Finally, in the Port Name dialog box that pops up, enter the UNC pathname that is used to designate the NetWare Printer resource (\\servername\printername).

The remainder of the Add Printer Wizard works just as it does for any other printer. You will have to select a driver for the printer and specify the name that will be used when it is offered as a share on the Microsoft network.

Directory Service Manager for NetWare (DSMN)

One of the nice things about a network that is based on the Windows NT domain model is the single logon feature. This enables a user to log on at a client workstation using a single username and password to gain access to resources throughout the network, provided that the appropriate rights and permissions have been established for the resources the user wants to connect to.

DSMN is another optional tool that you can use to extend the single logon feature to your NetWare clients. It provides a simple method to manage users in a mixed network of NT and NetWare clients from a single user database.

Like the File and Print Services for NetWare product, however, DSMN operates only with NetWare 2.x, 3.x, and 4.x clients in bindery emulation mode. Also, DSMN must be installed on a Windows NT server computer that is operating as a primary domain controller in the network, and you must first install the Gateway Service for NetWare before you perform the DSMN installation.

DSMN also can be used to copy account information between NetWare servers and Windows NT domain controllers and to keep user passwords synchronized between both systems. You can select users or groups of users that you want to move between each system.

You install DSMN as a service, using the Network applet in the Control Panel. Use the Have Disk option and specify a path to the CD that contains the source files. When the computer is rebooted, the service will start. In the Administrative Tools folder you will then see Directory Service Manager for NetWare (also called the Synchronization Manager), which you can use to specify which servers you want to manage. When you select a NetWare server that you want to manage from Windows NT, you can select users or groups of users whose accounts will be copied to the NT server and placed in the domain database. From then on you can manage these users using the User Manager for Domains. DSMN will propagate changes you make to these accounts back to the NetWare servers where the accounts originated.

To manage users and NetWare servers you will use two utilities. The Synchronization Manager is used to add a NetWare server to the domain. The User Manager for Domains can then be used to manage any user accounts that you choose to copy from the NetWare server to the domain. Changes made to user accounts using User Manager will be copied back to the NetWare server (synchronized) on a periodic basis so that you will no longer have to use NetWare utilities to manage these users.

Technical Note

Although you will manage NetWare users that you copy to the NT domain by using the User Manager for Domains, you will continue to manage other administrative functions that you would normally perform on the NetWare server using NetWare utilities. This includes things such as managing shared NetWare volumes, file permissions, printing, and so on. Additionally, a NetWare server can be added to only one Windows NT domain. If you want to change this domain association at a later time, remove it from the NT domain, and then use the Synchronization Manager to add it to another domain.

To add a NetWare server to the domain using the Synchronization Manager follow these steps:

1. From the NetWare Server menu select Add Server to Manage.

2. When prompted, enter the name of a NetWare server. Click OK.

3. Enter a username that is valid on the NetWare server and the password for the username. Note that this user account must have Supervisor privileges on the server.

4. In the Propagate NetWare Accounts to Windows NT Domain dialog box, select either Use Mapping File or Ignore Mapping File.

5. A prompt will warn you to first make a backup of the NetWare server's bindery. Click Yes to continue.

6. The Set Propagated Accounts on *servername* dialog box appears. You can select to propagate some or all groups or user accounts back to the NetWare server. You will then be asked if you want to delete any remaining users or groups from the NetWare server that you have not selected. Click either Yes or No. You can continue to manage any users that are left behind on the NetWare server using the ordinary NetWare tools.

After you add a NetWare server to the Windows NT domain it will appear in the main screen for the Synchronization Manager utility. Also, in the NetWare server's bindery you will see a new account, named WINNT_SYNC_AGENT. Do not delete this account because it is used by Windows NT when it synchronizes changes made to user accounts.

If you want to map NetWare usernames or groups to a different name on the NT server, you can use the Synchronization Manager to create a mapping file.

Client Services for NetWare (CSNW)

This service can be installed on Windows NT Workstation computers to allow the workstation to connect to file and print services provided by NetWare servers on the network. The installation process is simple. Bring up the Network applet in the Control Panel. Select the Services tab, and then click the Add button to add a new service. From the list that is displayed, select Client Services for NetWare. When the setup process has finished copying the necessary files, it will prompt you to enter the name of a NetWare server that will be used to authenticate the client. After you furnish this name, the workstation will need to be rebooted before the service takes effect.

When the workstation logs on to the NetWare server it will use the username of the user who is locally logged on to the workstation. If your password on the workstation is different than that on the NetWare server, you will be prompted to enter it. It is a good idea to keep these passwords the same to keep users happy.

If you must connect to servers other than the Preferred Server that was designated when the CSNW service was installed, use the Windows NT Explorer and select Map Network Drive from the Tools menu just as you would when connecting to a network drive offered by a Windows NT computer. You will have to enter a username and password that is valid on the NetWare server to make the connection.

NetWare Utilities

Not to be outdone by Microsoft, Novell has developed its own solutions for networks that are made up of products from both companies. This includes several versions of client software that Windows NT workstations can use to connect to Novell network resources and a more comprehensive solution called NDS for NT, which allows Windows NT domains to be administered from NDS.

Novell Client for Windows NT

The Novell Client for Windows NT is an easily installed application that allows the Windows NT client to log on to the NetWare network via NDS. It also provides password synchronization between Windows NT and NetWare so that users do not have to maintain multiple user accounts. To install the client, run the WINSETUP.EXE program on the source CD. Note that you can also run the setup program from a network file share. When prompted, select the language you want to use (such as English), and then select Windows NT Client. After the files are copied to the workstation, you will have to reboot. When the workstation has rebooted you will get a Novell logon prompt (see Figure 51.7).

In this figure you can see that you can specify an NDS tree and context or a NetWare server to use for the logon process. Other tabs on the Novell Logon dialog box enable you to run a logon script or use Dial-Up Networking to log on to the network.

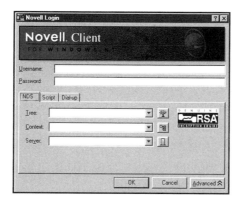

Figure 51.7 The client software allows the user to log on to the Novell network.

Technical Note

The program WINSETUP.EXE on the source CD for the client actually runs a program called SETUPNW.EXE, which is found in the \PRODUCTS\WINNT\I386 subdirectory. To perform a typical installation, use WINSETUP.EXE. If you want to customize the setup procedure, by using a configuration file for example, use SETUPNW.EXE. Use **SETUPNW** /? to obtain help about the options used with this command.

After the client software is installed, you can configure it by using the properties page. You can get to the Novell Client Configuration properties page by either

- Right-clicking the Network Neighborhood icon on the desktop and selecting Properties
- Selecting the Network icon in the Control Panel

From either of these, select the Services tab, highlight Novell Client for Windows NT, and then click Properties. The properties page consists of multiple tabs, as you can see in Figure 51.8.

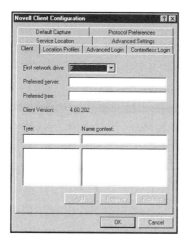

Figure 51.8 The Novell Client Configuration properties page enables you to further configure the client software after the installation is complete.

Each tab on the properties page enables you to configure different aspects of the client software. These include the following:

- **Client**—Here you can set the first drive letter that will be used to connect to network resources, the preferred server or NDS tree, and other NDS trees along with the context for this particular user.

- **Location Profiles**—Enables you to set up different configurations, such as NDS tree and context, so that a user can select the profile to use when moving from one workstation or location to another.

- **Advanced Login**—Control the information displayed by the login dialog box using this tab. You can change the bitmap and caption that is displayed, set a path for a particular policy, and decide whether the Advanced button is shown, among other things.

- **Contextless Login**—You can use this tab to configure a contextless login, which enables the user to log in without specifying an NDS context.

- **Service Location**—This tab enables you to set up scope names that are reported to SLP (Service Location Protocol) applications on the workstation. A *scope* is a collection of services in a logical group.

- **Advanced Settings**—This properties page contains a large list of parameters you can configure for the workstation. These include things like Auto Reconnect, which causes a connection to be reestablished if it is lost, or Burst Mode, which can improve performance by allowing larger network transfers.

- **Default Capture**—Specify printing parameters here, such as number of copies, whether to print a banner page, and whether a form-feed character is sent at the end of a print job.

- **Protocol Preferences**—Here you can configure the preferred network protocol (IP or IPX) and other settings for each protocol, such as DNS or SAP.

Of the preceding properties tabs, the Advanced Settings contains a wide range of parameters that can be configured for the client. For troubleshooting purposes, the information you can find here is invaluable. Table 51.6 lists each parameter and gives a brief description of its usage. Unless otherwise listed, each parameter can be configured as either *on* (enabled) or *off* (disabled).

Table 51.6   Parameters Configured Using the Advanced Settings Tab

Parameter	Usage
Auto Reconnect	Reconnect if network connection lost
Burst Mode	Use Packet Burst mode
DOS Long Name Support	Enables DOS application long name support
DOS Name	Name returned by the **%OS** variable (text string)
Give Up on Requests to SAs	Seconds to wait on SA requests (1–60,000 seconds)
Large Internet Packet Start Size	Starting value for negotiating Large Internet Packet Size (512–65,535 bytes)
Large Internet Packets	Enables the maximum packet size negotiated between NetWare server and workstation
Limit SAP Broadcast Queries	Disabling this will cause the use of SAP to locate servers if bindery queries fail
Link Support Layer Max Buffer Size	Maximum supported packet size (638–24,682 bytes)
Long Machine Type	Value for the **%MACHINE** environment variable (text string)

Parameter	Usage
Max Read Burst Size	Maximum value for read burst (1–65,536 bytes)
Max Write Burst Size	Maximum value for write burst (1–65,536 bytes)
Minimum Time to Net	Time to make connection across WAN link (0–65,536 milliseconds)
Name Resolution Timeout	Time to wait for name resolution for the configured namespace (1–180 seconds)
Opportunistic Locking	Enabling this improves performance by allowing exclusive file caching
Quit Idle Connects	Time for DAs and SAs to close idle TCP connections (1–60,000 minutes)
Receive Broadcast Message	Sets broadcast messages received (All, Server Only or None)
Replica Timeout	Replica timeout value (0–1,000 minutes)
Send Message	Enables the send message function
Set Station Time	If enabled, workstation's time and date are synchronized with first NetWare server connected
Short Machine Type	Determines the overlay file used for older NetWare utilities (text string)
Show Edit Login Script Item	Enables Edit DS Login Script item on the User Administration menu
Show Novell System Tray Icon	Enables the "N" Novell icon in the desktop system tray
Show Scheduler System Tray Icon	Enables the scheduler icon in the desktop system tray
Show User Administration Menu	Enables the menu item for user administration (in context menu of server or NDS tree)
Signature Level	Level for enhanced security support (numeric 0–3)
SLP Active Discovery	When enabled, SLP will use multicast or broadcast if Directory Agent unavailable
SLP Cache Replies	Time to cache replies by XID (1–60 minutes)
SLP Default Registration Lifetime	Time for default registration lifetime of a service (60–60,000 seconds)
SLP Maximum Transmission Unit	Maximum size of UDP packet (576–4,096 bytes)
SLP Multicast Radius	Number of routers (+1) that SLP multicast can traverse (numeric 1–32)
Use Broadcast for SLP Multicast	When enabled, use broadcast instead of IP multicasting
Use DHCP for SLP	When enabled, use DHCP to obtain SLP scope and Directory Agent configuration
Wait Before Giving Up On DA	Time to wait for DA requests (1–60,000 seconds)
Wait Before Registering on Passive DA	Time to wait before registering service on passive DA discovery (1–60,000 seconds)

As you can see, you can fine-tune the operation of the client software a great deal using this tab. For example, by setting the Large Internet Packet Start Size to a higher value, you might be able to shorten the time the client and server spend negotiating this size over a slow link. On a token-ring network you might change the value for Link Support Layer Max Buffer Size so that a packet size larger than the default is used, thus improving performance. Many of the timeout values can be manipulated to solve problems over slow links when users have problems connecting to resources.

NDS for NT

NDS for NT works by moving the information contained in the Windows NT Security Accounts Manager (SAM) database to NDS. The Domain Object Wizard extends the NDS schema to create new objects that will represent the NT domain and its users. NDS for NT then intercepts calls made to modify the SAM and redirects them to NDS. This allows the administrator to use either Windows NT administrative utilities, such as the User Manager for Domains, or the NetWare administrative utilities to manage both Windows NT and NetWare servers throughout the network.

The functionality provided by NDS for NT is similar to what you get with Microsoft's DSNW, in that it provides a single network logon for users. However, remember that DSNW works only with bindery-enabled NetWare servers and does not allow for administering NDS. Password synchronization can also be performed by selecting the Force Password Sync check box for each user. When the user or the administrator changes a password using a NetWare or any Windows NT utility, the Novell client software installed on the computer will look in NDS to determine whether the account exists in an NT domain that is stored in NDS. If so, it will make the password change for the domain and the NDS databases.

Another useful feature that NDS for NT provides is the capability to move a user from one domain object to another. In Windows NT this would require either creating trust relationships between domains so that users can access resources in domains other than where their user account exists, or you could create an account for the user in each domain he or she needs to access. This second method, however, defeats the single-logon feature.

Installing NDS for NT

Before installing NDS for NT you should have already installed the Novell Client for NT, using at least version 4.5 or higher. You can install NDS for NT only on a Primary Domain Controller (PDC) or a Backup Domain Controller (BDC). The installation procedure takes only a few minutes and requires that you have usernames and passwords for accounts that have administrative capabilities in both the Windows NT domain you are going to NDS-enable and in the NDS tree into which you will insert the domain object.

To begin the installation, insert the source CD to bring up the first screen, or run the WINSETUP.EXE program that comes with the source files. Figure 51.9 shows the first screen, which enables you to install NDS for NT as well as the administrative utilities that can be used on the NT server to manage NDS.

Click on NDS for NT to continue the installation. If you have not yet installed the Novell Client for NT, the setup procedure will do it for you (see Figure 51.10). The client software is the mechanism that NDS uses to communicate with the NT server when performing maintenance functions.

After the client software files have been copied to the NT server, you will have to reboot to continue. When the reboot has finished you will be prompted to first authenticate to the NDS tree using a username that has administrative privileges. This is necessary because the schema of NDS will be extended to add objects for NT. After you have been authenticated by NDS, the Domain Object Wizard will prompt you to continue and move information from the domain database to the NDS tree (see Figure 51.11). Other functions that the Domain Object Wizard can perform include creating an NDS replica on the local NT server. This can be useful if the NT server resides in a segment of the network that is connected to the main NDS network by a WAN link. Keeping a replica on a local server reduces traffic across the WAN link and improves performance for local users.

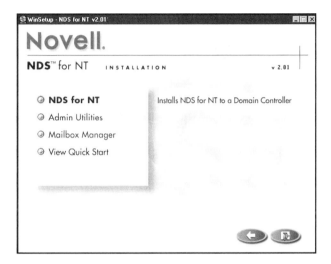

Figure 51.9   You can install both NDS for NT and NDS management utilities on the NT server.

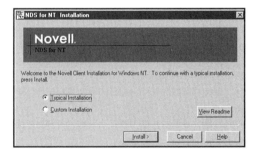

Figure 51.10   The Novell Client for NT software must be installed first.

The remaining screens presented by the installation utility will prompt you to select the NDS tree into which the domain will be inserted and to identify the container object (such as an organizational unit) that will hold the domain object. After you have selected the NDS tree, the NDS schema will be extended. The utility will also enable you to identify users that already exist in both the NDS tree and the Windows NT domain so that their accounts can be merged into one in the final database. When the utility has finished copying domain information to the NDS tree, you can view an error log to determine whether any further administrative tasks must be performed.

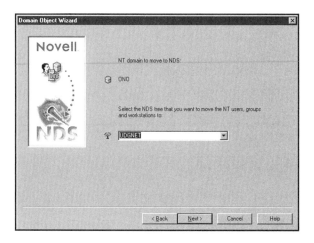

Figure 51.11   You can select the NDS tree used for this domain.

Administrative Utilities

Although it is not required, you can also install NDS administrative utilities on the NT server that can be used to administer the domain via NDS. You can still use the User Manager for Domains, Server Manager, and other Windows NT utilities to continue managing the domain users and resources, but if you install the NDS utilities, you will be able to administer other NDS resources that are not specific to the domain as well. The following tools will be installed:

- **NWAdmin**—This application, called the Netware Administrator, is used to manage objects in the NDS tree, such as users and resources.

- **NDS Manager**—This application is used to perform NDS partitioning and replication functions in NDS.

- **Domain Object Wizard**—This is the utility that you first used to transfer information from the domain to NDS. It can be used later to add or remove NDS replicas on NT servers or to remove NDS for NT if that is desired.

These two applications will be installed in the C:\Novell\Public\Win32 directory. You can also install the utilities on a NetWare server if that is more convenient. In that case they will be found in the Sys:Public\Win32 directory on the NetWare server.

Because NDS or NT essentially makes the existing Windows NT domain administrative utilities NDS-enabled, by intercepting calls to the SAM and updating NDS, existing Windows NT administrators do not have to be trained to use the NDS utilities. This can be very useful when integrating a Windows NT network into a NetWare network. Cross-training, if desired, can proceed at a pace you decide on and is not dictated by the time frame used to integrate the two networks. Each set of administrators can continue to perform their jobs as they always have. The exception is, however, that the Windows NT utilities cannot be used to administer other NDS objects that are not specific to the domain. NDS administrators can administer the entire network using their utilities.

Summary

Although both Microsoft and Novell continually fight for market share and would be quite happy if you chose to use only their products for your network, both companies provide solutions that allow their products to integrate with the other. If you have only a few clients that are from one vendor or the other, you might need only the client software to give users access to needed resources. If you have a large number of clients, using the more advanced utilities can make administration of users and resources an easier task for the administrator.

Integrating UNIX/Linux and Windows NT

Windows NT Support for UNIX Protocols and Utilities

Microsoft Windows NT Services for the UNIX Add-On Pack

SAMBA

Windows NT Terminal Server Edition

CHAPTER 52

It would be difficult to find two operating systems that are more different from each other than UNIX and Windows NT. UNIX has been around for a much longer time. What started out as a "developer's operating system" has evolved over the years into a stable platform that runs on more hardware platforms than perhaps any other operating system. Windows NT, on the other hand, is a graphically-oriented operating system that runs now on only two platforms: Intel or Alpha. Configuring Windows NT can be done using the GUI and in many cases command-line utilities at the command prompt. UNIX (and its younger cousin Linux) can also provide an optional GUI, using X Window, but is generally considered to be heavily oriented toward the command line when it comes to configuration.

Note

At the time this book was being prepared for publication both Compaq and Microsoft have indicated that the Alpha platform will not be supported by the next generation of Windows NT: Windows 2000. With support for the MIPS chip dropped before Windows NT 4.0, this means that future Windows platforms will run only on Intel chip-based computers.

Each operating system has its own strengths and weaknesses, and each can be used to solve different problems more effectively than the other. By integrating these two systems into the network, you can take advantage of each one's best capabilities and enhance performance of the services provided to users.

There are two approaches you can take to integrating these two kinds of systems in one network. First, you can use the features Windows NT provides, which were derived from standards that were developed in the UNIX world, such as TCP/IP and the suite of utilities that has been written for it. Second, you can use third-party applications, such as SAMBA, that have been created to allow Windows NT functionality to be installed onto UNIX/Linux platforms. This last approach seems to be the path that Microsoft will be taking in the near future, heralded by the release of the Microsoft Windows NT Services for UNIX Add-On Pack.

Windows NT Support for UNIX Protocols and Utilities

Many technologies that began in the UNIX world have evolved into standards that have been implemented on other platforms over the years. For example, the LPR/LPD printing system (see Chapter 27, "Network Printing Protocols"), which started out on UNIX, is supported not only by Windows NT, OpenVMS, and other operating systems, but also by printers from Hewlett-Packard and a number of other vendors. When adding Windows NT computers to a network that consists mainly of UNIX or Linux servers, printing can be the least of the network administrator's worries. It is a simple matter to configure Windows NT Server to direct printer output to a UNIX system that is responsible for maintaining print queues or to a printer that understands the lpr/lpd protocols.

Other technologies that were either first developed in or adopted by the UNIX world, which Windows NT supports, include the following:

- TCP/IP networking protocol suite, including the Telnet and FTP utilities
- Dynamic Host Configuration Protocol (DHCP)
- Domain Name System (DNS)
- Network File System (NFS)
- Remote Boot Protocol (BOOTP)

TCP/IP

When Windows 3.51 was introduced, the default network protocol was IPX/SPX. TCP/IP was there if you wanted to use it, but at that time Microsoft perceived that its main competitor in the client/server market was Novell. When NT 4.0 was released, the default had been changed to TCP/IP. Since the Internet had began to take on a higher degree of importance during the time frame in which NT 4.0 was being developed, this was a natural path for the operating system to take. TCP/IP is the network protocol suite that is used throughout the Internet to connect together computers from a wide range of manufacturers running many different operating systems. For example, you can find TCP/IP on every UNIX or Linux variant currently on the market, on the OpenVMS operating system, and every operating system from IBM to OS/2 to mainframes.

In a network that consists of UNIX servers, TCP/IP can be used by Windows NT clients to access resources on these servers. The two most common methods provided by TCP/IP are the Telnet and FTP applications.

Telnet

Windows NT Server and Workstation both come with a Telnet client. Microsoft did not choose to provide a Telnet server with either of these, however. So, while you can establish a Telnet session from a Windows NT client to a UNIX server, you cannot do the same to a plain vanilla installation of Windows NT from a UNIX platform. If you want to provide UNIX clients (or any other Telnet client for that matter) the capability to establish terminal sessions on Windows NT servers, you will have to either use a third-party product (of which there are many) or the Telnet server that comes with the Windows NT Services for UNIX Add-On Pack.

Telnet provides a character-cell terminal emulation that can be used to run applications that do not depend on the features provided by either the NT GUI or its equivalent in the UNIX world: X Window. For example, it is easy to Telnet into a UNIX system and perform system administration tasks using a command-line interface provided by a shell. Script files can be edited and run remotely by using a Telnet session.

If a Telnet server has been installed on the Windows NT Server, you can similarly perform some administration of Windows NT systems from a UNIX box by using command-line utilities.

File Transfer Protocol (FTP)

Windows NT does come with both an FTP client and FTP server. The FTP client can be easily used from the command prompt and uses the standard syntax that is common to other FTP clients. The FTP server is not part of the standard Windows NT Server installation, but instead was released as part of the Internet Information Server (IIS) which can be installed via the icon that appears on the desktop of a Windows NT Server. Since the release of Windows NT Server 4.0, Microsoft has enhanced IIS and the applications it provides, most especially the FTP server. If you want to run an FTP server on NT, it is recommended that you download IIS 4.0, which is part of the Windows NT Server 4.0 Option Pack, from Microsoft's Web site and use this version. It provides more flexibility in the management of users and is better enhanced in relation to security functions.

The Dynamic Host Configuration Protocol (DHCP) and BOOTP

Most UNIX environments that use TCP/IP for networking use DHCP servers to provide network configuration information to clients on the network. DHCP is not a proprietary solution but is based on standards defined in RFCs 2131 and 2132. Microsoft clients using TCP/IP can also use DHCP servers.

If you are bringing Windows-based client systems into an existing UNIX environment, it will be a simple matter to configure each Windows client with the address of a DHCP server. In an existing Windows network, you might want to stick with the Microsoft DHCP server. Because DHCP is based on Internet standards, most of the implementations you find will be compatible with both operating systems.

Bringing UNIX clients into a network that uses Microsoft DHCP servers can cause some seasoned UNIX administrators to worry. DHCP servers have been around for quite a while on UNIX networks; running on UNIX servers and Microsoft's DHCP server is a relatively new creature on the market.

However, the DHCP server that you can install on Windows NT 4.0 or Windows 2000 Advanced Server is a full-featured implementation that can be used to support clients no matter what their operating system. The configuration information that a DHCP server sends to clients is itself configurable through the use of DHCP options. Each option describes a parameter that can be configured for the client from information the DHCP server can provide.

Microsoft's DHCP server provides support for the options defined in RFC 1533, "DHCP Options and BOOTP Vendor Extensions." In addition, it allows the administrator to define custom options when needed. This capability to create customized options makes the server flexible in a networking environment that consists of different client types.

Before there was DHCP, there was BOOTP, which functions in a manner similar to DHCP. The BOOTP protocol is mainly used by diskless workstations, usually in a UNIX network, to request addressing configuration information and download an operating system. Microsoft's DHCP server enables the administrator to create records in a BOOTP table that can be used to satisfy requests from these kinds of clients. When the DHCP server receives a BOOTP request from a client, it looks up the client in the table. If a record for that client is found, the server will return to the client three pieces of information:

- **Boot Image**—A generic filename for the boot file.
- **Filename**—The path to the boot image on a TFTP (Trivial File Transfer Protocol) server.
- **TFTP Server**—The server from which the client can download the boot file.

The Microsoft DHCP server will respond to BOOTP clients with the information they need to download a boot file from another server. Unlike the standard DHCP lease, however, the BOOTP client does not have to renew the IP address periodically as regular DHCP clients do. Instead, a BOOTP client is managed like clients who use reserved DHCP addresses.

DNS

In Chapter 21, "Name Resolution," the implementation of DNS is examined. DNS is the standard method used on the Internet to resolve host IP addresses to "friendly names" that humans find easier to remember. Microsoft NT 4.0 provides a DNS server that is based on Internet Engineering Task Force (IETF) RFC 1053 and can be used by both Microsoft clients and other clients that have been created according to the standard. This includes, of course, most UNIX and Linux clients.

If you already have a DNS server running on your network, you might wonder why you would want to use Microsoft's version when you add clients that are not running UNIX or Linux. The answer is simple: Microsoft's DNS server provides a WINS (Windows Internet Name Service) lookup feature that can further simplify network administration chores. It provides a service similar to what DNS does, but with an interesting twist. Microsoft's DNS server has the capability to query the WINS server when it cannot resolve a name or address based on the information contained in its database.

Whereas DNS is basically used to perform IP address/name translations, WINS was developed to provide name resolution services for NetBIOS names. When a WINS client computer boots, it registers its NetBIOS names with the WINS server along with its current network address. If you incorporate DHCP into the network, you will be relieved of having to keep track of IP addresses for Microsoft clients, much less of maintaining an address space when clients move or new clients are added to the network. Enabling Microsoft clients to use the WINS service eliminates the manual task of administrating a name server to keep track of additions or changes to the network.

Because Microsoft's DNS server can make use of the name/address mappings stored in the WINS server, you can effectively automate both the administration of client addresses (using DHCP) and the administration of name resolutions (DNS/WINS) for Microsoft clients on the network.

Microsoft Windows NT Services for the UNIX Add-On Pack

Instead of trying to tackle the enormous job of developing still more applications to make it easier to integrate UNIX and Windows NT into a cohesive network, Microsoft chose to take advantage of developments by other vendors and instead released the Windows NT Services for UNIX Add-On Pack. This optional software, which sells for about $149, contains applications that were developed by other vendors but which can be bought as a single package. With the Add-On Pack you get

- Network File System (NFS) client and server software, developed by Integraph Corp.
- Commands based on the Korn Shell, developed by Mortice Kern Systems, Inc.
- One-way password synchronization
- New Telnet server and client software

Network File System (NFS)

The NFS server and client are based on NFS 3.0, and include authentication using pcnfsd or NIS. Since it uses Microsoft's native TCP/IP protocol stack, there is no need to load any additional components. Windows NT computers can use the client software to mount file systems exported by UNIX or Linux servers and those computers can likewise make use of file systems exported using NFS by Windows NT servers. By using NFS to make files and directories appear as if they were local to the client computer, you overcome the inherent problems associated with using FTP to copy files. When more than one copy of a file is created on the network, it is often a difficult endeavor to keep changes to the file coordinated among many users. When NFS users are accessing the same file, this problem does not come into play.

The NFS server can be used on file systems created under FAT, HPFS, CDFS, and NTFS.

Korn Shell

The Korn Shell commands that the Add-On Pack give to Windows NT allow you to use existing script files that run on UNIX systems to provide the same functions to Windows NT computers. The limited commands provided by Windows NT at the command prompt are based on older MS-DOS commands, along with new commands that were added to support Windows NT functions and services. For users trained on UNIX systems, the Korn Shell commands will make it much easier to add Windows NT computers to their flock of computers that need to be administered. Table 52.1 lists the commands that are provided by the Add-On Pack.

Table 52.1   Korn Shell UNIX Commands Provided by the Add-On Pack

Korn Shell Command	Usage
sh	Invokes the Korn Shell
basename	Removes a pathname and leaves just the filename
cat	Similar to **DIR**, shows files in the directory. Can also be used to concatenate files
chmod	Administers file permissions
chown	Administers file ownership
cp	Copies files
dirname	Extracts pathname from string
find	Searches directories to find files matching a Boolean expression
grep	Searches files for a pattern

Korn Shell Command	Usage
head	Copies *n* number of lines from a file to standard output
ln	Creates a link to a file (hard link)
ls	Lists a directory
mkdir	Creates named directory in mode 777
more	Displays contents of file, one screen at a time
mv	Moves a file
rm	Removes a file entry from a directory
rmdir	Removes a directory
sed	Copies a file to standard output while making edits according to a script
sort	Sorts contents of one or more files
tail	Similar to **head**, sends lines from a file to standard output, starting at a specified location in the file
tee	Transcribes standard input to standard output and makes copies in filename
touch	Updates the modification or access time of a file
uniq	Finds repeated lines in a file
wc	"Word Count," displays a count of lines, words, or characters in a file
vi	Screen-oriented text editor
perl	An interpreted language

Some of these commands are already familiar to Windows NT users, such as mkdir and find. However, their functions in the Korn Shell can differ from that provided by the standard Windows NT implementation.

Password Synchronization

This feature allows you to configure a group of UNIX servers so that when a user's password is changed on a Windows NT server the change is propagated to the user's accounts on those target UNIX servers. Because the application only runs on the Windows NT computer, it is a one-way service. That is, changes made on the UNIX servers are not sent back to the Windows NT computer. However, this utility can still provide useful functionality in a network for users that spend most of their time on the NT host. The changes can be sent across the network as clear text (not a good idea) or through encrypted means (better idea).

New Telnet Server and Client

The Add-On Pack also includes a Telnet Server for Windows NT, and a client application that greatly improves on the simple Telnet client that comes with the standard Windows NT Server or Workstation software. This makes it easy to use Telnet to log in to Windows NT computers to perform system administration tasks or run character-cell–based user applications.

SAMBA

SAMBA is a set of applications that is freely available on the Internet. It allows you to set up UNIX servers that can act as file servers for Microsoft clients that use the SMB protocol. In

Chapter 25, "File-Server Protocols," the Microsoft Server Message Block (SMB) protocol is covered along with SAMBA. More recent versions of SAMBA allow UNIX servers to act as domain controllers in a Microsoft network.

Using SAMBA you can make resources running on high performance UNIX servers available to Microsoft clients on the same network.

Windows NT Terminal Server Edition

Microsoft has entered into the market for thin clients with its terminal server edition of Windows NT. This version of the operating system allows client computers to run applications that reside on an NT server via a terminal emulator program that runs on the client. While Microsoft provides clients software for older Windows and MS-DOS clients, for UNIX clients you will have to use the client application from Citrix to make this connection.

If you already have a large installation of UNIX systems in your network and need to make moderate use of a few programs that run only on an NT platform, Terminal Server edition can be a good investment. If your network is composed of a more diverse set of clients, including Macintosh users, MS-DOS clients, or Windows for Workgroup clients, this solution can be used to provide access to applications for all these users without requiring you to purchase a copy of a Windows 98 or Windows NT client operating system for each.

Summary

Windows NT and UNIX computers can easily coexist on the same network. By using built-in functionality, such as the TCP/IP protocol and its related utilities, basic connectivity and data exchange can be accomplished. Other software products, such as the Add-On Pack from Microsoft, contain NFS servers, and the freely available SAMBA implementation of the SMB protocol can be used as well. The scripting commands based on the Korn Shell that come with the Add-On Pack make it easy for a seasoned UNIX administrator to begin managing Windows client and server computers.

Mixing UNIX/Linux, NetWare, and NT

CHAPTER 53

In this chapter, you will look at what is involved in providing a mixed network environment consisting of UNIX/Linux, NetWare, and Windows NT. Previous chapters talked about how to migrate or switch from one operating system to another. There might be cases, however, where you would need to have any two, or perhaps all three, network operating systems (NOSes) working together.

These four topics present the major concerns that arise when mixing these different operating systems into the same environment. For each operating system in use, users must log on to the system to gain access to the resources they need to perform their work. Each operating system has the same requirements but treat user accounts slightly different.

Each OS uses rights and permissions as well for allowing access to files and resources on the network. This is obviously a concern when accessing these resources from one OS to the other.

Protocols determine whether your computers will communicate. You must be aware of how these protocols function in each OS to get them to work together.

User Accounts

User accounts have one common denominator among all NOSes. They provide users with access to the system and network resources. Each system requires a username and a password. Although they all include this basic user account information, the permissions and rights assigned to users vary. To integrate these environments, you must know the similarities and differences between them. This is important to enable you to go from one platform to the other with an understanding of the permissions you are assigning.

Table 53.1 presents a side-by-side comparison of the permissions between each NOS.

Table 53.1   A Comparison of Permissions Between Three Network Operating Systems

Windows NT	NetWare	UNIX/Linux
Full Control	Supervisor (S)	rwx
Read Access	Read (R)	r
Change Access	Write (W), Erase (E), and Modify (M)	rw
Add	Create	rw
Take Ownership	Access Control (A)	rw

By using this table, you can determine which rights or permissions to assign to your users across the different platforms.

NetWare and NT

As far as providing user account access from a NetWare computer to an NT machine, you saw in Chapter 51, "Integrating NetWare with Windows NT," that the Migration Tool for NetWare provides a relatively easy way to transfer the user accounts along with the appropriate permissions.

The only catch with this process is the passwords. You need to re-create them because the migration tool does not transfer them over.

One of the easiest ways to provide the interoperability between user accounts and passwords is to use the Gateway Services for NetWare. As you saw earlier in Chapter 51, GSNW provides a single point of connection for Microsoft clients to connect to a NetWare server.

Using GSNW also has another distinct advantage when it comes to licensing. For example, suppose your NetWare server has only one client license available to be assigned. Assuming that you have the correct amount of client access licenses (CALs) for the NT server, you can have all your Microsoft clients connect to the one NetWare account through the GSNW service. This way, you do not have to purchase additional CALs for NetWare, and you don't violate your NetWare licensing agreement.

Accessing NT from NetWare

To accommodate existing NetWare user accounts on an NT server, you can use the NetWare Migration Tool to transfer the accounts. After you do so, you must install the File and Print Services for NetWare to let the NetWare clients gain access to the NT resources.

The File and Print Services for NetWare product is available separately from Microsoft. You can install it by running the Setup.exe program from the CD-ROM. The program comes with the Services for NetWare Administrator's Guide, which will walk you through the installation and setup of this product.

UNIX and NT User Accounts

Table 53.1, shown previously, enables you to compare the permissions between NT and UNIX and provides a means for you to set them accordingly when creating the new user accounts.

Now run through an example of each to see how they would integrate.

The user account root on the UNIX system is responsible for total system control. To gain that same permission on an NT system, you must make the user account a member of the Administrators group. The Administrators group provides total control over the NT computer. If you would like to give the user the capability to control all the Windows NT computers in the Domain, you need to assign the user to the Domain Admins group. This account does not permit you to administer non-Windows NT computers.

UNIX and Linux provide the Samba software package for sharing resources with a Windows computer. By editing the smb.conf file, you can allow the UNIX/Linux computer to act as a Domain Controller for Windows logons. This provides the advantage of enabling you to create user accounts on the UNIX server and supplying logon services for the Windows computers. The logon process is transparent to the user. He will have the capability to use the UNIX server files and resources as permitted by their account restrictions.

Understanding Rights and Permissions

Table 53.1 presented a side-by-side comparison of the available rights and permissions of each NOS. To implement them successfully on each platform within the integrated environment, you need a good understanding of how they compare to one another. Look at each in turn.

Full Control

Each OS has an equivalent permission or right that offers the same functionality on that specific platform. The permission that allows the most functionality is referred to as one that allows full control of the resource. Each OS utilizes this type of permission.

Windows NT

Full Control is actually an NT term that enables the user to view, modify, delete, and take ownership of the file.

Viewing, modifying, and deleting a file are relatively self-explanatory in that they allow the user to open the file in its native application, make changes to it, or even delete the file.

Ownership of a file or resource under NT refers to the creator of a file as the owner of that file. Ownership can be assigned by the owner of the file by granting another user the right to take ownership. This will grant the new user all the previously mentioned rights of that file.

An administrator can take ownership of any file or resource on the NT system.

NetWare

The NetWare equivalent of this permission is Supervisor. Supervisor permission provides complete access to the file or resource.

UNIX/Linux

UNIX assigns the r and w permissions to a file for creation, modification, and deletion. x is used to indicate that the file is an executable. Files will have these permissions assigned in three groups. The first group is used for the owner of the file, the second for the assigned group, and the last for others. For example, -rwxrwxrwx. The first character can be either a dash or the letter d, which indicates that the file is a directory. The dash indicates to the user that this is a regular file.

As you can see, there are three sets of rwx characters. Each assigns permissions to the owner, group, or others. In this way, the owner can retain full control over the file while simultaneously restricting the group and others to read-only access.

The permissions are assigned using a number scheme. Each permission flag has a number assigned to it as follows:

r	4
w	2
x	1

A file's permission is assigned by using the number scheme. The following code reproduces a file listing for your convenience:

```
-rw-rw-r-- gobrien users 512 Aug 8 10:50 testfile
```

A three-digit number is used to represent the file permissions. Each digit in the number represents a group in the file permission. The values of the assigned permissions are added to provide the number.

The file listing shown earlier indicates the permissions, the owner's username, the group that has permission to this file, the file size of 512 bytes, the date and time the file was created, and the name of the file.

In the preceding code, the file permissions expressed in numerical form would be 664. Here is how you arrive at that number. The first permission group has rw access. The value for r is 4 and the value for w is 2. By adding 4 and 2, you get 6. The next group has rw access as well, so it accounts for the second 6. The last group has only r permission; therefore, it totals the number 4.

When assigning permissions to files, the number syntax is what you will use so it pays to become familiar with it.

Read Access

Read access is the permission used to indicate that a user can read the file, which is to say that a user can open the file in the application that was used to create it but cannot make any changes to the file or delete it.

Windows NT

Under Windows NT, Read access provides the user with the capability to look at the file, and if it is an executable program, the user can run that program.

Note

Read access is not to be confused with the read-only file attribute. Although they essentially mean the same thing, there is a difference.

The read-only attribute of a file indicates that it cannot be deleted or modified by any user. You must remove the attribute using the command `attrib -r filename`.

Read access for file permissions determines the rights that users have to files on the network in general.

NetWare

NetWare uses the Read (R) access level as well. It is assigned to files and properties. When applied to a file, it permits the opening and reading of the file. If it is assigned to a property as a right, it grants the capability to read the values of the property.

UNIX/Linux

UNIX assigns the Read property using the r flag. Just as in the NT and NetWare scenarios, it enables a user to open and read a file. Unlike NT, it does not enable the user to execute the file. If the file were assigned r-x as permission, the user could execute it.

Change Access

To allow a user to make changes to a file, such as the ability to update the employee records database, that user must be assigned the right or permission of Change Access.

Windows NT

Windows NT uses Change Access to grant the user the right to open, modify, and delete the file.

When a user has this permission to a resource, they can open the file with the application used to create it or another application that will read the file. The user can then make modifications to the file in terms of additions and deletions, and then resave the modified version using the same filename.

NetWare

NetWare performs Change Access using the three following permissions:

- **Write (W)** is used to enable the opening and writing of a file.
- **Erase (E)** is used to permit, as you would expect, file and directory deletions.
- **Modify (M)** enables the changing of the attribute or name of the file or directory.

UNIX/Linux

UNIX must use the rw permissions in combination to enable the same idea of changing the file because the read permission must be assigned in order for the user to open the file in the first place. Read permission is not enough to allow the user to change the file's contents, so you must also assign the write permission for this ability.

ADD

Often, your users will need to be able to create new files on the server. These files can be created by users for their own use and placed into their own home directory or users can create new files that are shared in common directories.

Windows NT

NT actually uses two types of Add permission. The first one, listed as Add(WX)(Not Specified), enables you to add files and subdirectories to a directory. It does not provide you access to files unless the permissions are granted by other file/directory permissions. The second use is listed as Add & Read(RWX)(RX). This permission enables the addition of files and subdirectories as previously stated, but also provides for the following:

- Viewing files and subdirectory names
- Making changes to subdirectories within the given directory
- Viewing files and running applications

NetWare

The term Create (C) is used to indicate this right under NetWare. It provides for the creation of files and directories. It can also enable you to reclaim a file after it has been deleted.

UNIX/Linux

UNIX again uses the rw permissions to provide for the addition or creation of files into a directory. If a directory does not provide a user the w permission, the user cannot create a file or subdirectory under that directory.

Take Ownership

There is a permission that allows for complete control over a file or other resource. This permission has a different name under each operating system but essentially means the same thing. A user who has Take Ownership or its equivalent permission has complete control over that resource.

Windows NT

NT uses this permission to enable a user or group to take ownership of a resource. This can be a file or a printer share. By owning the resource, you control everything about that resource, including the capability to change the permissions and to assign ownership to others.

Ownership can only be held by one user at a time, so be careful when assigning this permission. If you are the administrator and assign ownership to another user, you will need to have that user reassign the ownership back to you for you to take control over the resource again.

The most common use for taking and assigning ownership in an NT network arises when a worker leaves the company, and another worker must take over his responsibilities.

Instead of re-creating all of the user's profile, the Administrator will do the following:

- Take ownership of all the previous user's resources.
- Change the name and password of the user's account.
- Instruct the new employee to sign into the renamed account and change the password.
- Assign ownership to the new user.

As you can see, this can be a great time saver.

NetWare

Take Ownership under NetWare is referred to as Access Control. This enables you to change the trustee assignments as well as the Inherited Rights Filter of the file or directory.

The Inherited Rights Filter (IRF) is created for every file, directory, and object and contains a list of rights. If the file is in a directory, the IRF will, by default, allow the file to inherit the rights from the parent directory.

Although the IRF can allow or revoke rights, it cannot grant them.

UNIX/Linux

If you are the owner of a file, you can change the ownership of that file. Only the owner can do so, and after you make the change, only the new owner can reassign ownership. Even if you don't have ownership of a file, that doesn't mean that you can't access the file. If the appropriate permissions are assigned in the group or other fields, you can still gain access to it as indicated by the permissions.

To change the ownership, you use the `chown` command. The syntax is as follows:

```
chown <owner> <file>
```

For example, use the file listing displayed earlier in this chapter. It is displayed here again for your convenience:

```
-rw-rw-r-- gobrien users 512 Aug 8 10:50 testfile
```

Note that the owner of this file is `gobrien`. To assign ownership to the user `bbunny`, you would issue this command:

```
chown bbunny testfile
```

A quick review of the file's new directory list entry would depict the changes shown here.

```
-rw-rw-r-- bbunny users 512 Aug 8 10:50 testfile
```

Note that no permissions have changed, only the file's owner.

Other Rights Not Listed

Although the permissions you just reviewed are complete when compared to similarities, NetWare and NT offer some extra, slightly different permissions not listed here. Take a look at them in the following sections.

NetWare

NetWare has one more permission that is assigned to files or directories: File Scan right. This enables the user to see a file and directory by using the `DIR` or `NDIR` commands.

Windows NT

Although it was mentioned in earlier in Table 53.1, the Add permission is not a file permission but rather a directory permission.

NT includes one other permission that is a part of directory permissions and not files. The List permission is used to enable browsing of a directory without any direct file access.

Networking Protocols

Each operating system has its own set of protocols. NetWare has used IPX/SPX for communication among computers on a NetWare network. UNIX uses TCP/IP. These protocols are necessary to ensure that the computers on the network can talk to each other in a common language.

Each NOS presented in this chapter has the capability to use more than one protocol. Correct configuration and selection of the appropriate protocol is central to setting up and maintaining communication among these different NOSes.

Windows NT supports nine network protocols:

- Network BIOS Extended User Interface (NetBEUI)
- Transmission Control Protocol/Internet Protocol (TCP/IP)
- NWLink IPX/SPX Compatible Transport
- Point-to-Point Tunneling Protocol (PPTP)
- Point-to-Point Protocol (PPP)
- Serial Line Internet Protocol (SLIP)
- AppleTalk
- DLC Protocol (Data Link Control Protocol used for Hewlett-Packard printers connected directly to the network)
- Streams Environment

Of these nine, NetBEUI, TCP/IP, and NWLink IPX/SPX Compatible Transport are the main areas of concern when integrating NT into a UNIX/NetWare environment. Of these three protocols, the one that is fully supported across UNIX, NT, and NetWare version 5.x and later platforms is TCP/IP. UNIX was built on the TCP/IP protocol and contains perhaps the most comprehensive suite of tools and utilities available for it.

Windows NT version 4.0 places a heavy emphasis on the TCP/IP protocol as well. This is mainly due to Microsoft's desire to integrate Internet and intranet technologies into its operating systems.

Installing TCP/IP in Windows NT

You install the TCP/IP protocol from the Network applet in Control Panel. The steps are listed as follows:

1. Open the Control Panel by choosing Start, Settings, Control Panel.
2. Double-click the Network applet icon (or right-click Network Neighborhood and choose Properties).
3. Select the Protocols tab.
4. Click the Add button.
5. Choose the TCP/IP Protocol from the available protocols list.
6. Click OK.

7. NT asks you to identify where the files are located. Enter the path to your i386 directory on the install media. This could be a CD-ROM or a network share.

8. NT copies the necessary files for TCP/IP support and then prompts you to configure RAS if it is already installed.

9. When the preceding step is complete, click the Close button on the bottom of the Network Properties dialog box. At this time, NT goes through a process of binding the protocol to the correct adapters in the system.

10. Restart your computer.

TCP/IP is now installed.

NetWare TCP/IP

Novell calls its implementation of TCP/IP *NetWare TCP/IP*, which consists of a group of NLM applications designed to work on TCP/IP. It is capable of IP routing. To accomplish this, NetWare makes use of the routing information protocol (RIP).

By using IPX/IP tunneling, NetWare TCP/IP allows communication to take place between IPX networks and IP networks that don't support the IPX protocol.

Although TCP/IP support is available, keep in mind that NetWare operates natively over IPX/SPX.

Making File and Print Shares Available to All Users

How do you ensure that all uses on the network can gain access to your files and printers? Well, the first step is obviously to make sure that all computers can communicate. The best way to do this is to provide a common protocol. TCP/IP is the one protocol that is truly supported across all platforms and provides routing capabilities.

You have already looked at how NetWare clients can access NT servers through the File and Print Services for NetWare. Basically, that solves part of the problem. Now you need to get UNIX to connect to these resources as well. This is discussed next.

The Samba Protocol

Microsoft operating systems share files with each other by using the Server Message Block (SMB) protocol. This protocol is also known as Samba. Under UNIX, Samba is a suite of components that provides file and print services to SMB clients. The main component is the smbd daemon. You can view and modify its configuration with the smb.conf file. To see what your smb.conf file looks like, you can use the more command to display it onscreen. You will find the file in the /etc directory. After you make any configuration changes, you should run the tesparm utility to test the file. The syntax for testparm is as follows:

```
testparm <config_file>
```

There is also an optional parameter, `<hostname hostIP>`, that can be used to determine whether the host has access to the services in the `smb.conf` file.

Note

The `<config_file>` parameter is an option as well and is needed only if your `smb.conf` file is not located in the default path.

Samba provides the smbclient for the purpose of getting UNIX/Linux to access file and print shares on NT. This client software accesses the file shares on an NT server with an interface that resembles an FTP client. It also provides the capability to print to an NT computer as well (actually, to any SMB server, even Windows 98).

Note

Samba also uses the **nmbd** daemon for browsing and as a name server service for NetBIOS.

Now, you have the capability to communicate with NT from all operating systems. This exercise shows a recommended method to set up a mixed network environment by using a Windows NT server computer as the common denominator. You can now see that Windows NT can function as the glue that holds together the entire network.

However, some might not buy into that scenario and choose not to follow my recommendation at all. If that is the case, there is still one unified communication protocol, TCP/IP, that Windows NT, UNIX, Linux, and NetWare can use and serve shares through that can simplify your life a great deal. As mentioned, NT, UNIX, Linux, and NetWare 5.x thoroughly support the TCP/IP protocol and Internet technologies. Furthermore, each can provide World Wide Web publishing capabilities for the Internet and intranets, which are discussed next.

Intranets

As is the norm with the computer industry, buzzwords and acronyms abound. The term intranet is used to describe an internal network utilizing Internet technologies.

In your normal everyday browsing of the World Wide Web, you never think to wonder what operating system is serving up this Web page or FTP file list. Most users don't think or care about this either. The fact is that the World Wide Web is made up of computers running UNIX, Linux, Windows NT, and NetWare, transparently providing the resources on each of them. If that task can be accomplished on the Internet, why not do it on your local network using an intranet? In this way, you are free to choose the NOS that you are most comfortable with.

If you are a Linux guru, set up the Apache Web server on your Linux box, and you have an intranet server. Another advantage to serving up shares in this way is that your administrative burden of file permissions and access can be reduced considerably. Using Web browsers to gain access to a server presents the user with only those available shares that you deem to make visible.

By setting an FTP root directory, users can be permitted only into that directory and any subdirectories that you make available via FTP. If they can't see it, they won't know it's there. If they don't know it's there, they are not likely to try to gain access to it.

Another reason for looking at an intranet type of scenario is that most offices have corporate procedure manuals, employees' information booklets, group insurance and pension brochures, and the list goes on. There is a fairly considerable expense in having these documents and manuals printed. You can save your company some of that expense by publishing these documents to a Web server on your intranet. This enables employees to view these documents through a familiar Web browser interface.

Summary

Mixing Windows NT, UNIX/Linux, and NetWare into one networking environment is no easy undertaking.

Your first concern is how to deal with user accounts. Each operating system requires a user to enter a username and password to log on to the system. Through this logon, the system can determine what resources the user has permission to access.

Next, you must be concerned with the comparison of similarities and differences between how each OS handles permissions and rights assigned to each user. By fully understanding this, you can ensure that no user has been assigned a permission on one system that might be greater than his or her assigned permission on another.

To incorporate Windows NT, UNIX, Linux, and NetWare into a common network effectively, they must be capable of communicating with each other, allowing resources to be shared over the network. You accomplish this by being aware of the protocols that each OS uses and setting them to correctly communicate with each other. This way you can make your resources on each OS available to users on the entire network.

Part XVII

APPENDIXES

The OSI Seven-Layer Networking Model

APPENDIX A

Following is a list of funny phrases. What do they all have in common?

- **P**lease **D**o **N**ot **T**hrow **S**ausage **P**izza **A**way
- **A**ll **P**eople **S**eem **T**o **N**eed **D**ata **P**rocessing
- **P**lease **D**o **N**ot **T**ouch **S**teve's **P**et **A**lligator

Each of these phrases is a commonly used mnemonic method for memorizing the layers that make up the OSI's seven-layer reference model. This reference model, which was developed in 1977 by the International Standards Organization, is called the *Open Systems Interconnection (OSI)* reference model. Its purpose is to define a communications model that can be used when designing network standards for creating technologies that can interoperate.

Overview of the OSI Model

Figure A.1 shows, conceptually, how the model is supposed to operate. Each layer in the model provides services to the layers that are adjacent to it. This means that the actual flow of information begins with the topmost Application Layer, which calls on services provided by the Presentation Layer, which uses services provided by the Session Layer, and so on. At the very bottom lie the physical portions of the network. How data is transmitted across the network—from the cabling to the network cards to the connectors used throughout the physical channel—are defined at this level.

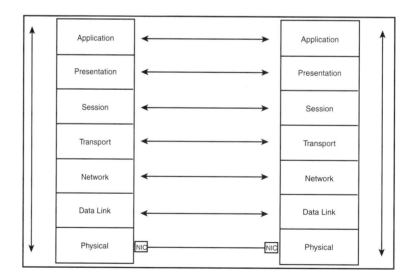

Figure A.1   The OSI seven-layer reference model.

When data arrives at another node at the Physical Layer, the data flows up the reference model. The software at each layer uses functions of the layer above it until, finally, the information reaches the Application Layer, where it can be dealt with by the user.

This is the physical flow of information through the model. From a logical perspective, each layer in the model communicates with its corresponding layer on the remote node. For example, the Application Layer software is only concerned with how to communicate with the Application Layer on the remote node. Software at this level does not have to understand the route the data takes to get to its destination, or whether it travels over fiber optic cable or 10BASE-T connections. Software that is working at the Physical Layer does not have to know that the information it is transmitting or receiving is ASCII text, binary encoded data, or graphics data. It is only concerned with working with the Physical Layer on the remote node to get the data to and from its system.

Physical Layer

The physical process of moving bits of data across a network medium is performed at this layer. Pieces of the network that are defined at this layer include

- Cabling
- Connectors
- Signaling techniques (electrical and optical)

This layer is perhaps the easiest to classify. It is composed of all the physical parts of the network that are concerned with sending and receiving the actual raw bits of information. How many pins a certain connector has is defined here; how a signal is interpreted (for example, Manchester and Differential Manchester Encoding) is also defined at this level.

Data Link Layer

Functions that are performed at this layer are targeted toward making sure that reliable data transmissions are made from one device to another on the network. Here lies the code that performs error checking on the basic frames of data that are transmitted between devices at the Physical Layer. The individual bits of a message arrive at the Physical Layer, and this layer organizes them into the proper frame format, which can be understood by upper-level protocols.

The IEEE specifications divide this layer into two sublayers: the Media Access Control (MAC) Layer and the Logical Link Control Layer (LLC). Although not a part of the original OSI model, these sublayers play an important part in most ethernet implementations. The upper layer (LLC) implements Service Access Points (SAPs) to which other devices can refer when sending information, and the MAC Layer is concerned with sending or receiving error-free data between nodes on the network.

Network Layer

Network connections between nodes on the network are controlled at this layer. A logical network connection between nodes is established and terminated at this layer. Functions that make up the services of the network layer include

- The translation of logical and physical addresses
- Routing, switching

- Flow control and network congestion
- Packet fragmentation and reassembly is done here if it is determined that a router or other device that the data passes through cannot handle the packet at its current size

This layer is the lowest layer in the reference model that has no knowledge of the underlying physical aspects of the network.

Transport Layer

This layer is the lowest layer in the model that provides user services to the layers above. One of the services performed at this layer is defining how data is exchanged. This includes

- Error-free data transport. Data in large packets is divided up here to make transmission more efficient. It is reassembled at this layer when they arrive from a remote system. The packet composition is dependent on the protocol that the two nodes are using for data exchange.
- Sequencing to make sure that packets are delivered to upper layers in the correct order.
- Acknowledgement of transfer or receipt of data packets.
- Flow control for the protocol in use.

Session Layer

Applications must recognize their counterparts on a remote system and establish a common *session* to handle their data exchanges. For example, at this layer, the NetBIOS protocol operates to establish sessions based on names. To control a session, software at this layer referees between the two computers, telling each one when it can transmit and for how long. Sessions between application software are created, maintained, and terminated at this level.

Presentation Layer

Information must be presented to users in such a way that it can be understood. Differences between nodes, such as how data is represented (EBCIDIC versus ASCII, for example), is taken care of here. Data compression and protocol conversion is performed at this layer. Encryption is also performed at this layer. This layer also includes the redirector, which "directs" input/output operations to resources outside the local system when necessary, such as when a request is made for data that resides on a network server. The networking client software installed on the system provides the redirector.

Application Layer

Users' application communications are handled here. Functions at this layer directly support user applications that use the network. Services that allow a program to access a database that resides on a server do so by making calls to functions at this level. Other application services that are implemented at this level include

- Directory services
- Email services

- File and print services
- Service advertisement

How Common Network Protocols Relate to the OSI Model

The OSI reference model is only a model. It is not a hard and fast standard into which you can neatly fit all (or any) of today's commonly used protocols. However, most protocols include the functions provided by one or more OSI layers, so it is possible to cross-reference them with the different OSI layers. In Table A.1 you can see a list of some of the more commonly used protocols and where they fall based on the functions they perform.

Table A.1   Common Protocols and the OSI Reference Model

OSI Layer	Protocol
Physical	IEEE 802.3
	IEEE 802.4
	IEEE 802.5
	RS-232
	RS-449
	V.35
Data Link (MAC)	IEEE 802.3
	IEEE 802.5
	CSMA/CD
	Token
Data Link (LLC)	Software Drivers
	LABP
	NDIS and ODI
	IEEE 802.2
Network	IP
	IPX
	X.25
	ICMP
Transport	SPX and IPX
	TCP
	UDP
Session	TCP
	IPX
	SMTP
	TFTP
	RPC

(continues)

Table A.1 Continued

OSI Layer	Protocol
	NetBIOS
	FTP
	Telnet
	RPC
	SNMP
Presentation	NCP
	NFS
	SMB
Application	X.400
	X.500
	Shell and Redirector
	NFS

In Table A.1, some protocols appear at more than one level. This is because they do not fit neatly into a particular layer, but instead perform functions that are defined at more than one layer in the model.

Another way to look at how the OSI model influences networking technologies is to see how specific technologies fit into the model. For example, routers perform functions that generally lie in the Network layer of the model. Gateways operate at the Transport Layer. Bridges and switches usually operate at a lower level: the Data Link Layer. Still simpler devices such as hubs, MAUs, and network cards can be found at the Physical Layer.

TCP and UDP Common Ports

SOME OF THE MAIN TOPICS IN THIS CHAPTER ARE

Well-Known Ports

Registered Ports

When one computer on a network must exchange data with another computer and both are configured to use the TCP/IP protocol suite, the IP address is used to address each computer. Because more than one application can use the networking facilities of a computer, there must be a method to distinguish communication paths between two systems other than just the simple IP address. If all applications that used the network only identified the destination for their data exchange as a single IP address, the information would arrive at the destination computer, but it would be almost impossible for the targeted system to figure out which process to give the data to.

Port numbers are an additional addressing mechanism that solves this problem. In addition to using an IP address, each application that communicates on the network using TCP/IP also specifies a *port* number on the target computer. The port numbers are endpoints for the communications path so that two applications communicating across the network can identify each other.

Well-Known Ports

The Internet Assigned Numbers Authority (IANA) is the organization that controls the first range of port numbers that are available (0–1023) and these are usually called *well-known ports*. The use for these ports has been defined in several RFCs (most recently RFC 1700), and change only occasionally. In Table B.1, you will find a list of these ports and a short description of their use.

Well-known ports are usually accessible on a given system by a privileged process or privileged users. For example, you can see that the FTP utility uses ports 20 and 21, while the Telnet utility uses port 23. Note that in most cases the User Datagram Protocol (UDP) and Transmission Control Protocol (TCP) make the same use for a particular port. This is not required, however, so when you are using this table be sure to check the protocol for each port when looking up its use.

Use this table to decide which ports to block when building a firewall. Some of these applications will never be used by your system, so no good reason exists to allow network traffic through the firewall that uses these ports.

Registered Ports

Ports numbered from 1024 to 65535 can also be used but are not reserved by IANA. These ports are called registered ports and can be used by most any user process on the system.

Table B.1   TCP and UDP Well-Known Port Numbers

Service	Port Number	Protocol	Description
	0	TCP	Reserved
	0	UDP	Reserved
tcpmux	1	TCP	TCP Port Service Multiplexer
tcpmux	1	UDP	TCP Port Service Multiplexer
compressnet	2	TCP	Management Utility
compressnet	2	UDP	Management Utility
compressnet	3	TCP	Compression Process

Service	Port Number	Protocol	Description
compressnet	3	UDP	Compression Process
rje	5	TCP	Remote Job Entry
rje	5	UDP	Remote Job Entry
echo	7	TCP	Echo
echo	7	UDP	Echo
discard	9	TCP	Discard
discard	9	UDP	Discard
systat	11	TCP	Active Users
systat	11	UDP	Active Users
daytime	13	TCP	Daytime (RFC 867)
daytime	13	UDP	Daytime (RFC 867)
qotd	17	TCP	Quote of the Day
qotd	17	UDP	Quote of the Day
msp	18	TCP	Message Send Protocol
msp	18	UDP	Message Send Protocol
chargen	19	TCP	Character Generator
chargen	19	UDP	Character Generator
ftp-data	20	TCP	File Transfer [Default Data]
ftp-data	20	UDP	File Transfer [Default Data]
ftp	21	TCP	File Transfer [Control]
ftp	21	UDP	File Transfer [Control]
ssh	22	TCP	SSH Remote Login Protocol
ssh	22	UDP	SSH Remote Login Protocol
telnet	23	TCP	Telnet
telnet	23	UDP	Telnet
	24	TCP	Any private mail system
	24	UDP	Any private mail system
smtp	25	TCP	Simple Mail Transfer
smtp	25	UDP	Simple Mail Transfer
nsw-fe	27	TCP	NSW User System FE
nsw-fe	27	UDP	NSW User System FE
msg-icp	29	TCP	MSG ICP
msg-icp	29	UDP	MSG ICP
msg-auth	31	TCP	MSG Authentication
msg-auth	31	UDP	MSG Authentication
dsp	33	TCP	Display Support Protocol
dsp	33	UDP	Display Support Protocol
	35	TCP	Any private printer server

(continues)

Service	Port Number	Protocol	Description
	35	UDP	Any private printer server
time	37	TCP	Time
time	37	UDP	Time
rap	38	TCP	Route Access Protocol
rap	38	UDP	Route Access Protocol
rlp	39	TCP	Resource Location Protocol
rlp	39	UDP	Resource Location Protocol
graphics	41	TCP	Graphics
graphics	41	UDP	Graphics
name	42	TCP	Hostname Server
name	42	UDP	Hostname Server
nameserver	42	TCP	Hostname Server
nameserver	42	UDP	Hostname Server
nicname	43	TCP	Who Is
nicname	43	UDP	Who Is
mpm-flags	44	TCP	MPM FLAGS Protocol
mpm-flags	44	UDP	MPM FLAGS Protocol
mpm	45	TCP	Message Processing Module [recv]
mpm	45	UDP	Message Processing Module [recv]
mpm-snd	46	TCP	MPM [default send]
mpm-snd	46	UDP	MPM [default send]
ni-ftp	47	TCP	NI FTP
ni-ftp	47	UDP	NI FTP
auditd	48	TCP	Digital Audit Daemon
auditd	48	UDP	Digital Audit Daemon
tacacs	49	TCP	Login Host Protocol (TACACS)
tacacs	49	UDP	Login Host Protocol (TACACS)
re-mail-ck	50	TCP	Remote Mail Checking Protocol
re-mail-ck	50	UDP	Remote Mail Checking Protocol
la-maint	51	TCP	IMP Logical Address Maintenance
la-maint	51	UDP	IMP Logical Address Maintenance
xns-time	52	TCP	XNS Time Protocol
xns-time	52	UDP	XNS Time Protocol
domain	53	TCP	Domain Name Server
domain	53	UDP	Domain Name Server
xns-ch	54	TCP	XNS Clearinghouse
xns-ch	54	UDP	XNS Clearinghouse
isi-gl	55	TCP	ISI Graphics Language
isi-gl	55	UDP	ISI Graphics Language
xns-auth	56	TCP	XNS Authentication
xns-auth	56	UDP	XNS Authentication

Service	Port Number	Protocol	Description
	57	TCP	Any private terminal access
	57	UDP	Any private terminal access
xns-mail	58	TCP	XNS Mail
xns-mail	58	UDP	XNS Mail
	59	TCP	Any private file service
	59	UDP	Any private file service
	60	TCP	Unassigned
	60	UDP	Unassigned
ni-mail	61	TCP	NI MAIL
ni-mail	61	UDP	NI MAIL
acas	62	TCP	ACA Services
acas	62	UDP	ACA Services
whois++	63	TCP	whois++
whois++	63	UDP	whois++
covia	64	TCP	Communications Integrator (CI)
covia	64	UDP	Communications Integrator (CI)
tacacs-ds	65	TCP	TACACS-Database Service
tacacs-ds	65	UDP	TACACS-Database Service
sql*net	66	TCP	Oracle SQL*NET
sql*net	66	UDP	Oracle SQL*NET
bootps	67	TCP	Bootstrap Protocol Server
bootps	67	UDP	Bootstrap Protocol Server
bootpc	68	TCP	Bootstrap Protocol Client
bootpc	68	UDP	Bootstrap Protocol Client
tftp	69	TCP	Trivial File Transfer
tftp	69	UDP	Trivial File Transfer
gopher	70	TCP	Gopher
gopher	70	UDP	Gopher
netrjs-1	71	TCP	Remote Job Service
netrjs-1	71	UDP	Remote Job Service
netrjs-2	72	TCP	Remote Job Service
netrjs-2	72	UDP	Remote Job Service
netrjs-3	73	TCP	Remote Job Service
netrjs-3	73	UDP	Remote Job Service
netrjs-4	74	TCP	Remote Job Service
netrjs-4	74	UDP	Remote Job Service
	75	TCP	Any private dial out service
	75	UDP	Any private dial out service

(continues)

Service	Port Number	Protocol	Description
deos	76	TCP	Distributed External Object Store
deos	76	UDP	Distributed External Object Store
	77	TCP	Any private RJE service
	77	UDP	Any private RJE service
vettcp	78	TCP	vettcp
vettcp	78	UDP	vettcp
finger	79	TCP	Finger
finger	79	UDP	Finger
http	80	TCP	World Wide Web HTTP
http	80	UDP	World Wide Web HTTP
www	80	TCP	World Wide Web HTTP
www	80	UDP	World Wide Web HTTP
www-http	80	TCP	World Wide Web HTTP
www-http	80	UDP	World Wide Web HTTP
hosts2-ns	81	TCP	HOSTS2 Name Server
hosts2-ns	81	UDP	HOSTS2 Name Server
xfer	82	TCP	XFER Utility
xfer	82	UDP	XFER Utility
mit-ml-dev	83	TCP	MIT ML Device
mit-ml-dev	83	UDP	MIT ML Device
ctf	84	TCP	Common Trace Facility
ctf	84	UDP	Common Trace Facility
mit-ml-dev	85	TCP	MIT ML Device
mit-ml-dev	85	UDP	MIT ML Device
mfcobol	86	TCP	Micro Focus Cobol
mfcobol	86	UDP	Micro Focus Cobol
	87	TCP	Any private terminal link
	87	UDP	Any private terminal link
kerberos	88	TCP	Kerberos
kerberos	88	UDP	Kerberos
su-mit-tg	89	TCP	SUMIT Telnet Gateway
su-mit-tg	89	UDP	SUMIT Telnet Gateway
dnsix	90	TCP	DNSIX Securit Attribute Token Map
dnsix	90	UDP	DNSIX Securit Attribute Token Map
mit-dov	91	TCP	MIT Dover Spooler
mit-dov	91	UDP	MIT Dover Spooler
npp	92	TCP	Network Printing Protocol
npp	92	UDP	Network Printing Protocol
dcp	93	TCP	Device Control Protocol
dcp	93	UDP	Device Control Protocol

Service	Port Number	Protocol	Description
objcall	94	TCP	Tivoli Object Dispatcher
objcall	94	UDP	Tivoli Object Dispatcher
supdup	95	TCP	SUPDUP
supdup	95	UDP	SUPDUP
dixie	96	TCP	DIXIE Protocol Specification
dixie	96	UDP	DIXIE Protocol Specification
swift-rvf	97	TCP	Swift Remote Virtual File Protocol
swift-rvf	97	UDP	Swift Remote Virtual File Protocol
tacnews	98	TCP	TAC News
tacnews	98	UDP	TAC News
metagram	99	TCP	Metagram Relay
metagram	99	UDP	Metagram Relay
newacct	100	TCP	[unauthorized use]
hostname	101	TCP	NIC Host Name Server
hostname	101	UDP	NIC Host Name Server
iso-tsap	102	TCP	ISO-TSAP Class 0
iso-tsap	102	UDP	ISO-TSAP Class 0
gppitnp	103	TCP	Genesis Point-to-Point Trans Net
gppitnp	103	UDP	Genesis Point-to-Point Trans Net
acr-nema	104	TCP	ACR-NEMA Digital Imag. & Comm. 300
acr-nema	104	UDP	ACR-NEMA Digital Imag. & Comm. 300
cso	105	TCP	CCSO Name Server Protocol
cso	105	UDP	CCSO Name Server Protocol
csnet-ns	105	TCP	Mailbox Name Nameserver
csnet-ns	105	UDP	Mailbox Name Nameserver
3com-tsmux	106	TCP	3COM-TSMUX
3com-tsmux	106	UDP	3COM-TSMUX
rtelnet	107	TCP	Remote Telnet Service
rtelnet	107	UDP	Remote Telnet Service
snagas	108	TCP	SNA Gateway Access Server
snagas	108	UDP	SNA Gateway Access Server
pop2	109	TCP	Post Office Protocol—Version 2
pop2	109	UDP	Post Office Protocol—Version 2
pop3	110	TCP	Post Office Protocol—Version 3
pop3	110	UDP	Post Office Protocol—Version 3
sunrpc	111	TCP	SUN Remote Procedure Call
sunrpc	111	UDP	SUN Remote Procedure Call
mcidas	112	TCP	McIDAS Data Transmission Protocol

(continues)

Service	Port Number	Protocol	Description
mcidas	112	UDP	McIDAS Data Transmission Protocol
ident	113	TCP	
auth	113	TCP	Authentication Service
auth	113	UDP	Authentication Service
audionews	114	TCP	Audio News Multicast
audionews	114	UDP	Audio News Multicast
sftp	115	TCP	Simple File Transfer Protocol
sftp	115	UDP	Simple File Transfer Protocol
ansanotify	116	TCP	ANSA REX Notify
ansanotify	116	UDP	ANSA REX Notify
uucp-path	117	TCP	UUCP Path Service
uucp-path	117	UDP	UUCP Path Service
sqlserv	118	TCP	SQL Services
sqlserv	118	UDP	SQL Services
nntp	119	TCP	Network News Transfer Protocol
nntp	119	UDP	Network News Transfer Protocol
cfdptkt	120	TCP	CFDPTKT
cfdptkt	120	UDP	CFDPTKT
erpc	121	TCP	Encore Expedited Remote Pro. Call
erpc	121	UDP	Encore Expedited Remote Pro. Call
smakynet	122	TCP	SMAKYNET
smakynet	122	UDP	SMAKYNET
ntp	123	TCP	Network Time Protocol
ntp	123	UDP	Network Time Protocol
ansatrader	124	TCP	ANSA REX Trader
ansatrader	124	UDP	ANSA REX Trader
locus-map	125	TCP	Locus PC-Interface Net. Map Ser.
locus-map	125	UDP	Locus PC-Interface Net. Map Ser.
nxedit	126	TCP	NXEdit
nxedit	126	UDP	NXEdit
locus-con	127	TCP	Locus PC-Interface Conn. Server
locus-con	127	UDP	Locus PC-Interface Conn. Server
gss-xlicen	128	TCP	GSS X License Verification
gss-xlicen	128	UDP	GSS X License Verification
pwdgen	129	TCP	Password Generator Protocol
pwdgen	129	UDP	Password Generator Protocol
cisco-fna	130	TCP	cisco FNATIVE
cisco-fna	130	UDP	cisco FNATIVE
cisco-tna	131	TCP	cisco TNATIVE
cisco-tna	131	UDP	cisco TNATIVE
cisco-sys	132	TCP	cisco SYSMAINT

Service	Port Number	Protocol	Description
cisco-sys	132	UDP	cisco SYSMAINT
statsrv	133	TCP	Statistics Service
statsrv	133	UDP	Statistics Service
ingres-net	134	TCP	INGRES-NET Service
ingres-net	134	UDP	INGRES-NET Service
epmap	135	TCP	DCE Endpoint Resolution
epmap	135	UDP	DCE Endpoint Resolution
profile	136	TCP	PROFILE Naming System
profile	136	UDP	PROFILE Naming System
netbios-ns	137	TCP	NETBIOS Name Service
netbios-ns	137	UDP	NETBIOS Name Service
netbios-dgm	138	TCP	NETBIOS Datagram Service
netbios-dgm	138	UDP	NETBIOS Datagram Service
netbios-ssn	139	TCP	NETBIOS Session Service
netbios-ssn	139	UDP	NETBIOS Session Service
emfis-data	140	TCP	EMFIS Data Service
emfis-data	140	UDP	EMFIS Data Service
emfis-cntl	141	TCP	EMFIS Control Service
emfis-cntl	141	UDP	EMFIS Control Service
bl-idm	142	TCP	Britton-Lee IDM
bl-idm	142	UDP	Britton-Lee IDM
imap	143	TCP	Internet Message Access Protocol
imap	143	UDP	Internet Message Access Protocol
uma	144	TCP	Universal Management Architecture
uma	144	UDP	Universal Management Architecture
uaac	145	TCP	UAAC Protocol
uaac	145	UDP	UAAC Protocol
iso-tp0	146	TCP	ISO-IP0
iso-tp0	146	UDP	ISO-IP0
iso-ip	147	TCP	ISO-IP
iso-ip	147	UDP	ISO-IP
jargon	148	TCP	Jargon
jargon	148	UDP	Jargon
aed-512	149	TCP	AED 512 Emulation Service
aed-512	149	UDP	AED 512 Emulation Service
sql-net	150	TCP	SQL-NET
sql-net	150	UDP	SQL-NET
hems	151	TCP	HEMS

(continues)

Service	Port Number	Protocol	Description
hems	151	UDP	HEMS
bftp	152	TCP	Background File Transfer Program
bftp	152	UDP	Background File Transfer Program
sgmp	153	TCP	SGMP
sgmp	153	UDP	SGMP
netsc-prod	154	TCP	NETSC
netsc-prod	154	UDP	NETSC
netsc-dev	155	TCP	NETSC
netsc-dev	155	UDP	NETSC
sqlsrv	156	TCP	SQL Service
sqlsrv	156	UDP	SQL Service
knet-cmp	157	TCP	KNET VM Command Message Protocol
knet-cmp	157	UDP	KNET VM Command Message Protocol
pcmail-srv	158	TCP	PCMail Server
pcmail-srv	158	UDP	PCMail Server
nss-routing	159	TCP	NSS-Routing
nss-routing	159	UDP	NSS-Routing
sgmp-traps	160	TCP	SGMP-TRAPS
sgmp-traps	160	UDP	SGMP-TRAPS
snmp	161	TCP	SNMP
snmp	161	UDP	SNMP
snmptrap	162	TCP	SNMPTRAP
snmptrap	162	UDP	SNMPTRAP
cmip-man	163	TCP	CMIP TCP Manager
cmip-man	163	UDP	CMIP TCP Manager
cmip-agent	164	TCP	CMIP TCP Agent
smip-agent	164	UDP	CMIP TCP Agent
xns-courier	165	TCP	Xerox
xns-courier	165	UDP	Xerox
s-net	166	TCP	Sirius Systems
s-net	166	UDP	Sirius Systems
namp	167	TCP	NAMP
namp	167	UDP	NAMP
rsvd	168	TCP	RSVD
rsvd	168	UDP	RSVD
send	169	TCP	SEND
send	169	UDP	SEND
print-srv	170	TCP	Network PostScript
print-srv	170	UDP	Network PostScript
multiplex	171	TCP	Network Innovations Multiplex
multiplex	171	UDP	Network Innovations Multiplex

Service	Port Number	Protocol	Description
cl/1	172	TCP	Network Innovations CL/1
cl/1	172	UDP	Network Innovations CL/1
xyplex-mux	173	TCP	Xyplex
xyplex-mux	173	UDP	Xyplex
mailq	174	TCP	MAILQ
mailq	174	UDP	MAILQ
vmnet	175	TCP	VMNET
vmnet	175	UDP	VMNET
genrad-mux	176	TCP	GENRAD-MUX
genrad-mux	176	UDP	GENRAD-MUX
xdmcp	177	TCP	X Display Manager Control Protocol
xdmcp	177	UDP	X Display Manager Control Protocol
nextstep	178	TCP	NextStep Window Server
nextstep	178	UDP	NextStep Window Server
bgp	179	TCP	Border Gateway Protocol
bgp	179	UDP	Border Gateway Protocol
ris	180	TCP	Intergraph
ris	180	UDP	Intergraph
unify	181	TCP	Unify
unify	181	UDP	Unify
audit	182	TCP	Unisys Audit SITP
audit	182	UDP	Unisys Audit SITP
ocbinder	183	TCP	OCBinder
ocbinder	183	UDP	OCBinder
ocserver	184	TCP	OCServer
ocserver	184	UDP	OCServer
remote-kis	185	TCP	Remote-KIS
remote-kis	185	UDP	Remote-KIS
kis	186	TCP	KIS Protocol
kis	186	UDP	KIS Protocol
aci	187	TCP	Application Communication Interface
aci	187	UDP	Application Communication Interface
mumps	188	TCP	Plus Five's MUMPS
mumps	188	UDP	Plus Five's MUMPS
qft	189	TCP	Queued File Transport
qft	189	UDP	Queued File Transport
gacp	190	TCP	Gateway Access Control Protocol
gacp	190	UDP	Gateway Access Control Protocol

(continues)

Service	Port Number	Protocol	Description
prospero	191	TCP	Prospero Directory Service
prospero	191	UDP	Prospero Directory Service
osu-nms	192	TCP	OSU Network Monitoring System
osu-nms	192	UDP	OSU Network Monitoring System
srmp	193	TCP	Spider Remote Monitoring Protocol
srmp	193	UDP	Spider Remote Monitoring Protocol
irc	194	TCP	Internet Relay Chat Protocol
irc	194	UDP	Internet Relay Chat Protocol
dn6-nlm-aud	195	TCP	DNSIX Network Level Module Audit
dn6-nlm-aud	195	UDP	DNSIX Network Level Module Audit
dn6-smm-red	196	TCP	DNSIX Session Mgt. Module Audit Redir
dn6-smm-red	196	UDP	DNSIX Session Mgt. Module Audit Redir
dls	197	TCP	Directory Location Service
dls	197	UDP	Directory Location Service
dls-mon	198	TCP	Directory Location Service Monitor
dls-mon	198	UDP	Directory Location Service Monitor
smux	199	TCP	SMUX
smux	199	UDP	SMUX
src	200	TCP	IBM System Resource Controller
src	200	UDP	IBM System Resource Controller
at-rtmp	201	TCP	AppleTalk Routing Maintenance
at-rtmp	201	UDP	AppleTalk Routing Maintenance
at-nbp	202	TCP	AppleTalk Name Binding
at-nbp	202	UDP	AppleTalk Name Binding
at-3	203	TCP	AppleTalk Unused
at-3	203	UDP	AppleTalk Unused
at-echo	204	TCP	AppleTalk Echo
at-echo	204	UDP	AppleTalk Echo
at-5	205	TCP	AppleTalk Unused
at-5	205	UDP	AppleTalk Unused
at-zis	206	TCP	AppleTalk Zone Information
at-zis	206	UDP	AppleTalk Zone Information
at-7	207	TCP	AppleTalk Unused
at-7	207	UDP	AppleTalk Unused
at-8	208	TCP	AppleTalk Unused
at-8	208	UDP	AppleTalk Unused
qmtp	209	TCP	The Quick Mail Transfer Protocol
qmtp	209	UDP	The Quick Mail Transfer Protocol
z39.50	210	TCP	ANSI Z39.50
z39.50	210	UDP	ANSI Z39.50
914c/g	211	TCP	Texas Instruments 914C/G Terminal

Service	Port Number	Protocol	Description
914c/g	211	UDP	Texas Instruments 914C/G Terminal
anet	212	TCP	ATEXSSTR
anet	212	UDP	ATEXSSTR
ipx	213	TCP	IPX
ipx	213	UDP	IPX
vmpwscs	214	TCP	VM PWSCS
vmpwscs	214	UDP	VM PWSCS
softpc	215	TCP	Insignia Solutions
softpc	215	UDP	Insignia Solutions
CAllic	216	TCP	Computer Associates Int'l. License Server
CAllic	216	UDP	Computer Associates Int'l License Server
dbase	217	TCP	dBASE UNIX
dbase	217	UDP	dBASE UNIX
mpp	218	TCP	Netix Message Posting Protocol
mpp	218	UDP	Netix Message Posting Protocol
uarps	219	TCP	Unisys ARPs
uarps	219	UDP	Unisys ARPs
imap3	220	TCP	Interactive Mail Access Protocol v3
imap3	220	UDP	Interactive Mail Access Protocol v3
fln-spx	221	TCP	Berkeley rlogind with SPX auth.
fln-spx	221	UDP	Berkeley rlogind with SPX auth.
rsh-spx	222	TCP	Berkeley rshd with SPX auth.
rsh-spx	222	UDP	Berkeley rshd with SPX auth.
cdc	223	TCP	Certificate Distribution Center
cdc	223	UDP	Certificate Distribution Center
masqdialer	224	TCP	masqdialer
masqdialer	224	UDP	masqdialer
direct	242	TCP	Direct
direct	242	UDP	Direct
sur-meas	243	TCP	Survey Measurement
sur-meas	243	UDP	Survey Measurement
dayna	244	TCP	Dayna
dayna	244	UDP	Dayna
link	245	TCP	LINK
link	245	UDP	LINK
dsp3270	246	TCP	Display Systems Protocol
dsp3270	246	UDP	Display Systems Protocol
subntbcst_tftp	247	TCP	SUBNTBCST_TFTP

(continues)

Service	Port Number	Protocol	Description
subntbcst_tftp	247	UDP	SUBNTBCST_TFTP
bhfhs	248	TCP	bhfhs
bhfhs	248	UDP	bhfhs
rap	256	TCP	RAP
rap	256	UDP	RAP
set	257	TCP	Secure Electronic Transaction
set	257	UDP	Secure Electronic Transaction
yak-chat	258	TCP	Yak Winsock Personal Chat
yak-chat	258	UDP	Yak Winsock Personal Chat
esro-gen	259	TCP	Efficient Short Remote Operations
esro-gen	259	UDP	Efficient Short Remote Operations
openport	260	TCP	Openport
openport	260	UDP	Openport
nsiiops	261	TCP	IIOP Name Service over TLS/SSL
nsiiops	261	UDP	IIOP Name Service over TLS/SSL
arcisdms	262	TCP	Arcisdms
arcisdms	262	UDP	Arcisdms
hdap	263	TCP	HDAP
hdap	263	UDP	HDAP
bgmp	264	TCP	BGMP
bgmp	264	UDP	BGMP
http-mgmt	280	TCP	http-mgmt
http-mgmt	280	UDP	http-mgmt
personal-link	281	TCP	Personal Link
personal-link	281	UDP	Personal Link
cableport-ax	282	TCP	Cable Port AX
cableport-ax	282	UDP	Cable Port AX
rescap	283	TCP	Rescap
rescap	283	UDP	Rescap
novastorbakcup	308	TCP	Novastor Backup
novastorbakcup	308	UDP	Novastor Backup
entrusttime	309	TCP	EntrustTime
entrusttime	309	UDP	EntrustTime
bhmds	310	TCP	bhmds
bhmds	310	UDP	bhmds
asip-webadmin	311	TCP	AppleShare IP WebAdmin
asip-webadmin	311	UDP	AppleShare IP WebAdmin
vslmp	312	TCP	VSLMP
vslmp	312	UDP	VSLMP
magenta-logic	313	TCP	Magenta Logic

Service	Port Number	Protocol	Description
magenta-logic	313	UDP	Magenta Logic
opalis-robot	314	TCP	Opalis Robot
opalis-robot	314	UDP	Opalis Robot
dpsi	315	TCP	DPSI
dpsi	315	UDP	DPSI
decauth	316	TCP	decAuth
decauth	316	UDP	decAuth
zannet	317	TCP	Zannet
zannet	317	UDP	Zannet
pkix-timestamp	318	TCP	PKIX TimeStamp
pkix-timestamp	318	UDP	PKIX TimeStamp
ptp-event	319	TCP	PTP Event
ptp-event	319	UDP	PTP Event
ptp-general	320	TCP	PTP General
ptp-general	320	UDP	PTP General
pip	321	TCP	PIP
pip	321	UDP	PIP
rtsps	322	TCP	RTSPS
rtsps	322	UDP	RTSPS
pdap	344	TCP	Prospero Data Access Protocol
pdap	344	UDP	Prospero Data Access Protocol
pawserv	345	TCP	Perf Analysis Workbench
pawserv	345	UDP	Perf Analysis Workbench
zserv	346	TCP	Zebra Server
zserv	346	UDP	Zebra Server
fatserv	347	TCP	Fatmen Server
fatserv	347	UDP	Fatmen Server
csi-sgwp	348	TCP	Cabletron Management Protocol
csi-sgwp	348	UDP	Cabletron Management Protocol
mftp	349	TCP	mftp
mftp	349	UDP	mftp
matip-type-a	350	TCP	MATIP Type A
matip-type-a	350	UDP	MATIP Type A
matip-type-b	351	TCP	MATIP Type B
matip-type-b	351	UDP	MATIP Type B
bhoetty	351	TCP	bhoetty
bhoetty	351	UDP	bhoetty
dtag-ste-sb	352	TCP	DTAG

(continues)

Service	Port Number	Protocol	Description
dtag-ste-sb	352	UDP	DTAG
bhoedap4	352	TCP	bhoedap4
bhoedap4	352	UDP	bhoedap4
ndsauth	353	TCP	NDSAUTH
ndsauth	353	UDP	NDSAUTH
bh611	354	TCP	bh611
bh611	354	UDP	bh611
datex-asn	355	TCP	DATEX-ASN
datex-asn	355	UDP	DATEX-ASN
cloanto-net-1	356	TCP	Cloanto Net 1
cloanto-net-1	356	UDP	Cloanto Net 1
bhevent	357	TCP	bhevent
bhevent	357	UDP	bhevent
shrinkwrap	358	TCP	Shrinkwrap
shrinkwrap	358	UDP	Shrinkwrap
tenebris_nts	359	TCP	Tenebris Network Trace Service
tenebris_nts	359	UDP	Tenebris Network Trace Service
scoi2odialog	360	TCP	scoi2odialog
scoi2odialog	360	UDP	scoi2odialog
semantix	361	TCP	Semantix
semantix	361	UDP	Semantix
srssend	362	TCP	SRS Send
srssend	362	UDP	SRS Send
rsvp_tunnel	363	TCP	RSVP Tunnel
rsvp_tunnel	363	UDP	RSVP Tunnel
aurora-cmgr	364	TCP	Aurora CMGR
aurora-cmgr	364	UDP	Aurora CMGR
dtk	365	TCP	DTK
dtk	365	UDP	DTK
odmr	366	TCP	ODMR
odmr	366	UDP	ODMR
mortgageware	367	TCP	MortgageWare
mortgageware	367	UDP	MortgageWare
qbikgdp	368	TCP	QbikGDP
qbikgdp	368	UDP	QbikGDP
rpc2portmap	369	TCP	rpc2portmap
rpc2portmap	369	UDP	rpc2portmap
codaauth2	370	TCP	codaauth2
codaauth2	370	UDP	codaauth2
clearcase	371	TCP	Clearcase
clearcase	371	UDP	Clearcase

Service	Port Number	Protocol	Description
ulistproc	372	TCP	ListProcessor
ulistproc	372	UDP	ListProcessor
legent-1	373	TCP	Legent Corporation
legent-1	373	UDP	Legent Corporation
legent-2	374	TCP	Legent Corporation
legent-2	374	UDP	Legent Corporation
hassle	375	TCP	Hassle
hassle	375	UDP	Hassle
nip	376	TCP	Amiga Envoy Network Inquiry Proto
nip	376	UDP	Amiga Envoy Network Inquiry Proto
tnETOS	377	TCP	NEC Corporation
tnETOS	377	UDP	NEC Corporation
dsETOS	378	TCP	NEC Corporation
dsETOS	378	UDP	NEC Corporation
is99c	379	TCP	TIA/EIA/IS-99 Modem Client
is99c	379	UDP	TIA/EIA/IS-99 Modem Client
is99s	380	TCP	TIA/EIA/IS-99 Modem Server
is99s	380	UDP	TIA/EIA/IS-99 Modem Server
hp-collector	381	TCP	hp Performance Data Collector
hp-collector	381	UDP	hp Performance Data Collector
hp-managed-node	382	TCP	hp Performance Data Managed Node
hp-managed-node	382	UDP	hp Performance Data Managed Node
hp-alarm-mgr	383	TCP	hp Performance Data Alarm Manager
hp-alarm-mgr	383	UDP	hp Performance Data Alarm Manager
arns	384	TCP	A Remote Network Server System
arns	384	UDP	A Remote Network Server System
ibm-app	385	TCP	IBM Application
ibm-app	385	UDP	IBM Application
asa	386	TCP	ASA Message Router Object Def.
asa	386	UDP	ASA Message Router Object Def.
aurp	387	TCP	Appletalk Update-Based Routing Pro.
aurp	387	UDP	Appletalk Update-Based Routing Pro.
unidata-ldm	388	TCP	Unidata LDM Version 4
unidata-ldm	388	UDP	Unidata LDM Version 4
ldap	389	TCP	Lightweight Directory Access Protocol
ldap	389	UDP	Lightweight Directory Access Protocol
uis	390	TCP	UIS
uis	390	UDP	UIS

(continues)

Service	Port Number	Protocol	Description
synotics-relay	391	TCP	SynOptics SNMP Relay Port
synotics-relay	391	UDP	SynOptics SNMP Relay Port
synotics-broker	392	TCP	SynOptics Port Broker Port
synotics-broker	392	UDP	SynOptics Port Broker Port
dis	393	TCP	Data Interpretation System
dis	393	UDP	Data Interpretation System
embl-ndt	394	TCP	EMBL Nucleic Data Transfer
embl-ndt	394	UDP	EMBL Nucleic Data Transfer
netcp	395	TCP	NETscout Control Protocol
netcp	395	UDP	NETscout Control Protocol
netware-ip	396	TCP	Novell NetWare over IP
netware-ip	396	UDP	Novell NetWare over IP
mptn	397	TCP	Multi Protocol Trans. Net.
mptn	397	UDP	Multi Protocol Trans. Net.
kryptolan	398	TCP	Kryptolan
kryptolan	398	UDP	Kryptolan
iso-tsap-c2	399	TCP	ISO Transport Class 2 Non-Control over TCP
iso-tsap-c2	399	UDP	ISO Transport Class 2 Non-Control over TCP
work-sol	400	TCP	Workstation Solutions
work-sol	400	UDP	Workstation Solutions
ups	401	TCP	Uninterruptible Power Supply
ups	401	UDP	Uninterruptible Power Supply
genie	402	TCP	Genie Protocol
genie	402	UDP	Genie Protocol
decap	403	TCP	decap
decap	403	UDP	decap
nced	404	TCP	nced
nced	404	UDP	nced
ncld	405	TCP	ncld
ncld	405	UDP	ncld
imsp	406	TCP	Interactive Mail Support Protocol
imsp	406	UDP	Interactive Mail Support Protocol
timbuktu	407	TCP	Timbuktu
timbuktu	407	UDP	Timbuktu
prm-sm	408	TCP	Prospero Resource Manager Sys. Man.
prm-sm	408	UDP	Prospero Resource Manager Sys. Man.
prm-nm	409	TCP	Prospero Resource Manager Node Man.
prm-nm	409	UDP	Prospero Resource Manager Node Man.
decladebug	410	TCP	DECLadebug Remote Debug Protocol
decladebug	410	UDP	DECLadebug Remote Debug Protocol
rmt	411	TCP	Remote MT Protocol

Service	Port Number	Protocol	Description
rmt	411	UDP	Remote MT Protocol
synoptics-trap	412	TCP	Trap Convention Port
synoptics-trap	412	UDP	Trap Convention Port
smsp	413	TCP	SMSP
smsp	413	UDP	SMSP
infoseek	414	TCP	InfoSeek
infoseek	414	UDP	InfoSeek
bnet	415	TCP	BNet
bnet	415	UDP	BNet
silverplatter	416	TCP	Silverplatter
silverplatter	416	UDP	Silverplatter
onmux	417	TCP	Onmux
onmux	417	UDP	Onmux
hyper-g	418	TCP	Hyper-G
hyper-g	418	UDP	Hyper-G
ariel1	419	TCP	Ariel
ariel1	419	UDP	Ariel
smpte	420	TCP	SMPTE
smpte	420	UDP	SMPTE
ariel2	421	TCP	Ariel
ariel2	421	UDP	Ariel
ariel3	422	TCP	Ariel
ariel3	422	UDP	Ariel
opc-job-start	423	TCP	IBM Operations Planning and Control Start
opc-job-start	423	UDP	IBM Operations Planning and Control Start
opc-job-track	424	TCP	IBM Operations Planning and Control Track
opc-job-track	424	UDP	IBM Operations Planning and Control Track
icad-el	425	TCP	ICAD
icad-el	425	UDP	ICAD
smartsdp	426	TCP	smartsdp
smartsdp	426	UDP	smartsdp
svrloc	427	TCP	Server Location
svrloc	427	UDP	Server Location
ocs_cmu	428	TCP	OCS_CMU
ocs_cmu	428	UDP	OCS_CMU
ocs_amu	429	TCP	OCS_AMU
ocs_amu	429	UDP	OCS_AMU
utmpsd	430	TCP	UTMPSD

(continues)

Service	Port Number	Protocol	Description
utmpsd	430	UDP	UTMPSD
utmpcd	431	TCP	UTMPCD
utmpcd	431	UDP	UTMPCD
iasd	432	TCP	IASD
iasd	432	UDP	IASD
nnsp	433	TCP	NNSP
nnsp	433	UDP	NNSP
mobileip-agent	434	TCP	MobileIP-Agent
mobileip-agent	434	UDP	MobileIP-Agent
mobilip-mn	435	TCP	MobilIP-MN
mobilip-mn	435	UDP	MobilIP-MN
dna-cml	436	TCP	DNA-CML
dna-cml	436	UDP	DNA-CML
comscm	437	TCP	comscm
comscm	437	UDP	comscm
dsfgw	438	TCP	dsfgw
dsfgw	438	UDP	dsfgw
dasp	439	TCP	dasp
dasp	439	UDP	dasp
sgcp	440	TCP	sgcp
sgcp	440	UDP	sgcp
decvms-sysmgt	441	TCP	decvms-sysmgt
decvms-sysmgt	441	UDP	decvms-sysmgt
cvc_hostd	442	TCP	cvc_hostd
cvc_hostd	442	UDP	cvc_hostd
https	443	TCP	http protocol over TLS/SSL
https	443	UDP	http protocol over TLS/SSL
snpp	444	TCP	Simple Network Paging Protocol
snpp	444	UDP	Simple Network Paging Protocol
microsoft-ds	445	TCP	Microsoft-DS
microsoft-ds	445	UDP	Microsoft-DS
ddm-rdb	446	TCP	DDM-RDB
ddm-rdb	446	UDP	DDM-RDB
ddm-dfm	447	TCP	DDM-RFM
ddm-dfm	447	UDP	DDM-RFM
ddm-ssl	448	TCP	DDM-SSL
ddm-ssl	448	UDP	DDM-SSL
as-servermap	449	TCP	AS Server Mapper
as-servermap	449	UDP	AS Server Mapper
tserver	450	TCP	TServer

Service	Port Number	Protocol	Description
tserver	450	UDP	TServer
sfs-smp-net	451	TCP	Cray Network Semaphore Server
sfs-smp-net	451	UDP	Cray Network Semaphore Server
sfs-config	452	TCP	Cray SFS Config. Server
sfs-config	452	UDP	Cray SFS Config. Server
creativeserver	453	TCP	CreativeServer
creativeserver	453	UDP	CreativeServer
contentserver	454	TCP	ContentServer
contentserver	454	UDP	ContentServer
creativepartnr	455	TCP	CreativePartnr
creativepartnr	455	UDP	CreativePartnr
macon-tcp	456	TCP	macon-tcp
macon-udp	456	UDP	macon-udp
scohelp	457	TCP	scohelp
scohelp	457	UDP	scohelp
appleqtc	458	TCP	Apple QuickTime
appleqtc	458	UDP	Apple QuickTime
ampr-rcmd	459	TCP	ampr-rcmd
ampr-rcmd	459	UDP	ampr-rcmd
skronk	460	TCP	skronk
skronk	460	UDP	skronk
datasurfsrv	461	TCP	DataRampSrv
datasurfsrv	461	UDP	DataRampSrv
datasurfsrvsec	462	TCP	DataRampSrvSec
datasurfsrvsec	462	UDP	DataRampSrvSec
alpes	463	TCP	alpes
alpes	463	UDP	alpes
kpasswd	464	TCP	kpasswd
kpasswd	464	UDP	kpasswd
digital-vrc	466	TCP	digital-vrc
digital-vrc	466	UDP	digital-vrc
mylex-mapd	467	TCP	mylex-mapd
mylex-mapd	467	UDP	mylex-mapd
photuris	468	TCP	proturis
photuris	468	UDP	proturis
rcp	469	TCP	Radio Control Protocol
rcp	469	UDP	Radio Control Protocol
scx-proxy	470	TCP	scx-proxy

(continues)

Service	Port Number	Protocol	Description
scx-proxy	470	UDP	scx-proxy
mondex	471	TCP	Mondex
mondex	471	UDP	Mondex
ljk-login	472	TCP	ljk-login
ljk-login	472	UDP	ljk-login
hybrid-pop	473	TCP	hybrid-pop
hybrid-pop	473	UDP	hybrid-pop
tn-tl-w1	474	TCP	tn-tl-w1
tn-tl-w2	474	UDP	tn-tl-w2
tcpnethaspsrv	475	TCP	tcpnethaspsrv
tcpnethaspsrv	475	UDP	tcpnethaspsrv
tn-tl-fd1	476	TCP	tn-tl-fd1
tn-tl-fd1	476	UDP	tn-tl-fd1
ss7ns	477	TCP	ss7ns
ss7ns	477	UDP	ss7ns
spsc	478	TCP	spsc
spsc	478	UDP	spsc
iafserver	479	TCP	iafserver
iafserver	479	UDP	iafserver
iafdbase	480	TCP	iafdbase
iafdbase	480	UDP	iafdbase
ph	481	TCP	Ph service
ph	481	UDP	Ph service
bgs-nsi	482	TCP	bgs-nsi
bgs-nsi	482	UDP	bgs-nsi
ulpnet	483	TCP	ulpnet
ulpnet	483	UDP	ulpnet
integra-sme	484	TCP	Integra Software Management Environment
integra-sme	484	UDP	Integra Software Management Environment
powerburst	485	TCP	Air Soft Power Burst
powerburst	485	UDP	Air Soft Power Burst
avian	486	TCP	avian
avian	486	UDP	avian
saft	487	TCP	saft Simple Asynchronous File Transfer
saft	487	UDP	saft Simple Asynchronous File Transfer
gss-http	488	TCP	gss-http
gss-http	488	UDP	gss-http
nest-protocol	489	TCP	nest-protocol
nest-protocol	489	UDP	nest-protocol
micom-pfs	490	TCP	micom-pfs

Service	Port Number	Protocol	Description
micom-pfs	490	UDP	micom-pfs
go-login	491	TCP	go-login
go-login	491	UDP	go-login
ticf-1	492	TCP	Transport Independent Convergence for FNA
ticf-1	492	UDP	Transport Independent Convergence for FNA
ticf-2	493	TCP	Transport Independent Convergence for FNA
ticf-2	493	UDP	Transport Independent Convergence for FNA
pov-ray	494	TCP	POV-Ray
pov-ray	494	UDP	POV-Ray
intecourier	495	TCP	intecourier
intecourier	495	UDP	intecourier
pim-rp-disc	496	TCP	PIM-RP-DISC
pim-rp-disc	496	UDP	PIM-RP-DISC
dantz	497	TCP	dantz
dantz	497	UDP	dantz
siam	498	TCP	siam
siam	498	UDP	siam
iso-ill	499	TCP	ISO ILL Protocol
iso-ill	499	UDP	ISO ILL rotocol
isakmp	500	TCP	isakmp
isakmp	500	UDP	isakmp
stmf	501	TCP	STMF
stmf	501	UDP	STMF
asa-appl-proto	502	TCP	asa-appl-proto
asa-appl-proto	502	UDP	asa-appl-proto
intrinsa	503	TCP	Intrinsa
intrinsa	503	UDP	Intrinsa
citadel	504	TCP	citadel
citadel	504	UDP	citadel
mailbox-lm	505	TCP	mailbox-lm
mailbox-lm	505	UDP	mailbox-lm
ohimsrv	506	TCP	ohimsrv
ohimsrv	506	UDP	ohimsrv
crs	507	TCP	crs
crs	507	UDP	crs
xvttp	508	TCP	xvttp
xvttp	508	UDP	xvttp
snare	509	TCP	snare

(continues)

Service	Port Number	Protocol	Description
snare	509	UDP	snare
fcp	510	TCP	FirstClass Protocol
fcp	510	UDP	FirstClass Protocol
passgo	511	TCP	PassGo
passgo	511	UDP	PassGo
exec	512	TCP	remote process execution;
comsat	512	UDP	
biff	512	UDP	Used by mail system to notify users
login	513	TCP	Remote login a la Telnet;
who	513	UDP	Maintains the who is databases
shell	514	TCP	cmd
syslog	514	UDP	
printer	515	TCP	spooler
printer	515	UDP	spooler
videotex	516	TCP	videotex
videotex	516	UDP	videotex
talk	517	TCP	Like tenex link, but across
talk	517	UDP	Like tenex link, but across
ntalk	518	TCP	
ntalk	518	UDP	
utime	519	TCP	unixtime
utime	519	UDP	unixtime
efs	520	TCP	Extended File Name Server
router	520	UDP	Local Routing Process (on site)
ripng	521	TCP	ripng
ripng	521	UDP	ripng
ulp	522	TCP	ULP
ulp	522	UDP	ULP
ibm-db2	523	TCP	IBM-DB2
ibm-db2	523	UDP	IBM-DB2
ncp	524	TCP	NCP
ncp	524	UDP	NCP
timed	525	TCP	timeserver
timed	525	UDP	timeserver
tempo	526	TCP	newdate
tempo	526	UDP	newdate
stx	527	TCP	Stock IXChange
stx	527	UDP	Stock IXChange
custix	528	TCP	Customer IXChange
custix	528	UDP	CustomerIXChange

Service	Port Number	Protocol	Description
irc-serv	529	TCP	IRC-SERV
irc-serv	529	UDP	IRC-SERV
courier	530	TCP	rpc
courier	530	UDP	rpc
conference	531	TCP	chat
conference	531	UDP	chat
netnews	532	TCP	readnews
netnews	532	UDP	readnews
netwall	533	TCP	For Emergency Broadcasts
netwall	533	UDP	For Emergency Broadcasts
mm-admin	534	TCP	MegaMedia Admin
mm-admin	534	UDP	MegaMedia Admin
iiop	535	TCP	iiop
iiop	535	UDP	iiop
opalis-rdv	536	TCP	opalis-rdv
opalis-rdv	536	UDP	opalis-rdv
nmsp	537	TCP	Networked Media Streaming Protocol
nmsp	537	UDP	Networked Media Streaming Protocol
gdomap	538	TCP	gdomap
gdomap	538	UDP	gdomap
apertus-ldp	539	TCP	Apertus Technologies Load Determination
apertus-ldp	539	UDP	Apertus Technologies Load Determination
uucp	540	TCP	uucpd
uucp	540	UDP	uucpd
uucp-rlogin	541	TCP	uucp-rlogin
uucp-rlogin	541	UDP	uucp-rlogin
commerce	542	TCP	commerce
commerce	542	UDP	commerce
klogin	543	TCP	
klogin	543	UDP	
kshell	544	TCP	krcmd
kshell	544	UDP	krcmd
appleqtcsrvr	545	TCP	appleqtcsrvr
appleqtcsrvr	545	UDP	appleqtcsrvr
dhcpv6-client	546	TCP	DHCPv6 Client
dhcpv6-client	546	UDP	DHCPv6 Client
dhcpv6-server	547	TCP	DHCPv6 Server
dhcpv6-server	547	UDP	DHCPv6 Server

(continues)

Service	Port Number	Protocol	Description
afpovertcp	548	TCP	AFP over TCP
afpovertcp	548	UDP	AFP over TCP
idfp	549	TCP	IDFP
idfp	549	UDP	IDFP
new-rwho	550	TCP	new-who
new-rwho	550	UDP	new-who
cybercash	551	TCP	cybercash
cybercash	551	UDP	cybercash
deviceshare	552	TCP	deviceshare
deviceshare	552	UDP	deviceshare
pirp	553	TCP	pirp
pirp	553	UDP	pirp
rtsp	554	TCP	Real Time Stream Control Protocol
rtsp	554	UDP	Real Time Stream Control Protocol
dsf	555	TCP	
dsf	555	UDP	
remotefs	556	TCP	rfs server
remotefs	556	UDP	rfs server
openvms-sysipc	557	TCP	openvms-sysipc
openvms-sysipc	557	UDP	openvms-sysipc
sdnskmp	558	TCP	SDNSKMP
sdnskmp	558	UDP	SDNSKMP
teedtap	559	TCP	TEEDTAP
teedtap	559	UDP	TEEDTAP
rmonitor	560	TCP	rmonitord
rmonitor	560	UDP	rmonitord
monitor	561	TCP	
monitor	561	UDP	
chshell	562	TCP	chcmd
chshell	562	UDP	chcmd
nntps	563	TCP	nntp protocol over TLS/SSL (was snntp)
nntps	563	UDP	nntp protocol over TLS/SSL (was snntp)
9pfs	564	TCP	Plan 9 File Service
9pfs	564	UDP	Plan 9 File Service
whoami	565	TCP	whoami
whoami	565	UDP	whoami
streettalk	566	TCP	streettalk
streettalk	566	UDP	streettalk
banyan-rpc	567	TCP	banyan-rpc
banyan-rpc	567	UDP	banyan-rpc

Service	Port Number	Protocol	Description
ms-shuttle	568	TCP	microsoft shuttle
ms-shuttle	568	UDP	microsoft shuttle
ms-rome	569	TCP	microsoft rome
ms-rome	569	UDP	microsoft rome
meter	570	TCP	demon
meter	570	UDP	demon
meter	571	TCP	udemon
meter	571	UDP	udemon
sonar	572	TCP	sonar
sonar	572	UDP	sonar
banyan-vip	573	TCP	banyan-vip
banyan-vip	573	UDP	banyan-vip
ftp-agent	574	TCP	FTP Software Agent System
ftp-agent	574	UDP	FTP Software Agent System
vemmi	575	TCP	VEMMI
vemmi	575	UDP	VEMMI
ipcd	576	TCP	ipcd
ipcd	576	UDP	ipcd
vnas	577	TCP	vnas
vnas	577	UDP	vnas
ipdd	578	TCP	ipdd
ipdd	578	UDP	ipdd
decbsrv	579	TCP	decbsrv
decbsrv	579	UDP	decbsrv
sntp-heartbeat	580	TCP	SNTP HEARTBEAT
sntp-heartbeat	580	UDP	SNTP HEARTBEAT
bdp	581	TCP	Bundle Discovery Protocol
bdp	581	UDP	Bundle Discovery Protocol
scc-security	582	TCP	SCC Security
scc-security	582	UDP	SCC Security
philips-vc	583	TCP	Philips Video-Conferencing
philips-vc	583	UDP	Philips Video-Conferencing
keyserver	584	TCP	Key Server
keyserver	584	UDP	Key Server
imap4-ssl	585	TCP	IMAP4+SSL (Use 993 instead)
imap4-ssl	585	UDP	IMAP4+SSL (Use 993 instead)
password-chg	586	TCP	Password Change
password-chg	586	UDP	Password Change

(continues)

Service	Port Number	Protocol	Description
submission	587	TCP	Submission
submission	587	UDP	Submission
cal	588	TCP	CAL
cal	588	UDP	CAL
eyelink	589	TCP	EyeLink
eyelink	589	UDP	EyeLink
tns-cml	590	TCP	TNS CML
tns-cml	590	UDP	TNS CML
http-alt	591	TCP	FileMaker, Inc.—HTTP Alternate (see Port 80)
http-alt	591	UDP	FileMaker, Inc.—HTTP Alternate (see Port 80)
eudora-set	592	TCP	Eudora Set
eudora-set	592	UDP	Eudora Set
http-rpc-epmap	593	TCP	HTTP RPC Ep Map
http-rpc-epmap	593	UDP	HTTP RPC Ep Map
tpip	594	TCP	TPIP
tpip	594	UDP	TPIP
cab-protocol	595	TCP	CAB Protocol
cab-protocol	595	UDP	CAB Protocol
smsd	596	TCP	SMSD
smsd	596	UDP	SMSD
ptcnameservice	597	TCP	PTC Name Service
ptcnameservice	597	UDP	PTC Name Service
sco-websrvrmg3	598	TCP	SCO Web Server Manager 3
sco-websrvrmg3	598	UDP	SCO Web Server Manager 3
acp	599	TCP	Aeolon Core Protocol
acp	599	UDP	Aeolon Core Protocol
ipcserver	600	TCP	Sun IPC server
ipcserver	600	UDP	Sun IPC server
urm	606	TCP	Cray Unified Resource Manager
urm	606	UDP	Cray Unified Resource Manager
nqs	607	TCP	nqs
nqs	607	UDP	nqs
sift-uft	608	TCP	Sender-Initiated/Unsolicited File Transfer
sift-uft	608	UDP	Sender-Initiated/Unsolicited File Transfer
npmp-trap	609	TCP	npmp-trap
npmp-trap	609	UDP	npmp-trap
npmp-local	610	TCP	npmp-local
npmp-local	610	UDP	npmp-local
npmp-gui	611	TCP	npmp-gui
npmp-gui	611	UDP	npmp-gui

Service	Port Number	Protocol	Description
hmmp-ind	612	TCP	HMMP Indication
hmmp-ind	612	UDP	HMMP Indication
hmmp-op	613	TCP	HMMP Operation
hmmp-op	613	UDP	HMMP Operation
sshell	614	TCP	SSLshell
sshell	614	UDP	SSLshell
sco-inetmgr	615	TCP	Internet Configuration Manager
sco-inetmgr	615	UDP	Internet Configuration Manager
sco-sysmgr	616	TCP	SCO System Administration Server
sco-sysmgr	616	UDP	SCO System Administration Server
sco-dtmgr	617	TCP	SCO Desktop Administration Server
sco-dtmgr	617	UDP	SCO Desktop Administration Server
dei-icda	618	TCP	DEI-ICDA
dei-icda	618	UDP	DEI-ICDA
digital-evm	619	TCP	Digital EVM
digital-evm	619	UDP	Digital EVM
sco-websrvrmgr	620	TCP	SCO WebServer Manager
sco-websrvrmgr	620	UDP	SCO WebServer Manager
escp-ip	621	TCP	ESCP
escp-ip	621	UDP	ESCP
collaborator	622	TCP	Collaborator
collaborator	622	UDP	Collaborator
aux_bus_shunt	623	TCP	Aux Bus Shunt
aux_bus_shunt	623	UDP	Aux Bus Shunt
cryptoadmin	624	TCP	Crypto Admin.
cryptoadmin	624	UDP	Crypto Admin.
dec_dlm	625	TCP	DEC DLM
dec_dlm	625	UDP	DEC DLM
asia	626	TCP	ASIA
asia	626	UDP	ASIA
passgo-tivoli	627	TCP	PassGo Tivoli
passgo-tivoli	627	UDP	PassGo Tivoli
qmqp	628	TCP	QMQP
qmqp	628	UDP	QMQP
3com-amp3	629	TCP	3Com AMP3
3com-amp3	629	UDP	3Com AMP3
rda	630	TCP	RDA
rda	630	UDP	RDA

(continues)

Service	Port Number	Protocol	Description
ipp	631	TCP	IPP (Internet Printing Protocol)
ipp	631	UDP	IPP (Internet Printing Protocol)
bmpp	632	TCP	bmpp
bmpp	632	UDP	bmpp
servstat	633	TCP	Service Status update (Sterling Software)
servstat	633	UDP	Service Status update (Sterling Software)
ginad	634	TCP	ginad
ginad	634	UDP	ginad
rlzdbase	635	TCP	RLZ DBase
rlzdbase	635	UDP	RLZ DBase
ldaps	636	TCP	ldap protocol over TLS/SSL (was sldap)
ldaps	636	UDP	ldap protocol over TLS/SSL (was sldap)
lanserver	637	TCP	lanserver
lanserver	637	UDP	lanserver
mcns-sec	638	TCP	mcns-sec
mcns-sec	638	UDP	mcns-sec
msdp	639	TCP	MSDP
msdp	639	UDP	MSDP
entrust-sps	640	TCP	entrust-sps
entrust-sps	640	UDP	entrust-sps
repcmd	641	TCP	repcmd
repcmd	641	UDP	repcmd
esro-emsdp	642	TCP	ESRO-EMSDP V1.3
esro-emsdp	642	UDP	ESRO-EMSDP V1.3
sanity	643	TCP	SANity
sanity	643	UDP	SANity
dwr	644	TCP	dwr
dwr	644	UDP	dwr
pssc	645	TCP	PSSC
pssc	645	UDP	PSSC
ldp	646	TCP	LDP
ldp	646	UDP	LDP
dhcp-failover	647	TCP	DHCP Failover
dhcp-failover	647	UDP	DHCP Failover
rrp	648	TCP	Registry Registrar Protocol (RRP)
rrp	648	UDP	Registry Registrar Protocol (RRP)
aminet	649	TCP	Aminet
aminet	649	UDP	Aminet
obex	650	TCP	OBEX
obex	650	UDP	OBEX

Service	Port Number	Protocol	Description
ieee-mms	651	TCP	IEEE MMS
ieee-mms	651	UDP	IEEE MMS
udlr-dtcp	652	TCP	UDLR_DTCP
udlr-dtcp	652	UDP	UDLR_DTCP
repscmd	653	TCP	RepCmd
repscmd	653	UDP	RepCmd
aodv	654	TCP	AODV
aodv	654	UDP	AODV
tinc	655	TCP	TINC
tinc	655	UDP	TINC
spmp	656	TCP	SPMP
spmp	656	UDP	SPMP
mdqs	666	TCP	
mdqs	666	UDP	
doom	666	TCP	doom Id Software
doom	666	UDP	doom Id Software
disclose Technologies	667	TCP	campaign contribution disclosures—SDR
disclose Technologies	667	UDP	campaign contribution disclosures—SDR
mecomm	668	TCP	MeComm
mecomm	668	UDP	MeComm
meregister	669	TCP	MeRegister
meregister	669	UDP	MeRegister
vacdsm-sws	670	TCP	VACDSM-SWS
vacdsm-sws	670	UDP	VACDSM-SWS
vacdsm-app	671	TCP	VACDSM-APP
vacdsm-app	671	UDP	VACDSM-APP
vpps-qua	672	TCP	VPPS-QUA
vpps-qua	672	UDP	VPPS-QUA
cimplex	673	TCP	CIMPLEX
cimplex	673	UDP	CIMPLEX
acap	674	TCP	ACAP
acap	674	UDP	ACAP
dctp	675	TCP	DCTP
dctp	675	UDP	DCTP
vpps-via	676	TCP	VPPS Via
vpps-via	676	UDP	VPPS Via

(continues)

Service	Port Number	Protocol	Description
vpp	677	TCP	Virtual PresenceProtocol
vpp	677	UDP	Virtual Presence Protocol
ggf-ncp	678	TCP	GNU Generation Foundation NCP
ggf-ncp	678	UDP	GNU Generation Foundation NCP
mrm	679	TCP	MRM
mrm	679	UDP	MRM
entrust-aaas	680	TCP	entrust-aaas
entrust-aaas	680	UDP	entrust-aaas
entrust-aams	681	TCP	entrust-aams
entrust-aams	681	UDP	entrust-aams
xfr	682	TCP	XFR
xfr	682	UDP	XFR
corba-iiop	683	TCP	CORBA IIOP
corba-iiop	683	UDP	CORBA IIOP
corba-iiop-ssl	684	TCP	CORBA IIOP SSL
corba-iiop-ssl	684	UDP	CORBA IIOP SSL
mdc-portmapper	685	TCP	MDC Port Mapper
mdc-portmapper	685	UDP	MDC Port Mapper
hcp-wismar	686	TCP	Hardware Control Protocol Wismar
hcp-wismar	686	UDP	Hardware Control Protocol Wismar
asipregistry	687	TCP	asipregistry
asipregistry	687	UDP	asipregistry
realm-rusd	688	TCP	REALM-RUSD
realm-rusd	688	UDP	REALM-RUSD
elcsd	704	TCP	errlog copy/server daemon
elcsd	704	UDP	errlog copy/server daemon
agentx	705	TCP	AgentX
agentx	705	UDP	AgentX
borland-dsj	707	TCP	Borland DSJ
borland-dsj	707	UDP	Borland DSJ
entrust-kmsh	709	TCP	Entrust Key Management Service Handler
entrust-kmsh	709	UDP	Entrust Key Management Service Handler
entrust-ash	710	TCP	Entrust Administration Service Handler
entrust-ash	710	UDP	Entrust Administration Service Handler
cisco-tdp	711	TCP	Cisco TDP
cisco-tdp	711	UDP	Cisco TDP
netviewdm1	729	TCP	IBM NetView DM/6000 Server/Client
netviewdm1	729	UDP	IBM NetView DM/6000 Server/Client
netviewdm2	730	TCP	IBM NetView DM/6000 send/tcp
netviewdm2	730	UDP	IBM NetView DM/6000 send/tcp

REMARK

Syntax
REM[ARK] [text]
* [text]
; [text]

This command is used to place remarks in the login script. Text following REMARK is not displayed on the user's screen. It is useful for documenting commands in the script. The asterisk (*) and semicolon (;) characters can also be used to indicate remark text, and the command REMARK can be shortened to REM.

Remark text should not span multiple lines and should not be placed on the same line as an executable script command. To create remark text that is more than one line, use a REMARK command or one of the symbols at the start of each line.

Example
* Map drives in this section.
; Test day of the week to determine text to display.
REM Run reminder program if this is Friday.

SCRIPT_SERVER

Syntax
SCRIPT_SERVER servername

This command is useful only for NetWare 2.x and 3.x users and does not have any effect on NetWare 4 users or NDS. It is used to indicate the home server that is used to store the login script.

Example
SCRIPT_SERVER acctng

SET

Syntax
[TEMP] SET variablename="value"

This command sets a DOS environment variable. Replace variablename with the name of the variable and value with the value to be associated with the variable. Note that values that must be enclosed in quotation marks. The optional [TEMP] command will allow the variable to be set for only the duration of the login script.

Example
SET PROMPT="pG"

NOSWAP

Syntax

NOSWAP

LOGIN swaps to extended or expanded memory by default. Using this command, you can prevent this from happening. This command is useful if you do not want LOGIN to be swapped out of conventional memory before an external program is run using the # command.

Example

NOSWAP

PAUSE

Syntax

PAUSE

This command displays the text Strike any key when ready... and waits until the user presses a key before continuing. It is useful for displaying a message on the screen and giving the user time to read it before continuing.

Example

DISPLAY SYS:PUBLIC\MESSAGES\WELCOME.TXT
PAUSE

PCCOMPATIBLE

Syntax

PCCOMPATIBLE

This command is used for computers that are IBM compatibles. It will allow the EXIT "*command*" command to work correctly if the computer's long machine name is not "IBM_PC." The long machine name should be set in the NET.CFG file.

Example

PCCOMPATIBLE
EXIT "C:\CALENDAR"

PROFILE

Syntax

PROFILE profile_objectname

Use this command to override a user's assigned profile script or one specified on the command line. This is usually used to specify a group profile.

MAP [option] [drive:=path]

MAP is used to map network drives and to search network directories. Substitute a valid drive letter or search drive number for *drive* and *path* with a full path or an NDS directory Map object. You can place more than one MAP command on the same line by separating each drive mapping with a semicolon (;) character.

option can be any of the following:

- DISPLAY ON or DISPLAY OFF—If ON is used, mappings are displayed on the user's screen during the login process. If OFF is used, they are not. The default is ON.
- ERRORS ON or ERRORS OFF—If ON is used, any errors encountered during drive mapping are displayed on the user's screen. If OFF, errors are not displayed. The default is ON.
- INS:—This option inserts a drive mapping between existing search mappings.
- DEL:—This option deletes a drive mapping. The drive letter associated with the mapping is again available for use.
- ROOT:—This option maps a fake root.
- C—The change option will change a search drive mapping to a regular drive mapping or vice versa.
- P—The physical option can be used to map a drive to the physical volume of a server instead of the volume object's name. It is useful when a physical volume name is the same as one used for an object volume's name.
- N—The next option can be used to specify the next available drive letter so that you do not have to specify the actual drive letter in the mapping command.

To map a search drive, use the letter S followed by a number. Up to 16 NetWare search drives can be specified. Drive letters for search drives are assigned starting with the letter Z and then working backwards through the alphabet. Search drive letters are placed into the DOS path statement.

Example

MAP S1:=SYS:PUBLIC

or

MAP *2=SYS:PUBLIC;*3=SYS:PUBLIC\MSDOS

NO_DEFAULT

Syntax

NO_DEFAULT

This command can be used in a container or profile login script to suppress running of the default user login script. This applies only to the default login script. If you have created an actual login script for a user, it will still run.

■ <== —less than or equal to

Example

```
IF DAY_OF_WEEK="Friday" THEN
WRITE "Get ready for the weekend!"
ELSE
WRITE "Good morning."
END
```

INCLUDE

Syntax

```
INCLUDE [path]filename
```

or

```
INCLUDE objectname
```

This command enables you to incorporate other text files into the script. This capability enables you to separate portions of login scripts into files that can be maintained independently of each other. When a change is needed, you can make it to just the one subscript file that will be included later into many other user login scripts. In this manner, administration is simplified because you only have to make the change in one location instead of having to edit numerous user login scripts.

Example

```
INCLUDE VOL9:\ADMIN\USERS\TUESDAY.TXT
```

LASTLOGINTIME

Syntax

```
LASTLOGINTIME
```

This command displays on the user's screen the date and time of his last login.

Example

```
LASTLOGINTIME
```

MACHINE

Syntax

```
MACHINE=machinename
```

This command sets the DOS machine name to the text machinename, which can be up to 15 characters of text.

Example

```
MACHINE=IBM_PS2
```

Syntax

FIRE n

This command will generate a "phaser" sound n number of times.

Example

FIRE 2

GOTO

Syntax

GOTO label

This command changes the order of execution of commands in the login script. Execution branches to the section of the script specified by label. This command is usually used in combination with a conditional command such as IF...THEN.

Example

IF DAY_OF_WEEK="Tuesday" THEN GOTO FINISHED
[other code]
FINISHED:
EXIT

IF...THEN

Syntax

IF condition [AND ¦ OR] [condition]] THEN
    commands
[ELSE
    commands]
[END]

You can use the IF...THEN construct to test conditions and determine which set of commands you want to execute. The AND and OR commands are optional and can be used to indicate more than one condition that must be tested. The ELSE and END commands are optional and are used to specify a set of commands to be executed when the conditions being tested are not met. THEN can be on the same line with IF, but the ELSE and END commands must be on a separate line. If the WRITE command is used in an IF...THEN construct, it must be on a separate line. You can nest IF...THEN commands up to 10 levels, but should not use a GOTO command to enter or exit a nested IF...THEN statement.

You can use the following symbols to test conditions:

- ■ = — equals
- ■ <> — not equal to
- ■ > — greater than
- ■ < — less than

DOS VERIFY OFF (default)

DRIVE

Syntax

DRIVE [drive: | *n:]

This command can be used to change the default disk drive during the execution of the login script. The first network drive, which is usually the one with the user's home directory, is the default drive for the user. Use this command to specify a *drive* (drive letter) or *n (drive number) to change the default drive. The drive letter or drive number you specify should already be mapped before this command is used.

Example

DRIVE X:

or

DRIVE *3:

EXIT

Syntax

EXIT ["filename [parameters]"]

This command terminates the login script and executes an external program. Enclose the program name (filename) and any command-line parameters in quotation marks. This command should be used at the end of the script because nothing following it will be executed. You can, however, use it in a conditional statement (IF...THEN) to cause the script to terminate and run the program based on variable information.

Example

EXIT "C:\WORD"

FDISPLAY

Syntax

FDISPLAY [path]filename

This command is similar to the DISPLAY command in that it displays a file on the user's screen. However, this version should be used when the file to be displayed is a word processing document. The DISPLAY command sends all the file's contents to the screen. This command removes any nonprintable characters and displays only text characters from the file.

Example

FDISPLAY SYS:PUBLIC\MESSAGES\TUESDAY.TXT

CONTEXT .SALES:ROUTING

or

CONTEXT .

DISPLAY

Syntax

DISPLAY [path]filename

You can use *path* and *filename* with the DISPLAY command to have the contents of a file sent to the user's screen during the login process. This is a useful command for giving users static or variable information when they log in to the network.

Example

DISPLAY SYS:PUBLIC\MESSAGES\WELCOME.TXT

or

IF DAY_OF_WEEK="Tuesday" THEN
    DISPLAY SYS:PUBLIC\MESSAGES\TUESDAY.TXT
END

DOS BREAK

Syntax

DOS BREAK [ON ¦ OFF]

This command enables the user to use the key combination Ctrl+Break (or Ctrl+C) to stop a program other than the login script. Although the BREAK command enables the user to stop the execution of the login script, it will not stop an executing program. Use this command to give the user that capability.

Example

DOS BREAK ON

or

DOS BREAK OFF (default)

DOS SET

See SET

DOS VERIFY

Syntax

DOS VERIFY [ON ¦ OFF]

This command causes DOS to verify that the data that was written to a local drive can be read without error.

Syntax

BREAK ON | OFF

This command can be used to give the user the capability to terminate a login script by using the Ctrl+C or Ctrl+Break key combination. To allow termination, use BREAK ON.

Example

BREAK ON

CLS

Syntax

CLS

This command will clear the user's screen during the login process. It is generally used for cosmetic purposes, such as clearing the screen after numerous commands that are executed in the script have produced output (screen clutter).

Example

CLS

COMSPEC

Syntax

COMSPEC=[path]COMMAND.COM

This command is used to specify the location of the DOS command processor program. If you are running DOS from a network location, first map the drive that contains the command processor, and then use this command to designate the location of COMMAND.COM. If the user's workstation will run DOS from a local drive, you do not need to use this command. *path* can be specified using an environment variable, and if so, the variable needs to be preceded by the percent sign character (%variable).

Example

COMSPEC=X:\DOS\COMMAND.COM

CONTEXT

Syntax

CONTEXT context

This command is used to set the user's context in the NDS directory tree. Follow the command with the actual context that you want the user to be able to use after the login completes. You can use the period character (.) to move up one level from the current context, two periods to move up two levels in the directory tree, and so on.

appendix provides a more complete listing of the available commands and variables that you can use to customize the login process for your NetWare clients.

NetWare Login Script Commands

Each command listed here is formatted using the following syntax:

- Actual commands are shown in uppercase.
- Italicized text indicates a variable, and you should replace the text with something that is appropriate to the command.
- Items enclosed in square brackets ([]) are optional.
- When items are separated by a vertical bar (|), you can use one or the other, but not both at the same time.

Commands

(Execute External Program)

Syntax

    # [path] filename [parameters]

The # command enables you to execute an external program from within the login script. *path* can be a drive letter, or if NOSWAP is specified in the script, *path* can be the the full directory path, starting with the name of a NetWare volume. *filename* is the name of an executable program, and it can be any file whose extension is .EXE, .COM, or .BAT. Any command-line parameters needed by the executable program can follow the executable program name in the *parameters* position.

Example

    #X:\MISC\MYPROGRAM

ATTACH

Syntax

    ATTACH [servername[/username[;password]]]

This command can be used to connect to a bindery-based NetWare server. *servername* indicates the NetWare to attach to, and if needed, you can specify a *username* and a *password* for that username. If the username is not specified, the user will be prompted for it when the script executes. If the username is the same as the primary login name, you can omit the password, and the user will not have to enter one. Use caution when placing passwords in any script file.

Example

    ATTACH ACCTNG/OGLETREE;YOKONO

NetWare Login Script Reference

SOME OF THE MAIN TOPICS IN THIS CHAPTER ARE

NetWare Login Script Commands

Variables

Table C.1   Ethernet Cabling Specifications

Cabling	Max. Segment	Max. Devices	Max. Length
10Base-2	185 m/607 ft.	30	925 m/3,035 ft.
10Base-5	500 m/1,640 ft.	100	2.1 km/1.56 miles
10Base-T	100 m/328 ft.	2	500 m
10Base-FL	2 km/1.2 miles	2	4 km
100Base-T4	100 m/328 ft.	2	200 m
100Base-TX	100 m/328 ft.	2	200 m
100Base-FX	412 m/ 1,351 ft.	2	2 km

100VG-AnyLAN

Table C.2   100VG-AnyLAN Cabling Specifications

Cable Type	Max. Segment	Max. Devices	Max. Length
Category 3 or 4	328 ft.	2	4,200 ft.
Category 5	700 ft.	2	4,200 ft.
Fiber	1,640 ft.	2	1.2 miles

Token-Ring Specifications

Table C.3   Token-Ring Cabling Specifications

IBM Cable Type Max.	Max. Devices	Station to MAU Max.	MAU to MAU
Types 1 & 2 (1 MAU)	260	300 m/975 ft.	n/a
Types 1 & 2 (multiple MAUs)	260	100 m/325 ft.	200 m/650 ft.
Type 3 (1 MAU)	96	100 m/325 ft.	n/a
Type 3 (multiple MAUs)	96	45 m/145 ft.	120 m/390 ft.

APPENDIX C

Cable Specifications

SOME OF THE MAIN TOPICS IN THIS CHAPTER ARE

IEEE 802 Ethernet Specifications

100VG-AnyLAN

Token-Ring Specifications

iclcnet-locate	886	TCP	ICL coNETion Locate Server
iclcnet-locate	886	UDP	ICL coNETion Locate Server
iclcnet_svinfo	887	TCP	ICL coNETion Server Info.
iclcnet_svinfo	887	UDP	ICL coNETion Server Info.
accessbuilder	888	TCP	AccessBuilder
accessbuilder	888	UDP	AccessBuilder
cddbp	888	TCP	CD Database Protocol
omginitialrefs	900	TCP	OMG Initial Refs.
omginitialrefs	900	UDP	OMG Initial Refs.
xact-backup	911	TCP	xact-backup
xact-backup	911	UDP	xact-backup
ftps-data	989	TCP	ftp protocol, data, over TLS/SSL
ftps-data	989	UDP	ftp protocol, data, over TLS/SSL
ftps	990	TCP	ftp protocol, control, over TLS/SSL
ftps	990	UDP	ftp protocol, control, over TLS/SSL
nas	991	TCP	Netnews Administration System
nas	991	UDP	Netnews Administration System
telnets	992	TCP	telnet protocol over TLS/SSL
telnets	992	UDP	telnet protocol over TLS/SSL
imaps	993	TCP	imap4 protocol over TLS/SSL
imaps	993	UDP	imap4 protocol over TLS/SSL
ircs	994	TCP	irc protocol over TLS/SSL
ircs	994	UDP	irc protocol over TLS/SSL
pop3s	995	TCP	pop3 protocol over TLS/SSL (was spop3)
pop3s	995	UDP	pop3 protocol over TLS/SSL (was spop3)
vsinet	996	TCP	vsinet
vsinet	996	UDP	vsinet
maitrd	997	TCP	
maitrd	997	UDP	
busboy	998	TCP	
puparp	998	UDP	
garcon	999	TCP	
applix	999	UDP	Applix ac
puprouter	999	TCP	
puprouter	999	UDP	
cadlock	1000	TCP	
ock	1000	UDP	
surf	1010	TCP	surf
surf	1010	UDP	surf
	1023	TCP	Reserved
	1023	UDP	Reserved

webster	765	TCP	
webster	765	UDP	
phonebook	767	TCP	Phone
phonebook	767	UDP	Phone
vid	769	TCP	
vid	769	UDP	
cadlock	770	TCP	
cadlock	770	UDP	
rtip	771	TCP	
rtip	771	UDP	
cycleserv2	772	TCP	
cycleserv2	772	UDP	
submit	773	TCP	
notify	773	UDP	
rpasswd	774	TCP	
acmaint_dbd	774	UDP	
entomb	775	TCP	
acmaint_transd	775	UDP	
wpages	776	TCP	
wpages	776	UDP	
multiling-http	777	TCP	Multiling HTTP
multiling-http	777	UDP	Multiling HTTP
wpgs	780	TCP	
wpgs	780	UDP	
concert	786	TCP	Concert
concert	786	UDP	Concert
qsc	787	TCP	QSC
qsc	787	UDP	QSC
mdbs_daemon	800	TCP	
mdbs_daemon	800	UDP	
device	801	TCP	
device	801	UDP	
fcp-udp	810	TCP	FCP
fcp-udp	810	UDP	FCP Datagram
itm-mcell-s	828	TCP	itm-mcell-s
itm-mcell-s	828	UDP	itm-mcell-s
pkix-3-ca-ra	829	TCP	PKIX-3 CA/RA
pkix-3-ca-ra	829	UDP	PKIX-3 CA/RA
rsync	873	TCP	rsync
rsync	873	UDP	rsync

netviewdm3	731	TCP	IBM NetView DM/6000 receive/tcp
netviewdm3	731	UDP	IBM NetView DM/6000 receive/tcp
netgw	741	TCP	netGW
netgw	741	UDP	netGW
netrcs	742	TCP	Network based Rev. Cont. Sys.
netrcs	742	UDP	Network based Rev. Cont. Sys.
flexlm	744	TCP	Flexible License Manager
flexlm	744	UDP	Flexible License Manager
fujitsu-dev	747	TCP	Fujitsu Device Control
fujitsu-dev	747	UDP	Fujitsu Device Control
ris-cm	748	TCP	Russell Info. Sci. Calendar Manager
ris-cm	748	UDP	Russell Info. Sci. Calendar Manager
kerberos-adm	749	TCP	kerberos Administration
kerberos-adm	749	UDP	kerberos Administration
rfile	750	TCP	
loadav	750	UDP	
kerberos-iv	750	UDP	kerberos Version iv
pump	751	TCP	
pump	751	UDP	
qrh	752	TCP	
qrh	752	UDP	
rrh	753	TCP	
rrh	753	UDP	
tell	754	TCP	send
tell	754	UDP	send
nlogin	758	TCP	
nlogin	758	UDP	
con	759	TCP	
con	759	UDP	
ns	760	TCP	
ns	760	UDP	
rxe	761	TCP	
rxe	761	UDP	
quotad	762	TCP	
quotad	762	UDP	
cycleserv	763	TCP	
cycleserv	763	UDP	
omserv	764	TCP	

(continues)

or

```
SET PATH="C:\ACCOUNTING\RECEIVABLES"
```

SET TIME

Syntax

```
SET TIME ON ¦ OFF
```

Use this command to control whether the workstation's clock is set to the time of the NetWare server used for login. SET TIME ON causes the clock to be set, whereas SET TIME OFF prevents this.

Example

```
SET TIME ON (default)
```

or

```
SET TIME OFF
```

SHIFT

Syntax

```
SHIFT [n]
```

The SHIFT command enables you to change the order in which %n variables in the login script are interpreted. Replace n with the number of variables to shift, with the default being 1.

Example

```
SHIFT 3
```

SWAP

Syntax

```
SWAP [path]
```

This command causes the LOGIN utility to be swapped out of conventional memory so that the # command can execute an external program at the same time. LOGIN is usually swapped to extended or expanded memory unless the NOSWAP command is used. You can use path to specify a directory to which LOGIN is swapped. If no path is specified, it will be swapped to higher memory or, if it is not available, to a local drive.

Example

```
SWAP
```

TREE

Syntax

```
TREE treename[/completename[;password]]
```

This command can be used to attach to another NDS tree on the network. After this command is executed, all other objects in the remaining part of the login script will refer to objects in the

NDS tree to which you have switched. Use can use the TREE command more than once to change between NDS trees in the login script.

Example

```
TREE ACME
```

WRITE

Syntax

```
WRITE "[text][%identifier]";[identifier]
```

This command is used to display information on the user's screen during the login script. You can specify any *text* to display, and you can display the values of *identifier* variables. Text should be enclosed in quotation marks. The semicolon character (;) can be used to concatenate the display of more than one identifier. When using multiple lines containing WRITE commands, by default each WRITE command is displayed on a separate line. Placing a semicolon character at the end of a line causes multiple WRITE commands to be displayed as continuous text. When doing this, do not put a semicolon at the end of the last WRITE command.

The text that you enclose in quotation marks can also use the following escape characters:

- /r—Carriage return character.
- /n—New line character.
- /"—Displays a quotation mark.
- /7—Causes the workstation to issue the "beep" sound.

Example

```
WRITE "Welcome to the Acme Network"
```

or

```
WRITE "Welcome to the Acme Network ";%LAST_NAME
```

Variables

Identifier variables provide you more flexibility in coding login scripts because you can use them to display information instead of having to hard code it into the script. For example, a user's name can be displayed using an identifier variable, enabling one script to be used for different users.

Table D.1 shows the most common identifier variables and gives a brief description of the information they contain.

Table D.1   NetWare Login Script Identifier Variables

Variable	Description
DAY	Number of day in the month (0–31)
DAY_OF_WEEK	Day of the week (Monday, Tuesday, and so on)
MONTH	Number of month in the year (01–12)

Variable	Description
MONTH_NAME	Name of the month (January, February, and so on)
NDAY_OF_WEEK	Number of day in the week (1–7)
SHORT_YEAR	Year in 2-digit format (98, 99, 00)
YEAR	Year in 4-digit format (1999, 2000)
AM_PM	AM or PM, depending on the time
GREETING_TIME	Time of the day expressed as morning, afternoon, or evening
HOUR	Number of the hour (1–12)
HOUR24	Number of the hour (00–23, 00=midnight)
MINUTE	Number of the minute (00–59)
SECOND	Number of the second (00–59)
%CN	The user's full login name (must exist in NDS)
LOGIN_ALIAS_CONTEXT	Y if REQUESTER_CONTEXT is an alias
FULL_NAME	Text from the FULL_NAME property for NDS and bindery-based NetWare, with spaces replaced by underscores
LAST_NAME	User's last name if NDS, or user's full login name if bindery-based NetWare
LOGIN_CONTEXT	User's context in NDS
LOGIN_NAME	User's login name, truncated to 8 characters
PASSWORD_EXPIRES	Number of days until user's password expires
REQUESTER_CONTEXT	Context when login process began
USER_ID	Numeric identifier of user
FILE_SERVER	Name of NetWare server
NETWORK_ADDRESS	IPX external network number, an 8-digit hexadecimal number
MACHINE	Type of computer
NETWARE_REQUESTER	Version of NetWare Requester for OS/2 or VLM users
OS	Workstation's operating system type
OS_VERSION	Workstation's operating system version
P_STATION	Workstation's node number, a 12-digit hexadecimal number
PLATFORM	Workstation's operating system platform (DOS, O2S, WIN, WNT, or W95)
SHELL_TYPE	If DOS, version of DOS shell
SMACHINE	Short machine name
STATION	Workstation's connection number
ACCESS_SERVER	TRUE or FALSE to show if access server is functional
ERROR_LEVEL	Error number, with 0=no error

In addition, you can generally use any DOS environment variable by enclosing it in angle-brackets (<>). If used with the MAP, COMSPEC, or FIRE command, add the percent sign (%) before the variable. You can also use NDS objects as variables using this method. If the object name contains a space, place quotation marks around it.

To use parameters that the user specifies on the command line with the LOGIN utility, use the percent sign (%) with the parameter number.

Overview of the X.500 and LDAP Protocols

SOME OF THE MAIN TOPICS IN THIS CHAPTER ARE

APPENDIX E

You have, no doubt, heard or read references that mention X.500 or LDAP. Any time you see either of these acronyms, it is in reference to some sort of directory. This appendix provides a general description of a directory service, a brief explanation of the X.500 and LDAP protocols, and several resources for additional information.

Directories and Namespace

Before starting any discussion on X.500 or LDAP, you must first understand the concept of directories. It is not a difficult topic to grasp because you use them almost every day. Consider your local phone book for example. A phone book is comprised of several main records: a name, an address, and a phone number. That data is collected and presented in a logical and orderly manner. This logical and orderly presentation of data can be thought of as a *namespace*. The namespace, as it applies to the phone book example, would be the alphabetical nature in which the names are organized. Imagine the horror if you were to pick up a new copy of the phone book and all the names and numbers were entered randomly throughout the book. It would be nearly impossible to find the information you were looking for! You can clearly see how important the presentation of data is to the directory. Without some sort of structure and order, finding information in the directory would take too long to be useful.

Electronic collections of data—a database, for example—can also be referred to as a directory. Consider email systems, file systems, or the list of users, printers, files, folders, and security attributes in your Windows NT or Novell NetWare domains. All these can be referred to or referenced by a directory. There are certainly obvious advantages to using the electronic model of a directory, including fast access to thousands or even millions of potential records, logical presentation of similar and dissimilar data, rapid execution of extremely complex queries, and many more.

X.500

With this basic understanding of a directory, you can delve into the meaning of X.500. X.500 is a protocol standard created by CCITT (now the ITU-T) in 1988 and 1992 to connect data from different information stores. As mentioned earlier, structure and order is crucial to the directory concept. X.500 is hierarchical in nature with a clear-cut and orderly namespace, which tends to make management and presentation of data to the user difficult. Figure E.1 is a visual representation of the hierarchical nature of an X.500 directory tree.

Records (or entries) in X.500 are composed of *attributes* (see RFC 1617 for naming and structuring guidelines). Attributes can be broken down into a type and one or more values associated with that type. Seventeen object classes have been defined in the standard. Forty basic attribute types can describe these 17 object classes. X.500 is expandable in that directories can include additional object classes as specified by those implementing the service.

A *Directory User Agent (DUA)* processes data access requests from users, applications, and services. A *Directory Systems Agent (DSA)* then receives the request from the DUA by way of the *Directory Access Protocol (DAP)*. Directories are made up of at least one DSA, which can be configured to communicate with other local DSAs (in the same directory) or can refer a request from a DUA to a specific DSA. A referral takes place when the DSAs are not configured to communicate with each other for security or other reasons.

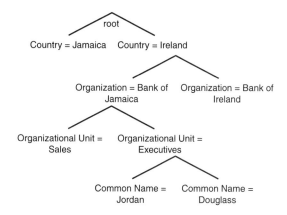

Figure E.1   The hierarchical nature of an X.500 directory tree.

In an environment that fully embraces the OSI model, DAP uses the entire OSI stack to process requests over a network. The OSI stack is large and complex and requires a huge amount of processing and memory overhead. Standard desktop computing hardware is adequate for this type of processing, but not without serious drawbacks in performance.

LDAP

LDAP, or *Lightweight Directory Access Protocol,* was originally intended to solve the problem of complexity and overhead on the client side. It was designed so that desktop computers could access X.500 directories without a tremendous performance hit. A client running TCP/IP could issue a request to an LDAP server, which in turn communicates with the desired X.500 directory via OSI protocols. Figure E.2 demonstrates the communication between an LDAP client and an LDAP server.

Although the initial issue of TCP/IP-based clients gaining access to the X.500 directory service had been addressed, performance issues still remained when a single LDAP server was used to access several large X.500 directories. The X.500 directory was growing increasingly more difficult to manage, so the developers of the LDAP standard got together to design a set of standalone directory services based solely on LDAP.

LDAPv2 was born through that effort (see RFC 1777, RFC 1778, and RFC 1779 for LDAPv2 specs). LDAPv2 allowed LDAP servers to run independently of X.500 directories while running a distributed directory-based topology. This distributed directory topology was less complex than the one used in native X.500 but remained compatible.

The namespace in LDAP is essentially identical to the namespace defined in X.500. Each record (entry) is comprised of an attribute, which is described by a type and one or more values.

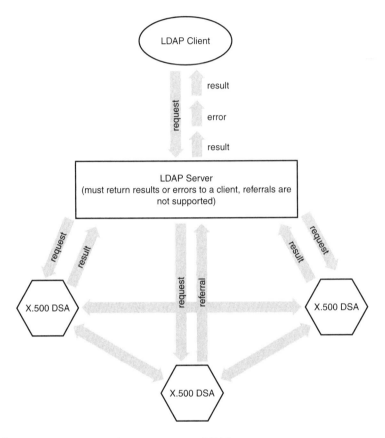

Figure E.2   An LDAP client sends a request to an LDAP server.

Summary

X.500 and LDAP provide access to directory information. X.500 tends to be more structured and difficult to manage. LDAP, though structured in nature, maintains its relative simplicity through the use of more common TCP/IP-based clients. X.500 remains popular in the large corporate intranet environments where "big" hardware and powerful clients are plentiful. LDAP has found a niche in Internet-driven database applications where the client-side hardware is an unknown. If you want a more thorough description of X.500 and LDAP, see the following references.

Additional Resources

LDAP/SLADP Resource

```
http://www.umich.edu/~dirsvcs/ldap/doc/guides/slapd
```

LDAP Mailing List

```
ldap-request@umich.edu
```

LDAP FAQ

http://www.critical-angle.com/ldapworld/ldapfaq.html

X.500 Resource

http://www.salford.ac.uk/its024

X.500 Resource

http://www.bcs.org.uk/publicat/ebull/feb96/books/book8.htm

LDAP and X.500 Resource

http://www.nexor.com/info/understandldap.htm

LDAP Resource

http://www.eema.org/understanding_ldap.html

NASA's X.500 Directory Service

http://x500.nasa.gov/

References

http://www.sunworld.com/swol-10-1996/swol-10-ldap.html

http://www.critical-angle.com/ldapworld/ldapfaq.html

M. Smith, "Definition of an X.500 Attribute Type and Object Class to Hold Uniform Resource Identifiers (URIs)," Internet Draft draft-ietf-asid-x500-url- 01.txt, March 1995.

University of Michigan at Ann Arbor, "SLAPD and SLURPD Administrators Guide," Internet Draft Release 3.3, April 1996.

Symbols

A

INDEX

Get FREE books and more...when you register this book online for our Personal Bookshelf Program

http://register.quecorp.com/

 Register online and you can sign up for our *FREE Personal Bookshelf Program...*unlimited access to the electronic version of more than 200 complete computer books—immediately! That means you'll have 100,000 pages of valuable information onscreen, at your fingertips!

 Plus, you can access product support, including complimentary downloads, technical support files, book-focused links, companion Web sites, author sites, and more!

 And you'll be automatically registered to receive a *FREE subscription to a weekly email newsletter* to help you stay current with news, announcements, sample book chapters, and special events, including sweepstakes, contests, and various product giveaways!

 We value your comments! Best of all, the entire registration process takes only a few minutes to complete, so go online and get the greatest value going—absolutely FREE!

Don't Miss Out On This Great Opportunity!

QUE® is a brand of Macmillan Computer Publishing USA.

For more information, please visit *www.mcp.com*

Other Related Titles

Upgrading and Repairing PCs, Eleventh Edition
Scott Mueller
ISBN: 0-7897-1903-7
$59.99 U.S./
$81.95 CAN

Special Edition Using Microsoft Windows 2000 Professional
Robert Cowart
ISBN: 0-7897-2125-2
$39.99 U.S./$59.95 CAN

Special Edition Microsoft Windows 2000 Server
Roger Jennings
ISBN: 0-7897-2122-8
$39.99 U.S./$59.95 CAN

Special Edition Using MS-DOS 6.22, Second Edition
Jim Cooper
ISBN: 0-7897-2040-x
$34.99 U.S./$52.95 CAN

Microsoft Windows 2000 Professional Installation and Configuration
Jim Boyce
ISBN: 0-7897-2133-3
$39.99 U.S./$59.95 CAN

Microsoft Windows 2000 Security Handbook
Jeff Schmidt
ISBN: 0-7897-1999-1
$39.99 U.S./$59.95 CAN

Network+ Exam Guide
Jonathan Feldman
ISBN: 0-7897-2157-0
$39.99 U.S./$59.95 CAN

Upgrading and Repairing PCs, Linux Edition
Joe DeVita
ISBN: 0-7897-2075-2
$59.99 U.S./
$74.95 CAN

Upgrading and Repairing PCs: A+ Certification Study Guide
Scott Mueller
ISBN: 0-7897-2095-7
$19.99 U.S./
$29.95 CAN

All prices are subject to change.

Installation Instructions

This disc is a very unique and powerful CD-ROM for PC gurus to add to their personal toolbox. The CD-ROM is designed to be bootable on any machine that allows booting from the CD-ROM device. This enables you to pop the CD into a machine you are trying to restore or repair, bringing up a live file system so you can navigate the system to troubleshoot any problem it might be having. Additionally, from the CD-ROM, you can access PowerQuest's ServerMagic 2.0 to diagnose and install software onto your system. Even if you use this only as a resource and not as a bootable diagnostic disc, you will surely find this CD a great addition to your hardware arsenal.

Bootable CD-ROM (Non-OS Dependent)

1. Insert the CD-ROM into your CD-ROM drive.
2. Reboot your computer, allowing your system to boot up off the CD-ROM.
3. Log on to the live file system by following the instructions on the screen.
4. When you are logged on, the system will give you a command menu that enables you to navigate the various options available to you.

Note

If your machine does not boot up to the LGS screen, check your manual for instructions on configuring your BIOS to recognize the CD-ROM as the primary BOOT device. Systems with older BIOS might not have this capability.

Linux and UNIX

Look in the individual directories for software and associated documentation. A README file in standard text format is available in the root directory of the CD-ROM for program descriptions.

Note

Although most of the software is intended for use in the Linux environment, some pieces (such as ServerMagic by PowerQuest) are best accessed via MS-DOS or Windows.

Windows 95, NT 4, and MS-DOS

Look in the /Non-GPL directory for various files that can be accessed and utilized from the Windows 9x/NT environment. The PowerQuest software (ServerMagic 2.0) is located in /Non-GPL/powerquest.

Read This Before Opening the Software